The Customary International Law of Human Rights

The Customary International Law of Human Rights

WILLIAM A. SCHABAS

OXFORD
UNIVERSITY PRESS

OXFORD
UNIVERSITY PRESS

Great Clarendon Street, Oxford, OX2 6DP,
United Kingdom

Oxford University Press is a department of the University of Oxford.
It furthers the University's objective of excellence in research, scholarship,
and education by publishing worldwide. Oxford is a registered trade mark of
Oxford University Press in the UK and in certain other countries

First Edition published in 2021

Published in the United States of America by Oxford University Press
198 Madison Avenue, New York, NY 10016, United States of America

British Library Cataloguing in Publication Data

Data available

Library of Congress Control Number: 2021932331

ISBN 978–0–19–284569–6

DOI: 10.1093/oso/9780192845696.001.0001

Printed and bound by
CPI Group (UK) Ltd, Croydon, CR0 4YY

Acknowledgements

This project was many years in gestation, but for most of them there was talk but little action, as my colleagues and students will confirm. To paraphrase Mark Twain, everybody talks about customary international law but nobody does anything about it, and I was no exception. My research in the area was regularly put aside in favour of other tasks including academic and professional duties. Ultimately, the restrictions on freedom of movement in reaction to COVID-19 created the conditions for its completion. My academic base, Middlesex University, locked my office and told me to work from home, and that's what I did. I even bought a t-shirt that said 'Work from home? I don't even work from work', attesting to the fact that research in human rights is an avocation rather than a vocation. Virtually every day of the lockdown, Penelope cracked the whip (figuratively), urging me to finish the job. Her companionship and support over the months of isolation was indispensable.

I also had some help along the way from Mohamed Elewa Bader, Christina Cerna, Milena Sterio, and Alfred de Zayas. Many thanks to you all.

William Schabas
London, 10 December 2020

Table of Contents

Table of Cases

AFRICAN COMMISSION ON HUMAN AND PEOPLES' RIGHTS

AFRICAN COURT ON HUMAN AND PEOPLES' RIGHTS

ARGENTINA

AUSTRALIA

BARBADOS

CANADA

COMMITTEE ON ECONOMIC, SOCIAL AND CULTURAL RIGHTS

EUROPEAN COMMISSION OF HUMAN RIGHTS

EUROPEAN COURT OF HUMAN RIGHTS

EUROPEAN COURT OF JUSTICE

EXTRAORDINARY CHAMBERS OF THE COURTS OF CAMBODIA

HUMAN RIGHTS COMMITTEE

INTER-AMERICAN COMMISSION ON HUMAN RIGHTS

INTER-AMERICAN COURT OF HUMAN RIGHTS

INTERNATIONAL CENTRE FOR SETTLEMENT OF INVESTMENT DISPUTES

INTERNATIONAL COURT OF JUSTICE

INTERNATIONAL CRIMINAL COURT

INTERNATIONAL CRIMINAL TRIBUNAL FOR RWANDA

INTERNATIONAL CRIMINAL TRIBUNAL FOR THE FORMER YUGOSLAVIA

INTERNATIONAL MILITARY TRIBUNAL

ISRAEL

PERMANENT COURT OF ARBITRATION

PERMANENT COURT OF INTERNATIONAL JUSTICE

SOUTH AFRICA

SPECIAL COURT FOR SIERRA LEONE

SPECIAL TRIBUNAL FOR LEBANON

UNITED KINGDOM

UNITED STATES

WORKING GROUP ON ARBITRARY DETENTION (WGAD)

Table of Legislation

DOMESTIC LEGISLATION

France

Germany

Mozambique

Myanmar

Pakistan

Peru

South Africa

South Sudan

United Arab Emirates

United Kingdom

United States

Introduction

The customary law of human rights is hiding in plain sight

Today, a huge body of international treaties governs the protection and promotion of human rights. None of these legal texts existed when the Charter of the United Nations was adopted, on 26 June 1945, although shadows of the system had begun to emerge following the First World War initiatives, and even earlier, on such matters as the rights of religious minorities, the protection of refugees, and the suppression of the slave trade. The Charter itself was rather understated on the substance of human rights. It failed to fulfil commitments to enshrine fundamental freedoms that had been made by the major powers earlier in the Second World War when victory over fascism had not looked so certain. The Charter confined itself to declaring that one of the purposes of the United Nations was 'promoting and encouraging respect for human rights and for fundamental freedoms'. This was to be 'without distinction as to race, sex, language, or religion'. The equality of men and women was also recognised.[1] At the closing session of the San Francisco Conference, President Truman promised the adoption of an 'international bill of rights'. He recalled that the Charter was 'dedicated to the achievement and observance of human rights and fundamental freedoms', adding that '[u]nless we can attain those objectives for all men and women everywhere—without regard to race, language or religion—we cannot have permanent peace and security'.[2]

Just as there were no comprehensive human rights treaties and no 'international bill of rights' prior to the establishment of the United Nations, there was no customary international law of human rights either. International law has two principal sources, treaties and custom, the latter identified on the basis of 'practice accepted as law'.[3] At one time, a century or more ago, customary law predominated. Writing in one of the first issues of the *American Journal of International Law*, in 1908, Professor Lassa Oppenheim of Cambridge University predicted that

[1] Charter of the United Nations, PP 1, arts. 1(3), 13(1)(b), 55, 56, 62(2), 68, 76. See Farrokh Jhabvala, 'The Drafting of the Human Rights Provisions of the UN Charter', (1997) 44 *Netherlands International Law Review* 1; Egon Schwelb, 'The International Court of Justice and the Human Rights Clauses of the Charter', (1972) 68 *American Journal of International Law* 337.

[2] Address by the President of the United States of America, *Documents of the United Nations Conference on International Organization, San Francisco, 1945*, Vol. I, pp. 713–718, at p. 717.

[3] Report of the International Law Commission, Seventieth session (30 April–1 June and 2 July–10 August 2018), A/73/10, pp. 124–126.

The Customary International Law of Human Rights. William A. Schabas, Oxford University Press.
© William A. Schabas 2021. DOI: 10.1093/oso/9780192845696.003.0001

customary international law would gradually 'be pushed into the background' although he thought it would not entirely disappear. 'The future of international law belongs to conventional and not customary law', he said.[4] But in 1945 there was no customary international law of human rights to be pushed into the background.

When the United Nations was established, human rights had occupied an important place in national law for a few hundred years. The English Bill of Rights of 1689, the French *Déclaration des droits de l'homme et du citoyen* of 1789, and the American Bill of Rights of 1791 are prominent examples of early recognition for human rights in domestic statutes and constitutions. But the human rights principles recognised in national texts had no real echo at the international level. The issues they addressed were viewed as being quintessentially matters of domestic concern. To the extent that there might have been some relevant customary law, it addressed matters that had an international dimension, such as the slave trade (as opposed to slavery per se), other forms of human trafficking, refugees, and treatment of civilians in occupied territory. Oppenheim's forecast of the gradual effacement of customary law by treaties was entirely accurate in areas like diplomatic immunities, the law of the sea, transport and telecommunications, the law of armed conflict, and even protection of the environment. However, this was not the case in the area of human rights. In international human rights law, custom did not precede treaty, it followed it.

From its earliest days, the United Nations devoted attention to the codification of human rights. The first tangible result was the Universal Declaration of Human Rights, adopted by the General Assembly on 10 December 1948.[5] A succinct manifesto of fundamental rights and freedoms, it comprised thirty laconic provisions totalling not quite 1,800 words. The norms in the Universal Declaration of Human Rights were derived from two main sources, the human rights provisions recognised in the law of the founding Member States of the United Nations and draft international declarations submitted by Cuba, Panama, Chile, and the American Federation of Labor.[6] Various United Nations organs, principally the Commission on Human Rights and the Third Committee of the General Assembly, crafted the final text, drawing upon the sources but adjusting them in light of contemporary values and, to a limited extent, with an eye to future development. This initial attempt at a genuinely universal codification took place during the early phases of the Cold War. Only about fifty States were involved. At the present day, there are nearly 200 members of the United Nations. But in the late 1940s, a majority of them did not yet exist as independent, sovereign political entities. Africa, which today

[4] Lassa Oppenheim, 'The Science of International Law: Its Task and Method', (1908) 2 *American Journal of International Law* 313, at p. 349.

[5] Universal Declaration of Human Rights, A/RES/217 (III).

[6] Drafting Committee on an International Bill of Human Rights, International Bill of Rights Documented Outline, E/CN.4/AC.1/3/Add.1.

accounts for not quite a third of the current membership of the United Nations, had only four Member States at the first session of the General Assembly in 1946.

Over the seventy-five years since its establishment, the United Nations has developed an enormous body of written law dealing with human rights. This takes the form of treaties, resolutions, and declarations of the General Assembly, the Human Rights Council, and other organs of the United Nations, together with a large number of 'guidelines', 'principles', 'safeguards', and similar documents. Three treaties were adopted to complement the Universal Declaration of Human Rights and complete the 'international bill of rights': the International Covenant on Civil and Political Rights, the International Covenant on Economic, Social and Cultural Rights, and the Optional Protocol to the International Covenant on Civil and Political Rights. Alongside the materials generated by the United Nations and its agencies, such as the International Labour Organisation and UNESCO, are similar texts from regional bodies like the Council of Europe, the European Union, the Organisation for Cooperation and Development in Europe, the African Union, the Organization of American States, the League of Arab States, and other intergovernmental organisations.

Writing in 2003, Ian Brownlie observed that '[t]he literature of human rights tends to neglect the role, or potential role, of customary law'.[7] Customary international law is occasionally invoked in human rights litigation before national courts, either because the constitution invites its application or because of the provisions of some specific domestic legislation. Human rights lawyers, activists, diplomats, and academics may point to customary international law as a source of obligation. It is particularly relevant when a State has not ratified or acceded to one of the relevant human rights treaties, or when a reservation has been made to one or more of the provisions of a treaty, or when its application has been subject to derogation because of a state of emergency. Customary international law is also an important component of the discourse of international human rights bodies. Manuals, guidelines, and similar documents issued by the Office of the United Nations High Commissioner for Human Rights list customary international law as one of the sources of human rights norms and principles.[8]

The prohibitions of torture, genocide, and racial discrimination are usually presented as examples of customary international law. In support, reference may be made to authoritative pronouncements of the International Court of Justice. But if the conversation moves beyond these core human rights issues to more specific legal problems, be it the relevance of customary international law to a broad range of other human rights norms and standards or details on what the prohibitions of

[7] Ian Brownlie, *Principles of Public International Law*, 6th ed., Oxford: Oxford University Press, 2003, p. 538. Hugh Thirlway noted that this sentence did not appear in subsequent editions (Hugh Thirlway, *The Sources of International Law*, Oxford: Oxford University Press, 2014, p. 177, fn. 19).

[8] For example, Office of the High Commissioner for Human Rights, Training Manual on Human Rights Monitoring, Geneva, 2011, Chapter 5, pp. 10–11.

torture, genocide, and racial discrimination actually require, the case law and other relevant materials generated by international bodies are rarely very helpful. Often enough, the norm will be described as being customary in nature without any attempt at serious justification, as if the description is self-evident. If an authority is provided, the reference is to nothing more than some other body or individual proclaiming the norm to be customary but without evidence in support. A chain of assertions may be created, as if a norm becomes customary because enough judges and academics repeat the claim, citing one another.

Pronouncements are prone to be couched in cautious language: ' … the norm is emerging … ';[9] there is a 'crystallising international norm … ';[10] a practice is 'contrary to the direction in which customary law is developing … '.[11] There are frequent suggestions that 'many provisions' in certain instruments constitute a codification of customary norms although without necessarily specifying what is and what is not. For example, the Special Rapporteur on extrajudicial, summary, and arbitrary executions said that the Standard Minimum Rules for the Treatment of Prisoners 'reflect customary international law in many respects'.[12] Sometimes, reference is made to the Universal Declaration of Human Rights, almost invariably with the caveat that much or even most of its content constitutes customary international law.[13] Judgments declare that a customary norm is emerging but without explaining what has to happen for that blessed event to take place.

By its very nature, treaty law offers more certainty than custom. The text of the relevant convention generally provides a good starting point, subject to verifying whether the provision in question has been enfeebled by a reservation or neutralised by a derogation. Greater precision is provided by judicial interpretation of a text, where the application of restriction or limitation clauses may narrow what initially appears as an absolute formulation, not to mention reliance on notions like a 'margin of appreciation' or deference to the policies of States and to national cultural features. Comprehensive academic commentary on relevant treaty provisions contributes further to this process of clarification. If a specialist is asked whether a relevant treaty addresses the right to marry, the prohibition of hate speech, or restrictions on use of the death penalty, reliable answers can usually be found quite quickly. Of course, human rights treaties exist in a dynamic environment. Courts

[9] *Roach and Pinkerton v. United States*, Case 9647, Merits, Resolution No. 3/87, Merits, 22 September 1987, para. 60.

[10] *Prosecutor v. Kallon et al.* (SCSL-04-15-AR72), Decision on Challenge to Jurisdiction: Lomé Accord Amnesty, 13 March 2004, para. 82.

[11] *Prosecutor v. Ieng Sary et al.* (002/19-09-2007/ECCC/TC), Decision on Ieng Sary's Rule 89 Preliminary Objections (amnesty and pardon and ne bis in idem), 3 November 2011, para. 27.

[12] Report of the Special Rapporteur on extrajudicial, summary, or arbitrary executions, Philip Alston, A/HRC/8/3, para. 74.

[13] See the references cited in Hurst Hannum, 'The Status of the Universal Declaration of Human Rights in National and International Law', (1995/96) 25 *Georgia Journal of International and Comparative Law* 287, at pp. 331–332.

and treaty bodies employ dynamic or evolutive interpretation, creating a degree of uncertainty about the reliability of precedent.

But what if the same question is asked with regard to customary international law? Where would one look it up? Obviously, the researcher cannot simply refer to a treaty text. One might comb through the case law of international courts, tribunals, and treaty bodies. But the pickings would be terribly slim. Only very occasionally has the International Court of Justice identified a norm of human rights law as being customary in nature.[14] In 1994, the United Nations Human Rights Committee adopted a succinct list of customary norms in the context of its General Comment on reservations,[15] but without explanation or authority. It has never returned to the subject. The Inter-American Court of Human Rights is typically bolder, although it has a preference for describing norms as being peremptory or *jus cogens* and tends to avoid reference to customary international law. In 2018, the International Law Commission completed a study on the identification of customary international law, but its draft conclusions and the preparatory materials offer no insight into the substantive human rights that may be customary in nature. An expert report prepared for the Commission was sceptical that such norms even existed.[16]

A more logical approach might be to start with scholarly materials. General textbooks on international human rights law largely ignore the subject of customary law, offering only perfunctory acknowledgement of its existence but providing little or no guidance as to its substance. There are several entries on aspects of 'human rights' in the authoritative *Max Planck Encyclopaedia of International Law* but none of them addresses the applicable customary international law. The main contribution, by Thomas Buergenthal, concludes with a laconic reference to 'an emerging customary international human rights law that may also be characterised as trans-national human rights law'.[17] The same *Encyclopaedia* contains a lengthy chapter on customary international law but devotes no particular attention to international human rights.[18] The *Cambridge Companion to Human Rights Law* offers one reference to customary international law dealing not with the content of the norms but rather with the idea of humanitarian intervention.[19] More promising

[14] *Questions relating to the Obligation to Prosecute or Extradite (Belgium v. Senegal), Judgment, ICJ Reports 2012*, p. 422, para. 99.

[15] General Comment 24, Issues Relating to Reservations Made upon Ratification or Accession to the Covenant or the Optional Protocols thereto, or in Relation to Declarations under art. 41 of the Covenant, CCPR/C/21/Rev.1/Add.6, para. 8.

[16] Hugh Thirlway, 'Human Rights in Customary Law: An Attempt to Define Some of the Issues', (2015) 28 *Leiden Journal of International Law* 495, at p. 497.

[17] Thomas Buergenthal, 'Human Rights', in Rüdiger Wolfrum, ed., *The Max Planck Encyclopaedia of Public International Law*, Oxford: Oxford University Press, 2012, pp. 1021–1031, at p. 1030.

[18] Tullio Treves, 'Customary International Law', in Rüdiger Wolfrum, ed., *The Max Planck Encyclopedia of Public International Law*, Vol. IV, Oxford: Oxford University Press, 2012, pp. 937–957.

[19] Conor Gearty and Costas Douzinas, eds., *Cambridge Companion to Human Rights Law*, Cambridge: Cambridge University Press, 2012, p. 138.

is the *Routledge Handbook of International Human Rights Law*, with a chapter entitled 'Customary law and human rights'.[20] But on closer inspection, this is a discussion about the relationship of international human rights norms to 'customary law' in the sense of traditional practices relating to the family and similar matters. The four-volume *Encyclopaedia of Human Rights*, published by Oxford University Press, contains a four-page entry entitled 'Customary International Law', most of which examines international humanitarian law rather than international human rights law.[21] Two chapters in the *Oxford Handbook of International Human Rights Law* briefly address the content and significance of customary international law.[22] One of the more substantial discussions in the textbooks, amounting to about four pages, can be found in the textbook by Ilias Bantekas and Lutz Oette. It points to the Universal Declaration and notes that 'some UDHR articles have undoubtedly become customary international law' but otherwise refrains from specifying the content.[23] Similar attention is given to customary international law in Olivier de Schutter's casebook.[24]

The great exception is Theodor Meron's seminal monograph, *Human Rights and Humanitarian Norms as Customary Law*, published in 1989.[25] It refers to a summary list of customary law norms proposed by the American Law Institute a few years earlier and suggests a few additions, but without detailed explanation as to why certain rights and not others should be considered customary. It is a huge contribution to the subject. But after more than thirty years this study needs to be re-examined and refreshed. The treaty law applicable to human rights and the institutions involved in monitoring and enforcement have been transformed during that period. Why would it be any different with respect to the corresponding customary international law?

A quarter of a century ago, the International Committee of the Red Cross began work on the codification of the customary international law of armed conflict. International humanitarian law, as it is now often referred to, originates in rules that are customary in nature. By 1995 many treaties, some of them ratified more or less universally, provided detailed codification of the laws and customs of war. The

[20] Scott Sheeran and Sir Nigel Rodley, eds., *Routledge Handbook of International Human Rights*, London and New York: Routledge, 2013, pp. 303–322.

[21] Connie de la Vega, 'Customary International Law', in David Forsythe, ed., *Encyclopaedia of Human Rights*, Vol. 1, Oxford: Oxford University Press, 2009, pp. 451–455.

[22] Michael O'Boyle and Michelle Lafferty, 'General Principles and Constitutions as Sources of Human Rights Law', in Dinah Shelton ed., *The Oxford Handbook of International Human Rights Law*, Oxford: Oxford University Press, 2013, pp. 194–221; Bertrand G. Ramcharan, 'The Law-making Process: From Declaration to Treaty to Custom to Prevention', in Dinah Shelton ed., *The Oxford Handbook of International Human Rights Law*, Oxford: Oxford University Press, 2013, pp. 499–526.

[23] Ilias Bantekas and Lutz Oette, *International Human Rights, Law and Practice*, 3rd. ed., Cambridge: Cambridge University Press, 2020, pp. 60–64.

[24] Olivier de Schutter, *International Human Rights Law, Cases, Materials, Commentary*, 3rd. ed., Cambridge: Cambridge University Press, 2019, pp. 59–63.

[25] Theodor Meron, *Human Rights and Humanitarian Norms as Customary Law*, Oxford: Clarendon Press, 1989, pp. 79–135.

vast majority of their provisions applied only to international armed conflict. With the prohibition of the use of force to settle disputes, entrenched in the Charter of the United Nations and confirmed in the judgment of the International Military Tribunal, the number and the scale of international armed conflicts had declined dramatically. The focus had shifted to non-international armed conflict, yet the applicable treaties were often not substantial or detailed enough. Moreover, in 1995 the principal treaty applicable to non-international armed conflict, Additional Protocol II to the Geneva Conventions, had not been widely ratified. These factors prompted renewed interest in the role of customary law. The result was a three-volume study built around a compendium of 160 rules or norms applicable to armed conflict regardless of whether or not there was an applicable treaty.[26] Many experts were involved in various parts of the work. One of the challenges in assessing State practice was reliance upon materials produced by countries that had not actively participated in an international armed conflict for many decades, and that had little or no experience of non-international armed conflict. Today's legal researchers interested in the substance of the customary law of armed conflict almost automatically turn to the study of the International Committee of the Red Cross. It is so thorough, well-researched, and exhaustively documented that there is rarely any need for further inquiry. The sources to which it refers, in national military manuals and domestic case law, in a range of languages, are not readily accessible, and this means there are no real alternatives available to the researcher other than to resort to the customary law study on humanitarian law. It immediately became the gold standard on the subject. The study has its critics,[27] but there are no rivals.

The essence of this project on the customary law of human rights is much the same as that of the study undertaken by the International Committee of the Red Cross. The ambition is to provide a compendium of the law of human rights, admittedly one that is more modest in scope. There are some important differences. In contrast with the law of armed conflict, which was born in custom and was only codified by treaty in later life, the pattern of international human rights law takes the opposite trajectory. In contrast with the situation of international humanitarian law, the sources of international human rights law are in some respects both richer and more accessible. For many States, the law of armed conflict is a largely theoretical matter. There are, of course, a few laboratories, such as Israel and Palestine, Syria, the former Yugoslavia, and Iraq, which provide fuel for legal debate and

[26] Jean-Marie Henckaerts and Louise Doswald-Beck, *Customary International Humanitarian Law*, Vol. I, Cambridge: Cambridge University Press, 2005.

[27] Yoram Dinstein, 'The ICRC Customary International Humanitarian Law Study', (2006) 36 *Israel Yearbook of Human Rights* 1; George H. Aldrich, 'Customary International Humanitarian Law—An Interpretation on behalf of the International Committee of the Red Cross', (2005) 76 *British Yearbook of International Law* 503; John B. Bellinger III and William J. Haynes II, 'A US Government Response to the International Committee of the Red Cross Study Customary International Humanitarian Law', (2007) 89 *International Review of the Red Cross* 443.

development. Human rights law, on the other hand, is daily fare in public discussion, parliamentary debate, and domestic legal practice in virtually every country. Every year, many hundreds of 'periodic reports' on human rights compliance, or the lack of it, are generated by States in fulfilment of their obligations under international treaties. Several of the treaties have now achieved near-universal ratification, strengthening the claim that they amount to codifications of rules that are also customary in nature. Moreover, for more than a decade the United Nations Human Rights Council has hosted a process known as the Universal Periodic Review by which all Member States of the organisation submit reports on the law and practice of human rights in their country. The reporting by States that are not parties to the important treaties is especially helpful, providing indications as to their opinions on the scope of international legal obligations in the absence of an applicable treaty, as well as to the practice that reflects or manifests this legal understanding.

Drawing upon all of these materials, this project endeavours to address a vacuum in the academic literature. The study is less prescriptive than that of the International Committee of the Red Cross, in that its objective is not a list of short, definitive texts setting out the applicable rules. Some attempt to summarise the norms of customary international law has been made in the conclusions of each chapter, largely to facilitate access by those who consult this work. However, most of the discussion attempts to weigh the relative strength of a norm rather than produce a list of commandments. Language is used to convey this—words like 'probably', 'perhaps', 'certainly', 'likely', 'improbable', 'unlikely'—rather than a binary approach premised upon definitions, as if the exercise were one of drafting yet another treaty. The task of reaching definitive conclusions is left, inevitably, to the courts and others whose task it is to interpret and implement international human rights law. Chapter 3 of this monograph explains the methodology in more detail.

From a scholarly perspective, the function of this work will, hopefully, be to stimulate a broader debate and more extensive research in the area. Unlike the humanitarian law study of the International Committee of the Red Cross, with its teams of experts, its working groups, and its conferences, this is the product of a single researcher. The simple explanation for such individualism is that there were no resources for an alternative approach. The author has many ideas about progressive development of international human rights law, some of them quite provocative, and his personal assessments are not entirely avoided. Nevertheless, while the study itself may identify the inadequacies of the current legal framework, it is not really directed at law reform but rather at description of the status quo. Although the identification of customary law requires evidence of State practice, the great paradox of this exercise is that States do not always deliver upon their obligations. It will be enough if this study can incite greater observance of the rules that now exist, without in any way losing sight of the imperative for progressive development.

1
The belated emergence of the customary international law of human rights

In his treatise on public international law published in 1905, Lassa Oppenheim wrote of the 'so-called rights of mankind', comprising 'the right of existence, the right to protection of honour, life, health, liberty, and property, the right of practising any religion one likes, the right of emigration, and the like'. But, he said, such rights 'do not in fact enjoy any guarantee whatever from the Law of Nations'.[1] Just as he denied the reality of any human rights under customary law, Oppenheim was prepared to acknowledge some evidence to the contrary in treaty law. For example, he noted the guarantees imposed on the Balkan states at the Congress of Berlin in 1878 and treaties suppressing the slave trade. But he could not see in these exceptional provisions any 'guarantee of the so-called rights of mankind'.[2] Oppenheim had detected what we now know to be the beginnings of the recognition of human rights within treaty law. But he could see nothing that might suggest that human rights could be found in custom.

The minorities treaties and declarations adopted in the First World War's aftermath engaged States throughout central and eastern Europe as well as parts of the Middle East to ensure '[f]ull and complete protection of life and liberty' regardless of 'birth, nationality, language, race or religion' as well as '[e]quality before the law and enjoyment of the same civil and political rights without distinction as to race, language or religion'.[3] Writing many years after their adoption, Jacob Robinson described how '[a]t the end of World War I, a Regional Bill of Rights emerged for a contiguous territory between the Baltic (Estonia) and the Eastern Mediterranean (Iraq), for the most endangered groups of individuals in our age—minorities or race, religion and language—in the form of minorities treaties, minorities provisions in peace treaties, and minorities declarations'.[4] These texts are antecedents of the post-Second World War declarations and treaties.

[1] Lassa Oppenheim, *International Law, A Treatise*, Vol. I, *Peace*, London: Longmans, Green, 1905, p. 346.

[2] Ibid., p. 347.

[3] *E.g.* Treaty between the Principal Allied and Associated Powers and Poland, (1919) 112 BSP 232, arts. 2, 7.

[4] Jacob Robinson, *Human Rights and Fundamental Freedoms in the Charter of the United Nations, A Commentary*, New York: Institute of Jewish Affairs, 1946, p. 1.

The Customary International Law of Human Rights. William A. Schabas, Oxford University Press.
 DOI: 10.1093/oso/9780192845696.003.0002

An effort at a more comprehensive codification of fundamental rights was undertaken by the Institut de Droit International, a prestigious professional body of international legal experts. At its 1929 session, held in Briarcliff Manor just north of New York City, the Institut adopted a Declaration of the International Rights of Man. The preamble began as follows: 'That the juridical conscience of the civilised world demands the recognition for the individual of rights preserved from all infringement on the part of the State.'[5] It went on to cite the French and American constitutions adopted at the end of the eighteenth century as well as the Fourteenth Amendment to the American Constitution as interpreted by the United States Supreme Court, a rather pathetic example given the Court's 'separate but equal' justification for racial segregation.[6] The preamble concluded with a reference to 'a certain number of treaties [that] stipulate the recognition of the rights of man', concluding that 'it is important to extend to the entire world international recognition of the rights of man'.[7] The Institut's Declaration emphasised equality and non-discrimination, including the right to language, reflecting the interests of the Rapporteur, André Mandelstam. The Declaration was understood not as an attempt at codification of customary law but rather as a departure from traditional doctrines based on State sovereignty. Writing about its significance, the editor of the *American Journal of International Law* described it as a 'revolutionary document' that constituted a 'liberal development of international law'.[8] René Cassin credited the Institut de Droit International with playing an important role in the history of the Universal Declaration of Human Rights, noting in particular that the right to life was included as part of the 1929 Declaration.[9]

[5] Institut de Droit International, 'Declaration of the International Rights of Man', (1941) 35 *American Journal of International Law* 663.

[6] *Plessy v. Ferguson*, 163 US 537 (1896).

[7] George A. Finch, 'The International Rights of Man', (1941) 35 *American Journal of International Law* 662, at pp. 663–664. See also the commentary on the Declaration by the rapporteur, André Mandelstam, 'La déclaration des droits internationaux de l'homme adoptée par l'Institut de Droit International', (1930) 5 *Revue de Droit International* 59. On Mandelstam, see Helmut Philipp Aust, 'From Diplomat to Academic Activist: André Mandelstam and the History of Human Rights', (2014) 25 *European Journal of International Law* 1105; Hülya Adak, 'The Legacy of André Nikolaievitch Mandelstam (1869–1949) and the Early History of Human Rights', (2018) 70 *Zeitschrift für Religions- und Geistesgischichte* 117.

[8] Philip Marshall Brown, 'The New York Session of the Institut de Droit International', (1930) 24 *American Journal of International Law* 126, at p. 127.

[9] René Cassin, 'La déclaration universelle et la mise en œuvre des droits de l'homme', (1951) 79 *Recueil des cours* 241, at p. 272. The 1929 Declaration was also considered by the drafters of the American Declaration of the Rights and Duties of Man: Inter-American Council of Jurists, *Recommendaciones e Informes, Documentos Oficiales, 1945–1947*, Washington, D.C.: Organization of American States, 1948, pp. 18–19.

A. Drafting an international bill of rights

A campaign for a more comprehensive formulation of human rights as well as mechanisms for their enforcement only really emerged during the Second World War. Very broad principles were proposed by President Roosevelt in his January 1941 'four freedoms speech'.[10] These were affirmed in the Atlantic Charter, in a somewhat different form, by Roosevelt and Churchill later that year.[11] Meanwhile, various individuals and institutions made efforts to draft a declaration of human rights.[12] H.G. Wells, the English writer and public intellectual, convened a group of prominent personalities and produced a widely publicised draft international bill of rights.[13]

The London International Assembly, a non-governmental body, although it contained many government representatives, convened during the early years of the Second World War as a kind of think tank on the social and legal order to follow the conflict. Its Third (Legal) Committee, chaired by University of Oxford law professor Arthur Lehman Goodhart, produced a draft declaration of rights in February 1943. The Committee's report explained that it had attempted to deal with the issue of fundamental rights 'from the strictly legal standpoint', the aim being 'to formulate these various maxims as positive legal principles'. As sources, it referred to English, American, and French domestic law, the post-First World War principles concerning protection of minorities, and the proposals from the Institut de Droit International. 'Its guiding principle has been to limit itself to the principles concerning the protection of the individual which can be of such a fundamental nature that every civilised State wishes and must respect them in so far as it wishes to be recognised as a civilised State', said the report.[14] There was no suggestion of any role for customary international law.

The most interesting of these precursors of the Universal Declaration of Human Rights may well be the text proposed by Hersch Lauterpacht, given his status as one of the world's pre-eminent international lawyers. Lauterpacht had been commissioned by the American Jewish Committee to prepare a book on the international law of human rights.[15] *An International Bill of the Rights of Man* was published by Columbia University Press in early 1945. Lauterpacht did not refer to customary international law as a source of the human rights that he set out. Acknowledging

[10] Congressional Record, 1941, Vol. 87, Pt. I, 6 January 1941.

[11] 'Joint Statement by President Roosevelt and Prime Minister Churchill, 14 August 1941', FRUS 1941 I, pp. 367-369 .

[12] Jan Herman Burgers, 'The Road to San Francisco: The Revival of the Human Rights Idea in the Twentieth Century', (1992) 14 *Human Rights Quarterly* 447.

[13] Herbert G. Wells, *The Rights of Man*, London: Penguin, 1940.

[14] London International Assembly, Report of the Third Commission (Legal Commission) on individual rights, TNA LNU 6/7.

[15] Elihu Lauterpacht, *The Life of Hersch Lauterpacht*, Cambridge: Cambridge University Press, 2010, pp. 251–264.

the growing protection of human rights in domestic legislation, Lauterpacht considered that 'the individual became only to an imperfect degree the object of the law of nations'. He explained that 'the fundamental claims of human personality to equality, liberty, and freedom against the arbitrary will of the State remained outside the orbit of international law save for the precarious and controversial principle of humanitarian intervention'.[16] He added that 'international law does not at present recognise, apart from treaty, any fundamental rights of the individual guaranteed and protected by international society as against the State of which he is a national'.[17]

Lauterpacht rooted the principles he set out within 'the law of nature and the inherent rights of man'.[18] The preamble of his draft spoke of 'the natural rights of man to freedom and equality before the law'.[19] His ambition was to promote a Bill of Rights inspired by natural law and thereby introduce fundamental rights into positive international law. The draft Bill was 'an instrument creating legal rights and obligations' rather than one confirming those that already existed, at least under international law.[20] Although this was 'to a large extent an affirmation of the general principles of constitutional law of civilised States in the matter of the fundamental rights of man', it was at the same time 'a radical innovation in international practice'.[21]

At about the same time, Edwin Borchard, an international law professor at Yale University, published an article in *The Annals of the American Academy of Political and Social Science* on the origins of the international protection of human rights. After noting the recognition of fundamental rights in various national constitutions, Borchard wrote that '[w]hen it comes to international law, substantive or procedural, we find somewhat more difficulty in proving that the rights of man, however appealing to every human instinct, were ever taken under its protection'.[22] He signalled the 'general principles of law recognised by civilised nations', describing them as 'a form of natural law'.[23] He also pointed to some international conventions, but he made no mention whatsoever of customary international law.[24]

All of these early efforts at identification and codification of international human rights law are striking for the absence of references to customary international law as a source. This was not neglect, or an oversight. The drafters understood that the protection of fundamental rights of the individual had not previously been

[16] Hersch Lauterpacht, *An International Bill of the Rights of Man*, New York: Columbia University Press, 1945, p. 5.
[17] Ibid., pp. 47–48.
[18] Ibid., pp. 16–40.
[19] Ibid., p. 69.
[20] Ibid., p. 78.
[21] Ibid., p. 81.
[22] Edwin Borchard, 'Historical Background of International Protection of Human Rights', (1946) 243 *Annals of the American Academy of Political and Social Science* 112, at p. 112.
[23] Ibid., p. 113.
[24] Ibid.

addressed by international law. The subject had been viewed as an internal matter premised on respect for the sovereignty of States, a situation that could only be modified by their consent. The contrast with the development of international humanitarian law cannot be more striking. The declarations and treaties on the law of armed conflict adopted since the mid-nineteenth century had often been expressly referred to using the nomenclature of 'laws and *customs* of war'.[25] The preamble of the 1899 Hague Convention on the Laws and Customs of War described its object as being 'to revise the laws and general customs of war, either with the view of defining them more precisely, or of laying down certain limits for the purpose of modifying their severity as far as possible'.[26] By contrast, none of the early efforts at codifying international human rights ever contemplated 'revising' or 'defining more precisely' the scope of international law.

How are we to understand these quite different histories of international humanitarian law and international human rights law? There is a dimension of reciprocity in international humanitarian law that is relatively absent in international human rights law. Rules of conduct during international armed conflict, as yet unwritten, were nevertheless respected to the extent that both sides abided by them. There was mutual interest in their observance. To this extent, international humanitarian law has resembled other areas of international law where custom developed well before treaty law, like diplomatic immunities and the extent of the territorial sea. Maurice Mendelson noted how '[d]iscussions of the formulation of customary international law concentrate on bilateral relationships whereby one State reacts, or doesn't react, to an act or an omission of another State'.[27] Hugh Thirlway observed that 'the relationship of a State with its own subjects . . . has been generally immune from the impact of developing customary law'.[28] That is because '[c]ustom derives from the *de facto* adjustment of conflicting claims and interests of the subjects of international law, and it has always been—and probably still is—one of the most fundamental tenets of international law that individuals and private corporations are not subjects of international law',[29] although he added that '[t]his appears to be no longer the case'.[30]

Activity in the field of international criminal law also sheds light on the subject of the recognition of a customary international law in the area of human rights. That international law might be the basis for prosecution of State officials

[25] The earliest use of the term may have been in the Brussels Declaration of 1874, which was based upon a draft convention 'concernant les lois et coutumes de la guerre' proposed by the Russian government. See, for example, *Actes de la Conférence de Bruxelles*, Brussels: Hayez, 1874.

[26] Convention (II) with respect to the Laws and Customs of War on Land, 29 July 1899, US Treaty Series 403, PP 3.

[27] See, *e.g.* Maurice Mendelson, 'State Acts and Omissions as Explicit or Implicit Claims', (1993) in International Law Association, *Report of the Sixty-Fifth Conference, Cairo, Egypt*, London: International Law Association, 1993 pp. 370–379.

[28] Hugh Thirlway, *International Customary Law and Codification*, Leiden: Sijthoff, 1972, p. 7.

[29] Ibid., p. 78.

[30] Hugh Thirlway, *The Sources of International Law*, Oxford: Oxford University Press, 2014, p. 177.

for atrocities perpetrated against their own nationals was an idea that had first been advanced in the *démarche* of the British, French, and Russian governments in May 1915, at the height of what we now call the genocide of the Armenians. They informed the Ottoman rulers that they would be held accountable for 'these new crimes of Turkey against humanity and civilisation'.[31] The threat was made concrete in Article 230 of the Treaty of Sèvres, in August 1920,[32] but Turkey's refusal to ratify brought an end to the initiative. During 1944, the United Nations War Crimes Commission studied the possible legal framework for prosecutions of those responsible for Nazi atrocities. The Commission proposed a new category of 'war crime' in order to address atrocities committed against Jews and other minorities. The United Kingdom Foreign Office indicated that it had no objection to addressing acts perpetrated in occupied territories but felt there were 'serious difficulties' if the prosecutions were also to involve acts perpetrated within Germany itself.[33] At the London Conference in 1945, where the Nuremberg trial was planned, the American representative, Robert Jackson, made it clear that 'the internal affairs of another government are not ordinarily our business; that is to say, the way Germany treats its inhabitants, or any other country treats its inhabitants is not our affair any more than it is the affair of some other government to interpose itself in our problems'.[34]

Although the Charter of the United Nations contains important general references to human rights,[35] the task of 'putting flesh on the bare bones of the Charter'[36] was left to the Commission on Human Rights. In 1947, the Commission decided that work would progress along three strands: a manifesto or declaration, a treaty or covenant, and measures of implementation. Drafting of the manifesto or declaration progressed rapidly. The General Assembly decided to proceed immediately with its adoption, postponing completion of the other parts of the international bill of rights for what was then expected to take another year or two. On 10 December 1948, the General Assembly adopted the Universal Declaration of

31 Sharp to Secretary of State, 28 May 1915, FRUS 1915 Supplement, The World War, p. 981; Morgenthau to Secretary of State, 18 June 1915, FRUS 1915 Supplement, The World War, p. 982. The British issued a slightly different version that did not refer to 'Crimes Against Humanity and Civilisation': Press Release, 23 May 1915, TNA FO 146/4471; 'Allies Stern Warning to Turkey', *The Times*, 25 May 1915.

32 Treaty of Peace with Turkey, signed at Sèvres, 10 August 1920, [1920] TS 11, art. 230.

33 'Correspondence Between the War Crimes Commission and HM Government in London Regarding the Punishment of Crimes Committed on Religious, Racial or Political Grounds', UNWCC Doc. C.78, 15 February 1945.

34 'Minutes of Conference Session of 23 July 1945', in *Report of Robert H. Jackson, United States Representative to the International Conference on Military Trials*, Washington: US Government Printing Office, 1949, pp. 328–347, at p. 331.

35 See Farrokh Jhabvala, 'The Drafting of the Human Rights Provisions of the UN Charter', (1997) 44 *Netherlands International Law Review* 1; Louis B. Sohn, 'The Human Rights Law of the Charter', (1977) 12 *Texas International Law Journal* 129.

36 Mark Mazower, 'The Strange Triumph of Human Rights', (2004) 47 *The Historical Journal* 379, at p. 395.

Human Rights.[37] Consisting of a preamble and thirty articles, it provided succinct formulations of a catalogue of fundamental rights. The treaty and measures of implementation would wait another eighteen years. In 1966, the General Assembly approved two international covenants, the International Covenant on Civil and Political Rights and the International Covenant on Economic, Social and Cultural Rights, as well as an Optional Protocol providing for individual petitions alleging violations of civil and political rights.[38]

In June 1947, John P. Humphrey of the United Nations Secretariat prepared an initial draft bill of rights as a basis for debate within the Commission on Human Rights. His forty-eight-article text was derived from a detailed study of national constitutional provisions. A document of several hundred pages was prepared, collating the formulations of rights in the national constitutional law of the United Nations member states.[39] It did not even look at the legal culture and traditions of countries without written constitutions, in particular the United Kingdom and some other members of the Commonwealth like Canada, Australia, and New Zealand. Thus, for example, no account was taken of the English Bill of Rights. There was no suggestion that this was an attempt to codify human rights norms under international law. The idea that such norms existed would have been hotly contested. To the extent that any source of international law was involved, the Secretariat draft of the Universal Declaration might be said to have been influenced by 'general principles of law'.[40]

Today, it would not be uncommon in negotiations of an international treaty, particularly one dealing with human rights, for delegates to refer to customary international law. But there were virtually no such references during the drafting of the Universal Declaration of Human Rights in 1946, 1947, and 1948. In the Third Committee of the General Assembly the Belgian delegate, Fernand Dehousse, made a formal statement 'on the Legal Significance of the Declaration'. He said that some of the principles in the Universal Declaration 'would only repeat rules already in the customary law of nations and were, in consequence, recognised in unwritten international law. The act of inscribing them in an international declaration could not deprive these rules of the binding character they already possessed'. Although without any specification, he explained that '[o]ther principles which would be included in the declaration did not belong to customary international

[37] Universal Declaration of Human Rights, A/RES/217 (III).

[38] International Covenant on Economic, Social and Cultural Rights, International Covenant on Civil and Political Rights and Optional Protocol to the International Covenant on Civil and Political Rights, A/RES/2200 (XXI).

[39] Drafting Committee on an International Bill of Human Rights, International Bill of Rights Documented Outline, E/CN.4/AC.1/3/Add.1.

[40] Michael O'Boyle and Michelle Lafferty, 'General Principles and Constitutions as Sources of Human Rights Law', in Dinah Shelton, ed., *The Oxford Handbook of International Human Rights Law*, Oxford: Oxford University Press, 2013, pp. 194–221, at p. 198.

law and the fact of their inclusion in an international declaration would certainly not make them obligatory'.[41]

The only other mention of customary law during the drafting of the Universal Declaration related to the principle of legality and the non-retroactivity of criminal law. The concern was not whether some or all of the norms in the Declaration were customary in nature but rather whether such a thing as international crimes could be said to exist. Dehousse of Belgium stated: 'International law included an extremely important customary section which it was essential to take into account.'[42] Radevanovic of Yugoslavia said that 'from the penal point of view, international law had not been codified; it was based on custom'.[43] Finally, René Cassin of France 'confirmed that his delegation understood by "international law", positive law, both customary and written'.[44]

Shortly after the adoption of the Declaration, Hersch Lauterpacht was critical of Dehousse's comments on its legal significance, insisting that prior to adoption of the Charter of the United Nations, 'apart from the precarious doctrine of humanitarian intervention, international law considered these matters to be within the exclusive domestic jurisdiction of the state'.[45] Lauterpacht examined various theories of the legal status of the Declaration, notably the argument that it codified 'general principles of law' and that it was an authoritative interpretation of the Charter of the United Nations. He made only a single, and exceedingly dismissive, reference to customary international law as a possible basis for attributing legal force to the Universal Declaration: 'The student of international law may find it difficult to subscribe to the view that it is a rule of customary international law that, to mention some of the least controversial pronouncements of the Declaration, "everyone has the right to life, liberty and security of person" (Art. 3 of the Declaration); or that "no one shall be held in slavery or servitude" (Art. 4); or that "no one shall be subjected to torture or to cruel, inhuman, or degrading treatment or punishment" (Art. 5).'[46] Lauterpacht also rejected the thesis that the provisions of the Universal Declaration might constitute binding legal rules as 'general principles of law recognised by civilised nations', which is the formulation in Article 38(1)(c) of the Statute of the International Court of Justice. He conceded that '[t]he Declaration

[41] Summary Record of the hundred and eighth meeting [of the Third Committee of the General Assembly], 20 October 1948, *Official Records of the General Assembly*, Third Session, 1948, p. 200.

[42] Summary Record of the hundred and sixteenth meeting [of the Third Committee of the General Assembly], 29 October 1948, *Official Records of the General Assembly*, Third Session, 1948, p. 270.

[43] Ibid., p. 272.

[44] Ibid., p. 275.

[45] Hersch Lauterpacht, 'The Universal Declaration of Human Rights', (1948) 25 *British Yearbook of International Law* 354, at p. 365. Also: Hersch Lauterpacht, *International Law and Human Rights*, London: Stevens and Sons, 1950, p. 407.

[46] Hersch Lauterpacht, 'The Universal Declaration of Human Rights', (1948) 25 *British Yearbook of International Law* 354, pp. 364–365.

gives expression to what, in the fullness of time, ought to become principles of law generally recognised and acted upon by States Members of the United Nations.'[47]

Writing decades later, John Humphrey, who headed the Secretariat of the Commission on Human Rights for two decades starting in 1947, claimed that from the time of its adoption he subscribed to the view that the Universal Declaration of Human Rights constituted a codification of customary law, but he added that he could not 'remember anyone in 1948 who shared my views.'[48] Nor is there any evidence of anyone else remembering that Humphrey held the view. 'That substantial portions of the Universal Declaration of Human Rights, adopted in 1948, eventually might become customary international law, and therefore binding on all states, was beyond the comprehension and vision of all but a few of the participants,'[49] wrote Richard Lillich nearly fifty years after the Declaration's adoption.

There was certainly a debate in 1948 about the legal status of the Declaration but, according to the record, apart from the isolated comment by the Belgian delegate cited above, claims about customary law did not figure in the conversations. Many delegations felt deceived that the Declaration was to proceed to adoption without an accompanying binding treaty, for which the text was far from ready. They were therefore somewhat contemptuous of the Declaration, treating it as a pale and inadequate substitute for the Covenant that they had been promised. One of the most eloquent voices for this view was Hersch Lauterpacht. He said bluntly that '[n]ot being a legal instrument, the Declaration would appear to be outside international law. Its provisions cannot properly be the subject-matter of legal interpretation.'[50] Humphrey was furious with Lauterpacht, but he wrote much later that it was 'only fair' to note that Lauterpacht's comments were made 'shortly after the adoption of the Declaration, before it began to have any real impact and before the subtle processes began to work which would make it part of the customary law of nations.'[51]

More than a decade after the Declaration's adoption, Egon Schwelb, then Deputy Director of the Division of Human Rights of the United Nations Secretariat, spoke at the annual meeting of the American Society of International Law on the influence of the Universal Declaration in national and international law. He said 'that while the substance of most, though by no means all, of the provisions of the Declaration may well be said to be identical with general principles of law recognised by civilised nations, the proposition that the Declaration is a codification of

[47] Hersch Lauterpacht, *International Law and Human Rights*, London: Stevens and Sons, 1950, p. 408.

[48] John P. Humphrey, *Human Rights and the United Nations: A Great Adventure*, Dobbs Ferry, NY: Transnational Publishers, 1984, p. 65.

[49] Richard Lillich, 'The Growing Importance of Customary International Human Rights Law', (1996) 25 *Georgia Journal of International and Comparative Law* 1, at p. 1.

[50] Hersch Lauterpacht, 'The Universal Declaration of Human Rights', (1948) 25 *British Yearbook of International Law* 354, at p. 369. Along similar lines, Josef L. Kunz, 'The United Nations Declaration of Human Rights', (1949) 43 *American Journal of International Law* 316, at p. 321: 'it is not law'.

[51] John P. Humphrey, *Human Rights and the United Nations: A Great Adventure*, Dobbs Ferry, NY: Transnational Publishers, 1984, p. 74.

these general principles is not warranted'.[52] Schwelb provided many compelling examples of the influence of the Declaration, citing its role in treaty-making and in constitutional law, but he did not mention customary international law. Schwelb appeared to discount any claim to a relationship of the Universal Declaration with customary international law.

The inescapable conclusion is that in 1948, when the Universal Declaration of Human Rights was adopted, there was little or no customary international law of human rights. It even seems audacious to contend that it was 'emerging' or 'crystallising'. Rather, the Universal Declaration launched a process that proceeded along two strands: the detailed codification of international human rights law in the many treaties and other instruments that it spawned directly or indirectly, and the gradual and less tangible appearance of state practice and *opinio juris* leading, some years later, to the establishment of a corpus worthy of being described as customary international law.

B. The debate about customary human rights law emerges

It was only in the mid-1960s that judges, academic lawyers, and activists began to speak of the customary law of human rights. When the Universal Declaration was adopted by the General Assembly, in 1948, there was some expectation that the Covenant would arrive a year or perhaps two later. But the work dragged on. In 1951, the General Assembly decided to split the draft Covenant, whose content closely tracked the Universal Declaration, into two separate instruments, based upon the nature of the rights that they contained. In 1954, the Commission on Human Rights submitted texts of the draft covenants on civil and political rights and on economic, social, and cultural rights for consideration by the General Assembly. The negotiations continued for more than a decade and the two Covenants were only adopted in 1966. It took another ten years before the thirty-five ratifications necessary for their entry into force were obtained.

There was understandable frustration about the pace of adoption and entry into force of these missing components of the international bill of rights. This provoked consideration of other pathways to the development of human rights law, stimulating interest in the potential of customary international law. In 1965, Humphrey Waldock, the British judge at the European Court of Human Rights and later at the International Court of Justice, wrote that the Universal Declaration of Human Rights was clothed 'in the character of customary international law'.[53] Nobel Peace

52 Egon Schwelb, 'The Influence of the Universal Declaration of Human Rights on International and National Law', (1959) 53 *Proceedings of the American Society of International Law* 217, at p. 218.

53 Humphrey Waldock, 'Human Rights in Contemporary International Law and the Significance of the European Convention', (1965) 11 *International and Comparative Law Quarterly Supplementary Publication* 1, p. 15.

Prize laureate Seán MacBride wrote in the *UNESCO Courier*, on the twentieth anniversary of the adoption of the Universal Declaration, that 'there is a growing view among international lawyers that some of its provisions, which are justiciable, now form part of customary international law ... The Universal Declaration does now represent in written form the basis for the law of nations, the laws of humanity and the dictates of the public conscience as accepted in the twentieth century.'[54] The language was borrowed from the preambles of the two Hague Conventions on the laws and customs of war. The same year, a conference of non-governmental organisations adopted the 'Montreal Statement', affirming that the 'Universal Declaration of Human Rights ... has over the years become part of customary international law'.[55] In the same vein, but without an explicit claim about customary international law, the Declaration of Tehran, adopted by the 1968 International Conference on Human Rights, said that the Universal Declaration 'constitutes an obligation for members of the international community'.[56]

Recognition that human rights had entered the domain of customary international law received important judicial recognition in 1966 from Judge Kōtarō Tanaka of the International Court of Justice. Referring to Article 38(1)(b) of the Statute of the Court, Judge Tanaka said although customary law had traditionally developed as part of an historical process over a long period of time, the establishment of the League of Nations and the United Nations had brought changes. 'In the contemporary age of highly developed techniques of communication and information, the formation of a custom through the medium of international organisations is greatly facilitated and accelerated; the establishment of such a custom would require no more than one generation or even far less than that', he wrote.[57] Judge Tanaka said that '[t]he method of the generation of customary international law is in the stage of transformation from being an individualistic process to being a collectivistic process'.[58] He concluded that a norm prohibiting racial discrimination had emerged through an 'accumulation of authoritative pronouncements' in the form of resolutions, trust territory agreements, and above all the Universal Declaration of Human Rights.

In 1976, John Humphrey wrote that '[i]n the more than a quarter of a century since its adoption, however, the Declaration has been invoked so many times both within and without the United Nations that lawyers now are saying that, whatever the intention of its authors may have been, the Declaration is

[54] Seán MacBride, 'The New Frontiers of International Law', *UNESCO Courier*, January 1968, p. 26.

[55] 'Montreal Statement of the Assembly for Human Rights', (1968) 9 *Journal of the International Commission of Jurists* 94, at p. 95.

[56] Final Act of the International Conference on Human Rights, Tehran, 22 April to 13 May 1968, A/CONF.32/41, para. 2.

[57] *South West Africa, Second Phase, Judgment, ICJ Reports 1966*, Dissenting opinion of Judge Tanaka, p. 293.

[58] Ibid., p. 294.

now part of the customary law of nations and therefore is binding on all states'.[59] Humphrey added, in a footnote: 'This claim is applicable only to those provisions that are justiciable. Philosophical assertions, such as those set forth in article 1, are not justiciable.'[60] Louis Sohn described the Declaration as 'a binding instrument in its own right'.[61] In 1980, Myres McDougal, Harold Lasswell, and Lung-chu Chen discussed 'the evolution of the Universal Declaration of Human Rights from its first status as mere common aspiration to its present wide acceptance as authoritative legal requirement',[62] concluding that it constituted 'established customary international law, having the attributes of *jus cogens* and constituting the heart of a global bill of rights'.[63] Writing in 1982, although he would later adjust his position,[64] Philip Alston said there was 'a large and growing body of evidence' favouring the claim that at least the first twenty-one articles of the Declaration were part of customary law.[65] Oscar Schachter, without invoking the Declaration as such, described the 'hard core' of human rights as being part of customary international law.[66] Frederic L. Kirgis wrote that 'the Universal Declaration of Human Rights has come to be regarded as an authoritative articulation of customary international law, at least with respect to the most fundamental human rights, no matter how widespread or persistent the nonconforming state conduct may be'.[67] In the early 1990s, several distinguished Scandinavian scholars stated that 'plentiful evidence of general and specific practice by the international community and its components has led several statesmen and scholars to conclude that the UDHR constitutes binding law as international custom in accordance with article 38 of the Statute of the International Court of Justice'. They acknowledged that other writers had suggested 'that at least many of the rights spelled out in the UDHR have emerged as rules of customary law'.[68] And a decade later,

[59] John P. Humphrey, 'The International Bill of Rights: Scope and Implementation', (1976) 17 *William and Mary Law Review* 527, at p. 529 (internal references omitted).

[60] Ibid., fn. 13.

[61] Louis B. Sohn, 'The Human Rights Law of the Charter', (1977) 12 *Texas International Law Journal* 129, at p. 133. See also: Louis B. Sohn, 'John A. Sibley Lecture: The Shaping of International Law', (1978) 8 *Georgia Journal of International and Comparative Law* 1, at pp. 18–22; Louis B. Sohn, 'The New International Law: Protection of the Rights of Individuals Rather than States', (1982) 32 *American University Law Review* 1, at p. 17.

[62] Myres S. McDougal, Harold Lasswell, and Lung-Chu Chen, *Human Rights and World Public Order*, New Haven: Yale University Press, 1980, p. 272.

[63] Ibid., p. 274.

[64] A '*volte face*' that Richard Lillich described as 'passing strange': Richard Lillich, 'The Growing Importance of Customary International Human Rights Law', (1996) 25 *Georgia Journal of International and Comparative Law* 1, at p. 11, fn. 61.

[65] Philip Alston, 'The Universal Declaration at 35: Western and Passée or Alive and Universal', (1982) 31 *ICJ Review* 60, at p. 69.

[66] Oscar Schachter, 'International Law in Theory and Practice: General Course in Public International Law', (1982) 178-V *Receuil des cours* 21, at pp. 333–342.

[67] Frederic L. Kirgis, 'Custom on a Sliding Scale', (1987) 81 *American Journal of International Law* 146, 147–148.

[68] 'Introduction', in Asbjørn Eide, Gudmunder Alfredsson, Göran Melander, Lars Adam Rejof, and Allan Rosas, eds., *The Universal Declaration of Human Rights: A Commentary*, Oslo: Scandinavian

in the early 2000s, Manfred Nowak wrote of the Universal Declaration that '[n]o doubt some of its provisions, such as the prohibition of torture and slavery, today enjoy the status of customary international law, yet despite certain legal opinions to the contrary, it is still doubtful whether the Declaration as a whole can be considered as having achieved this status'.[69]

C. American lawyers and alien torts

In the early 1980s, creative human rights lawyers in the United States invoked an ancient and essentially dormant piece of legislation, the Alien Torts Claims Act or the Alien Tort Statute, adopted in the aftermath of the Revolutionary War. The Statute authorises a civil action by an alien for a tort 'committed in violation of the law of nations'. At the time, the United States had a dismal record of ratification of human rights conventions, so there was little in the way of treaties to which to turn as a source of applicable international law. Customary international law provided an answer, to the extent that its existence could be demonstrated and its content ascertained. The United States Court of Appeals for the Second Circuit upheld the admissibility of a claim based upon the prohibition of state-sponsored torture under customary international law: 'Having examined the sources from which customary international law is derived the usage of nations, judicial opinions and the works of jurists we conclude that official torture is now prohibited by the law of nations'.[70] The Court noted that '[t]his prohibition has become part of customary international law, as evidenced and defined by the Universal Declaration of Human Rights'.[71] Subsequently, cases decided under the Alien Tort Claims Statute by American courts found that other human rights violations were also prohibited by the law of nations including cruel, inhuman, or degrading treatment,[72] arbitrary detention,[73] summary execution or murder,[74] enforced disappearance,[75] and genocide.[76] But United States courts also declined to make similar findings

University Press, 1992, pp. 7–8. Along the same lines: 'Introduction', in Gudmunder Alfredsson and Asbjørn Eide, eds., *The Universal Declaration of Human Rights, A Common Standard of Achievement*, The Hague/Boston/London: Martinus Nijhoff, 1999, pp. xxxi–xxxii.

[69] Manfred Nowak, *Introduction to the International Human Rights Regime*, Leiden/Boston: Martinus Nijhoff, 2003, p. 76.

[70] *Filártiga v. Peña-Irala*, 630 F.2d 876, 885 (2d Cir. 1980) (internal references omitted).

[71] Ibid.

[72] *Xuncax v. Gramajo*, 886 F.Supp. 162, 185–189 (D. Mass. 1995).

[73] *Fernandez v. Wilkinson*, 505 F.Supp. 787, 798 (D. Kan. 1980).

[74] *Forti v. Suarez-Mason*, 672 F.Supp. 1531, 1542 (N.D. Cal. 1987).

[75] *Forti v. Suarez-Mason*, 694 F.Supp. 707, 709–711 (N.D. Cal. 1988).

[76] *Xuncax v. Gramajo*, 886 F.Supp. 162, 187, n. 35 (D. Mass. 1995).

with respect to other human rights, such as the right to education,[77] the right to property,[78] and freedom of speech.[79]

In 1987, the American Law Institute, a prestigious body composed of senior lawyers and judges, addressed the customary international law of human rights in its Restatement on foreign relations law. The Restatements of the American Law Institute are authoritative codifications intended to reflect an expert consensus on the state of the law within the United States. The Restatement on the subject of the 'Customary Law of Human Rights' is frequently referred to in the literature. It reads as follows:

> ***§702. Customary International Law of Human Rights***
> A state violates international law if, as a matter of state policy, it practices, encourages or condones
> (a) genocide,
> (b) slavery or slave trade,
> (c) the murder or causing the disappearance of individuals,
> (d) torture or other cruel, inhuman, or degrading treatment or punishment,
> (e) prolonged arbitrary detention,
> (f) systematic racial discrimination or
> (g) a consistent pattern of gross violations of internationally recognised human rights.[80]

This short text is accompanied by a lengthy Comment, by Reporter's Notes, and by short summaries of relevant cases decided by the courts of the United States. The Comment explains that the Restatement recognises 'only those human rights whose status as customary law is generally accepted (as of 1987) and whose scope and content are generally agreed. The list is not necessarily complete, and is not closed: human rights not listed in this section may have achieved the status of customary law, and some rights might achieve that status in the future.'

The Reporter's Notes explain that it applies to the human rights violations indicated, if the violations are state policy. 'This view is accepted by virtually all states; with the exception of the Republic of South Africa in respect of apartheid, no state claims the right to commit the practices set forth in this section as state policy, and few, if any, would deny that they are violations of international law', the Reporter's Notes state. 'Other rights may already have become customary law and international law may develop to include additional rights. It has been argued that

[77] *In re Alien Children Educ. Litig.*, 501 F.Supp. 544, 596 (S.D. Tex. 1980), *aff'd unreported memo.*, (5th Cir. 1981), *affid sub nom. Plyer v. Doe*, 457 US 202 (1982).
[78] *De Sanchez v. Banco Central de Nicaragua*, 770 F.2d 1385, 1397 (5th Cir. 1985).
[79] *Guinto v. Marcos*, 654 F. Supp. 276, 280 (S.D. Cal. 1986).
[80] Restatement (Third) of the Foreign Relations Law of the United States, St. Paul, MN: American Law Institute, 1987, para. 702.

customary international law is already more comprehensive than here indicated and forbids violation of any of the rights set forth in the Universal Declaration.'[81]

The final category in the list of the Restatement, which refers very broadly to 'internationally recognised human rights', contemplates violations of customary law even if the practice is not consistent or not part of a pattern, but only committed singly or sporadically, according to the Comment. However, the violation must also be 'particularly shocking'. It explains that

> [a]ll of the rights proclaimed in the Universal Declaration and protected by the principal International Covenants are internationally recognised human rights, but some rights are fundamental and intrinsic to human dignity. Consistent patterns of violation of such rights as state policy may be deemed 'gross' *ipso facto*. These include, for example, systematic harassment, invasions of the privacy of the home, arbitrary arrest and detention (even if not prolonged); denial of fair trial in criminal cases; grossly disproportionate punishment; denial of freedom to leave a country; denial of the right to return to one's country; mass uprooting of a country's population; denial of freedom of conscience and religion; denial of personality before the law; denial of basic privacy such as the right to marry and raise a family; and invidious racial or religious discrimination.[82]

The Comment also notes that with the exception of paragraph (g), all of the norms in the list are also peremptory (*jus cogens*).[83] Furthermore, violations are *erga omnes*, thereby permitting any State to invoke 'the ordinary remedies available to a state when its rights under customary law are violated'.[84]

In an academic publication, the chief reporter for the Restatement, Louis Henkin, wrote that it 'supports the non-conventional human rights law it restates by invoking the traditional indicia of traditional customary law—state practice with a sense of legal obligation'. But Henkin admitted that 'the state practice supporting non-conventional human rights law looks different, is different ...'.[85] Henkin said that 'international non-conventional human rights law is ... not the result of practice but the product of common consensus from which few dare dissent ...'.[86]

Three decades later, the American Law Institute revised parts of the Restatement but did not deal with the customary law of human rights.[87] Commentators have

[81] Ibid., Reporter's Notes, para. 1.
[82] Ibid., Comment, para. m.
[83] Ibid., para. n.
[84] Ibid., para. o.
[85] Louis Henkin, 'Human Rights and State "Sovereignty"', (1995/96) 25 *Georgia Journal of International and Comparative Law* 31, at p. 38.
[86] Ibid.
[87] Restatement (Fourth) of the Foreign Relations Law of the United States, St. Paul, MN: American Law Institute, 2018.

noted that the Fourth Restatement generally takes 'a more cautious approach to restating rules of customary international law'.[88]

D. Theodor Meron's study of customary law

Shortly after adoption of the Restatement, Professor Theodor Meron published his seminal study, *Human Rights and Humanitarian Norms as Customary Law*.[89] Meron first focussed on international humanitarian law. He noted the near-universal acceptance of the four Geneva Conventions of 1949 as well as the quite ancient manifestations of some of the laws and customs of war and their recognition in the Hague Conventions of 1899 and 1907. The same type of observation could not be made about international human rights law, where the main instruments had been ratified by far fewer States, he observed.[90] Meron listed the nine human rights treaties that had been adopted within the United Nations system. At the time, several important United Nations human rights instruments that are now widely ratified had not even been adopted. For example, the Convention on the Rights of the Child, adopted in 1989 and in force since 1990, now has 196 States Parties. The Convention on the Rights of Persons with Disabilities, adopted in 2006 and in force since 2008, has 182 ratifications and accessions.

Professor Meron thought the list of customary norms proposed in the Restatement was 'somewhat too cautious'.[91] He began his discussion with the words '[a]mong other customary human rights, or general principles of law, I would include . . .', as if customary law and general principles were synonymous or, at any rate, indistinguishable. Meron included the prohibition of retroactive criminal prosecution as a customary norm, justifying this with the fact that it is non-derogable in the International Covenant on Civil and Political Rights, the American Convention on Human Rights, and the European Convention of Human Rights.[92] The rationale, apparently, is that non-derogability implies some special, intangible status within a hierarchy of human rights. But the non-derogability of certain rights in a treaty

[88] William S. Dodge, 'Jurisdiction, State Immunity, and Judgments in the Restatement (Fourth) of US Foreign Relations Law', (2020) 19 *Chinese Journal of International Law* 101, para. 8.

[89] Theodor Meron, *Human Rights and Humanitarian Norms as Customary Law*, Oxford: Clarendon Press, 1989.

[90] Ibid., p. 79.

[91] Ibid., p. 95. Some years later, Professor Louis Henkin, who was the rapporteur for the Restatement, confirmed that he would be prepared to include the right to property, freedom from gender discrimination, the right to personal autonomy, and the right to live in a democratic society. See Richard Lillich, 'The Growing Importance of Customary International Human Rights Law', (1996) 25 *Georgia Journal of International and Comparative Law* 1, at p. 7, fn. 43.

[92] Theodor Meron, *Human Rights and Humanitarian Norms as Customary Law*, Oxford: Clarendon Press, 1989, p. 95.

may have other explanations, as the Human Rights Committee has pointed out.[93] Meron also included 'the right of self-determination'. He added that he would also include the right to humane treatment of detainees, citing in support a General Comment of the Human Rights Committee that described '[t]he humane treatment and the respect for the dignity of all persons deprived of their liberty [as] a basic standard of universal application'.[94]

Professor Meron said he believed 'at least the core of a number of the due process guarantees stated in Article 14 of the Covenant have a strong claim to customary law status', referring specifically to the right to be tried by a competent, independent, and impartial tribunal established by law; the presumption of innocence; the right not to be compelled to testify against oneself or to confess guilt; the right to be present at trial and to defence in person or through legal assistance of one's choosing; the right to examine witnesses; and to have conviction and sentence reviewed by a higher tribunal.[95] He said the principle *ne bis in idem* could be regarded as 'emerging customary law', but without explanation as to why he was more equivocal than with the other fair trial rights. Meron cited 'the rapid, continued development of international human rights', saying it was 'undergoing a stage of continuing evolution', and he criticised 'the static picture of human rights as reflected by the Restatement. Many other rights will be added in the course of time.'[96]

Meron discussed the work of some of the leading scholars as well as the views of experts within the United Nations system who had supported the contention that some provisions of the Universal Declaration of Human Rights could be deemed binding customary international law. He explained that 'an attempt to endow customary law status instantly upon norms approved by consensus or near-consensus at international conferences raises serious concerns'. It was 'far from certain' that participating States intended to be bound by such manifestations, noting that they might be motivated by other considerations. Moreover, those making the declarations or supporting the consensus at diplomatic gatherings might well be without authority to bind the State.[97] Meron turned briefly to 'general principles of law recognised by civilised nations', noting the importance in international human rights law of questions of due process and the administration of justice. In this area, national legislation and judicial activity could provide useful indications. He expressed surprise that greater attention had not be devoted to general principles of law, which is the third source listed in Article 38 of the Statute of the International

[93] General Comment 24, Issues relating to reservations made upon ratification or accession to the Covenant or the Optional Protocols thereto, or in relation to declarations under art. 41 of the Covenant, CCPR/C/21/Rev.1/Add.6, para. 10.

[94] Theodor Meron, *Human Rights and Humanitarian Norms as Customary Law*, Oxford: Clarendon Press, 1989, p. 95.

[95] Ibid., pp. 96–97.

[96] Ibid., p. 99.

[97] Ibid., pp. 86–88.

Court of Justice, 'as a method for obtaining greater legal recognition for the principles of the Universal Declaration and other human rights instruments'.[98] He predicted that the distinction between customary law and general principles 'will gradually become blurred'.[99] Regardless of the extent of ratification, Meron saw difficulty in an assumption that human rights conventions constituted authoritative codifications of customary law. He noted the difficulty in identifying so-called codification treaties, explaining that in practice 'treaties can only seldom be categorised as either codifying existing law, crystallising the emergent law, generating new rules of customary law, or merely creating conventional obligations. A normative multilateral treaty characteristically mixes provisions falling into each of these categories.'[100]

The early human rights treaties could not easily be described as codifying custom, he said, '[g]iven the relatively recent birth of international human rights as positive law for the international community'.[101] An exception, said Professor Meron, was the Convention on the Prevention and Punishment of the Crime of Genocide, adopted by the United Nations General Assembly in 1948. By contrast, 'most human rights instruments state largely new or conventional norms'.[102] He cited the 1977 report of the International Law Commission on State responsibility: '[W]ithout in any way disregarding the existence of a few customary international rules on the subject, and without ruling out the possibility—even the likelihood—that such rules will increase in number, we are bound to conclude that, today, the international obligations of the State in regard to the treatment of its own nationals are almost exclusively of a conventional nature . . .'.[103] But these words of the International Law Commission were '[e]xcessive even in 1977' and were 'becoming less and less true', he said. Acceptance of norms in human rights treaties, especially by non-party States, was generating new customary rules. Moreover, '[n]ew human rights instruments have been adopted that already embody certain customary rules', wrote Meron, although without providing greater specificity. He pointed to the repetition of certain norms in human rights instruments as 'an important articular of state practice [that] may serve as evidence of customary international law'.[104]

Professor Meron endorsed the list of evidentiary sources for the identification of customary international law proposed in the Restatement of the American Law Institute. He also agreed with Oscar Schachter, who had referred to the importance of 'actual state practice and the intensity and depth of third-party condemnations of

[98] Ibid., p. 88.
[99] Ibid., p. 89.
[100] Ibid., p. 90.
[101] Ibid., p. 91.
[102] Ibid.
[103] Ibid., p. 92, citing, *Yearbook . . . 1977*, Vol. II (Part 2), p. 46.
[104] Ibid., p. 92.

violations'.[105] He said that his own 'preferred indicators' were 'the degree to which a statement of a particular right in one human rights instrument, especially a human rights treaty, has been repeated in other human rights instruments, and second, the confirmation of the right in national practice, primarily through the incorporation of the right in national laws'.[106] On the negative side of the balance, Meron said 'the degree to which a particular right is subject to limitations (clawback clauses) and the extent of contrary practice' needed to be taken into account.[107] Meron insisted that '[e]mpiric studies of state practice are therefore of the highest importance in establishing whether a particular right has matured into customary law'. He said that 'rights which are most crucial to the protection of human dignity and of universally accepted values of humanity, and whose violation triggers broad condemnation by the international community, will require a lesser amount of confirmatory evidence'.[108]

E. Critics of the American school

Reviewing Theodor Meron's book in the *Michigan Journal of International Law*, Martti Koskenniemi remarked that it 'is more intended to show American lawyers how to plead when pressing a human rights case in American courts than to reveal much about international law'.[109] He noted the virtual absence of discussion of the customary status attached to economic, social, and cultural rights.[110] Koskenniemi thought that 'the difficulty of justifying conceptions of natural justice in modern society' had led some international lawyers 'to relegate into "customs" all those important norms that cannot be supported by treaties. In this way, they might avoid arguing from an essentially naturalistic—and thus suspect—position.' Custom was less difficult to verify and more justifiable to apply than abstract maxims of international justice, he thought. One alternative approach was the category of general principles of law, but Koskenniemi said it had been neglected by the International Court of Justice. He acknowledged that Meron had contemplated but not pursued the possibility of fitting human rights within general principles of law rather than custom.[111]

Koskenniemi did not quarrel much with Meron's attempt to impose certain legal norms on States in the absence of treaty obligations but he seemed unimpressed with the methodology. Meron was searching for 'irreproachable legal methods' in

105 Ibid., p. 93.
106 Ibid., p. 94.
107 Ibid.
108 Ibid.
109 Martti Koskiennemi, 'The Pull of the Mainstream', (1990) 88 *Michigan Law Review* 1946, at p. 1951.
110 Ibid., p. 1958.
111 Ibid., pp. 1947–1948.

a search for custom, and this required him to demonstrate the two elements that are required by Article 38(1)(b) of the Statute of the International Court of Justice, *opinio juris* and practice. 'His hope was that these would provide a noncontroversial litmus test that would finally convince everyone of the certainty of his conclusions', wrote Koskenniemi.[112] The test was 'useless', said Koskenniemi, because discerning the behaviour or will of States was complex and the exercise could 'usually allow one to argue either way'. But in any case, he said, 'it is really our certainty that genocide or torture is illegal that allows us to understand state behaviour and accept or rejects its legal message, not state behaviour itself that allows us to understand that these practices are prohibited by law'.[113] Koskenniemi considered that Meron's conclusions were 'usually intuitively acceptable', but not because of his demonstration of State practice, rather because they, 'for the most part, appear reasonable and coincide with our moral imagination'.[114]

Bruno Simma and Philip Alston were also critical of Meron's book, which they understood to be a detailed scholarly justification for the Restatement of the American Law Institute. Both were products of the United States 'customary-law-of-human rights school'.[115] Meron offered an 'elaborate and carefully-reasoned support for the Restatement view without challenging in any significant way its theoretical foundation', they wrote.[116] Simma and Alston reasoned that it was better to look to domestic legislation for evidence of commitment to international human rights norms. This would fall under general principles of law rather than under custom. They acknowledged that 'general principles have not fared too well as a source of international law', attributing this to their 'natural law flavour and the uncertainties surrounding the ways in which they are to be established and applied'.[117] The general principles of law category seem to have appealed to them because it did not require evidence of practice. As Simma and Alston explained, 'in the development of human rights law principles have always preceded practice'.[118]

Simma and Alston observed the 'remarkable correlation between the norms identified as customary rules, and the range of rights which has been incorporated into the US Bill of Rights'.[119] It was, they said, a form of 'normative chauvinism, albeit of an unintentional or sub-conscious variety'.[120] Alston and Simma said the end result of the Restatement's analysis was 'suspiciously convenient' because '[t]he great majority of rights considered important under U.S. law, as well as virtually

[112] Ibid., p. 1952.
[113] Ibid.
[114] Ibid., p. 1953.
[115] Bruno Simma and Philip Alston, 'The Sources of Human Rights Law: Custom, Jus Cogens, and General Principles', (1992) 12 *Australian Yearbook of International Law* 82, at p. 106.
[116] Ibid., p. 85.
[117] Ibid., p. 107.
[118] Ibid.
[119] Ibid., p. 94.
[120] Ibid.

every right which recent US governments have been prepared to criticise other governments for violation, are held to be part of customary international law. By contrast, none of the rights which the US fails to recognise in its domestic law, is included.'[121] Simma and Alston asked 'whether any theory of human rights law which singles out race but not gender discrimination, which condemns arbitrary imprisonment but not death by starvation, and which finds no place for a right of access to primary health care is not flawed in terms both of the theory of human rights and of United Nations doctrine'.[122] They believed the emphasis on customary international law by American lawyers could be explained by the reluctance of the Government of the United States to ratify international human rights treaties.[123]

Surveying the spectrum of approaches, Simma and Alston considered that the American Law Institute and Theodor Meron were to be found in the middle, recognising customary human rights norms in principle, but bestowing the honour on a relatively short list. This was the 'mainstream position', favoured in the United States, which 'satisfies its appetite by resorting to a progressive, streamlined theory of customary law, more or less stripped of the traditional practice requirement, and through this dubious operation is able to find a customary law of human rights'. A more extreme position took the view that most or all of the Universal Declaration of Human Rights could be considered customary law. Describing its proponents as 'wishful thinkers', Simma and Alston labelled this the 'customary-law-of-human rights school',[124] a sobriquet its members seem to have graciously accepted.[125] Finally, on the other extreme, was 'an embattled group of writers' who are unable to conclude that there exist such customary norms 'in a large part of a field so torn by ideology and politics, and so replete with hypocrisy, double standards and second thoughts'.[126] In this camp, they pointed to Antonio Cassese, 'an author certainly not to be accused of avoiding pronounced humanitarian stands', who remained firm that 'in formal terms, [the Universal Declaration] is not legally binding, but possesses only moral and political force'.[127] Some years earlier, Cassese had written that '... very few rules on human rights have acquired universal validity (*i.e.* have become customary law). Most have remained mere treaty rules, with all the inherent limitations that this entails ...'.[128] Eventually, Cassese would become much more comfortable making pronouncements about customary international law.

[121] Ibid., p. 95.

[122] Ibid. See also Hilary Charlesworth and Christine Chinkin, 'The Gender of Jus Cogens', (1993) 15 *Human Rights Quarterly* 63, at pp. 68–69.

[123] Bruno Simma and Philip Alston, 'The Sources of Human Rights Law: Custom, Jus Cogens, and General Principles', (1992) 12 *Australian Yearbook of International Law* 82, at p. 87.

[124] Ibid., p. 106.

[125] Richard Lillich, 'The Growing Importance of Customary International Human Rights Law', (1996) 25 *Georgia Journal of International and Comparative Law* 1, at p. 30.

[126] Bruno Simma and Philip Alston, 'The Sources of Human Rights Law: Custom, Jus Cogens, and General Principles', (1992) 12 *Australian Yearbook of International Law* 82, at p. 85.

[127] Ibid., p. 85, citing Antonio Cassese, *International Law in a Divided World*, Oxford: Oxford University Press, 1986, p. 299.

[128] Antonio Cassese, *Human Rights in a Changing World*, Cambridge: Polity, 1990, p. 165.

The critique by Simma and Alston was answered in a symposium held at the University of Georgia in 1994 and published subsequently in the *Georgia Journal of International and Comparative Law*. One of its organisers, Richard Lillich, explained in his opening remarks that 'the Simma–Alston critique comes as something of a surprise to anyone familiar with their past writings'.[129] Lillich explained that Simma and Alston's approach to customary international law emphasised past practice rather than the *opinio juris*, including that which does not necessarily involve interaction with other States. He noted their preference for general principles of international law, saying that this 'sidesteps the problems associated with proving customary international law'.[130] Lillich continued: 'It is true, of course, that general principles may play a role in the human rights area; this role, however, traditionally has been regarded as one of "promoting the passage of human rights into customary law", not of metamorphosing them into free-standing, independent rules of international law.'[131] Lillich said that the consensus of the Georgia conference rejected the Simma–Alston critique. Rather, 'along with the Restatement, it looks not only to traditional but also to new sources of state practice and new expressions of opinio juris to determine and develop the content and contours of the emerging customary international law of human rights'.[132]

Several other participants in the symposium were also very critical of Simma and Alston. Joan Fitzpatrick observed that Simma and Alston saw 'a peculiar American pathology at work in over-generous claims for the existence of customary human rights norms by both scholars and litigants in recent years'.[133] The symposium also included a seminal article by Hurst Hannum on the domestic implementation of the Universal Declaration of Human Rights.[134] Hannum had been the rapporteur of the International Law Association's study on the status of the Universal Declaration. Presented to the Association's Buenos Aires Conference, also held in 1994, the Committee's report concluded that 'there would seem to be little argument that many provisions of the Declaration today do reflect customary international law'.[135]

[129] Richard B. Lillich, 'The Growing Importance of Customary International Human Rights Law', (1995/96) 25 *Georgia Journal of International and Comparative Law* 1, at p. 11.

[130] Ibid., p. 15.

[131] Ibid., p. 16. The internal citation is to Theodor Meron, *Human Rights and Humanitarian Norms as Customary Law*, Oxford: Clarendon Press, 1989, p. 88.

[132] Richard B. Lillich, 'The Growing Importance of Customary International Human Rights Law', (1995/96) 25 *Georgia Journal of International and Comparative Law* 1, at p. 18.

[133] Joan Fitzpatrick, 'The Relevance of Customary International Norms to the Death Penalty in the United States', (1995/96) 25 *Georgia Journal of International and Comparative Law* 165, at p. 168.

[134] Hurst Hannum, 'The Status of the Universal Declaration of Human Rights in National and International Law', (1995/96) 25 *Georgia Journal of International and Comparative Law* 287.

[135] International Law Association, Committee on the Enforcement of Human Rights Law, Final Report on the Status of the Universal Declaration of Human Rights in National and International Law, International Law Association, Report of the Sixty-Sixth Conference, Buenos Aires: International Law Association, 1994.

Louis Henkin delivered the keynote lecture at the Georgia Conference. He distinguished the 'significant, and increasing, amount of such non-conventional law of human rights' from 'traditional customary law', which Henkin said 'was not made', 'it resulted'.[136] He said that American Law Institute's Restatement supported this modern 'non-conventional law of human rights' by using 'the traditional indicia of traditional customary law', although the Reporters of the Restatement had admitted 'that the state practice supporting non-conventional human rights law looks different, is different ....'[137] Henkin continued: 'The international system, having identified contemporary human values, has adopted and declared them to be fundamental law, international law. But, in a radical derogation from the axiom of "sovereignty", that law is not based on consent: at least, it does not honour or accept dissent, and it binds particular states regardless of their objection.'[138]

F. The Human Rights Committee's General Comment

The United Nations Human Rights Committee, the treaty body established by the International Covenant on Civil and Political Rights, undertakes a number of functions relating to the treaty's interpretation, application, and enforcement. One of these is the preparation of 'general comments'. These consist of relatively succinct summaries of the law concerning specific provisions of the Covenant or issues related to its implementation generally. In 1994, the Committee addressed the issue of reservations to the Covenant, a subject on which the treaty itself is silent. The Committee confirmed that the principles set out by the International Court of Justice[139] and subsequently codified in the Vienna Convention on the Law of Treaties applied, in particular the impermissibility of reservations that are incompatible with the 'object and purpose' of the Covenant.[140] The Committee proposed a test whereby the 'object and purpose' of treaty provisions can be determined with reference to customary international law.

> Although treaties that are mere exchanges of obligations between States allow them to reserve *inter se* application of rules of general international law, it is otherwise in human rights treaties, which are for the benefit of persons within their jurisdiction. Accordingly, provisions in the Covenant that represent customary international law (and a fortiori when they have the character of peremptory norms) may not be the subject of reservations. Accordingly, a State may not reserve the right to engage in

[136] Louis Henkin, 'Human Rights and State "Sovereignty"', (1995/96) 25 *Georgia Journal of International and Comparative Law* 31, p. 37.
[137] Ibid., p. 38.
[138] Ibid.
[139] *Reservations to the Convention on Genocide, Advisory Opinion, ICJ Reports 1951*, p. 15, pp. 25–27.
[140] Vienna Convention on the Law of Treaties, (1980) 1155 UNTS 31, art. 19(c).

> slavery; to torture; to subject persons to cruel, inhuman, or degrading treatment or punishment; to arbitrarily deprive persons of their lives; to arbitrarily arrest and detain persons; to deny freedom of thought, conscience, and religion; to presume a person guilty unless he proves his innocence; to execute pregnant women or children; to permit the advocacy of national, racial, or religious hatred; to deny to persons of marriageable age the right to marry; or to deny to minorities the right to enjoy their own culture, profess their own religion, or use their own language. And while reservations to particular clauses of Article 14 may be acceptable, a general reservation to the right to a fair trial would not be.[141]

No attempt was made to provide sources or justification for the customary law status of certain of the rights set out in the Covenant, any more than explanation provided for the exclusion of other rights. Nor do the *travaux préparatoires* of the General Comment that are available to the public elucidate things.

The Human Rights Committee had begun considering a draft of the General Comment at its fifty-first session.[142] A draft was prepared by Rosalyn Higgins that was subsequently revised by a working group.[143] The draft was studied over several meetings during the fifty-second session.[144] However, the Committee's consideration of the list of customary norms remains quite opaque. After an initial discussion, Higgins affirmed that it was wrong to contend that rules of customary international law could not be subject to reservation, thereby implying that the proposition was added by the working group and was not in her original draft. She said that if the Committee wished to say this was not the case, it should justify this contention based on the special nature of international human rights law.[145] A redraft prepared by Higgins contained a phrase noting that while it was permissible to make reservations to 'rules of general international law' with respect to treaties that were 'mere exchanges of obligations between States', human rights treaties were in a special category because they were 'for the benefit of persons' within the jurisdiction of States.[146] In the debate on the revised paragraph, the only comment was by Higgins herself, who said that a new introductory sentence was required dealing with peremptory norms.[147] At no point in the entire discussion, as far as the public record is concerned, did the Committee give any attention to the list of rights deemed to be customary in nature. Where did it come from? What methodology was employed? Was it meant to be an exhaustive list, thereby indicating that

141 General Comment 24, Issues Relating to Reservations Made upon Ratification or Accession to the Covenant or the Optional Protocols thereto, or in Relation to Declarations under art. 41 of the Covenant, CCPR/C/21/Rev.1/Add.6, para. 8.
142 Report of the Human Rights Committee, Vol. I, A/49/40, para. 373; CCPR/C/SR.1356/Add.1, para. 71.
143 CCPR/C/SR.1366, para. 53.
144 Report of the Human Rights Committee, Vol. I, A/50/40, para. 477.
145 CCPR/C/SR.1368, para. 36.
146 CCPR/C/52/CRP.1/Rev.1.
147 CCPR/C/SR.1381, paras. 2–5.

the rights that were not on this list, such as freedom of expression or the prohibition of retroactive criminal law, were not customary in nature?

The General Comment said that that it would be contrary to customary international law 'to execute ... children', a statement that imprecisely reformulates Article 6(5) of the Covenant, which prohibits the death penalty for 'crimes committed by persons below eighteen years of age'. There are two things wrong with the Committee's formulation. First, the prohibition must be based upon the age when the crime was committed, not the age at the time of execution. The Covenant also prohibits execution of adults for crimes committed when they were juveniles. Second, the term 'children' looks like a deliberate attempt to avoid indicating the age with precision. Only seven years earlier, the Inter-American Commission on Human Rights had accepted the argument of the United States that there was no customary norm setting eighteen as the minimum age but rather that such a norm was 'emerging'.[148]

Professor Richard Lillich promptly hailed the General Comment as a 'resounding endorsement' of the approach to customary international law of the American Law Institute's Restatement.[149] The list proposed by the Committee was in fact more extensive than what was in the restatement. But it is hard to compare the 'approaches' of the two bodies in the absence of any explanation by the Human Rights Committee of its methodology. Other writers about General Comment 24 did not really address the issue of customary norms of human rights.[150]

The United States, which had only recently ratified the International Covenant, reacted harshly to the General Comment. Its ratification had been accompanied by a number of reservations and these provoked many objections from States Parties. Indeed, it seems probable that it was the reservations by the United States that inspired the Committee to issue the General Comment. The United States described the proposition that a reservation that contravened a norm of customary international law was per se incompatible with the object and purpose as a 'significant

[148] *Roach and Pinkerton v. United States*, Case 9647, Resolution No. 3/87, Merits, 22 September 1987, para. 60.

[149] Richard Lillich, 'The Growing Importance of Customary International Human Rights Law', (1996) 25 *Georgia Journal of International and Comparative Law* 1, at p. 19.

[150] *E.g.* Catherine J. Redgwell, 'Reservations to Treaties and Human Rights Committee General Comment No. 24(52)', (1997) 46 *International and Comparative Law Quarterly* 390; Elena A. Baylis, 'General Comment 24: Confronting the Problem of Reservations to Human Rights Treaties', (1999) 17 *Berkeley Journal of International Law* 277; Akbar Rasulov, 'The Life and Times of the Modern Law of Reservations: The Doctrinal Genealogy of General Comment No. 24', (2009) 14 *Austrian Review of International and European Law* 103; Giorgio Gaja, 'Le riserve al Patto sui diritti civili e politici e il diritto consuetudinario', (1996) 79 *Rivista di diritto internazionale* 451; Martin Scheinin, 'Reservations by States under the International Covenant on Civil and Political Rights and Its Optional Protocols, and the Practice of the Human Rights Committee', in Inete Ziemele, ed., *Reservations to Human Rights Treaties and the Vienna Convention Regime*, Dordrecht: Springer, 2004, pp. 41–58; Ulf Linderfalk, 'Reservations to Treaties and Norms of Jus Cogens—A Comment on Human Rights Committee General Comment No. 24', in Inete Ziemele, ed., *Reservations to Human Rights Treaties and the Vienna Convention Regime*, Dordrecht: Springer, 2004, pp. 213–234.

and sweeping premise' that was 'wholly unsupported and is in fact contrary to international law'.[151] It said that the Committee 'asserts in a wholly conclusory fashion that a number of propositions are customary international law which, to speak plainly, are not'. For example, said the United States, 'while many are opposed to the death penalty in general and the juvenile death penalty in particular, the practice of States demonstrates that there is currently no blanket prohibition in customary law'. It said the Committee's treatment of customary international human rights law manifested a 'cavalier approach to international law'.[152]

Several months later, the United Kingdom formulated its own critique of the General Comment. The language was more restrained than that of the United States, but the United Kingdom agreed that the customary law of human rights was not an appropriate criterion for determination of the object and purpose of the treaty. The United Kingdom said it was 'less convinced' by the argument that 'because human rights treaties are for the benefit of individuals, provisions in the Covenant that represent customary international law may not be the subject of reservations'. It described as 'doubtful' whether 'such a proposition represents existing customary international law; it is not a view shared by most commentators, and States have not expressly objected to reservations on this ground'. The United Kingdom made no comment on the list of rights that the Committee had proposed were part of customary international law.[153]

France, too, formally objected to General Comment 24. With respect to the Committee's assertions about customary international law, France said '[i]t must be acknowledged that it is difficult—however regrettable that may be—to identify practices in the human rights area that fit this definition exactly. It would be premature, to say the least, to claim that all the examples cited in the report fit the definition of international custom cited above.' France said that although certain human rights treaties might formalise customary principles, this did not mean the State's duty to observe a general customary principle should be confused with its agreement to be bound by the expression of that principle in a treaty.[154]

The General Comment was also criticised by the International Law Commission in the context of its study of reservations. The guidelines on reservations adopted by the Commission in 2011 contain the following: 'The fact that a treaty provision reflects a rule of customary international law does not in itself constitute an obstacle to the formulation of a reservation to that provision.'[155] The accompanying

[151] 'Observations on General Comment No. 24 (52), on issues relating to reservations made upon ratification or accession to the Covenant or the Optional Protocols thereto, or in relation to declarations under article 41 of the Covenant', Report of the Human Rights Committee, Vol. I, A/50/40, Annex VI, pp. 126–134, at p. 127.

[152] Ibid., p. 128.

[153] Ibid., p. 131.

[154] 'Observations of States Parties under article 40, paragraph 5, of the Covenant', Report of the Human Rights Committee, Vol. I, A/51/40, Annex VI, pp. 104–106, at p. 104.

[155] Guide to Practice on Reservations to Treaties, A/66/10, para. 75 (3.1.5.3).

Commentary rejects the proposition in General Comment 24 that this rule is set aside when human rights treaties are concerned.[156] Only in a footnote is the enumeration of human rights norms that are deemed to be customary by the Committee discussed. The Commentary says of the list that it is 'certainly true', but adds that 'it does not automatically mean that reservations to the relevant provisions of the International Covenant on Civil and Political Rights are prohibited; if these rights must be respected, it is because of their customary and, in some cases, peremptory nature, not because of their inclusion in the Covenant'.[157]

The Human Rights Committee has never returned to its effort at the identification of norms of customary international law. In its concluding observations on State Party reports, the Committee regularly calls upon States to withdraw reservations. It never even hints at the impermissibility of a reservation because it contemplates one of the customary law rights listed in the General Comment. The British observations that States do not invoke customary international law when they object to reservations are not without merit. For example, Qatar ratified the International Covenant on Civil and Political Rights with a reservation to Article 7, the prohibition of torture and cruel, inhuman, or degrading treatment or punishment.[158] There were many objections, including some that referred to the impermissibility of reservation to the Covenant's 'central provisions',[159] its 'most essential provisions',[160] and its 'essential'[161] or 'core elements'.[162] In objecting to the Maldives's reservation to the freedom of religion provision,[163] Canada said Article 18 was 'one of the most essential provisions'.[164] Denmark said that Pakistan's reservation to several provisions, including the right to life, the prohibition of torture, freedom of religion and expression, and the right to participate in government,[165] concerned 'essential obligations'.[166] Finland objected to the reservations by the United States to Articles 6 and 7 of the Covenant,[167] citing their 'fundamental importance in the Covenant'.[168] But no State has alluded to paragraph 8 of General Comment 24, directly or indirectly, or argued that a reservation was inadmissible because it concerned a norm of customary international law. In the entire corpus of United Nations human rights treaties, there would appear to be only one instance

[156] Report of the International Law Commission on the work of its sixty-third session (26 April–3 June and 4 July–12 August 2011) (Addendum), A/66/10/Add.1, pp. 220–223.
[157] Ibid., p. 222, fn. 1696.
[158] C.N.262.2018.TREATIES-IV.4.
[159] Austria, C.N.195.2019.TREATIES-IV.4.
[160] Canada, C.N.223.2019.TREATIES-IV.4.
[161] Norway, C.N.211.2019.TREATIES-IV.4; Moldova, C.N.217.2019.TREATIES-IV.4.
[162] Latvia, C.N.200.2019.TREATIES-IV.4.
[163] C.N.741.2006.TREATIES-14.
[164] C.N.893.2007.TREATIES-29.
[165] C.N.405.2010.TREATIES-17.
[166] C.N.446.2011.TREATIES-22.
[167] C.N.250.1992.TREATIES-14.
[168] C.N.377.1993.TREATIES-21.

of an objection to a reservation invoking the customary nature of the norm in question.[169] General Comment 24 has only rarely been cited as authority for the content of the customary international law of human rights.[170]

G. Subsequent developments

Richard Lillich entitled his remarks at the 1994 University of Georgia Conference 'the growing importance of customary international human rights law'. He acknowledged that support for this came principally from American legal and academic sources. He hoped that 'our colleagues overseas' would 'join us in this great adventure, the U.S. "customary-law-of-human-rights-school"'.[171] But if truth be told, there was probably more interest and activity on the subject in the quarter century prior to 1994 than in the quarter century that followed. The General Comment of the Human Rights Committee was somewhat of a high water mark, although there have been some significant developments subsequent to 1994, such as the finding of the International Court of Justice that the prohibition of torture was a norm of customary international law. Also, the international criminal tribunals have devoted a great deal of attention to customary international law.[172] Nevertheless, their focus has been primarily on the scope of war crimes, and on ancillary issues such as claims of immunity to heads of State[173] and the contention that amnesty is prohibited,[174] and not on the substance of human rights. Writing in 1995, Ian Brownlie said that '[t]he vast majority of States and authoritative writers would now recognise that the fundamental principles of human rights form part of

[169] Hungary objected to Malaysia's reservation to the Convention on the Rights of Persons with Disabilities, (2008) 2515 UNTS 3 in the following terms (C.N.510.2011.TREATIES-15): 'The Government of the Republic of Hungary is of the view that Articles 15 and 18 of the Convention address core human rights values that are not only reflected in several multilateral treaties, such as the UN Convention against Torture and Other Cruel, Inhuman or Degrading Treatment or Punishment, and the International Covenant on Civil and Political Rights but also form part of the international customary law.'

[170] Integrity of the judicial system, Report of the United Nations High Commissioner for Human Rights, A/HRC/43/35, para. 4.

[171] Richard Lillich, 'The Growing Importance of Customary International Human Rights Law', (1996) 25 *Georgia Journal of International and Comparative Law* 1, at p. 30.

[172] Micaela Frulli, 'The Contribution of International Criminal Tribunals to the Development of International Law: the Prominence of Opinio Juris and the Moralization of Customary Law', (2015) 14 *The Law and Practice of International Courts and Tribunals* 80; Noora Arajärvi, *The Changing Nature of Customary International Law: Methods of Interpreting the Concept of Custom in International Criminal Tribunals*, London: Routledge, 2014; Birgit Schlütter, *Developments in Customary International Law, Theory and the Practice of the International Court of Justice and the International ad hoc Criminal Tribunals for Rwanda and Yugoslavia*, The Hague: Brill/Nijhoff, 2010.

[173] For example, *Prosecutor v. Al-Bashir*, ICC-02/05-01/09 OA2, Judgment in the Jordan Referral re Al-Bashir Appeal, 6 May 2019, paras. 100–119.

[174] For example, *Prosecutor v. Gaddafi* (ICC-01/11-01/11), Judgment on the appeal of Mr Saif Al-Islam Gaddafi against the decision of Pre-Trial Chamber I entitled 'Decision on the "Admissibility Challenge by Dr. Saif Al Islam Gaddafi pursuant to Articles 17(1)(c), 19 and 20(3) of the Rome Statute"' of 5 April 2019, 9 March 2020, para. 96.

customary or general international law' but, he added presciently, 'they would not necessarily agree on the identity of the fundamental principles'.[175]

The customary law of human rights was at issue before the International Court of Justice in the *Belgium v. Senegal* case, and led to its remarkable pronouncement on the customary nature of the prohibition of torture. Belgium accused Senegal not only of violating the Convention against Torture by its failure to try or extradite the former head of state of Chad, to whom it had given asylum, but also of violating norms of customary international law. Belgium contended that 'pursuant to the obligation to combat impunity, international law requires Senegal to prosecute the alleged perpetrator of such crimes as long as he is in its territory or, if it does not prosecute, to extradite him to a State which wishes to prosecute'.[176] Belgium said the legal basis of its complaint was 'the obligation, imposed on States by international law, to combat impunity for persons present in their territory who are suspected of having committed serious crimes under international law'.[177] Belgium did not actually argue that the prohibition of torture, as such, was a crime under customary law, focussing all of its attention on the obligation to try or extradite persons suspected of responsibility for crimes against humanity, war crimes, and genocide. The Court declined to rule on the customary law issue because it said that there was no dispute between the parties.[178] During the proceedings, Judge Donohue questioned the parties about the temporal scope of the Convention against Torture.[179] The Court observed that in their answer, the parties had indicated their agreement 'that acts of torture are regarded by customary international law as international crimes, independently of the Convention'.[180] This provided the Court with the occasion to make its celebrated obiter dictum about the prohibition of torture (and not its status as an international crime) under customary international law.

[175] Ian Brownlie, *The Rule of Law in International Affairs: International Law at the Fiftieth Anniversary of the United Nations*, The Hague: Martinus Nijhoff, 1998, pp. 77, and 83.

[176] *Questions relating to the Obligation to Prosecute or Extradite (Belgium v. Senegal)*, Memorial of Belgium, para. 4.61. Also *Questions relating to the Obligation to Prosecute or Extradite (Belgium v. Senegal), Judgment, ICJ Reports 2012*, p. 422, para. 53. On the Habré trial, see Sharon Weill, Kim Thuy Seelinger, and Kerstin Bree Carlson, eds., *The President on Trial*, Oxford: Oxford University Press, 2020.

[177] *Questions relating to the Obligation to Prosecute or Extradite (Belgium v. Senegal)*, Memorial of Belgium, para. 4.88. See also Ibid., Transcript, CR 2009/08, 6 April 2009, Morning sitting, Submissions of Prof. Eric David, paras. 19–21; Ibid., Transcript, CR 2012/3, 13 March 2012, Submissions of Prof. Eric David, paras. 10–27.

[178] *Questions relating to the Obligation to Prosecute or Extradite (Belgium v. Senegal), Judgment, ICJ Reports 2012*, p. 422, para. 55.

[179] *Questions relating to the Obligation to Prosecute or Extradite (Belgium v. Senegal)*, Transcript, CR 2012/5, 16 March 2012, morning sitting, p. 35.

[180] *Questions relating to the Obligation to Prosecute or Extradite (Belgium v. Senegal), Judgment, ICJ Reports 2012*, p. 422, para. 97. This is apparently a reference to *Belgium v. Senegal*, Supplementary written replies of the Government of Senegal to the questions put by judges at the close of the hearing held on 16 March 2012. See also *Belgium v. Senegal*, Further written comments of the Government of Senegal on the supplementary replies of the Belgian Government to the question put to Belgium by Judge Greenwood at the close of the hearing held on 16 March 2012, presented by Mr. Cheikh Tidiane Thiam, Ambassador and Agent of Senegal.

On the subject of customary law in general, in recent years the main act has been the work of the International Law Commission, led by its rapporteur, Michael Wood. Wood's study was on the 'identification of customary international law' rather than on its content. His five reports to the International Law Commission make no mention of General Comment 24. The effort of the Human Rights Committee to identify norms of customary law of human rights was not considered. In his first report to the Commission, Wood said that one of the issues to be addressed was whether there were 'different approaches to the formation and evidence of customary international law in different fields of international law, such as international human rights law'.[181] From the outset of his work, Wood said that 'it is neither helpful nor in accordance with principle, for the purposes of the present topic, to break the law up into separate specialist fields. The same basic approach to the formation and identification of customary international law applies regardless of the field of law under consideration.'[182] One of the issues that concerned Wood was the theory of 'modern customary law' or 'new customary law', by which the two constitutive elements of custom set out in Article 38(1)(b) of the Statute of the International Court of Justice become merged or, in reality, the *opinio juris* becomes the only element. This was said to be the case particularly with respect to human rights law, international criminal law, and international humanitarian law, where there were powerful moral and ideological imperatives for development. But, said Wood, the better view is that the two-element requirement must apply to all areas of public international law.[183]

The reinforcement of the traditional approach by the International Law Commission contrasts with innovative theories proposed by scholars. For example, Brian Lepard took an ethics-based perspective that largely set aside the role of State practice. It was especially relevant in the field of human rights. According to Professor Lepard, customary norms are created when 'states generally believe that it is desirable now or in the near future to have an authoritative legal principle or rule prescribing, permitting, or prohibiting certain conduct'.[184] He described this as a revised definition of *opinio juris* that captured the 'essence' of custom. In a broadside directed at the International Law Commission, B.S. Chimni proposed a 'third world' approach to custom, whereby 'the historical role of [customary international law] has been to facilitate the functioning of global capitalist

[181] First report on formation and evidence of customary international law by Michael Wood, Special Rapporteur, A/CN.4/663, para. 19.

[182] Formation and evidence of customary international law, Note by Michael Wood, Special Rapporteur, A/CN.4/653, para. 22.

[183] First report on formation and evidence of customary international law by Michael Wood, Special Rapporteur, A/CN.4/663, para. 19; Second report on formation and evidence of customary international law by Michael Wood, Special Rapporteur, A/CN.4/672, para. 24.

[184] Brian D. Lepard, *Customary International Law: A New Theory with Practical Applications*, Cambridge: Cambridge University Press, 2010, p. 151. Also Brian D. Lepard, 'Toward a New Theory of Customary International Human Rights Law', in Brian D. Lepard, ed., *Re-examining Customary International* Law, Cambridge: Cambridge University Press, 2017, pp. 233–265.

system by filling crucial gaps in the international legal system'.[185] Chimni singled out international human rights law, saying that customary international law was 'performing the function of sustaining its systemic interests through legitimising global capitalism', although he did not provide useful examples.[186] Andreas Paulus and Matthias Lippold challenged Chimni, insisting that 'much of contemporary human rights law, including economic and social rights, attempts, with mixed success, to tame rather than to strengthen capitalism'.[187]

Generally, the important debate about custom as a source of human rights law that took place during the 1980s and the first half of the 1990s has largely died out. However, although customary human rights law has not subsequently received as much academic and judicial attention as such, it has continued to develop, quietly and sometimes imperceptibly, in a manner parallel to that of the human rights formulated in treaties. From the 1960s, when claims about the customary international law of human rights began, there was a tendency to emphasise *opinio juris*, manifested in resolutions and similar sources, and to down-play or even deny a role for State practice. The primary impetus for this was a perceived shortage of evidence for the second of the two elements. However, the conservative position recently taken by the International Law Commission is much less of an obstacle to the identification of customary law in the field of human rights than it once might have been. A challenge to the two-element approach or a demand for some exceptional treatment dictated by the special features of international human rights law is unnecessary. Evidence of both elements has become immensely richer over the years. Two factors are of central importance: the trend towards universality of the major human rights treaties and the establishment of the Universal Periodic Review, by which States report on their compliance with human rights norms without reference, as a general rule, to specific treaty obligations. The chapter that follows considers the role that these sources, amongst others, now play in facilitating the identification of evidence of both elements of custom in the area of human rights.

[185] Bhupinder S. Chimni, 'Customary International Law: A Third World Perspective', (2018) *112 American Journal of International Law* 1, at p. 4.
[186] Ibid., p. 5.
[187] Andreas Paulus and Matthias Lippold, 'Customary Law in the Postmodern World (dis)Order', (2018) 112 *AJIL Unbound* 308, at p. 310.

2
Identifying the norms of the customary international law of human rights

Much of the debate about customary international law in the 1980s and early 1990s, discussed in the previous chapter, was concerned with determining whether the identification of custom followed the general approach, requiring evidence both of *opinio juris* and of State practice, or whether novel principles applied in the field of human rights law by way of exception. The basis of such an approach was recognition that human rights law was somehow different from international law in general in that it did not really address reciprocal obligations of States but rather obligations applicable to individual States in their relationship to individuals and groups within their territory and subject to their jurisdiction. As the European Commission on Human Rights explained, in one of its earliest decisions, the human rights obligations are 'essentially of an objective character ... designed rather to protect the fundamental rights of individual human beings from infringements ... than to create subjective and reciprocal rights ... '.[1] According to the Human Rights Committee, the human rights treaties are not to be viewed as 'a web of inter-State exchanges of mutual obligations. They concern the endowment of individuals with rights. The principle of inter-State reciprocity has no place ... '.[2]

For example, in some familiar areas of public international law where custom is well developed, such as the recognition of immunities to diplomats and others, and the delimitation of maritime boundaries, the direct interest that States have in mutual respect for various rules is obvious. But even in an area that is in many respects a cognate of human rights, the law of armed conflict or international humanitarian law, the reciprocal dimension has been quite fundamental to development of the rules and to their successful application. That States have a mutual interest in how they treat prisoners in an international armed conflict is quite obvious. They have no similar shared interest with respect to their own political prisoners in peacetime or during a civil war.

[1] *Austria v. Italy*, no. 788/60, Commission decision of 11 January 1961, (1961) 4 YB 116, at p. 140.

[2] General Comment 24, Issues relating to reservations made upon ratification or accession to the Covenant or the Optional Protocols thereto, or in relation to declarations under art. 41 of the Covenant, CCPR/C/21/Rev.1/Add.6, para. 17. Also *The Effect of Reservations on the Entry into Force of the American Convention on Human Rights (Arts. 74 and 75)*, Advisory Opinion OC-2/82, Series A, No. 2, 24 September 1982, para. 29.

The Customary International Law of Human Rights. William A. Schabas, Oxford University Press.
 DOI: 10.1093/oso/9780192845696.003.0003

The International Law Commission gave short shrift to the suggestion that special rules governed the identification of customary rules of international human rights law. It rejected proposals that the 'two-element approach' derived from Article 38(1)(b) of the Statute of the International Court of Justice might be abandoned or attenuated, either generally or for special bodies of law, such as international human rights law. The term 'human rights' does not appear in the Draft Conclusions of the Commission, and the references to human rights in the reports of the Special Rapporteur, Michael Wood, are quite sparse.[3] The debates in the Commission reveal that human rights law as a distinct field of public international law was only occasionally considered.[4] In his first report to the Commission, the Special Rapporteur questioned whether the formation of custom might vary depending on the branch of law concerned, giving human rights law as an example.[5] The Special Rapporteur commissioned a study from Hugh Thirlway on the customary law of human rights. Thirlway seemed unenthusiastic, indeed sceptical, beginning his analysis by asserting that it was 'still a perfectly tenable view that there is in fact no general international customary law of human rights'.[6] He noted the 'virtual absence of state practice in the traditional sense', explaining that this was due to the 'domination of the field by treaty instruments'.[7] His study reached no conclusions. It asked a series of rhetorical questions that were, predictably, left unanswered by the Special Rapporteur.

A. International case law and other authorities

The International Court of Justice is the definitive voice on the subject of customary international law. Taken as a whole, its contribution to the customary international law of human rights is modest. Its first judgment in a contentious case spoke of 'elementary considerations of humanity, even more exacting in peace than in war'.[8] A few years later, the Court explained that the Convention on the Prevention and Punishment of the Crime of Genocide had been adopted 'for a purely humanitarian and civilising purpose. It is indeed difficult to imagine a convention that

[3] Formation and evidence of customary international law, Note by Michael Wood, Special Rapporteur, A/CN.4/653, para. 22; First report on formation and evidence of customary international law, by Michael Wood, Special Rapporteur, A/CN.4/663, paras. 19, 53, 98, 101; Second report on identification of customary international law, by Michael Wood, Special Rapporteur, A/CN.4/672, para. 28; Third report on identification of customary international law, by Michael Wood, Special Rapporteur, A/CN.4/682, paras. 15, 17.

[4] A/CN.4/SR.3252, pp. 13–14 (Pavel Šturma).

[5] First report on formation and evidence of customary international law, by Michael Wood, Special Rapporteur, A/CN.4/663, para. 19.

[6] Hugh Thirlway, 'Human Rights in Customary Law: An Attempt to Define Some of the Issues', (2015) 28 *Leiden Journal of International Law* 495, at p. 497.

[7] Ibid.

[8] *Corfu Channel (United Kingdom v. Albania), Judgment, ICJ Reports 1949*, p. 4, at p. 22.

might have this dual character to a greater degree, since its object on the one hand is to safeguard the very existence of certain human groups and on the other to confirm and endorse the most elementary principles of morality.' The Court explained that in such a convention, 'the contracting States do not have any interests of their own; they merely have, one and all, a common interest, namely, the accomplishment of those high purposes which are the raison d'être of the convention.'[9] The Court said that 'the principles underlying the Convention are principles which are recognised by civilised nations as binding on States, even without any conventional obligation.'[10] But at best, the statements in *Corfu Channel* and the Advisory Opinion on the Genocide Convention are only implied references to customary international law.

Two decades later, in 1971, the International Court of Justice held that South Africa's 'denial of fundamental human rights is a flagrant violation of the purposes and principles of the Charter [of the United Nations]'.[11] In his separate opinion, Vice-President Ammoun wrote that although 'the affirmations of the [Universal Declaration of Human Rights] are not binding qua international convention ... , they can bind States on the basis of custom within the meaning of paragraph 1(b) of [Article 38 of the Statute of the Court] ... because they constituted a codification of customary law... or because they have acquired the force of custom through a general practice accepted as law'.[12]

In 1980, in the case concerning the hostages in the American embassy in Tehran, the Court made a somewhat more explicit pronouncement: 'Wrongfully to deprive human beings of their freedom and to subject them to physical constraint in conditions of hardship is in itself manifestly incompatible with the principles of the Charter of the United Nations, as well as with the fundamental principles enunciated in the Universal Declaration of Human Rights.'[13] The United States had argued the point in its memorial, claiming a violation of the rights of the hostages that it said were 'now reflected, inter alia, in the Charter of the United Nations, the Universal Declaration of Human Rights and corresponding portions of the International Covenant on Civil and Political Rights, regional conventions and other instruments defining basic human rights.'[14] At the time, the United States had signed but not ratified the Covenant. Some scholars urged that the words of

[9] *Reservations to the Convention on Genocide, Advisory Opinion, ICJ Reports 1951*, p. 15, at p. 24.

[10] Ibid., p. 23.

[11] *Legal Consequences for States of the Continued Presence of South Africa in Namibia (South West Africa) Notwithstanding Security Council Resolution 276 (1970), Advisory Opinion, ICJ Reports 1971*, p. 16, at p. 57.

[12] *Legal Consequences for States of the Continued Presence of South Africa in Namibia (South West Africa) Notwithstanding Security Council Resolution 276 (1970), Advisory Opinion, ICJ Reports 1971*, p. 16, Separate Opinion of Vice-President Ammoun, p. 76.

[13] *United States Diplomatic and Consular Staff in Tehran (United States of America v. Iran), Judgment, ICJ Reports 1980*, p. 2, at p. 42.

[14] *United States Diplomatic and Consular Staff in Tehran (United States of America v. Iran)*, Memorial of the United States of America, p. 182 (internal references omitted).

the Court should not be interpreted narrowly, and that the Court's pronouncement be understood as confirmation that the Universal Declaration 'as a whole propounds fundamental principles recognised by general international law'.[15] A few years later, in 1986, the Court issued an important decision on customary international law in the *Nicaragua v. United States* case. The judgment dealt with the law on the use of force and not human rights, however.[16]

The International Court of Justice did not expressly declare a human rights norm to be customary international law until 2012. In the *Belgium v. Senegal* case, dealing with Senegal's failure to either prosecute or extradite a former tyrant from Chad, the Court stated that 'the prohibition of torture is part of customary international law'. To support this pronouncement, the Court offered a brief paragraph explaining that the prohibition was 'grounded in a widespread international practice and on the *opinio juris* of States'. Some of the relevant treaties and declarations were cited, including Article 5 of the Universal Declaration of Human Rights. Furthermore, the Court noted that the prohibition of torture 'has been introduced into the domestic law of almost all States' and the 'acts of torture are regularly denounced within national and international fora'.[17]

The sparse pronouncements of the International Court of Justice on the customary law of human rights may come as no surprise. More striking is the relative absence of consideration of customary human rights law by specialised international courts and treaty bodies. References to the customary law of human rights by the European Court of Human Rights, which is the pre-eminent judicial body charged with jurisdiction over fundamental human rights, are almost as rare as those of the International Court of Justice. The European Court has referred to customary law in order to apply the principle of legality, set out in Article 7 of the Convention, but that is because the scope of the term 'international law' in the text of the treaty provision is understood to concern customary law as well as treaty law.[18] On one occasion, the European Court cited with approval the view of the Committee on the Elimination of Discrimination against Women about

[15] Nigel S. Rodley, 'Human Rights and Humanitarian Intervention: The Case Law of the World Court', (1989) 38 *International and Comparative Law Quarterly* 321, at p. 326. Also: Richard Lillich, 'The Growing Importance of Customary International Human Rights Law', (1996) 25 *Georgia Journal of International and Comparative Law* 1, at p. 4.

[16] *Military and Paramilitary Activities in and against Nicaragua (Nicaragua v. United States of America), Merits, Judgment, ICJ Reports 1986*, p. 14.

[17] *Questions relating to the Obligation to Prosecute or Extradite (Belgium v. Senegal), Judgment, ICJ Reports 2012*, p. 422, para. 99.

[18] *Kononov v. Latvia* [GC], no. 36376/04, §§ 203, 211, 215, 221, ECHR 2010-IV and Dissenting opinion of Judge Costa joined by Judges Kalaydjieva and Poalelungi, §§ 4, 9, 11; *Korbely v. Hungary* [GC], no. 9174/02, § 90, ECHR 2008-IV and Dissenting opinion of Judge Loucaides; *Kononov v. Latvia*, no. 36376/04, §§ 120, 122, 131, 24 July 2008 and Joint dissenting opinion of Judges Fura-Sandström, David Hór Björgvinsson, and Ziemele, §§ 6, 7, 13; *Vasiliauskas v. Lithuania* [GC], no. 35343/05, §§ 175 and 178, ECHR 2015-VII; *K.-H. W. v. Germany* [GC], no. 37201/97, ECHR 2001-II, Concurring opinion of Judge Loucaides; *Streletz, Kessler, and Krenz v. Germany* [GC], nos. 34044/96, 35532/97, and 44801/98, ECHR 2001-II, Concurring opinion of Judge Loucaides.

the customary nature of the prohibition of violence against women.[19] Like the International Court of Justice, the European Court of Human Rights has affirmed that 'the prohibition of torture has achieved the status of a peremptory norm in international law'.[20] It has also held that there is no rule under customary international law requiring the criminalisation of genocide denial.[21] Sometimes the parties or the *amici curiae* invoke customary international law norms in their submissions. The European Court may take due notice of this but make no comment on the issue in its conclusions.[22] There are also a number of references to the customary law of human rights by a rather limited cohort of individual judges.[23] Otherwise, the references to customary international law by the European Court are confined to corollary issues of public international law, such as State

[19] *Volodina v. Russia*, no. 41261/17, § 110, 9 July 2019.

[20] *Al-Adsani v. the United Kingdom* [GC], no. 35753/97, § 61, ECHR 2001-XI.

[21] *Perinçek v. Switzerland* [GC], no. 27510/08, §§ 266, 268, 15 October 2015.

[22] *E.g. Al-Saadoon and Mufdhi v. United Kingdom* (dec.), no. 61498/08, §§ 101, 109, 30 June 2009; *Ramzy v. Netherlands* (dec.), no. 25424/05, § 133, 27 May 2008; *Jorgić v. Germany*, no. 74613/01, §§ 59, 62, 12 July 2007; *Öcalan v. Turkey* [GC], no. 46221/99, § 82, 12 May 2005; *Öcalan v. Turkey*, no. 46221/99, § 85, 12 March 2003; *Öcalan v. Turkey* (dec.), no. 46221/99, 14 December 2000; *Isayeva, Yusupova, and Bazayeva v. Russia*, nos. 57947/00, 57948/00, and 57949/00, § 102, 24 February 2005; *Isayeva v. Russia*, no. 57950/00, § 104, 24 February 2005; *Prince Hans-Adam II of Liechtenstein v. Germany* [GC], no. 42527/98, 12 July 2001, § 41; *Loizidou v. Turkey* [GC], no. 15318/89, § 36, 18 December 1996.

[23] *Volodina v. Russia*, no. 41261/17, 9 July 2019, Separate Opinion of Judge de Albuquerque, joined by Judge Dedov, para. 3; *Ilnseher v. Germany* [GC], nos. 10211/12 and 27505/14, 4 December 2018, Dissenting opinion of Judge Pinto de Albuquerque, joined by Judge Dedov, §§ 75, 88; *Lopes de Sousa Fernandes v. Portugal* [GC], no. 56080/13, 19 December 2017, Partly concurring, partly dissenting opinion of Judge Pinto de Albuquerque, §§ 71, 92; *Trivkanović v. Croatia*, no. 12986/13, 6 July 2017, Partly dissenting and partly concurring opinion of Judge Wojtyczek; *Koprivnikar v. Slovenia*, no. 67503/13, 24 January 2017, Dissenting opinion of Judge Sajó; *J. et al. v. Austria*, no. 58215/12, 17 January 2017, Concurring opinion of Judge Pinto de Albuquerque, joined by Judge Tsotsoria; *Khlaifia et al. v. Italy* [GC], 15 December 2016, Partly dissenting opinion of Judge Serghides, § 24; *A. and B. v. Norway* [GC], no. 24130/11 and 29758/11, 15 November 2016, Dissenting opinion of Judge Pinto de Albuquerque, §§ 6–15; *Muršić v. Croatia* [GC], no. 7334/13, 20 October 2016, Partially dissenting opinion of Judge Pinto de Albuquerque, § 23; *Al-Dulimi and Montana Management Inc. v. Switzerland* [GC], no. 5809/08, 21 June 2016, Concurring opinion of Judge Pinto de Albuquerque, joined by Judges Hajiyev, Pejchal, and Dedov, §§ 3, 28, 34; *Ramadan v. Malta*, no. 76136/12, 21 June 2016, Dissenting opinion of Judge Pinto de Albuquerque, § 7; *F.G. v. Sweden* [GC], no. 43611/11, 23 March 2016, Joint separate opinion of Judges Ziemele, de Gaetano, Pinto de Albuquerque, and Wojtyczek; *Chiragov et al. v. Armenia* [GC], no. 13218/05, 16 June 2015, Dissenting opinion of Judge Pinto de Albuquerque, §§ 34, 40, 42; *Sargsyan v. Azerbaijan* [GC], no. 40167/06, ECHR 2015-IV, Dissenting opinion of Judge Pinto de Albuquerque, §§ 21–29; *Moanu et al. v. Moldova* [GC], nos. 10865/09, 45886/07, and 32431/08, 17 September 2014, Concurring opinion of Judge Pinto de Albuquerque, Joined by Judge Vučinić; *Perinçek v. Switzerland*, no. 27510/08, 17 December 2013, Joint partly dissenting opinion of Judges Vučinić and Pinto de Albuquerque, § 6; *Maktouf and Damjanović v. Bosnia and Herzegovina* [GC], nos. 2312/08 and 34179/08, ECHR 2013-IV, Concurring opinion of Judge Pinto de Albuquerque, Joined by Judge Vučinić, § 9; *Valiulienė v. Lithuania*, no. 33234/07, 26 March 2013, Concurring opinion of Judge Pinto de Albuquerque; *Tautkus v. Lithuania*, no. 29474/09, 27 November 2012, Dissenting opinion of Judge Pinto de Albuquerque; *Kurić et al. v. Slovenia*, no. 26828/06, 26 June 2012, Partly concurring, party dissenting opinion of Judge Vučinić; *Hirsi Jamaa et al. v. Italy* [GC], no. 27765/09, ECHR 2012-II, Concurring opinion of Judge Pinto de Albuquerque. See Ineta Ziemele, 'Customary International Law in the Case Law of the European Court of Human Rights', in Liesbeth Lijnzaad, ed., *The Judge and International Custom*, Strasbourg: Council of Europe, 2012, pp. 73–85.

responsibility,[24] the use of force,[25] the law of treaties,[26] State succession,[27] immunities,[28] the law of the sea,[29] statutory limitation,[30] and jurisdictional questions.[31]

The relative absence of pronouncements on the substance of fundamental human rights by the European Court of Human Rights, with the exception of the individual opinions of judges, might be explained by the fact that its jurisdiction is circumscribed by the European Convention on Human Rights with no explicit role for customary law. Yet relying upon Article 31(3)(c) of the Vienna Convention on the Law of Treaties the European Court of Human Rights has taken the view that for purposes of interpretation it must 'take into account any relevant rules and principles of international law applicable in relations between the Contracting Parties'.[32] This is an open invitation to refer to rules of customary international law, albeit one the Court has not taken up. In a conference presentation, Judge Ineta Ziemele explained that 'the Court is evidently open to paying attention to all sources of international law which include norms of customary international law and general principles'.[33] The same judge, in a decision of the Court, said that

[24] *Čikanović v. Croatia*, no. 27630/07, § 53, 5 February 2015; *Bureš v. the Czech Republic*, no. 37679/08, § 34, 18 October 2012; *Makuchyan and Minasyan v. Azerbaijan and Hungary*, no. 17247/13, § 114, 26 May 2020.

[25] *Behrami and Behrami v. France*, no. 71412/01 and *Saramati v. France, Germany and Norway* [GC] (dec.), no. 78166/01, §§ 19, 148, 2 May 2007.

[26] *Stoll v. Switzerland* [GC], no 69698/01, § 59, ECHR 2007-V; *Janowiec et al. v. Russia* [GC], nos. 55508/07 and 29520/09, ECHR 2013-V, Partly concurring and party dissenting opinion of Judge Wojtyczek.

[27] *Ålišić et al. v. Bosnia and Herzegovina, Croatia, Serbia, Slovenia, and the former Yugoslav Republic of Macedonia* [GC], no. 60642/08, § 59, ECHR 2014-IV; *Ališić et al. v. Bosnia and Herzegovina, Croatia, Serbia, Slovenia, and the former Yugoslav Republic of Macedonia*, no. 60642/08, § 46, 6 November 2012.

[28] *Cudak v. Lithuania* [GC], no. 15869/02, §§ 64–66, ECHR 2010-III; *Radunović et al. v. Montenegro*, nos. 45197/13, 53000/13, and 73404/13, §§ 41, 69, 73, 25 October 2016; *Naku v. Lithuania and Sweden*, no. 26126/02, 8 November 2016, Concurring opinion of Judge Motoc; *Wallishauser v. Austria*, no. 156/04, §§ 30, 66, 69, 70, 17 July 2012; *Sabeh El Leil v. France* [GC], no. 34869/05, §§ 54, 57, 58, 29 June 2011; *Oleynikov v. Russia*, no. 36703/04, § 66–68, 14 March 2013; *Wallishauser v. Austria (No. 2)*, no. 14497/06, §§ 39, 71, 72, 20 June 2013; *Hirschhorn v. Romania*, no. 29294/02, 26 July 2007, Concurring opinion of Judge Caflisch, joined by Judge Ziemele, § 8; *Treska v. Albania and Italy* (dec.), no. 26937/04, 29 June 2006; *Manoilescu and Dobrescu v. Romania* (dec.), no. 60861/00, § 81, 3 March 2005; *Kalegoroupoulou et al. v. Greece and Germany* (dec.), no. 59021/00, 12 December 2002; *Al-Adsani v. the United Kingdom* [GC], no. 35753/97, §§ 61–67, ECHR 2001-XI; *Fogarty v. United Kingdom*, no. 37112/97, ECHR 2001-XI, Dissenting opinion of Judge Loucaides.

[29] *Medvedev v. France* [GC], no. 3394/03, §§ 85, 92, ECHR 2010-III.

[30] *Mocanu et al. v. Romania* [GC], nos. 10865/09, 45888/07, and 32431/08, ECHR 2014-V, Concurring opinion of Judge Pinto de Albuquerque, joined by Judge Vučinić, para. 5.

[31] *Nait-Liman v. Switzerland*, no. 51357/07, § 120, 21 June 2016; *Medvedev et al. v. France* [GC], no. 3394/03, §§ 65, 92, ECHR 2010-III and Joint partly dissenting opinion of Judges Costa, Casadevall, Bîrsan, Garlicki, Hajiyev, Šimuta, and Nicolaou, § 8; *Banković et al. v. Belgium et al.* (dec.), no. 52207/99, § 73, 12 December 2001; *Al-Saadoon and Mufdhi v. United Kingdom* (dec.), no. 61498/08, § 85, 30 June 2009.

[32] *Jones et al. v. the United Kingdom*, nos. 34356/06 and 40528/06, § 195, 14 January 2014; *Al-Saadoon and Mufdhi v. the United Kingdom*, no. 61498/08, § 126, ECHR 2010 (extracts); *Catan et al. v. the Republic of Moldova and Russia* [GC], nos. 43370/04, 8252/05, and 18454/06, § 136, ECHR 2012 (extracts).

[33] Ineta Ziemele, 'Customary International Law in the Case Law of the European Court of Human Rights', in Liesbeth Lijnzaad, ed., *The Judge and International Custom*, Strasbourg: Council of Europe, 2012, pp. 73–85, at p. 77.

'[w]here the customary rule turns out to be different from the Convention provision, at least in its original form and intent, that rule may indeed affect the subsequent reading of the Convention provision'.[34]

The pattern of neglect with respect to customary international law is much the same at the Inter-American Court of Human Rights. It usually includes a standard paragraph in its judgments affirming that under customary law any violation of an international obligation that has produced damage entails the obligation to provide adequate reparation.[35] In its first judgments with such pronouncements, the Court referred to precedent of the Permanent Court of International Justice where reparation was described as a 'a principle of international law'[36] and 'even a general conception of law'[37] rather than as a customary norm.[38] In those early decisions the Court also spoke of 'the applicable principles of international law'.[39] The Inter-American Court has also referred to 'the customary norm according to which a State that has acceded to an international treaty must amend its domestic law as necessary in order to ensure the execution of the obligations assumed'.[40] On a few occasions, the Inter-American Court of Human Rights has stated that it may base itself on the corpus juris of international human rights law including customary international law.[41] The reluctance of the Inter-American Court to identify rules of

[34] *Lalmahomed v. the Netherlands*, no. 26036/08, Concurring opinion of Judge Ziemele, 22 February 2011.

[35] For example, *Fermín Ramírez v. Guatemala*, Judgment (Merits, reparations, and costs), 20 June 2005, Series C, No. 126, para. 122; *Girls Yean and Bosico v. Dominican Republic*, Judgment (Preliminary objections, merits, reparations, and costs), 8 September 2005, Series C, No. 130, paras. 208–209; *Massacres of El Mozote and nearby places v. El Salvador*, Judgment (Merits, reparations, and costs), 25 October 2012, Series C, No. 252, para. 302; *Expelled Dominicans and Haitians v. Dominican Republic*, Judgment (Preliminary objections, merits, reparations, and costs), 28 August 2014, Series C, No. 282, para. 444; *Azul Rojas Marín et al. v. Peru*, Judgment (Preliminary objections, merits, reparations, and costs), 12 March 2020, Series C, No. 402, para. 224; *Noguera et al. v. Paraguay*, Judgment (Merits, reparations, and costs), 9 March 2020, Series C, No. 401, para. 88; *Carranza Alarcón v. Ecuador*, Judgment (Preliminary objections, merits, reparations, and costs), 3 February 2020, Series C, No. 399, para. 98; *Cabrera García and Montiel Flores v. Mexico*, Judgment (Preliminary objections, merits, reparations, and costs), 26 November 2010, Series C, No. 220, para. 208.

[36] *Factory at Chorzów*, Judgment (Jurisdiction), 26 July 1927, PCIJ Series A, No. 9, p. 21.

[37] *Factory at Chorzów*, Judgment (Merits), 13 September 1928, PCIJ Series A, No. 17, p. 29.

[38] *Factory at Chorzów*, Judgment (Jurisdiction), 26 July 1927, PCIJ Series A, No. 9, p. 21.

[39] *Velásquez Rodríguez v. Honduras*, Judgment (Compensatory damages), 21 July 1989, Series C, No. 7, para. 25; *Godínez Cruz v. Honduras*, Judgment (Compensatory damages), 21 July 1989, Series C, No. 8, para. 23; *Aloeboetoe et al. v. Suriname*, Judgment (Reparations and costs), 10 September 1993, Series C, No. 15, para. 27.

[40] *Osorio Rivera and Family Members v Peru*, Judgment (Preliminary objections, merits, reparations, and costs), 26 November 2013, Series C, No. 274, para. 24.

[41] *The Environment and Human Rights (State obligations in relation to the environment in the context of the protection and guarantee of the rights to life and to personal integrity: interpretation and scope of articles 4(1) and 5(1) in relation to articles 1(1) and 2 of the American Convention on Human Rights)*, Advisory Opinion OC-23/17, Series A, No. 23, 15 November 2017, para. 45; *State Obligations Concerning Change of Name, Gender Identity, and Rights Derived from a Relationship Between Same-Sex Couples (Interpretation and Scope of Articles 1(1), 3, 7, 11(2), 13, 17, 18, and 24, in relation to Article 1, of the American Convention on Human Rights)*, Advisory Opinion OC-24/17, Series A, No. 24, 24 November 2017, para. 54.

customary international law stands in juxtaposition to its unsurpassed enthusiasm for anointing norms with the status of *jus cogens*.[42]

The African Court on Human and Peoples' Rights has made occasional pronouncements on the scope of customary international law. As is the case with the other international human rights courts, the issues tend to be those of general international law, such as the rule of exhaustion of domestic remedies[43] and the law of treaties.[44] The African Court has recognised the Universal Declaration of Human Rights as 'forming part of customary law'.[45] It has made specific reference to customary international law in dealing with the right to life[46] and the right to a nationality.[47]

In addition to strictly judicial pronouncements on the scope of the customary law of human rights, quasi-judicial and expert sources, such as the United Nations treaty bodies, the commissions of the regional human rights systems, and the special procedures of the Human Rights Council have made their contributions. The legal significance of such sources is sometimes disputed. Unfortunately, they are not infrequently dismissed as 'non-binding'. But even the judgments of the International Court of Justice only 'bind' the parties to the dispute, as its Statute makes clear.[48] The quasi-judicial and expert materials are authoritative and persuasive. For example, referring to the 'jurisprudence' of the Human Rights Committee, the International Court of Justice said 'it should ascribe great weight to the interpretation adopted by this independent body that was established specifically to supervise the application' of the International Covenant on Civil and Political Rights, all with a view to achieving 'the necessary clarity and the essential consistency of international law, as well as legal security'.[49] The treaty bodies, human rights commissions, and special procedures have unequalled expertise in the area of international human rights law generally. The weight that the pronouncements from these sources on customary international law deserve varies considerably depending upon the composition of the institution and the quality of its analysis.

[42] See the many examples discussed *infra* pp. 53–67.

[43] *Shukrani Masagenya Mango et al. v. Tanzania*, No. 001/2015, Judgment (Merits and reparations), 26 September 2019, Separate Opinion of Judge Blaise Tchikala, para. 5.

[44] *Alfred Agbesi Woyome v. Ghana*, No. 001/2017, Judgment (Merits and reparations), 28 June 2019, para. 32.

[45] *Thobias Mangara Mango and Shukrani Masegenya Mango v. Tanzania*, No. 005/2015, Judgment, 11 May 2018, para. 33; *Shukrani Masagenya Mango et al. v. Tanzania*, No. 008/2015, Judgment (Merits and reparations), 26 September 2019, para. 29; *Anudo Ochieng Anudo v. Tanzania*, No. 012/2015, Judgment, 22 March 2018, para. 76; *Ally Rajabu et al. v. Tanzania*, No. 007/2019, Judgment, 28 November 2019, para. 113, fn. 33.

[46] *Ally Rajabu et al. v. Tanzania*, No. 007/2019, Judgment, 28 November 2019, para. 113, fn. 33.

[47] *Robert John Penessis v. Tanzania*, No. 013/2015, Judgment, 28 November 2019, paras. 85–88.

[48] Statute of the International Court of Justice, art. 59.

[49] *Ahmadou Sadio Diallo(Republic of Guinea v. Democratic Republic of the Congo), Merits, Judgment, ICJ Reports 2010*, p. 639, para. 66.

The most significant statement on customary international law from the United Nations treaty bodies is the enumeration of customary human rights norms in the General Comment of the United Nations Human Rights Committee on the subject of reservations, adopted in late 1994.[50] There is no indication in the General Comment or in its *travaux* of the sources or the methodology used by the Committee. A few years later, in a decision on a petition submitted against Australia in which the parties made submissions on the scope of customary international law applicable to detention of asylum seekers, the Committee said it could not 'find any support for the contention that there is a rule of customary international law which would render all such detention arbitrary'.[51] Since then, it does not appear that it has ever revisited the issue of customary international law. On occasion, individual members of the Committee have turned their attention to customary international law, but with respect to ancillary issues, such as immunities, and not to the substance of fundamental rights.[52]

The other treaty body to venture into the area of customary international law is the Committee for the Elimination of Discrimination against Women. In 2017, it declared that 'the prohibition of gender-based violence against women has evolved into a principle of customary international law'. Twenty-five years earlier, the Committee issued a General Recommendation stating that discrimination against women, as defined in Article 1 of the Convention on the Elimination of All Forms of Discrimination against Women, includes gender-based violence, defined as 'violence which is directed against a woman because she is a woman or that affects women disproportionately'.[53] The 2017 General Recommendation said that '[f]or over 25 years, the practice of States Parties has endorsed the Committee's interpretation. The *opinio juris* and State practice suggest that the prohibition of gender-based violence against women has evolved into a principle of customary international law.'[54]

[50] General Comment 24, Issues Relating to Reservations Made upon Ratification or Accession to the Covenant or the Optional Protocols thereto, or in Relation to Declarations under art. 41 of the Covenant, CCPR/C/21/Rev.1/Add.6, para. 8. The drafting of the General Comment is discussed in the previous chapter, at pp. 31–35.

[51] *A v. Australia*, no. 560/1993, Views, 3 April 1997, CCPR/C/59/D/560/1993, para. 9.3.

[52] *Sechremelis et al. v. Greece*, no. 1507/2006, Views, 30 November 2012, CCPR/C/100/D/1507/2006, Individual opinion by Committee member Mr. Ivan Shearer concerning admissibility (dissenting) and Individual opinion by Committee members Mr. Lazhari Bouzid, Mr. Rajsoomer Lallah, and Mr. Fabián Salvioli concerning merits (dissenting); *Sayadi and Vinck v. Belgium*, no. 1472/2006, Views, 22 October 2008, CCPR/C/94/D/1472/2006, Individual opinion (dissenting) of Ms. Ruth Wedgwood and Individual opinion of Committee member Mr. Ivan Shearer (dissenting); *Koi v. Portugal*, no. 925/2000, Decision, 22 October 2001, CCPR/C/73/D/925/2000, Individual opinion of Committee member Mr. Nisuke Ando (partly dissenting); *Dumont v. Canada*, no. 1467/2006, Views, 16 March 2010, CCPR/C/98/D/1467/2006, Partially dissenting individual opinion by Mr. Fabián Omar Salvioli, para. 11.

[53] General Recommendation 19: Violence against women, A/47/38, p. 1, para. 6.

[54] General Recommendation 35 on gender-based violence against women, updating General Recommendation 19, CEDAW/C/GC/35, para. 2.

The European Commission of Human Rights began its activities in the early 1950s following entry into force of the European Convention on Human Rights. It was replaced in 1998 by the essentially new European Court of Human Rights created by Protocol 11 to the Convention. In the more than forty years of its existence, the European Commission referred to customary international law on only a few occasions. The references were to treaty law,[55] jurisdictional issues,[56] and immunities,[57] and not the substantive content of human rights law. In one decision, the Commission said that the term 'general principles of international law' in Article 1 of Protocol 1 to the European Convention 'incorporates a large body of customary international law, including both the principles of jurisdiction that allocate competence among states to make and apply law, and the well-established principles known as the responsibility of states for injuries to aliens or denial of justice'.[58]

The Inter-American Commission of Human Rights has expressed the view that many of the 'core provisions' of the American Declaration of the Rights and Duties of Man reflect customary international law.[59] It has issued two very significant decisions that consider the scope of customary international law. Both of them involved petitions by persons sentenced to death for crimes committed while under the age of eighteen. In the 1987 decision in *Roach and Pinkerton v. United States*, the Inter-American Commission rejected a challenge to the juvenile death penalty based upon the right to life provision of the American Declaration, whose interpretation, according to the applicants, was to be 'informed by customary law'.[60] 'The Commission is convinced by the U.S. Government's argument that there does not now exist a norm of customary international law establishing 18 to be the minimum age for imposition of the death penalty', it said, although the Commission considered that such a norm was 'emerging'.[61] This decision was reversed by the Commission in its 2002 decision in *Domingues v. United States*. The Commission referred to '[d]evelopments in the corpus of international human rights law relevant to interpreting and applying the American Declaration' that could be drawn from various sources including customary international law.[62]

[55] *Launder v. United Kingdom*, no. 27279/95, Commission decision of 8 December 1997.

[56] *X v. Federal Republic of Germany*, no. 1611/62, Commission decision of 25 September 1965, (1965) 8 *Yearbook of the European Convention on Human Rights* 158 and 169; *X v. the United Kingdom*, no. 7547/76, Commission decision of 15 December 1977, DR 12, p. 73; *WM v. Denmark*, no. 17392/90, Commission decision of 14 October 1993, DR 73, p. 193.

[57] *N., C., F. and A.G. v. Italy*, no. 24236/94, Commission decision of 4 December 1995.

[58] *H. v. the United Kingdom*, no. 10000/82, Commission decision of 4 July 1983, DR 33, p. 24.

[59] *Mary and Carrie Dann v. United States*, Case 11.140, Report No. 75/02, Merits, 27 December 2002, para. 163.

[60] *Roach and Pinkerton v. United States*, Case 9647, Resolution No. 3/87, Merits, 22 September 1987, para. 6. The Commission ruled in favour of the applicants, but on grounds of a violation of the right to equality.

[61] Ibid., para. 60.

[62] *Domingues v. United States*, Case 12.285, Report No. 62/02, Merits, 22 October 2002, para. 45. Also, see the subsequent cases of *Beazley v. United States*, Case No. 12.412, Report No. 101/03, Merits, 29 December 2003, para. 48; *Graham v. United* States, Case No. 11.193, Report No. 97/03, Merits, 29 December 2003, para. 52; *Thomas v. United States*, Case No. 12.240, Report No. 100/03, Merits, 29

In addition to the juvenile death penalty cases, the Inter-American Commission has considered customary law with respect to irreducible life sentences of juveniles.[63] It has said the prohibition of slavery and similar practices, such as trafficking, are customary norms.[64] It has also held that the definition of statelessness, contained in Article 1.1 of the Convention relating to the Status of Stateless Persons, 'is part of customary international law'.[65] The Inter-American Commission has invoked customary international law with respect to the right to life,[66] the prohibition of arbitrary detention, and the right to a fair trial.[67]

The African Commission of Human and Peoples' Rights has said that '[t]he right to life constitutes a norm of customary international law . . . '.[68] The African Commission has also referred to customary law with respect to the rule of exhaustion of domestic remedies,[69] conditions of detention,[70] protection of property in armed conflict,[71] statelessness,[72] and the impermissibility of amnesty.[73]

The mandates of the special procedures of the Human Rights Council can be said to involve the implementation of customary international law. They are intended to apply to all United Nations Member States, without distinction based upon whether or not a State has ratified any particular human rights treaty. In 2012

December 2003; *Patterson v. United States*, Case No. 12.439 (2005), Report No. 25/05, Merits, 7 March 2005, para. 24.

[63] *Hill et al. v. United States*, Petition 161-06, Report No. 18/12, Admissibility, 20 March 2012, para. 35.

[64] Human Rights of Migrants, Refugees, Stateless Persons, Victims of Human Trafficking and Internally Displaced Persons: Norms and Standards of the Inter-American Human Rights System, OEA/Ser.L/V/II, Doc. 46/15, para. 219; Captive Communities: Situation of the Guaraní Indigenous People and Contemporary Forms of Slavery in the Bolivian Chaco, OEA/Ser.L/V/II, Doc. 58, para. 54.

[65] Report on the Situation of Human Rights in the Dominican Republic, OEA/Ser.L/V/II, Doc. 45/15, para. 276.

[66] *Mario Aflredo Lares-Reyes et al. v. United States*, Case 12.379, Report No. 19/02, Inadmissibility, 27 February 2002, para. 46, fn. 23; *Victims of the Tugboat '13 de Marzo' v. Cuba*, Case 11.436, Report 47/96, Merits, 16 October 1996, para. 79.

[67] *Mario Aflredo Lares-Reyes et al. v. United States*, Case 12.379, Report No. 19/02, Inadmissibility, 27 February 2002, para. 46, fn. 23.

[68] *Noah Kazingachire, John Chitsenga, Elias Chemvura, and Batanai Hadzisi (represented by Zimbabwe Human Rights NGO Forum) v. Zimbabwe*, No. 295/04, 12 October 2013, para. 137. Also General Comment 3 on the African Charter on Human and Peoples' Rights: The right to life (art. 4), para. 5.

[69] *Mamboleo M. Itundamilamba v. Democratic Republic of Congo*, No. 302/05, 18 October 2013, para. 48; *Institute for Human Rights and Development in Africa v. Angola*, No. 292/04, 22 May 2008, para. 38; *Luke Munyandu Tembani and Benjamin John Freeth (represented by Norman Tjombe) et al. v. Angola*, No. 409/12, 30 April 2014, para. 96; *Article 19 v. Eritrea*, No. 275/03, 30 May 2007, para. 45; *The Nubian Community in Kenya v. Kenya*, No. 317/2006, 30 May 2016, para. 25; *Zimbabwe Lawyers for Human Rights and Associated Newspapers of Zimbabwe v. Zimbabwe*, No. 284/03, 3 April 2009, para. 99; *Institute for Human Rights and Development in Africa (on behalf of Sierra Leonean refugees in Guinea) v. Guinea*, No. 249/02, 7 December 2004, para. 32.

[70] *Thomas Kwoyelo v. Uganda*, No. 431/12, 17 October 2018, paras. 251, 271.

[71] *Democratic Republic of Congo v. Burundi, Rwanda, Uganda*, No. 227/99, 29 May 2003, para. 85.

[72] *The Nubian Community in Kenya v. Kenya*, No. 317/2006, 30 May 2016, para. 146.

[73] *Zimbabwe Human Rights NGO Forum v. Zimbabwe*, No. 245/02, 15 May 2006, para. 201; *Thomas Kwoyelo v. Uganda*, No. 431/12, 17 October 2018, para. 289; *Mouvement ivoirien des droits humains (MIDH) v. Côte d'Ivoire*, No. 246/02, 29 July 2008, para. 91.

the Working Group on Arbitrary Detention, one of the Council's special procedures, issued a significant study on the customary law relating to arbitrary detention entitled 'Deliberation No. 9 concerning the definition and scope of arbitrary deprivation of liberty under customary international law'.[74] It remains the most substantial consideration of the scope of customary international law by any of the special procedures. The Working Group reviewed the relevant provisions in human rights treaties of universal and regional application, the references to arbitrary detention in the case law of the International Court of Justice, and the legislative provisions on this subject in the domestic law of some of the States that are not parties to the International Covenant on Civil and Political Rights.

Other mandate holders have sometimes commented on the scope of customary international law. For example, the Special Rapporteur on torture and other cruel, inhuman, or degrading treatment or punishment pointed to an 'evolving standard ... developing into a norm of customary law' prohibiting the death penalty.[75] Basing herself on the precedents established in the Inter-American, European, and universal human rights systems, The Special Rapporteur on violence against women, its causes and consequences wrote that 'on the basis of the practice and *opinio juris* [...], it can be concluded that there is a rule of customary international law that obliges States to prevent and respond to acts of violence against women with due diligence'.[76] The Special Rapporteur on the rights of indigenous peoples has noted 'the emergence of customary international law in the area of indigenous peoples' rights'.[77] The Special Rapporteur on the rights to freedom of peaceful assembly and association has said that customary international law enshrines the right to strike.[78]

International criminal tribunals occasionally pronounce themselves on the subject of the customary law of human rights. They may do this where there is an international crime, such as the recruitment of child soldiers, which is in part derived from norms of human rights law. The Special Court for Sierra Leone identified the recruitment of children for participation in armed conflict as a violation of customary international law.[79] The Appeals Chamber of the International Criminal Tribunal for the former Yugoslavia said that the 'inherent right to life' was a norm of customary international

[74] Report of the Working Group on Arbitrary Detention, A/HRC/22/44, paras. 37–75.

[75] Interim report of the Special Rapporteur on torture and other cruel, inhuman, or degrading treatment or punishment, A/67/279, para. 74; Observations on communications transmitted to Governments and replies received, A/HRC/31/57/Add.1, para. 33

[76] Missing and Murdered Indigenous Women in British Columbia, Canada, OEA/Ser.L/V/II, Doc. 30/14, para. 181. Also *María Isabel Véliz Franco et al. v. Guatemala*, Case 12,578, Report No. 170/11, Merits, 3 November 2011, para. 83; *Claudina Isabel Velasquez Paiz et al. v. Guatemala*, Case 12.777, Report No. 53/13, Merits, 4 November 2013, para. 90.

[77] Report of the Special Rapporteur on the rights of indigenous peoples, A/HRC/33/42, para. 14.

[78] Report of the Special Rapporteur on the rights to freedom of peaceful assembly and of association, A/71/385, para. 56.

[79] *Prosecutor v. Norman* SCSL-04-14-AR72(E), Decision on Preliminary Motion Based on Lack of Jurisdiction (Child Recruitment), 31 May 2004, paras. 17–24.

law.[80] In several decisions chambers of the International Criminal Tribunal for the former Yugoslavia held that torture[81] and cruel, inhuman, or degrading treatment[82] are prohibited by customary international law. That the prohibition of slavery is a norm of customary international law has found support in case law of the Special Court for Sierra Leone[83] and the International Criminal Court.[84]Many punishable acts falling within the definition of crimes against humanity, including enslavement, imprisonment, torture, enforced disappearance, and apartheid are closely aligned with serious human rights violations.[85] The International Criminal Court has referred to 'the customary rule of *non-refoulement*'.[86] It has said that there is no right to compensation for an acquitted defendant under customary international law.[87]

Finally, national courts may also apply customary human rights law or refer to it for the purposes of interpreting domestic legal provisions. International law is applicable law before both international and national courts. It 'percolates down from the international to the domestic sphere, but it also bubbles up', Anthea Roberts has written.[88] The frequent reference to customary human rights law by the courts of the United States in the application of the Alien Tort Claims Act stands as perhaps the supreme example. Decisions have recognised that the prohibition of forced labour[89] and torture[90] are norms of customary international law. There are also many examples of the customary law of human rights being debated before courts in the United Kingdom,[91] Australia,[92]

[80] *Prosecutor v. Blaškić* (IT-94/14-A), Judgment, 29 July 2004, para. 143; *Prosecutor v. Kordić and Čerkez* (IT-95-14/2-A), Judgment, 17 December 2004, para. 106.

[81] *Prosecutor v. Furundžija* (IT-95-17/1), Judgment, 10 December 1998, para. 147; *Prosecutor v. Delalić et al.* (IT-96-21-T), Judgment, 16 November 1998, paras. 454, 459; *Prosecutor v. Kunarac et al.* (IT-96-23-T and IT-96-23/1-T), Judgment, 22 February 2001, para. 466; *Prosecutor v. Simić* (IT-95-9/2-S), Sentencing judgment, 17 October 2002, para. 34.

[82] *Prosecutor v. Blaškić* (IT-94/14-A), Judgment, 29 July 2004, para. 143; *Prosecutor v. Kordić and Čerkez* (IT-95-14/2-A), Judgment, 17 December 2004, para. 106.

[83] *Prosecutor v. Brima et al.* (SCSL-04-16-T), Judgment, 20 June 2007, para. 705.

[84] *Prosecutor v. Ntaganda* (ICC-01/04-02/06), Second decision on the Defence's challenge to the jurisdiction of the Court in respect of Counts 6 and 9, 4 January 2017, para. 51.

[85] Rome Statute of the International Criminal Court, (2002) 2187 UNTS 689, art. 7.

[86] *Prosecutor v. Katanga* et al. (ICC-01/04-01/07), Decision on an Amicus Curiae application and on the 'Requête tendant à obtenir présentations des témoins DRC-D02-P-0350, DRC-D02-P-0236, DRC-D02-P-0228 aux autorités néerlandaises aux fins d'asile' (arts. 68 and 93(7) of the Statute), 9 June 2011. Also paras. 67, 68.

[87] *Prosecutor v. Bemba* (ICC-01/05-01/08), Decision on Mr. Bemba's claim for compensation and damages, 18 May 2020, para. 47.

[88] Anthea Elizabeth Roberts, 'Comparative International Law? The Role of National Courts in Creating and Enforcing International Law', (2011) 60 *International and Comparative Law Quarterly* 57, at p. 69.

[89] *Doe v. Unocal*, 395 F.3d 932, paras. 44–52 and 114–116 (*per* Reinhardt).

[90] *Filártiga v. Peña-Irala*, 630 F.2d 876 (2d Cir. 1980), paras. 24–32.

[91] For example, *R (European Roma Rights Centre) v. Immigration Officer at Prague Airport*, [2005] 2 AC 1, paras. 18–28, 46; *Keyu et al. (Appellants) v. Secretary of State for Foreign and Commonwealth Affairs and another (Respondents)*, [2015] UKSC 69, para. 116 (*per* Lord Neuberger); *Elgizouli (Appellant) v. Secretary of State for the Home Department (Respondent)*, [2020] UKSC 10, paras. 89–94, 148–151.

[92] *Nulyarimma et al. v. Thompson, Buzzacott et al. v. Minister for the Environment*, [1999] FCA 1192, paras. 18–20.

Canada,[93] Barbados,[94] and elsewhere, sometimes with positive outcomes. National case law has a dual function; not only is it a source of judicial authority but it is also relevant as evidence of general practice or of *opinio juris*. In that sense it provides evidence of customary international law.

B. Peremptory norms (*jus cogens*)

In his keynote address at the 1994 University of Georgia conference on customary international law and human rights, Louis Henkin spoke of 'non-conventional' norms that 'may have sneaked into the law on the back of another idea', *jus cogens*.[95] He was careful to distinguish customary law from *jus cogens* or peremptory norms, noting that the latter 'does not reflect ancient custom or traditional natural law; it has not been built by State practice'.[96] Henkin explained that 'international non-conventional human rights law is ... like *ius cogens* ... [I]t is not the result of practice but the product of common consensus from which few dare dissent ... '.[97] Many others have treated customary law and *jus cogens* as if they are synonymous[98] or described *jus cogens* norms as a 'subset' of customary international law[99] and as a 'higher form of customary international law'.[100] Michael Wood has referred to the 'aura of mystery' that still surrounds the source of *jus cogens* rules: 'some international lawyers consider them to be a special category of customary international law; others deny that they can derive from custom; still others are of the view that customary international law is merely one possible source of jus cogens'.[101] The draft Conclusions adopted by the International Law Commission in 2019 explain that '[c]ustomary international law is the most common basis for peremptory norms of general international law (*jus cogens*)', but that they may also be derived from '[t]reaty provisions and general principles of law'.[102] One of the flaws

[93] *Nevsun Resources Ltd. v. Araya et al.*, 2020 SCC 5, paras. 60–132; *Minister of Citizenship and Immigration v. Mugesera et al.*, 2005 SCC 40, paras. 132–159; *Baker v. Canada (Minister of Citizenship and Immigration)*, [1999] 2 SCR. 817, paras. 69–71; *R. v. Hape*, 2007 SCC 26, 35–46.

[94] *Attorney General of Barbados et al. v. Joseph and Boyce*, CCJ Appeal No. CV 2 of 2005, paras. 60–68.

[95] Ibid., p. 38.

[96] Ibid.

[97] Ibid., p, 39.

[98] For example, *Prosecutor v. Brima et al.* (SCSL-2004-16-T), Judgment, 20 June 2007, para. 705.

[99] *Nevsun Resources Ltd. v. Araya*, 2020 SCC 5, para. 83; *Siderman de Blake v. Republic of Argentina*, 965 F.2d 699 (1992), p. 715. See also John Tasioulas, 'Custom, Jus Cogens, and Human Rights', in Curtis A. Bradley, ed., *Custom's Future: International Law in a Changing World*, New York: Cambridge University Press, 2016, pp. 95–116, at p. 107.

[100] *Kazemi Estate v. Iran*, [2014] 3 SCR 176, para. 151.

[101] First report on formation and evidence of customary international law by Michael Wood, Special Rapporteur, A/CN.4/663, para. 25 (internal references omitted).

[102] Report of the International Law Commission, Seventy-first session (29 April–7 June and 8 July–9 August 2019), A/74/10, p. 158.

in viewing *jus cogens* as 'very strong rule[s] of customary international law'[103] is the implication that ordinary customary norms are not so 'strong'.

The Vienna Convention on the Law of Treaties defines a peremptory norm of general international law (*jus cogens*) as being 'accepted and recognised by the international community of States as a whole as a norm from which no derogation is permitted and which can be modified only by a subsequent norm of general international law having the same character'.[104] Although *jus cogens* norms may be associated with various areas of public international law, they are of particular importance in the area of human rights law, where most of the relevant case law has been generated.[105]

Modern human rights law has a degree of resistance to hierarchy. The Vienna Declaration and Programme of Action, adopted at the World Conference on Human Rights in 1993, states: 'All human rights are universal, indivisible and interdependent and interrelated. The international community must treat human rights globally in a fair and equal manner, on the same footing, and with the same emphasis.'[106] At the heart of this concern is the subordination of economic, social, and cultural rights to civil and political rights that is reflected in the asymmetric provisions of the two International Covenants. Nevertheless, *jus cogens* norms are by their very essence in a position of superiority to all other human rights rules and principles, and the concept has been endorsed by the international human rights courts.[107] Norms of *jus cogens* 'enjoy the highest status in international law and prevail over both customary international law and treaties'.[108] Prosper Weil labelled them 'elite' norms.[109] They stand above 'ordinary customary or conventional rules'[110] in somewhat the same way as a national constitution prevails over ordinary statutes. The draft Conclusions of the International Law Commission declare that *jus cogens* norms are 'hierarchically superior to other rules of international law and are universally applicable'.[111] Article 103 of the Charter of the United Nations

[103] Anthony D'Amato, *The Concept of Custom in International Law*, Ithaca, NY: Cornell University Press, 1971, p. 132, n. 73.

[104] Vienna Convention on the Law of Treaties, (1980) 1155 UNTS 31, art. 53. Also Report of the International Law Commission, Seventy-first session (29 April–7 June and 8 July–9 August 2019), A/74/10, p. 142.

[105] Andrea Bianchi, 'Human Rights and the Magic of *Jus Cogens*', (2008) 19 *European Journal of International Law* 491, at p. 491.

[106] Vienna Declaration and Programme of Action, A/CONF.157/23, para. 5.

[107] *Al-Adsani v. the United Kingdom* [GC], no. 35763/97, § 60, ECHR 2001-XI; *García Lucero et al. v. Chile* (Preliminary objection, merits, and reparations), 28 August 2013, Series C, No. 267, para. 123, fn. 39.

[108] *Committee of United States Citizens Living in Nicaragua v. Reagan*, 859 F.2d 929 (DC Cir. 1988), para. 19.

[109] Prosper Weil, 'Towards Relative Normativity in International Law', (1983) 77 *American Journal of International Law* 413, at p. 423.

[110] Report of the International Law Commission on the work of its twenty-eighth session, 3 May–23 July 1976, A/31/10, p. 92.

[111] Report of the International Law Commission, Seventy-first session (29 April–7 June and 8 July–9 August 2019), A/74/10, p. 150.

provides a similar hierarchical rule: 'In the event of a conflict between the obligations of the Members of the United Nations under the present Charter and their obligations under any other international agreement, their obligations under the present Charter shall prevail.' The provision does not refer explicitly to customary law but the reference to 'international agreement' arguably applies to both treaty and custom. Problems arise notably with respect to Security Council resolutions that may infringe upon fundamental human rights in the obligations that they impose upon States, where it seems that *jus cogens* prevails even over the Charter of the United Nations.[112]

Given the affinities with customary international law, it seems somewhat ironic that the concept of *jus cogens* emerged in public international law entirely within the context of treaty law. Analogies were made with the law of contract in domestic law, whereby freedom of contract is limited to the extent that agreements are not enforceable if they violate principles of public policy or public order (*ordre public*). The *Code civil* adopted in 1803 declares: 'On ne peut déroger, par des conventions particulières, aux lois qui intéressent l'ordre public . . . '. English common law considers agreements contrary to public policy to be void.[113] The notion of *ordre public* in international law can be traced at least as far back as legal scholarship in the mid-nineteenth century and the opinions of Judge Schücking at the Permanent Court of International Justice.[114] In the *Krupp* trial, following the Second World War, the defendants invoked an agreement between Germany and the Vichy government to justify the use of French prisoners of war in the armaments industry. The American military tribunal said such an agreement 'was manifestly *contra bonus mores* and hence void', and that it was 'void under the law of nations'.[115] In its study of fragmentation of international law, the Working Group of the International Law Commission noted that 'the development of the international law notion of jus cogens has undoubtedly been influenced by domestic laws that provide for the nullity of agreements conflicting with ordre public or public policy objectives'.[116]

Writing as Special Rapporteur of the International Law Commission, in 1953, Hersch Lauterpacht considered that a treaty could be deemed illegal, and therefore

[112] See, for example *Kadi and Al Barakaat International Foundation v. Council and Commission*, [2008] ECR I-6351, para. 327, reversing *Kadi v. Council and Commission*, [2005] ECR II-3649, para. 230 and *Yusuf and Al Barakaat International Foundation v. Council and Commission*, [2005] ECR II-3533, para. 277. Also *Sayadi and Vinck v. Belgium*, no. 1472/2006, Views, 22 October 2008, CCPR/C/94/D/1472/2006, Individual opinion of Committee member Sir Nigel Rodley (concurring).

[113] Frederick Pollock, *Principle of Contract at Law and Equity*, London: Stevens and Sons, 1876, p. 222.

[114] The *Oscar Chinn* case, Judgment, 12 December 1934, PCIJ Series A/B, No. 63, Separate opinion of M. Schücking, p. 149. See also Egon Schwelb, 'Some Aspects of International *jus cogens* as Formulated by the International Law Commission', (1967) 61 *American Journal of International Law* 946, at pp. 949–950.

[115] *United States of America v. Krupp et al.*, Judgment, (1950) 9 TWC 1327, at p. 1395.

[116] Fragmentation of international law: Difficulties arising from the diversification and expansion of international law, Report of the Study Group of the International Law Commission finalised by Martti Koskenniemi, A/CN.4/L.682, para. 361.

void, if it were to violate the Slavery Convention of 1926. He said that the obligation the Convention imposed to prevent and suppress trade in slaves had become 'expressive of a principle of customary international law' with the consequence that 'a treaty obliging the parties to violate these principles would be void on account of the illegality of its object'.[117] Lauterpacht used formulations analogous to those of contract law, speaking of treaty provisions that were contrary to 'international public policy (*ordre international public*)'.[118] He said that voidance of contractual agreements with an illegal object was a general principle of law that 'must find a place in a codification of the law of treaties'.[119] Some years later, Gerald Fitzmaurice endorsed the same view, this time using the term *jus cogens*. The examples he provided related to such matters as aggression and piracy.[120]

The Inter-American Commission on Human Rights has explained that *jus cogens* is derived from ancient law concepts of a 'superior order of legal norms, which the laws of man or nations may not contravene' and as the 'rules which have been accepted, either expressly by treaty or tacitly by custom, as being necessary to protect the public morality recognised by them'.[121] Special Rapporteur Dire Tladi wrote of 'the idea that there are some rules of international law that apply independent of the will of States'[122] and of 'the doctrine of higher norms'.[123] The academic literature advances two approaches, one premised on natural law, the other on positivism, to explain the theoretical basis of *jus cogens*. Martti Koskenniemi has written that neither position is satisfactory on its own 'because they also rely on each other'.[124]

Jus cogens norms 'reflect and protect fundamental values of the international community'.[125] The International Law Commission traced the origins of 'fundamental values of the international community' to the Advisory Opinion of the International Court of Justice on *Reservations to the Convention on the Prevention and Punishment of the Crime of Genocide* with its references to 'moral law' and 'the conscience of mankind'.[126] The Court had taken those formulations from the

[117] Report on the Law of Treaties by Mr. H. Lauterpacht, Special Rapporteur, A/CN.4/63, in *Yearbook... 1953*, Vol. II, pp. 154–155.

[118] Ibid., p. 155.

[119] Ibid.

[120] Third Report on the Law of Treaties by Mr. G.G. Fitzmaurice, Special Rapporteur, A/CN.4/115 and Corr. 1, para. 76.

[121] *Roach and Pinkerton v. United States*, Resolution No. 3/87, Merits, 22 September 1987, para. 55; *Domingues v. United States*, Case 12.285, Report No. 62/02, Merits, 22 October 2002, para. 49. See also First report on *jus cogens* by Dire Tladi, Special Rapporteur, A/CN.4/693, para. 19.

[122] Ibid., para. 21.

[123] Ibid., para. 24.

[124] Martti Koskenniemi, *From Apology to Utopia: The Structure of Legal Argument (Reissue with New Epilogue)*, Cambridge: Cambridge University Press, 2006, pp. 307–308. Also Martti Koskenniemi, *The Politics of International Law*, Oxford: Oxford University Press, 2011, p. 52.

[125] Report of the International Law Commission, Seventy-first session (29 April–7 June and 8 July–9 August 2019), A/74/10, p. 150.

[126] Ibid., p. 151.

preamble of the 1946 General Assembly resolution declaring the punishment of the crime of genocide to be 'a matter of international concern'.[127]

The other distinguishing characteristic of *jus cogens* norms is their immunity to derogation, as Article 53 of the Vienna Convention makes clear. The International Law Commission has said a third characteristic is that *jus cogens* norms are 'universally applicable', but this seems to be more of a corollary or consequence of their non-derogability: 'The fact that a norm is non-derogable, by extension, means that it is applicable to all since States cannot derogate from it by creating their own special rules that conflict with it.'[128] The criterion of non-derogability has a clear application to treaty law. The Special Rapporteur of the International Law Commission, Dire Tladi, wrote that 'non-derogation is at the heart of the idea of *jus cogens*.'[129] Article 53 of the Vienna Convention says that a treaty is void if it conflicts with *jus cogens* norms at the time of its adoption. If a new peremptory norm emerges, an existing treaty that is in conflict with that norm becomes void and terminates.[130]

In the first explicit reference to possible norms of *jus cogens* in the work of the International Law Commission, in 1966, the Special Rapporteur gave the rather implausible example, at least in modern times, of 'a treaty contemplating or conniving at the commission of acts, such as trade in slaves, piracy or genocide'.[131] Human rights case law provides only one example where such a conflict is even conceivable. In *Aloeboetoe et al. v. Suriname*, the Government invoked an ancient agreement between the Netherlands and the Saramakas community by which the latter undertook to capture escaped slaves and to return them to slavery. The Inter-American Court of Human Rights said that even if the agreement had been an international treaty, it would be 'null and void because it contradicts the norms of *jus cogens superveniens*'.[132] Theodor Meron has dismissed examples of conflicts between human rights treaty norms and *jus cogens* as nothing more than *hypothèses d'école*.[133]

Because one of the defining characteristics of *jus cogens* is non-derogability, there is sometimes confusion with the phenomenon of derogation in the human

[127] The Crime of Genocide, A/RES/96(I). The reference to 'moral law' was not in the original draft, whose author is thought to have been Rafael Lemkin: Draft resolution relating to the crime of genocide, proposed by the delegations of Cuba, India, and Panama, A/BUR/50.

[128] Report of the International Law Commission, Seventy-first session (29 April–7 June and 8 July–9 August 2019), A/74/10, p. 155.

[129] First report on *jus cogens* by Dire Tladi, Special Rapporteur, A/CN.4/693, para. 62. See also Robert Kolb, *Peremptory International Law: Jus Cogens*, Oxford and Portland: Hart, 2015, p. 2.

[130] Vienna Convention on the Law of Treaties, (1980) 1155 UNTS 31, art. 64. See the discussion in Report of the International Law Commission, Seventy-first session (29 April–7 June and 8 July–9 August 2019), A/74/10, pp. 174–177.

[131] Report of the International Law Commission on the work of its eighteenth session, 4 May–19 July 1966, *Yearbook*... 1966, Vol. II, p. 248.

[132] *Aloeboetoe et al. v. Suriname*, Judgment (Reparations and costs), 10 September 1993, Series C, No. 15, para. 56.

[133] Theodor Meron, 'A Hierarchy of Human Rights', (1986) 80 *American Journal of International Law* 1, at p. 14.

rights treaties, whereby a State Party may temporarily suspend the application of some provisions in time of emergency.[134] The treaties that so provide also contain lists of provisions for which derogation is not authorised. The selection of non-derogable norms in the various treaties is not consistent although there is a hard core of them that is common to all: the right to life, the prohibitions of torture and slavery, and the protection against retroactive criminal prosecution. French scholars have described this is as the *noyau dur* of fundamental rights.[135] This common body of norms not subject to derogation provides an element in support of their claim to *jus cogens* status. However, there can be no presumption that the non-derogability of a rule entitles the *jus cogens* qualification. The Human Rights Committee, in its General Comment on reservations, rejected the idea, explaining that 'not all rights of profound importance' were immune to derogation, giving as examples the protection against arbitrary detention and the rights of minorities. Moreover, it explained, some non-derogable rights, such as the prohibition of imprisonment for debt, were irrelevant to national emergencies, while for others, such as freedom of conscience, derogation was simply impossible.[136] The Reporter of the American Law Institute explained that '[n]onderogability in emergency and *jus cogens* are different principles, responding to different concerns, and they are not necessarily congruent'.[137] According to Michael Wood, it is 'highly questionable to reach conclusions' about *jus cogens* based on sources dealing with 'quite different concepts such as . . . non-derogable treaty obligations'.[138]

If conflicts between *jus cogens* and human rights treaty law sit on a distant horizon, more theoretical than real, the impact of *jus cogens* on customary international law is at the vanishing point. In its draft Conclusions on *jus cogens*, the International Law Commission stated that '[a] rule of customary international law does not come into existence if it conflicts with a peremptory norm of general international law *(jus cogens)*'.[139] Furthermore, '[a] rule of customary international law not of a peremptory character ceases to exist if and to the extent that it

[134] International Covenant on Civil and Political Rights, (1976) 999 UNTS 171, art. 4; European Convention on Human Rights, (1953) 213 UNTS 221, art. 15; American Convention on Human Rights, (1978) 1144 UNTS 123, art. 27; Arab Charter on Human Rights, art. 4. For an example of this confusion, see Deliberation No. 9 concerning the definition and scope of arbitrary deprivation of liberty under customary international law, A/HRC/22/44, para. 50.

[135] Gérard Cohen-Jonathan, 'Les droits de l'homme, une valeur internationalisée', (2001) 1 *Droits fondamentaux* 157, at p. 159.

[136] General Comment 24, Issues Relating to Reservations Made upon Ratification or Accession to the Covenant or the Optional Protocols thereto, or in Relation to Declarations under art. 41 of the Covenant, CCPR/C/21/Rev.1/Add.6, para. 10. Also General Comment 29, art. 4: Derogations during a State of Emergency, CCPR/C/21/Rev.1/Add.11, para. 11 and the debate within the Committee, CCPR/C/SR.1874, paras. 24–45.

[137] Restatement (Third) of the Foreign Relations Law of the United States, St. Paul, MN: American Law Institute, 1987, Reporter's Notes, para. 11.

[138] A/CN.4/SR.3459, p. 9.

[139] Report of the International Law Commission, Seventy-first session (29 April–7 June and 8 July–9 August 2019), A/74/10, p. 189.

conflicts with a new peremptory norm of general international law (*jus cogens*)'.[140] The International Law Commission offered no examples. The Special Rapporteur cited several national court decisions as support for the view that a norm of *jus cogens* may conflict with a rule of customary law, but they were nothing more than statements recalling the hierarchy and did not in fact indicate how custom and *jus cogens* could conceivably be in contradiction.[141] If it is easy to understand how *jus cogens* norms may emerge out of custom, the possibility of conflicts between *jus cogens* and either emergent or existing custom is unfathomable.

Over time, *jus cogens* has lost its focus on direct conflicts with other norms of international law. It has come to be closely linked with fundamental human rights norms where it has taken on a sense of obligation. Thus, the consequence of identifying the prohibition of torture as *jus cogens* is not about invalidating treaties that authorise torture but rather challenging whether its absolute status has the effect of excluding ordinary exceptions, restrictions, and limitations. The debate is about such matters as access to justice despite State immunities,[142] the obligation to investigate and prosecute,[143] statutory limitation,[144] amnesty,[145] and refoulement to a State where there is a risk of torture.[146] John Dugard, writing as an ad hoc judge of the International Court of Justice, has explained that *jus cogens* norms 'are a blend of principle and policy'. According to Professor Dugard, 'they affirm the high principles of international law, which recognise the most important rights of the international order—such as the right to be free from aggression, genocide, torture and slavery and the right to self-determination; while, on the other hand, they give legal form to the most fundamental policies or goals of the international community—the prohibitions on aggression, genocide, torture and slavery and the

[140] Ibid.

[141] Third report on peremptory norms of general international law (*jus cogens*) by Dire Tladi, Special Rapporteur, A/CN.4/714, para. 140, *Committee of United States Citizens Living in Nicaragua v. Reagan*, 859 F.2d 929 (DC Cir. 1988), p. 940. See also *Siderman de Blake v. Republic of Argentina*, 965 F.2d 699 (9th Cir. 1992) at 715; *Sabbithi v. Al Saleh*, 605 F.Supp. 2d 122 (D.D.C. 2009), p. 129; *R (Mohamed) v. Secretary of State for Foreign and Commonwealth Affairs*, [2009] 1 WLR 2579, p. 142(ii); *Simón, Julio Héctor and others*, No. 17.768, 14 June 2005, Supreme Court of Argentina; *Kenya Section of the International Commission of Jurists v. Attorney-General and others*, [2011] eKLR, 28 November 2011, p. 14.

[142] *Al-Adsani v. the United Kingdom* [GC], no. 35753/97, §§ 61–67, ECHR 2001-XI; Lee M. Caplan, 'State Immunity, Human Rights, and Jus Cogens: A Critique of the Normative Hierarchy Theory', (2003) 97 *American Journal of International Law* 741.

[143] Antonio A. Cançado Trindade, 'Enforced Disappearances of Persons as a Violation of Jus Cogens: the Contribution of the Inter-American Court of Human Rights', (2012) 81 *Nordic Journal of International Law* 507.

[144] *Mocanu et al. v. Romania* [GC], nos. 10865/09, 45888/07, and 32431/08, ECHR 2014-V, Concurring opinion of Judge Pinto de Albuquerque, joined by Judge Vučinić, para. 5.

[145] *Marguš v. Croatia*, no. 4455/10, § 74, 13 November 2012; *Marguš v. Croatia* [GC], no. 4455/10, § 130, 27 May 2014.

[146] Elihu Lauterpacht and Daniel Bethlehem, 'The Scope and Content of the Principle of *Non-Refoulement*: Opinion', in Erika Feller, Volker Türk, and Frances Nicholson, eds., *Refugee Protection in International Law: UNHCR's Global Consultations on International Protection*, Cambridge: Cambridge University Press, 2003, pp. 87–177; *Rights and Guarantees of Children in the Context of Migration and/or in need of International Protection*, Advisory Opinion OC-21/14, 19 August 2014, para. 227.

advancement of self-determination... The fact that norms of *jus cogens* advance both principle and policy means that they must inevitably play a dominant role in the process of judicial choice.'[147]

There is a close relationship between *jus cogens* and *erga omnes* norms.[148] The latter are 'obligations of a State towards the international community of a whole' and 'all States can be held to have a legal interest in their protection'.[149] According to the International Court of Justice, obligations *erga omnes* 'derive, for example, in contemporary international law, from the outlawing of acts of aggression, and of genocide, as also from the principles and rules concerning the basic rights of the human person, including protection from slavery and racial discrimination'.[150] The terms *jus cogens* and *erga omnes* are often confused or treated as if they are nothing more than two elegant Latin formulations to describe the same phenomenon. A judgment of the House of Lords refers to 'the *jus cogens erga omnes* nature of the prohibition of torture'.[151] Sometimes the famous enumeration of *erga omnes* norms by the International Court of Justice in the *Barcelona Traction* case is described as a list of *jus cogens* norms.[152] The International Law Commission has explained that although all peremptory norms of general international law (*jus cogens*) give rise to obligations *erga omnes*, not all obligations *erga omnes* arise from peremptory norms of general international law (*jus cogens*). As an example it referred to rules relating to common spaces, in particular common heritage regimes, explaining that they may 'produce *erga omnes* obligations independent of whether they have peremptory status'.[153] Sean Murphy offered examples of *erga omnes* rules dealing with the sea and with outer space. He noted that in *Legal Consequences of the Separation of the Chagos Archipelago from Mauritius in 1965*, the International Court of Justice did not declare the right to self-determination to be *jus cogens*, despite being urged to do so by several States, and instead confined itself to noting its *erga omnes* character.[154] Eduardo Valencia-Ospina provided the example of

[147] *Armed Activities on the Territory of the Congo (New Application: 2002) (Democratic Republic of the Congo v. Rwanda), Jurisdiction and Admissibility, Judgment, ICJ Reports 2006*, p. 6, Separate Opinion of Judge *ad hoc* Dugard, para. 10.

[148] Report of the International Law Commission on the work of its fifty-third session, 23 April–1 June and 2 July–10 August 2001, A/56/10, p. 111. Also A/CN.4/SR.3465, p. 6 (Dire Tladi).

[149] *Barcelona Traction, Light and Power Company, Limited, Judgment, ICJ Reports 1970*, p. 3, para. 33.

[150] Ibid., para. 34.

[151] *A, Amnesty International and Commonwealth Lawyers Association v. Secretary of State for the Home Department*, [2005] UKHL 7, [2006] 1 All ER 575, para. 34.

[152] *Prosecutor v. Ntaganda* (ICC-01/04-02/06), Second decision on the Defence's challenge to the jurisdiction of the Court in respect of Counts 6 and 9, 4 January 2017, para. 51; *Al Dulimi and Montana Management Corporation v. Switzerland* [GC], no. 5809/08, 21 June 2016, Concurring opinion of Judge Pinto de Albuquerque, joined by Judges Hajiev, Pejchal, and Dedov, para. 28, fn. 15.

[153] Report of the International Law Commission, Seventy-first session (29 April–7 June and 8 July–9 August 2019), A/74/10, p. 192.

[154] A/CN.4/SR.3460, p. 9, referring to *Legal Consequences of the Separation of the Chagos Archipelago from Mauritius in 1965, Advisory Opinion, ICJ Reports 2019*, para. 180. See also *East Timor (Portugal v. Australia), Judgment, ICJ Reports 1995*, p. 102, para. 29; *Legal Consequences of the Construction of a Wall in the Occupied Palestinian Territory, Advisory Opinion, ICJ Reports 2004*, p. 136, para. 88.

norms of international environmental law to show that *erga omnes* should not be equated with *jus cogens*.[155] Alain Pellet has noted that the right of innocent passage is an *erga omnes* norm but not one of *jus cogens*.[156] On the other hand, Judge Kooijmans assumed that the consequences of violating one or the other category were identical.[157]

Peremptory or *jus cogens* norms must be accepted by 'a very large majority of States'.[158] Forms of evidence of acceptance and recognition may include 'public statements made on behalf of States; official publications; government legal opinions; diplomatic correspondence; legislative and administrative acts; decisions of national courts; treaty provisions; and resolutions adopted by an international organisation or at an intergovernmental conference'.[159] The International Law Commission has said that 'subsidiary means' for the determination of *jus cogens* status could be decisions of international courts and tribunals, in particular of the International Court of Justice, the works of expert bodies established by States or international organisations (presumably including the International Law Commission) and 'the teachings of the most highly qualified publicists'.[160] When Courts, tribunals, treaty bodies, international experts, and academics declare that norms are *jus cogens* they rarely offer much, if any, demonstration to support the claim. To the extent that they provide anything, the sources tend to be the very same ones that are used to make the claim that a norm is customary in nature.

In 1966, in the commentaries on its draft articles on the law of treaties, the International Law Commission reported on the examples of *jus cogens* norms that had been suggested: '(a) a treaty contemplating an unlawful use of force contrary to the principles of the Charter, (b) a treaty contemplating the performance of any other act criminal under international law, and (c) a treaty contemplating or conniving at the commission of acts, such as trade in slaves, piracy or genocide, in the suppression of which every State is called upon to co-operate'.[161] A much broader list, including 'dispersion of germs' and 'hostile modification of weather' was advanced in 1977 by a distinguished American international lawyer.[162] The American Law Institute Restatement of 1987 which enumerated customary norms of human rights proposed the following should also be labelled *jus cogens*: genocide; slavery or slave trade; the murder or causing the disappearance of individuals; torture or

155 A/CN.4/SR.3463, p. 14.
156 A/CN.4/SR.2902, para. 27.
157 *Legal Consequences of the Construction of a Wall in the Occupied Palestinian Territory, Advisory Opinion, ICJ Reports 2004*, p. 136, Separate opinion of Judge Kooijmans, para. 41.
158 Report of the International Law Commission, Seventy-first session (29 April–7 June and 8 July–9 August 2019), A/74/10, p. 143.
159 Ibid.
160 Ibid.
161 Report of the International Law Commission on the work of its eighteenth session, Geneva, 4 May—19 July 1966, in *Yearbook . . . 1966*, Vol. II, p. 248.
162 Marjorie Whiteman, 'Jus Cogens in International Law, with a Projected List', (1977) 7 *Georgia Journal of International and Comparative Law* 609, at pp. 626–626.

other cruel, inhuman, or degrading treatment or punishment; prolonged arbitrary detention; and systematic racial discrimination. The Restatement explained that '[n]ot all human rights norms are peremptory norms (jus cogens)' although its list was virtually identical to the one it offered for customary norms in general, the one exception being 'a consistent pattern of gross violations of internationally recognised human rights'.[163]

Production of a list of *jus cogens* norms is a controversial business and many States challenged this being attempted by the International Law Commission in the context of its recent study.[164] But the Commission went ahead, adopting a draft 'exemplary' list in 2019: the prohibitions of aggression, genocide, and crimes against humanity, basic rules of international humanitarian law, the prohibitions of racial discrimination and apartheid, slavery, and torture, and the right of self-determination.[165] It took care to explain that its list was 'non-exhaustive' and that it was derived from previous efforts at enumeration undertaken by the Commission.[166] '[S]ince the idea of norms of general international law that cannot be derogated from is exceptional, it should be the case that such norms are few in number', said Dire Tladi, the Commission's Special Rapporteur.[167] The norms are in no particular order; there is no suggestion of a hierarchy.[168] The Commission warned that its silence with respect to some norms should not be taken to indicate that they did not also have peremptory status. Nevertheless, the debates within the Commission during its 2019 session provide many helpful insights as to the extent to which the unenumerated norms that the Commission did not include might be deserving candidates.

A popular proposal in the International Law Commission was to designate environmental protection as a *jus cogens* norm.[169] The Special Rapporteur thought it might be an obvious choice given 'the importance of the subject matter and the catastrophic consequence that could result from the destruction of the environment', but he said there was little evidence of the required 'acceptance and

[163] Restatement (Third) of the Foreign Relations Law of the United States, St. Paul, MN: American Law Institute, 1987, para. 702.

[164] First report on *jus cogens* by Dire Tladi, Special Rapporteur, A/CN.4/693, para. 9.

[165] Report of the International Law Commission, Seventy-first session (29 April–7 June and 8 July–9 August 2019), A/74/10, p. 203. The only change to the list proposed by the Special Rapporteur was the addition of 'racial discrimination'.

[166] For earlier efforts at an enumeration, see *Yearbook … 2001*, Vol. II, Part 2, pp. 84–85, 112–113; Fragmentation of international law: Difficulties arising from the diversification and expansion of international law, Report of the Study Group of the International Law Commission finalised by Martti Koskenniemi, A/CN.4/L.682, para. 374.

[167] Fourth report on peremptory norms of general international law (*jus cogens*) by Dire Tladi, Special Rapporteur, A/CN.4/727, para. 57.

[168] Report of the International Law Commission, Seventy-first session (29 April–7 June and 8 July–9 August 2019), A/74/10, p. 207.

[169] A/CN.4/SR.3461, p. 9 (Charles Jalloh); A/CN.4/SR.3459, p. 20 (Maria Lehto); A/CN.4/SR.3460, p. 7 (Nilüfer Oral).

recognition of the international community of States as a whole'.[170] There was also support for non-refoulement, which has been identified as *jus cogens* in some judgments.[171] Members of the Commission pointed out that non-refoulement in the Refugee Convention was subject to exceptions, undermining its claim to peremptory status.[172] Human rights tribunals recognise a protection against refoulement without exception, but only where there is a risk of violation of the right to life and the protection against torture and cruel, inhuman, or degrading treatment or punishment. The Refugee Convention has a broader scope, sheltering refugees from being sent to a country where they would be subject to persecution for reasons of race, religion, nationality, membership of a particular social group, or political opinion. Human rights law probably does not protect someone who is not a refugee to the same degree. At the same time, the Refugee Convention brooks exceptions to the general rule, allowing refoulement for convicted criminals and national security risks.[173]

Enforced disappearance was also excluded from the list after being considered by the International Law Commission.[174] The Inter-American Court of Human Rights has found the prohibition of enforced disappearance, and the corresponding duty on the State to investigate and prosecute the crime, to be a norm of *jus cogens*.[175] There is also support for this from national courts.[176]

Some members of the International Law Commission supported inclusion of the right to life on the list.[177] Case law of the Inter-American Commission on Human Rights holds the right to life to be a *jus cogens* norm.[178] The African

[170] Fourth report on peremptory norms of general international law (*jus cogens*) by Dire Tladi, Special Rapporteur A/CN.4/727, para. 136.

[171] *Prosecutor v. Katanga* (ICC-01/04-01/07), Decision on the application for the interim release of detained Witnesses DRC-D02-P-0236, DRC-D02-P-0228, and DRC-D02-P-0350, 1 October 2013, para. 30; *Hirsi Jamaa et al. v. Italy* [GC], no. 27765/09, ECHR 2012-II, Concurring opinion of Judge Pinto de Albuquerque; *Djamel Ameziane v. United States of America*, Case 12.865, Report No. 29/20, Merits, 22 June 2020, paras. 256, 258.

[172] A/CN.4/SR.3460, p. 16 (Hussein Hassouna); A/CN.4/SR.3461, pp. 14–15 (Aniruddha Rajput).

[173] See the discussion *infra* at pp. 112, 136, 137.

[174] Fourth report on peremptory norms of general international law (*jus cogens*) by Dire Tladi, Special Rapporteur, A/CN.4/727, paras. 125–127. See also: A/CN.4/SR.3459, p.18, (Ki-Gab Park); A/CN.4/SR.3460, p. 16 (Hussein Hassouna); A/CN.4/SR.3461, p. 13 (Huang Huikang); A/CN.4/SR.3462, p. 11 (Carlos Arguëllo Gómez); A/CN.4/SR.3462, p. 17 (Juan José Ruda Santolaria); A/CN.4/SR.3465, para. 9 (Dire Tladi).

[175] *García and family members v. Guatemala*, Judgment (Merits, reparations, and costs), 29 November 2012. Series C, No. 258, para. 96; *Río Negro Massacres v. Guatemala*, Judgment (Preliminary objection, merits, reparations, and costs), 4 September 2012, Series C, No. 250, para. 114; *González Medina and family members v. Dominican Republic* (Preliminary objections, merits, reparations, and costs), 27 February 2012, Series C, No. 240, para. 130; *Osorio Rivera and Family Members v. Peru*, Judgment (Preliminary objections, merits, reparations, and costs), 26 November 2013, Series C, No. 274, para. 112; *Blake v. Guatemala*, Merits (Merits), 24 January 1998, Series C, No. 36, Separate opinion of Judge Cançado Trindade, paras. 15, 25.

[176] *Simón (Julio Héctor) v. Office of the Public Prosecutor*, Judgment, Supreme Court of Argentina, 14 June 2005, para. 38; *Siderman de Blake v. Republic of Argentina*, 965 F.2d 699 (1992), p. 714.

[177] A/CN.4/SR.3462, p. 4 (Bogdan Aurescu); A/CN.4/SR.3462, p. 11 (Carlos Argüello Gómez).

[178] *Victims of the Tugboat '13 de Marzo' v. Cuba*, Case 11.436, Report 47/96, Merits, 16 October 1996, para. 79.

Commission on Human and Peoples' Rights has also described the right to life as a norm of *jus cogens*.[179] In General Comment 29, the United Nations Human Rights Committee explained that although not all the rights that were non-derogable under Article 4 of the International Covenant on Civil and Political Rights were *jus cogens*, the right not be arbitrarily deprived of life was a peremptory norm.[180] The Commission did not include the right to life on its list, perhaps out of awkwardness in addressing the issue of the death penalty.[181]

The International Law Commission linked two related concepts, listing the *jus cogens* prohibition of 'racial discrimination and apartheid'. Initially, the Special Rapporteur had proposed 'apartheid and racial discrimination'[182] but he subsequently shortened the formulation to 'apartheid', dropping racial discrimination altogether.[183] The Drafting Committee reinstated the term and returned to the original proposal by the Special Rapporteur, explaining that this was done so as 'to align the formulation with that previously used by the Commission'.[184] By way of explanation, the Special Rapporteur said the phrase 'racial discrimination and apartheid' was not meant 'in this context, to indicate separate prohibitions, namely the prohibition of racial discrimination *and* the prohibition of apartheid (or for that matter the prohibition of racial discrimination or the prohibition of apartheid). Rather it was intended to signify a composite act, namely the prohibition of apartheid with racial discrimination as an integral part of that.'[185] Some members of the Commission noted that the Special Rapporteur had made no reference to the International Convention on the Elimination of All Forms of Racial Discrimination.[186] The Restatement of the American Law Institute declared 'systematic racial discrimination' to be a *jus cogens* prohibition but did not mention apartheid.[187] The International Court of Justice identified the prevention of racial discrimination as an *erga omnes* norm in *Barcelona Traction*.[188]

[179] General Comment 3 on the African Charter on Human and Peoples' Rights: The right to life (art. 4), para. 5.

[180] General Comment 29, art. 4: Derogations during a State of Emergency, CCPR/C/21/Rev.1/Add.11, para. 11.

[181] Fourth report on peremptory norms of general international law (*jus cogens*) by Dire Tladi, Special Rapporteur, A/CN.4/727, paras. 128–130.

[182] Ibid., para. 137.

[183] A/CN.4/SR.3465, pp. 10–11.

[184] A/CN.4/SR.3472, p. 12. The term 'racial discrimination and apartheid' was used in Fragmentation of international law: difficulties arising from the diversification and expansion of international law, report of the Study Group of the International Law Commission finalised by Martti Koskenniemi (A/CN.4/L.682 and Corr.1 and Add.1), para. 374. The commentary on the draft articles on State responsibility makes reference both to 'racial discrimination', without the term apartheid, and to 'racial discrimination and apartheid' as norms of *jus cogens: Yearbook . . . 2001*, Vol. II, Part 2, pp. 85, 112.

[185] Fourth report on peremptory norms of general international law (*jus cogens*) by Dire Tladi, Special Rapporteur, A/CN.4/727, para. 91.

[186] A/CN.4/SR.3459, p. 10 (Michael Wood); A/CN.4/SR.3462, p. 7 (Gilberto Saboia).

[187] Restatement (Third) of the Foreign Relations Law of the United States, St. Paul, MN: American Law Institute, 1987, para. 702.

[188] *Barcelona Traction, Light and Power Company, Limited, Judgment, ICJ Reports 1970*, p. 3, para. 33.

The International Law Commission might have chosen to treat racial discrimination and apartheid separately, because there was also a basis for doing this in the previous work of the Commission. In so doing, it dodged the difficult issue of addressing other specific forms of discrimination, notably against women, and even discrimination in general. One member of the Commission, Shinya Murase, had raised this issue, warning that independent reference to 'racial discrimination' might encourage calls to consider other categories, such as women, children, older persons, and persons with disabilities.[189] Hussein Hassouna said that although 'there was some support for the peremptory status of the principle of non-discrimination ... there seemed to be no universal recognition regarding the prohibition of discrimination in general, including gender discrimination'.[190] The Inter-American Court of Human Rights has said 'the principle of equality before the law, equal protection before the law and non-discrimination belongs to *jus cogens*, because the whole legal structure of national and international public order rests on it and it is a fundamental principle that permeates all laws'.[191] Similar views have been expressed by individual judges of the International Court of Justice[192] and the European Court of Human Rights,[193] and by the Inter-American Commission on Human Rights.[194]

During the 2019 debate in the International Law Commission, Charles Jalloh, said it was 'troubling' that gender-based discrimination was not considered.[195] The Special Rapporteur spoke directly to the issue of discrimination against women as a norm of *jus cogens*. The Special Rapporteur, Dire Tladi, addressed the issue directly. He said he believed, 'as a normative proposition, that gender discrimination should be prohibited in the same way as other *jus cogens* norms' but that 'one of the hurdles that this proposition would have to overcome is the significant number of reservations that are attached to the principal instrument on gender discrimination, namely the Convention on the Elimination of All Forms of Discrimination against Women'.[196] The explanation is not very compelling. There are 189 ratifications of the Convention. Many of the reservations are of course quite objectionable, but they concern the detailed obligations that the Convention imposes rather than women's equality as such. If States truly contested this underlying principle, which is also enshrined in the Charter of the United Nations, they would not have

[189] A/CN.4/SR.3459, p. 15.

[190] A/CN.4/SR.3460, p. 16.

[191] *Juridical Condition and Rights of Undocumented Migrants*, Advisory Opinion OC-18/03, 17 September 2003, Series A, No. 18, para. 101.

[192] *Jurisdictional Immunities of the State (Germany v. Italy), Counter-Claim, Order of 6 July 2010, ICJ Reports 2010*, p. 310, Dissenting opinion of Judge Cançado Trindade, para. 134.

[193] *Georgia v. Russia* [GC], no. 13255/07, 3 July 2014, Partially dissenting opinion of Judge Tsotsoria.

[194] *Djamel Ameziane v. United States of America*, Case 12.865, Report No. 29/20, Merits, 22 June 2020, para. 249.

[195] A/CN.4/SR.3461, p. 10.

[196] Fourth report on peremptory norms of general international law (*jus cogens*) by Dire Tladi, Special Rapporteur, A/CN.4/727, para. 135.

ratified the Convention on discrimination against women in the first place. The International Law Commission will account for this omission from its 2019 list with the rather feeble explanation that it was only compiling a consolidated list of *jus cogens* norms that had already been identified by the Commission, and women's equality was not among them. But that only directs attention to the historic neglect of discrimination against women by the International Law Commission, something that might in part be explained by the tradition of gender imbalance in the institution. Women were first elected to the Commission in 2001 and even now only four of the thirty-four members are women.

Some good candidates for *jus cogens* status were barely considered by the Commission or overlooked altogether. The prohibition of arbitrary detention, for example, has been declared a *jus cogens* norm by the United Nations Working Group of Arbitrary Detention,[197] the Inter-American Court of Human Rights,[198] and the United Nations Human Rights Committee.[199] There is also support for including the prohibition of retroactive criminal prosecution.[200] The right of access to justice has also been identified by several authorities to be a norm of *jus cogens*.[201] The United Nations Human Rights Committee has identified 'deviating from fundamental principles of fair trial, including the presumption of innocence' as a *jus cogens* norm.[202]

[197] Deliberation No. 9 concerning the definition and scope of arbitrary deprivation of liberty under customary international law, A/HRC/22/44, paras. 51, 75.

[198] *Osorio Rivera and Family Members v. Peru*, Judgment (Preliminary objections, merits, reparations, and costs), 26 November 2013, Series C, No. 274, para. 112; *Goiburú et al. v. Paraguay*, Judgment (Merits, reparations, and costs), 22 September 2006, Series C, No. 153, para. 84, and paras. 93, 128; *Tiu Tojín v. Guatemala*, Judgment (Merits, reparations, and costs), 26 November 2008, Series C, No. 190, para. 91; *La Cantuta v. Peru*, Judgment (Merits, reparations, and costs), 29 November 2006, Series C, No. 162, para. 157.

[199] General Comment 29, art. 4: Derogations during a State of Emergency, CCPR/C/21/Rev.1/Add.11, para. 11.

[200] *Unnamed defendant* (STL-11-01/I), Interlocutory Decision on the Applicable Law: Terrorism, Conspiracy, Homicide, Perpetration, Cumulative Charging, 16 February 2011, para. 76; *Maktouf and Damjanović v. Bosnia and Herzegovina* [GC], nos. 2312/08 and 34179/08, ECHR 2013-IV, Concurring opinion of Judge Pinto de Albuquerque, joined by Judge Vučinić, para. 9; *Ilnseher v. Germany* [GC], nos. 10211/12 and 27505/14, 4 December 2018, Dissenting opinion of Judge Pinto de Albuquerque, joined by Judge Dedov, para. 75.

[201] *Prosecutor v. El Sayed* (CH/PRES/2010/01), Order assigning Matter to Pre-Trial Judge, 15 April 2010, para. 29; *Goiburú et al. v. Paraguay* , Judgment (Merits, reparations, and costs), 22 September 2006, Series C, No. 153, Separate opinion of Judge A.A. Cançado Trindade, para. 68; *La Cantuta v. Peru* , Judgment (Merits, reparations, and costs), 29 November 2006. Series C, No. 162, para. 160; *Al Dulimi and Montana Management Corporation v. Switzerland* [GC], no. 5809/08, 21 June 2016, Concurring opinion of Judge Pinto de Albuquerque, joined by Judges Hajiyev, Pejchal, and Dedov, paras. 28, 33–37; A/CN.4/SR.3461, p. 4 (Gregor Nolte).

[202] General Comment 29, art. 4: Derogations during a State of Emergency, CCPR/C/21/Rev.1/Add.11, para. 11. See also *Prosecutor v. Ayyash et al.* (STL-11-01/AC.AR90.1), Decision on the Defence Appeals against the Trial Chamber's 'Decision on the Jurisdiction and Legality of the Tribunal', 24 October 2012, para. 68, which refers to 'the jus cogens character of fair trial'. It cites only an earlier ruling of the Tribunal, *Unnamed defendant* (STL-11-01/I), Interlocutory Decision on the Applicable Law: Terrorism, Conspiracy, Homicide, Perpetration, Cumulative Charging, 16 February 2011, para. 76, which does not, on inspection, support the proposition.

Human rights law proclaims the indivisibility of fundamental rights yet seems to do the opposite to the extent that economic, social, and cultural rights are totally absent from the discussion of peremptory (*jus cogens*) norms. During the debates in the International Law Commission in 2019 the issue did not even arise. To be entirely accurate, there was an isolated reference by a member of the Commission, who challenged the methodology of the Special Rapporteur, arguing that if the prohibition of apartheid were included in a list of *jus cogens* norms then the right to safe drinking water might just as well be added. The sense of the observation as not to lament the exclusion of economic, social, and cultural rights but rather to warn that without a more rigorous methodology insignificant or trivial matters might be deemed *jus cogens*.[203]

The exclusion of economic, social, and cultural rights is nothing more than a remnant of conservative and even archaic visions of fundamental human rights. In contemporary society, there is a consensus that certain entitlements, many of them codified in Articles 22 to 26 of the Universal Declaration of Human Rights, in the International Covenant on Economic, Social and Cultural Rights, and in a range of specialised and regional instruments, are as fundamental to modern life as the prohibitions of torture and slavery. The COVID-19 pandemic manifested a global understanding of the significance of public health and of the right to a minimal level of medical care. The right to education, at least at the primary level, is acknowledged universally as something that is not subject to derogation and that all States aspire to fulfil, without exception. Some States remain unable to ensure universal primary education, but this is a consequence of resource limitations. None of them would contend that the situation is acceptable or satisfactory, and nobody would challenge the fact that any shortcoming could be addressed through international cooperation and assistance.

C. Apocryphal customary law

International human rights tribunals and treaty bodies are often the source of pronouncements about the norms of customary law that provide no substantiation or references. It is as if they have descended from the Mount Sinai of human rights bearing stone tablets on which the norms of customary law are etched. Like Moses, the authority is unquestioned. The pronouncements then ricochet through the case law, the expert reports, and the academic authorities. The list of customary norms in the General Comment of the Human Rights Committee on reservations is a good example. In some cases, such declarations are uncontroversial and there may be no need to question the origin of the assertion. Yet the credibility of the

203 A/CN.4/SR.3461, p. 5 (Gregor Nolte).

entire exercise rests on the substantiation of claims to customary status based upon real sources providing evidence both of *opinio juris* and State practice. The tendency to pontification leaves the unfortunate impression that claims to customary status are often mere expressions of wishful thinking, of the *lex ferenda*, and not of the law as it really is.

Sometimes confident affirmations about customary law do not stand up to scrutiny. There is no shortage of examples. In 2005, a prestigious commission of inquiry headed by Professor Antonio Cassese considered the definition set out in Article 2 of the 1948 Convention on the Prevention and Punishment of the Crime of Genocide. It was troubled by the restriction of the prohibition of genocide to 'national, ethnical, racial or religious groups' because its mandate was focussed on groups 'that do not perfectly match the definitions'. The Commission chose to endorse an interpretation that had been developed by a trial chamber of the International Criminal Tribunal for Rwanda by which genocide could be perpetrated against any 'stable and permanent group'.[204] It wrote that 'the interpretative expansion of one of the elements of the notion of genocide (the concept of protected group) by the two International Criminal Tribunals is in line with the object and scope of the rules on genocide (to protect from deliberate annihilation essentially stable and permanent human groups, which can be differentiated on one of the grounds contemplated by the Convention and the corresponding customary rules)'. The Commission said that 'perhaps more importantly, this broad interpretation has not been challenged by States. It may therefore be safely held that that interpretation and expansion has become part and parcel of international customary law'.[205] But this was an unsafe conclusion, premised on incorrect assumptions about the case law. The 'stable and permanent group' thesis emanated from only one Trial Chamber of the Rwanda Tribunal but was never endorsed by the other judges. Contrary to the claim of the Commission, it was not adopted by the International Criminal Tribunal for the former Yugoslavia. And that explains why no States objected. There was nothing for them to object to.

On several occasions, the African Court of Human and Peoples' Rights has declared that the Universal Declaration of Human Rights is 'part of customary law'.[206] The most recent judgments simply cite the first statement by the Court as authority for the proposition. In *Anudo v. Tanzania*, the Court supported its view of the

[204] *Prosecutor v. Akayesu* (ICTR-96-4-T), Judgment, 2 September 1998, paras. 428–429; *Prosecutor v. Rutaganda* (Case No. ICTR-96-3-T), Judgment and Sentence, 6 December 1999, para. 57; *Prosecutor v. Musema* (Case No. ICTR-96-13-T), Judgment and Sentence, 27 January 2000, para. 162.

[205] Report of the International Commission of Inquiry on Violations of International Humanitarian Law and Human Rights Law in Darfur, UN Doc. S/2005/60, para. 501.

[206] *Anudo Ochieng Anudo v. Tanzania*, No. 012/2015, Judgment, 22 March 2018, para. 76; *Thobias Mangara Mango and Shukrani Masegenya Mango v. Tanzania*, No. 005/2015, Judgment, 11 May 2018, para. 33; *Shukrani Masagenya Mango et al. v. Tanzania*, No. 008/2015, Judgment (Merits and reparations), 26 September 2019, para. 29; *Ally Rajabu et al. v. Tanzania*, No. 007/2019, Judgment, 28 November 2019, para. 113, fn. 33.

Declaration with two references to case law of the International Court of Justice. The Court cited the *United States v. Iran* case, but without a paragraph reference. That decision states that 'wrongfully to deprive human beings of their freedom and to subject them to physical constraint in conditions of hardship is in itself manifestly incompatible . . . with the fundamental principles enunciated in the Universal Declaration of Human Rights'.[207] It is useful authority for the proposition that arbitrary detention is contrary to customary international law, but hardly supports the claim that the entire Universal Declaration is 'part of customary law'. The African Court ruling also cites a separate opinion of Judge Bustamente in *South-West Africa*. Therein, Judge Bustamente made two references to the Universal Declaration, one linking it to the 'same process of legal advance under which the abolition of slavery was first proclaimed'[208] and the other noting that 'the right of defence before the law is expressly mentioned'.[209] There are many good authorities for contending that the Universal Declaration of Human Rights is a codification of customary law but the African Court didn't cite them.

Something similar can be seen at the Special Tribunal for Lebanon, where the Appeals Chamber spoke of 'the *jus cogens* character of fair trial'.[210] The footnote reference states: '[a]s recognised by the unanimous Appeals Chamber in Interlocutory Decision on the Applicable Law, para. 76'. Paragraph 76 of the Interlocutory Decision reads as follows: 'The principle of legality (*nullum crimen sine lege*), whereby individuals may not be punished if their conduct had not been previously criminalised by law, has been so extensively proclaimed in international human rights treaties with regard to domestic legal systems and so frequently upheld by international criminal courts with regard to international prosecution of crimes, that it is warranted to hold that by now it has the status of a peremptory norm (jus cogens), imposing its observance both within domestic legal orders and at the international level.'[211] The Interlocutory Decision provided a number of references to support the *jus cogens* character of the rule against retroactive prosecution but nothing, of course, on 'the *jus cogens* character of fair trial'.

A 2015 report of the Inter-American Commission of Human Rights provides an example of what might be called the 'ricochet phenomenon'. The Commission declared that '[t]he prohibition of slavery and similar practices, such as the trafficking, are part of customary international law and *jus cogens*'.[212] The authority supporting

[207] *United States Diplomatic and Consular Staff in Tehran, Judgment, ICJ Reports 1980*, p. 3, para. 91.

[208] *South West Africa Cases (Ethiopia v. South Africa; Liberia v. South Africa), Preliminary Objections, Judgment, 21 December 1962, ICJ Reports 1962*, p. 319, Separate Opinion of Judge Bustamente, p. 356.

[209] Ibid., p. 379.

[210] *Prosecutor v. Ayyash et al.* (STL-11-01/AC.AR90.1), Decision on the Defence Appeals against the Trial Chamber's 'Decision on the Jurisdiction and Legality of the Tribunal', 24 October 2012, para. 68.

[211] *Unnamed defendant* (STL-11-01/I), Interlocutory Decision on the Applicable Law: Terrorism, Conspiracy, Homicide, Perpetration, Cumulative Charging, 16 February 2011, para. 76.

[212] Human Rights of Migrants, Refugees, Stateless Persons, Victims of Human Trafficking and Internally Displaced Persons: Norms and Standards of the Inter-American Human Rights System, OEA/Ser.L/V/II, Doc. 46/15, para. 219.

this claim is a 2009 report of the Commission: 'The prohibition on slavery and similar practices is part of customary international law and of jus cogens.'[213] The 2009 report cites an academic, David Weissbrodt.[214] But Professor Weissbrodt's statement in the report is actually a quotation from an article published in 1991 by another academic, M. Cherif Bassiouni.[215] Bassiouni's article, as the title confirms, is about enslavement as a war crime and does not make a case for slavery as such being prohibited by customary international law. The Weissbrodt study also cites a 1963 report of the International Law Commission, but the reference is to a discussion of *jus cogens* norms in the context of the drafting of the Vienna Convention on the Law of Treaties. The International Law Commission referred to 'a treaty contemplating or conniving at the commission of acts, such as trade in slaves, piracy or genocide, in the suppression of which every State is called upon to co-operate', and not to customary international law as such.[216] Finally, at the end of the footnote, preceded by a 'see also', Professor Weissbrodt also cited an article by Yasmine Rassam, then a teaching fellow at Columbia University. And Yasmine Rassam cited as authority for the customary law prohibition of slavery the 1987 Restatement of the American Law Institute.[217] Essentially, her article was devoted to identifying contemporary forms of slavery, examining whether they can be included within the scope of the prohibition of slavery in the modern treaties. It was really an exercise in interpretation of treaty texts condemning slavery as a violation of human rights. Great reliance was placed on materials from the Working Group on Contemporary Forms of Slavery. She cited the conclusions of the Working Group to the effect 'that slavery, in all its contemporary forms, is a crime against humanity'. Consequently, any acquiescence, through complicity or omission, by a state in such practices, 'irrespective of whether it has accede[d] to the convention on slavery or any other relevant conventions, is a violation of basic human rights'.[218] Rassam concluded: 'In other words, contemporary forms of slavery are considered by the Working Group to be prohibited by customary international law.'[219] Except that the Working Group did not reach such a conclusion in its 1996 Report.

[213] Captive Communities: Situation of the Guaraní Indigenous People and Contemporary Forms of Slavery in the Bolivian Chaco, OEA/Ser.L/V/II, Doc. 58, para. 54.

[214] David Weissbrodt and Anti-Slavery International, Abolishing Slavery and Its Contemporary Forms HR/PUB/02/4, para. 6.

[215] M. Cherif Bassiouni, 'Enslavement as an International Crime', (1991) *23 New York University Journal of International Law and Politics* 445.

[216] Report of the International Law Commission covering the work of its fifteenth session, 6 May–12 July 1963, A/5509, para. 17.

[217] A. Yasmine Rassam, 'Contemporary Forms of Slavery and the Evolution of the Prohibition of Slavery and the Slave Trade Under Customary International Law', (1999) 39 *Virginia Journal of International Law* 303, at p. 310.

[218] Ibid., pp. 341–342, citing Report of the Working Group on Contemporary Forms of Slavery on its twenty-first session, E/CN.4/Sub.2/1996/24, para. 110.

[219] Ibid., p. 342.

This examination of the sources is not meant as a challenge to the proposition that slavery and the slave trade are prohibited by customary international law, but rather as an example of how a claim about customary law made in 2015 by an authoritative body like the Inter-American Commission of Human Rights rests on a nebulous chain of footnotes and cross-references that ultimately do not provide the requisite confirmation. The syndrome of unsubstantiated claims that norms are customary in nature is familiar to all who work in the field of human rights law. Many such statements, perhaps most, are not necessarily inaccurate, but it is frequently difficult to untangle the *lex lata* from the *lex ferenda*.

D. Identifying the two elements of customary international law

International custom is identified, according to the Statute of the International Court of Justice, 'as evidence of a general practice accepted as law'. The text is taken from the Statute of the Permanent Court of International Justice, drafted in 1920.[220] The Special Rapporteur of the International Law Commission, Michael Wood, said that the formulation 'now almost a century old, continues to be widely relied upon and has lost none of its relevance'.[221] In one of its seminal decisions, the Permanent Court paraphrased this as 'usages generally accepted as expressing principles of law'.[222] The first of the two components of the definition, 'a general practice', is sometimes referred to as 'State practice', and is described as the objective element. According to the International Law Commission, forms of State practice include, but are not limited to: 'diplomatic acts and correspondence; conduct in connection with resolutions adopted by an international organisation or at an intergovernmental conference; conduct in connection with treaties; executive conduct, including operational conduct "on the ground"; legislative and administrative acts; and decisions of national courts'.[223]

The second element, 'accepted by law', is frequently associated with the Latin phrase *opinio juris sive necessitates* or more simply *opinio juris*, and is subjective in nature.[224] It is, explained Hugh Thirlway, 'the psychological element in the formation of custom, the philosopher's stone which transmutes the inert mass of accumulated usage into the gold of binding legal rules'.[225] Evidence that a rule or norm

[220] Statute of the Permanent Court of International Justice, (1920) 6 LNTS 390, art. 38(2).

[221] Second report on identification of customary international law by Michael Wood, Special Rapporteur, A/CN.4/672, para. 17.

[222] *S.S. Lotus (France v. Turkey)*, Judgment (Merits), 7 September 1927, PCIJ Series A, No. 10, p. 18.

[223] Report of the International Law Commission, Seventieth session (30 April–1 June and 2 July–10 August 2018), A/73/10, pp. 135–138.

[224] Not infrequently, the term *opinion juris* is also used, but this is nothing more than a perversion resulting from automatic text correction functions in word processing programmes.

[225] Hugh Thirlway, *International Customary Law and Codification*, Leiden: Sijthoff, 1972, p. 47.

is accepted as law (*opinio juris*) may include, but is not limited to, 'public statements made on behalf of States; official publications; government legal opinions; diplomatic correspondence; decisions of national courts; treaty provisions; and conduct in connection with resolutions adopted by an international organisation or at an intergovernmental conference'.[226]

Efforts to emphasise the subjective element at the expense of the objective element have been especially significant in the area of human rights. Identifying State practice was inconvenient because those engaged in human rights tend to be more concerned with denouncing violations than praising compliance. On the other hand, evidence of *opinio juris* was readily available in the form of noble-sounding resolutions of international bodies that are, in Hamlet's immortal words, honoured more in the breach than in the observance. Although the International Law Commission has resisted this trend, it seems to have been gently encouraged by the International Court of Justice. In the *Nicaragua* case, the Court focussed on the *opinio juris* rather than practice in determining that the prohibition on the use of force was customary as well as treaty-based. Speaking of his 'softening of custom', Bruno Simma thought it had opened the door to the expansive view of customary international human rights law adopted by the American Law Institute in its 1987 Restatement.[227] When the International Court of Justice identified the prohibition of torture as a norm of customary international law, in *Belgium v. Senegal*, it focussed on the subjective dimension. The Court noted that the prohibition 'appears in numerous international instruments of universal application', that it 'has been introduced into the domestic law of almost all States' and that 'finally, acts of torture are regularly denounced within national and international fora'.[228]

Nicaragua v. United States was also important for rationalising the insignificance of contrary practice. Theodor Meron thought this to be 'essential, in my view, to the effectiveness of customary law' in the area of human rights.[229] In *Nicaragua*, the International Court of Justice said 'instances of State conduct inconsistent with a given rule should generally have been treated as breaches of that rule, not as indications of the recognition of a new rule'.[230] The Court said that practice need not be perfect, 'in the sense that States should have refrained, with complete consistency' from violation, manifesting conduct 'in absolutely rigorous conformity with the rule'. What was required was that 'the conduct of States should, in general, be

[226] Report of the International Law Commission, Seventieth session (30 April–1 June and 2 July–10 August 2018), A/73/10, pp. 140–142.

[227] 'Remarks by Bruno Simma', (1988) 82 *Proceedings of the Annual Meeting (American Society of International Law)* 377, at p. 379.

[228] *Questions relating to the Obligation to Prosecute or Extradite (Belgium v. Senegal), Judgment, ICJ Reports 2012*, p. 422, para. 99.

[229] Theodor Meron, *The Humanisation of International Law*, Leiden/Boston: Martinus Nijhoff, 2006, pp. 403–404.

[230] *Military and Paramilitary Activities in and against Nicaragua (Nicaragua v. United States of America), Merits, Judgment, ICJ Reports 1986*, p. 14, para. 186.

consistent with such rules, and that instances of State conduct inconsistent with a given rule should generally have been treated as breaches of that rule, not as indications of the recognition of a new rule. If a State acts in a way prima facie incompatible with a recognised rule, but defends its conduct by appealing to exceptions or justifications contained within the rule itself, then whether or not the State's conduct is in fact justifiable on that basis, the significance of that attitude is to confirm rather than to weaken the rule.'[231] Even before the Court's discussion of this issue, Oscar Schachter, who was one of the pioneers of the American school of customary international law, argued that 'when violations of these strongly held basic rights of the person take place, they are to be regarded as violations, not as "State practice" that nullifies the legal force of the right'.[232] Schachter also attached relevance to the attitude of the offending State because its response to charges that it had violated the norm might well contest the description of its conduct rather than its recognition that there was a rule of law that it was required to respect.[233] Addressing this issue of inconsistent State practice, Elihu Lauterpacht and Daniel Bethlehem observed that 'such practice appears to be regarded as a breach of the law rather than as an indication of the emergence of a rule of different content'.[234]

Acts of torture and of cruel, inhuman, or degrading treatment or punishment are regularly perpetrated by many States. The European Court of Human Rights, which exercises jurisdiction over forty-seven Member States of the Council of Europe, has in the course of its history found 7,600 violations of the prohibition of torture and ill-treatment. A large majority of these violations took place in the twenty-first century. In the first six months of 2020 alone, the Court registered violations of Article 3 of the European Convention by thirteen Member States of the Council of Europe: Albania,[235], Azerbaijan,[236] Belgium,[237] Bosnia and Herzegovina,[238] Bulgaria,[239] France,[240] Georgia,[241] Moldova,[242] North Macedonia,[243] Romania,[244] Russia,[245]

[231] Ibid.

[232] Oscar Schachter, 'International Law in Theory and Practice: General Course in Public International Law', (1982) 178-V *Recueil des cours* 21, at p. 336.

[233] Ibid., p. 338.

[234] Elihu Lauterpacht and Daniel Bethlehem, 'The Scope and Content of the Principle of *Non-Refoulement*: Opinion', in Erika Feller, Volker Türk and Frances Nicholson, eds., *Refugee Protection in International Law: UNHCR's Global Consultations on International Protection*, Cambridge: Cambridge University Press, 2003, pp. 87–177, para. 228.

[235] *Strazimir v. Albania*, no. 34602/16, § 97, 21 January 2020.

[236] *Ibrahimov and Mammadov v. Azerbaijan*, nos. 63571/16, and five others, 13 February 2020.

[237] *Jeanty v. Belgium*, no. 82284/17, §§ 120, 129, 31 March 2020.

[238] *Pranjić-M-Lukić v. Bosnia and Herzegovina*, no. 4938/16, § 83, 2 June 2020.

[239] *Y v. Bulgaria*, no. 41990/18, § 96, 20 February 2020.

[240] *Association Innocence en Danger et Association Enfance et Partage v. France*, nos. 15343/15 and 16806/15, § 176, 4 June 2020; *Castellani v. France*, no. 43207/16, § 67, 30 April 2020.

[241] *Kadagishvili v. Georgia*, no. 12391/06, § 133, 14 May 2020.

[242] *Cantaragiu v. Moldova*, no. 13013/11, § 53, 24 March 2020.

[243] *L.R. v. North Macedonia*, no. 38067/15, § 95, 23 January 2020.

[244] *Buturugă v. Romania*, no. 56817/15, § 79, 11 February 2020.

[245] *Murdalovy v. Russia*, no. 51933/08, § 93, 31 March 2020.

Slovakia,[246] and Ukraine.[247] Indeed, it seems that only six of the forty-seven Member States have never been found to be in violation of Article 3: Andorra, Iceland, Liechtenstein, Luxembourg, Monaco, and San Marino. As a general rule, when charged with such violations States vehemently contest the facts or, rather less frequently, admit the circumstances and hang their heads in shame. But even when States have no treaty obligation with respect to torture and ill-treatment, they treat accusations of torture in much the same way as those who are bound by treaty. When the International Court of Justice explained, in *Belgium v. Senegal*, that acts of torture were regularly condemned at the international level it might have added that with few exceptions those charged with such violations never respond by invoking a lack of international legal obligation. The Universal Periodic Review materials confirm this.

In *Belgium v. Senegal*, the International Court of Justice also invoked the fact that the prohibition of torture 'has been introduced into the domestic legislation of almost all States'.[248] The Court overstated the situation. The Concluding Observations of the Human Rights Committee for many of the States Parties to the International Covenant on Civil and Political Rights indicate a total absence of legislative provision for the crime of torture or else definitions of the crime that are inconsistent with international law.[249] Even if the Court's statement had been accurate, the presence of a crime in national legislation does not necessarily support

[246] *A.P. v. Slovakia*, no. 10465/17, §§ 63, 84, 28 January 2020.

[247] *Sukachov v. Ukraine*, no. 14057/17, § 125, 30 January 2020.

[248] *Questions relating to the Obligation to Prosecute or Extradite (Belgium v. Senegal), Judgment, ICJ Reports 2012*, p. 422, para. 99.

[249] Angola, Concluding observations, CCPR/C/AGO/CO/1, para. 15; Barbados, Concluding observations, CCPR/C/BRB/CO/3, para. 11; Belarus, Concluding observations, CCPR/C/BLR/CO/5, para. 30; Bolivia, Concluding observations, CCPR/C/BOL/CO/3, para. 16; Botswana, Concluding observations, CCPR/C/BWA/CO/1, para. 15; Bulgaria, Concluding observations, CCPR/C/BGR/CO/3, para. 13; Democratic Republic of the Congo, Concluding observations, CCPR/C/COD/CO/3, para. 16l; Denmark, Concluding observations, CCPR/C/DNK/CO/6, para. 10; Eswatini, Concluding observations, CCPR/C/SWZ/CO/1, para. 33(b); Haiti, Concluding observations, CCPR/C/HTI/CO/1, para. 12; Indonesia, Concluding observations, CCPR/C/IDN/CO/1, para. 14; Iraq, Concluding observations, CCPR/C/IRQ/CO/5, para. 29; Israel, Concluding observations, CCPR/C/ISR/CO/4, para. 14; Jordan, Concluding observations, CCPR/C/JOR/CO/5, para. 16; Kazakhstan, Concluding observations, CCPR/C/KAZ/CO/2, paras. 21–22; Kenya, Concluding observations, CCPR/C/KEN/CO/3, para. 16; Kuwait, Concluding observations, CCPR/C/KWT/CO/3, para. 24; Laos, Concluding observations, CCPR/C/LAO/CO/1, para. 23; Lebanon, Concluding observations, CCPR/C/LBN/CO/3, para. 28; Liechtenstein, Concluding observations, CCPR/C/LIE/CO/2, para. 29; Madagascar, Concluding observations, CCPR/C/MDG/CO/3, para. 19; Mauritania, Concluding observations, CCPR/C/MRT/CO/1, para. 14; Mexico, Concluding observations, CCPR/C/MEX/CO/5, para. 13; Mongolia, Concluding observations, CCPR/C/MNG/CO/5, para. 13; Pakistan, Concluding observations, CCPR/C/PAK/CO/1, para. 20; Republic of Korea, Concluding observations, CCPR/C/KOR/CO/4, para. 26; Serbia, Concluding observations, CCPR/C/SRB/CO/3, para. 26; Sierra Leone, Concluding observations, CCPR/C/SLE/CO/1, para. 16; Suriname, Concluding observations, CCPR/C/SUR/CO/3, para. 24; Sweden, Concluding observations, CCPR/C/SWE/CO/7, para. 27; Sudan, Concluding observations, CCPR/C/SDN/CO/4, para. 15; Turkmenistan, Concluding observations, CCPR/C/TKM/CO/1, para. 9; Uzbekistan, Concluding observations, CCPR/C/UZB/CO/4, para. 13; Yemen, Concluding observations, CCPR/C/YEM/CO/5, para. 19.

the existence of a rule of international law. The crime of torture, or crimes underlying the crime such as assault and abduction or kidnapping, was present in domestic criminal justice long before international human rights law existed. Perhaps the criminalisation of certain acts can nourish an argument premised on general principles of law rather than international custom. That national legislation may contribute to the proof of custom seems relevant when States indicate that they have enacted such measures out of a sense of international obligation. This is the case when they refer to legislature on torture in their reports to the Human Rights Council in the context of the Universal Periodic Review.

The International Law Commission recognised that 'the same material may be used to ascertain practice and acceptance as law (*opinio juris*)'.[250] It also acknowledged that the two elements might sometimes be 'intertwined', in that 'practice may be accompanied by a certain motivation'.[251] When States report on their practice within the context of an international mechanism of accountability for human rights, the 'certain motivation' is obvious. As the International Law Commission explained, 'an official report issued by a State may serve as practice (or contain information as to that State's practice) as well as attest to the legal views underlying it'.[252]

Recent developments in international law and practice in the area of human rights greatly facilitates the identification of customary norms. The first is the Universal Periodic Review mechanism, which began in 2008 under the aegis of the Human Rights Council. The Universal Periodic Review materials constitute an immense and invaluable repository of State practice. In addition, they are particularly important to the extent that they may manifest, especially for States that are not party to applicable treaties, indications of the *opinio juris*. The second is the growing recognition of the Universal Declaration of Human Rights as a source of binding legal obligation. These two developments are related because the Universal Declaration of Human Rights is one of the bases for the Universal Periodic Review. The third is the near-universality of several major human rights treaties, a phenomenon of the past ten to fifteen years. The two human rights Covenants, the Convention on the Rights of the Child, and the three non-discrimination conventions dealing with women, persons with disabilities, and racism, are now ratified by between 170 and 196 States. Every Member State of the United Nations and most of the entities that have yet to join are party to at least one of these treaties. Each of these three sources for the identification of custom will be addressed in turn.

[250] Report of the International Law Commission, Seventieth session (30 April–1 June and 2 July–10 August 2018), A/73/10, p. 129.
[251] Ibid., pp. 128–129.
[252] Ibid., p. 129.

E. Universal Periodic Review as evidence of custom

Universal Periodic Review is one of the principal mechanisms of the United Nations Human Rights Council. It emerged from the reform proposals made by Secretary-General Kofi Annan in 2005. Annan's idea was to replace the Commission on Human Rights, which was created pursuant to Article 68 of the Charter of the United Nations, with a more robust institution, a standing body that would operate throughout the year rather than for several weeks early each year.[253] Annan said the new Council's 'main task' was to be a mechanism of peer review. 'This would give concrete expression to the principle that human rights are universal and indivisible', he said. Furthermore, '[e]qual attention will have to be given to civil, political, economic, social and cultural rights, as well as the right to development'. Annan said that every Member State would be subject to review on a periodic basis.

The General Assembly created the new Human Rights Council in March 2006. It decided that the Council was to '[u]ndertake a universal periodic review, based on objective and reliable information, of the fulfilment by each State of its human rights obligations and commitments in a manner which ensures universality of coverage and equal treatment with respect to all States; the review shall be a cooperative mechanism, based on an interactive dialogue, with the full involvement of the country concerned and with consideration given to its capacity-building needs; such a mechanism shall complement and not duplicate the work of treaty bodies; the Council shall develop the modalities and necessary time allocation for the universal periodic review mechanism within one year after the holding of its first session'.[254] The first four-year cycle of the Universal Periodic Review began in 2008.

[253] In larger freedom: towards development, security and human rights for all, A/59/2005, paras. 181–183. See Hilary Charlesworth and Emma Larking, eds., *Human Rights and the Universal Periodic Review*, Cambridge: Cambridge University Press, 2014; Valentina Carraro, 'The United Nations Treaty Bodies and Universal Periodic Review: Advancing Human Rights by Preventing Politicization', (2017) 39 *Human Rights Quarterly* 943; Frederick Cowell, 'Understanding the Legal Status of Universal Periodic Review Recommendations', (2018) 7 *Cambridge International Law Journal* 164; Elvira Dominguez Redondo, 'The Universal Periodic Review of the UN Human Rights Council: An Assessment of the First Session', (2008) 7 *Chinese Journal of International Law* 21; Elvira Dominguez Redondo, 'The Universal Periodic Review—Is There Life Beyond Naming and Shaming in Human Rights Implementation?', (2012) 34 *New Zealand Law Review* 673; Rochelle Terman and Erik Voeten, 'The Relational Politics of Shame: Evidence from the Universal Periodic Review', (2018) 13 *Review of International Organizations* 1; Karolina Milewicz and Robert Goodin, 'Deliberative Capacity Building through International Organizations: The Case of the Universal Periodic Review of Human Rights' (2016) 46 *British Journal of Political Science* 1; Rhona Smith, 'Pacific Island States: Themes Emerging from the United Nations Human Rights Council's Inaugural Universal Periodic Review' (2012) 13 *Melbourne Journal of International Law* 569; Edward McMahon and Marta Ascherio, 'A Step Ahead in Promoting Human Rights? The Universal Periodic Review of the UN Human Rights Council', (2012) 18 *Global Governance* 231; Eric Tistounet, *The Human Rights Council*, Cheltenham: Elgar, 2020.

[254] Human Rights Council, A/RES/60/251, OP 5(e).

For each Member State, three documents are prepared at the outset of the cycle. The most important is the State's own National report, limited in length to twenty pages. This is where the State confirms its own understanding of the substance of its human rights obligations. States do not explicitly acknowledge their obligations with reference to customary international law. In fact, they almost never refer to any source of obligations at all. States present reports that imply an understanding that there is a body of general international human rights law for which they are being called to account but without explaining its basis. The National report is complemented by two other documents prepared by the Office of the High Commissioner for Human Rights, a ten-page compilation of information generated by the United Nations human rights institutions and mechanisms, and a ten-page summary of information from 'stakeholders' who are mainly non-governmental organisations and national human rights institutions. These two sources are helpful in examining the country but they do not provide much insight into the formation or recognition of customary international law.

The State is reviewed in a public session of the Working Group, which consists of the forty-seven Member States sitting on the Council. The process takes place under the supervision of a 'troika', consisting of three States designated by the Human Rights Council. After a presentation by the State being reviewed, other States make observations that consist of a mixture of praise and criticism. In this way, they indicate their approval or disapproval of features of the human rights regime within the State being examined. In this way, the Review provides useful indications not only of the views on fundamental rights taken by the State being examined but also of those participating in the examination. If, for example, a large number of States commend a State for its approach to equality rights for persons with disabilities, insight is provided into the existence of a broader consensus on the subject. Recommendations are made by many of the States that participate. The State being reviewed may accept or reject specific recommendations.

The 'basis of the review' according to a decision of the Human Rights Council is the Charter of the United Nations, the Universal Declaration of Human Rights, human rights instruments to which a State is party, and voluntary pledges and commitments made by States, including those undertaken when presenting their candidatures for election to the Human Rights Council.[255] The word 'obligation' is not used in the Council's resolution but the General Assembly resolution that launched the process said that the Review would consider 'the fulfilment by each State of its human rights obligations and commitments'.[256]

At least explicitly, the 'basis of the review' does not include customary international law, although it might be said to enter through the back door as a

[255] Institution-building of the United Nations Human Rights Council, A/HRC/RES/5/1, Annex, para. 1. Endorsed by the General Assembly: Report of the Human Rights Council, A/RES/62/219.

[256] Human Rights Council, A/RES/60/251, OP 5(e).

consequence of the reference to the Universal Declaration of Human Rights. The Council resolution setting out the basis of the review also says that '[i]n addition to the above and given the complementary and mutually interrelated nature of international human rights law and international humanitarian law, the review shall take into account applicable international humanitarian law'. The relevant international humanitarian law unquestionably has a customary component. In practice, international humanitarian law plays a very small role in the Universal Periodic Review.

Most United Nations Member States are parties to both of the International Covenants. Although provisions of the Covenants are rarely referred to, there is little doubt that most of the reporting to the Council by such States is done in light of the legal obligations imposed by treaty law. The situation is different for those States, numbering about twenty-five, that have not ratified one or both of the Covenants. With the exception of a few Arab States that are parties to the Arab Charter on Human Rights, these States are not bound by any comprehensive treaties setting out human rights obligations. Their reporting to the Human Rights Council is therefore of particular interest in the identification of norms of customary international law because there can be no other source to explain the scope of their obligations. What emerges from the Universal Periodic Review is that even States without comprehensive treaty obligations consider themselves to be subject to a considerable body of international norms. Formally, it might be said that the source is the Universal Declaration of Human Rights, as this is expressly referred to in the relevant resolution on the basis of the Universal Periodic Review. But the conclusion that they are in fact reporting on their obligations under customary international law seems inescapable.

For example, the People's Republic of China has not ratified the International Covenant on Civil and Political Rights. It does not have any treaty obligations that specifically concern implementation of the death penalty, other than Article 37(a) of the Convention on the Rights of the Child that prohibits its imposition for crimes committed by persons under the age of eighteen. Some aspects of the imposition of capital punishment, such as conditions on death row, also fall within the ambit of the Convention against Torture.[257] China's reports under the Universal Periodic Review mechanism have addressed the issue of the imposition of capital punishment, including the crimes for which it may be imposed, the procedural guarantees, and the categories of persons who are excluded from its imposition.[258] China's reports to the Council manifest its own understanding that the use of capital punishment is subject to international legal standards that, broadly speaking, echo those found in Article 6 of the International Covenant on Civil and Political Rights.

[257] China, Concluding observations, CAT/C/CHN/CO/4, para. 34.

[258] China, National report, A/HRC/WG.6/4/CHN/1, para. 43; China, National report, A/HRC/WG.6/17/CHN/1, paras. 44–47; China, national report, A/HRC/WG.6/31/CHN/1, paras. 37–38.

The obligations concerning implementation of the death penalty that China acknowledges must be rooted in customary international law.

The United States of America is not a party to the International Covenant on Economic, Social and Cultural Rights. It has no comprehensive treaty obligations with respect to economic, social, and cultural rights. Yet, its reports to the Human Rights Council describe measures taken in the United States to ensure access to education, health care, and housing.[259] The United States might well object that it has no international legal obligations in this respect. It is significant that during the Review the United States made a point of stating that it did not consider General Assembly resolutions on the right to water and sanitation to be legally binding.[260] Evidently, it will indeed object when it considers certain subjects to fall outside the scope of its international legal obligations. It does not make similar objections with respect to most economic, social, and cultural rights. To a recommendation that it '[g]uarantee the right to family reunification of migrants held in detention and continue with the efforts to protect the human rights of migrant persons, particularly their economic, social and cultural rights',[261] the United States indicated its support 'insofar as it recommends compliance with our international human rights obligations'.[262] Surely the source of its obligations in the area of economic, social, and cultural rights is customary international law.

In this way, the reporting under the Universal Periodic Review provides significant indications of the *opinio juris* of States, that is, of their understanding of the extent of their international human rights obligations. The Reports by States as well as their remarks during the public sessions ('interactive dialogue') also provide information about State practice. When States volunteer information about their domestic legislation, including constitutional provisions, this is because they consider it to be relevant to international obligations. During the Universal Periodic Review, States often confirm that specific fundamental rights are enshrined in their constitutions. This might suggest that a compendium of norms of customary international law could be done by simply collating various national constitutions and looking for the common denominator. To some extent this is what the Secretariat of the Commission on Human Rights did in early 1947 in order to prepare the original draft of the International Bill of Rights.[263]

But there is a special significance to the constitutional references when they are included in reporting to the Human Rights Council. States are confirming that they not only provide protection to such rights within the domestic legal order but that

[259] United States of America, National report, A/HRC/WG.6/9/USA/1, paras. 68–76; United States of America, National report, A/HRC/WG.6/22/USA/1, paras. 100–108.
[260] United States of America, Views on conclusions, A/HRC/30/12/Add.1, para. 12.
[261] United States of America, Report of the Working Group, A/HRC/30/12, para. 176.338.
[262] United States of America, Views on conclusions, A/HRC/30/12/Add.1, para. 12.
[263] Drafting Committee on an International Bill of Human Rights, International Bill of Rights Documented Outline, E/CN.4/AC.1/3/Add.1.

they also consider the rights to be a matter of international concern and even of international obligation. For example, the United States has told the Human Rights Council that freedom of religion is protected by the constitution as well as by state and federal laws.[264] But it does not report on all 'rights' issues in national law. The United States does not provide information about 'the right to keep and bear arms', which has an important place in its constitution and in the public debate but which has no purchase at the international level. Similarly, European Union Member States do not provide information about 'freedom to conduct a business', which is a peculiarly European right comprised within the Charter of Fundamental Rights but without equivalent in other human rights treaties.[265]

Although not as important as the National reports to the Human Rights Council, the materials on the participation of other Member States in the Universal Periodic Review also provide indications of their own views on the scope of international human rights law. For example, Canada has not addressed the right to a clean environment in its National reports but it commended Maldives for its efforts 'to promote human rights internationally, particularly human rights and climate change'.[266] Sudan has not referred to the Standard Minimum Rules for the Treatment of Prisoners in its reports to the Council but it recommended that Cuba abide by them.[267]

F. Significance of the Universal Declaration of Human Rights

The reference to the Universal Declaration of Human Rights as the second component of the 'basis' of the Universal Periodic Review in the resolution of the Human Rights Council marks an important development respecting the instrument's legal significance. It is of special relevance for the twenty-five-odd States that are not parties to one or both of the International Covenants and that do not have comprehensive human rights treaty obligations from some other source. Many of these States have made explicit reference to the Universal Declaration in their National reports to the Human Rights Council. For example, Bhutan told the Council that 'many provisions of the Universal Declaration of Human Rights had been incorporated into the Constitution'.[268] Brunei Darussalam, informed the Council that it 'upholds the values of the 1948 United Nations Universal Declaration of Human Rights'.[269] Cuba explained to the Council that human rights are secured through its constitution and other legislation, 'in accordance with the rights enshrined in the

264 United States of America, National report, A/HRC/WG.6/9/USA/1, para. 20.
265 Charter of Fundamental Rights of the European Union, OJ C 326/391, art. 16.
266 Maldives, Report of the Working Group, A/HRC/16/7, para. 54.
267 Sudan, in Cuba, Report of the Working Group, A/HRC/39/16, para. 24.127.
268 Bhutan, Report of the Working Group, A/HRC/27/8, para. 5.
269 Brunei Darussalam, A/HRC/WG.6/6/BRN/1, para. 23.

Universal Declaration of Human Rights and all other international human rights instruments'.[270] Kiribati reported that it 'adheres to the United Nations Charter and the Universal Declaration on Human Rights'.[271] Micronesia explained that it 'subscribed to the Universal Declaration of Human Rights'.[272] Myanmar described national legislation aimed at 'creat[ing] a society where human rights are respected and protected in recognition of the Universal Declaration of Human Rights'.[273] Oman said that it 'included the fundamental principles of human rights, as enunciated in the Charter of the United Nations and the Universal Declaration of Human Rights, in its Constitution and legislation'.[274] Palau 'affirm[ed] its commitment towards the advancement and protection of fundamental principles and values of universal human rights enshrined in the *Universal Declaration of Human Rights*'.[275] St. Kitts and Nevis said it 'espouses human rights practices enshrined in the United Nations Charter, the Universal Declaration of Human Rights . . .'.[276] Saint Lucia told the Council that its constitution guarantees the protection of fundamental rights and freedoms 'in a similar manner as contained in the Universal Declaration of Human Rights'.[277] Singapore said it 'fully subscribes to the principles enshrined in the Universal Declaration of Human Rights'.[278] The United Arab Emirates reported that it had 'taken care to incorporate the fundamental human rights principles enshrined in the Charter of the United Nations and the Universal Declaration of Human Rights into its Constitution and laws'.[279] Tuvalu stated that it 'adheres to the United Nations Charter and the Universal Declaration on Human Rights'.[280]

A few States are parties to the International Covenant on Economic, Social and Cultural Rights but not the International Covenant on Civil and Political Rights. One of them, China, said it respects 'the basic spirit of the Universal Declaration of Human Rights'.[281] Fiji 'affirm[ed] its commitment towards the advancement and protection of fundamental principles and values of universal human rights enshrined in the *Universal Declaration of Human Rights*'.[282]

[270] Cuba, Report of the Working Group, A/HRC/24/16, para. 13. Also Cuba, National report, A/HRC/WG.6/4/CUB/1, para. 33.

[271] Kiribati, National report, A/HRC/WG.6/8/KIR/1, para. 19.

[272] Micronesia, Report of the Working Group, A/HRC/16/16, para. 22. Also Micronesia, National report, A/HRC/WG.6/9/FSM/1, para. 13.

[273] Myanmar, National report, A/HRC/WG.6/23/MMR/1, para. 25.

[274] Oman, Report of the Working Group, A/HRC/10/75, para. 41.

[275] Palau, National report, A/HRC/WG.6/24/PLW/1, para. 1. Also Palau, National report, A/HRC/WG.6/11/PLW/1, para. 29.

[276] St. Kitts and Nevis, National report, A/HRC/WG.6/10/KNA/1, para. 16.

[277] Saint Lucia, National report, A/HRC/WG.6/23/LCA/1, para. 60. Also Saint Lucia, Report of the Working Group, A/HRC/17/6, para. 8 and Views on conclusions, A/HRC/17/6/Add.1, para. 89.35.

[278] Singapore, National report, A/HRC/WG.6/11/SGP/1, para. 33. Also ibid., para. 20 and Singapore, National report, A/HRC/WG.6/24/SGP/1, para. 4.

[279] United Arab Emirates, National report, A/HRC/WG.6/3/ARE/1, p. 12.

[280] Tuvalu, National report, A/HRC/WG.6/16/TUV/1, para. 35 and National report, A/HRC/WG.6/3/TUV/1, para. 29.

[281] China, National report, A/HRC/WG.6/17/CHN/1, para. 4.

[282] Fiji, National report, A/HRC/WG.6/20/FJI/1, para. 1.

The Marshall Islands said it 'adhere[d] to the Universal Declaration on Human Rights'.[283]

During the Universal Periodic Review, some States have taken the opportunity to vaunt their contribution to the adoption of the Universal Declaration. France reminded the Human Rights Council that it was in Paris, 'at the Palais de Chaillot where the General Assembly of the United Nations was being held in 1948, that the Universal Declaration of Human Rights was adopted. One of the main architects of the Declaration was the eminent French jurist, René Cassin, who went on to become Chairman of the United Nations Commission on Human Rights, President of the European Court of Human Rights, and a Nobel Peace Prize Laureate.'[284] Myanmar reported that it 'was the first to vote and voted for the Declaration. It represents Myanmar's landmark position in the history of United Nations in promoting and protecting of human rights.'[285] Indeed, on 10 December 1948 the President of the General Assembly announced that a roll call vote was to be taken on the final draft. He drew the name of Burma by lot, and the others followed in alphabetical order.[286] The first National report by the United States to the Human Rights Council '[e]cho[ed] Eleanor Roosevelt, whose leadership was crucial to the adoption of the Universal Declaration of Human Rights'.[287] Lebanon recalled that it 'participated in drafting the Universal Declaration of Human Rights',[288] an understatement given the central role played by its delegate, Charles Malik.[289] Saudi Arabia told the Council that it 'was among the first States to participate in the drafting of the Universal Declaration'.[290] This was not full disclosure of its role, as Saudi Arabia was one of the notorious abstainers when the final vote was taken in the General Assembly on 10 December 1948.

There is today considerable authority for the view that much if not all of the Declaration constitutes a codification of customary international law. Indeed, this is a relatively uncontroversial proposition although there is little discussion about the provisions of the Declaration that are not to be considered customary. In his exhaustive review of political, judicial, and scholarly pronouncements on the status of the Universal Declaration undertaken in the mid-1990s, Hurst Hannum said that those who held that it consisted *in toto* of customary norms were in the minority. He gave three examples of rights set out in the Declaration that he thought

[283] Marshall Islands, Views on conclusions, A/HRC/WG.6/9/MHL/1/Rev.1, para. 86.
[284] France, National report, A/HRC/WG.6/2/FRA/1, para. 3.
[285] Myanmar, National report, A/HRC/WG.6/23/MMR/1, para. 94.
[286] Hundred and Eighty-Third Plenary Meeting [of the General Assembly], 10 December 1948, *Official Records of the General Assembly*, Third Session, 1948, p. 933.
[287] United States of America, National report, A/HRC/WG.6/9/USA/1, para. 5.
[288] Lebanon, National report, A/HRC/WG.6/9/LBN/1, para. 13.
[289] Habib C. Malik, ed., *The Challenge of Human Rights, Charles Malik and the Universal Declaration*, Oxford: Centre for Lebanese Studies, 2000.
[290] Saudi Arabia, National report, A/HRC/WG.6/4/SAU/1, para. 19.

would not be generally accepted: periodic holidays with pay, full equality of rights upon dissolution of a marriage, and protection against unemployment.[291]

Vice-President Ammoun of the International Court of Justice wrote that although 'the affirmations of the Declaration are not binding qua international convention ... , they can bind States on the basis of custom within the meaning of paragraph l(b) of [Article 38 of the Statute of the Court] ... because they constituted a codification of customary law... or because they have acquired the force of custom through a general practice accepted as law'.[292] Perhaps inspired by these remarks, the Court as a whole invoked the Universal Declaration as a normative standard in assessing Iran's compliance with international law following the hostage-taking at the United States embassy: 'Wrongfully to deprive human beings of their freedom and to subject them to physical constraint in conditions of hardship is in itself manifestly incompatible with the principles of the Charter of the United Nations, as well as with the fundamental principles enunciated in the Universal Declaration of Human Rights.'[293]

G. Near-universal ratification of human rights treaties

In contrast with many areas of international law, including international humanitarian law, where a body of customary law existed prior to any codification, human rights law was codified before customary norms were identified. There is clearly a synergy between treaties and custom. The International Court of Justice has explained that the 'provisions and the process of their adoption and implementation [of multilateral treaties] shed light on the content of customary international law'.[294] Moreover, 'multilateral conventions may have an important role to play in recording and defining rules deriving from custom, or indeed in developing them'.[295] The Court has said that 'even without the passage of any considerable period of time, a very widespread and representative participation in [a] convention might suffice of itself' to indicate the existence of custom.[296] In *Nicaragua v. United States*, the Court treated provisions of the Charter of the United Nations and of the Charter of the Organization of American States dealing with the prohibition of the use of force as, in effect, codifications of customary international law.[297]

[291] Hurst Hannum, 'The Status of the Universal Declaration of Human Rights in National and International Law', (1995) 25 *Georgia Journal of International and Comparative Law* 287, p. 340.

[292] *Legal Consequences for States of the Continued Presence of South Africa in Namibia (South West Africa) Notwithstanding Security Council Resolution 276 (1970)*, *ICJ Reports 1971*, p. 16, Separate Opinion of Vice-President Ammoun, p. 76.

[293] *United States Diplomatic and Consular Staff in Tehran, Judgment, ICJ Reports 1980*, p. 3, para. 91.

[294] *Jurisdictional Immunities of the State (Germany v. Italy: Greece intervening), Judgment, ICJ Reports 2012*, p. 99, para. 66.

[295] *Continental Shelf (Libyan Arab Jamahiriya/Malta), Judgment, ICJ Reports 1985*, p. 13, para. 27.

[296] *North Sea Continent Shelf, Judgment, ICJ Reports 1969*, p. 3, para. 73.

[297] *Military and Paramilitary Activities in and against Nicaragua (Nicaragua v. United States of America), Merits, Judgment, ICJ Reports 1986*, p. 14, paras. 183–184.

In its study of customary law, the International Law Association said that a multilateral treaty may provide evidence of existing custom. Although there is no general presumption that this is the case, it may assist in the 'crystallisation' of emerging custom, and may 'even give rise to new custom of "its own impact" if the rule concerned is of a fundamentally norm-creating character and is widely adopted by States with a view to creating a new general legal obligation'.[298] It has been held that 'there is no obstacle in international law to the expression of the will of States through treaties being at the same time an expression of practice and of the opinio juris necessary for the birth of a customary rule if the conditions for it are met'.[299] The Draft Conclusions of the International Law Commission affirm that a rule set forth in a treaty 'may reflect a rule of customary international law if it is established that the treaty rule: (*a*) codified a rule of customary international law existing at the time when the treaty was concluded; (*b*) has led to the crystallisation of a rule of customary international law that had started to emerge prior to the conclusion of the treaty; or (*c*) has given rise to a general practice that is accepted as law (*opinio juris*), thus generating a new rule of customary international law'.[300]

One of the factors that initially generated interest in the customary law of human rights was the slow pace not so much of codification as of the acceptance of human rights treaty obligations. The two Covenants on human rights, designed to complement the Universal Declaration of Human Rights in the package known as the International Bill of Rights, took a decade to obtain the required thirty-five ratifications for entry into force. The country where there was probably the most interest in the customary law of human rights, the United States, did not ratify any of the important international conventions until the 1990s. Its participation in the treaty system still remains somewhat incomplete.

Today, many of the major human rights conventions have achieved near-universal ratification, providing very compelling evidence that the norms they contain are customary in nature. The Convention on the Rights of the Child, with 196 ratifications, is at the head of the pack. The Convention on the Elimination of All Forms of Discrimination against Women has 189 ratifications, followed by the Convention on the Rights of Persons with Disabilities and the International Convention on the Elimination of All Forms of Racial Discrimination, both with 182. The two general treaties of global application, the International Covenant on Civil and Political Rights and the International Covenant on Economic, Social and Cultural Rights, have 173 and 170 States Parties respectively.

[298] International Law Association, Final Report of the Committee on the Formation of Customary (General) International Law, Statement of Principles Applicable to the Formation of General Customary International Law, Report of the Sixty-Ninth Conference, London, 2000, pp. 43–44, 49–50.

[299] *Camuzzi International S.A. v. The Argentine Republic*, ICSID Case No. ARB/03/2, Decision on Objections to Jurisdiction, 11 May 2005, para. 144, citing Julio A. Barberis, 'Reflexions sur la coutume internationale', (1990) 36 *Annuaire Français de Droit International* 9.

[300] Report of the International Law Commission, Seventieth session (30 April–1 June and 2 July–10 August 2018), A/73/10, pp. 143–146.

In his study of customary international law, published in 1989, Theodor Meron examined the level of ratification of the major human rights treaties.[301] At the time there were eighty-seven States Parties to the Covenant on Civil and Political Rights and ninety-one to the Covenant on Economic, Social, and Cultural Rights. The Convention on the Elimination of All Forms of Discrimination against Women had ninety-four States Parties in 1989. These numbers have now about doubled, although it should be borne in mind that there are about forty more Member States in the United Nations than there were then. Meron's principal critics, Bruno Simma and Philip Alston, did not think that reference to treaty ratifications as evidence of custom was very helpful. They pointed to what they considered to be the low rate of ratification of the Covenants and concluded that 'a certain plateau seems to have been reached'.[302] The point here is that the world has changed dramatically from what it was when these early debates about customary law and human rights took place. Today, the near-universal treaties provide very compelling evidence of custom.

All States are equal, as the Charter of the United Nations reminds us, but in a search for near-universality it is not without relevance to note that more than half of the States that have not ratified one or both of the Covenants record a population of less than one million. Indeed, nine of them taken together have a total population of about one million inhabitants. If they were grouped together in a city, they would rank about 540th in size in the world, comparable to Odessa, Ukraine, or Marrakesh, Morocco. Sometimes these small States indicate that they have no difficulty in principle with ratification of the Covenants and that the obstacles to ratification or accession are technical in nature.[303] Six large States, with populations well in excess of one million, have not signed, ratified, or acceded to either of the two international covenants: Malaysia, Oman, Saudi Arabia, Singapore, South Sudan, and the United Arab Emirates. Their combined population is about 140 million, or not quite 2% of the world's total. With the exception of South Sudan, a new State that recently split from a State that is a party to the two Covenants, they are all confined to two regions, the Gulf and Southeast Asia. In its National report to the Human Rights Council South Sudan actually claimed, by mistake, that it was a party to the Covenants.[304] At the conclusion of the Universal Periodic Review, South Sudan accepted several recommendations that it proceed to ratification

[301] Theodor Meron, *Human Rights and Humanitarian Norms as Customary Law*, Oxford: Oxford University Press, 1989, p. 97, fn. 1.

[302] Bruno Simma and Philip Alston, 'The Sources of Human Rights Law: Custom, Jus Cogens, and General Principles', (1992) 12 *Australian Yearbook of International Law* 82, at p. 87.

[303] Bhutan, Report of the Working Group, A/HRC/27/8/Add.1, para. 2.1 and Views on conclusions, A/HRC/42/8/Add.1, p. 2; Comoros, Report of the Working Group, A/HRC/41/12, para. 118.1; Kiribati, Views on conclusions, A/HRC/15/3/Add.1, para. 11; Marshall Islands, Report of the Working Group, A/HRC/16/12/Add.1, Addendum, para. 55.1; Micronesia, Views on conclusions, A/HRC/31/4/Add.1, para. 2; Palau, A/HRC/32/11/Add.1, para. 3; Tonga, Report of the Working Group, A/HRC/38/5, para. 6.

[304] South Sudan, National report, A/HRC/WG.6/26/SSD/1, para. 17.

although it said it would appreciate 'technical assistance and resources' in order to fully implement its obligations.[305] Taiwan with its population of twenty million, signed the two covenants in the late 1960s but has been prevented from ratifying them because of the one-China policy followed by the United Nations. Taiwan prepares periodic reports on compliance with the two Covenants, as if it were actually a State party. These are reviewed by independent experts who issue concluding observations. There is no doubt that if ratification were allowed by the depository of the treaties, Taiwan would not hesitate to do so.

Reservations to treaties must be taken into account in assessing their universal or near-universal character. A reservation is 'a unilateral statement, however phrased or named, made by a State, when signing, ratifying, accepting, approving or acceding to a treaty, whereby it purports to exclude or to modify the legal effect of certain provisions of the treaty in their application to that State'.[306] States sometimes disguise what amount to reservations by labelling them interpretative declarations.[307] Reservations to treaties are often met with objections from other States Parties.

Most provisions in the major international human rights treaties have actually been subject to very few reservations. Such provisions, when they are accompanied by near-universal ratification, and by statements recognising the norm in the Reports of non-party States to the Human Rights Council, prompt a relatively firm conclusion that they define a norm of customary international law. On the other hand, where there are a significant number of reservations to a provision, this weakens any claim to customary status.

Reservations to the treaties require severe scrutiny as their formulation is often quite vague. This is one of the common explanations for objections to the reservation. But this problem is not so important with respect to the identification of customary international law because the issue is not the legality or permissibility of the reservation. Whether the reservation is compatible with the object and purpose of the treaty is a concern for the other States Parties but it is not really germane to the determination of customary law. The reservation, whether or not it is legally valid, is a manifestation of the *opinio juris* of a State. This is what makes it relevant to research into customary law. Several States have made reservations whereby they subject the ratification of the treaty subject to consistency with their own constitutional law. This may be a source of uncertainty for other treaty partners, rendering it objectionable, but for the purposes of identifying customary law it becomes necessary to examine the State's constitution. Examination of the constitution may indicate that there are no significant conflicts with many of the provisions in the

305 South Sudan, Views on conclusions, A/HRC/34/13/Add.1, para. 4(a).

306 Vienna Convention on the Law of Treaties, (1980) 1155 UNTS 31, art. 1(d).

307 General Comment 24, Issues Relating to Reservations Made upon Ratification or Accession to the Covenant or the Optional Protocols thereto, or in Relation to Declarations under art. 41 of the Covenant, CCPR/C/21/Rev.1/Add.6, para. 3.

treaty. Where this is the case, the reservation should not be taken as evidence that the norm in the treaty affected by the reservation is not customary in nature.

A significant number of States have made reservations requiring that their obligations under certain treaties be consistent with Islamic law or the Shariah. For example, when it ratified the Convention on the Rights of the Child Iran reserved 'the right not to apply any provisions or articles of the Convention that are incompatible with Islamic Laws and the internal legislation in effect'.[308] The scope is intolerably nebulous, of course, and there were several objections from States who complained that made difficult the determination of Iran's obligations under the Convention.[309] But at the same time it is certain that the reservation has no application or relevance, for example, to the right of the child to a nationality enshrined in Article 7 of the Convention, amongst other provisions. This is confirmed in Iran's reports to the Committee on the Rights of the Child, which make no reference to Islamic law in comments on many of the provisions of the Convention.[310] Iran told the Committee that it was subject to the provisions of the Convention 'provided that they do not contradict the principles of the Sharia (Holy Laws)',[311] but only on rare occasions has it actually invoked Islamic law in its reports to the Committee. It said that under 'the lofty Islamic Sharia ... an undiscerning minor is not liable to prosecution and punishment'.[312] There does not seem to be any meaningful difference with Article 40(3)(a) of the Convention requiring '[t]he establishment of a minimum age below which children shall be presumed not to have the capacity to infringe the penal law'.

Saudi Arabia made a reservation along the same lines to the Convention on the Elimination of All Forms of Discrimination against Women: 'In case of contradiction between any term of the Convention and the norms of Islamic Law, the Kingdom is not under obligation to observe the contradictory terms of the Convention.'[313] The 'norms of Islamic Law' may have some relevance to certain provisions of the Convention but they are also quite irrelevant to many of them. With respect to equal opportunity in terms of education and employment, Saudi Arabia told the Committee on the Elimination of Discrimination against Women that it has 'since its creation, taken all measures to ensure equality of women with men in respect of rights, including the right to obtain education and work, and training to acquire the skills necessary to qualify women for access to the job market and equip them to raise their children and care for their health'.[314] It does not seem that Saudi Arabia considers that its reservation in any way limits or

[308] C.N.235.1994.TREATIES-4.
[309] C.N.321.1995.TREATIES -6.
[310] On art. 7 of the Convention, see: Iran, Initial report, CRC/C/41/Add.5, paras. 28–37.
[311] Iran, Initial report, CRC/C/41/Add.5, para. 1.
[312] Iran, Second periodic report, CRC/C/104/Add.3, para. 204.
[313] C.N.925.2000.TREATIES-8.
[314] Saudi Arabia, Combined initial and second periodic report, CEDAW/C/SAU/2, p. 15.

restrains these rights. There may well be shortcomings in its implementation of women's equality in the area of education and employment in Saudi Arabia, but the same might be said of many other States Parties, some of them with no reservations to the Convention.

When the Human Rights Committee, in its General Comment on reservations, claimed that it was contrary to customary international law 'to permit the advocacy of national, racial or religious hatred',[315] the United States challenged the conclusion that 'on the basis of practice or other authority, for example, that the mere expression (albeit deplorable) of national, racial or religion hatred (unaccompanied by any overt action of preparation) is prohibited by customary international law'. It said that the Committee 'seems to be suggesting here that the reservations which a large number of States Parties have submitted to article 20 are per se invalid'.[316] A similar observation appears in a partly dissenting opinion from a judgment of the Appeals Chamber of the International Criminal Tribunal for Rwanda. Judge Theodor Meron contended that 'mere hate speech' did not fall within the scope of the crime against humanity of persecution, contrary to the conclusion of the Trial Chamber, which had invoked provisions of the International Covenant on Civil and Political Rights and the International Convention on the Elimination of all Forms of Racial Discrimination in support of its position.[317] Meron acknowledged that these instruments required States Parties to prohibit hate speech but he noted that 'various states have entered reservations with respect to these provisions', giving France and the United States as examples. 'Critically, no state party has objected to such reservations', wrote Meron. 'The number and extent of the reservations reveal that profound disagreement persists in the international community as to whether mere hate speech is or should be prohibited, indicating that Article 4 of the CERD and Article 20 of the ICCPR do not reflect a settled principle. Since a consensus among states has not crystallised, there is clearly no norm under customary international law criminalising mere hate speech.'[318]

Under closer examination, the assessments by the United States and by Judge Meron appear greatly exaggerated. It is true that the provisions in question provoked a not insignificant reaction from States Parties at the time of ratification, but in most cases this took the form of interpretative declarations or understandings

[315] General Comment 24, Issues Relating to Reservations Made upon Ratification or Accession to the Covenant or the Optional Protocols thereto, or in Relation to Declarations under art. 41 of the Covenant, CCPR/C/21/Rev.1/Add.6, para. 8.

[316] 'Observations on General Comment No. 24 (52), on issues relating to reservations made upon ratification or accession to the Covenant or the Optional Protocols thereto, or in relation to declarations under article 41 of the Covenant', Report of the Human Rights Committee, Vol. I, A/50/40, Annex VI, pp. 126–134, at p. 128.

[317] *Prosecutor v. Nahimana et al.* (ICTR-99-52-T), Judgment and Sentence, 3 December 2003, paras. 985–990.

[318] *Prosecutor v. Nahimana et al.* (ICTR-99-52-TA), Partly dissenting opinion of Judge Meron, 28 November 2007, para. 5.

rather than genuine reservations.[319] Meron pointed specifically to France as a State that 'objected' to any obligation that would encroach upon freedom of expression, citing its statement upon ratification of the International Convention on the Elimination of All Forms of Racial Discrimination. But it is obvious that France only made an interpretative declaration, not a reservation.[320] In reports to the Committee on the Elimination of Racial Discrimination, France has insisted that it 'did not formulate a reservation to article 4 of the Convention, but made a declaration, the purpose of which is not to reduce the scope of the obligations provided for by the Convention but only to record its interpretation of article 4 of the Convention.'[321] France has regularly demonstrated a commitment to the enactment and enforcement of robust legislation dealing with 'mere hate speech.'[322] It has referred to a 'legislative arsenal' that includes criminal penalties for incitement to discrimination and racial hatred.[323] Meron also cited the four States, other than the United States, with reservations to Article 20(2) of the Covenant. But those four States, Australia, New Zealand, Malta, and the United Kingdom, only reserved the right not to introduce additional legislation on the grounds that they had already addressed the obligation.

[319] To art. 20 of the International Covenant on Civil and Political Rights: Australia, C.N.230.1980.TREATIES-6; Belgium, C.N.113.1983.TREATIES-4; Luxembourg, C.N.265.1983.TREATIES-3/8/2; Malta, C.N.304.1990.TREATIES-4/11/4; New Zealand, C.N.329.1978.TREATIES-15; United Kingdom, C.N.193.1976.TREATIES-6; United States of America, C.N.250.1992.TREATIES-14. To art. 20(1) only of the Covenant: Denmark, C.N.10.1972.TREATIES-1; Finland, C.N.210.1975.TREATIES-7; France, C.N.335.1980.TREATIES-10; Iceland, C.N.189.1979.TREATIES-6; Ireland, C.N.344.1989.TREATIES-2/17/4; Netherlands, C.N.316.1978.TREATIES-l4; Norway, C.N.188.1972.TREATIES-7; Sweden, C.N.198.1971.TREATIES-6; Switzerland, C.N.223.1992.TREATIES-7/12; Thailand, CN.381.1996.TREATIES-8. To art. 4 of the International Convention on the Elimination of All Forms of Racial Discrimination: Antigua and Barbuda, C.N.264.1988.TREATIES-2; Australia, C.N.272.1975.TREATIES-8; Austria, C.N.71.1972.TREATIES-4; Bahamas, C.N.220.1975.TREATIES-6; Barbados, C.N.225.1972.TREATIES-16; Belgium, C.N.213.1975.TREATIES-5; France, C.N.151.1971.TREATIES-17; Grenada, C.N.278.2013.TREATIES-IV.2; Guyana, C.N.50.1977.TREATIES-1; Ireland, C.N.1460.2000.TREATIES-10; Italy, C.N.3.1976.TREATIES-1; Jamaica, C.N.98.1971.TREATIES-12; Malta, C.N.148.1968. TREATIES-5 (upon signature); Nepal, C.N.16.1971.TREATIES-3; Papua New Guinea, C.H.32.1982.TREATIES-1; Switzerland, C.N.356.l994.TREATIES-3; Tonga, C.N.35.1972.TREATIES-2; United Kingdom, C.N.219.1966.TREATIES-5 (upon signature); United States of America, C.N.356.l994.TREATIES-3.

[320] 'With regard to article 4, France wishes to make it clear that it interprets the reference made therein to the principles of the Universal Declaration of Human Rights and to the rights set forth in article 5 of the Convention as releasing the States Parties from the obligation to enact anti-discrimination legislation which is incompatible with the freedoms of opinion and expression and of peaceful assembly and association guaranteed by those texts.'

[321] France, Combined twenty-second and twenty-third periodic reports submitted by France under art. 9 of the Convention, due in 2017, CERD/C/FRA/22-23, para. 65.

[322] For example, France, Fourteenth periodic reports of States Parties due in 1998, CERD/C/337/Add.5, paras. 121–151; France, Sixteenth periodic reports of States Parties due in 2002, CERD/C/430/Add.4, paras. 289–325; France, Seventeenth, eighteenth, and nineteenth periodic reports of the States Parties due in 2008, CERD/C/FRA/17-19, paras. 224–235.

[323] France, Eleventh periodic reports of States Parties due in 1992, CERD/C/225/Add.2, paras. 2–3. See also: France, Fourteenth periodic reports of States Parties due in 1998, CERD/C/337/Add.5, paras. 121–151; France, Sixteenth periodic report of States Parties due in 2002, CERD/C/430/Add.4, paras. 289–325; France, Seventeenth, eighteenth, and nineteenth periodic reports of the States Parties due in 2008, CERD/C/FRA/17-19, paras. 224–235.

There is a great deal of overlap in the core human rights treaties. The duplication of rights in various treaties contributes to the certainty that the norm is customary as well as conventional. For example, the right to freedom of expression enjoys a general formulation in the International Covenant on Civil and Political Rights.[324] It is also set out in a virtually identical fashion in the Convention on the Rights of the Child, except that the right is reserved to 'the child' given the nature of the instrument.[325] There are a few insignificant interpretative declarations to the Convention provision and no genuine reservations. Of the twenty-four States that have not ratified the International Covenant on Civil and Political Rights but that have ratified the Convention on the Rights of the child, can it be said that to the extent that they recognise a treaty obligation to ensure freedom of expression to children, they also accept a customary obligation with respect to adults? There would not seem to be any logical justification for accepting an international legal obligation to ensure freedom of expression for children, only to deny it when they turn eighteen. Similarly, the Convention on the Rights of the Child enshrines the principle of legality: 'No child shall be alleged as, be accused of, or recognised as having infringed the penal law by reason of acts or omissions that were not prohibited by national or international law at the time they were committed.'[326] Do States that accept this right for children as parties to the Convention on the Rights of the Child but who are not parties to the International Covenant on Civil and Political Rights, and therefore have not accepted the treaty norm in Article 15 of the Covenant, really consider that they are not also bound to respect this right for adults?

Under the International Convention on the Elimination of All Forms of Racial Discrimination, States undertake 'to guarantee the right of everyone, without distinction as to race, colour, or national or ethnic origin, to equality before the law, notably in the enjoyment of the following rights ... '.[327] A quite detailed summary list of fundamental rights follows. With such a formulation, the Convention proclaims a full recognition of the rights in question. For example, Article 5(c) of the Convention affirms a right 'to participate in elections—to vote and to stand for election—on the basis of universal and equal suffrage'. China is not a party to the Covenant but it acceded to the Racial Discrimination Convention without reservation to Article 5(c). The Convention on the Elimination of All Forms of Discrimination against Women is somewhat different, in that it provides that States Parties are to ensure many rights to women 'on equal terms with men'. For example, Article 7 of the Convention requires that women be allowed '[t]o vote in all elections and public referenda and to be eligible for selection to all publicly elected bodies'. But this cannot really justify the claim that States Parties thereby recognise

[324] International Covenant on Civil and Political Rights, (1976) 999 UNTS 171, art. 19(2) and (3).
[325] Convention on the Rights of the Child, (1990) 1571 UNTS 3, art. 13.
[326] Ibid. 3, art. 40(2)(a).
[327] International Convention on the Elimination of All Forms of Racial Discrimination, (1969) 660 UNTS 195, art. 5(d)(viii).

the right generally. It is only to the extent that they recognise the right that they must ensure that women are not victims of discrimination. The Convention on the Rights of Persons with Disabilities is similar in approach. Article 29 requires States Parties to 'guarantee to persons with disabilities political rights and the opportunity to enjoy them on an equal basis with others . . . '.

H. Particular or regional customary norms

Regional customary norms are one aspect of what has been called 'particular custom', as opposed to 'general custom'. Particular custom may apply to a group of States that share a geographic region although it may also exist for States that share some community of interest. Bilateral custom, between two States, is also possible.[328] The draft Conclusions of the International Law Commission state that '[a] rule of particular customary international law, whether regional, local or other, is a rule of customary international law that applies only among a limited number of States. To determine the existence and content of a rule of particular customary international law, it is necessary to ascertain whether there is a general practice among the States concerned that is accepted by them as law among themselves (*opinio juris*).'[329] But if the phenomenon of regional custom is well accepted in public international law, its application to human rights law is problematic. In the cognate field of international humanitarian law, the detailed study of customary law by the International Committee of the Red Cross does not appear to have even contemplated the possibility of regional rules, applicable in one part of the world and not another. The 1993 World Conference on Human Rights affirmed that '[t]he universal nature of these rights and freedoms is beyond question'.[330] The Universal Periodic Review, whose name is itself not without relevance to this discussion, provides no indication that States consider there to be regional differences in the application of human rights principles.

Yet there can be no question of the existence of regional human rights law. Regional institutions have played an extremely important role. The most familiar are the Council of Europe, the Organization of American States, and the African Union, because these bodies have highly-developed judicial and quasi-judicial mechanisms for the enforcement of human rights. Human rights law has also been enriched by contributions from the European Union, the Organisation for Security and Cooperation in Europe, and the Association of Southeast Asian Nations. Organisations that are not strictly regional in scope, but that are comprised

[328] *Right of Passage over Indian Territory (Merits), Judgment, 12 April 1960, ICJ Reports 1960*, p. 6, at p. 39.

[329] Fifth report on identification of customary international law, by Michael Wood, Special Rapporteur A/CN.4/717, p. 60.

[330] Vienna Declaration and Programme of Action, A/CONF.157/23, para. 1.

of States with common interests, should not be overlooked. They include the League of Arab States, the Commonwealth, the Organisation internationale de la Francophonie, the Organization of Islamic Cooperation, and the Comunidade dos Países de Língua Portuguesa. Inspection of the relevant legal instruments shows that in a general sense there is a common approach, confirming the message of universality of the Vienna Conference and the Universal Declaration of Human Rights.

The European Court of Human Rights frequently interprets the European Convention on Human Rights with respect to practice within the Member States of the Council of Europe. The Court displays considerable deference for national legislation pursuant to its 'margin of appreciation' doctrine, because 'national authorities have direct democratic legitimation and are, as the Court has held on many occasions, in principle better placed than an international court to evaluate local needs and conditions'.[331] The Court will intervene when it can identify 'common ground amongst the member States of the Council of Europe'[332] or a 'European consensus',[333] although sometimes it also refers to an 'international consensus'[334] or to one 'in Europe and internationally'.[335] Judge Ineta Ziemele wrote that when the European Court of Human Rights examines domestic laws and practices of European States, it is 'in fact looking for a particular regional practice that the States consider it necessary to follow, in other words, regional custom ... If the Court establishes the existence of a practice which the European States by and large follow (for instance, soft custom), there is no question but that it needs to keep that State practice in mind when interpreting the Convention in the light of modern-day developments.'[336]

There is a synergy in the case law of the regional human rights courts and commissions manifested in their increasingly enthusiastic reference to each other's precedents. There is little or no evidence that any of these courts overlooks or rejects authority from another region on the grounds that it is in some way culturally inapplicable. Often differences in approach are explained by the individuals who make up the tribunal and its 'culture' in an institutional rather than an ethnic

[331] *Maurice v. France* [GC], no. 11810/03, § 117, ECHR 2005-IX. Also *Handyside v. the United Kingdom*, 7 December 1976, p. 22, § 48, Series A no. 24; *James and Others v. the United Kingdom*, 21 February 1986, § 46, Series A no. 98, p. 32.

[332] *Khamtokhu and Aksenchik v. Russia* [GC], nos. 60367/08 and 961/11, § 85, 24 January 2017; *X, Y, and Z v. the United Kingdom* [GC], no. 21830/93), § 44, 22 April 1997.

[333] *Magyar Kétfarkú Kutya Párt v. Hungary* [GC], no. 201/17, § 80, 20 January 2020; *Murtazaliyeva v. Russia* [GC], no. 36658/05, § 57, 18 December 2018; *Vo v. France* [GC], no. 53924/00, § 82, ECHR 2004-VIII.

[334] *Strand Lobben and Others v. Norway* [GC], no. 37283/13, § 207, 10 September 2019; *Naït-Liman v. Switzerland* [GC], no. 51357/07, § 97, 15 March 2018.

[335] *Scoppola v. Italy (no. 2)* [GC], no. 102/49/03, § 106, 17 September 2009.

[336] *Rohlena v. Czech Republic* [GC], no. 59552/08, 27 January 2015, Concurring opinion of Judge Ziemele, para. 2. See also Ineta Ziemele, 'Customary International Law in the Case Law of the European Court of Human Rights', in Liesbeth Lijnzaad, ed., *The Judge and International Custom*, Strasbourg: Council of Europe, 2012, pp. 73–85.

sense. For example, the European Court of Human Rights and the United Nations Human Rights Committee reached different conclusions about the French legislation prohibiting women from wearing the *burqa*.[337] Sometimes reasonable people simply disagree.

The International Law Commission debated whether to recognise the existence of a regional *jus cogens*. There were differences of opinion and the issue has been left in abeyance.[338] One member pointed out that '[s]cholars who claimed that regional jus cogens existed appeared to be referring to regional customary law, rather than to regional jus cogens, as such'.[339] In his report to the Commission, the Special Rapporteur noted regional differences in human rights treaty law, giving the example of the African system with 'its distinctive appeal to the collective', the European Court's focus on 'European public order' and the Inter-American system's emphasis on declaring the existence of *jus cogens* norms.[340] The Special Rapporteur said '[t]he existence of a common set of unifying and binding norms in different regions does not, however, translate into a recognition of regional *jus cogens*. It is simply a reflection of the general structure of international law, namely that States are free to have particular rules different and distinct from general rules of international law'.[341]

In *Roach and Pinkerton*, the Inter-American Commission on Human Rights contemplated the possibility of regional *jus cogens*. The Commission held that 'in the member States of the [Organisation of American States] there is recognised a norm of *jus cogens* which prohibits the State execution of children. This norm is accepted by all the States of the inter-American system, including the United States.'[342] But it is a poor precedent for the existence of regional *jus cogens*. When the Commission returned to the issue in 2002, it did not repeat the claim to regional *jus cogens* that it had made earlier.[343] The *Roach and Pinkerton* decision actually endorsed the view of the United States that there was no customary norm prohibiting the death penalty for crimes committed by persons under the age of eighteen. The pronouncement on *jus cogens* only recognised *jus cogens* with respect to 'children', which is not the same as applying the death penalty for crimes

[337] *S.A.S. v. France* [GC], no. 43835/11, §§ 137–159, ECHR 2014 (extracts); *Yaker v. France*, no. 2747/2016, Views, 22 February 2016, CCPR/C/123/D/2747/2016, para.7; *Hebbadj v. France*, no. 2807/2016, Views, 3 March 2016, CCPR/C/123/D/2807/2016, para. 7.7.

[338] Draft report of the International Law Commission on the work of its seventy-first session, A/CN.4/L.929/Add.1, p. 7; A/CN.4/SR.3499, pp. 9–10; Topical summary of the discussion held in the Sixth Committee of the General Assembly during its seventy-fourth session, prepared by the Secretariat, A/CN.4/734, para. 39.

[339] A/CN.4/SR.3461, p. 13 (Aniruddha Rajput).

[340] Fourth report on peremptory norms of general international law (*jus cogens*) by Dire Tladi, Special Rapporteur, A/CN.4/727, para. 45.

[341] Ibid., para. 46.

[342] *Roach and Pinkerton v. United States*, Case 9647, Resolution No. 3/87, Merits, 22 September 1987, para. 56.

[343] *Domingues v. United States*, Case 12.285, Report No. 62/02, Merits, 22 October 2002.

committed by children. In United States practice for the past half-century, persons sentenced to death for juvenile offences were invariably adults by the time execution was imposed. The claim by the Commission that the prohibition of executing children was 'regional' might just as well have been said of the world as a whole. In 1987, when it made the statement, there was no country on the planet that did not prohibit execution of 'children' below a certain age, although several allowed the execution for crimes committed by adolescents above a certain age.

I. Emerging or crystallising norms and the persistent objector

It is often said that custom is 'emerging', 'ripening', or 'crystallising'. Judgments speak of 'emergent customary law'.[344] Sometimes, judges and commentators seem to favour such terms when they feel unable to confirm the existence of a custom. It is a convenient way of proclaiming a preference for the formation of the rule. But can it really be known whether a norm is emerging or crystallising until the process is complete? All that can really be said is that there appears to be a direction of travel. There is no certainty that the process will be completed. To pursue the chemistry metaphor, not all substances do in fact crystallise. The chemist who is attempting to achieve the crystallisation of something that will not crystallise might describe the experiment with the word 'crystallising' but others would find it more suitable to speak of a failure or inability to crystallise.

The 'emerging' or 'crystallising' notion is of legal relevance to the phenemenon of the 'persistent objector'. A State that resists the formation of customary norm may, but only if the norm is found to have emerged or crystallised, claim that the new norm cannot be set up or invoked against it. According to the International Law Commission, '[w]here a State has objected to a rule of customary international law while that rule was in the process of formation, the rule is not opposable to the State concerned for so long as it maintains its objection'.[345] It warned of confusing the persistent objector exception from situations 'where the objection of a significant number of States to the emergence of a new rule of customary international law prevents its crystallisation altogether (because there is no general practice accepted as law)'.[346] The International Law Commission has explained that 'the objection must be communicated internationally; it cannot simply be voiced internally'.[347]

The International Law Commission said that the persistent objector is 'not infrequently invoked and recognised, both in international and domestic case law'.[348]

[344] *South China Sea Arbitration (The Republic of Philippines v. The People's Republic of China)* (PCA 2013-19), Award, 12 July 2016, para. 258.

[345] Report of the International Law Commission, Seventieth session (30 April–1 June and 2 July–10 August 2018), A/73/10, p. 152.

[346] Ibid.

[347] Ibid.

[348] Ibid., p. 153.

The footnote to this assertion contained five examples, three of them dealing with human rights issues. But careful reading of the two decisions does not point to the conclusion drawn by the International Law Commission. In the first, the Inter-American Commission considered that the United States could not invoke the persistent objector exception given that it had not objected persistently.[349] In the second and third, it does not appear from the judgments that the respondent State had even invoked the principle. All that the Courts were doing was explaining that the persistent objector rule did not apply to norms of *jus cogens*.[350] In reality, the persistent objector rule is invoked with respect to customary norms of human rights very rarely.

The persistent objector issue has arisen in cases decided by the Inter-American Commission on Human Rights on applications directed against the United States based upon the American Declaration of the Rights and Duties of Man. Strictly speaking, the Commission was interpreting provisions of the Declaration and not exercising jurisdiction over customary law human righs violations as such. In *Roach and Pinkerton*, which concerned imposition of the death penalty for crimes committed when the offenders were under the age of eighteen, the United States claimed to have objected to such a norm. It contended that it had abstained from participating in the debate and vote on the draft International Covenant on Civil and Political Rights, and that the President had formulated a reservation on the issue when the Covenant was submitted to the Senate for advice and consent.[351] The Commission did not rule on the objection because it accepted the argument of the United States that there was no such norm.[352] When the issue returned fifteen years later, the United States did not appear before the Commission and therefore made no objection based on being a persistent objector. The Commission nevertheless chose to address the issue, concluding that the United States had not in fact been consistent in its objection and that it could not benefit from the exception. Furthermore, it held that because the prohibition of juvenile executions is a rule of *jus cogens*, the persistent objector rule could not apply.[353] In a subsequent case, the United States contended that its practice did not reflect the prohibition of juvenile executions although it did not explicitly invoke the persistent objector rule.[354] The Commission repeated what it had said in

[349] *Domingues v. United States*, Case 12.285, Report No. 62/02, Merits, 22 October 2002, para. 85.

[350] *Sabeh El Leil v. France* [GC], no. 34869/05, § 54, 29 June 2011; *Siderman de Blake v. Republic of Argentina*, 965 F.2d 699 (1992), p. 715. On the exclusion of the persistent object exception to the formation of *jus cogens* norms, see Third report on peremptory norms of general international law (*jus cogens*) by Dire Tladi, Special Rapporteur, A/CN.4/714, paras. 142–145.

[351] *Roach and Pinkerton v. United States*, Case 9647, Resolution No. 3/87, Merits, 22 September 1987, para. 38(i).

[352] Ibid., para. 60.

[353] *Domingues v. United States*, Case 12.285, Report No. 62/02, Merits, 22 October 2002, para. 85. See also *Beazley v. United States*, Case No. 12.412, Report No. 101/03, Merits, 29 December 2003, para. 48; *Graham v. United* States, Case No. 11.193, Report No. 97/03, Merits, 29 December 2003, para. 52; *Thomas v. United States*, Case No. 12.240, Report No. 100/03, Merits, 29 December 2003.

[354] *Patterson v. United States*, Case No. 12.439, Report No. 25/05, Merits, 7 March 2005, para. 24.

Domingues.[355] The United States also invoked the persistent objector rule in a case concerning sentencing of juvenile offenders to irreducible terms of life imprisonment. The United States argued that 'it had consistently reserved its right to sentence minors to life imprisonment without parole when they commit serious breaches of criminal laws, and thus has continuously objected to the practice having acquired the status of obligation'.[356] The United States has also claimed to be a persistent objector with respect to the Inter-American Commission's construction of the Charter of the Organization of American States and the American Declaration on the Rights and Duties of Man.[357] This seems to be a confused understanding of the persistent objector claim, which is confined to the application of custom and has no relevance to issues of interpretation.

A State that establishes itself as a persistent objector must maintain the objection once the customary rule has emerged.[358] According to the International Law Commission, 'the objection should be reiterated when the circumstances are such that a restatement is called for (that is, in circumstances where silence or inaction may reasonably lead to the conclusion that the State has given up its objection)'.[359] The United States appears to have abandoned its objections with respect to juvenile executions and irreducible life sentences for young offenders. Both of these practices have been declared unconstitutional by the United States Supreme Court.[360] The United States has included information on the relevant judgments in its reports to the Human Rights Council and to the applicable treaty bodies.[361]

The abolition of the death penalty is probably an 'emerging norm'. The quinquennial reports of the Secretary General of the United Nations indicate a consistent trend towards abolition.[362] Every second year, the General Assembly adopts a resolution calling for a moratorium on capital punishment, with steadily increasing majorities.[363] The bi-annual resolution is followed by the issuance of a statement

[355] Ibid., para. 45.

[356] *Hill et al. v. United States*, Petition 161-06, Report No. 18/12 Admissibility, 20 March 2012, para. 35.

[357] *Mitchell v. United States*, Case No. Report No. 211/20, Admissibility and Merits, 24 August 2020, para. 14.

[358] Report of the International Law Commission, Seventieth session (30 April–1 June and 2 July–10 August 2018), A/73/10, p. 153.

[359] Ibid.

[360] *Roper v. Simmons*, 543 US 551 (2005); *Graham v. Florida*, 560 US 48 (2010); *Miller v. Alabama*, 567 US 460 (2012).

[361] United States of America, Fourth periodic report, CCPR/C/USA/4, paras. 212, 679; United States of America, Third to fifth periodic report, CAT/C/USA/3-5, paras. 162, 202; United States of America, Seventh to ninth periodic report, CERD/C/USA/7-9, para. 71; United States, National report, A/HRC/WG.6/9/USA/1, para. 63.

[362] *E.g.* Capital punishment and implementation of the safeguards guaranteeing protection of the rights of those facing the death penalty, E/2020/53; Capital punishment and implementation of the safeguards guaranteeing protection of the rights of those facing the death penalty, E/2015/49.

[363] Moratorium on the use of the death penalty, A/RES/62/147 (104 in favour, 54 against and 29 abstentions), Moratorium on the use of the death penalty, A/RES/63/168 (106-46-34); Moratorium on

of dissociation from States in opposition. They declare that they 'wish to place on record that they are in persistent objection to any attempt to impose a moratorium on the use of the death penalty or its abolition in contravention of existing stipulations under international law'. The statements have emphasised the permissibility of capital punishment under international law, and have contested the issue being considered as a matter of human rights rather than as one of criminal justice policy falling within the sovereign authority of States.[364] The September 2019 statement was signed by thirty States.[365] For purposes of comparison, a similar declaration issued in 2009 obtained fifty-three signatures in 2009.[366]

To the extent that States wish to object to an emerging customary norm, the Universal Periodic Review would appear to be the ideal forum. Only very occasionally, during the Universal Periodic Review process, do States reply to allegations of human rights violations by claiming that they do not consider themselves to be bound by such a norm. One issue that is regularly considered by the Council and that confronts some difficulty is the elimination of discrimination based upon sexual orientation. There is sometimes rather shocking resistance to progressive reform although this can hardly be called 'persistent objection'. Comoros described the subject as a 'taboo',[367] and said there was not a majority in the legislature for decriminalisation.[368] Malawi said 'there was no international consensus on gay rights or on the right of gay persons to marry. Malawi should not be unduly singled out and unnecessarily pressured to legalise homosexuality.'[369] Antigua and Barbuda described a 'certain amount of public

the use of the death penalty, A/RES/65/206 (109-41-35); Moratorium on the use of the death penalty, A/RES/67/176 (111-41-34); Moratorium on the use of the death penalty, A/RES/69/186 (117-37-34); Moratorium on the use of the death penalty, A/RES/71/187 (117-40-31); Moratorium on the use of the death penalty, A/RES/ 73/175 (121-35-32).

[364] For example, Annex to the note verbale dated 13 September 2019 from the Permanent Representative of Egypt to the United Nations addressed to the Secretary-General, A/73/1004.

[365] Bahrain, Bangladesh, Botswana, Brunei Darussalam, Chad, China, Democratic People's Republic of Korea, Egypt, Ethiopia, Grenada, Iran, Iraq, Jamaica, Kuwait, Libya, Nigeria, Oman, Pakistan, Papua New Guinea, Qatar, Saint Kitts and Nevis, Saint Lucia, Saint Vincent and the Grenadines, Saudi Arabia, Singapore, Sudan, Syrian Arab Republic, United Arab Emirates, Yemen, Zimbabwe.

[366] Note verbale dated 10 February 2009 from the Permanent Missions to the United Nations of Afghanistan, the Bahamas, Bahrain, Bangladesh, Barbados, Botswana, Brunei Darussalam, the Central African Republic, Chad, China, the Comoros, the Democratic People's Republic of Korea, Dominica, Egypt, Equatorial Guinea, Eritrea, Ethiopia, Fiji, the Gambia, Grenada, Guinea, Guyana, Indonesia, Iran (Islamic Republic of), Iraq, Kuwait, the Lao People's Democratic Republic, the Libyan Arab Jamahiriya, Malaysia, Maldives, Mongolia, Myanmar, Niger, Nigeria, Papua New Guinea, Qatar, St Kitts and Nevis, Saint Lucia, Saint Vincent and the Grenadines, Saudi Arabia, Singapore, Solomon Islands, Somalia, the Sudan, Swaziland, the Syrian Arab Republic, Thailand, Tonga, Trinidad and Tobago, Uganda, the United Arab Emirates, Yemen, and Zimbabwe addressed to the Secretary-General, A/63/716.

[367] Comoros, Report of the Working Group, A/HRC/12/16, para. 56.

[368] Comoros, Report of the Working Group, A/HRC/26/11, para. 73.

[369] Malawi, Report of the Working Group, A/HRC/16/4, para. 39.

acceptance of homosexual conduct, although generally in a silent way. Antigua and Barbuda, however, did not have a political mandate with respect to changing the law, notwithstanding the fact that enforcement of those laws was not actually sought.'[370] Tunisia said there was a national debate but that the country was not ready to take a decision on decriminalisation.[371]

Many of the statements can hardly be deemed unequivocal rejection of the increasing attention given by international human rights law to the prohibition of discrimination based upon sexual orientation. Uganda told the Human Rights Council how anti-homosexuality legislation had been declared unconstitutional, adding that the Government 'would not accept or tolerate discrimination and/or harassment, including of lesbian, gay, bisexual, transgender and intersex persons. All Ugandans were treated equally, without discrimination.'[372] Kiribati told the Council that it 'appreciated the existence of homosexuality and the need to include it as a prohibited discriminatory ground in the Constitution' but explained that a high threshold was required for such an amendment.[373] Botswana spoke of its 'openness' towards advocacy for decriminalisation.[374] St. Kitts and Nevis told the Council that 'the former Prime Minister had publicly advocated a review of the country's anti-sodomy laws and tolerance for lesbian, gay, bisexual and transgender individuals'.[375] Singapore reported that '[s]egments of Singapore society continue to hold strong views against homosexuality',[376] but also explained that the criminal law provisions are not applied in practice.[377] Nauru accepted a recommendation of decriminalisation.[378] Ghana answered a challenge about decriminalisation by stating that its laws do not discriminate.[379] Brunei Darussalam reported that it does not 'criminalise a person's status based on sexual orientation or belief', and that the people of the country have, 'regardless of their sexual orientation, continued to live and to pursue their activities in their own private space. There was no discrimination against citizens or permanent residents in any way in their access to services, such as employment, education and health care.'[380] Some countries do not rise to the bait, and when they get the inevitable questions they offer no

370 Antigua and Barbuda, Report of the Working Group, A/HRC/19/5, para. 48.
371 Tunisia, Report of the Working Group, A/HRC/21/5, para. 40.
372 Uganda, Report of the Working Group, A/HRC/34/10, para. 56.
373 Kiribati, Report of the Working Group, A/HRC/15/3, para. 61.
374 Botswana, Report of the Working Group, A/HRC/10/69, para. 42. See also Botswana, National report, A/HRC/WG.6/29/BWA/1, para. 121.
375 St. Kitts and Nevis, National report, A/HRC/WG.6/23/KNA/2, para. 15.
376 Singapore, National report, A/HRC/WG.6/24/SGP/1, para. 111.
377 Singapore, Report of the Working Group, A/HRC/18/11, para. 82.
378 Nauru, Views on conclusions, A/HRC/17/3/Add.1, para. 31.
379 Ghana, Report of the Working Group, A/HRC/22/6, para. 75.
380 Brunei Darussalam, Report of the Working Group, A/HRC/42/11, para. 20 and Views on conclusions, A/HRC/42/11/Add.1, p. 4.

explanation other than declining recommendations on the subject.[381] But such silence can hardly qualify as persistent objection.

A favourite subject of the 'crystallising' or 'emerging' paradigm is the question of amnesty. For many years, there have been claims of the crystallising of a norm of international law prohibiting amnesty. The actual extent of the norm is unclear. Some suggest that it applies to the core international crimes of genocide, crimes against humanity, and war crimes. The Appeals Chamber of the Special Court for Sierra Leone endorsed the Prosecutor's submission that there was a 'crystallising international norm that a government cannot grant amnesty for serious violations of crimes under international law', although it recognised that the opinion of the *amici curiae* 'that it has crystallised may not be entirely correct'.[382] Several years later, the Extraordinary Chambers of the Courts of Cambodia stated that 'an emerging consensus prohibits amnesties in relation to serious international crimes, based on a duty to investigate and prosecute these crimes and to punish their perpetrators'.[383] This view was picked up by a Chamber of the European Court of Human Rights: 'Granting amnesty in respect of "international crimes"—which include crimes against humanity, war crimes and genocide—is increasingly considered to be prohibited by international law. This understanding is drawn from customary rules of international humanitarian law, human rights treaties, as well as the decisions of international and regional courts and developing State practice.'[384] But when the decision was reconsidered, the Grand Chamber took a somewhat different position. It spoke of a 'growing tendency in international law ... to see such amnesties as unacceptable because they are incompatible with the unanimously recognised obligation of States to prosecute and punish grave breaches of fundamental human rights', rather than 'international crimes'. Without reaching any definite conclusion, the Grand Chamber appeared to acknowledge the legitimacy of a view that amnesties might be possible 'where there are some particular circumstances, such as a reconciliation process and/or a form of compensation to the victims'.[385]

The Inter-American Court of Human Rights developed a doctrine whereby amnesty provisions are prohibited 'because they are intended to prevent the investigation and punishment of those responsible for serious human rights violations such as torture, extrajudicial, summary or arbitrary execution and forced

[381] Oman, Report of the Working Group, A/HRC/17/7, para. 66; Saint Lucia, National report, A/HRC/WG.6/23/KNA/2, para. 63.

[382] *Prosecutor v. Kallon et al.*, Cases Nos. SCSL-2004-15-AR72(E) and SCSL-2004-16-AR72(E), Decision on Challenge to Jurisdiction: Lomé Accord Amnesty, 13 March 2004, para. 82.

[383] *Prosecutor v. Ieng Sary* (no. 002/19-09-2007/ECCC/TC), Decision on Ieng Sary's Rule 89 Preliminary Objections (*ne bis in idem* and amnesty and pardon), 3 November 2011, para. 53.

[384] *Marguš v. Croatia*, no. 4455/10, § 74, 13 November 2012.

[385] *Marguš v. Croatia* [GC], no. 4455/10, § 130, 27 May 2014.

disappearance',[386] rather than because they are 'international crimes'. But in 2012, the seemingly absolute view of the Inter-American Court of Human Rights was toned down, with a majority of the Court noting that none of its rulings had considered amnesty laws adopted 'in the context of a process aimed at ending, through negotiations, a non-international armed conflict'.[387] The judges recognised that limitations on the obligation to investigate and prosecute could not be ruled out when this was part of a broader process of post-conflict peace-building and accountability.

At the International Criminal Court, three judges of a Pre-Trial Chamber wrote that 'granting amnesties and pardons for serious acts such as murder constituting crimes against humanity is incompatible with internationally recognised human rights'.[388] The term 'internationally recognised human rights' is employed in the applicable law provision of the Rome Statute[389] and is probably a cognate of customary international law. In a separate opinion, Judge Perrin de Brichambault noted that there was an 'ongoing political debate' on the subject, citing an academic who pointed to the widespread acceptance of South Africa's amnesty.[390] The Appeals Chamber did not endorse the Trial Chamber's position, which it characterised as *obiter dictum*. '[I]t suffices to say only that international law is still in the developmental stage on the question of acceptability of amnesties', said the Appeals Chamber.

A similarly equivocal position on amnesties emerges from recent work of the International Law Commission on the draft articles on crimes against humanity. Special Rapporteur Sean Murphy noted that '[c]onflicting views exist as to the permissibility of amnesties under international law'.[391] He noted that State practice did not confirm a general condemnation of amnesties, even for international crimes.[392] Murphy also pointed to an acknowledgement that customary law had not 'crystallised' found in the statements of the Special Court for Sierra Leone and

[386] *Barrios Altos v. Peru*, Judgment (Merits), 14 March 2001, Series C, No. 75, para. 41.

[387] *Massacres of El Mozote and nearby places v. El Salvador*, Judgment (Merits, reparations, and costs), 25 October 2012, Series C, No. 252, Concurring Opinion of Judge Diego Garcia-Sayán, para. 9.

[388] *Prosecutor v. Saif Al-Islam Gaddafi* (ICC-01/11-01/11), Decision on the 'Admissibility Challenge by Dr. Saif Al-Islam Gadafi pursuant to Articles 17(1)(c), 19 and 20(3) of the Rome Statute', 5 April 2019, para. 77.

[389] Rome Statute of the International Criminal Court, (2002) 2187 UNTS 689, art. 21(3).

[390] *Prosecutor v. Saif Al-Islam Gaddafi* (ICC-01/11-01/11), Separate concurring opinion by Judge Marc Perrin de Brichambault, 5 April 2019, para. 136.

[391] Third report on crimes against humanity, by Sean D. Murphy, Special Rapporteur, A/CN.4/704, para. 286. His views received support from many members of the Commission: A/CN.4/SR.3349, p. 7 (Hassouna); A/CN.4/SR.3349, p. 10 (Park); ibid., p. 13 (Nguyen); A/CN.4/SR.3350, p. 11 (Jalloh); A/CN.4/SR.3351, p. 4 (Kolodkin); A/CN.4/SR.3351, p. 9 (Jalloh); A/CN.4/SR.3351, p. 12 (Šturma); A/CN.4/SR.3352, p. 4 (Wood); A/CN.4/SR.3353, pp. 11–12 (Rajput). *Contra* A/CN.4/SR.3351, pp. 8–9 (Hmoud); A/CN.4/SR.3352, p. 3 (Ruda Santolaria); A/CN.4/SR.3353, pp. 6–7 (Vázquez-Bermúdez); A/CN.4/SR.3353, pp. 12–13 (Hmoud).

[392] Third report on crimes against humanity, by Sean D. Murphy, Special Rapporteur, A/CN.4/704, paras. 288, 290.

the Extraordinary Chambers of the Courts of Cambodia.[393] Consequently, he said, 'many publicists have found it difficult to conclude that there is a consensus on whether a complete prohibition on amnesties, even for serious crimes, has attained the status of customary international law'.[394] The Commission reached no conclusion on the issue of amnesty and did not include a provision requiring their prohibition in its draft articles.[395]

[393] Ibid., para. 292.
[394] Ibid., para. 296.
[395] Report of the International Law Commission Seventy-first session (29 April–7 June and 8 July–9 August 2019), A/74/10, pp. 95–96.

3
Methodological considerations

The chapters that follow address the evidence of custom for a range of fundamental rights. The catalogue of human rights has been broken down into eight categories in an original manner, although one inspired by similar attempts in legal instruments like the Charter of Fundamental Rights of the European Union. Given the novelty of the exercise, the author felt unconstrained to follow other types of classification, such as the dichotomy reflected in the two International Covenants or the unofficial grouping into the three generations proposed in the academic literature. The starting point, of course, is the Universal Declaration of Human Rights. All of the rights set out in the Declaration are considered. A few categories of rights, such as the right of peoples to self-determination and the rights of persons belonging to minorities, do not appear in the Universal Declaration but are nevertheless found in the International Covenant on Civil and Political Rights, and they too are examined. Some fundamental rights are not adequately addressed in either the Universal Declaration of Human Rights or in the two Covenants. For example, the right to a healthy environment is at best implicit in most of the major universal, regional, and specialised human rights treaties. That it has a good claim to be a fundamental right under customary law receives considerable support in the National reports and other documents of the Universal Periodic Review.

A cautionary note is in order about the observations and conclusions in this book on the scope of the customary law of human rights. Detailed codification is beyond the scope of this study. The intention is not to provide a definitive list of norms of customary international law, a project that would be unrealistic and rather arrogant. The International Law Commission has warned of writers who 'sometimes seek not merely to record the state of the law as it is (*lex lata*) but to advocate its development (*lex ferenda*). In doing so, they do not always distinguish (or distinguish clearly) between the law as it is and the law as they would like it to be.'[1] The Commission recalled the *Paquete Habana* case, in which the United States Supreme Court recognised the contribution of scholars and academic lawyers whose writings 'are resorted to by judicial tribunals, not for the speculations of their authors concerning what the law ought to be, but for trustworthy evidence of what the law really is.'[2]

[1] Report of the International Law Commission, Seventieth session (30 April–1 June and 2 July–10 August 2018), A/73/10, p. 151.
[2] *The Paquete Habana and The Lola*, 175 US 677 (1900), p. 700.

The Customary International Law of Human Rights. William A. Schabas, Oxford University Press.
 DOI: 10.1093/oso/9780192845696.003.0004

The pages that follow only endeavour to present relevant information drawn from evidence of State practice and *opinio juris*. Verdicts on whether or not a norm or principle can be labelled 'customary' are avoided in favour of conclusions framed using the subtlety of language, with words such as 'probable', 'likely', 'possible', 'improbable', 'extravagant', 'almost certain', and so on. The exercise is one of measuring the temperature of the norm. Readers and, hopefully, judges will find these materials helpful. Furthermore, detailed examination of the scope and application of the norms is a job for those who interpret and apply the law at the judicial and the political level. The most that can or should be done here is to identify norms with a level of precision comparable to what is found in the relevant treaties, nothing more. Some of the interpretative debates are touched upon although no effort is made to provide a detailed analysis of every norm of customary international law. Volumes could be written about most of them. There are certain very general understandings of the scope of the rights. An effort is made to describe them, relying upon such materials as the case law of international and national courts, the studies by expert mechanisms of the intergovernmental organisations and the work of scholars.

For example, States can agree to respect freedom of expression but not on whether or not to prohibit hate speech, genocide denial, blasphemy, and pornography, to what extent and by what means. They can accept the outlawing of slavery without necessarily agreeing on whether this encompasses certain forms of contract labour, or whether there should be payment for housework. Human rights treaties provide that there be a minimum age for work, criminal liability, the right to vote and to marry, but they do not specify what that age might be. It is unrealistic to expect a study of customary law to do more. To the extent that human rights treaties permit capital punishment, its application must be limited to those convicted of the 'most serious crimes', although of what this category consists is left to interpretation. Customary law cannot really go any further. Ongoing controversies about some issues prevent firm conclusions about the extent of customary international law: the death penalty, elections, abortion, rights of non-citizens. On other issues, however, there is no dispute: the right to health and to medical care, education, rest, and leisure. Not only is the principle of equality and non-discrimination universally recognised, there is general agreement about identification of many of the prohibited grounds: race, gender, ethnicity, and even age, disability, and sexual orientation. Where disagreement arises is not on the principle of non-discrimination but on its implementation. Some States insist on maintaining legislation criminalising forms of sexual activity between adults of the same sex, and refuse extending to them the right to marry and to found a family, yet they would insist that they do not discriminate on the basis of sexual orientation. Similarly, States agree upon women's equality but there is no consensus on the right of women to wear the veil, or not to wear it. After all, even the European

Court of Human Rights and the Human Rights Committee cannot agree on that issue.[3]

The recognition of fundamental rights under customary international law is the subject. Not compliance with them. This distinction is fundamental. If conclusions about the validity of customary law could be successfully challenged simply because many or even most States do not fully respect them then the entire exercise would be rather futile. Failure to comply with standards does not prove that they do not exist. Ultimately, the same problem arises with respect to treaties. Many States Parties to the important international human rights treaties fall short of their obligations in a number of respects. If there is any doubt about this, reference might be made to the examination of their periodic reports.

The analysis draws primarily on four sources. The starting point is the Universal Declaration of Human Rights, adopted nearly three-quarters of a century ago yet still preserving its vitality and resonance while the world has changed around it. Regardless of the debate about its precise legal status, something discussed in the previous chapter,[4] the Declaration runs like a *leitmotif* through all modern human rights law, at both the domestic and the international level. There is a rebuttable presumption that all rights in the Declaration are norms of customary international law. In a few cases, there is insufficient evidence to permit a firm conclusion, but they are very much the exception to the general rule.

For each right, the study considers its formulation in treaties that enjoy near-universal ratification. Although the two Covenants are the direct progeny of the Universal Declaration, certain rights they contain are also formulated in regional and specialised treaties. Essentially every State in the world is a party to one or more human rights treaty. A pattern may emerge indicating a global consensus, especially because many fundamental rights are recognised in one form or another in most if not all of the treaties. For example, some States that have not ratified the International Covenant on Civil and Political Rights are nevertheless party to the Arab Charter on Human Rights. Even more significant is the role played by two of the specialised treaties, the Convention on the Rights of the Child and the Convention on the Elimination of All Forms of Discrimination against Women, because these two treaties are virtually universally accepted. An exercise in interpretation is required here because these specialised treaties apply to children and to women, not to everyone. Although rights affirmed in the Convention on the Rights of the Child may only be invoked by persons under the age of eighteen, it is irrational that a State would acknowledge to children the right to freedom of expression or religion, for example, yet deny it to adults. This extrapolation cannot

[3] *S.A.S. v. France* [GC], no. 43835/11, §§ 137–159, ECHR 2014 (extracts); *Yaker v. France*, no. 2747/2016, Views, 22 February 2016, CCPR/C/123/D/2747/2016, para.7; *Hebbadj v. France*, no. 2807/2016, Views, 3 March 2016, CCPR/C/123/D/2807/2016, para. 7.7.

[4] See *supra* pp. 80–83.

be made for all rights in the Convention, where the application to children is quite unique, but it is a reasonable inference for many of them. Similarly, the Convention on the Elimination of All Forms of Discrimination against Women affirms that various rights should be recognised for women under a condition of equality with men rather than in an absolute sense. However, when the Convention declares that women have the right to vote in all elections and public referendums on terms of equality this amounts to indirect acknowledgement of the fundamental right to participate in government through periodic elections.

Consideration of the pattern of treaty ratification requires that reservations and interpretative declarations be examined. In some cases, a significant number of reservations to a specific norm may raise doubts about its universal acceptance. It is quite notorious that the two specialised treaties referred to in the previous paragraph bring with them a large number of reservations. But even if reservations may weaken the legal scope of a treaty, their significance should not be exaggerated unnecessarily. The many reservations to the Convention on the Elimination of all Forms of Discrimination against Women mitigate the application to specific aspects of the subject matter, but cannot totally obscure the fact that 189 States are prepared to confirm, by assuming a treaty obligation, their recognition of many features of the prohibition of gender-based discrimination.

Analysis of near-universal treaties nevertheless leaves significant gaps. About twenty-five States, including several large ones, have not ratified both of the Covenants. Many have not ratified either of them. Previously, it was extremely difficult to locate evidence permitting the identification of either practice or *opinio juris* of these States. The thesis of this study is that the Universal Periodic Review mechanism launched by the Human Rights Council in 2008 and now completing its third cycle of reporting and recommendations provides unprecedented access to such evidence. The Universal Periodic Review materials for these States have been examined intensively in order to establish their position about the substance of fundamental rights as well as their practice in implementation.

Case law, especially the decisions and judgments of international courts and tribunals, has been canvassed for pronouncements on customary international law. However, it has proven to be of limited assistance. Most of the case law deals with a small number of fundamental rights about which there is little controversy, such as the prohibitions of torture and of slavery. This shortcoming of the international jurisprudence is relatively easy to comprehend. The international courts and tribunals do not generally have jurisdiction to rule on violations of the customary law of human rights. Their mandate is usually determined by a treaty. Litigants invoke a breach of the treaty and not a violation of customary international law. Although the International Court of Justice has the authority to deal with violations of customary international law pursuant to Article 38(1)(b) of its Statute, it is not without interest that the judgments where it made pronouncements customary norms of human rights were premised upon compromissory clauses in special treaties rather than on the general jurisdiction.[5]

The various pronouncements by authoritative bodies, such as treaty bodies and other expert institutions, are also assessed. The General Comments and similar instruments of the treaty bodies are particularly useful because although in a formal sense they are addressed to conventional provisions, in substance they do much more than merely provide interpretative guidance for a text but rather set out substantive conclusions about the content of human rights norms in a general sense. Some caution is required because these sources do not provide, strictly speaking, evidence of customary international law. With the possible exception of resolutions and declarations of bodies like the United Nations General Assembly and the Human Rights Council,[6] they do not amount to either State practice or *opinio juris*. Nevertheless, such materials provide important confirmation of the content of the customary international law of human rights. They warrant serious consideration. It would be negligent to disregard them.

Most if not all rights are subject to restrictions and limitations. As Article 29(2) of the Universal Declaration of Human Rights explains, '[i]n the exercise of his rights and freedoms, everyone shall be subject only to such limitations as are determined by law solely for the purpose of securing due recognition and respect for the rights and freedoms of others and of meeting the just requirements of morality, public order and the general welfare in a democratic society'. Some of the human rights treaties have adapted this text and included clauses that are specifically tailored to the right in question. For example, Article 18(2) of the International Covenant on Civil and Political Rights states that '[f]reedom to manifest one's religion or beliefs may be subject only to such limitations as are prescribed by law and are necessary to protect public safety, order, health, or morals or the fundamental rights and freedoms of others'. When States report to the Human Rights Council, they may confirm that they respect freedom to manifest religion and while they often provide examples of exceptions to the right they do not spell out exhaustively the manner in which the right may be limited. A study of customary law can do no more. All that can be said is that when customary norms are identified it must be borne in mind that they are not absolute or unlimited in their application, and may be subject to limitations.

[5] *Questions relating to the Obligation to Prosecute or Extradite (Belgium v. Senegal), Judgment, ICJ Reports 2012*, p. 422, para. 99 (a claim based upon customary law was declared inadmissible, see para. 55); *United States Diplomatic and Consular Staff in Tehran, Judgment, ICJ Reports 1980*, p. 3, para. 91.

[6] Report of the International Law Commission, Seventieth session (30 April–1 June and 2 July–10 August 2018), A/73/10, pp. 147–149.

4
Dignity

Several rights dealing with the physical and psychological integrity of the human person are discussed here under the rubric 'dignity'. Echoing the first preambular paragraph of the Charter of the United Nations, which speaks of 'the dignity and worth of the human person', the preamble of the Universal Declaration of Human Rights begins with reference to 'recognition of the inherent dignity and of the equal and inalienable rights of all members of the human family'. It explains this to be 'the foundation of freedom, justice and peace in the world'. Dignity may well be used to confirm the secular nature of the Declaration, although it can also be argued that it is there as an ecumenical compromise that gracefully avoids reference to 'God'.[1] Further on, the preamble recognises that 'the peoples of the United Nations have in the Charter reaffirmed their faith in fundamental human rights, in the dignity and worth of the human person and in the equal rights of men and women'. Article 1 of the Declaration opens with these words: 'All human beings are born free and equal in dignity and rights.' The substantive provisions of the Declaration use the word dignity in two places. Article 22 speaks of 'the economic, social and cultural rights indispensable for his dignity and the free development of his personality'. Article 23(3) affirms that '[e]veryone who works has the right to just and favourable remuneration ensuring for himself and his family an existence worthy of human dignity'.[2]

Human rights law treaties and declarations are permeated with references to 'dignity', or to 'human dignity'. The preambles to the two International Covenants recognise that human rights 'derive from the inherent dignity of the human person'. The International Covenant on Economic, Social and Cultural Rights states that 'education shall be directed to the full development of the human personality and the sense of its dignity'.[3] Article 10(1) of the International Covenant on Civil and Political Rights declares that '[a]ll persons deprived of their liberty shall be treated with humanity and with respect for the inherent dignity of the human person'. Dignity is also invoked in several of the specialised United Nations treaties.[4]

[1] See, for example, Summary Record of the ninety-eighth meeting [of the Third Committee of the General Assembly], 9 October 1948, *Official Records of the General Assembly*, Third Session, 1948, p. 113.

[2] See Klaus Dicke, 'The Founding Function of Human Dignity in the Universal Declaration of Human Rights', in David Kretzmer and Eckart Klein, eds., *The Concept of Human Dignity in Human Rights Discourse*, The Hague: Kluwer Law International, 2002, pp. 111–120.

[3] International Covenant on Economic, Social and Cultural Rights, (1976) 993 UNTS 3, art. 13(1).

[4] International Convention on the Elimination of All Forms of Racial Discrimination, (1969) 660 UNTS 195, PPs 1, 2, 5; Convention on the Elimination of All Forms of Discrimination against Women,

The Customary International Law of Human Rights. William A. Schabas, Oxford University Press.
 DOI: 10.1093/oso/9780192845696.003.0005

The universality of human dignity is confirmed by the use of the term in many of the regional instruments. The African Charter on Human and Peoples' Rights refers, in the preamble, to the duty 'to achieve the total liberation of Africa, the peoples of which are still struggling for their dignity', and a substantive provision recognises that '[e]very individual shall have the right to the respect of the dignity inherent in a human being and to the recognition of his legal status'.[5] The Arab Charter on Human Rights begins by acknowledging 'the faith of the Arab nation in the dignity of the human person'. Several substantive provisions of the Arab Charter refer to dignity and to human dignity.[6] References to dignity are also to be found in the American Convention on Human Rights[7] and in the European Convention on Human Rights, whose preamble speaks of 'the inherent dignity of all human beings'. The Charter of the European Union begins by presenting dignity as an autonomous right, as well as a sub-title for the rights to life, the integrity of the person, the prohibition of torture and inhuman or degrading treatment or punishment, and the prohibition of slavery and forced labour: 'Article 1. Human dignity is inviolable. It must be respected and protected.'[8]

The African Court on Human and Peoples' Rights has described the protection of the dignity of the human person as 'a cardinal principle under international law'. Aside from its recognition in most international human rights instruments, the Court observed that dignity is also enshrined in most modern constitutions. 'The protection of human dignity is therefore considered as a fundamental human right', it concluded.[9]

The Universal Periodic Review materials do not, as a general rule, approach human dignity as a fundamental right but rather as an overarching principle to be invoked in the context of other rights.[10] Dignity may be better understood as being adjectival rather than substantive.[11] The choice here has been to treat it as a category rather than as a distinct right.

(1981) 1249 UNTS 13, PPs 1, 2, 6; Convention against Torture and Other Cruel, Inhuman or Degrading Treatment of Punishment, (1987) 1465 UNTS 85, PP 2; Convention on the Rights of the Child, (1990) 1571 UNTS 3, PPs 1, 2, 7, arts. 23(1), 28(2), 37(c), 39, 40(1); International Convention on the Protection of the Rights of all Migrant Workers and Members of their Families, (2003) 2220 UNTS 3, arts. 17(1), 70; Convention on the Rights of Persons with Disabilities, (2008) 2515 UNTS 3, PPs (a), (h), (y), arts. 1, 3(a), 8(a), 16(4), 24(a), 25(d); International Convention for the Protection of All Persons from Enforced Disappearance, (2010) 2716 UNTS 3, arts. 19(2), 24(5)(c).

[5] African Charter on Human and Peoples' Rights, (1986) 1520 UNTS 271, art. 5.

[6] Arab Charter on Human Rights, arts. 2(3), 3(3), 7, 20, 33(3), 40(1).

[7] American Convention on Human Rights, (1978) 1144 UNTS 123, arts. 5(2), 6(2), 11(1).

[8] Charter of Fundamental Rights of the European Union, OJ C 326/391.

[9] *Robert John Penessis v. Tanzania*, No. 013/2015, Judgment, 28 November 2019, para. 87.

[10] There are a few references to a 'right to dignity', but in the context of domestic constitutional provisions or legislation: *e.g.* France, National report, A/HRC/WG.6/15/FRA/1, para. 127; Gambia, National report, A/HRC/WG.6/34/GMB/1, para. 41; Israel, National report, A/HRC/WG.6/3/ISR/1, para. 25, A/HRC/WG.6/17/ISR/1, para. 65, and A/HRC/WG.6/29/ISR/1, para. 82; Nigeria, National report, A/HRC/WG.6/17/NGA/1, para. 56.

[11] See, for example, Mary Neal, 'Respect for Human Dignity as "Substantive Basic Norm"', (2014) 10 *International Journal of Law in Context* 26; Nicoleta-Ramona Predescu, 'Human Dignity—A

A. Right to life

In the 'little treaty of Versailles', adopted at the Paris Peace Conference at the same time as the main peace treaty with Germany, Poland undertook 'to assure full and complete protection of life' to its inhabitants.[12] A decade later, Article 1 of the draft declaration adopted by the Institut de Droit International stated that '[i]t is the duty of every State to recognise the equal right of every individual to life . . . '.[13] A right to life was also formulated in the declaration proposed by the London International Assembly,[14] but not in Hersch Lauterpacht's draft or in the submissions by Cuba and Panama to the San Francisco Conference.

The right to life is affirmed succinctly in Article 3 of the Universal Declaration of Human Rights: 'Everyone has the right to life.' A more elaborate formulation of the right, focussed largely on the limitation of capital punishment, appears in the International Covenant on Civil and Political Rights. The Covenant does not offer an absolute protection of life; rather, it states that nobody is to be 'arbitrarily' deprived of life.[15] The regional instruments also have provisions that recognise the right to life.[16] All of these instruments with the exception of the African Charter on Human and Peoples' Rights explicitly acknowledge the death penalty as an exception to the protection of the right to life. Protocols to the Covenant and to the European and American conventions prohibit the use of the death penalty.[17] The right to life is also protected by some specialised conventions,[18] including the

Right or a Principle of Human Rights', [2018] *Conferinta Internationala de Drept, Studii Europene si Relatii Internationale* 137; Conor O'Mahony, 'There is no Such Thing as a Right to Dignity', (2012) 10 *International Journal of Constitutional Law* 551; Emily Kidd White, 'There is no Such Thing as a Right to Human Dignity: A Reply to Conor O'Mahony', (2012) 10 *International Journal of Constitutional Law* 575; Christopher McCrudden, 'Human Dignity and Judicial Interpretation of Human Rights', (2008) 19 *European Journal of International Law* 655; Paolo Carozza, 'Human Dignity and Judicial Interpretation of Human Rights: A Reply', (2008) 19 *European Journal of International Law* 931.

12 Treaty between the Principal Allied and Associated Powers and Poland, (1919) 112 BSP 232, art. 2.

13 Institut de Droit International, 'Declaration of the International Rights of Man', (1941) 35 *American Journal of International Law* 663.

14 London International Assembly, Report of the Third Commission (Legal Commission) on individual rights, TNA LNU 6/7, art. I.

15 International Covenant on Civil and Political Rights, (1976) 999 UNTS 171, art. 6.

16 European Convention on Human Rights, (1953) 213 UNTS 221, art. 2; American Declaration on the Rights and Duties of Man, Final Act of the Ninth International Conference of American States, Res. XXX, art. I; American Convention on Human Rights, (1978) 1144 UNTS 123, art. 4; African Charter on Human and Peoples' Rights, (1986) 1520 UNTS 271, art. 4; Arab Charter on Human Rights, art. 5.

17 Second Optional Protocol to the International Covenant on Civil and Political Rights, aiming at the abolition of the death penalty, (1991) 1642 UNTS 414; Protocol 6 to the Convention for the Protection of Human Rights and Fundamental Freedoms concerning the Abolition of the Death Penalty, CETS 114; Protocol 13 to the Convention for the Protection of Human Rights and Fundamental Freedoms, concerning the abolition of the death penalty in all circumstances, CETS 187; Protocol to the American Convention on Human Rights to Abolish the Death Penalty, OASTS 73.

18 International Convention on the Suppression and Punishment of the Crime of Apartheid, (1976) 1015 UNTS 243, art. II(a); Convention on the Rights of Persons with Disabilities, (2008) 2515 UNTS 3, art. 10; International Convention on the Protection of the Rights of all Migrant Workers and Members of their Families, (2003) 2220 UNTS 3, art. 9; Inter-American Convention on the Prevention,

Convention on the Rights of the Child, which declares that 'every child has the inherent right to life'.[19]

There have been three reservations to Article 6 of the International Covenant on Civil and Political Rights, of which two, by Norway[20] and Pakistan,[21] have been withdrawn. The United States reserved the right, 'subject to its Constitutional constraints, to impose capital punishment on any person (other than a pregnant woman)'.[22] The two interpretative declarations concerning Article 6, by Ireland[23] and Thailand,[24] have been withdrawn. With respect to the Convention on the Rights of the Child, there are a few reservations and declarations concerning family planning and related issues.[25] The broad general reservations formulated by some States do not appear to be addressed to the right to life as such, but rather to aspects of its interpretation.[26] Thus, the reservations and declarations to the right to life provision in the Covenant and the Convention on the Rights of the Child do not challenge the right in such a way as to raise questions about its customary nature.

Nothing in the Universal Periodic Review materials raises any doubt that States that are not party to the Covenant or to the Arab Charter question whether they

Punishment and Eradication of Violence against Women, 'Convention of Belem do Para', OASTS 61, art. 4(a).

19 Convention on the Rights of the Child, (1990) 1571 UNTS 3, art. 6(1).

20 C.N.188.1972.TREATIES-7 ('with regard to the obligation to keep accused juvenile persons and juvenile offenders segregated from adults'), C.N.298.1979.TREATIES-9.

21 C.N.405.2010.TREATIES-17, (2011) 2786 UNTS 97 ('the provisions of [article 6] shall be so applied to the extent that they are not repugnant to the Provisions of the Constitution of Pakistan and the Sharia laws'), C.N.604.2011.TREATIES-41.

22 C.N.250.1992.TREATIES-14. On the reservation by the United States, see *Domingues v. United States*, Case No. 12.285, Report No. 62/02, Merits, 22 October 2002, paras. 61–62.

23 C.N.344.1989.TREATIES-2/17/4 ('Pending the introduction of further legislation to give full effect to the provisions of paragraph 5 of Article 6, should a case arise which is not covered by the provisions of existing law, the Government of Ireland will have regard to its obligations under the Covenant in the exercise of its power to advise commutation of the sentence of death.'), C.N.112.1994.TREATIES-2.

24 C.N.381.1996.TREATIES-8 (' … though in theory, sentence of death may be imposed for crimes committed by persons below eighteen years, but not below seventeen years of age, the Court always exercises its discretion under Section 75 to reduce the said scale of punishment, and in practice the death penalty has not been imposed upon any person below eighteen years of age. Consequently, Thailand considers that in real terms it has already complied with the principles enshrined herein'), C.N.356.2012.TREATIES-IV.4. See the discussion of Thailand's declaration in *Domingues v. United States*, Case 12.285, Report No. 62/02, Merits, 22 October 2002, para. 59.

25 China, C.N.92.1992.TREATIES-6 ('[T]he People's Republic of China shall fulfil its obligations provided by article 6 of the Convention under the prerequisite that the Convention accords with the provisions of article 25 concerning family planning of the Constitution of the People's Republic of China and in conformity with the provisions of article 2 of the Law of Minor Children of the People's Republic of China.'); France, Luxembourg, C.N.85.1994.TREATIES-1 (' … that this Convention, particularly article 6, cannot be interpreted as constituting any obstacle to the implementation of the provisions of … legislation relating to the voluntary interruption of pregnancy'); Tunisia, C.N.32.1992.TREATIES-2 (' … that the Preamble to and the provisions of the Convention, in particular article 6, shall not be interpreted in such a way as to impede the application of Tunisian legislation concerning voluntary termination of pregnancy'.).

26 General Comment 24, Issues Relating to Reservations Made upon Ratification or Accession to the Covenant or the Optional Protocols thereto, or in Relation to Declarations under art. 41 of the Covenant, CCPR/C/21/Rev.1/Add.6, para. 10, fn. 3.

have an obligation to respect and protect the right to life. Confirmation can be found in many of the reports by these States to the Human Rights Council.[27]

The right to life has been described as 'the supreme right'[28] and 'the most fundamental of the rights'.[29] The Human Rights Council's Special Rapporteur on extrajudicial, summary, or arbitrary executions has spoken of 'the supremacy and non-derogability of the right to life under both treaty and customary international law'.[30] According to the Special Rapporteur, '[w]henever a State is responsible for an unlawful killing, international law requires reparations in the form of compensation and/or satisfaction. This obligation is based in general customary international law.'[31] The list of customary norms in the Third Restatement of the American Law Institute included 'the murder or causing the disappearance of individuals'. The accompanying Comment explained that 'it is a violation of international law for a state to kill an individual other than as lawful punishment pursuant to conviction in accordance with due process of law, or as necessary under exigent circumstances, for example by police officials in line of duty in defence of themselves or of other innocent persons, or to prevent serious crime'.[32]

In its General Comment on reservations, the Human Rights Committee said that customary international law prohibited arbitrary deprivation of life.[33] This was reformulated, in more detail, in its third General Comment on the right to life. The Committee said reservations were not allowed 'to the prohibition against arbitrary deprivation of life of persons and to the strict limits provided in Article 6

[27] Bhutan, National report, A/HRC/WG.6/33/BTN/1, para. 7; China, National report, A/HRC/WG.6/17/CHN/1, paras. 44–47 and National report, A/HRC/WG.6/4/CHN/1, paras. 42–44; Fiji, National report, A/HRC/WG.6/20/FJI/1, para. 8; Kiribati, National report, A/HRC/WG.6/35/KIR/1, para. 75 and Views on conclusions, A/HRC/15/3/Add.1, para. 46; Micronesia, Report of the Working Group, A/HRC/16/16, paras. 8, 21; Nauru, National report, A/HRC/WG.6/10/NRU/1, paras. 16, 18–19, 28 and National report, A/HRC/WG.6/23/NRU/1, para. 27; St Kitts and Nevis, National report, A/HRC/WG.6/10/KNA/1, para. 8; Saint Lucia, National report, A/HRC/WG.6/10/LCA/1, para. 17 and Report of the Working Group, A/HRC/31/16, para. 18; Saudi Arabia, National report, A/HRC/WG.6/17/SAU/1, para. 57; Singapore, National report, A/HRC/WG.6/11/SGP/1, para. 22; Solomon Islands, National report, A/HRC/WG.6/11/SLB/1, para. 24; South Sudan, National report, A/HRC/WG.6/11/SDN/1, para. 123; Tuvalu, National report, A/HRC/WG.6/3/TUV/1, para. 33; United Arab Emirates, National report, A/HRC/WG.6/29/ARE/1, para. 13 and National report, A/HRC/WG.6/29/ARE/2, p. 3.

[28] General Comment 36, art. 6: right to life, CCPR/C/GC/36, para. 2.

[29] *Elgizouli (Appellant) v. Secretary of State for the Home Department (Respondent)*, [2020] UKSC 10, para. 14 (per Lady Hale).

[30] Report of the Special Rapporteur on extrajudicial, summary, or arbitrary executions, Christof Heyns, A/HRC/23/47, para. 36. Also Report of the Special Rapporteur on extrajudicial, summary, or arbitrary executions, Christof Heyns, A/HRC/20/22, para. 41; Report of the Special Rapporteur on extrajudicial, summary, or arbitrary executions, Christof Heyns, A/HRC/17/28, para. 43.

[31] Report of the Special Rapporteur on extrajudicial, summary, or arbitrary executions, Philip Alston, A/HRC/14/24, para. 56.

[32] Restatement (Third) of the Foreign Relations Law of the United States, St. Paul, MN: American Law Institute, 1987, para. 702 and Comment, para. f.

[33] General Comment 24, Issues Relating to Reservations Made upon Ratification or Accession to the Covenant or the Optional Protocols thereto, or in Relation to Declarations under art. 41 of the Covenant, CCPR/C/21/Rev.1/Add.6, para. 8.

with respect to the application of the death penalty'.[34] It wrote that the right to life has 'crucial importance both for individuals and for society as a whole. It is most precious for its own sake as a right that inheres in every human being, but it also constitutes a fundamental right whose effective protection is the prerequisite for the enjoyment of all other human rights and whose content can be informed by other human rights.'[35]

There is also support for viewing the right to life as a norm of *jus cogens*.[36] The Inter-American Commission on Human Rights has said that the right to life had 'attained the status of customary, and indeed peremptory, norms of international law'.[37] The African Commission on Human and Peoples' Rights has described the right to life as a norm of customary law[38] and of *jus cogens*.[39] The Appeals Chamber of the International Criminal Tribunal for the former Yugoslavia said that the 'inherent right to life' was a norm of customary international law.[40] The Human Rights Committee has explained that although not all the rights that are non-derogable under Article 4 of the International Covenant on Civil and Political Rights are *jus cogens*, the right not to be arbitrarily deprived of life was a peremptory norm. The International Law Commission did not include the right to life in the draft list of *jus cogens* norms that it adopted in 2019,[41] although some members of the Commission supported its inclusion.[42]

The right to life has both positive and negative dimensions. The negative aspect is the obligation of the State not to deprive arbitrarily persons within its jurisdiction of their lives. The positive aspect requires that States take measures to protect human life, including both the enactment of appropriate legislation and its effective enforcement. In making homicide a crime and ensuring that killings are investigated and, where appropriate, prosecuted, the State ensures the protection of the right to life. It is difficult to go beyond general principles in this respect because national legislation varies considerably, at least at the technical level. Where killings are either ignored by the authorities or, even worse, deliberately sheltered

[34] General Comment 36, art. 6: right to life, CCPR/C/GC/36, para. 68.

[35] Ibid., para. 2.

[36] General Comment 29, art. 4: Derogations during a State of Emergency, CCPR/C/21/Rev.1/Add.11, para. 11.

[37] *Mario Alfredo Lares-Reyes et al. v. United States*, Case 12.379, Report No. 19/02, 27 February 2002, para. 46, fn. 23; *Victims of the Tugboat '13 de Marzo' v. Cuba*, Case 11.436, Report 47/96, 16 October 1996, para. 79.

[38] *Noah Kazingachire, John Chitsenga, Elias Chemvura, and Batanai Hadzisi (represented by Zimbabwe Human Rights NGO Forum) v. Zimbabwe*, No. 295/04, 12 October 2013, para. 137.

[39] General Comment 3 on the African Charter on Human and Peoples' Rights: The right to life (art. 4), para. 5.

[40] *Prosecutor v. Blaškić* (IT-94/14-A), Judgment, 29 July 2004, para. 143; *Prosecutor v. Kordić and Čerkez* (IT-95-14/2-A), Judgment, 17 December 2004, para. 106.

[41] Report of the International Law Commission, Seventy-first session (29 April–7 June and 8 July–9 August 2019), A/74/10, p. 274; Fourth report on peremptory norms of general international law (*jus cogens*) by Dire Tladi, Special Rapporteur, A/CN.4/727, paras. 128–130.

[42] A/CN.4/SR.3462, p. 4 (Bogdan Aurescu); A/CN.4/SR.3462, p. 11 (Carlos Argüello Gómez).

from investigation, the question of violation of the right to life arises. A Special Rapporteur has explained that 'lack of accountability for a violation of the right to life is itself a violation of that right, and transparency is an integral part of accountability'.[43] There is a presumption that when loss of life is attributable to acts of violence, administrative sanctions and inquiries outside the context of criminal justice are not sufficient. The obligation is one of means and not one of result. Lord Neuberger of the United Kingdom Supreme Court said he thought it 'unlikely' that customary international law imposed a duty to investigate 'any suspicious death, which amounts to a violation of human rights law or of humanitarian law'.[44]

Although human rights obligations generally apply within the borders of a State and not outside them, there is a notable exception in cases of expulsion, extradition, and deportation. The principle of non-refoulement protects persons from being sent to another State where there are substantial grounds to believe they would be in danger of violations of the right to life. The Special Rapporteur on extrajudicial, summary, and arbitrary executions has referred to 'the principle of non-refoulement as a matter of customary law' in the context of transfer to a State where there was a risk of the death penalty.[45] It is common practice for States to obtain assurances that capital punishment will not be imposed before consenting to extradition, if the laws of the receiving State allow for this. In General Comment 36, the Human Rights Committee referred to the principle of non-refoulement more generally, stating that '[w]hen the alleged risk to life emanates from non-state actors or foreign States operating in the territory of the receiving State, credible and effective assurances for protection by the authorities of the receiving State may be sought and internal flight options could be explored. When relying upon assurances from the receiving State of treatment upon removal, the removing State should put in place adequate mechanisms for ensuring compliance with the issued assurances from the moment of removal onwards.'[46]

Issues may also arise regarding excuses or justifications that are invoked by perpetrators when charged with the crime of homicide. Lethal use of force by a person acting in self-defence is widely accepted by courts and is, indeed, in one sense a manifestation of the right to life to the extent it is directed at preserving life. The European Convention on Human Rights explicitly recognises that 'defence of any person from unlawful violence' does not constitute a violation of the right to life.[47] On the other hand, lenient treatment of so-called 'honour crimes', whose only

[43] Report of the Special Rapporteur on extrajudicial, summary, or arbitrary executions, A/67/275, para. 105.

[44] *Keyu et al. (Appellants) v. Secretary of State for Foreign and Commonwealth Affairs and another (Respondents)*, [2015] UKSC 69, para. 116 (per Lord Neuberger).

[45] Report of the Special Rapporteur on extrajudicial, summary, or arbitrary executions, A/67/275, para. 87.

[46] General Comment 36, art. 6: right to life, CCPR/C/GC/36, para. 30.

[47] European Convention on Human Rights, (1953) 213 UNTS 221, art. 2(2)(a).

justification is rooted in primitive notions of inequality and non-discrimination, is unacceptable.[48]

Amnesty is a subject of great controversy, and many have contended that it is prohibited under all circumstances, in particular when crimes involving the right to life are characterised as the international crimes of genocide, crimes against humanity, and war crimes. 'Amnesties that preclude accountability measures for gross violations of human rights and serious violations of humanitarian law, particularly for individuals with senior command responsibility, also violate customary international law', the African Commission has held.[49] But this position is too absolute, and it may well be necessary for amnesty to be accorded as part of a necessary compromise related to the conclusion of a peace agreement. This is an area in which no firm rule of international law can be identified.[50]

Breaches of the right to life often do not involve violent crime by individuals, whether or not they are acting on behalf of the State. Many violations of the right to life result from the failure to take adequate measures to protect health and safety. States are required to ensure minimum standards of living, including access to food, to potable water, to medical care, and to an environment that is not life-threatening.[51]

1. Prohibition of genocide

Genocide constitutes the ultimate attack upon the right to life. According to the very widely accepted definition, set out in Article 2 of the 1948 Convention on the Prevention and Punishment of the Crime of Genocide,[52] it consists of the physical destruction of a national, ethnic, racial, or religious group. At its first session, in 1946, the United Nations General Assembly described genocide as 'a denial of the right of existence of entire human groups, as homicide is the denial of the right to live of individual human beings'.[53] Although the term 'genocide' had only existed for a few years when the General Assembly declared it to be 'a matter of international concern' and subsequently adopted the Convention, almost immediately it found recognition as a crime under customary international law. In 1951, the International Court of Justice said genocide was contrary to 'moral law' and that

[48] Report submitted by Mr. Abdelfattah Amor, Special Rapporteur, in accordance with Commission on Human Rights resolution 2001/42, E/CN.4/2002/73/Add.2, paras. 155–158.

[49] *Thomas Kwoyelo v. Uganda*, No. 431/12, 17 October 2018, para. 289. Also *Zimbabwe Human Rights NGO Forum v. Zimbabwe*, No. 245/02, 15 May 2006, para. 201; *Mouvement ivoirien des droits humains (MIDH) v. Côte d'Ivoire*, No. 246/02, 29 July 2008, para. 91.

[50] For a more detailed discussion, see *supra*, pp. 98–100

[51] General Comment 36, art. 6: right to life, CCPR/C/GC/36, para. 26.

[52] Convention on the Prevention and Punishment of the Crime of Genocide, (1951) 78 UNTS 277, art. 2.

[53] The Crime of Genocide, A/RES/96(I), PP 1.

'the principles underlying the Convention are principles which are recognised by civilised nations as binding on States, even without any conventional obligation'. Although the Court did not say this explicitly, its statement has been understood to refer to customary international law.[54]

The advisory opinion of the International Court of Justice has also been cited as authority for the proposition that the prohibition of genocide is a norm of *jus cogens*.[55] This is obviously inaccurate, if only because the entire concept of *jus cogens* was still quite undeveloped in 1951. Although the International Court of Justice identified 'outlawing of acts … of genocide' as an *erga omnes* obligation in 1970,[56] only in 2006, more than half a century after the Advisory Opinion, did it finally use the label *jus cogens* with respect to genocide, saying this was 'assuredly the case'.[57] Subsequently, the European Court of Human Rights also affirmed the *jus cogens* nature of the prohibition of genocide.[58] It also appeared on the draft list of *jus cogens* norms adopted by the International Law Commission in 2019.[59] The prohibition of genocide has also been identified as *jus cogens* in judgments of national courts.[60] Judge Pinto de Albuquerque of the European Court of Human Rights said that prevention and punishment of genocide, as well as crimes against humanity and war crimes, 'is a *jus cogens* obligation of a non-derogable, imperative nature, in times of both peace and war'.[61]

[54] For example, *A.G. Israel v. Eichmann*, (1968) 36 ILR 5 (DC), para. 21; *A.G. Israel v. Eichmann*, (1968) 36 ILR 277 (SC), at p. 297; Report of the Secretary-General pursuant to paragraph 2 of Security Council Resolution 808(1993) S/25704, para. 45; *Prosecutor v. Akayesu* (ICTR-96-4-T), Judgment, 2 September 1998, para. 494; *Prosecutor v. Rutaganda* (ICTR-96-3-T) Judgment and Sentence, 6 December 1999, para. 46; *Prosecutor v. Jelisić* (IT-95-10-T), Judgment, 14 December 1999, para. 60; *Prosecutor v. Bagilishema* (ICTR-95-1A-T), Judgment, 7 June 2001, para. 124; *Prosecutor v. Sikirica et al.* (IT-95-8-I), Judgment on Defence Motions to Acquit, 3 September 2001, para. 55, fn. 160; *Prosecutor v. Tolimir* (IT-05-88/2-T), Judgment, 12 December 2012, para. 733; *Prosecutor v. Karadžić*, IT-95-5/18-T, Public redacted version of Judgment, 24 March 2016, para. 539.

[55] *Roach and Pinkerton v. United States*, Case 9647, Resolution No. 3/87, Merits, 22 September 1987, para. 55; *Application of the Convention on the Prevention and Punishment of the Crime of Genocide, Provisional Measures, Order of 13 September 1993, ICJ Reports 1993*, p. 325, Separate opinion of Judge Lauterpacht, para. 100; *Prosecutor v. Jelisić* (IT-95-10-T), Judgment, 14 December 1999, para. 60.

[56] *Barcelona Traction, Light and Power Company, Limited, Judgment, ICJ Reports 1970*, p. 3, para. 33.

[57] *Armed Activities on the Territory of the Congo (New Application: 2002) (Democratic Republic of the Congo v. Rwanda), Jurisdiction and Admissibility, Judgment, ICJ Reports 2006*, p. 6, para. 64. Also *Application of the Convention on the Prevention and Punishment of the Crime of Genocide (Bosnia and Herzegovina v. Serbia and Montenegro), Judgment, ICJ Reports 2007 (I)*, pp. 110–111, para. 161; *Application of the Convention on the Prevention and Punishment of the Crime of Genocide (Croatia v. Serbia), Judgment, ICJ Reports 2015*, p. 3, para. 87.

[58] *Jorgic v. Germany*, no. 74613/01, § 68, ECHR 2007-III.

[59] Report of the International Law Commission, Seventy-first session (29 April–7 June and 8 July–9 August 2019), A/74/10, p. 274. See also the explanation of the Special Rapporteur, ibid., p. 205; Fourth report on peremptory norms of general international law (*jus cogens*) by Dire Tladi, Special Rapporteur, A/CN.4/727, paras. 78–83.

[60] *Nulyarimma et al. v. Thompson, Buzzacott et al. v. Minister for the Environment*, [1999] FCA 1192, para. 18.

[61] *Sargsyan v. Azerbaijan* [GC], no. 40167/06, 16 June 2016, Dissenting opinion of Judge Pinto de Albuquerque, para. 22.

The American Law Institute Restatement is also authority for the *jus cogens* classification of genocide. The Restatement says that a State violates customary international law if it 'practices, encourages or condones' genocide, and if it 'fails to make genocide a crime or to punish persons guilty of it, or otherwise condones genocide. Parties to the Genocide Convention are bound also by the provisions requiring states to punish persons guilty of conspiracy, direct and public incitement, or attempt to commit genocide, or complicity in genocide, and to extradite persons accused of genocide.'[62] At the time the Restatement was adopted, the United States had not yet ratified the Genocide Convention and the Genocide Convention Implementation Act of 1987, also known as the 'Proxmire Act', had yet to enter into force.

The definition in the 1948 Convention has been held to refer to physical (or biological) destruction of the group and to exclude what is sometimes referred to as 'cultural genocide'.[63] Chambers of the International Criminal Tribunal for the former Yugoslavia ruled that customary international law limits the definition of genocide to acts seeking the physical or biological destruction of all or part of the group.[64] Although the definition in the Convention confines the scope of genocide to national, ethnic, racial, and religious groups, the 1946 General Assembly resolution was broader, extending genocide to 'racial, religious, political and other groups'.[65] The Grand Chamber of the European Court of Human Rights rejected the argument that under customary international law genocide included the targeting of political groups.[66]

2. Death penalty

The death penalty has been at the centre of debate about the scope of the right to life since the drafting of the Universal Declaration of Human Rights. The Declaration itself is silent on the subject of capital punishment. It states succinctly that '[e]veryone has the right to life ... '. This was a compromise between those who anticipated progressive development directed at abolition and the realities of

[62] Restatement (Third) of the Foreign Relations Law of the United States, St. Paul, MN: American Law Institute, 1987, para. 702, Comment, para. d.

[63] *Application of the Convention on the Prevention and Punishment of the Crime of Genocide (Bosnia and Herzegovina v. Serbia and Montenegro), Judgment, ICJ Reports 2007 (I)*, pp. 110–111, para. 344; *Application of the Convention on the Prevention and Punishment of the Crime of Genocide (Croatia v. Serbia), Judgment, ICJ Reports 2015*, p. 3, para. 136.

[64] *Prosecutor v. Krstić* (IT-98-33-T), Judgment, 2 August 2001, para. 580; *Prosecutor v. Stakić* (IT-97-24-T), Judgment, 31 July 2003, para. 519; *Prosecutor v. Krstić* (IT-98-33-A), Judgment, 19 April 2004, para. 25.

[65] The Crime of Genocide, A/RES/96(I), PP 2; also para. 1.

[66] *Vasiliauskas v. Lithuania* [GC], no. 35303/05, 20 October 2015, paras. 171–175.

State practice at that time.[67] In 1948, a large majority of United Nations Member States continued to employ the death penalty. Moreover, the 'international community' had recently endorsed its use for several of the war criminals convicted by the International Military Tribunal in October 1946.

When the Universal Declaration's laconic reference to the right to life was transposed into human rights treaties, explicit reference to the death penalty as a limited exception was included. In one sense, this was an admission that in the absence of a formal mention of capital punishment as a limitation, the practice of State-sanctioned murder as punishment for serious crimes would be vulnerable to challenge as an arbitrary deprivation of the right to life. Four of the major human rights treaties, the International Covenant on Civil and Political Rights, the European Convention on Human Rights, the American Convention on Human Rights, and the Arab Charter of Human Rights, all recognise the death penalty as a permissible exception to the protection of the right to life. With the exception of the European Convention, they subject this exception to a number of conditions concerning the quality of justice, the nature of the crimes for which it may be imposed, and categories of persons who may not be executed under any circumstances. Although Article 6 of the International Covenant on Civil and Political Rights recognises that States that had not yet abolished capital punishment are permitted to conduct executions subject to a number of conditions, it also insists that '[n]othing in this article shall be invoked to delay or to prevent the abolition of capital punishment by any State Party to the present Covenant'.[68]

The United Nations Secretary-General began the issuance of periodic reporting on the global status of the death penalty in the early 1970s. Initially, he was sceptical about the existence of any trend towards abolition of the death penalty.[69] Subsequent reports, issued every five years, were ambivalent.[70] But by 1990, the Secretary-General considered that 'that the movement towards abolition had progressed somewhat'.[71] His report that year noted that seventy-seven countries had abolished the death penalty in law or in practice as opposed to ninety-two that retained it.[72] In the three decades that followed, the trend continued without relapse. By 2020, there were 167 abolitionist States as opposed to thirty-one that continued to use the death penalty. Moreover, most of the thirty-one retentionist States manifested dramatic reductions in the number of executions and in the crimes for

[67] For a summary of the debates on capital punishment during the drafting of the Universal Declaration of Human Rights, see William A. Schabas, *The Abolition of the Death Penalty in International Law*, 3rd ed., Cambridge: Cambridge University Press, 2003, pp. 27–39.

[68] International Covenant on Civil and Political Rights, (1976) 999 UNTS 171, art. 6(6).

[69] Capital punishment, E/5616, para. 48.

[70] Capital punishment, E/1980/9, paras. 10, 83; Capital punishment, E/1985/43/Corr.1, para. 28.

[71] Capital punishment and implementation of the safeguards guaranteeing the protection of those facing the death penalty, E/1990/38/Rev.1, para. 10.

[72] Ibid., para. 15.

which capital punishment could be imposed.[73] The persistence of the death penalty is largely confined to Asia. It has virtually disappeared in much of Africa, while in Europe and the Western Hemisphere there is only one State of each region where capital punishment continues to be imposed, Belarus and the United States. In the United States, most of the executions in recent years have taken place in only a few of the fifty states. This pattern may indicate the existence of regional customary norms in many parts of the world. The European Court of Human Rights has already suggested as much in judgments that view the reference to the death penalty in the right to life provision of the European Convention on Human Rights as essentially obsolete and inoperative.[74]

Thus, this is an area in which there have been very marked changes in State practice in recent decades pointing to the emergence of a customary norm prohibiting the death penalty in the not too distant future. In the International Law Commission, Charles Jalloh has pointed to 'an emerging custom', but noted that the number of abolitionist countries 'might therefore fall short'.[75] Juan Méndez, the United Nations Special Rapporteur on torture and other cruel, inhuman, or degrading treatment or punishment, referred to the '[p]ossible emergence of a customary norm' prohibiting capital punishment. He spoke of a 'growing concern at the irreconcilable conflict between the legally imposed death penalty and the infliction of torture or cruel, inhuman or degrading treatment or punishment'.[76] The Special Rapporteur concluded that 'there is an evolving standard whereby States and judiciaries consider the death penalty to be a violation per se of the prohibition of torture or cruel, inhuman or degrading treatment'. He said he was 'convinced that a customary norm prohibiting the death penalty under all circumstances, if it has not already emerged, is at least in the process of formation'.[77] Even if the formation of the customary norm prohibiting capital punishment altogether has not yet occurred, wrote the Special Rapporteur, in most cases its imposition is 'tantamount to torture' or to cruel, inhuman or degrading treatment.'[78]

The Special Rapporteur on extrajudicial, summary, and arbitrary executions, in an expert report submitted to the Supreme Court of the United Kingdom, said 'there is an emerging norm of customary international law that the death penalty as such is a violation of the absolute right against torture and cruel, inhuman and degrading treatment of punishment, and that a norm against the facilitation of the

[73] Capital punishment and implementation of the safeguards guaranteeing the protection of those facing the death penalty, E/2020/53, para. 6.

[74] *Al Nashiri v. Poland*, no. 28761/11, §§ 576–577, 24 July 2014. Also *Al Nashiri v. Romania*, no. 33234/12, §§ 726–727, 31 May 2018.

[75] A/CN.4/SR.3461, p. 10.

[76] Interim report of the Special Rapporteur on torture and other cruel, inhuman, or degrading treatment or punishment, A/67/279, para. 66.

[77] Ibid., para. 71.

[78] Observations on communications transmitted to Governments and replies received, A/HRC/31/57/Add.1, para. 33.

death penalty follows from that'.[79] But in a 2020 judgment, the Court said it was unconvinced, concluding that '[i]n the absence of firm, tangible evidence that the process of evolution has been completed or that there is a general practice . . . , it is impossible to accept the appellant's argument based on customary international law'.[80] Also, in assessing the claim that an abolitionist norm has emerged the bi-annual statements signed by a significant number of States affirming their objection to any such customary norm must also be taken into account.[81]

Beyond any question, customary international law imposes important restrictions on the use of capital punishment. Limitations on the use of capital punishment are set out in Article 6 of the International Covenant on Civil and Political Rights. Of the two dozen States that are not parties to the Covenant, about half have abolished the death penalty in law[82] while another seven are deemed to be *de facto* abolitionist because they have not conducted an execution for at least ten years.[83] There is evidence in the reports to the Human Rights Council from these *de facto* abolitionist States that they accept the limitations on capital punishment imposed by the Covenant.[84] Some of them declare this explicitly.[85] The six States that continue to impose capital punishment and that are not parties to the Covenant often indicate in their reporting to the Human Rights Council that they comply with the norms set out in Article 6 of the Covenant. [86] Malaysia reported that in death penalty cases, it 'maintains that such safeguards are in line with international standards, in particular Article 6 of ICCPR'.[87] Saudi Arabia said that although international law had not abolished the death penalty, there exist 'established norms governing its imposition'.[88] The United Arab Emirates told the Human Rights Council that

[79] *Elgizouli (Appellant) v. Secretary of State for the Home Department (Respondent)*, [2020] UKSC 10, para. 148.

[80] Ibid., paras. 148–151 (per Lord Kerr), para. 190(iii) (per Lord Carnwath). For an earlier decision to the same effect by the United States Court of Appeals, Sixth Circuit, see *Buell v. Mitchell*, 274 F.3d 337 (6th Cir. 2001), at pp. 372–373.

[81] Annex to the note verbale dated 13 September 2019 from the Permanent Representative of Egypt to the United Nations addressed to the Secretary-General, A/73/1004. See *supra*, p. C.2 P105.

[82] Bhutan, Cook Islands, Holy Sea, Fiji, Kiribati, Marshall Islands, Micronesia, Nauru, Niue, Palau, Samoa, Solomon Islands, Tuvalu, Vanuatu.

[83] Brunei Darussalam, Cuba, Myanmar, Oman, St Kitts and Nevis, Saint Lucia, Tonga.

[84] Myanmar, National report, A/HRC/WG.6/10/MMR/1, para. 37 and National report A/HRC/WG.6/23/MMR/1, para. 165; Oman, National report, A/HRC/WG.6/10/OMN/1, paras. 76–78 and Views on conclusions, A/HRC/31/11/Add.1, p. 9; Saint Lucia, Report of the Working Group, A/HRC/17/12, paras. 8–12; Tonga, National report, A/HRC/WG.6/15/TON/1, para. 136.

[85] Tonga, National report, A/HRC/WG.6/15/TON/1, para. 136 and Report of the Working Group, A/HRC/38/5, para. 6; Myanmar, National report, A/HRC/WG.6/10/MMR/1, para. 37.

[86] China, National report, A/HRC/WG.6/4/CHN/1, paras. 43–44, 54, National report, A/HRC/WG.6/17/CHN/1, paras. 44–47, Report of the Working Group, A/HRC/11/25, paras. 11, 67, and Report of the Working Group, A/HRC/25/5, para. 16; Malaysia, National report, A/HRC/WG.6/17/MYS/1, paras. 45–47 and National report, A/HRC/WG.6/4/MYS/1/Rev.1, paras. 89–90; Saudi Arabia, Report of the Working Group, A/HRC/25/3, para. 97(a) and National report, A/HRC/WG.6/17/SAU/1, para. 37; South Sudan, Views on conclusions, A/HRC/34/13/Add.1, para. 7, National report, A/HRC/WG.6/11/SDN/1, para. 124, Report of the Working Group, A/HRC/18/16, paras. 46, 82.

[87] Malaysia, National report, A/HRC/WG.6/17/MYS/1, para. 45 and National report, A/HRC/WG.6/4/MYS/1/Rev.1, para. 89.

[88] Saudi Arabia, Views on conclusions, A/HRC/40/4/Add.1, para. 18.

its law ensures respect for the Safeguards Guaranteeing Protection of the Rights of Those Facing the Death Penalty,[89] which constitute an authoritative elaboration of Article 6 of the Covenant prepared by the UN Committee on Crime Prevention and Control in the early 1980s and since endorsed and amended by the Economic and Social Council.[90] Singapore is the real outlier. In its early reports to the Council, where little information on the practice of capital punishment was provided, it declared that it considered 'capital punishment as a criminal justice issue, rather than a human rights issue'.[91] Subsequently, Singapore provided details on the practice of the death penalty, suggesting that its view had evolved.[92]

Article 6 of the Covenant, coupled with the Safeguards Guaranteeing Protection of the Rights of Those Facing the Death Penalty as well as information gleaned from reporting to the Human Rights Council, points to several features of customary international law governing application of capital punishment. The death penalty may only be imposed for the 'most serious crimes'. The formulation, which is taken from Article 6(2) of the International Covenant on Civil and Political Rights, is generally accepted despite the fact that its somewhat vague wording has sometimes invited unacceptably broad understandings. The Safeguards Guaranteeing Protection of those Facing the Death Penalty declare that the ambit of the term most serious crimes 'should not go beyond intentional crimes, with lethal or other extremely grave consequences'.[93] According to the Human Rights Committee, the death penalty may not be imposed for crimes that do not result directly and intentionally in death.[94] The Third Restatement of the American Law Institute said that capital punishment could constitute cruel or inhuman punishment 'if grossly disproportionate to the crime', supporting this with reference to a United States Supreme Court judgment prohibiting the death penalty for rape.[95] In its first report to the Human Rights Council for the Universal Periodic Review, China explained that '[t]he Criminal Law provides that the death penalty is to be applied only to criminals who commit the most heinous crimes'.[96] In its National report to the

[89] Safeguards Guaranteeing Protection of the Rights of Those Facing the Death Penalty, E/RES/1984/50.

[90] United Arab Emirates, National report A/HRC/WG.6/29/ARE/1, para. 24.

[91] Singapore, National report, A/HRC/WG.6/11/SGP/1, para. 120. Also Singapore, Report of the Working Group, A/HRC/18/11, para. 87.

[92] Singapore, National report, A/HRC/WG.6/24/SGP/1, para. 103. Also Singapore, Report of the Working Group, A/HRC/32/17, paras. 61–63.

[93] E/RES/1984/50, para. 1. Also Human rights in the administration of justice, A/RES/39/118.

[94] Iran, Comments of the Human Rights Committee, CCPR/C/79/Add.25, para. 8.

[95] Restatement (Third) of the Foreign Relations Law of the United States, St. Paul, MN: American Law Institute, 1987, para. 702, Comment, para. f, citing *Coker v. Georgia*, 433 U.S. 584, 97 S.Ct. 2861, 53 L.Ed.2d 982 (1977).

[96] China, UPR National report, A/HRC/WG.6/4/CHN/1, para. 43. Also: China, UPR Working Group Report, A/HRC/11/25, para. 67; China, National report, A/HRC/WG.6/17/CHN/1, paras. 44–47; China, Working Group Report, A/HRC/25/5, paras. 16, 84; China, Working Group Report, Addendum, A/HRC/25/5/Add.1, para. 186.17.

Human Rights Council, Saudi Arabia explained that the death penalty 'is imposed only for the most serious crimes and in the narrowest of circumstances'.[97]

Certain categories of individuals may not be made subject to the death penalty. It is universally recognised that offences committed by persons under the age of eighteen may not result in a capital sentence. The rule appears in several treaties, including the Convention on the Rights of the Child.[98] There are no reservations to the relevant provision. The United States is the only Member State of the United Nations that has not ratified the Convention on the Rights of the Child. Its Supreme Court, with reference to international law sources, has held imposition of the death penalty for crimes committed by persons under eighteen to be unconstitutional.[99] The United Nations Sub-Commission on the Protection and Promotion of Human Rights declared that the imposition of a death sentence on a person who was aged under eighteen at the time of the offence is forbidden by customary international law.[100] The Inter-American Commission on Human Rights has also held that customary international law prohibits execution for a crime committed when under the age of eighteen.[101] The Commission reversed an earlier decision in which it concluded that there was a customary norm prohibiting execution of 'children', one of *jus cogens* moreover.[102] In that ruling the Commission said it had been convinced by the United States that there was not then a norm of customary international law establishing eighteen as the minimum age, although one was 'emerging'.[103] The Human Rights Committee took a similar position in General Comment 24, issued in 1994, including the prohibition of the execution of 'children' in its list of customary norms but without specifying the age.[104] Reassessing its position in 2002, the Inter-American Commission referred to 'several notable

[97] Saudi Arabia, National report, A/HRC/WG.6/17/SAU/1, para. 35.

[98] Convention on the Rights of the Child, (1990) 1571 UNTS 3, art. 37(a).

[99] *Roper v. Simmons*, 543 US 551 (2005),

[100] The death penalty in relation to juvenile offenders, E/C.4/Sub.2/RES/2000/17, PP 8.

[101] *Domingues v. United States*, Case 12.285, Report No. 62/02, Merits, 22 October 2002, para. 55. The Inter-American Commission was interpreting art. I of the American Declaration on the Rights and Duties of Man, Final Act of the Ninth International Conference of American States, Res. XXX. Like the Universal Declaration of Human Rights, the 'core provisions' of the American Declaration on the Rights and Duties of Man, adopted in May 1948, are said to represent customary norms: *Mary and Carrie Dann v. United States*, Case 11.140, Report No. 75/02, Merits, 27 December 2002, para. 163; *Mario Alfredo Lares-Reyes et al. v. United States*, Case 12.379, Report No. 19/02, Merits, 27 February 2002, para. 46; Human Rights Situation of Refugee and Migrant Families and Unaccompanied Children in the United States of America, OAS/Ser.L/V/II.155, Doc. 16, para. 40; Missing and Murdered Indigenous Women in British Columbia, Canada, OEA/Ser.L/V/II, Doc. 30/14, para. 104; Towards the Closure of Guantanamo, OAS/Ser.L/V/II, Doc. 20/15, para. 19.

[102] *Roach and Pinkerton v. United States*, Case 9647, Resolution No. 3/87, Merits, 22 September 1987, para. 56. For a discussion of this case as well as examination of the difficult issue of regional *jus cogens*, see Fourth report on peremptory norms of general international law (*jus cogens*) by Dire Tladi, Special Rapporteur, A/CN.4/727, para. 39.

[103] *Roach and Pinkerton v. United States*, Case 9647, Resolution No. 3/87, Merits, 22 September 1987, para. 60.

[104] General Comment 24, Issues Relating to Reservations Made upon Ratification or Accession to the Covenant or the Optional Protocols thereto, or in Relation to Declarations under art. 41 of the Covenant, CCPR/C/21/Rev.1/Add.6, para. 8.

developments' with respect to treaties, including the entry into force of new instruments like the Convention on the Rights of the Child as well as 'broadened ratifications of existing treaties'.[105]

Execution of pregnant women is also prohibited, an implied acknowledgment that the unborn child may benefit from some protection of the right to life. Several countries also prohibit the death penalty for young mothers, although it is difficult to confirm the existence of a universal rule. The two Additional Protocols to the Geneva Conventions somewhat inconsistently proscribe pronouncing the death penalty on 'mothers having dependent infants, for an offence related to the armed conflict' in the case of international armed conflict, and that it 'shall not be carried out on pregnant women or mothers of young children' in the context of non-international armed conflict.[106] The International Committee of the Red Cross study on customary law did not address this norm specifically, providing only that '[t]he specific protection, health and assistance needs of women affected by armed conflict must be respected' and discussing the issue of execution of pregnant women and mothers in the accompanying commentary.[107] The Arab Charter on Human Rights forbids execution of 'a nursing mother within two years from the date of her delivery'.[108] In practice, executions of pregnant women and mothers of young children are virtually unknown.

There seems also to be uniform State practice prohibiting the execution of persons who are insane, including those who have become so since conviction. The Safeguards Guaranteeing Protection of Those Facing the Death Penalty prohibit execution of 'persons who have become insane'.[109] They were amended in 1988 with addition of the words 'persons suffering from mental retardation or extremely limited mental competence'.[110]

Imposition of the death penalty following a trial characterised by unfairness to the accused constitutes in itself a violation of the right to life.[111] According to the United Nations Sub-Commission on the Protection and Promotion of Human Rights, 'under customary international law the death penalty cannot be

[105] *Domingues v. United States*, Case 12.285, Report No. 62/02, Merits, 22 October 2002, para. 55.

[106] Additional Protocol to the 1949 Geneva Conventions and Relating to the Protection of Victims of International Armed Conflicts, (1979) 1125 UNTS 3, art. 76(3); Additional Protocol to the 1949 Geneva Conventions and Relating to the Protection of Victims of Non-International Armed Conflicts, (1979) 1125 UNTS 3, art. 6(4).

[107] Jean-Marie Henckaerts and Louise Doswald-Beck, *Customary International Humanitarian Law*, Vol. I, Cambridge: Cambridge University Press, 2005, pp. 473–479.

[108] Arab Charter on Human Rights, art. 7(2).

[109] Safeguards Guaranteeing Protection of the Rights of Those Facing the Death Penalty, E/RES/1984/50, para. 3.

[110] Implementation of the Safeguards Guaranteeing Protection of the Rights of Those Facing the Death Penalty, E/RES/1989/64, art. 1(c) and (d).

[111] General Comment 32, art. 14: Right to equality before courts and tribunals and to a fair trial, CCPR/C/GC/32, para. 59.

imposed except after proceedings that provide all the guarantees required for a fair trial, including a competent, independent and impartial tribunal'.[112] The Sub-Commission also said that imposing the death penalty on a civilian tried by a military tribunal or a tribunal whose composition includes one or more members of the armed forces is contrary to customary international law.[113] Fair trial issues are dealt with more comprehensively elsewhere in this volume. The death penalty may only be pronounced to the extent that it is already provided for in legislation, a specific formulation of the more general rule of *nulla poena sine lege*. Moreover, if legislation is amended subsequent to the offence so as to provide for a more clement sentence, the accused person must benefit according to the *lex mitior* principle.

The possibility of pardon or commutation must be available. Special Rapporteur Philip Alston said the right to seek pardon or commutation to a less draconian penalty was reflected in international and regional instruments as well as in the domestic practice of almost every country that applies capital punishment. 'Indeed its recognition is so widespread that it would be difficult to deny its status as a norm of customary international law', he wrote.[114]

Human history shows a general trend towards the adoption of increasingly 'humane' forms of execution. Underlying this development is the sense that, according to the European Court of Human Rights, '[w]hatever the method of execution, the extinction of life involves some physical pain'.[115] Medieval forms of execution, involving public dismemberment of the body of the victim, crucifixion and burning alive, much of it in public, have long been abandoned with the aim of minimising the brutality and horror. There is judicial authority condemning as cruel, inhuman, and degrading such forms of punishment as gas asphyxiation[116] and lapidation.[117] The English Court of Appeal has refused to declare that hanging is contrary to customary international law.[118] In many jurisdictions, execution is delayed seemingly indefinitely as death row detention cells become increasingly overcrowded. The lengthy wait for execution is itself a form of cruel, inhuman, or degrading treatment.[119]

[112] Imposition of the death penalty on civilians by military tribunals or by tribunals whose composition includes one or more members of the armed forces, E/C.4/Sub.2/RES/2004/25, PP 1.

[113] Ibid., para. 1.

[114] Report of the Special Rapporteur on extrajudicial, summary, or arbitrary executions, Philip Alston, A/HRC/8/3, para. 59.

[115] *Al Nashiri v. Poland*, no. 28761/11, § 576, 24 July 2014. Also *Al Nashiri v. Romania*, no. 33234/12, § 726, 31 May 2018.

[116] *Ng. v. Canada*, no. 469/1991, Views, 7 January 1994, CCPR/C/49/D/469/1991, paras. 16.1–16.5.

[117] Iran, Concluding observations, CCPR/C/IRN/CO/3, para. 12; Sudan, Concluding observations, CCPR/C/SDN/CO/5, para. 29; Yemen, Concluding observations, CCPR/C/YEM/CO/5, para. 14.

[118] *Al-Saadoon et al., R (on the application of) v. Secretary of State for Defence* [2009] EWCA Civ 7.

[119] *Soering v. the United Kingdom and Germany*, 7 July 1989, § 111, Series A no. 161; *Pratt and Morgan v. Attorney-General for Jamaica et al.*, [1994] 2 AC 1.

3. Armed conflict

In recent centuries, the most massive violations of the right to life have resulted from armed conflict. The Human Rights Committee, in its third General Comment on the right to life, stated that '[w]ars and other acts of mass violence continue to be a scourge of humanity resulting in the loss of many thousands of lives every year. Efforts to avert the risks of war, and any other armed conflict, and to strengthen international peace and security, are among the most important safeguards for the right to life.'[120] It added that States that 'fail to take all reasonable measures to settle their international disputes by peaceful means might fall short of complying with their positive obligation to ensure the right to life'.[121] Although the effective enjoyment of fundamental human rights, including the right to life, can only be ensured by world peace, this does not mean that human rights law is irrelevant during armed conflict. International courts have confirmed the continued application of human rights law during armed conflict.[122]

A specialised body of law, known as the law of armed conflict or international humanitarian law, has developed over the centuries in order to govern conduct during war. Originally, it was entirely customary in nature. It is now highly codified in treaties like the Hague Conventions on the Laws and Customs of War and the Geneva Conventions although the customary dimension retains great importance. In some circumstances, international humanitarian law provides useful guidance with respect to the application and interpretation of rules of human rights law. An example is provided by prisoners of war, who are not subject to the ordinary rules applicable in peacetime that govern detention and appearance before criminal courts.[123] Moreover, and this is of particular relevance to the right to life, prisoners of war are in principle not prosecuted for killing during wartime to the extent that their conduct can be considered 'lawful acts of war'.

Much of international humanitarian law concerns the treatment of persons who have fallen under the control of one of the parties to the conflict, notably civilian non-combatants as well as prisoners and wounded soldiers. Here the overlap with human rights law is particularly evident. The Venice Commission of the Council of Europe has referred to 'the rule of customary international law that the well-being of the population in occupied areas has to be a basic concern of those involved in a conflict'.[124] The other main area addressed by the law of armed conflict concerns the means and methods of warfare, where the application of human rights law is

[120] General Comment 36, art. 6: right to life, CCPR/C/GC/36, para. 69 (internal references omitted).
[121] Ibid., para. 70 (internal references omitted).
[122] *Armed Activities on the Territory of the Congo (Democratic Republic of the Congo v. Uganda), Judgment, ICJ Reports 2005*, p. 168, para. 216; *Legal Consequences of the Construction of a Wall in the Occupied Palestinian Territory, Advisory Opinion, ICJ Reports 2004*, p. 136, para. 106.
[123] *Hassan v. the United Kingdom* [GC], no. 29750/09, §§ 101–102, ECHR 2014-VI.
[124] European Commission for Democracy through Law (Venice Commission), Draft Annual Report of Activities 2009, CDL(2010)018, p. 22.

less straightforward and there has been some tendency to exclude its application in favour of a *lex specialis* reserved to international humanitarian law. Yet, even the means and methods of warfare raise issues that are germane to human rights law. The European Court of Human Rights has held that poison gas, whose use was widespread during the First World War, is prohibited by customary international law.[125]

There is clearly a tension between respect for the right to life and the tolerance of large-scale killing during wartime. To some extent this is addressed through concepts of self-defence in the sense that the killing by those who have been wrongfully attacked is necessary to save and protect life. The principle works much as it does to individual acts of self-defence during peacetime. The same does not apply, however, where the killing is a result of aggression. As the Human Rights Committee explained in its General Comment on the right to life, States that engage in acts of aggression, 'as defined in international law, resulting in deprivation of life, violate *ipso facto*' the right to life.[126] In other words, although killing during armed conflict may not run afoul of international humanitarian law regardless of the legality of the conflict itself, to the extent that principles of targeting and proportionality are respected, the same cannot be said of international human rights law.

International humanitarian law makes an important distinction between combatants and civilians who do not participate actively in hostilities. Nevertheless, even soldiers themselves are entitled to protection of the right to life. They may not be targeted with lethal force or summarily executed merely because of their status. The prohibition of the killing of captured prisoners is not disputed. The same cannot be said for gratuitous killing of those identified as combatants even if they pose no threat to the other party. Where combatants may be captured without great risk, their lives are entitled to protection. One of the eminent authorities on international humanitarian law, Jean Pictet, wrote that '[i]f we can put a soldier out of action by capturing him, we should not wound him; if we can obtain the same result by wounding him, we must not kill him. If there are two means to achieve the same military advantage, we must choose the one which causes the lesser evil.'[127]

4. When does the right to life begin?

The substantive provisions of the Universal Declaration of Human Rights open with the words '[a]ll human beings are born free and equal in dignity and rights'.

[125] *Van Anraat v. Netherlands* (dec.), no. 65389/09, §§ 90–92, 6 July 2010.

[126] General Comment 36, art. 6: right to life, CCPR/C/GC/36, para. 70.

[127] Jean Pictet, *Development and Principles of International Humanitarian Law*, Dordrecht: Martinus Nijhoff, 1985, p. 75. See also Nils Meltzer, *Interpretive Guidance on the Notion of Direct Participation in Hostilities under International Humanitarian Law*, Geneva: International Committee of the Red Cross, 2009, pp. 77–82.

This has been taken as confirmation that human rights protection begins with birth and not before, and that the right to life does not benefit an unborn child. But there are other signals in human rights law that suggest a degree of recognition of the right to life of the unborn child. One of them is found in the right to life provisions of the major treaties on the prohibition of the execution of pregnant women.[128] The American Convention on Human Rights affirms that the right to life begins 'in general, from the moment of conception'.[129] It does not seem possible to identify a rule of customary international law that clarifies whether or not the unborn child benefits from the right to life.

Right to life issues arise, nevertheless, with respect to expectant mothers to the extent that their own lives are endangered by pregnancy. Regulations governing the voluntary termination of pregnancy must not threaten their lives and well-being. The State must ensure safe, legal, and effective access to abortion in circumstances where the mother's life and health are at risk. Legislation that is too restrictive may compel women and girls to seek illegal means of terminating pregnancy under conditions that are dangerous to themselves.[130] The unavailability of voluntary termination of pregnancy also raises issues with other fundamental rights, in particular the right to privacy and the right to equality.

5. Voluntary termination of life

In principle, fundamental rights may be waived by the individual who benefits from them, including the right to life. Personal autonomy entitles individuals to decide to bring an end to their lives. At present, views on the subject vary considerably and it is not possible to conclude that there is a 'right to die' under customary law.[131]

However, protection of the right to life requires the State to take measures directed at the prevention of suicide. This is particularly the case with vulnerable persons, including those in detention of one form or another. Where States opt to facilitate the voluntary termination of life, for example of those who are terminally ill or in an unbearable situation, this may be subject to strict regulations in order to ensure that the consent is free, informed, explicit, and unambiguous. Such measures are necessary in order to protect against abuse.[132]

* * *

[128] International Covenant on Civil and Political Rights, (1976) 999 UNTS 171, art. 6(5); American Convention on Human Rights, (1978) 1144 UNTS 123, art. 4(5); Arab Charter on Human Rights, art. 7(2).

[129] American Convention on Human Rights, (1978) 1144 UNTS 123, art. 4(1).

[130] General Comment 35, art. 9 (Liberty and security of person), CCPR/C/GC/35, para. 8.

[131] For example, *Pretty v. United Kingdom* no. 2346/02, ECHR 2002-III.

[132] General Comment 36, art. 6: right to life, CCPR/C/GC/36, para. 9 (internal references omitted).

Conclusions. The right to life is enshrined in customary international law. No person may be deprived arbitrarily of his or her life. Genocide, which amounts to violation of the right to life of a national, ethnic, racial, or religious group, is a crime under customary international law. The right to life and the prohibition of genocide are also norms of *jus cogens*. Protection against arbitrary deprivation of life continues to apply during armed conflict, even with respect to combatants. No person may be subject to refoulement to a country where there is a real risk of arbitrary deprivation of life. States have an obligation to investigate and prosecute violations of the right to life. In States where the death penalty has not yet been abolished, it may only be imposed for the most serious crimes, following a trial in which procedural guarantees have been scrupulously observed. Certain categories of persons may not be executed.

It is not possible to reach firm conclusions about the application of the right to life to the unborn. Nor is it possible to identify applicable rules of customary international law concerning voluntary cessation of life.

B. Torture and cruel, inhuman, or degrading treatment or punishment

Torture's prohibition by customary international law is hardly controversial. It is the only rule of customary human rights law to be endorsed clearly and unequivocally by the International Court of Justice. In support of its holding, the Court cited 'numerous international instruments of universal application', including the International Covenant on Civil and Political Rights, the Universal Declaration of Human Rights, the 1949 Geneva Conventions, and General Assembly resolution 3452 (XXX). Furthermore, said the Court, the prohibition of torture 'has been introduced into the domestic law of almost all States; finally, acts of torture are regularly denounced within national and international fora'.[133] The prohibition of torture has been identified as a customary norm by many other international courts and tribunals. For example, a Trial Chamber of the International Criminal Tribunal for the former Yugoslavia said that the definition of torture contained in the Convention against Torture and Other Cruel, Inhuman or Degrading Treatment or Punishment 'reflects a consensus ... representative of customary international law'.[134]

Given its status today as the iconic customary law norm, the neglect of the prohibition of torture in the early attempts at codification of human rights norms is

[133] *Questions relating to the Obligation to Prosecute or Extradite (Belgium v. Senegal), Judgment, ICJ Reports 2012*, p. 422, para. 99.

[134] *Prosecutor v. Delalić et al.* (IT-96-21-T), Judgment, 16 November 1998, para. 459.

striking. There is no mention of the issue in the 1929 draft of the Institut de Droit International[135] and the 1943 draft of the London International Assembly.[136] Similarly, Hersch Lauterpacht did not refer to torture in his 1945 draft bill of rights although it did proscribe 'inhuman and cruel punishment'.[137] Torture is not referred to in the amendments to the Charter of the United Nations submitted by Cuba and Panama at the San Francisco Conference, or in the early drafts of the International Bill of Rights submitted in 1946 and early 1947, with the exception of that of the American Federation of Labor.[138] The American Declaration on the Rights and Duties of Man, of May 1948, is also silent on the subject. The relative neglect of the prohibition of torture at this early stage in the codification of international human rights norms stands in marked contrast with the preeminent status it now possesses.

Article 5 of the Universal Declaration of Human Rights states that '[n]o one shall be subjected to torture or to cruel, inhuman or degrading treatment or punishment'. The text can be traced to John Humphrey's initial draft for the Drafting Committee of the Commission on Human Rights that he placed at the beginning of the instrument immediately following the right to life.[139] The International Covenant on Civil and Political Rights reprises the words of Declaration but adds a second sentence specifying that 'no one shall be subjected without his free consent to medical or scientific experimentation'.[140] There have been a few reservations to Article 7 of the Covenant,[141] but they do not attempt to reserve right to engage in torture.[142]

The prohibition of torture and other cruel, inhuman, or degrading treatment or punishment is set out in many other regional and specialised human rights treaties.[143] Several of the States that are not parties to the Covenant have ratified the

[135] Institut de Droit International, 'Declaration of the International Rights of Man', (1941) 35 *American Journal of International Law* 663.

[136] London International Assembly, Report of the Third Commission (Legal Commission) on individual rights, TNA LNU 6/7.

[137] Hersch Lauterpacht, *An International Bill of the Rights of Man*, New York: Columbia University Press, 1945, p. 70.

[138] International Bill of Rights, Proposal Submitted by American Federation of Labor, E/CT.2/2, para. 12(e).

[139] Draft Outline of International Bill of Rights (prepared by the Division of Human Rights), E/CN.4/AC.1/3: 'No one shall be subjected to torture, or to any unusual punishment or indignity.'

[140] International Covenant on Civil and Political Rights, (1976) 999 UNTS 171, art. 7.

[141] Botswana, C.N.978.2000.TREATIES-14; Pakistan, C.N.405.2010.TREATIES-17; Qatar, C.N.15.2019.TREATIES-IV.4; United States of America, C.N.250.1992.TREATIES-14.

[142] General Comment 24, Issues Relating to Reservations Made upon Ratification or Accession to the Covenant or the Optional Protocols thereto, or in Relation to Declarations under art. 41 of the Covenant, CCPR/C/21/Rev.1/Add.6, para. 10, fn. 3.

[143] European Convention on Human Rights, (1953) 213 UNTS 221, art. 3; American Convention on Human Rights, (1978) 1144 UNTS 123, art. 5(2); African Charter on Human and Peoples' Rights, (1986) 1520 UNTS 217, art. 5; Arab Charter on Human Rights, art. 8; Charter of Fundamental Rights of the European Union, OJ C 326/391, art. 4; Convention against Torture and Other Cruel, Inhuman or Degrading Treatment of Punishment, (1987) 1465 UNTS 85; European Convention for the Prevention of Torture and Inhuman or Degrading Treatment or Punishment, (1989) 1561 UNTS 363; Inter-American Convention to Prevent and Punish Torture, OASTS 67; Convention on the Rights of the

specialised instrument, the Convention against Torture and Other Cruel, Inhuman or Degrading Treatment or Punishment.[144] Others have expressed their commitment to the prevention of torture in submissions to the Human Rights Council.[145] In its National report to the Human Rights Council, Tonga cited a statement by its Chief Justice that 'the prohibition against torture is part of customary international law, and furthermore it is a *jus cogens* rule from which States cannot derogate whether they are a party to the various treaties which prohibit it or not'.[146]

The pronouncement of the International Court of Justice in *Belgium v. Senegal* refers only to torture and not to cruel, inhuman, or degrading treatment or punishment.[147] The prohibition in customary law, like the treaty provisions, extends to cruel, inhuman, or degrading treatment or punishment. Although it did not refer explicitly to customary international law, the General Assembly has affirmed 'the existing prohibition under international law of every form of cruel, inhuman or degrading treatment or punishment'.[148] The Human Rights Council has signalled the fact 'that a number of international, regional and domestic courts have held the prohibition of cruel, inhuman or degrading treatment or punishment to be customary international law'.[149] The Appeals Chamber of the International Criminal Tribunal for the former Yugoslavia said that the right 'to be free from cruel, inhuman or degrading treatment or punishment' was a norm of customary international law.[150] In its enumeration of customary human rights norms, the Human Rights Committee

Child, (1990) 1571 UNTS 3, art. 37(a); African Charter on the Rights and Welfare of the Child, art. 16; International Convention on the Suppression and Punishment of the Crime of Apartheid, (1976) 1015 UNTS 243, art. II(a)(ii); Convention on the Rights of Persons with Disabilities, (2008) 2515 UNTS 3, art. 15; International Convention on the Protection of the Rights of all Migrant Workers and Members of their Families, (2003) 2220 UNTS 3, art. 10.

[144] China, C.N.228.1988.TREATIES-13; Comoros, C.N.295.2017.TREATIES-IV.9; Cuba, C.N.167.1995.TREATIES-3; Fiji, C.N.93.2016.TREATIES-IV.9; Holy See, C.N.696.2002.TREATIES-8; Kiribati, C.N.696.2002.TREATIES-8; Marshall Islands, C.N.696.2002.TREATIES-8; Nauru, C.N.549.2012.TREATIES-IV.9; Saudi Arabia, C.N.406.1997.TREATIES-3; South Sudan, C.N.279.2015.TREATIES-IV.9; United Arab Emirates, C.N.388.2012.TREATIES-IV.9; Brunei Darussalam, C.N.493.2015.TREATIES-IV.9 and A/HRC/42/11/Add.1, paras. 121.1 and 121.10; and Palau, C.N.558.2011.TREATIES-35, have signed the Convention.

[145] Bhutan, National report, A/HRC/WG.6/33/BTN/1, para. 7; Views on conclusions, A/HRC/27/8/Add.1, para. 120.4; Malaysia, National report, A/HRC/WG.6/31/MYS/1, paras. 27–28; Myanmar, National report, A/HRC/WG.6/10/MMR/1, para. 38; Report of the Working Group, A/HRC/17/9, para. 52; Oman, National report, A/HRC/WG.6/23/OMN/1, para. 94(b) and Report of the Working Group, A/HRC/31/11, paras. 7, 8; Saint Lucia, National report, A/HRC/WG.6/23/LCA/1, paras. 60–64 and Views on conclusions, A/HRC/17/6/Add.1, para. 89.6; Solomon Islands, Report of the Working Group, A/HRC/32/14, para. 58; Tuvalu, National report, A/HRC/WG.6/30/TUV/1, para. 25.

[146] Tonga, National report, A/HRC/WG.6/15/TON/1, paras. 32, 138, and Tonga, National report, A/HRC/WG.6/29/TON/1, para. 16, citing *Tavake v. Kingdom of Tonga*, [2008] Tonga LR 304.

[147] *Questions relating to the Obligation to Prosecute or Extradite (Belgium v. Senegal), Judgment, ICJ Reports 2012*, p. 422, para. 99.

[148] Human rights in the administration of justice, A/RES/39/118, OP 1.

[149] Torture and other cruel, inhuman, or degrading treatment or punishment, A/HRC/RES/8/8, PP 4.

[150] *Prosecutor v. Blaškić* (IT-94/14-A), Judgment, 29 July 2004, para. 143; *Prosecutor v. Kordić and Čerkez* (IT-95-14/2-A), Judgment, 17 December 2004, para. 106.

listed both torture and cruel, inhuman, or degrading treatment or punishment.[151] The list of the Third Restatement of the American Law Institute included 'torture or other cruel, inhuman, or degrading treatment or punishment'.[152] After a detailed review of the authorities, Elihu Lauterpacht and Daniel Bethlehem concluded that 'evidence in favour of a broad formulation of the prohibition under discussion to include torture and other cruel, inhuman or degrading treatment or punishment is overwhelming'.[153] The Universal Periodic Review materials tend to abbreviate the formulation of the norm, speaking of 'torture' and often omitting the phrase 'cruel, inhuman or degrading treatment or punishment'.

Early interpreters of the treaty provisions considered that these different notions sat in a hierarchy, distinguishing 'torture' from ill-treatment by its gravity.[154] The Convention against Torture appears to confirm this understanding. However, the modern view rejects this understanding, and considers that the decisive criteria for distinguishing torture from cruel, inhuman, and degrading treatment 'may best be understood to be the purpose of the conduct and the powerlessness of the victim, rather than the intensity of the pain or suffering inflicted', according to the Special Rapporteur on torture.[155]

The prohibition of torture is said to have a particularly absolute status. 'There exists today universal revulsion against torture', wrote a Trial Chamber of the International Criminal Tribunal for the former Yugoslavia in 1998. 'This revulsion, as well as the importance States attach to the eradication of torture, has led to a cluster of treaty and customary rules on torture acquiring a particularly high status in the international, normative system.'[156] No exceptions to the prohibition of torture and ill-treatment are contemplated. By contrast, even the right to life is subject to limitations or restrictions, as can be seen in the prohibition of 'arbitrary' deprivation of life, and the paragraphs dealing with capital punishment in Article 6(1) of the International Covenant on Civil and Political Rights. The prohibition of torture is not subject to derogation in time of national emergency. Logically, this suggests that torture is always 'arbitrary'. Not only is it non-derogable in the various regional and universal treaties, it is also ensured without any restriction whatsoever.

[151] General Comment 24, Issues Relating to Reservations Made upon Ratification or Accession to the Covenant or the Optional Protocols thereto, or in Relation to Declarations under art. 41 of the Covenant, CCPR/C/21/Rev.1/Add.6, para. 8.

[152] Restatement (Third) of the Foreign Relations Law of the United States, St. Paul, MN: American Law Institute, 1987, para. 702, Comment, para. g.

[153] Elihu Lauterpacht and Daniel Bethlehem, 'The Scope and Content of the Principle of *Non-Refoulement*: Opinion', in Erika Feller, Volker Türk and Frances Nicholson, eds., *Refugee Protection in International Law: UNHCR's Global Consultations on International Protection*, Cambridge: Cambridge University Press, 2003, pp. 87–177, para. 229.

[154] *Ireland v. the United Kingdom*, 18 January 1978, § 167, Series A no. 25.

[155] Report of the Special Rapporteur on torture and other cruel, inhuman, or degrading treatment of punishment, E/CN.4/2006/6, para. 39. Also *Selmouni v. France* [GC], no. 25803/94, §§ 101–105, ECHR 1999-V.

[156] *Prosecutor v. Furundžija* (IT-95-17/1), Judgment, 10 December 1998, para. 147.

The famous pronouncement of the International Court of Justice on the customary status of the prohibition of torture also declared it to be a norm of *jus cogens*.[157] Many other authorities confirm this assessment. The prohibition of torture was included in the draft list of *jus cogens* norms adopted in 2019 by the International Law Commission.[158] Other international courts and tribunals have made a similar finding, including the European Court of Human Rights,[159] the Inter-American Court of Human Rights,[160] the International Criminal Tribunal for the former Yugoslavia,[161] the Committee Against Torture,[162] the Committee on the Elimination of Discrimination against Women,[163] the African Commission on Human and Peoples' Rights,[164] and many national courts.[165] The Special Rapporteur on torture said '[t]he prohibition against torture and other cruel, inhuman or degrading treatment or punishment enjoys the enhanced status of a *jus cogens* or peremptory norm of general international law and requires States not merely to refrain from authorising or conniving at torture or other ill-treatment but also to suppress, prevent and discourage such practices. States have not only

[157] *Questions relating to the Obligation to Prosecute or Extradite (Belgium v. Senegal), Judgment, ICJ Reports 2012*, p. 422, para. 99.

[158] Report of the International Law Commission, Seventy-first session (29 April–7 June and 8 July–9 August 2019), A/74/10, p. 207. See also Fourth report on peremptory norms of general international law (*jus cogens*) by Dire Tladi, Special Rapporteur, A/CN.4/727, paras. 69–77; A/CN.4/SR.3463, pp. 8–9 (Grossmann Guiloff).

[159] *Al-Adsani v. the United Kingdom* [GC], no. 35763/97, § 61, ECHR 2001-XI; *Naït-Liman v. Switzerland* [GC], no. 51357/07, 15 March 2018, Partly dissenting opinion of Judge Wojtyczek.

[160] *Women Victims of Sexual Torture in Atenco v. Mexico*, Judgment (Preliminary objection, merits, reparations, and costs), 28 November 2018, Series C, No. 371, para. 178; *Herzog et al. v. Brazil*, Judgment (Preliminary objections, merits, reparations, and costs), 15 March 2018. Series C, No. 353, para. 220; *Mendoza et al. v. Argentina*, Judgment (Preliminary objections, merits, and costs), 14 May 2013, Series C, No. 260, para. 199; *Baldeón-García v. Peru*, Judgment (Merits, reparations, and costs), 6 April 2006, Series C, No. 147, para. 117; *Fermín-Ramírez v. Guatemala*, Judgment (Merits, reparations, and costs), 20 June 2005, Series C, No. 126, para. 117; *Caesar v. Trinidad and Tobago*, Judgment (Merits, reparations, and costs), 11 March 2005, Series C No. 123, para. 100; *Tibi v. Ecuador*, Judgment (Preliminary objections, merits, reparations, and costs), 7 September 2004, Series C, No. 114, para. 143; *Gómez-Paquiyauri Brothers v. Peru*, Judgment (Merits, reparations, and costs), 8 July 2004, Series C, No. 110, para. 112; *Maritza Urrutia v. Guatemala*, Judgment (Merits, reparations, and costs), 27 November 2003, Series C, No. 103, para. 92. Also *Blake v. Guatemala* (Merits), 24 January 1998, Series C, No. 36, Separate opinion of Judge Cançado Trindade, paras. 15, 25.

[161] *Prosecutor v. Furundžija* (IT-95-17/1-T), Judgment, 10 December 1998, paras. 153–157; *Prosecutor v. Simić* (IT-95-9/2-S), Sentencing judgment, 17 October 2002, para. 34; *Prosecutor v. Kunarac et al.* (IT-96-23-T and IT-96-23/1-T), Judgment, 22 February 2001, para. 466.

[162] General Comment 2, Implementation of art. 2 by States Parties, CAT/C/GC/2, para. 1. Also Observations of the Committee Against Torture on the revision of the United Nations Standard Minimum Rules for the Treatment of Prisoners (SMR), CAT/C/51/4, para. 11.

[163] General Recommendation 35 on gender-based violence against women, updating general recommendation 19, CEDAW/C/GC/35, para. 25.

[164] *Mohammed Abdullah Saleh Al-Asad v. Djibouti*, No. 383/10, 14 October 2014, para. 179.

[165] *A, Amnesty International and Commonwealth Lawyers Association v. Secretary of State for the Home Department*, [2005] UKHL 7, [2006] 1 All ER 575, para. 31; *R v. Bow Street Metropolitan Stipendiary Magistrate, Ex p Pinochet Ugarte (No. 3)*, [2000] 1 AC 147, paras. 197–199; *National Commissioner of the South African Police Service v. the Southern African Human Rights Litigation Centre and Others*, [2014] (12) BCLR 1428 (CC), para. 4.

the obligation to "respect", but to "ensure respect" for, the absolute prohibition against torture.'[166]

To the extent that detention is imposed lawfully, the conditions must nevertheless respect the prohibition of cruel, inhuman, or degrading treatment. Conditions of detention that are intended to humiliate or that aggravate insecurity,[167] or that arouse 'feelings of fear, anguish or inferiority capable of breaking an individual's moral and physical resistance',[168] may violate this requirement.[169] In this respect, the UN Standard Minimum Rules for the Treatment of Prisoners, now known as the Nelson Mandela Rules, provide a universally accepted benchmark, governing such matters as the size of cells, sanitary facilities, clothing, ventilation, and food.[170] Judge Pinto de Albuquerque of the European Court of Human Rights wrote that the Rules 'reflect customary international law in many respects'.[171] It is not without significance that many of the States that are not parties to the International Covenant proclaim their adherence to the Standard Minimum Rules in reporting to the Human Rights Council.[172] The practice of solitary confinement may amount to ill-treatment where it is prolonged, especially when young prisoners are concerned.[173]

The prohibition of torture and cruel, inhuman, or degrading treatment or punishment imposes upon States a duty not only to refrain from such acts but also to prevent their perpetration by others. Moreover, there is also an obligation to ensure that acts of torture and ill-treatment are effectively investigated and prosecuted.[174] This applies not only when there is an allegation of ill-treatment by the police or other agents of the State, but also when the acts themselves cannot be imputed to the State at all.[175] According to the Human Rights Committee, States have a duty 'to afford everyone protection through legislative and other measures

[166] Report of the Special Rapporteur on torture and other cruel, inhuman, or degrading treatment or punishment, Juan E. Méndez, A/HRC/25/60, para. 40.

[167] *Arutyunyan v. Russia*, no. 48977/09, § 81, 10 January 2012.

[168] *Dedovskiy et al. v. Russia*, no. 7178/03, § 85, ECHR 2008 (extracts). Also *Members of the Gldani Congregation of Jehovah's Witnesses et al. v. Georgia*, no. 71156/01, §§ 102–105, 3 May 2007.

[169] *Hiber Conteris v. Uruguay*, no. 139/1983, Views, 17 July 1985, A/40/40, p. 196. § 9.2; *Martínez Portorreal v. Dominican Republic*, no. 188/1984, Views, 5 November 1987, A/43/40, p. 207, para. 11.

[170] United Nations Standard Minimum Rules for the Treatment of Prisoners (the Mandela Rules), E/CN.15/2015/L.6/Rev.1, Annex.

[171] *Tautkus v. Lithuania*, no. 29474/09, 27 November 2012, Dissenting opinion of Judge Pinto de Albuquerque.

[172] Cuba, Report of the Working Group, A/HRC/11/22, para. 123; Malaysia, Report of the Working Group, A/HRC/40/11, para. 74; Myanmar, Report of the Working Group, A/HRC/17/9, para. 53; Saudi Arabia, Report of the Working Group, A/HRC/40/4/Add.1, para. 9; Solomon Islands, National report, A/HRC/WG.6/11/SLB/1, para. 77; Sudan, in Cuba, Report of the Working Group, A/HRC/39/16, para. 24.127; Tonga, National report, A/HRC/WG.6/15/TON/1, para. 38.

[173] General Comment 20, A/47/40, p. 193, para. 6. See, for example, Argentina, Concluding observations, CCPR/C/ARG/CO/5, para. 13.

[174] *V.C. v. Slovakia*, no. 18968/07, § 123, ECHR 2011 (extracts); *Assenov et al. v. Bulgaria*, 28 October 1998, § 102, *Reports of Judgments and Decisions* 1998-VIII; *Biçici v. Turkey*, no. 30357/05, § 39, 27 May 2010.

[175] *M.C. v. Bulgaria*, no. 39272/98, § 151, ECHR 2003-XII; *Ay v. Turkey*, no. 30951/96, § 59, 22 March 2005; *Gülbahar et al. v. Turkey*, no. 5264/03, § 72, 21 October 2008.

as may be necessary' against acts of torture and ill-treatment, 'whether inflicted by people acting in their official capacity, outside their official capacity or in a private capacity'.[176] Of course, it is an obligation of means, and the State cannot be held responsible simply because inhuman or degrading treatment is inflicted by one individual on another or, if it is, that criminal proceedings necessarily lead to a particular sanction. Although treaty bodies regularly encourage States to provide specifically for the crime of torture in their criminal justice system this does not seem to be really necessary as the underlying acts are invariably dealt with in criminal codes.

Medical or scientific experimentation without the free consent of the person concerned is prohibited by the International Covenant on Civil and Political Rights as an aspect of the broader norm concerning torture and ill-treatment.[177] The Arab Charter on Human Rights has a similar and more elaborate provision. It adds that '[t]rafficking in human organs is prohibited in all circumstances'.[178] It seems unlikely that the States that are not party to the Covenant or the Arab Charter would dispute the prohibition of experimentation upon humans without their consent. There does not appear to be evidence of their views or their practice on the subject capable of strengthening the claim that this is a norm of customary international law.

1. Cruel, inhuman, or degrading punishments

With the development of human rights and recognition of human dignity as the principal value underlying human rights, most traditional punishments have been re-evaluated and gradually restrained. This is particularly obvious in the case of corporal and capital punishment, but also banishment, expulsion, and deprivation of political rights meet with increasing reprobation. Even with respect to the most common punishment, deprivation of personal liberty, the prohibition of cruel, inhuman, and degrading punishment imposes certain limits. Although life imprisonment is usually prescribed as a replacement when States abolish capital punishment, there is much support for the view that it too constitutes cruel, inhuman, or degrading punishment to the extent that early release is not permitted under any circumstances.[179] The Convention on the Rights of the Child recognises the inhumanity of life sentences if there is no possibility of early release by prohibiting this absolutely for offences perpetrated by minors. It seems only a small step in the progressive development of human rights law to extend this to adult offenders. The

[176] General Comment 20, A/47/40, p. 193, para. 2.
[177] International Covenant on Civil and Political Rights, (1976) 999 UNTS 171, art. 7(2).
[178] Arab Charter on Human Rights, art. 9.
[179] Dirk van Zyl Smit and Catherine Appleton, *Life Imprisonment, A Global Human Rights Analysis*, Cambridge, MA: Harvard University Press, 2019.

European Court of Human Rights has held that an 'irreducible' life sentence, by which there is no realistic prospect of release, is not compatible with human dignity and therefore a breach of the prohibition of torture and ill-treatment.[180]

Corporal punishments are increasingly viewed as being incompatible with customary international law. Nevertheless, it is difficult to contend that they are absolutely impermissible in principle. In the Universal Periodic Review,[181] Singapore rather robustly insists that its use of corporal punishment for adult offenders is 'within internationally accepted norms',[182] and it receives relatively mild rebukes from a few other States.[183] Singapore employs 'caning' as a punishment for certain crimes. Other forms of corporal punishment, such as amputation of limbs,[184] flogging,[185] and stoning,[186] come in for more severe scrutiny. Some States appear to condemn these forms of punishment when imposed on children yet remain silent with respect to adults.[187] In comments on Saudi Arabia's Report to the Human Rights Council, Switzerland said 'corporal punishment, such as flogging and amputations, is incompatible with ... international customary law'.[188] The Human Rights Committee has held that whipping amounts to cruel, inhuman, or degrading treatment or punishment.[189] The Committee Against Torture has said that

[180] *Vinter et al. v. the United Kingdom* [GC], nos. 66069/09, 130/10, and 3896/10, § 113, 9 July 2013; ibid., Concurring opinion of Judge Power-Forde. Followed in *Öcalan v. Turkey (No. 2)*, nos. 24069/03, 197/04, 6201/06, and 10464/07, § 197, 18 March 2014; *László Magyar v. Hungary*, no. 73593/10, § 58, 20 May 2014.

[181] See this detailed discussion of the corporal punishment issue in the Universal Periodic Review: Frederick Cowell, 'Understanding the Legal Status of Universal Periodic Review Recommendations', (2018) 7 *Cambridge International Law Journal* 164, at pp. 175–177.

[182] Singapore, Report of the Working Group, A/HRC/18/11, para. 88. Also Singapore, Report of the Working Group, A/HRC/32/17, para. 64.

[183] Singapore, Report of the Working Group, A/HRC/18/11, paras. 62, 96.32, 97.7, 97.8; Singapore, Report of the Working Group, A/HRC/32/17, paras. 166.33, 166.80, 166.170.

[184] Saudi Arabia, Report of the Working Group, A/HRC/25/3, para. 138.129 and Report of the Working Group, A/HRC/11/23, para. 27; Brunei Darussalam, Report of the Working Group, A/HRC/25/3, para. 92 and Report of the Working Group, A/HRC/42/11, paras. 92, 121.37, 121.39; Yemen, Report of the Working Group, A/HRC/26/8, para. 109; Mali, Report of the Working Group, A/HRC/23/6, para. 72; Somalia, National report, A/HRC/WG.6/11/SOM/1, para. 24 and Report of the Working Group, A/HRC/18/6, paras. 49, 98.71; Maldives, Report of the Working Group, A/HRC/16/7, para. 100.58, fn. 2; Iran, Report of the Working Group, A/HRC/14/12, para. 32; Mauritania, Report of the Working Group, A/HRC/16/17, paras. 92.39, 92.42.

[185] Brunei Darussalam, Report of the Working Group, A/HRC/13/14, para. 15 and Report of the Working Group, A/HRC/42/11, para. 121.39; Report of the Working Group, A/HRC/11/23, para. 27; Somali, Report of the Working Group, A/HRC/18/6, para. 24.

[186] Brunei Darussalam, Report of the Working Group, A/HRC/25/3, para. 92 and Report of the Working Group, A/HRC/42/11, paras. 92, 97, 121.37, 121.39; Yemen, Report of the Working Group, A/HRC/26/8, paras. 115, 55, 117.7; Mali, Report of the Working Group, A/HRC/23/6, para. 72; Somali, Report of the Working Group, A/HRC/18/6, para. 98.69; Iran, Report of the Working Group, A/HRC/14/12, paras. 24, 91.6, 91.18, 92.22.

[187] Montenegro, in Brunei Darussalam, Report of the Working Group, A/HRC/42/11, para. 121.96; Montenegro, in Saudi Arabia, Report of the Working Group, A/HRC/40/4, para. 122.109; Chile, in Brunei Darussalam, Report of the Working Group, A/HRC/42/11, para. 121.202.

[188] Saudi Arabia, Report of the Working Group, A/HRC/11/23, para. 65.

[189] *Osbourne v. Jamaica*, no. 759/1997, Views, 13 April 2000, CCPR/C/68/D/759/1997, para. 9.1; *Higginson v. Jamaica*, no. 792/1998, Views, 19 May 1995, CCPR/C/74/D/792/1998, para. 4.6; *Sooklal v. Trinidad and Tobago*, no. 928/2000, Views, 25 October 2001, CCPR/C/73/D/928/2000, para. 9.1. See also General Comment 34, art. 19: Freedoms of opinion and expression, CCPR/C/GC/34, para. 26.

in assessing whether there is a real risk in expelling someone to a country where corporal punishment might be imposed, consideration must be given to whether it would amount to 'torture or cruel, inhuman or degrading treatment or punishment according to customary international law'.[190] A Pre-Trial Chamber of the International Criminal Court has held that penalties of whipping and amputation, imposed in public, constitute violations of human dignity and torture.[191]

The most extreme form of corporal punishment is the death penalty. Because some international human rights treaties have recognised capital punishment as an exception to the right to life, tribunals and treaty bodies involved in the application of those treaties have been reluctant to declare that the death penalty is contrary to the prohibition of cruel, inhuman, or degrading punishment in all circumstances. The consequence is a bit of a conundrum, whereby measures that injure a person are prohibited as a form of torture or ill-treatment unless the injury is fatal, in which case there is no violation. Within the Council of Europe, where no Member State has conducted an execution for more than two decades, the European Court of Human Rights eventually concluded that the death penalty is indeed incompatible with the prohibition of inhuman or degrading punishment.[192] It is more difficult for the Human Rights Committee to adopt such an interpretation given the continuing practice of capital punishment in several of the States Parties to the International Covenant on Civil and Political Rights.

Noting that several national constitutional courts and political instances have pronounced 'their conviction that the death penalty is a cruel, inhuman and degrading treatment not reconcilable with the inherent right to physical and mental integrity and human dignity', the United Nations Special Rapporteur on torture has written of 'an evolving standard whereby States and judiciaries consider the death penalty to be a violation per se of the prohibition of torture or cruel, inhuman or degrading treatment'. He expressed his conviction 'that a customary norm prohibiting the death penalty under all circumstances, if it has not already emerged, is at least in the process of formation'.[193]

In a 2020 judgment the Supreme Court of the United Kingdom rejected the submission that capital punishment per se was a form of inhuman or degrading treatment or punishment, and therefore prohibited by customary international law. Lord Kerr seriously contemplated the possibility but said that '[i]n the absence of firm, tangible evidence that the process of evolution has been completed or that

[190] General Comment 4 on the implementation of art. 3 of the Convention in the context of art. 22, CAT/C/GC/4, para. 29(f).

[191] *Prosecutor v. Al Hassan* (ICC-01/12-01/18), Rectificatif à la Décision relative à la confirmation des charges portées contre Al Hassan Ag Abdoul Aziz Ag Mohamed Ag Mahmoud, 13 November 2019, paras. 348, 350.

[192] *Al Saadoon and Mufdhi v. the United Kingdom*, no. 61498/08, § 120, 2 March 2010.

[193] Interim report of the Special Rapporteur on torture and other cruel, inhuman, or degrading treatment or punishment, A/67/279, para. 69. Also Observations on communications transmitted to Governments and replies received, A/HRC/31/57/Add.1, para. 33.

there is a general practice' it was 'impossible to accept the appellant's argument based on customary international law'.[194] Even if it is premature to conclude that capital punishment as such is prohibited by customary international law, a good case can be made that certain aspects of its imposition, such as excessive brutality in the method of execution and protracted delay in imposition, can amount to cruel, inhuman, or degrading punishment.[195]

2. Admissibility of evidence

The prohibition of torture and other cruel, inhuman, or degrading treatment or punishment is associated with rules prohibiting the admission of evidence in criminal prosecutions. The Convention against Torture lists one of the purposes of torture to be the obtaining from the victim or a third person of 'information or a confession'.[196] No confession obtained as a result of torture to a crime by a person accused of an offence can be used as evidence of guilt.[197] In any event, a confession obtained by torture is inherently unreliable, and should not be the basis of a conviction because of the presumption of innocence.[198] But the principle applies more broadly because it requires the exclusion of statements made by persons other than the accused to the extent that they were obtained through torture or ill-treatment.[199] This is generally known as the 'exclusionary rule'. The Special Rapporteur on torture and other cruel, inhuman, or degrading treatment or punishment has said that the exclusionary rule is a norm of customary international law.[200]

Testimony obtained through torture should be disregarded because of its inherent unreliability, something upon which campaigners against torture often insist. But where torture leads to the identification of material evidence, such as the location of a body or a weapon, there may be no reason to question its authenticity. The prohibition must be rooted in the need to deter the use of torture

[194] *Elgizouli (Appellant) v. Secretary of State for the Home Department (Respondent)*, [2020] UKSC 10, para. 151.

[195] See the detailed discussion of the death penalty under customary international law in the previous chapter, on the right to life, at pp. 115–122.

[196] Convention against Torture and Other Cruel, Inhuman and Degrading Treatment or Punishment, (1984) 1465 UNTS 85, art. 1(1).

[197] General Comment 32, art. 14: Right to equality before courts and tribunals and to a fair trial, CCPR/C/GC/32, para. 41. Also General Comment 36, art. 6: right to life, CCPR/C/GC/36, para. 54. The formulations of the Human Rights Committee are derived from the Convention against Torture and Other Cruel, Inhuman and Degrading Treatment or Punishment, (1984) 1465 UNTS 85, art. 15.

[198] *Al Nashiri v. Romania*, no. 33234/12, § 718, 31 May 2018; *Söylemez v. Turkey*, no. 46661/99, § 122, 21 September 2006.

[199] Report of the Special Rapporteur on torture and other cruel, inhuman, or degrading treatment or punishment, Juan E. Méndez, A/HRC/25/60, para. 28.

[200] Report of the Special Rapporteur on torture and other cruel, inhuman or degrading treatment or punishment, Juan E. Méndez, A/HRC/25/60, para. 17.

by law enforcement authorities. In an early General Comment, the Human Rights Committee called for the inadmissibility not only of confessions but also of 'other evidence' obtained through torture or ill-treatment.[201] It subsequently confined its position on this matter to 'statements or confessions',[202] a rule that is aligned with the text of Article 15 of the Convention against Torture. The Committee Against Torture, nevertheless, has taken the view that 'strict enforcement' of Article 15 of the Convention requires that 'all evidence obtained directly or indirectly by torture' be excluded from the court record.[203] The Grand Chamber of the European Court of Human Rights concluded that 'there is no clear consensus in the States Parties to the Convention on the scope of the exclusionary rule'[204] although it appeared, but hesitantly, to support the principle of exclusion.[205] The Inter-American Court of Human Rights has held that evidence generated by torture as well as statements or confessions must be excluded.[206]

3. Non-refoulement

An important corollary of the norm against torture and other cruel, inhuman, or degrading treatment or punishment is the prohibition of refoulement, a French word used to describe expulsion, return, or extradition to a State where there are substantial grounds to believe that a person would be subjected to torture.[207] The rule is codified in Article 3 of the Convention against Torture but it has been upheld in case law of international human rights courts and treaty bodies even in the absence of an explicit provision in relevant treaties such as the European Convention on Human Rights[208] and the International Covenant on Civil and Political Rights.[209] In their study of the question, Lauterpacht and Bethlehem explained that 'a prohibition on expulsion or return in circumstances in which there is a real risk of torture or cruel, inhuman or degrading treatment or punishment is inherent

[201] General Comment 7, A/37/40, p. 94, para. 1.

[202] General Comment 20, A/47/40, p. 193, para. 12; General Comment 32, art. 14: Right to equality before courts and tribunals and to a fair trial, CCPR/C/GC/32, para. 41.

[203] Germany, Concluding observations, A/53/44, para. 193. Also Concluding observations, Iceland, CAT/C/ISL/CO/3, para. 13; Poland, Concluding observations, CAT/C/POL/CO/7, para. 12(a).

[204] *Gäfgen v. Germany* [GC], no. 22978/05, § 69, ECHR 2010.

[205] Ibid., § 178. See also *Bykov v. Russia* [GC], no. 4378/02, Concurring opinion of Judge Cabral Barretto, 10 March 2009, para. 2.

[206] *Cabrera García and Montiel Flores v. Mexico*, Judgment (Preliminary objections, merits, reparations, and costs), 26 November 2010, para. 167.

[207] See the detailed analysis of non-refoulement as a customary norm in Elihu Lauterpacht and Daniel Bethlehem, 'The Scope and Content of the Principle of *Non-Refoulement*: Opinion', in Erika Feller, Volker Türk and Frances Nicholson, eds., *Refugee Protection in International Law: UNHCR's Global Consultations on International Protection*, Cambridge: Cambridge University Press, 2003, pp. 87–177.

[208] *Soering v. the United Kingdom and Germany*, 7 July 1989, § 88, Series A no. 161; *Chahal v. the United Kingdom*, 15 November 1996, §§ 74–75, 79–81, *Reports of Judgments and Decisions* 1996-V.

[209] General Comment 20, A/47/40, p. 193, para. 9.

in the prohibition of such acts', noting that this was consistent with the views of the European Court of Human Rights and the Human Rights Committee.[210] Theo van Boven, the United Nations Special Rapporteur on torture, described the non-refoulement principle as 'an inherent part of the overall fundamental obligation to avoid contributing in any way to a violation of the prohibition of torture and other cruel, inhuman or degrading treatment or punishment'.[211]

The protection against refoulement in the case of torture and ill-treatment is not subject to exceptions, in contrast with the situation contemplated by Article 33 of the Convention on the Status of Refugees.[212] Under that treaty, a refugee may be returned to the country of origin even when there is a real risk of persecution in circumstances of criminal activity or where there is a threat to national security. As the European Court of Human Rights has explained, whenever substantial grounds exist to believe that an individual would face a real risk of being subjected to torture or ill-treatment, the State must safeguard him or her against such treatment. 'In these circumstances, the activities of the individual in question, however undesirable or dangerous, cannot be a material consideration' it said.[213] Finding that the non-refoulement principle in torture cases is absolute, the Inter-American Court of Human Rights described it as 'a peremptory norm of customary international law', adding that it 'seeks, above all, to ensure the effectiveness of the prohibition of torture in any circumstance and with regard to any person, without any discrimination'.[214]

4. Enforced disappearance

The phenomenon of enforced disappearance was familiar enough to the drafters of the Universal Declaration of Human Rights and the International Covenant on Civil and Political Rights. It had been practised by the Nazi regime pursuant to the 'night and fog decree', the *Nacht und Nebel Erlass*. The expression comes from the Tarnhelm spell, pronounced by Alberich to his brother Mime in *Das Rheingold*,

[210] Elihu Lauterpacht and Daniel Bethlehem, 'The Scope and Content of the Principle of *Non-Refoulement*: Opinion', in Erika Feller, Volker Türk and Frances Nicholson, eds., *Refugee Protection in International Law: UNHCR's Global Consultations on International Protection*, Cambridge: Cambridge University Press, 2003, pp. 87–177, para. 235.

[211] Report of the newly appointed Special Rapporteur on torture, Mr. Theo van Boven, E/CN.4/2002/137, 26 February 2002, para. 14.

[212] Elihu Lauterpacht and Daniel Bethlehem, 'The Scope and Content of the Principle of *Non-Refoulement*: Opinion', in Erika Feller, Volker Türk and Frances Nicholson, eds., *Refugee Protection in International Law: UNHCR's Global Consultations on International Protection*, Cambridge: Cambridge University Press, 2003, pp. 87–177, paras. 250, 253(a).

[213] *Chahal v. the United Kingdom*, 15 November 1996, § 80, *Reports of Judgments and Decisions* 1996-V.

[214] *Rights and Guarantees of Children in the Context of Migration and/or in need of International Protection*, Advisory Opinion OC-21/14, 19 August 2014, Series A, No. 21, para. 227.

the first of Richard Wagner's four Ring Cycle works: 'Nacht und Nebel, niemand gleich! Siehst du mich, Bruder?' During the International Military Tribunal trial, prosecution witness Marie Claude Vaillant-Couturier described being taken to the NN or *Nacht und Nebel* block at Ravensbrück concentration camp.[215]

According to the Human Rights Committee, 'while the Covenant does not explicitly use the term "enforced disappearance" in any of its articles, enforced disappearance constitutes a unique and integrated series of acts that represent continuing violation of various rights recognised in that treaty'.[216] Human rights courts and treaty bodies have often treated 'enforced disappearance' as falling within the scope of the prohibition of torture and other cruel, inhuman, or degrading treatment, although it is also relevant to the right to life, the right to liberty and security of the person, and the right to recognition as a person before the law.[217] Article 2 of the International Convention for the Protection of All Persons from Enforced Disappearance states: 'For the purposes of this Convention, "enforced disappearance" is considered to be the arrest, detention, abduction or any other form of deprivation of liberty by agents of the State or by persons or groups of persons acting with the authorisation, support or acquiescence of the State, followed by a refusal to acknowledge the deprivation of liberty or by concealment of the fate or whereabouts of the disappeared person, which place such a person outside the protection of the law.'[218]

The Commission of Inquiry appointed by the Human Rights Council for Syria stated that a practice of forcible disappearance is prohibited under customary international humanitarian law. It said the 1992 United Nations Declaration for the Protection of All Persons from Enforced Disappearance and the International Convention for the Protection of All Persons from Enforced Disappearance 'crystallise custom'.[219]

5. Violence against women

International human rights law has devoted special attention to the issue of violence against women. This is manifested in the adoption of specialised treaties to

[215] *France et al. v. Goering et al.*, Transcript, 28 January 1946, (1947) 6 IMT 203, at p. 220.

[216] *Dhakal et al. v. Nepal*, no. 2185/2012, Views, 21 July 2017, CCPR/C/120/D/2170/2012, para. 11.5; *Katwal et al. v. Nepal*, no. 2000/2010, Views, 5 May 2015, CCPR/C/113/D/2000/2010, para. 11.3; *Serna et al. v. Colombia*, no. 2134/2012, Views, 9 July 2015, CCPR/C/114/D/2134/2012, para. 9.4.

[217] Declaration on the Protection of all Persons from Enforced Disappearance, A/RES/47/133, PP 7.

[218] International Convention for the Protection of All Persons from Enforced Disappearance, (2010) 2716 UNTS 3.

[219] Report of the independent international commission of inquiry on the Syrian Arab Republic, Annex II, A/HRC/25/65, para. 5. See also Detailed findings of the commission of inquiry on human rights in Eritrea, A/HRC/32/CRP.1, para. 106; Situation of human rights in the temporarily occupied Autonomous Republic of Crimea and the city of Sevastopol (Ukraine), A/HRC/36/CRP.3, para. 99.

address the issue.[220] In 2006, the Special Rapporteur on violence against women, its causes and consequences referred to practice and *opinio juris*, essentially consisting of statements by United Nations bodies and decisions of human rights courts, in concluding 'that there is a rule of customary international law that obliges States to prevent and respond to acts of violence against women with due diligence'.[221] This pronouncement has been cited with approval by other international legal authorities.[222] Judge Pinto de Albuquerque of the European Court of Human Rights referred to the obligation to bring to justice perpetrators of domestic violence, and to prevent recidivism, saying this 'must be acknowledged, in view of the broad and long-lasting consensus mentioned above, as a principle of customary international law'.[223]

In 2014, arguing that there was a 'normative gap', a different Special Rapporteur on violence against women lamented the lack of a legally binding instrument on violence against women, although it is apparent from the context that she acknowledged the three regional instruments, cited in the previous paragraph. Rashida Manjoo said there were many 'soft law' documents that address the issue, explaining that such 'soft law' materials may be influential in developing norms, but 'their non-binding nature effectively means that States cannot be held responsible for violations'. She concluded that 'none of the soft law developments on violence against women has moved into the realm of customary international law as yet'.[224]

In 2017, the Committee for the Elimination of Discrimination against Women declared that 'the prohibition of gender-based violence against women has evolved into a principle of customary international law'. Twenty-five years earlier, the Committee had issued a General Recommendation stating that discrimination against women, as set out in Article 1 of the Convention on the Elimination of All Forms of Discrimination against Women, includes gender-based violence,

[220] Inter-American Convention on the Prevention, Punishment and Eradication of Violence against Women, 'Convention of Belem do Para', OASTS 61; Council of Europe Convention on preventing and combating violence against women and domestic violence, CETS 210; Protocol to the African Charter on Human and Peoples' Rights on the Rights of Women in Africa. Note also the Declaration on the Elimination of Violence against Women in the ASEAN Region, 12 October 2012.

[221] Report of the Special Rapporteur on violence against women, its causes, and consequences, Yakin Ertürk, E/CN.4/2006/61, para. 29.

[222] *Bevacqua and S. v. Bulgaria*, no. 71127/01, § 53, 12 June 2008; *Opuz v. Turkey*, no. 33401/02, § 79, 9 June 2009; *Valiulienė v. Lithuania*, no. 33234/07, 26 March 2013, Dissenting opinion of Judge Jočienė, para. 4; *González et al. ('Cotton Field') v. Mexico*, Judgment (Preliminary objection, merits, reparations, and costs), 16 November 2009, Series C, No. 205, para. 254; *María Isabel Véliz Franco et al. v. Guatemala*, Case 12,578, Report No. 170/11, Merits, 3 November 2011, para. 83; *Claudina Velasquez Paiz et al. v. Guatemala*, Case 12.777, Report No. 53/13, Merits, 4 November 2013, para. 90; Missing and Murdered Indigenous Women in British Columbia, Canada, OEA/Ser.L/V/II, Doc. 30/14, para. 181.

[223] *Valiulienė v. Lithuania*, no. 33234/07, 26 March 2013, Concurring opinion of Judge Pinto de Albuquerque.

[224] Report of the Special Rapporteur on violence against women, its causes, and consequences, Rashida Manjoo, A/HRC/26/38, para. 68.

defined as 'violence which is directed against a woman because she is a woman or that affects women disproportionately'. The 2017 General Recommendation said that '[f]or over twenty-five years, the practice of States Parties has endorsed the Committee's interpretation. The *opinio juris* and State practice suggest that the prohibition of gender-based violence against women has evolved into a principle of customary international law.'[225]

The Universal Periodic Review materials are replete with evidence, far too numerous to list here, of a global commitment to the prohibition of violence against women. As a sampling, those States that are not party to the International Covenant on Civil and Political Rights were examined. Almost all of them manifest recognition of the prohibition and the importance of specific efforts to address the phenomenon.[226]

* * *

Conclusions. Torture and cruel, inhuman, or degrading treatment or punishment are prohibited by customary international law under all circumstances. This prohibition is a norm of *jus cogens*. Cruel, inhuman, or degrading treatment encompasses a range of phenomena, including forms of corporal punishment, enforced disappearance, and violence against women. No person may be subject to refoulement to a country where there is a real risk of torture and cruel, inhuman, or degrading treatment or punishment. States have an obligation to investigate and prosecute violations. Medical or scientific experimentation without consent is prohibited. Evidence obtained through torture may not be used in criminal proceedings, although customary law may not exclude possible exceptions.

[225] General Recommendation 35 on gender-based violence against women, updating general recommendation 19, CEDAW/C/GC/35, para. 2.

[226] Bhutan, National report, A/HRC/WG.6/33/BTN/1, paras. 96–99, 103; Brunei Darussalam, National report, A/HRC/WG.6/33/BRN/1, para. 69; China, National report, A/HRC/WG.6/17/CHN/1, para. 69; Comoros, National report, A/HRC/WG.6/18/COM/1, para. 94, National report, A/HRC/WG.6/32/COM/1, para. 152 and Report of the Working Group, A/HRC/41/12, para. 20; Cuba, National report, A/HRC/WG.6/30/CUB/1, paras. 21, 64; Kiribati, National report, A/HRC/WG.6/35/KIR/1, paras. 42, 124, 125, 144, 149, 152; Malaysia, National report, A/HRC/WG.6/31/MYS/1, paras. 102–105; Micronesia, Report of the Working Group, A/HRC/16/16, paras. 11, 13, 37 and Views on recommendations, A/HRC/31/4/Add.1, para. 17; Myanmar, National report, A/HRC/WG.6/10/MMR/1, para. 54 and National report, A/HRC/WG.6/23/MMR/1, paras. 80–81; Nauru, National report, A/HRC/WG.6/10/NRU/1, paras. 44, 47, 111; Oman, Views on recommendations, A/HRC/31/11/Add.1, para. 129.85; Palau, National report, A/HRC/WG.6/24/PLW/1, paras. 18, 19, 29, 94, 95, 99–101; Saint Lucia, National report, A/HRC/WG.6/10/LCA/1, para. 46 and National report, A/HRC/WG.6/23/LCA/1, paras. 40–41; St Kitts and Nevis, Report of the Working Group, A/HRC/17/12, paras. 15–16; Saudi Arabia, National report, A/HRC/WG.6/4/SAU/1, para. 21, National report, A/HRC/WG.6/17/SAU/1, paras. 64–67, and Report of the Working Group, A/HRC/40/4, para. 9; Singapore, Views on recommendations, A/HRC/32/17/Add.1, para. 17; Solomon Islands, Report of the Working Group, A/HRC/18/8 , paras. 12, 16, 20; South Sudan, National report, A/HRC/WG.6/26/SSD/1, paras. 36, 54; Tonga, National report, A/HRC/WG.6/15/TON/1, paras. 79–88; Tuvalu, National report, A/HRC/WG.6/16/TUV/1, paras. 62, 71, 91, 93, 94, 98.

C. Slavery and servitude

One of the pioneers of international law, Hugo Grotius, wrote favourably about the practice of slavery, confirming its wide acceptance as recently as the seventeenth century.[227] This all changed with the Enlightenment. Grotius was attacked by Jean-Jacques Rousseau, who wrote: 'Ainsi, de quelque sens qu'on envisage les choses, le droit d'esclave est nul, non seulement parce qu'il est illégitime, mais parce qu'il est absurde et ne signifie rien. Ces mots, esclavage et droit, sont contradictoires; ils s'excluent mutuellement.'[228] The slave trade was only prohibited by the British Parliament in 1807 although the practice persisted in most of the Empire until 1833. In an 1821 judgment of the United States Supreme Court, Chief Justice John Marshall wrote that although the slave trade might be judged an abhorrent practice, it could not be considered contrary to international law.[229] France abolished slavery and the slave trade at the time of the Revolution but the practice was subsequently restored and only definitively ended in 1848. Russia continued the related practice of serfdom until 1861. Slavery was abolished a few years later in the United States of America. It persisted in South America until early in the twentieth century.

In the course of the transatlantic slave trade, which lasted over about three centuries, more than ten million Africans were enslaved. Because the slave trade is trans-border, the struggle against slavery and the slave trade in the late eighteenth century became one of the most important historical antecedents of the international protection of human rights. Early international prohibitions of the slave trade are found in a number of bilateral treaties stemming from the period of the Congress of Vienna at the end of the Napoleonic Wars. These were followed by the multilateral treaty between Austria, Great Britain, Prussia, and Russia for the Suppression of the African Slave Trade of 1841, as well as the 1885 Acts of the Berlin Congress and the 1890 General Acts of the Brussels Conference.[230] In 1926, the Slavery Convention was adopted under the auspices of the League of Nations. It entered into force the following year. The States Parties undertook to prevent and suppress the slave trade, to progressively bring about the complete elimination of slavery in all its forms, and to promulgate 'severe penalties for slave trading, slave-holding, and enslavement'.[231]

[227] See, *e.g.* Hugo Grotius, *On the Law of War and Peace*, Oxford: Clarendon Press, 1925, pp. 255–258.

[228] Jean-Jacques Rousseau, *Du contrat social*, in *Œuvres complètes*, Vol. III, Paris: Gallimard, 1964, pp. 347–469, at p. 356.

[229] *The Antelope*, 23 US 66, 115 (1825).

[230] Renee Colette Redman, 'The League of Nations and the Right to be Free from Enslavement: The First Human Right to be Recognized as Customary International Law', (1994) 17 *Chicago-Kent Law Review* 759.

[231] Slavery Convention, (1927) 60 LNTS 253, arts. 2, 6. The Convention was amended in 1953 so as to make its provision applicable to the United Nations: Protocol amending the Slavery Convention, signed at Geneva on 25 September 1926, (1953) 182 UNTS 51.

Slavery returned to Europe during the 1940s, practised by the Nazi regime during the Second World War. The International Military Tribunal said that the Nazi government planned 'to exploit the inhabitants of the occupied countries for slave labour on the very greatest scale', considering that slave labour was 'an integral part of the war economy'. According to the Tribunal, '[w]hole populations were deported to Germany for the purposes of slave labour upon defence works, armament production and similar tasks connected with the war effort'.[232] An estimated five million people were moved by force to Germany to work as slaves in this way.[233] Leading Nazis were condemned for the crime against humanity of enslavement in accordance with Article 6(c) of the Charter of the International Military Tribunal and Article II(1)(c) of Control Council Law No. 10.[234]

Although classic chattel slavery like that of the transatlantic slave trade is assuredly a thing of the past,[235] slavery takes on other dimensions in all corners of the world as a result of modern forms of economic exploitation, such as the international migration of workers, sex tourism in countries of the South, and trade and trafficking in human beings.[236] These modern forms of slavery are in principal unlawful, in contrast with the early manifestations of slavery that were enforced by the courts according to law. Despite the official abolition of and international ban on slavery and the slave trade, more subtle forms, often practised underground, have persisted. The modern forms of slavery cry out for vigilance and strict enforcement of law. Their existence can in no way suggest that they are not contemplated by the customary legal prohibition. Speaking of contemporary forms of slavery, the Appeals Chamber of the International Criminal Tribunal for the former Yugoslavia noted that 'the victim is not subject to the exercise of the more extreme rights of ownership associated with "chattel slavery", but in all cases, as a result of the exercise of any or all of the powers attaching to the right of ownership, there is some destruction of the juridical personality'.[237] The Appeals Chamber said that whether a particular phenomenon is a form of enslavement depends upon the operation of such factors as 'control of someone's movement, control of physical environment, psychological control, measures taken to prevent or deter escape, force, threat of force or coercion, duration, assertion of exclusivity, subjection to cruel treatment

[232] *France et al. v. Goering et al.*, (1948) 22 IMT 411, at p. 470.

[233] See, for example, Associazione Nazionale Reduci Dalla Prigionia dall'Internamento e dalla Guerra di Liberazione and 275 Others v. Germany (dec.), no. 45563/04, 4 September 2007.

[234] *United States of America v. Krupp et al.*, Opinion and Judgment, (1950) 9 TWC 1327, at pp. 667–1314.

[235] Mauritania is said to be perhaps the only remaining State where chattel slavery exists. It was only abolished formally in 1981, but provisions to criminalise slavery came much later and are reportedly not being enforced. See Mauritania, Concluding observations, CCPR/C/MRT/CO/1, para. 17; Mauritania, National report, A/HRC/WG.6/23/MRT/1, paras. 22–23, 76–81.

[236] Emmanuel Decaux, *Les formes contemporaines de l'esclavage*, Leiden/Boston: Martinus Nijhoff, 2009.

[237] *Prosecutor v. Kunarac et al.* (IT-96-23-A and IT-96-23/1-a), Judgment, 12 June 2002, para. 117.

and abuse, control of sexuality and forced labour'.[238] The Chamber also recalled a post-Second World War judgment that addressed the issue of 'benevolent' slavery:

> Slaves may be well fed, well clothed, and comfortably housed, but they are still slaves if without lawful process they are deprived of their freedom by forceful restraint. We might eliminate all proof of ill-treatment, overlook the starvation, beatings, and other barbarous acts, but the admitted fact of slavery—compulsory uncompensated labour—would still remain. There is no such thing as benevolent slavery. Involuntary servitude, even if tempered by humane treatment, is still slavery.[239]

The prohibition of slavery is not addressed in the 1929 declaration of the Institut de Droit International.[240] The 1943 draft declaration of the London International Assembly declared: 'Slavery shall be prohibited. Involuntary servitude shall only be permitted as a punishment for crime whereof the party shall have been duly convicted.'[241] Hersch Lauterpacht's 1945 draft bill of rights proscribed 'slavery, or traffic in slaves, or compulsory labour in any form other than public service, equally incumbent upon all, or as part of punishment pronounced by a court of law'.[242] There was nothing about slavery in the draft human rights declarations submitted to the United Nations by Chile, Cuba, and Panama, nor in the American Declaration on the Rights and Duties of Man, of May 1948.[243]

The Universal Declaration of Human Rights states: 'No one shall be held in slavery or servitude; slavery and the slave trade shall be prohibited in all their forms.'[244] This succinct formulation was amplified to nearly 200 words in the corresponding provision of the International Covenant on Civil and Political Rights because of the perceived need to offer not only a detailed definition of 'servitude' but also to spell out limitations on the prohibition of forced or compulsory labour. The Covenant treats imprisonment with hard labour as an exception, as well as work or service associated with the sentence of a court, compulsory military service, service exacted in time of emergency, and work or service that are part of

[238] Ibid., para. 119, citing *Prosecutor v. Kunarac et al.* (IT-96-23-T and IT-96-23/1-T), Judgment, 22 February 2001, paras. 542–543.

[239] *United States of America v. Pohl et al.*, Judgment, (1950) 5 TWC 958, at p. 970.

[240] Institut de Droit International, 'Declaration of the International Rights of Man', (1941) 35 *American Journal of International Law* 663. In 1931, the Institut adopted a resolution recognising the right of any State to exercise universal jurisdiction over 'une infraction contre des intérêts généraux protégés par le droit international (tels que la piraterie, la traite des noirs, la traite des blanches ...': Le conflit des lois pénales en matière de compétence, 3 August 1931.

[241] London International Assembly, Report of the Third Commission (Legal Commission) on individual rights, TNA LNU 6/7.

[242] Hersch Lauterpacht, *An International Bill of the Rights of Man*, New York: Columbia University Press, 1945, p. 70.

[243] International Bill of Rights Documented Outline, E/CN.4/AC.1/3/Add.1, p. 60.

[244] Universal Declaration of Human Rights, A/RES/217 (III), art. 4.

normal civic obligations.[245] There are no reservations or interpretative declarations to Article 8 of the International Covenant.

All of the regional human rights treaties contain provisions on slavery and servitude, with varying degrees of detail.[246] There are also provisions prohibiting slavery in some of the specialised treaties.[247] The Supplementary Convention on the Abolition of Slavery, the Slave Trade, and Institutions and Practices Similar to Slavery, 1956, provides for the complete abolition of debt bondage and serfdom.[248] International Labour Organisation Convention 29 concerning Forced or Compulsory Labour, which was adopted in 1930, obliges States 'to suppress the use of forced or compulsory labour in all its forms within the shortest possible period'.[249] Convention 29 has been ratified by 178 States, several of them not parties to the International Covenant on Civil and Political Rights.[250] Convention 105 on the Abolition of Forced Labour, adopted in 1957 and now with 175 ratifications, builds upon the earlier instrument, prohibiting the use of forced labour as a means of political coercion or repression, for economic development, for labour discipline and punishment for strikes, and as a means of racial, social, national, or religious discrimination.[251]

The Declaration adopted at the World Conference against Racism, Racial Discrimination, Xenophobia and Related Intolerance, in 2001, states: 'We acknowledge that slavery and the slave trade, including the transatlantic slave trade, were appalling tragedies in the history of humanity not only because of their abhorrent barbarism but also in terms of their magnitude, organised nature and especially their negation of the essence of the victims, and further acknowledge that slavery and the slave trade are a crime against humanity and should always have been so, especially the transatlantic slave trade and are among the major sources and manifestations of racism, racial discrimination, xenophobia and related intolerance, and that Africans and people of African descent, Asians and people of Asian descent and indigenous peoples were victims of these acts and continue to be victims of their consequences.'[252]

Although Hersch Lauterpacht had included the prohibition of slavery in his own 1945 draft bill of rights, writing a decade later, in the eighth edition of *Oppenheim's International Law*, he said that it was 'difficult to say that customary International Law condemns two of the greatest curses which man has ever imposed upon his fellow-man, the institution of

245 International Covenant on Civil and Political Rights, (1976) 999 UNTS 171, art. 8.

246 European Convention on Human Rights, (1953) 213 UNTS 221, art. 4; American Convention on Human Rights, (1978) 1144 UNTS 123, arts. 5 and 6; Arab Charter on Human Rights, art. 10; Charter of Fundamental Rights of the European Union, OJ C 326/391, art. 5.

247 Convention on the Rights of Persons with Disabilities, (2008) 2515 UNTS 3, art. 27(2); International Convention on the Protection of the Rights of all Migrant Workers and Members of their Families, (2003) 2220 UNTS 3, art. 11(1).

248 Supplementary Convention on the Abolition of Slavery, the Slave Trade, and Institutions and Practices Similar to Slavery, (1957) 226 UNTS 3.

249 Convention 29 concerning Forced or Compulsory Labour, (1946) 39 UNTS 55.

250 Comoros, Cook Islands, Cuba, Fiji, Kiribati, Malaysia, Myanmar, Oman, St Kitts and Nevis, Saint Lucia, Saudi Arabia, Singapore, Solomon Islands, South Sudan, United Arab Emirates.

251 Convention 105 concerning the Abolition of Forced Labour, (1959) 320 UNTS 291, art. 1.

252 Declaration, Report of the World Conference against Racism, Racial Discrimination, Xenophobia and Related Intolerance Durban, 31 August–8September 2001, A/CONF.189/12, p. 5, para. 13.

slavery and the traffic in slaves.'[253] Eight years later, reporting on the law of treaties to the International Law Commission, Humphrey Waldock gave the slave trade as an example of an act or omission in the suppression or punishment of which every State is required by international law to co-operate.[254] Today there is no shortage of support for the view that the prohibition of slavery is a norm of customary international law,[255] from such bodies as the Human Rights Committee,[256] the Special Court for Sierra Leone,[257] and the International Criminal Court.[258] The International Court of Justice has described 'protection from slavery' as an *erga omnes* norm.[259] The International Law Commission listed the prohibition of slavery in its 2019 draft norms of *jus cogens*.[260] A study published by the Office of the High Commissioner for Human Rights said that 'it is now a well-established principle of international law' that the 'prohibition against slavery and slavery-related practices have achieved the level of customary international law and have attained "*jus cogens*" status.'[261] The Inter-American Commission on Human Rights has described the prohibition of slavery as a norm of *jus cogens*,[262] as have national courts.[263] There is a tendency to extrapolate the *jus cogens* categorisation so as to include 'modern' or 'contemporary' forms of slavery, such as sexual slavery,[264] although members of the International Law Commission have warned of overbreadth.[265]

[253] Hersch Lauterpacht, *Oppenheim's International Law*, Vol. I, 8th ed., London: Longmans, Green, 1955, pp. 733–734. See also Hugo Fischer, 'The Suppression of Slavery in International Law', (1950) 3 *International Law Quarterly* 28, at p. 41: 'it can be said that in customary international law slave-holding is not unlawful'; ibid., p. 42: 'In 1885 customary international law did not forbid the slave-trade.'

[254] Second report on the law of treaties, by Sir Humphrey Waldock, Special Rapporteur, in *Yearbook . . . 1963*, Vol. II, p. 53.

[255] General Comment 24, Issues Relating to Reservations Made upon Ratification or Accession to the Covenant or the Optional Protocols thereto, or in Relation to Declarations under art. 41 of the Covenant, CCPR/C/21/Rev.1/Add.6, para. 8.

[256] Ibid.

[257] *Prosecutor v. Brima et al.* (SCSL-04-16-T), Judgment, 20 June 2007, para. 705.

[258] *Prosecutor v. Ntaganda* (ICC-01/04-02/06), Second decision on the Defence's challenge to the jurisdiction of the Court in respect of Counts 6 and 9, 4 January 2017, para. 51.

[259] *Barcelona Traction, Light and Power Company, Limited, Judgment, ICJ Reports 1970*, p. 3, para. 34.

[260] Report of the International Law Commission, Seventy-first session (29 April–7 June and 8 July–9 August 2019), A/74/10, p. 206. Also Fourth report on peremptory norms of general international law (*jus cogens*) by Dire Tladi, Special Rapporteur, A/CN.4/727, paras. 102–107.

[261] David Weissbrodt and Anti-Slavery International, Abolishing Slavery and its Contemporary Forms, HR/PUB/02/4, p. 3.

[262] Captive Communities: Situation of the Guaraní Indigenous People and Contemporary Forms of Slavery in the Bolivian Chaco, OEA/Ser.L/V/II, Doc. 58, para. 54.

[263] *Nevsun Resources Ltd. v. Araya*, 2020 SCC 5, para. 101.

[264] *Prosecutor v. Brima et al.* (SCSL-2004-16-T), Judgment, 20 June 2007, para. 705; *Prosecutor v. Ntaganda* (ICC-01/04-02/06), Second decision on the Defence's challenge to the jurisdiction of the Court in respect of Counts 6 and 9, 4 January 2017, para. 51; Systematic rape, sexual slavery, and slavery-like practices during armed conflict Final report submitted by Ms. Gay J. McDougall, Special Rapporteur, E/CN.4/Sub.2/1998/13, para. 28. See however the critique by Cóman Kenny and Yvonne McDermott, 'The Expanding Protection of Members of a Party's own Armed Forces under International Criminal Law', (2019) 68 *International and Comparative Law Quarterly* 943, at pp. 952–953.

[265] A/CN.4/SR.3459, p. 15 (Shinya Murase); A/CN.4/SR.3462, p. 18 (Hong Thao Nguyen); A/CN.4/SR.3462, p. 18 (Rudo Santolaria). See also Anthony D'Amato, 'Human Rights as Part of Customary

A Commission of Experts appointed pursuant to the International Labour Organisation Constitution to examine Myanmar's compliance with Convention 29 held that 'a State which supports, instigates, accepts or tolerates forced labour on its territory commits a wrongful act and engages its responsibility for the violation of a peremptory norm of international law'.[266] This view was subsequently endorsed by the Organisation's Committee of Experts: 'Freedom from forced or compulsory labour was among the first basic human rights subjects within the Organisation's mandate to be dealt with in international labour standards. The principles embodied in the ILO Conventions in this field have since been incorporated in various international instruments, both universal and regional, and have therefore become a peremptory norm of international law.'[267] The Committee of Experts considered that by labelling the prohibition of forced labour as *jus cogens*, it was no longer possible for a State to invoke what was essentially a transitional provision of ILO Convention 29.[268] Referring to the International Labour Organisation's determination, the Supreme Court of Canada has said '[t]o the extent that debate may exist about whether forced labour is a peremptory norm, there can be no doubt that it is at least a norm of customary international law'.[269]

Slavery is defined, in the sense of Article 1(1) of the Slavery Convention of 1926, as the 'status or condition of a person over whom any or all of the powers attaching to the right of ownership are exercised'.[270] According to Article 1(2) of this Convention, the slave trade includes 'all acts involved in the capture, acquisition or disposal of a person with intent to reduce him to slavery; all acts involved in the acquisition of a slave with a view to selling or exchanging him; all acts of disposal by sale or exchange of a slave acquired with a view to being sold or exchanged, and, in general, every act of trade or transport in slaves'. Serfdom, servitude, forced labour,

International Law: A Plea for Change of Paradigms', (1995–96) 25 *Georgia Journal of International and Comparative Law* 47, at p. 48.

[266] International Labour Organisation. International Labour Office, 'Forced Labour in Myanmar (Burma), Report of the Commission of Inquiry Appointed under Article 26 of the Constitution of the International Labour Organization to Examine the Observance by Myanmar of the Forced Labour Convention, 1930 (No. 29)', *ILO Official Bulletin*: Special Supplement, vol. LXXXI, 1998, Series B, special supplement, paras. 528, 531, 538.

[267] General Survey concerning the Forced Labour Convention, 1930 (No. 29), and the Abolition of Forced Labour Convention, 1957 (No. 105), Report III (Part 1B), 2007, para. 192.

[268] Ibid., para. 10. See the opinion of the Legal Advisor of the Secretary-General on this question: 'Characterisation of the Prohibition of Forced or Compulsory Labour as a Peremptory Norm by the Supervisory Bodies of the ILO—Article 53 of the 1969 Vienna Convention on the Law of Treaties', *United Nations Juridical Yearbook 2014*, p. 348. Also, see the critique of the International Labour Organisation's approach in Jean Allain, *Slavery in International Law: Of Human Exploitation and Trafficking*, Leiden: Martinus Nijhoff, 2012, pp. 246–252.

[269] *Nevsun Resources Ltd. v. Araya*, 2020 SCC 5, para. 102.

[270] The generally accepted definition is also used, *e.g.* in the interpretation of the term 'slavery' in art. 4 of the European Convention on Human Rights. See William A. Schabas, *The European Convention on Human Rights, A Commentary*, Oxford: Oxford University Press, 2015, p. 207.

and debt bondage are related practices that fall generally under the prohibition of slavery.

Of States that have no treaty norm prohibiting slavery, there does not appear to be much doubt that they understand that they are under an international obligation derived from customary law. Few of them seem to report on this to the Human Rights Council.[271] That this is not really a controversial issue can be seen in the absence of questions or recommendations from other States during the Universal Periodic Review. Forced labour attracts more attention. A limited number of States are not subject to a treaty provision prohibiting forced labour, as they are not parties to either the International Covenant on Civil and Political Rights or the International Labour Organisation conventions on forced labour. During the Universal Periodic Review these States, including China, have been generally unresponsive to questions and recommendations on the subject of forced labour, suggesting that they may not consider it to fall within their obligations under international law.[272]

* * *

Conclusions. Slavery and servitude, including the slave trade, are prohibited by customary international law. This prohibition is a norm of *jus cogens*.

D. Liberty and security

The notions of 'liberty and security' play an important part in human rights law. Hersch Lauterpacht, in his 1945 draft, proposed the following: 'The liberty of the person shall be inviolate within the limits of the law.' Lauterpacht traced the right back to the Magna Carta and the Habeas Corpus Acts, stating that '[p]ersonal freedom, that is, freedom from arbitrary physical restraint on the part of governmental authority, is the first claim of man in his struggle against the arbitrariness of the State.' This was the very first right in Lauterpacht's enumeration. He broke it down into several components: prohibition of administrative detention; protection from arbitrary arrest; pre-trial detention not to be unduly prolonged, nor unreasonable or excessive bail imposed; protection of the writ of habeas corpus; a right to trial by jury; safeguards of evidence and procedure in criminal trials;

[271] Myanmar, National report, A/HRC/WG.6/10/MMR/1, para. 59; Myanmar, National report, A/HRC/WG.6/10/MMR/1, para. 38; Oman, National report, A/HRC/WG.6/10/OMN/1, para. 15 and Report of the Working Group, A/HRC/17/7, paras. 74–75; Singapore, National report, A/HRC/WG.6/11/SGP/1, para. 23.

[272] Bhutan, Report of the Working Group, A/HRC/42/8, paras. 103, 157.137; Brunei Darussalam, Report of the Working Group, A/HRC/27/11, paras. 34, 113.51 and Views on recommendations, A/HRC/27/11/Add.1, para. 113.51; China, Report of the Working Group, A/HRC/11/25, paras. 43, 84, 97; Micronesia, Report of the Working Group, A/HRC/31/4, para. 25.

prohibition of retroactive operation of criminal law; prohibition of cruel and inhuman punishment.[273]

Article 3 of the Universal Declaration of Human Rights proclaims that 'Everyone has the right to … liberty and security of person.' It is complemented by Article 9: 'No one shall be subjected to arbitrary arrest, detention or exile.' These provisions are combined in Article 9(1) of the International Covenant on Civil and Political Rights, which adds that nobody 'shall be deprived of his liberty except on such grounds and in accordance with such procedure as are established by law.' The four paragraphs that follow set out detailed aspects of the protection against arbitrary detention: the right of a person who is arrested to be informed, at the time of arrest, of the reasons for arrest and to be promptly informed of any charges; to be brought promptly before a judge or other judicial official, and to be tried within a reasonable time or to be released; as a general rule, not to be detained while awaiting trial; to take proceedings to determine the lawfulness of detention; to compensation for unlawful arrest or detention. Guarantees against arbitrary detention are also set out in many other regional and specialised treaties.[274] In the *Diallo* case, the International Court of Justice observed that the prohibition of arbitrary deprivation of liberty appears in all major human rights instruments and is widely enshrined in national constitutions. Furthermore, '[t]he prohibition of arbitrary detention is not limited to criminal justice proceedings. It also applies to other forms of detention such as administrative proceedings governing forcible removal of refugees, asylum seekers and immigrants from the national territory.'[275]

There have only been a few reservations to Article 9 of the International Covenant on Civil and Political Rights. None concern the right in a general sense. The reservations and some interpretative declarations deal with exceptions for forms of administrative detention,[276] military discipline,[277] compensation for unlawful arrest,[278] and peculiarities of national legislation.[279]

[273] Hersch Lauterpacht, *An International Bill of the Rights of Man*, New York: Columbia University Press, 1945, pp. 93–100.

[274] European Convention on Human Rights, (1953) 213 UNTS 221, art. 5; American Convention on Human Rights, (1978) 1144 UNTS 123, arts. 5(4) and (5), 7; African Charter on Human and Peoples' Rights, (1986) 1520 UNTS 271, art. 6; Arab Charter on Human Rights, art. 14; Charter of Fundamental Rights of the European Union, OJ C 326/391, art. 6; International Convention on the Protection of the Rights of all Migrant Workers and Members of their Families, (2003) 2220 UNTS 3, arts. 16, 17; Convention on the Rights of the Child, (1990) 1571 UNTS 3, art. 37; Convention on the Rights of Persons with Disabilities, (2008) 2515 UNTS 3, art. 14; International Convention on the Elimination of All Forms of Racial Discrimination, (1969) 660 UNTS 195, art. 5(b); International Convention on the Suppression and Punishment of the Crime of Apartheid, (1976) 1015 UNTS 243, art. II(a); African Convention on the Rights and Duties of the Child, art. 17(2).

[275] *Ahmadou Sadio Diallo (Republic of Guinea v. Democratic Republic of the Congo), Merits, Judgment, ICJ Reports 2010*, p. 639, para. 77.

[276] Austria, (1978) 1103 UNTS 394; Finland, C.N.210.1975.TREATIES-7, now withdrawn, C.N.236.1990.TREATIES-10.

[277] France, C.N.335.1980.TREATIES-10.

[278] India, C.N.81.1979.TREATIES-2; Bahrain, C.N.1140.2006.TREATIES-24; Mexico, C.N.81.1981.TREATIES-8; United States of America, C.N.250.1992.TREATIES-14.

[279] Italy, C.N.231.1978.TREATIES-11, now withdrawn, C.N.1291.2005.TREATIES-27; Thailand, C.N.381.1996.TREATIES-8, now withdrawn, C.N.356.2012.TREATIES-IV.4.

Despite the fact that the guarantee against arbitrary detention is of 'profound importance', in the words of the Human Rights Committee,[280] the Covenant authorises its derogation. It is probably one of the provisions that is most subject to derogation. Some fifteen States Parties have made general derogations to Article 9, often on several occasions.[281] Israel made a general derogation to Article 9 that has been in force for almost thirty years, since it ratified the Covenant in 1991. In its Concluding Observations on Israel's initial report, the Human Rights Committee said that despite the derogation 'a State Party may not depart from the requirement of effective judicial review of detention'.[282] The Human Rights Committee has taken the view that the requirement of court review over the lawfulness of detention (right to habeas corpus) forms a non-derogable element of Article 9.[283] No State Party has ever made an explicit derogation to the right to judicial review of detention.

The Universal Periodic Review materials demonstrate that the right to liberty and security of the person is recognised as an obligation owed under international law even by States that have not ratified a relevant treaty.[284] The references are often

[280] General Comment 24, Issues Relating to Reservations Made upon Ratification or Accession to the Covenant or the Optional Protocols thereto, or in Relation to Declarations under art. 41 of the Covenant, CCPR/C/21/Rev.1/Add.6, para. 10.

[281] Argentina, C.N.170.1989.TREATIES-7; Azerbaijan, C.N.424.1994.TREATIES-13, C.N.90.1995. TREATIES-2; Bahrain, C.N.261.2011.TREATIES-5; Chile, C.N.306.1976.TREATIES-9, C.N.221.1986. TREATIES-11; Guatemala, C.N.145.2010.TREATIES-2, C.N.146.2010.TREATIES-3, etc.; Israel, C.N.222.1991.TREATIES-4/14; Jamaica, C.N.51.2018.TREATIES-IV-4; Peru, C.N.254.2006. TREATIES-9, etc.; Poland, C.N.37.1982.TREATIES-2, C.N.327.1982.TREATIES-13; Russia, C.N.24.1990.TREATIES-2, C.N.91.1990.TREATIES-4, etc.; Serbia, C.N.274.2003.TREATIES-3; Trinidad and Tobago, C.N.314.1990.TREATIES-13, C.N.303.1995.TREATIES-7, C.N.680.2011. TREATIES-43; Turkey, C.N.424.2017.TREATIES-IV.4 of 27 July 2017, C.N.4.2017.TREATIES-IV.4, etc.; United Kingdom, C.N.319.1988.TREATIES-17, C.N.343.1989.TREATIES-16, etc.; Venezuela, C.N.98.1989.TREATIES-5, C.N.88.1992.TREATIES-5, etc. There are also reservations to specific paragraphs: (1) Ecuador, C.N.68.1984.TREATIES-5; (2) Ecuador, C.N.68.1984.TREATIES-5; Namibia, C.N.969.1999.TREATIES-7; Sri Lanka, C.N.373.2000.TREATIES-5, C.N.400.2010.TREATIES-16; (3) Algeria, C.N.155.1991.TREATIES-10, C.N.47.1992.TREATIES-3; Namibia, C.N.969.1999. TREATIES-7; Sri Lanka, C.N.122.1984.TREATIES-9, C.N.171.1984.TREATIES-12, C.N.373.2000. TREATIES-5.

[282] Israel, Concluding observations, CCPR/C/79/Add.93, para. 21; Israel, Concluding observations, CCPR/CO/78/ISR, para. 12; Israel, Concluding observations, CCPR/C/ISR/CO/3, para. 7; Israel, Concluding observations, CCPR/C/ISR/CO/4, para. 10.

[283] General Comment 29, art. 4: Derogations during a State of Emergency, CCPR/C/21/Rev.1/ Add.11, para. 16.

[284] Bhutan, National report, A/HRC/WG.6/33/BTN/1, paras. 7, 146; China, National report, A/ HRC/WG.6/4/CHN/1, para. 45–48 and Report of the Working Group, A/HRC/11/25, para. 66; Cuba, National report, A/HRC/WG.6/4/CUB/1, para. 30 and Report of the Working Group, A/HRC/11/ 22, para. 19; Kiribati, National report, A/HRC/WG.6/21/KIR/1, para. 41 and Views on conclusions, A/HRC/15/3/Add.1, para. 46; Malaysia, National report, A/HRC/WG.6/4/MYS/1/Rev.1, para. 9 and National report, A/HRC/WG.6/17/MYS/1, para. 93; Micronesia, Report of the Working Group, A/ HRC/31/4, para. 8; Myanmar, National report, A/HRC/WG.6/10/MMR/1, para. 38; St Kitts and Nevis, National report, A/HRC/WG.6/10/KNA/1, para. 8; Nauru, National report, A/HRC/WG.6/ 10/NRU/1, para. 16; Palau, National report, A/HRC/WG.6/24/PLW/1, para. 5 and National report, A/HRC/WG.6/11/PLW/1, para. 30; Singapore, National report, A/HRC/WG.6/11/SGP/1, paras. 22, 126–130 National report, A/HRC/WG.6/11/SGP/1, para. 113; Solomon Islands, National report, A/

quite perfunctory, amounting to nothing more than confirmation that the right is included in the constitution.

Although it did not explicitly refer to customary international law, the International Court of Justice, in the case concerning the hostages at the embassy in Tehran, declared that 'wrongfully to deprive human beings of their freedom and to subject them to physical constraint in conditions of hardship is in itself manifestly incompatible with the principles of the Charter of the United Nations, as well as with the fundamental principles enunciated in the Universal Declaration of Human Rights'.[285] The United Nations General Assembly has condemned 'any form of deprivation of liberty that amounts to placing a detained person outside the protection of the law', urging States 'to respect the safeguards concerning the liberty, security and dignity of the person and to treat all prisoners in all places of detention in accordance with international law, including human rights law and international humanitarian law'.[286] One of the difficulties in assessing the strength of the norm, from the standpoint of customary international law, is that all States detain people. The levels of detention vary from one country to another, but they are significant everywhere and violations of the protection against arbitrary detention are frequent. For example, the European Court of Human Rights has found breaches of the right in all but one of the Member States of the Council of Europe, Andorra.

In General Comment 24, the Human Rights Committee identified the prohibition of arbitrary arrest and detention as a rule of customary international law.[287] The Restatement of the American Law Institute includes 'prolonged arbitrary detention' among norms of customary law.[288] In a study of the customary law concerning arbitrary deprivation of liberty, the Working Group on Arbitrary Detention concluded that 'widespread ratification of international treaty law on arbitrary deprivation of liberty, as well as the widespread translation of the prohibition into national laws, constitute a near universal State practice evidencing the customary nature of the arbitrary deprivation of liberty prohibition'.[289] The Working Group pointed to various United Nations Security Council resolutions

HRC/WG.6/11/SLB/1, paras. 23, 24; South Sudan, National report, A/HRC/WG.6/26/SSD/1, para. 18 and Report of the Working Group, A/HRC/34/13, para. 7; Tuvalu, National report, A/HRC/WG.6/3/TUV/1, para. 33.

285 *United States Diplomatic and Consular Staff in Tehran, Judgment, ICJ Reports 1980*, p. 3, para. 91.

286 Protection of human rights and fundamental freedoms while countering terrorism, A/RES/62/159, para. 10, adopted without a vote (A/62/PV.76, p. 20).

287 General Comment 24, Issues Relating to Reservations Made upon Ratification or Accession to the Covenant or the Optional Protocols thereto, or in Relation to Declarations under art. 41 of the Covenant, CCPR/C/21/Rev.1/Add.6, para. 8.

288 Restatement (Third) of the Foreign Relations Law of the United States, St. Paul, MN: American Law Institute, 1987.

289 Deliberation No. 9 concerning the definition and scope of arbitrary deprivation of liberty under customary international law, A/HRC/22/44, para. 43.

condemning arbitrary deprivation of liberty in States that were not parties to relevant treaty norms at the time,[290] as well as resolutions of a general nature and of a universal nature regardless of treaty obligations, as evidence of 'the consensus that the prohibition of arbitrary deprivation of liberty is of a universally binding nature under customary international law'.[291]

In a decision on a petition submitted against Australia, in which the parties made submissions on the scope of customary international law applicable to detention of asylum seekers, the Human Rights Committee said it could not 'find any support for the contention that there is a rule of customary international law which would render all such detention arbitrary'.[292] The Working Group on Arbitrary Detention has identified several situations where the prohibition on arbitrary deprivation of liberty imposed by customary law may apply: when it is clearly impossible to invoke any legal basis justifying the deprivation of liberty; when the deprivation of liberty results from the exercise of the rights or freedoms guaranteed by the Universal Declaration of Human Rights, such as the freedoms of religion and belief, expression, association and peaceful assembly, the right to equality before the law, freedom of movement and the right to seek and enjoy asylum from persecution; the total or partial non-observance of fair trial rights of such gravity as to give the deprivation of liberty an arbitrary character; the subjection of asylum seekers, immigrants, or refugees to prolonged administrative custody without the possibility of administrative or judicial review of remedy; and circumstances where liberty is deprived for reasons of discrimination based on birth; national, ethnic, or social origin; language; religion; economic condition; political or other opinion; gender; sexual orientation; disability or other status, 'and which aims towards or can result in ignoring the equality of human rights'.[293] At the request of the Human Rights Council, the Working Group on Arbitrary Detention prepared the Basic Principles and Guidelines on Remedies and Procedures on the Right of Anyone Deprived of Their Liberty to Bring Proceedings Before a Court.[294]

The Working Group on Arbitrary Detention has also concluded that arbitrary deprivation of liberty constitutes a peremptory or *jus cogens* norm.[295] The Working Group provided no justification or authority for its conclusion, although it might have been based on the holding by the Working Group that 'derogation from customary international law's prohibition of arbitrary deprivation of liberty is not

[290] For example, S/RES/417 (1977), para. 3(b) and S/RES/473 (1980), para. 8.

[291] Deliberation No. 9 concerning the definition and scope of arbitrary deprivation of liberty under customary international law, A/HRC/22/44, para. 43.

[292] *A v. Australia*, no. 560/1993, Views, 30 April 1997, CCPR/C/59/D/560/1993, para. 9.3.

[293] Deliberation No. 9 concerning the definition and scope of arbitrary deprivation of liberty under customary international law, A/HRC/22/44, para. 38.

[294] United Nations Basic Principles and Guidelines on Remedies and Procedures on the Right of Anyone Deprived of Their Liberty to Bring Proceedings Before a Court, A/HRC/30/37.

[295] Ibid., para. 51. Also Opinion No. 41/2017 concerning ten individuals associated with the newspaper Cumhuriyet (Turkey), A/HRC/WGAD/2017/41, para. 76.

possible' in the paragraph immediately preceding the statement about peremptory norms. But the relevance of the issue of derogation to the customary law environment is not evident. Not only is derogation possible to Article 9 of the Covenant, many States Parties have availed themselves of the possibility. Nevertheless, the holding of the Working Group received an endorsement from Lord Sumption of the United Kingdom Supreme Court who did not think that the possibility of derogation from the norm raised any difficulty.[296]

There is some support for the *jus cogens* determination from the Human Rights Committee[297] and the Inter-American Commission on Human Rights.[298] On the other hand, a Trial Chamber of the International Criminal Court said that '[s]ince there are numerous exceptions to the right to liberty (and its corollary, the prohibition on arbitrary arrest and detention), it cannot be considered an intransgressible or peremptory norm of international law'.[299] In its study of *jus cogens*, the International Law Commission noted the position taken by the Working Group on Arbitrary Detention, but as an example of a trend of 'determining the existence of a *jus cogens* norm on the basis of customary international law when the norm in question also exists in treaty law', and otherwise ignored it.[300] There was never any suggestion from members of the Commission that the prohibition of arbitrary detention should figure in its list of *jus cogens* norms.

The right of a person deprived of liberty to apply to a court in order to determine the legality of the detention is widely known by the term it is given in English law, habeas corpus, or in Spanish law, where it is known as *amparo*. Recognition of the specific right to a mechanism for judicial challenge to detention is a specific example of the more general right to a remedy. The Working Group on Arbitrary Detention noted that it is deemed non-derogable in several of the treaties, thereby signalling its fundamental character.[301] The notion of derogability, by which States temporarily suspend certain of their treaty obligations, is not really applicable to the customary law context. States that are not parties to the International Covenant on Civil and Political Rights and relevant regional treaties that guarantee habeas corpus nevertheless confirm its availability under national law in their reports to the Human Rights Council, providing evidence of its customary status.[302]

[296] *Belhaj et al. v. Straw et al., Rahmatullah (No. 1) v. Ministry of Defence et al.*, [2017] UKSC 3, para. 271.

[297] General Comment 29, art. 4: Derogations during a State of Emergency, CCPR/C/21/Rev.1/Add.11, para. 11.

[298] *Mario Aflredo Lares-Reyes et al. v.* United States, Case 12.379, Report No. 19/02, Merits, 27 February 2002, para. 46, fn. 23.

[299] *Prosecutor v. Katanga et al.* (ICC-01/04-01/07), Decision on the application for the interim release of detained Witnesses DRC-D02-P-0236, DRC-D02-P-0228, and DRC-D02-P-0350, 1 October 2013, para. 33.

[300] Second report on *jus cogens* by Dire Tladi, Special Rapporteur, A/CN.4/706, para. 58.

[301] Deliberation No. 9 concerning the definition and scope of arbitrary deprivation of liberty under customary international law, A/HRC/22/44, para. 47.

[302] Cuba, National Report, A/HRC/WG.6/30/CUB/1, para. 18; Marshall Islands, National report, / HRC/WG.6/9/MHL/1/Rev.1, para. 10(h); Myanmar, National report, A/HRC/WG.6/10/MMR/1, para.

1. Right to security

The right to liberty is often formulated together with the right to security, both in international law instruments and national constitutions. Because of the focus on arbitrary detention, an autonomous right to security has found little purchase in international human rights law. In General Comment 35, the Human Rights Committee said that security of person 'concerns freedom from injury to the body and the mind, or bodily and mental integrity'.[303] Accordingly, the right to security of person protects individuals from 'intentional infliction of bodily or mental injury, regardless of whether the victim is detained or non-detained. For example, officials of States Parties violate the right to personal security when they unjustifiably inflict bodily injury.'[304] The Committee has invoked the right to security with respect to failure by States to protect against violence based upon sexual orientation or gender identity,[305] against persons with disabilities,[306] and human rights defenders.[307] The European Court of Human Rights has not attributed any independent significance beyond personal liberty to the right to security.[308]

2. Imprisonment for debt

Imprisonment for debt may be viewed as a form of arbitrary detention. It is also related to debt bondage, an issue that arises within the framework of the prohibition of slavery and servitude. The International Covenant on Civil and Political Rights provides that no one shall be imprisoned merely on the ground of inability to fulfil a contractual obligation.[309] Provisions to the same effect are found in the American Convention on Human Rights,[310] Protocol 4 to the European Convention on Human Rights,[311] and the Arab Charter on Human Rights,[312] but not in the Universal Declaration of Human Rights. The Covenant deems it a non-derogable

107; Malaysia, National report, A/HRC/WG.6/4/MYS/1/Rev.1, paras. 87–88; Tonga, National report, A/HRC/WG.6/15/TON/1, para. 29.

303 General Comment 35, art. 9 (Liberty and security of person), CCPR/C/GC/35, para. 3.

304 Ibid., para. 9.

305 El Salvador, Concluding observations, CCPR/CO/78/SLV, para. 16.

306 Norway, Concluding observations, CCPR/C/NOR/CO/6, para. 10.

307 *Marcellana et al. v. Philippines*, no. 1560/2007, Views, 30 October 2008, CCPR/C/94/D/1560/2007, para. 7.7.

308 See, *e.g.* the judgment of the European Court of Human Rights in *Bozano v. France*, 18 December 1986, § 23, Series A no. 111.

309 International Covenant on Civil and Political Rights, (1976) 999 UNTS 171, art. 11.

310 American Convention on Human Rights, (1978) 1144 UNTS 123, art. 7(7).

311 Protocol 4 to the Convention for the Protection of Human Rights and Fundamental Freedoms, securing certain rights and freedoms other than those already included in the Convention and in the first Protocol thereto, CETS 46, art. 1.

312 Arab Charter on Human Rights, art. 18.

right, immune from suspension in time of national emergency. In its General Comment on reservations, the Human Rights Committee referred to the prohibition of imprisonment for debt as an indication that some rights are non-derogable not because of their fundamental status but merely because 'their suspension is irrelevant to the legitimate control of the state of national emergency'.[313]

According to the South African Constitutional Court, international human rights law repudiates 'the core element of the institution of civil imprisonment, namely, the locking-up of people merely because they fail to pay contractual debts' but 'there is a penumbra relating to money payments in which imprisonment can be used in appropriately defined circumstances'.[314] The Human Rights Committee has held that the prohibition of prosecutions for fraudulent bankruptcy and similar corruption-related offences where an offender may be punished with imprisonment even when no longer able to pay debts.[315] Moreover, it is inapplicable to imprisonment related to the non-payment of maintenance or alimentary support.

Reports to the Human Rights Council by States that are not party to the Covenant, and therefore have no explicit treaty obligation with respect to imprisonment for failure to fulfil a contractual obligation, contain no references that would make it possible to indicate whether they have a view about the position of customary international law or to identify their practice.

* * *

Conclusions. Everyone has the right to liberty and security. Arbitrary detention is prohibited. A judicial remedy must be available to verify the lawfulness of detention. Imprisonment for failure to fulfil a contractual obligation is prohibited.

E. Recognition as a person before the law

The right to recognition as a person before the law has been described as 'undoubtedly one of the most direct expressions of the principle of respect for the dignity of the human person in international human rights law: the very fact of being human entails the right to recognition of legal personality, independently of even the legal capacity accorded to the person (for example, infants have the right to legal personality even if they have a limited capacity that means that they do not enjoy all

[313] General Comment 24, Issues Relating to Reservations Made upon Ratification or Accession to the Covenant or the Optional Protocols thereto, or in Relation to Declarations under art. 41 of the Covenant, CCPR/C/21/Rev.1/Add.6, para. 10.

[314] *Coetzee v. Government of the Republic of South Africa, Matiso et al. v. Commanding Officer Port Elizabeth Prison et al.*, [1995] ZACC 7.

[315] *Foumbi v. Cameroon*, no. 2325/2013, Views, 28 October 2014, CCPR/C/112/D/2325/2013, para. 8.7; *Zogo Andela v. Cameroon*, no. 2764/2016, Views, 8 November 2017, CCPR/C/121/D/2764/2016, para. 6.1.

rights)'.[316] For the Inter-American Court of Human Rights, 'the failure to recognise juridical personality harms human dignity, because it denies absolutely an individual's condition of being a subject of rights and renders him vulnerable to non-observance of his rights by the State or other individuals'.[317]

Everyone has the right to recognition everywhere as a person before the law, states Article 6 of the Universal Declaration of Human Rights. This formulation can be traced to a proposal from Eleanor Roosevelt.[318] The provision is repeated verbatim in Article 16 of the International Covenant on Civil and Political Rights.[319] It assumes slightly different forms in the American Declaration of the Rights and Duties of Man,[320] the American Convention on Human Rights,[321] the African Charter on Human and Peoples' Rights,[322] and the Arab Charter on Human Rights.[323] Article 12(1) of the Convention on the Rights of Persons with Disabilities reprises the text of the Universal Declaration but with specific application to persons with disabilities. It goes on to require recognition that persons with disabilities 'enjoy legal capacity on an equal basis with others in all aspects of life' and that they 'take appropriate measures to provide access by persons with disabilities to the support they may require in exercising their legal capacity'.[324] The drafters of the European Convention on Human Rights opted to omit the right. Apparently they felt it was unnecessary and could be deduced from other provisions in the treaty.[325] Premised upon the equality of women with men 'before the law', a detailed text in the Convention on the Elimination of All Forms of Discrimination against Women addresses legal capacity in civil matters, the right to conclude contracts and to administer property, and equality in all stages of procedure in courts and tribunals.[326] Implicit in the affirmation of equal legal capacity with men is the recognition as a person before the law. Most of the States that have not ratified the Covenant are nevertheless parties to the Women's Convention. To

[316] *Hamulić v. Bosnia and Herzegovina*, no. 2022/2011, Views, 30 March 2015, CCPR/C/113/D/2022/2011, Separate opinion of Committee members Olivier de Frouville, Mauro Politi, Victor Manuel Rodríuez-Rescia, and Fabián Omar Salvioli (partly dissenting), para. 3. Also *Ičić et al. v. Bosnia and Herzegovina*, no. 2028/2011, Views, 30 March 2015, CCPR/C/113/D/2028/2011, Joint opinion of Committee members Olivier de Frouville, Mauro Politi, Victor Manuel Rodríguez-Rescia, and Fabián Omar Salvioli (partly dissenting).

[317] *Girls Yean and Bosico v. Dominican Republic*, 8 September 2005 (Preliminary Objections, Merits, Reparations, and Costs), Series C, No. 130, para. 179.

[318] E/CN.4/AC.2/SR.5, p. 10.

[319] International Covenant on Civil and Political Rights, (1976) 999 UNTS 171, art. 16.

[320] American Declaration on the Rights and Duties of Man, Final Act of the Ninth International Conference of American States, Res. XXX, art. XVII.

[321] American Convention on Human Rights, (1978) 1144 UNTS 123, art. 3.

[322] African Charter on Human and Peoples' Rights, (1986) 1520 UNTS 271, art. 5.

[323] Arab Charter on Human Rights, art. 22.

[324] Convention on the Rights of Persons with Disabilities, (2008) 2515 UNTS 3, art. 12.

[325] CE Doc. H(70)7, para. 41. See *Kurić et al. v. Slovenia*, no. 26828/06, 26 June 2012, Partly concurring, party dissenting opinion of Judge Vučinić.

[326] Convention on the Elimination of All Forms of Discrimination against Women, (1981) 1249 UNTS 13, art. 15(2) and (3).

the extent that Article 15 of that instrument is understood to confirm the norm of recognition as a person before the law, those States can be considered to have accepted it. Four States, the Holy See, Niue, Palau, and Tonga, with a population of slightly more than 100,000 taken together, are parties to neither the International Covenant nor the Women's Convention. Two of them, the Holy See and Niue, do not report to the Human Rights Council making it difficult to establish their legal position. Acceptance of equality before the law appears in reports to the Human Rights Council from Palau[327] and Tonga.[328]

There have been no reservations or interpretative declarations with respect to Article 16 of the International Covenant on Civil and Political Rights. The United Arab Emirates has ratified the Women's Convention, but with a reservation to Article 15(2), which concerns legal capacity in civil matters, invoking Sharia law.[329] Saudi Arabia has a notoriously broad reservation to the entire Women's Convention: 'In case of contradiction between any term of the Convention and the norms of Islamic law, the Kingdom is not under obligation to observe the contradictory terms of the Convention.'[330] Nevertheless, in their reports to the Human Rights Council within the framework of the Universal Periodic Review, these States provide evidence that they recognise the right to recognition before the law. Saudi Arabia reported to the Council that 'women are full citizens in their own right and are endowed with independent financial and full legal capacity under which they enjoy freedom to dispose of their property and manage their affairs in a totally independent manner without seeking permission from anyone'.[331]Taken as a whole, these elements provide robust confirmation that the right to recognition as a person before the law is a norm of customary international law.

Recognition before the law is deemed a non-derogable right in the International Covenant, the American Convention, and the Arab Charter.

The right to recognition as a person before the law 'protects the absolute and non-derogable right to be recognised as someone having the capacity to be a bearer of rights and duties, and thus is the most fundamental of all rights insofar as recognition of legal personality is [...] a necessary prerequisite to all other rights of the

[327] Palau, National report, A/HRC/WG.6/11/PLW/1, para. 69; Palau, Report of the Working Group, A/HRC/18/5, para. 55; Palau, Views on conclusions, A/HRC/18/5/Add.1, p. 6; Palau, National report, A/HRC/WG.6/24/PLW/1, paras. 95–98.

[328] Tonga, National report, A/HRC/WG.6/2/TON/1, para. 68; Tonga, Report of the Working Group, A/HRC/8/48, para. 13; Tonga, National report, A/HRC/WG.6/15/TON/1, paras. 101–109; Tonga, Report of the Working Group, A/HRC/23/4, para. 22; Tonga, National report, A/HRC/WG.6/29/TON/1, para. 112–120.

[329] C.N.I223.2004.TREATIES-11.

[330] C.N.925.2000.TREATIES-8.

[331] Saudi Arabia, Report of the Working Group A/HRC/25/3, para. 11. See also Saudi Arabia, National report, A/HRC/WG.6/4/SAU/1, para. 46; Saudi Arabia, Views on conclusions, A/HRC/11/23/Add.1, para. 34; Saudi Arabia, National report, A/HRC/WG.6/31/SAU/1, paras. 21, 99; Saudi Arabia, Report of the Working Group, A/HRC/40/4, para. 8; United Arab Emirates, National report, A/HRC/WG.6/3/ARE/1, paras. 17–19; United Arab Emirates, National report, A/HRC/WG.6/29/ARE/1, paras. 26, 32.

individual', wrote Walter Kälin as a member of the United Nations Human Rights Committee.[332] According to the General Comment on the right to recognition before the law adopted by the Committee on the Rights of Persons with Disabilities, '[l]egal capacity is an inherent right accorded to all people, including persons with disabilities' consisting of 'two strands'. The first is 'legal standing to hold rights and to be recognised as a legal person before the law' and may include, for example, having a birth certificate, seeking medical assistance, registering to be on the electoral role, or applying for a passport. The second is 'legal agency to act on those rights and to have those actions recognised by the law'.[333] The capacity to be a person before the law must be distinguished from the capacity to act, *i.e.*, to establish rights and duties by way of one's own conduct.

The Commissioner for Human Rights of the Council of Europe has described legal capacity 'as a person's power or possibility to act within the framework of the legal system'. The Commissioner explained that it is 'a legal concept, a construct, assigned to most people of majority age enabling them to have rights and obligations, to make binding decisions and have them respected. As such, it facilitates personal freedom.' Legal capacity enables such other rights as taking up a job and getting married, and enables the refusal of unwanted medical treatment.[334] Whereas the essence of the capacity to be a person before the law is linked to the recognition of legal personality, the two variants of the capacity to act—capacity to incur contractual liability and capacity for tortious liability—do not necessarily follow from the recognition of legal personality.

In its General Comment on the equality of women and men, the Human Rights Committee wrote that the right to recognition as a person is of special importance for women, who often find it curtailed because of their gender or marital status. 'It implies that women may not be treated as objects to be given, together with the property of the deceased husband, to his family.'[335]

The International Convention on the Protection of All Persons from Enforced Disappearance defines an enforced disappearance as an act that places the victim outside the protection of the law.[336] The case law of the Human Rights Committee supports the view that enforced disappearances may amount to a violation of the right to recognition as a person before the law. The Committee has reasoned that

[332] *Aboufaied et al. v. Libya*, no. 1782/2008, Views, 21 March 2012, CCPR/C/104/D/1782/2008, Individual opinion of Committee member Mr. Walter Kälin (partly dissenting).

[333] General Comment No. 1 (2014), art. 12: Equal recognition before the law, CRPD/C/GC/1, para. 14.

[334] Who gets to decide? Right to legal capacity for persons with intellectual and psychosocial disabilities, CommDH/IssuePaper(2012)2, p. 7.

[335] General Comment 28, Equality of rights between men and women (art. 3), CCPR/C/21/Rev.1/Add.10, para. 16.

[336] (2010) 2716 UNTS 3, art. 2. Also Declaration on the Protection of All Persons from Enforced Disappearance, A/RES/47/133, art. 1(2); Inter-American Convention on the Forced Disappearance of Persons, OASTS 60, art. II. Enforced disappearance is also discussed in the context of the prohibition of torture; see *supra*, pp. 137–138.

'disappeared persons are in practice deprived of their capacity to exercise entitlements under law, including all their other rights under the Covenant, and of access to any possible remedy as a direct consequence of the actions of the State, which must be interpreted as a refusal to recognise such victims as persons before the law'.[337]

Decisions of the Inter-American Court of Human Rights have recognised a collective dimension to the right to recognition set out in Article 3 of the American Convention on Human Rights, a text that is identical to Article 6 of the Universal Declaration of Human Rights. The Court found that Article 3 of the Convention was breached by Suriname because its domestic laws did not recognise the collective exercise of the juridical personality of the indigenous and tribal peoples, specifically the Kaliña and Lokono.[338] In another case, the Court said that 'the right that the State recognise their juridical personality is one of the special measures that should be granted to the indigenous and tribal groups in order to ensure that they may enjoy their territories according to their traditions. This is the natural consequence of the recognition of the right of the members of the indigenous and tribal groups to enjoy certain rights collectively.'[339]

The Human Rights Council has associated birth registration with the right to recognition as a person before the law.[340] Birth registration is closely linked to the exercise by children of other rights, including access to education, social services, and medical care. The obligation to register all children immediately after birth is set out in the International Covenant on Civil and Political Rights,[341] the Convention on the Rights of the Child,[342] the International Convention on the Rights of All Migrant Workers and Members of their Families,[343] and the regional conventions.[344] The fact that the Convention on the Rights of the Child has achieved virtually universal participation, without reservations to the requirement in Article 7 of birth registration[345] should be enough to ensure its customary status.

[337] *Kimouche et al. v. Algeria*, no. 1328/2004, Views, 10 July 2007, CCPR/C/90/D/1328/2004, para. 7.8; *Grioua et al. v. Algeria*, no. 1327/2004, Views, 10 July 2007, CCPR/C/90/D/1327/2004, para. 7.8.

[338] *Kaliña and Lokono Peoples v. Suriname* , Judgment (Merits, reparations, and costs), 25 November 2015, Series C, No. 309, para. 113.

[339] *Saramaka People v. Suriname*, Judgment (Preliminary objections, merits, reparations, and costs), 28 November 2007, Series C, No. 172, para. 172. *Moiwana Community v. Suriname*, Judgment (Preliminary Objections, Merits, Reparations, and Costs), 15 June 2005, Series C, No. 124, para. 86.5.

[340] Birth registration and the right of everyone to recognition everywhere as a person before the law, A/HRC/RES/22/7.

[341] International Covenant on Civil and Political Rights, (1976) 999 UNTS 171, art. 24.

[342] Convention on the Rights of the Child, (1990) 1571 UNTS 3, art. 7.

[343] International Convention on the Protection of the Rights of all Migrant Workers and Members of their Families, (2003) 2220 UNTS 3, art. 29.

[344] American Convention on Human Rights, (1978) 1144 UNTS 123; African Charter on Human and Peoples' Rights, (1986) 1520 UNTS 271; Arab Charter on Human Rights.

[345] This is clear from the explanations provided to the Committee on the Rights of the Child from Luxembourg (CRC/C/41/Add.2, paras. 130–135), Malaysia (CRC/C/MYS/1, para. 82) and Saudi Arabia (CRC/C/61/Add.2, paras. 90–96).

The only exception to participation in the Convention on the Rights of the Child is the United States and it is bound by Article 24(2) of the Covenant.

Article 7 of the Convention on the Rights of the Child declares that '[t]he child shall have the right from birth to a name'. Article 7 also provides for acquisition of nationality by the child, and this part of the provision has provoked reservations.[346] The requirement of registration and the right to a name does not appear to be contemplated by these reservations. The right to a name is also recognised in several other international instruments, including the International Covenant on Civil and Political Rights.[347] Thus, essentially all countries are bound by treaty to ensure the right of every child to a name from birth, confirming its status as a customary norm.

According to the Inter-American Court of Human Rights, the right to a name, which is explicitly set out in Article 18 of the American Convention,[348] 'constitutes a basic and essential element of the identity of each individual'.[349] Name is important because it links an individual to the family. It is also germane to the identity of the individual within a community defined by nationality, ethnicity, and religion. The role of the name extends to the given name as well as to the family name, where names are composed of both elements.[350] The duty to ensure the child's right to a name is primarily directed at the parents, legal guardians, or other persons who are legally responsible for the child. Nevertheless, States have positive obligations to establish an appropriate legal framework.

* * *

Conclusions. Everyone has the right to recognition as a person before the law. Everyone has the right to a name. Birth registration is mandatory.

[346] Luxembourg, C.N.85.1994.TREATIES-1; Kuwait, C.N.252.1991.TREATIES-12; Malaysia, C.N.58.1995.TREATIES-1; Monaco, C.N.203.1993.TREATIES-6; United Arab Emirates, C.N.92.1997. TREATIES-1.

[347] International Covenant on Civil and Political Rights, (1976) 999 UNTS 171, art. 24(2). Also African Charter on the Rights and Welfare of the Child, art. 6(1); International Convention on the Protection of the Rights of all Migrant Workers and Members of their Families, (2003) 2220 UNTS 3, art. 29; Convention on the Rights of Persons with Disabilities, (2008) 2515 UNTS 3, art. 18(2). Although the European Convention on Human Rights does not provide explicitly for the right to a name, the European Court of Human Rights has said this is ensured by art. 8 of the Convention, on the right to private and family life: *Negrepontis-Giannisis v. Greece*, no. 56759/08, § 55, 3 May 2011; *Znamenskaya v. Russia*, no. 77785/01, § 23, 2 June 2005; *Cerva Osorio de Moscoso et al. v. Spain* (dec.), nos. 41127/98, 41503/98, 41717/98, and 45726/99, 28 October 1999; *Mentzen v. Latvia* (dec.), no. 71074/01, 7 December 2004.

[348] 'Every person has the right to a given name and to the surnames of his parents or that of one of them. The law shall regulate the manner in which this right shall be ensured for all, by the use of assumed names if necessary.'

[349] *Girls Yean and Bosico v. Dominican Republic*, Judgment (Preliminary objections, merits, reparations, and costs), 8 September 2005, Series C, No. 130, para. 182.

[350] *Guillot v. France*, 24 October 1996, §§ 21–22, *Reports of Judgments and Decisions* 1996-V.

5
Equality

Protection of religious minorities appears in treaties dating back centuries. As early as 1648, at the dawn of public international law as we know it, the Treaty of Westphalia guaranteed rights to German Protestants. Article XIV of the Treaty of Utrecht of 1713 ceded territory in North America from France to Britain, but at the same time ensured that French-speaking Catholics who wished to remain were entitled 'to enjoy the free exercise of their religion, according to the usage of the church of Rome, as far as the laws of Great Britain do allow the same'. Similar provisions appeared in many other treaties of the time.[1] Texts prohibiting discrimination based upon religion, race, and ethnicity also began to appear in constitutions and other domestic legislation, beginning with Article 1 of the *Déclaration des droits de l'homme et du citoyen*, adopted in the early days of the French Revolution: 'Men are born and remain free and equal in respect of rights.' The French Revolution launched the process of Jewish emancipation and the abolition of slavery. Equality came somewhat later to the United States. The Fourteenth Amendment to the Constitution, which dates to 1868 and the inchoate attempts to end the vestiges of slavery, affirmed 'the equal protection of the laws'. Two years later, the Fifteenth Amendment secured the right to vote without discrimination 'on account of race, color, or previous condition of servitude'.

The right to equality and the prohibition of discrimination emerged as an important theme in international law following the First World War. The treaty by which the Allied and Associated Powers recognised an independent Poland imposed human rights standards on the new State directed mainly at the protection of minorities. Poland undertook 'to assure full and complete protection of life and liberty to all inhabitants of Poland without distinction of birth, nationality, language, race or religion'. It provided that '[a]ll inhabitants of Poland shall be entitled to the free exercise, whether public or private, of any creed, religion or belief, whose practices are not inconsistent with public order or public morals'.[2] The language should sound familiar to modern-day human rights practitioners. The text is the ancestor of provisions in the Universal Declaration of Human Rights and the treaties that it inspired.

[1] Natan Lerner, *Group Rights and Discrimination in International Law*, Dordrecht/Boston/London: Martinus Nijhoff, 1991, pp. 7–22.

[2] Treaty between the Principal Allied and Associated Powers and Poland, (1919) 112 BSP 232.

The Customary International Law of Human Rights. William A. Schabas, Oxford University Press.
 DOI: 10.1093/oso/9780192845696.003.0006

Explaining the rationale for the inclusion of such clauses in the treaty recognising the State of Poland, French Prime Minister Georges Clemenceau wrote to the Polish President, Jan Paderewski. Clemenceau said this was 'no fresh departure', and that '[i]t has for long been the established procedure of the public law of Europe that when a state is created, or even when large accessions of territory are made to an established state, the joint and formal recognition by the great Powers should be accompanied by the requirement that such state should, in the form of a binding international convention, undertake to comply with certain principles of government'. He described the text as guaranteeing 'those elementary rights, which are, as a matter of fact, secured in every civilised State'.[3] Clemenceau pointed to nineteenth-century treaties containing clauses dealing with religious freedom. But the texts adopted in 1919 went much further, protecting 'life and liberty' and prohibiting discrimination based upon birth, nationality, language, and race, as well as religion. The treaty also addressed the rights of Jews to public funding of parochial schools and respect for the Jewish Sabbath. Similar provisions appeared in the other minorities treaties and unilateral declarations adopted during the 1920s.

Only weeks before Clemenceau's letter to Paderewski, Japan failed in an attempt to add a reference to 'the principle of equality of nations and just treatment of their nationals' in the preamble of the Covenant of the League of Nations.[4] The refusal of the 'Great Powers' to include a non-discrimination clause in the Covenant of the League of Nations provides confirmation that if new legal norms were emerging this was not out of any sense that they existed already as a matter of custom. Woodrow Wilson and his European Allies insisted that others respect the right to equality but they declined imposing the same obligation upon themselves.

One of the earliest efforts at codification of international human rights norms, the 1929 Declaration of the Institut de Droit International, proclaimed the full and entire protection of the 'equal right of every individual to life, liberty and property ... without distinction as to nationality, sex, race, language, or religion'.[5] The preamble of the 1929 Declaration cited the Fourteenth Amendment to the American Constitution and an allegedly expansive interpretation it had been given by the United States Supreme Court. It was an odd reference given the reactionary approach of the Court's case law that prevailed at the time.[6] The draft

[3] Draft of the Covering Letter to be Addressed to M. Paderewski in Transmitting to Him the Treaty to be Signed by Poland under art. 93 of the Treaty of Peace with Germany, FRUS VI, p. 629, (1919) 13 *American Journal of International Law* (supplement) 416.

[4] David Hunter Miller, *The Drafting of the Covenant*, Vol. I, New York: G.P. Putnam, 1928, pp. 461–466. See also Naoko Shimazu, *Japan, Race and Equality: The Racial Equality Proposal of 1919*, London: Routledge, 2009; Paul Gordon Lauren, *The Evolution of Human Rights, Visions Seen*, Philadelphia: University of Pennsylvania, 1998, pp. 268–275; Margaret McMillan, *Paris 1919, Six Months That Changed the World*, New York: Random House, 2001, pp. 302–321.

[5] Institut de Droit International, 'Declaration of the International Rights of Man', (1941) *35 American Journal of International Law* 663.

[6] *Plessy v. Ferguson*, 163 US 537 (1896). *Plessy* was reaffirmed by the Court in 1927, in *Lum v. Rice*, 275 US 78 (1927), only two years before the Institut adopted its Declaration.

Declaration adopted by the London International Assembly in 1943 contained no right to equality although it recognised protection against deprivation of property 'in particular because of the nationality, race, religion or political condition of the holder'.[7] Hersch Lauterpacht's 1945 draft affirmed that '[a]ll nationals of the State shall enjoy full equality before the law and equal treatment in all respects by the authorities of the State. In particular, there shall be no discrimination on account of religion, race, colour, language, or political creed.'[8]

The Charter of the United Nations, adopted in June 1945, contains provisions recognising the right to equality. In the first recital of the preamble to the Charter, the 'Peoples of the United Nations ... reaffirm faith ... in the equal rights of men and women'. The Purposes of the United Nations set out in Article 1 of the Charter include 'promoting and encouraging respect for human rights and for fundamental freedoms for all without distinction as to race, sex, language, or religion'. Over the decades, equality and non-discrimination have remained central themes in the protection of fundamental human rights.

A. Equality and non-discrimination

The Universal Declaration of Human Rights enlarges the categories listed in the Charter of the United Nations ('race, sex, language, or religion') so as to protect equality and prohibit discrimination based upon grounds 'such as race, colour, sex, language, religion, political or other opinion, national or social origin, property, birth or other status'.[9] To prepare for the drafting of the Universal Declaration, in early 1947 the Secretariat of the Commission for Human Rights prepared a compilation of grounds of discrimination found in various draft declarations. In addition to those that were finally incorporated into Article 2 of the Declaration were 'professed belief', 'citizenship', 'civil status', 'wealth', 'culture', and 'other reasons'.[10] The American Declaration of the Rights and Duties of Man, adopted seven months before the Universal Declaration, states that '[a]ll persons are equal before the law and have the rights and duties established in this Declaration, without distinction as to race, sex, language, creed or any other factor'.[11]

[7] London International Assembly, Report of the Third Commission (Legal Commission) on individual rights, TNA LNU 6/7, art. III.

[8] Hersch Lauterpacht, *An International Bill of the Rights of Man*, New York: Columbia University Press, 1945, p. 71.

[9] Universal Declaration of Human Rights, A/RES/217 (III), art. 2.

[10] List of Types of Rights Contained in Drafts of Proposed International Bills of Rights, A/CN.4/W.18.

[11] American Declaration on the Rights and Duties of Man, Final Act of the Ninth International Conference of American States, Res. XXX, art. II.

The two International Covenants follow the formulation of the Universal Declaration in their non-discrimination provisions.[12] The International Covenant on Civil and Political Rights departs from the enumeration somewhat in its treatment of derogation, which proscribes discrimination 'on the ground of race, colour, sex, language, religion or social origin',[13] and the text dealing with protection of children ('race, colour, sex, language, religion, national or social origin, property or birth').[14] There is some variation in the specialised instruments, however. The text of the Universal Declaration is reprised in the preamble of the Convention on the Rights of the Child.[15] But in a substantive provision on non-discrimination, the Convention on the Rights of the Child makes small modifications, inserting 'ethnic' between 'national or social origin', and adding 'disability' after 'property'.[16] The Convention on the Rights of Migrant Workers and Members of their Families includes 'or conviction' after religion, 'ethnic' between 'national or social origin', 'age' and 'economic position' following 'nationality', and 'marital status' after 'property'.[17] The Convention on the Rights of Persons with Disabilities, in the preamble, introduces 'ethnic, indigenous' to 'national or social origin' and 'age' after 'birth'.[18]

Texts on equality and non-discrimination in the regional human rights treaties show the influence of the list in the Universal Declaration, although many add one or more categories. The European Convention on Human Rights changes the order, putting 'sex' ahead of race and adding 'association with a national minority'.[19] The American Convention on Human Rights replaces 'property' with 'economic status' and 'other status' with 'any other social condition'.[20] The African Charter includes 'ethnic group', replaces 'or' with 'and' between national and social origin, and substitutes 'fortune' for 'property'.[21] The Arab Charter on Human Rights substitutes 'religious belief' for 'religion', removes 'political or other' before 'opinion', replaces 'property' with 'wealth' and changes 'other status' for 'physical or mental disability'.[22] The Charter of Fundamental Rights of the European Union is more innovative, referring to 'sex, race, colour, ethnic or social origin, genetic features, language, religion or belief, political or any other opinion, membership of a national minority, property, birth, disability, age or sexual orientation'.[23] Probably

[12] International Covenant on Civil and Political Rights, (1976) 999 UNTS 171, arts. 2(1) and 26; International Covenant on Economic, Social and Cultural Rights, (1976) 993 UNTS 3, art. 2(2).
[13] International Covenant on Civil and Political Rights, (1976) 999 UNTS 171, art. 4(1).
[14] Ibid., art. 44(1).
[15] Convention on the Rights of the Child, (1990) 1571 UNTS 3, PP 3.
[16] Ibid., art. 2.
[17] International Convention on the Protection of the Rights of all Migrant Workers and Members of their Families, (2003) 2220 UNTS 3, art. 1(1).
[18] Convention on the Rights of Persons with Disabilities, (2008) 2515 UNTS 3, PP (p).
[19] European Convention on Human Rights, (1953) 213 UNTS 221, art. 14.
[20] American Convention on Human Rights, (1978) 1144 UNTS 123, art. 1(1).
[21] African Charter on Human and Peoples' Rights, (1986) 1520 UNTS 271, art. 2.
[22] Arab Charter on Human Rights, art. 3(a).
[23] Charter of Fundamental Rights of the European Union, OJ C 326/391, art. 21(1).

the longest list is in the Istanbul Convention of the Council of Europe, adopted in 2011: 'The implementation of the provisions of this Convention by the Parties, in particular measures to protect the rights of victims, shall be secured without discrimination on any ground such as sex, gender, race, colour, language, religion, political or other opinion, national or social origin, association with a national minority, property, birth, sexual orientation, gender identity, age, state of health, disability, marital status, migrant or refugee status, or other status.'[24]

Clearly, the list of grounds in Article 2 of the Universal Declaration enjoys consensus. There is a core of grounds on which there seems to be universal agreement. Reformulating the word 'property' as 'fortune' or 'wealth' does not operate a substantive change of any significance. The recent addition of 'ethnic' to the list in some versions is more of a 'belt and braces' phenomenon than genuine gap-filling. The meaning of 'ethnic' has changed over time. In 1948, when the Universal Declaration of Human Rights was adopted, people regularly spoke of 'racial groups' in the sense that today is ascribed to 'ethnic groups'. The memorable final phrase of James Joyce's *A Portrait of the Artist as a Young Man* refers to the 'conscience of my race' rather than the 'conscience of my ethnic group'. Today, nobody would describe the Irish as a 'race'. The very notion of 'race' is itself a controversial topic, although 'racial discrimination' is understood to include not only 'colour' but also 'ethnicity'[25] and, arguably, 'caste'.[26] Use of the term race does not imply the acceptance of theories that attempt to determine the existence of separate human races.[27] The only categories to be added in some of the human rights treaties that quite definitely do not figure in the Universal Declaration under another label are 'disability', 'age' and 'sexual orientation'.

The first judicial argument favouring recognition of equality and non-discrimination as a norm of customary law is found in Judge Tanaka's dissent in the South-West Africa case. Kōtarō Tanaka said he considered that 'the norm of non-discrimination or non-separation on the basis of race has become a rule of customary international law', citing in support the Charter of the United Nations, resolutions of the General Assembly condemning apartheid, agreements respecting the trust territories and, above all, the Universal Declaration of Human Rights.[28] In, the International *Barcelona Traction*, the International Court of Justice

[24] Council of Europe Convention on preventing and combating violence against women and domestic violence, CETS 210, art. 4(3).

[25] International Convention on the Elimination of All Forms of Racial Discrimination, (1976) 1015 UNTS 243, art. 1: 'In this Convention, the term "racial discrimination" shall mean any distinction, exclusion, restriction or preference based on race, colour, descent, or national or ethnic origin ...'.

[26] Bangladesh, Concluding observations, CCPR/C/BGD/CO/1, para. 11; Nepal, Concluding observations, CCPR/C/SWZ/CO/1, para. 9; India, Concluding observations, CCPR/C/79/Add.81, paras. 8, 10, 15.

[27] Outcome Document of the Durban Review Conference, A/C.3/64/L.55, para. 6; General Comment 20, Non-discrimination in economic, social and cultural rights, E/C.12/GC/20, para. 19.

[28] *South West Africa, Second Phase, Judgment, ICJ Reports 1966*, p. 6, pp. 250–322, Dissenting opinion of Judge Tanaka, p. 293.

spoke of 'the principles and rules concerning the basic rights of the human person, including protection from . . . racial discrimination'.[29]

The 1987 Restatement of the American Law Institute listed 'systematic racial discrimination' as a customary norm. The word 'systematic' means that '[o]ccasional official practices of racial discrimination would not violate this section'.[30] The Restatement did not include discrimination based upon gender or religion. The accompanying Comment explained that '[g]ender-based discrimination is still practised in many states in varying degrees, but freedom from gender discrimination as state policy, in many matters, may already be a principle of customary international law'.[31] With respect to 'systematic religious discrimination', the Comment noted that '[t]here is as yet no convention on the elimination of religious discrimination, and there has been no concerted attack against discrimination comparable to that on apartheid, but there is a strong case that systematic discrimination on grounds of religion as a matter of state policy is also a violation of customary law'.[32] Many years later, Bertram Ramcharan wrote that the list of the American Law Institute might be updated with the addition of 'systematic general discrimination'.[33]

The Human Rights Committee did not include equality and non-discrimination in the list of customary norms it proposed in General Comment 24, adopted in 1994.[34] However, it said that a reservation to the obligation to ensure rights under the Covenant without discrimination, formulated in Article 2(1), would be contrary to its object and purpose.[35] In General Comment 29, it observed that Article 26 and other non-discrimination provisions of the Covenant were not included in Article 4(2) and were therefore subject to derogation although it added that 'there are elements or dimensions of the right to non-discrimination that cannot be derogated from in any circumstances'.[36]

The Inter-American Court of Human Rights has described the principles of equality and non-discrimination as peremptory norms of international law:

> Accordingly, this Court considers that the principle of equality before the law, equal protection before the law and non-discrimination belongs to *jus cogens*,

[29] *Barcelona Traction, Light and Power Company, Limited, Judgment, ICJ Reports 1970*, p. 3, para. 34.

[30] Restatement (Third) of the Foreign Relations Law of the United States, St. Paul, MN: American Law Institute, 1987, para. 702, Comment, para. i.

[31] Ibid., para. l.

[32] Ibid., para. j. See also ibid., Reporter's Notes, para. 8.

[33] Bertrand G. Ramcharan, 'The Law-making Process: From Declaration to Treaty to Custom to Prevention', in Dinah Shelton, ed., *The Oxford Handbook of International Human Rights Law*, Oxford: Oxford University Press, 2013, pp. 499–526, at p. 509.

[34] General Comment 24, Issues Relating to Reservations Made upon Ratification or Accession to the Covenant or the Optional Protocols thereto, or in Relation to Declarations under Article 41 of the Covenant, CCPR/C/21/Rev.1/Add.6, para. 8.

[35] Ibid., para. 9.

[36] General Comment 29, Article 4: Derogations during a State of Emergency, CCPR/C/21/Rev.1/Add.11, para. 8.

> because the whole legal structure of national and international public order rests on it and it is a fundamental principle that permeates all laws. Nowadays, no legal act that is in conflict with this fundamental principle is acceptable, and discriminatory treatment of any person, owing to gender, race, color, language, religion or belief, political or other opinion, national, ethnic or social origin, nationality, age, economic situation, property, civil status, birth or any other status is unacceptable. This principle (equality and non-discrimination) forms part of general international law. At the existing stage of the development of international law, the fundamental principle of equality and non-discrimination has entered the realm of *jus cogens*.[37]

Commenting on the Court's advisory opinion, Judge Cançado Trindade of the International Court of Justice said that 'States can no longer subordinate or condition the observance of the principle of equality before the law and non-discrimination to the objectives of their migratory or other policies... Without such principles, there is ultimately no legal order at all.'[38] Prohibition of discrimination has 'crystallised into a norm of *jus cogens*', wrote Judge Tsotsoria of the European Court of Human Rights.[39]

The International Law Commission, in the draft list of *jus cogens* norms that it adopted at its 2019 session, declined to go as far. Not only did it confine itself to 'racial discrimination' but it linked this to apartheid.[40] One of the members of the Commission, Shinya Murase, warned that by linking racial discrimination with apartheid 'people might mistakenly understand the term "racial discrimination"

[37] *Juridical Condition and Rights of Undocumented Migrants*, Advisory Opinion OC-18/03, 17 September 2003, Series A, No. 17, para. 101. Also *Expelled Dominicans and Haitians v. Dominican Republic*, Judgment (Preliminary objections, merits, reparations, and costs), 28 August 2014, Series C, No. 282, para. 264; *Article 55 of the American Convention on Human Rights*, Advisory Opinion OC-20/09, 29 September 2009, Series A, No. 20, para. 54; *Nadege Dorzema et al. v. Dominican Republic*, Judgment (Merits, reparations, and costs), 24 October 2012, Series C, No. 282, para. 225; *Atala Riffo and daughters v. Chile*, Judgment (Merits, reparations, and costs), 24 February 2012, Series C, No. 239, para. 79; *Indigenous Community Xákmok Kásek v. Paraguay*, Judgment (Merits, reparations, and costs), 24 August 2010, Series C, No. 214, para. 269; *Yatama v. Nicaragua*, Judgment (Preliminary objections, merits, reparations, and costs), 23 June 2005, Series C, No. 127, para. 184; *Servellón-García et al. v. Honduras*, Judgment (Merits, reparations, and costs), 21 September 2006, Series C, No. 152, para. 94; *Norín Catrimán et al. (Leaders, Members and Activist of the Mapuche Indigenous People) v. Chile*, Judgment (Merits, reparations, and costs), 29 May 2014, Series C, No. 279, para. 197; *Veliz Franco et al. v. Guatemala*, Judgment (Preliminary objections, merits, reparations, and costs), 19 May 2014, Series C, No. 277, para. 205.

[38] *Application of the International Convention on the Elimination of All Forms of Racial Discrimination (Qatar v. United Arab Emirates), Provisional Measures, Order of 23 July 2018, ICJ Reports 2018*, p. 406, Separate Opinion of Judge Cançado Trindade, paras. 19–20. Also *Jurisdictional Immunities of the State (Germany v. Italy), Counter-Claim, Order of 6 July 2010, ICJ Reports 2010*, Dissenting opinion of Judge Cançado Trindade.

[39] *Georgia v. Russia (I)* [GC], no. 13255/07, 3 July 2014, Partially dissenting opinion of Judge Tsotsoria.

[40] Report of the International Law Commission, Seventy-first session (29 April–7 June and 8 July–9 August 2019), A/74/10, p. 206. Also Fourth report on peremptory norms of general international law (*jus cogens*) by Dire Tladi, Special Rapporteur, A/CN.4/727, para. 101.

to be a separate and independent notion and suggest including other vulnerable groups, such as women, children, older persons and persons with disabilities'.[41] Hussein Hassouna observed that 'there was some support for the peremptory status of the principle of non-discrimination, but there seemed to be no universal recognition regarding the prohibition of discrimination in general, including gender discrimination'.[42] On the other hand, Charles Jalloh believed it 'very troubling' that the Commission did not include gender discrimination.[43] Jalloh considered that *jus cogens* norms included the prohibition of gender discrimination and even the right to same-sex marriage.[44]

Apartheid is described as practices of racial segregation and discrimination, similar to those in Southern Africa during the twentieth century, for the purpose of establishing and maintaining domination by one racial group of persons over any other racial group of persons and systematically oppressing them. It may consist of measures intended to prevent groups based upon race from participation in the political, social, economic, and cultural life of a country. It is also characterised by the creation of separate reserves and ghettos for the members of a racial group and the prohibition of mixed marriages based upon race.[45] Apartheid is a crime against humanity punishable under international law.[46] The prohibition of the crime of apartheid is considered a norm of *jus cogens*.[47]

International law acknowledges that not all distinctions that are predicated on prohibited grounds constitute prohibited forms of discrimination. For example, legislation usually restricts voting rights to citizens for a country's central government or its Head of State, thereby imposing a distinction based upon nationality. It also sets a minimum voting age, something that does not seem questionable. The general rule is that distinctions applied to protected categories are not prohibited to the extent that they are justified by objective and reasonable criteria. Denying the right to vote in national elections to tourists or to small children surely passes this test. While it may be relatively easy to identify acceptable distinctions grounded in nationality or age, it is difficult to imagine exceptions in the case of categories such as race and ethnicity or gender. In assessing reasonableness, specific circumstances need to be taken into account including the cultural and religious background, social traditions, and customs, bearing in mind how quickly values and moral standards evolve. The Committee on Economic, Social and Cultural Rights

[41] A/CN.4/SR.3459, p. 15.
[42] A/CN.4/SR.3460, p. 16.
[43] A/CN.4/SR.3461, p. 10.
[44] Ibid.
[45] International Convention on the Suppression and Punishment of the Crime of Apartheid, (1976) 1015 UNTS 243, art. II.
[46] Rome Statute of the International Criminal Court, (2002) 2187 UNTS 689, art. 7(1)(j) and (2)(h).
[47] Report of the International Law Commission, Seventy-first session (29 April–7 June and 8 July–9 August 2019), A/74/10, p. 203.

has observed how the nature of discrimination 'varies according to context and evolves over time'.[48]

States are required not only to ensure that they do not violate the right to equality and do not discriminate in their own actions but also must enact legislation and take measures to protect those within their jurisdiction from such violations by others. In the treaties, these concepts are described as 'equality before the law' and 'equal protection of the law'. Early efforts at identification of customary norms, such as the Restatement of the American Law Institute, specified that '[a] state violates international law if, as a matter of state policy, it practices, encourages or condones ... systematic racial discrimination'.[49] This only hints at a dimension of the protection against racial discrimination that is today more robust, in that States must take positive measures, through legislation and government activity, to prevent and prohibit manifestations of racism as well as other forms of discrimination. Legislation and acts that may appear on their face to be neutral in nature may in fact have the clear effect of discriminating based upon prohibited grounds. Any determination about discrimination requires a comparison with persons who are 'similarly situated'.

1. Protected categories

There is no hierarchy among the categories of prohibited discrimination set out in Article 2 of the Universal Declaration of Human Rights. Nevertheless, the attention given to racial discrimination by bodies like the International Law Commission suggests its special significance. The centrality of the condemnation of racial discrimination within modern international human rights law is confirmed by specialised instruments such as the Convention on the Prevention and Punishment of the Crime of Genocide,[50] the International Convention on the Elimination of All Forms of Racial Discrimination,[51] and the International Convention on the Prevention and Suppression of the Crime of Apartheid.[52] The United Kingdom House of Lords held that a 'moral norm' prohibiting racial discrimination, 'has ripened into a rule of customary international law. It is binding on all states'.[53]

[48] General Comment 20, Non-discrimination in economic, social and cultural rights, E/C.12/GC/20, para. 27.

[49] Restatement (Third) of the Foreign Relations Law of the United States, St. Paul, MN: American Law Institute, 1987, para. 702.

[50] Convention on the Prevention and Punishment of the Crime of Genocide, (1951) 78 UNTS 277.

[51] International Convention on the Elimination of All Forms of Racial Discrimination, (1969) 660 UNTS 195.

[52] International Convention on the Suppression and Punishment of the Crime of Apartheid, (1976) 1015 UNTS 243.

[53] *R (European Roma Rights Centre) v. Immigration Officer at Prague Airport*, [2005] 2 AC 1, par. 46.

Specialised treaties dealing with discrimination on the basis of gender and disability also point to certain priorities. The European Court of Human Rights has spoken of 'suspect grounds',[54] proposing sex, sexual orientation, ethnic origin, and nationality as examples.[55] Other grounds don't necessarily make the grade. In the 1960s, it was intended that the adoption of the International Convention on the Prevention of All Forms of Racial Discrimination be followed by a similar instrument dealing with religion. A draft prepared by the Commission on Human Rights was transmitted to the General Assembly but it failed to achieve sufficient support.[56] Clearly, it is more difficult to reach consensus about the prohibition of discrimination based upon religion than race.

Discrimination based upon religion overlaps with the protection of freedom of religion as a fundamental right. The identification of individuals based upon religion may often have little to do with their practices and beliefs and amount, in practice, to discrimination founded upon ethnicity, race, or nationality. According to the Committee on Economic, Social and Cultural Rights, in its General Comment on discrimination, 'this prohibited ground of discrimination covers the profession of religion or belief of one's choice (including the non-profession of any religion or belief), that may be publicly or privately manifested in worship, observance, practice and teaching'.[57]

'Sex' or 'gender' is a suspect ground for which it is difficult to imagine distinctions that are based on reasonable and objective criteria. Originally, the principle was addressed to women's equality, and much attention was focussed on political rights—universal suffrage—as well as unequal treatment compared to men during marriage and upon its dissolution. Nevertheless, the Universal Declaration of Human Rights also recognised the rule of 'equal pay for work of equal value'.[58] The equal pay norm is reaffirmed in the International Covenant on Economic, Social and Cultural Rights[59] as well as the Convention on the Elimination of All Forms of Discrimination against Women.[60] Canada, Ireland, and Mauritius all formulated

[54] *Clift v. the United Kingdom*, no. 7205/07, § 72, 13 July 2010.

[55] *Eweida et al. v. the United Kingdom*, no. 48420/10, § 71, ECHR 2013 (extracts). See also *C et al. v. Australia*, no. 2216/2012, Views, 28 March 2017, CCPR/C/119/D/2216/2012, Individual opinion of Committee member Sarah Cleveland (concurring), para. 8, citing *X et al. v. Austria* [GC], no. 19010/07, § 99, ECHR 2013.

[56] Draft Declaration on the Elimination of all Forms of Religious Intolerance and draft International Convention on the Elimination of all Forms of Religious Intolerance, A/RES/2020 (XX); Elimination of all forms of racial intolerance, A/RES/2295 (XXII). For the draft articles prepared by the Commission, see: Commission on Human Rights, Report on the Twenty-Third Session, 20 February–23 March 1967, E/4322, E/CN.4/940, paras. 26–134.

[57] General Comment 20, Non-discrimination in economic, social and cultural rights, E/C.12/GC/20, para. 22.

[58] Universal Declaration of Human Rights, A/RES/217 (III), art. 23(2).

[59] International Covenant on Economic, Social and Cultural Rights, (1976) 993 UNTS 3, art. 7(1)(a)(i).

[60] Convention on the Elimination of All Forms of Discrimination against Women, (1981) 1249 UNTS 13, art. 11(1)(d).

reservations to the equal pay provisions of the Women's Convention[61] but not to the corresponding recognition in the International Covenant. Singapore has a reservation to the Women's Convention provision[62] but it is also a party to International Labour Organisation Convention 100 on Equal Remuneration where the norm is enshrined.[63] Micronesia's reservation to the Women's Convention stated it was 'not at present in a position' to apply Article 11(1)(d).[64] In the Universal Periodic Review, Micronesia supported a recommendation that it 'promote equal remuneration in the workplace'.[65] Tonga, which is a party to none of the relevant treaties, expressed support for equal pay for equal work in its report to the Human Rights Council.[66] The only other States that apparently have no treaty obligation to ensure equal pay for equal work are the Holy See, Niue, and Palau, with a total population of about 20,000. In their reports to the Human Rights Council, many States make claims that they are implementing the principle of equal pay, thereby confirming their recognition of the norm.[67] Other States indicate their attachment to the norm in questions during the Universal Periodic Review process.[68]

It has been barely a century since women in developed countries obtained the right to vote. Issues of women's equality have evolved quickly and continue to do so. Often actual conduct and practice lag well behind legal standards, as the example of violence against women demonstrates. While abortion remains a controversial issue about which it is difficult to find enough consensus to be able to speak confidently of customary norms, it seems unarguable that the applicable law must be informed by the right to equality. Criminalisation of abortion may subject women to 'a gender-based stereotype of the reproductive role of women primarily

[61] Canada, C.N.385.1981.TREATIES-17, withdrawn, C.N.202.1992.TREATIES-5; Ireland, C.N.360.1985.TREATIES-16; Mauritius, C.N.166.1984.TREATIES-7, withdrawn, C.N.176.1998.TREATIES-5.

[62] C.N.358.1995.TREATIES-5.

[63] Convention 100 on Equal Remuneration, (1953) 165 UNTS 303, art. 2.

[64] C.N.904.2004.TREATIES-10.

[65] Micronesia, Report of the Working Group, A/HRC/16/16, para. 61.51 and Views on conclusions, A/HRC/16/16/Add.1, p. 6.

[66] Tonga, National report, A/HRC/WG.6/15/TON/1, para. 129.

[67] Andorra, National report, A/HRC/WG.6/9/AND/1, para. 64 and National report, A/HRC/WG.6/22/AND/1, paras. 85–89; Angola, National report, A/HRC/WG.6/20/AGO/1, para. 66; Cameroon, Report of the Working Group, A/HRC/24/15, para. 89; Eritrea, National report, A/HRC/WG.6/18/ERI/1, para. 54; Ethiopia, National report, A/HRC/WG.6/33/ETH/1, para. 118; Equatorial Guinea, National report, A/HRC/WG.6/19/GNQ/1, para. 28; Jamaica, Report of the Working Group, A/HRC/16/14, para. 97; Laos, National report, A/HRC/WG.6/8/LAO/1, para. 26; Qatar, National report, A/HRC/WG.6/19/QAT/1, para. 53; St Kitts and Nevis, Report of the Working Group, A/HRC/17/12, para. 67; South Sudan, National report, A/HRC/WG.6/26/SSD/1, para. 51; Sudan, National report, A/HRC/WG.6/11/SDN/1, paras. 57, 69 and Report of the Working Group, A/HRC/18/16, para. 48; Syria, A/HRC/WG.6/12/SYR/1, para. 67; United Arab Emirates, National report, A/HRC/WG.6/3/ARE/1, pp. 12, 17; United States of America, National report, A/HRC/WG.6/22/USA/1, para. 75 and National report, A/HRC/WG.6/9/USA/1, para. 37.

[68] Argentina, Report of the Working Group, A/HRC/16/5, para. 63; Bolivia, Report of the Working Group, A/HRC/25/5, para. 186.92; Ghana, Report of the Working Group, A/HRC/16/4, paras. 81 and 105.31; Netherlands, Report of the Working Group, A/HRC/23/3, para. 120.59; Norway, Report of the Working Group, A/HRC/16/5, para. 84.2.

as mothers', treating them as reproductive instruments and thereby subjecting them to discrimination.[69] The Human Rights Committee has noted that 'discrimination against women is often intertwined with discrimination on other grounds such as race, colour, language, religion, political or other opinion, national or social origin, property, birth or other status'.[70]

The Convention on the Rights of Persons with Disabilities, adopted in 2006, refers to 'sex' in a preambular paragraph modelled on Article 2 of the Universal Declaration of Human Rights but uses 'gender' in its substantive provisions.[71] The International Convention for the Protection of All Persons from Enforced Disappearance, adopted in 2007, also uses both words in different contexts.[72] These recent treaties appear to regard that the two terms appear as synonyms. The Universal Periodic Review reports and related documents confirm that most States use sex and gender interchangeably. But the term 'gender' does more than simply act as a replacement for 'sex'. For example, the Istanbul Convention on violence against women uses both terms in the same enumeration ('... such as sex, gender, race, colour, ...'),[73] implying that the meanings of 'sex' and 'gender' may not be the same. The Convention defines gender as 'the socially constructed roles, behaviours, activities and attributes that a given society considers appropriate for women and men'.[74] Gender may be taken to encompass issues of gender identity and sexual orientation, often designated using variations on the acronym LGBT, for Lesbian-gay-bisexual-transgender.

The earliest codified human rights provisions included 'language' as a prohibited ground of discrimination. Discrimination on this ground generally concerns minority languages and is often addressed in the context of the rights of national or ethnic minorities. Denial of the use of the mother tongue of a linguistic minority in its dealings with the public administration, the justice system, and education may amount to discrimination based upon language.[75]

[69] *Mellet v. Ireland*, no. 2324/2013, Views, 6 September 2016, CCPR/C/116/D/2324/2013, para. 7.11. See also *Whelan v. Ireland*, no. 2425/2014, Views, 12 June 2017, CCPR/C/119/D/2425/2014, para. 7.12; Concluding observations, Ireland, CCPR/C/IRL/CO/4, para. 9.

[70] General Comment 28, Equality of rights between men and women (art. 3), CCPR/C/21/Rev.1/Add.10, para. 30.

[71] Convention on the Rights of Persons with Disabilities, (2008) 2515 UNTS 3, arts. 16, 25.

[72] International Convention for the Protection of All Persons from Enforced Disappearance, (2010) 2716 UNTS 3, arts. 13(7), 26(1).

[73] Council of Europe Convention on preventing and combating violence against women and domestic violence, CETS 210, art. 4(3).

[74] Ibid., art. 3(c). Note also the definition in the Rome Statute of the International Criminal Court, (2002) 2187 UNTS 689, art. 7(3): 'For the purpose of this Statute, it is understood that the term "gender" refers to the two sexes, male and female, within the context of society. The term "gender" does not indicate any meaning different from the above.' See also the 'gender' issue at the Fourth World Conference on Women: Statement by the President of the Conference on the Commonly Understood Meaning of the Term 'Gender', A/CONF.177/20/Rev.1, Annex IV.

[75] *Diergaardt et al. v. Namibia*, no. 760/1997, Views, 25 July 2000, CCPR/C/69/D/760/1996, para. 10.10.

The Committee on Economic, Social and Cultural Rights has described the ground of political or other opinion as including 'both holding and not-holding, as well as expression of views or membership within opinion-based associations, trade unions or political parties'.[76]

Discrimination based upon 'national origin' may also be dealt with under race and colour. Confirmation of this relationship can be found in the preamble of the International Convention on the Suppression and Punishment of the Crime of Apartheid, which speaks of 'distinction of any kind, such as race, colour or national origin'.[77] There is a significant difference between 'national origin' and 'nationality', the latter term referring to citizenship. Article 1(1) of the International Convention on the Elimination of All Forms of Racial Discrimination confirms that racial discrimination applies to distinctions based upon 'national or ethnic origin' whereas Article 1(2) declares that the Convention 'shall not apply to distinctions, exclusions, restrictions or preferences made by a State Party to this Convention between citizens and non-citizens'. In its General Comment on the status of aliens under the International Covenant on Civil and Political Rights, the Human Rights Committee emphasised that, non-citizens are entitled to equal protection by the law and equality before the law.[78] Distinctions between citizens and non-citizens must be based on reasonable and objective criteria. The Committee on Economic, Social and Cultural Rights has given as an example the right of all children within a State, even those with undocumented status, to receive education, to have adequate food, and to access affordable health care.[79] Moreover, it seems obvious that distinctions based upon citizenship may produce discriminatory effects upon individuals based on race, ethnicity, and national origin, regardless of whether this was the intent. Furthermore, it would be unacceptable for States Parties to discriminate against persons based upon race, ethnicity, or national origin merely by labelling the distinction one based upon citizenship or nationality.

'Social origin', according to the Committee on Economic, Social and Cultural Rights, 'refers to a person's inherited social status'. It overlaps with the grounds of 'property' and 'birth'.[80] The International Labour Organisation Committee of Experts has defined 'social origin' as situations involving 'an individual's membership of a class, socio-occupational category or caste', without apparently any notion that this is inherited.[81]

[76] Ibid., para. 23.

[77] International Convention on the Suppression and Punishment of the Crime of Apartheid, (1976) 1015 UNTS 244, PP 1.

[78] General Comment 15, The position of aliens under the Covenant, A/41/40, paras. 2, 7, 9.

[79] General Comment 20, Non-discrimination in economic, social and cultural rights, E/C.12/GC/20, para. 30.

[80] Ibid., para. 23.

[81] Report of the Committee of Experts on the Application of Conventions and Recommendations (arts. 19, 22, and 35 of the Constitution), Report III (Part 1B), 2012, paras. 802–804.

According to the Committee on Economic, Social and Cultural Rights, property status, as a prohibited ground of discrimination, 'is a broad concept and includes real property (*e.g.* land ownership or tenure) and personal property (*e.g.* intellectual property, goods and chattels, and income), or the lack of it'.[82] 'Property' may be viewed broadly as covering 'socio-economic status'.[83] It might be more accurate to describe the ground as 'lack of property'.

The drafters of the Universal Declaration of Human Rights appear to have understood 'birth' as comprising notions of 'class' or 'caste'.[84] Discrimination based on birth may cover children of unmarried parents and stateless parents as well as persons who are adopted and those who constitute the families of such persons. In a celebrated case dealing with the status of ex-nuptial children, the European Court of Human Rights applied the 'birth' ground of the non-discrimination provision of the European Convention, in conjunction with the right to private and family life.[85] According to the Committee on Economic, Social and Cultural Rights, 'the prohibited ground of birth also includes descent, especially on the basis of caste and analogous systems of inherited status', referring to 'members of descent-based communities'.[86]

2. Unenumerated categories

The enumeration of protected categories set out in the Universal Declaration and the two Covenants is preceded by the words 'such as … ', indicating that discrimination based upon grounds that are not listed is also contemplated. Candidates for other categories might today include disability, age, and sexual orientation. The two Covenants, the European Convention, the European Charter, and the African Charter also precede the enumeration with the words 'such as'. The non-discrimination provisions in the American Convention and the Arab Charter do not explicitly invite the addition of analogous or similar grounds.

The Committee on Economic, Social and Cultural Rights has suggested that 'other status' should be 'of a comparable nature to the expressly recognised grounds … These additional grounds are commonly recognised when they reflect the experience of social groups that are vulnerable and have suffered and continue to suffer marginalisation.'[87] Indicators of unenumerated categories may be derived

[82] General Comment 20, Non-discrimination in economic, social and cultural rights, E/C.12/GC/20, para. 23.

[83] *Mellet v. Ireland*, no. 2324/2013, Views, 6 September 2016, CCPR/C/116/D/2324/2013, Individual opinion of Committee member Sarah Cleveland (concurring), para. 3.

[84] Summary Record of the hundred and first meeting [of the Third Committee of the General Assembly], 13 October 1948, *Official Records of the General Assembly*, Third Session, 1948, pp. 137–139.

[85] *Marckx v. Belgium*, 13 June 1979, § 34, Series A no. 31.

[86] General Comment 20, Non-discrimination in economic, social and cultural rights, E/C.12/GC/20, para. 23.

[87] Ibid., para. 27.

from new specialised treaties, such as the Convention on the Rights of Persons with Disabilities, as well as from the establishment of thematic mandates for special procedures by the Human Rights Council, on such issues as albinism,[88] older persons,[89] persons with leprosy and their family members,[90] people of African descent,[91] and sexual orientation and gender identity.[92] Also relevant are the specific grounds found in newer treaties such as the European Charter of Fundamental Rights (genetic features, disability, age, and sexual orientation)[93] and the Istanbul Convention (gender identity, state of health, marital status, migrant or refugee status).[94] The Committee on Economic, Social and Cultural Rights considers that 'other grounds' include economic and social situation as well as place of residence, such as whether an individual resides or is registered in an urban or a rural area, in a formal or an informal settlement, is internally displaced or leads a nomadic lifestyle.[95] It also extends 'other grounds' to cover economic and social situation, such as living in poverty or being homeless.

There are now 182 States Parties to the Convention on the Rights of Persons with Disabilities. Bhutan, Cameroon, Lebanon, Solomon Islands, Tajikistan, Tonga, and the United States of America have signed the treaty, manifesting their agreement in principle with the prohibition of discrimination based upon disability. Nothing in the Universal Periodic Review reporting suggests that the handful of States that have neither signed nor ratified the Convention are in disagreement with the fundamental principle of non-discrimination based upon disability that is its *raison d'être*. Without significant exception, they have reported to the Council that the process of accession to the Convention is underway.[96] There can be no doubt that were the Universal Declaration of Human Rights to be adopted today, disability would appear as one of the grounds of prohibited discrimination.

Measures of protection for disabled persons who have special needs should not be deemed discriminatory to the extent that they are intended to enable the

88 Independent Expert on the enjoyment of human rights by persons with albinism, A/HRC/RES/28/6; Report of the Human Rights Council Advisory Committee on the study on the situation of human rights of persons living with albinism, A/HRC/28/75.

89 The human rights of older persons, A/HRC/RES/24/20.

90 Elimination of discrimination against persons affected by leprosy and their family members, A/HRC/RES/35/9; Study on the implementation of the principles and guidelines for the elimination of discrimination against persons affected by leprosy and their family members, A/HRC/35/38.

91 Mandate of the Working Group of Experts on People of African Descent, A/HRC/RES/36/23.

92 Protection against violence and discrimination based on sexual orientation and gender identity, A/HRC/RES/32/2.

93 Charter of Fundamental Rights of the European Union, OJ C 326/391, art. 21.

94 Council of Europe Convention on preventing and combating violence against women and domestic violence, CETS 210, art. 4(3).

95 General Comment 20, Non-discrimination in economic, social and cultural rights, E/C.12/GC/20, para. 34.

96 Botswana, National report, A/HRC/WG.6/29/BWA/1, para. 56; Equatorial Guinea, A/HRC/WG.6/33/GNQ/1, para. 13; Eritrea, Report of the Working Group, A/HRC/41/14, 26, para. 26; Lebanon, Views on conclusions, A/HRC/31/5/Add.1, para. 132.23; Liechtenstein, Report of the Working Group, A/HRC/38/16, para. 17; Timor Leste, National report, A/HRC/WG.6/26/TLS/1, para. 8.

achievement of equality. Like the other specialised treaties dealing with the elimination of forms of discrimination,[97] the Convention on the Rights of Persons with Disabilities declares that '[s]pecific measures which are necessary to accelerate or achieve de facto equality of persons with disabilities shall not be considered discrimination under the terms of the present Convention'.[98]

Age as a ground of discrimination is not listed in the Universal Declaration of Human Rights but appears in some of the treaties. Unlike grounds in the 'suspect category', like race or gender, where explicitly discriminatory measures are very exceptional, we are surrounded by restrictions premised on age, most of them at the two ends of the spectrum of the human lifespan. In many parts of the world persons under the age of eighteen are denied the right to vote, to drive motor vehicles, to pilot aeroplanes, to consume certain substances, to volunteer for military service, to marry, to contract loans and other legal engagements, to apply for citizenship, and to engage in sexual activity. Yet the most widely-ratified human rights treaty, the Convention on the Rights of the Child applies, with a few exceptions, only to persons under the age of eighteen. Older persons confront limitations on the right to work in the form of mandatory retirement, ineligibility for a range of elected or appointed functions, insurance premiums that are higher than those that younger people enjoy, and restrictions on the ability to drive motor vehicles. Very often, such measures are considered justifiable on reasonable and objective grounds that are usually related to mental and physical capacity, which is thought to increase during adolescence and diminish in old age. Even human rights treaties have provisions that impose questionable limitations based upon age, such as the requirement in the European Convention on Human Rights that judges of the European Court of Human Rights be no older than seventy.[99] René Cassin was eighty-one when, as president of the European Court of Human Rights, he was awarded the Nobel Peace Prize. Six of the fifteen judges of the International Court of Justice are more than seventy years old. Many heads of State and government are well above the ordinary retirement age. While it seems possible to conclude that discrimination based upon age is prohibited by customary international law, the difficulty is in the interpretation and application of the rule.

There is also some recognition in international human rights law of special measures to protect older persons. For example, the African Charter on Human and Peoples' Rights provides that 'the aged' are to have 'special measures of protection in keeping with their physical or moral needs'.[100] Similar provisions are

[97] International Convention on the Elimination of All Forms of Racial Discrimination, (1969) 660 UNTS 195, art. 1(4); Convention on the Elimination of All Forms of Discrimination against Women, (1981) 1249 UNTS 13, art. 4.

[98] Convention on the Rights of Persons with Disabilities, (2008) 2515 UNTS 3, art. 5(4).

[99] Protocol 11 to the Convention for the Protection of Human Rights and Fundamental Freedoms, restructuring the control machinery established thereby, ETS 155, art. 1 (new art. 23(6)). The provision was renumbered art. 23(2) by Protocol 14 to the Convention for the Protection of Human Rights and Fundamental Freedoms, amending the control system of the Convention, ETS 194.

[100] African Charter on Human and Peoples' Rights, (1986) 1520 UNTS 271, art. 18(4).

found in the Arab Charter on Human Rights,[101] the Additional Protocol to the American Convention on Human Rights in the area of Economic, Social and Cultural Rights,[102] and the European Social Charter.[103] According to the American Convention on Human Rights, the death penalty may not be imposed on persons over seventy years of age, regardless of age at the time of commission of the crime.[104] The implementation of special measures for older persons should not be considered a form of discrimination to the extent that this is reasonable and objective.

The prohibition of discrimination based upon gender under customary law is uncontroversial, and benefits from a dedicated treaty, the Convention on the Elimination of All Forms of Discrimination against Women. Nevertheless, the term 'gender' may encompass categories based upon sexual orientation and gender identity. It is obviously more difficult to identify customary law norms applicable to this expanded understanding of 'gender'. Many issues concerning sexual orientation and gender identity remain controversial, with State practice and attitudes of the general public undergoing rapid change. Many States retain legal measures that are widely regarded as discriminatory, such as the criminalisation of same-sex consensual relations, yet at the same time they claim they do not condone discrimination based upon sexual orientation and that they respect equality.[105] This is a distinction whose importance should not be understated. The fact that they repudiate discrimination based upon sexual orientation and gender identity is important from the standpoint of recognising customary norms, even if the same States continue to engage in practices that are inconsistent with such a perspective. States provide evidence of evolving norms when they report on efforts to decriminalise homosexual activity.[106] Open defence of discrimination based upon sexual orientation and gender identity is rare.[107]

* * *

[101] Arab Charter on Human Rights, art. 33(2).

[102] Additional Protocol to the American Convention on Human Rights in the area of Economic, Social and Cultural Rights, OASTS 69, art. 17.

[103] European Social Charter, CETS 35, art. 23; European Social Charter (revised), CETS 163, art. 23.

[104] American Convention on Human Rights, (1978) 1144 UNTS 123, art. 4(5).

[105] For example, Botswana, National report, A/HRC/WG.6/29/BWA/1, para. 52; China, National report, A/HRC/WG.6/17/CHN/3, para. 19; Comoros, Report of the Working Group, A/HRC/12/16, para. 56; Guyana, Report of the Working Group, A/HRC/15/14, para. 17; Jamaica, Report of the Working Group, A/HRC/16/14, para. 31 and Views on conclusions, A/HRC/16/14/Add.1, p. 6; Malaysia, Report of the Working Group, A/HRC/25/10, para. 9; Mongolia, Report of the Working Group, A/HRC/16/5, paras. 22, 24; Peru, National report, A/HRC/WG.6/14/PER/1, para. 27; St Kitts and Nevis, Report of the Working Group, A/HRC/17/12, para. 35; Singapore, Report of the Working Group, A/HRC/18/11, para. 82; Saint Lucia, National report, A/HRC/WG.6/10/LCA/1, para. 123.

[106] Bhutan, Views on conclusions, A/HRC/42/8/Add.1, p. 3; Kiribati, Report of the Working Group, A/HRC/15/3/Add.1, para. 29; Nauru, Report of the Working Group, A/HRC/17/3, para. 9; Tunisia, Report of the Working Group, A/HRC/21/5, para. 40.

[107] For example, Uganda, National report, A/HRC/WG.6/12/UGA/1, para. 105; Maldives, Report of the Working Group, A/HRC/16/7, para. 34.

Conclusions. Everyone has the right to equality without discrimination on grounds such as race, colour, sex, gender, language, religion, political or other opinion, national or social origin, property, birth or other status, disability, age, and sexual orientation. Temporary special measures aimed at rectifying situations of inequality shall not be deemed impermissible distinctions. Apartheid is a crime under customary international law and its prohibition constitutes *jus cogens*.

B. Special protection of children

Children, like adults, enjoy the right to equality and are entitled to protection against discrimination based upon race, language, religion, gender, and other aspects of their identity. The right to equality has a particular application to children that is set out in the Universal Declaration of Human Rights expressly. It affords children, 'whether born in and out of wedlock', an entitlement to equal protection and equal rights.[108] Questions about the customary status of this norm arise because the provision is not repeated, at least expressly, in either the International Covenant on Civil and Political Rights or the Convention on the Rights of the Child. Nevertheless, it is understood to fall within the general prohibition of discrimination, with reference to the ground of 'birth or other status' in the enumerated categories.[109] Today, as the treaty body materials and the reporting to the Human Rights Council under the Universal Periodic Review process indicate, there are no longer any serious attempts by States Parties to defend such distinctions although remnants of historic prejudice remain in some domestic legislation. The Human Rights Committee has expressed concern that some States Parties have not abolished 'the status of illegitimacy'[110] and it has welcomed initiatives with this purpose.[111] It has called upon States that still make such distinctions in their legislation to remove such an 'obsolete distinction'.[112] When questioned on the issue

[108] Universal Declaration of Human Rights, A/RES/217 (III), art. 25(2). The expression 'out of wedlock' was no doubt preferred by the drafters of the Universal Declaration of Human Rights to more pejorative expressions, like 'illegitimate', but it is not used in the Covenant. The word 'wedlock' has become increasingly obsolete and the expression 'ex-nuptial children' is preferred in this volume. The Human Rights Committee has suggested that mere use of the term 'illegitimate' amounts to discrimination (A/33/40, para. 312). The Committee on the Rights of the Child seems to prefer the expression 'ex-nuptial children' (see, *e.g.* A/55/41, para. 101).

[109] See, for example, Comoros, Concluding observations, CRC/C/15/Add.141, paras. 23–24; Brunei Darussalam, Concluding observations, CRC/C/15/Add.219, para. 24; United Arab Emirates, Concluding observations, CRC/C/ARE/CO/2, paras. 23–24. Also *Marckx v. Belgium*, 13 June 1979, § 38, Series A no. 31; *Johnston et al. v. Ireland*, 18 December 1986, § 70, Series A no. 112.

[110] Concluding observations, United Kingdom (Overseas Territories), CCPR/CO/73/UKOT, para. 30.

[111] Concluding observations, Germany, CCPR/CO/80/DEU, para. 4; Concluding observations, Iceland, CCPR/CO/83/ISL, para. 4.

[112] Concluding observations, Luxembourg, CCPR/CO/77/LUX, para. 9; Concluding observations, Japan, CCPR/C/JPN/CO/5, para. 28.

during the Universal Periodic Review, Tonga said that addressing the issue would require 'cultural changes'.[113]

Children occupy a unique place in international human rights law. They have special protections that are rooted in their vulnerability, such as the requirement that when accused of crimes they be judged by special tribunals or not at all, depending upon their age. While adults may benefit from a right to work, children below a certain age are not only denied the right but actually prohibited from working. Some rights are given special formulations such as the right of children 'to engage in play', although this right is also implied with respect to adults where it is recognised as a right to rest and leisure. The existence of a legal regime of exception for children, that is, those under eighteen years of age, is all the more striking in light of the fact that they represent approximately 30% of the world's population. Rights reserved to adults, such as voting, are actually recognised for only 70% of the population. The differences in human rights when children are concerned seem mainly justified by their 'physical and mental immaturity', to use the words of the Declaration on the Rights of the Child, which are cited in the preamble to the Convention on the Rights of the Child. Special measures of protection are contemplated in the case of particularly vulnerable categories of children, in particular orphans, children separated from their parents or deprived of the family environment,[114] refugee children,[115] children with disabilities,[116] and children who are members of ethnic, religious, and linguistic minorities.[117]

Attention to the distinct rights of children dates to the earliest phase of the codification of human rights. The Declaration on the Rights of the Child was adopted by the General Assembly of the League of Nations in 1924. The United Nations General Assembly produced a more elaborate version in 1959.[118] Children enjoy special protection pursuant to the International Covenant on Civil and Political Rights,[119] and many specialised and regional conventions.[120]

[113] Tonga, National report, A/HRC/WG.6/29/TON/1, para. 100.
[114] Convention on the Rights of the Child, (1990) 1571 UNTS 3, art. 20.
[115] Ibid., art. 22.
[116] Ibid., art. 23.
[117] Ibid., art. 30.
[118] Declaration on the Rights of the Child, A/RES/1386(XIV).
[119] International Covenant on Civil and Political Rights, (1976) 999 UNTS 171, art. 24.
[120] African Charter on Human and Peoples' Rights, (1986) 1520 UNTS 271, art. 18(3); African Charter on the Rights and Duties of the Child; American Convention on Human Rights, (1978) 1144 UNTS 123, arts. 17(5), 19; Arab Charter on Human Rights, arts. 10(2), 17, 33, 34; European Social Charter, CETS 35, arts. 7, 17; European Social Charter (revised), CETS 163, arts. 7, 17; Additional Protocol to the American Convention on Human Rights in the area of Economic, Social and Cultural Rights, OASTS 69, art. 16; International Convention for the Protection of All Persons from Enforced Disappearance, (2010) 2716 UNTS 3, art. 25; International Convention on the Protection of the Rights of all Migrant Workers and Members of their Families, (2003) 2220 UNTS 3, arts. 21, 22; Convention on the Rights of Persons with Disabilities, (2008) 2515 UNTS 3, art. 7; Council of Europe Convention on the Protection of Children against Sexual Exploitation and Sexual Abuse, CETS No. 201; International Labour Organisation Convention 182 concerning the Prohibition and Immediate Action for the Elimination of the Worst Forms of Child Labour.

The central instrument is the 1989 Convention on the Rights of the Child.[121] With 196 States Parties, the Convention is the human rights treaty with the most ratifications. The United States of America, which has signed the Convention, stands alone among United Nations Member States in its failure to ratify the instrument. Additional rights and protections are contained in two protocols to the Convention, concerning armed conflict[122] and the sale of children, child prostitution, and child pornography,[123] both of which have been very widely ratified. The virtually universal status of the Convention on the Rights of the Child gives it a strong claim to be a codification of customary international law.

Nevertheless, a large number of reservations have to be borne in making such an assessment. Most are precisely targeted at specific provisions or aspects of them. Nevertheless, a number are extremely broad or vague, by Brunei Darussalam,[124] Iran,[125] Kuwait,[126] Mauritania,[127] Saudi Arabia,[128] Somalia,[129] and Syria.[130] These cast some doubt on their acceptance of the rights set out in the Convention, as the many objections have noted.[131] Although very damaging to the treaty regime, the significance of these reservations as evidence of customary law, or rather the lack of it, tends to be exaggerated. Islamic law appears to have little or no relevance for many of the rights in the Convention. Moreover, the States that have made such reservations are often bound to respect many of the rights found in the Convention by virtue of their ratification of other treaties, to which they have not attached similar reservations.

Several of the rights recognised to the child are actually ensured to everyone by customary international human rights law, obviating the need for any separate

[121] Convention on the Rights of the Child, (1990) 1571 UNTS 3.

[122] Optional Protocol to the Convention on the Rights of the Child on the involvement of children in armed conflict, (2002) 2173 UNTS 222.

[123] Optional Protocol to the Convention on the Rights of the Child on the sale of children, child prostitution and child pornography, (2002) 2171 UNTS 227.

[124] C.N.478.1995.TREATIES-11: 'Brunei Darussalam expresses its reservations on the provisions of the said Convention which may be contrary to the Constitution of Brunei Darussalam and to the beliefs and principles of Islam.'

[125] C.N.235.1994.TREATIES: 'The Islamic Republic of Iran reserves the right not to apply and provisions or articles of the Convention that are incompatible with Islamic Laws and the international legislation in effect.'

[126] C.N.252.1991.TREATIES-12: ' … reservations on all provisions of the Convention that are incompatible with the laws of Islamic Shari'a and the local statutes in effect'.

[127] C.N.116.1991.TREATIES-4: ' … the Islamic Republic of Mauritania is making reservations to articles or provisions which may be contrary to the beliefs and values of Islam, the religion of the Mauritania People and State'.

[128] C.N.22.1996.TREATIES-1: ' … reservations with respect to all such articles as are in conflict with the provisions of Islamic law'.

[129] C.N.528.2015.TREATIES-IV.11: 'The Federal Republic of Somalia does not consider itself bound by … provisions of the Convention contrary to the General Principles of Islamic Sharia.'

[130] C.N.267.1993.TREATIES-8: 'The Syrian Arab Republic has reservations on the Convention's provisions which are not in conformity with the Syrian Arab legislations and with the Islamic Shariah's principles.'

[131] For example, Ireland, C.N.432.2016.TREATIES-IV.11; Netherlands, C.N.87.2016. TREATIES-IV.11.

discussion in this study. For example, the 1959 Declaration highlighted the right of the child to adequate nutrition, housing, medical care, and education. The Convention on the Rights of the Child guarantees freedom of expression, of religion, and of association and peaceful assembly. To the extent that there is any special dimension to these rights required by the status of the child it may be the principle that '[i]n all actions concerning children, whether undertaken by public or private social welfare institutions, courts of law, administrative authorities or legislative bodies, the best interests of the child shall be a primary consideration', enshrined in Article 3(1) of the Convention on the Rights of the Child.[132] According to the Human Rights Committee, 'the principle that in all decisions affecting a child, its best interests shall be a primary consideration, forms an integral part of every child's right to such measures of protection as required by his or her status as a minor, on the part of his or her family, society and the State'.[133] Judge Pinto de Albuquerque of the European Court of Human Rights described the principle of the best interests as one of customary international law.[134] Although not referring explicitly to customary law, the Grand Chamber of the European Court has spoken of 'a broad consensus, including in international law, in support of the idea that in all decisions concerning children, their best interests are of paramount importance'.[135]

International human rights treaties are mainly directed at the obligations of the States Parties, but they may also impose obligations or duties on individuals. As the Universal Declaration makes explicit, '[e]veryone has duties to the community in which alone the free and full development of his personality is possible'.[136] The Convention on the Rights of the Child declares that 'both parents have common responsibilities for the upbringing and development of the child' and that '[p] arents or, as the case may be, legal guardians, have the primary responsibility for the upbringing and development of the child'.[137] There have been no reservations to the provision, providing confirmation for its universal recognition as a norm of customary international law. The State has obligations to ensure that parental duties are entrenched in laws that are enforced. States are also required to 'render appropriate assistance to parents and legal guardians in the performance of their child-rearing responsibilities and shall ensure the development of institutions, facilities and services for the care of children'.

132 Convention on the Rights of the Child, (1990) 1571 UNTS 3, art. 3(1).

133 *Bakhtiyari et al. v. Australia*, no. 1069/2002, Views, 6 November 2003, CCPR/C/79/D/1069/2002, para. 9.7; *D.T. et al. v. Canada*, no. 2081/2011, Views, 15 July 2016, CCPR/C/117/D/2081/2011, para. 7.10.

134 *X. v. Latvia* [GC], no. 27853/09, 26 November 2013, Concurring opinion of Judge Pinto de Albuquerque.

135 *Strand Lobben et al. v. Germany* [GC], no. 37283/13, § 204, 10 September 2019.

136 Universal Declaration of Human Rights, A/RES/217 (III), art. 29(1).

137 Convention on the Rights of the Child, (1990) 1571 UNTS 3, art. 18(1).

The Convention on the Rights of the Child prohibits the recruitment into the armed forces of any person who has not attained the age of fifteen.[138] The formulation in the Convention may appear somewhat equivocal, in that it speaks of taking 'all feasible measures to ensure that persons who have not attained the age of fifteen years do not take a direct part in hostilities'. The language is understandable, because while States may be able to control the age of recruitment into their own armed forces, where paramilitary or non-state militias are involved they can only undertake an obligation of means. A Protocol to the Convention, ratified by nearly 170 States, raises the age of active participation in hostilities to eighteen, although it allows recruitment below that age subject to certain safeguards, including parental authorisation.[139] The Rome Statute of the International Criminal Court defines as a war crime the conscripting or enlisting of children under fifteen or using them to participate actively in hostilities.[140] There have been several convictions by international criminal tribunals for this offence.[141] The Special Court for Sierra Leone identified the recruitment of children as a violation of customary international law.[142]

The scourge of child labour has received attention from international human rights law from its earliest days, in the period prior to the Second World War. Treaties prohibiting child labour were among the initial conventions adopted at the first session of the International Labour Organisation, in 1919.[143] The Convention on the Rights of the Child requires protection 'from economic exploitation and from performing any work that is likely to be hazardous or to interfere with the child's education, or to be harmful to the child's health or physical, mental, spiritual, moral or social development'.[144] States are required to provide for a minimum age for admission to employment, to provide 'appropriate regulation of the hours and conditions of employment', and to enforce these measures.[145]

The Convention on the Rights of the Child does not, however, specify what the minimum age for admission to employment should be. An International Labour Organisation Convention sets this at fifteen, allowing it at thirteen for 'light work' but prohibiting it until eighteen for 'hazardous work'. The age may be slightly lower

[138] Ibid., art. 38(3).

[139] Optional Protocol to the Convention on the Rights of the Child on the involvement of children in armed conflict, (2002) 2173 UNTS 222.

[140] (2002) 2187 UNTS 3, arts. 8(2)(b)(xxvi) and 8(2)(e)(vii).

[141] *Prosecutor v. Lubanga* (ICC-01/04-01/06), Judgment pursuant to art. 74 of the Statute, 14 March 2012; *Prosecutor v. Brima et al.* (SCSL-04-16-T), Judgment, 20 June 2007; *Prosecutor v. Sesay et al.* (SCSL-04-15-T), Judgment, 2 March 2009; *Prosecutor v. Taylor* (SCSL-03-1-T), Judgment, 26 April 2012; *Prosecutor v. Ntaganda* (ICC-01/04-02/06), Judgment, 8 July 2019.

[142] *Prosecutor v. Norman* (SCSL-04-14-AR72(E)), Decision on Preliminary Motion Based on Lack of Jurisdiction (Child Recruitment), 31 May 2004, paras. 17–24.

[143] Minimum Age (Industry) Convention, (1919) 38 LNTS 81; Night Work of Young Persons (Industry) Convention, (1919) 38 LNTS 93.

[144] Convention on the Rights of the Child, (1990) 1571 UNTS 3, art. 32(1).

[145] Ibid., art. 32(2).

in countries where the economy and educational facilities are insufficiently developed. The Minimum Age Convention has 172 ratifications.[146] A few States that have not ratified the Convention appear to have no minimum age for child labour. One of them, Australia, has explained that its failure to ratify the Convention is based upon its assessment that there is no need to set a minimum age because it considers that its existing legislation to protect children from abuse is adequate.[147] New Zealand, which made a reservation to Article 32 of the Convention on the Rights of the Child,[148] has noted that although it has no minimum age, employment of persons under sixteen during school hours is forbidden.[149] Iran reports children working who are as young as ten but also indicates that their number is declining. It has legislation aimed at protecting persons under eighteen who work.[150] The United States appears to allow children to work, in agriculture, from the age of twelve.[151] When India ratified the Convention on the Rights of the Child, it made a declaration confirming its recognition of the objectives and purposes of the Convention but acknowledging that 'for several reasons children of different ages do work in India', that a minimum age for employment in hazardous occupations and in certain other areas was prescribed by law, and 'that it is not practical immediately to prescribe minimum ages for admission to each and every area of employment in India'.[152] India agreed 'to take measures to progressively implement the provisions of Article 32, particularly paragraph 2(a)' and, in 2017, India ratified the Minimum Age Convention and declared the minimum age to be fourteen. Upon accession to the Convention on the Rights of the Child in 1995, Singapore made a reservation to Article 32, noting its legislation prohibited employment of children below twelve;[153] in 2005 it ratified the Minimum Age Convention, specifying an age of fifteen. To conclude, while the picture is not entirely consistent, and while there are a few stubborn exceptions, like Australia and New Zealand, even those States that are not parties to the Minimum Age Convention would not dispute the fact that were they to allow children to work below the age of twelve and possibly fourteen that they would be in breach of international legal obligations.

The International Labour Organisation refers to the 'worst forms of child labour'. These are enumerated in the Worst Forms of Child Labour Convention: all forms of slavery or practices similar to slavery, such as the sale and trafficking of children, debt bondage and serfdom and forced or compulsory labour, including forced or compulsory recruitment of children for use in armed conflict; the use,

[146] Convention 138 concerning Minimum Age for Admission to Employment, (1976) 1015 UNTS 297.
[147] Australia, Second and third periodic reports, CRC/C/129/Add.4, paras. 477–482.
[148] C.N.135.1993.TREATIES-4.
[149] New Zealand, Initial report, CRC/C/28/Add.3, para. 24.
[150] Iran, Third and fourth periodic reports, CRC/C/IRN/3-4, paras. 264–277.
[151] United States, Initial report, CCPR/C/81/Add.4, para. 718.
[152] C.N.457.1992.TREATIES-19.
[153] C.N.370.1995.TREATIES-9.

procuring, or offering of a child for prostitution; and generally work that is likely to harm the health, safety, or morals of children.[154] The practices listed in the Worst Forms of Child Labour Convention have a very strong claim to being prohibited by customary international law.

* * *

Conclusions. Children are entitled to special rights and protections under customary international law, with their best interests being a primary consideration. Discrimination against ex-nuptial children is prohibited. Children under the age of fifteen may not be recruited into the armed forces or used in armed conflict. States must set a minimum age for child labour and ensure that children are protected against work that is likely to harm their health, safety, or morals.

C. Minority rights and rights of indigenous peoples

The protection of the rights of minorities by treaty constitutes one of the first initiatives of the international law of human rights. Following the First World War, treaties and other instruments were adopted that provided for the protection of ethnic, linguistic, and religious minorities in the new entities that resulted from the breakup of the empires in Eastern Europe and the Middle East.[155] The 'little treaty of Versailles' contained an Article specifying that Polish nationals who were members of 'racial, religious or linguistic minorities shall enjoy the same treatment and security in law and in fact as the other Polish nationals. In particular they shall have an equal right to establish, manage and control at their own expense charitable, religious and social institutions, schools and other educational establishments, with the right to use their own language and to exercise their religion freely therein.'[156] These principles, however, did not find their way into the Universal Declaration of Human Rights. Proposals to include specific protection for minorities were dropped, the rationale being that the rights of such groups were adequately ensured by the guarantees of equality and non-discrimination. There is a widely-held belief that minority rights were excluded from the Universal Declaration because of dissatisfaction with the inter-war minority treaties system, but the better view is that States of the 'new world' were the real opponents of such a provision, concerned that this would discourage assimilation and prevent development of a new national identity.[157]

[154] Convention 182 on the World Forms of Child Labour, art. 3.
[155] Treaty between the Principal Allied and Associated Powers and Poland, (1919) 112 BSP 23, art. 2.
[156] Ibid., art. 8. See Felix Ermacora, 'The Protection of Minorities before the United Nations', (1985) 182 *Recueil des cours* 250.
[157] William A. Schabas, 'Les droits des minorités: Une déclaration inachevée', in *Déclaration universelle des droits de l'homme 1948–98, Avenir d'un idéal commun*, Paris: La Documentation française, 1999, pp. 223–242.

The omission of minority rights from the Universal Declaration was remedied to a degree by the inclusion of a relatively weak provision in the International Covenant on Civil and Political Rights. Article 27 of the Covenant provides that '[i]n those States in which ethnic, religious or linguistic minorities exist, persons belonging to such minorities shall not be denied the right, in community with the other members of their group, to enjoy their own culture, to profess and practise their own religion, or to use their own language'. The provision has had a rather modest impact and in practice it offers little or no 'value added' to the equality and non-discrimination clauses of the Covenant, principally Article 26, as case law of the Human Rights Committee has demonstrated.[158] In its Concluding Observations on periodic reports by States Parties, the Human Rights Committee frequently addresses minority rights issues with a general reference to Articles 26 and 27, as if the two provisions fulfil the same function.[159] A clause similar to Article 27 of the Covenant can be found in the Convention on the Rights of the Child[160] as well as in the Arab Charter on Human Rights,[161] but not in the American Convention on Human Rights or the African Charter on Human and Peoples' Rights. The European Convention on Human Rights includes association with a national minority among the enumerated grounds of prohibited discrimination but is otherwise silent on the subject. During the 1990s, the Council of Europe reacted to the newly emerging minority conflicts with the adoption of the European Charter for Regional or Minority Languages in 1992[162] and the European Framework Convention for the Protection of National Minorities in 1995.[163]

Despite this patchwork of recognition of the rights of minorities among the core principles of international human rights law, the fact remains that it is comprised within the Covenant and applies as a matter of treaty law to all of its States Parties. In the list of customary law norms that it prepared in its General Comment on reservations, the Committee included denial to minorities of 'the right to enjoy their own culture, profess their own religion, or use their own language', echoing

[158] *Diergaardt et al. v. Namibia*, no. 760/1997, Views, 7 July 1998, CCPR/C/69/D/760/1997, paras. 10.10, 11.

[159] *E.g.* Greece, Concluding observations, CCPR/C/GRC/CO/2, para. 43; Rwanda, Concluding observations, CCPR/C/RWA/CO/4, para. 37; Serbia, Concluding observations, CCPR/C/SRB/CO/3, para. 8; Bangladesh, Concluding observations, CCPR/C/BGD/CO/1, para. 11.

[160] Convention on the Rights of the Child, (1990) 1577 UNTS 3, art. 30.

[161] Arab Charter on Human Rights, art. 25.

[162] ETS 148. See Robert Dunbar, 'The Council of Europe's European Charter for Regional or Minority Languages', in Kristin Henrard and Robert Dunbar, eds., *Synergies in Minority Protection*, Cambridge: Cambridge University Press, 2008, pp. 1556–1586.

[163] ETS 157. See Asbjørn Eide, 'The Council of Europe's Framework Convention for the Protection of National Minorities', in Kristin Henrard and Robert Dunbar, eds., *Synergies in Minority Protection. European and International Law Perspectives*, Cambridge: Cambridge University Press, 2008, pp. 119–154; Mark Weller, ed., *The Rights of Minorities in Europe, A Commentary on the European Framework Convention for the Protection of National Minorities*, Oxford: Oxford University Press, 2005.

the formulation in Article 27 of the Covenant.[164] It also recalled that Article 27 did not appear on the list of non-derogable norms, despite being a right 'of profound importance'.[165]

There has been only one genuine reservation to Article 27, by Turkey, with respect to application of provisions of the Treaty of Lausanne.[166] In objecting to the reservation, Finland 'emphasise[d] the great importance of the rights of minorities provided for in Article 27 of the International Covenant on Civil and Political Rights'.[167] Despite the reservation, Turkey's reports to the Human Rights Council make it clear that it considers the protection of minorities to be included in its obligations under human rights law.[168] Upon ratification of the Covenant, in 1980, France 'declared' that it did not consider Article 27 to be applicable, given its Constitution's recognition of equality of all citizens.[169] During the Universal Periodic Review, France explained that this was an 'interpretative declaration', as opposed to a reservation, and, moreover, that 'the provisions of article 27 of the Covenant, including those on religious, linguistic and cultural freedom, are guaranteed to all citizens, without discrimination'.[170] France has declined invitations to withdraw its declaration, stating that 'collective rights cannot be acknowledged to particular groups, be they "ethnic, religious or linguistic minorities"'.[171] Qatar issued a 'statement' that is in reality an interpretative declaration: 'The State of Qatar shall interpret Article 27 of the Covenant that professing and practising one's own religion require that they do not violate the rules of public order and public morals, the protection of public safety and public health, or the rights of and basic freedoms of others.'[172] Although Qatar's reservations provoked some twenty objections, most of the objecting States ignored the innocuous statement about Article 27,[173] which appears to do nothing more than reproduce the text of Article 18 of the Covenant. Qatar's 'statement' does not undermine its commitment to the obligations set out in Article 27 even if the interpretation it adopts may be viewed as unacceptable.

[164] General Comment 24, Issues Relating to Reservations Made upon Ratification or Accession to the Covenant or the Optional Protocols thereto, or in Relation to Declarations under Article 41 of the Covenant, CCPR/C/21/Rev.1/Add.6, para. 8.

[165] Ibid., para. 10.

[166] Treaty of Lausanne, (1923) 28 LNTS 11, arts. 37–45.

[167] C.N.1183.2004.TREATIES-15.

[168] Turkey, National report, A/HRC/WG.6/35/TUR/1, paras. 67–72, Report of the Working Group, A/HRC/44/14, paras. 28, 31, National report, A/HRC/WG.6/21/TUR/1, paras. 46–54, and Report of the Working Group, A/HRC/29/15, para. 51.

[169] C.N.335.1980.TREATIES-10.

[170] France, Response, A/HRC/8/47/Add.1, paras. 9–10. See also A/HRC/8/47, para. 54. See also France, Views on conclusions, A/HRC/23/3/Add.1, para. 8.

[171] France, National report, A/HRC/WG.6/29/FRA/1, para. 5.

[172] C.N.262.2018.TREATIES-IV.4.

[173] There were objections, on varying grounds, from the United Kingdom, C.N.218.2019.TREATIES-IV.4; Norway, C.N.211.2019.TREATIES-IV.4; Ireland, C.N.207.2019.TREATIES-IV.4; Hungary, C.N.203.2019.TREATIES-IV.4; Poland, C.N.116.2019.TREATIES-IV.4. Some of them appear to have misread the statement.

Of States that are not parties to the Covenant, and that are therefore not bound by Article 27 of the Covenant, Saudi Arabia and the United Arab Emirates are parties to the Arab Charter on Human Rights which has an equivalent provision. Many of the States that are not parties to the Covenant indicate in their reports to the Human Rights Council that they take measures specifically directed at the protection of the rights of those belonging to ethnic, linguistic, and religious minorities.[174] A few appear to reject or are at least indifferent to the issue of protection of the rights of members of minority groups, or contend it is not an issue for them because there are no minorities within their borders.[175] Furthermore, all United Nations Members States are parties to the Convention on the Rights of the Child. Article 30 of the Convention is essentially identical to Article 27 of the Covenant. France and Turkey have made interpretative declarations or reservations to Article 30 of the Convention that are to the same effect as what they have done for the Covenant.[176] Otherwise, it seems possible to speak of universal acceptance of the rights of children belonging to ethnic, linguistic, and religious minorities. It makes no sense that States would acknowledge such a right to children only to challenge or question it for adults.

The ultimate challenge to minorities is the attempt at their destruction. In the most extreme cases, this may amount to physical extermination. The 1948 Convention on the Prevention and Punishment of the Crime of Genocide was the first human rights treaty to be adopted within the United Nations. The Convention defines the crime of genocide as the international destruction of a national, ethnic, racial, or religious group. Judicial interpretation has held that the crime of genocide requires the intent to destroy the group physically.[177] There is ample authority for the identification of genocide as an international crime under customary international law.[178] Cultural genocide, which refers to the destruction of the culture of a group with the purpose of its disappearance, falls outside the scope of the 1948 Convention, although measures directed at destroying a group's culture may

[174] China, Report of the Working Group, A/HRC/11/25, paras. 13, 102, 110, National report, A/HRC/WG.6/17/CHN/1, paras. 77–83, 115–116 and Report of the Working Group, A/HRC/25/5, paras. 19, 86; Malaysia, National report, A/HRC/WG.6/31/MYS, paras. 25–26, 43(c); Myanmar, Report of the Working Group, A/HRC/18/11, para. 18 and Report of the Working Group, A/HRC/17/9, para. 100; Saint Lucia, Views on conclusions, A/HRC/17/6/Add.1, para. 89.108; Saudi Arabia, Report of the Working Group, A/HRC/11/23, paras. 9, 83; Singapore, National report, A/HRC/WG.6/11/SGP/, paras. 11, 24, 134–140; Tuvalu, National report, A/HRC/WG.6/3/TUV/1, para. 51; United Arab Emirates, Report of the Working Group, A/HRC/23/13, para. 125.

[175] Bhutan, Report of the Working Group, A/HRC/42/8, paras. 19, 116; Comoros, A/HRC/WG.6/18/COM/1, National report, para. 70; Saudi Arabia, Report of the Working Group, A/HRC/11/23, paras. 9, 83 and National report, A/HRC/WG.6/17/SAU/1, para. 24.

[176] France: (1990) 1577 UNTS 171; Turkey, C.N.148.1995.TREATIES-4. There are also two interpretative declarations, by Canada, C.N.320.1991.TREATIES-16, and Venezuela.

[177] Convention on the Prevention and Punishment of the Crime of Genocide, (1951) 78 UNTS 277.

[178] The crime of genocide, A/RES/96 (I); *Application of the Convention on the Prevention and Punishment of the Crime of Genocide (Croatia v. Serbia), Judgment, ICJ Reports 2015*, p. 3, para. 87. See *supra*, pp. 113–115, for further authorities.

contribute to evidence of genocidal intent. Cultural genocide is addressed through the protection of the rights of members of minorities to the use of their language and to the protection of various features of their cultural life. In that sense, cultural genocide can be said to be prohibited under customary international law.

Indigenous peoples are not specifically referred to in the Universal Declaration of Human Rights and in most of the main specialised and regional human rights conventions. The Convention on the Rights of the Child adds the words 'or persons of indigenous origin' to the minority rights provision of the International Covenant and Civil and Political Rights.[179]

The principal treaty is the International Labour Organisation Indigenous and Tribal Peoples Convention, 1989, which has been ratified by only twenty-three States. But as with the case of minorities generally, a comprehensive universal treaty has yet to emerge. Indigenous peoples have obtained some protection under human rights law through such vehicles as the rights of minorities, although they legitimately object to being classified as a minority. In terms of codification, the two most important instruments are the United Nations Declaration on the Rights of Indigenous Peoples and the American Declaration on the Rights of Indigenous Peoples of the Organisation of American States.

The United Nations General Assembly adopted the Declaration on the Rights of Indigenous Peoples in 2007. It received 143 votes in favour, with four against (Australia, Canada, New Zealand, and the United States) and eleven abstentions (Azerbaijan, Bangladesh, Bhutan, Burundi, Colombia, Georgia, Kenya, Nigeria, Russian Federation, Samoa, and Ukraine).[180] Those who voted against have since changed their position.[181] However, the United States has insisted that the Declaration was not intended to create new international law, describing it as an 'aspirational statement of political and moral commitment' that is 'not binding under international law'.[182] Canada has said it does not consider the UN Declaration to 'reflect customary international law'.[183] In its National report to the Human Rights Council, New Zealand described the Declaration as a statement of 'aspirations'.[184]

The preamble of the United Nations Declaration notes that indigenous peoples 'have suffered from historic injustices as a result of, inter alia, their colonisation and dispossession of their lands, territories and resources, thus preventing them

[179] Convention on the Rights of the Child, (1990) 1571 UNTS 3, art. 30.

[180] A/61/PV.107, p. 19.

[181] Australia, National report, A/HRC/WG.6/10/AUS/1, para. 59 and National report, A/HRC/WG.6/23/AUS/1, para. 39; Canada, National report, A/HRC/WG.6/16/CAN/1, para. 16; New Zealand, National report, A/HRC/WG.6/18/NZL/1, para. 20; United States of America, National report, A/HRC/30/12, para. 6.

[182] *Mitchell v. United States*, Case No. Report No. 211/20, Admissibility and Merits, 24 August 2020, para. 14.

[183] Missing and Murdered Indigenous Women in British Columbia, Canada, OEA/Ser.L/V/II, Doc. 30/14, para. 122, citing State of Canada, Response to the IACHR's Report on the Situation of Missing and Murdered Indigenous Women in British Columbia, Canada. Note PRMOAS—0232, 30 October 2014.

[184] New Zealand, National report, A/HRC/WG.6/32/NZL/1, para. 21.

from exercising, in particular, their right to development in accordance with their own needs and interests ...'.[185] The Declaration recognises that indigenous peoples have the right to self-determination and that 'in exercising their right to self-determination [they] have the right to autonomy or self-government in matters relating to their internal and local affairs, as well as ways and means for financing their autonomous functions'. Furthermore, they have 'the right to maintain and strengthen their distinct political, legal, economic, social and cultural institutions, while retaining their right to participate fully, if they so choose, in the political, economic, social and cultural life of the State'.[186]

The American Declaration on the Rights of Indigenous Peoples was adopted in 2016 by the General Assembly of the Organization of American States following negotiations that lasted for more than a quarter of a century.[187] The Inter-American Commission of Human Rights has expressed the view that there is a 'customary international law norm which affirms the rights of indigenous peoples to their traditional lands'.[188] As early as 2002, the Inter-American Commission invoked the draft Declaration's protection of traditional forms of ownership and cultural survival and rights to land, territories, and resources.[189] It situated the draft Declaration in the context of 'the evolving rules and principles of human rights law in the Americas and in the international community more broadly, as reflected in treaties, custom and other sources of international law' concerning the rights of indigenous peoples.[190] It said that 'general international legal principles' included 'the right of indigenous peoples to legal recognition of their varied and specific forms and modalities of their control, ownership, use and enjoyment of territories and property; the recognition of their property and ownership rights with respect to lands, territories and resources they have historically occupied; and where property and user rights of indigenous peoples arise from rights existing prior to the creation of a state, recognition by that state of the permanent and inalienable title of indigenous peoples relative thereto and to have such title changed only by mutual consent between the state and respective indigenous peoples when they have full knowledge and appreciation of the nature or attributes of such property'.[191]

Referring to the United Nations Declaration and the International Labour Organisation Convention, the Special Rapporteur on the rights of indigenous peoples has noted 'the universal applicability of those instruments ... signalling

[185] A/RES/61/295, PP 6.

[186] Ibid., paras. 3–5.

[187] American Declaration on the Rights of Indigenous Peoples, AG/RES. 2888 (XLVI-O/16).

[188] Indigenous and Tribal People's Rights over their Ancestral Lands and Natural Resources, Norms and Jurisprudence of the Inter-American Human Rights System, OEA/Ser.L/V/II, Doc. 56/09, para. 18. See also *Mayagna (Sumo) Awas Tingni community v. Nicaragua*, Judgment (Merits, reparations and costs), 31 August 2001, Series C, No. 79, para. 140(d).

[189] *Mary and Carrie Dann v. United States*, Case 11.140, Report No. 75/02, Merits, 27 December 2002, para. 129.

[190] Ibid., para. 124.

[191] Ibid., para. 130.

the emergence of customary international law in the area of indigenous peoples' rights'.[192]

The Universal Periodic Review materials frequently refer to indigenous peoples, confirming their place within the customary law of human rights. Most States do not have specific treaty obligations concerning the rights of indigenous persons. The Declaration of 2007 is a fundamental document capable of propelling the recognition of customary law. In the course of the Universal Periodic Review, many States recognise obligations that they owe to indigenous peoples as such, often describing their initiatives in great detail.[193] They acknowledge the rights of indigenous peoples to their land, to the protection of traditional economies, and to the survival of their culture. This is an area of customary international law that is evolving quickly.

* * *

Conclusions. Persons belonging to ethnic, religious, or linguistic minorities, in community with the other members of their group, have the right to enjoy their own culture, to profess and practise their own religion, or to use their own language. Indigenous peoples are entitled to special protection, in particular with respect to their land, to their traditional economies, and to the survival of their language and culture.

[192] Report of the Special Rapporteur on the rights of indigenous peoples, A/HRC/33/42, para. 14.

[193] For example, Australia, National report, A/HRC/WG.6/10/AUS/1, paras. 54–67 and National report, A/HRC/WG.6/23/AUS/1, paras. 39–58; Brazil, National report, A/HRC/WG.6/13/BRA/1, paras. 66–71; Brazil, National report, A/HRC/WG.6/27/BRA/1, paras. 58–66; Canada, National report, A/HRC/WG.6/4/CAN/1, paras. 64–79; Canada, National report, A/HRC/WG.6/16/CAN/1, paras. 12–44; Canada, National report, A/HRC/WG.6/30/CAN/1, paras. 9–36; Denmark, National report, A/HRC/WG.6/11/DNK/1, paras. 108–111; Malaysia, National report, A/HRC/WG.6/17/MYS/1, paras. 67–72; Malaysia, National report, A/HRC/WG.6/31/MYS/1, paras. 46–54; Mexico, National report, A/HRC/WG.6/4/MEX/1, paras. 114–121; Mexico, A/HRC/WG.6/17/MEX/1, National report, paras. 119–124; New Zealand, National report, A/HRC/WG.6/5/NZL/1, paras. 98–100; New Zealand, National report, A/HRC/WG.6/32/NZL/1, para. 21; Norway, National report, A/HRC/WG.6/6/NOR/1, paras. 79–85; Norway, National report, A/HRC/WG.6/19/NOR/1, paras. 37–42; Norway, National report, A/HRC/WG.6/33/NOR/1, paras. 91–97; Russia, National report, A/HRC/WG.6/16/RUS/1, paras. 184–191; Russia, National report, A/HRC/WG.6/30/RUS/1, paras. 256–257.

6
Fundamental freedoms

Human rights are often associated with 'fundamental freedoms'. Article 1 of the Charter of the United Nations speaks of 'promoting and encouraging respect for human rights and for fundamental freedoms for all'. Perhaps use of the term was a nod of respect to the late American President, Franklin D. Roosevelt, and the 'four freedoms' he set out in his 1941 State of the Union Address.[1] There were echoes of the four freedoms in the Atlantic Charter, adopted by Roosevelt and Churchill later in 1941,[2] and they are alluded to in the preambles of the Universal Declaration of Human Rights and the two International Covenants. The Charter of the United Nations describes one of the purposes of the organisation as 'promoting and encouraging respect for human rights and for fundamental freedoms for all'.[3]

The term 'fundamental freedoms' probably has no legal significance that distinguishes it from 'human rights'.[4] The two formulations may be used separately, as synonyms, or they may be used together as a more eloquent statement. Article 1 of the American Convention on Human Rights speaks of 'rights and freedoms' whereas Article 2 refers to 'rights or freedoms'. The explanation would seem to be nothing more than careless drafting of the instrument. The other language versions make no distinction. The Spanish text uses 'los derechos y libertades', the Portuguese refers to 'direitos e liberdades', and the French 'droits et libertés', in both Articles 1 and 2.

The first of the major regional instruments to be adopted was named the 'Convention for the Protection of Human Rights and Fundamental Freedoms' but the institution that it created is the 'European Court of Human Rights', not the 'European Court of Human Rights and Fundamental Freedoms'. Today, most people refer to the treaty as the 'European Convention on Human Rights' and omit the reference to 'fundamental freedoms' altogether. The other major European rights instrument is the Charter of Fundamental Rights of the European Union. In many respects, the Charter tracks the language of the European Convention. Its title seems a bit of a hybrid, taking the words 'rights' and 'fundamental' and dropping the words 'human' and 'freedoms'. Some of the substantive provisions of the

[1] Congressional Record, 1941, Vol. 87, Pt. I, 6 January 1941.

[2] 'Joint Statement by President Roosevelt and Prime Minister Churchill, 14 August 1941', FRUS 1941 I, pp. 367–369.

[3] Charter of the United Nations, art. 1(3). Also arts. 31(1)(b), 55, 62(2), and 76(c).

[4] Theodor Meron, 'A Hierarchy of Human Rights', (1986) 80 *American Journal of International Law* 1, at pp. 5–6, citing Hans Kelsen, *The Law of the United Nations*, London: Stevens and Sons, 1966, p. 29.

The Customary International Law of Human Rights. William A. Schabas, Oxford University Press.
 DOI: 10.1093/oso/9780192845696.003.0007

Charter refer to 'rights and freedoms'. The preamble claims that the Charter consists of 'rights, freedoms and principles'.

Roosevelt's first two freedoms, of speech or expression and religion or belief, fall under the 'fundamental freedoms' here, along with their cognates, notably peaceful assembly and association. However, freedom from want, in Roosevelt's nomenclature, is dealt with under the heading economic, social, and cultural rights, and freedom of fear falls under solidarity. It was always understood that the four freedoms were not intended to exclude other fundamental rights or to relegate them to some subordinate status. The term 'freedoms' is used here as somewhat of a default, in that the various customary law norms addressed in this section do not fit conveniently under the other rubrics, such as dignity, equality, and political rights.

A. Opinion and expression

The Institut de Droit International had no proper freedom of expression provision in the draft declaration of rights that it adopted in 1929. Article III of the Declaration said it was 'the duty of every State to recognise the right of every individual both to the free use of the language of his choice and to the teaching of such language', but this is more of a minority language than a freedom of expression provision.[5] The first of the 'four essential freedoms' proclaimed by Franklin D. Roosevelt's was 'freedom of speech and expression—everywhere in the world'. The 1943 draft declaration of the London International Assembly contained the following: 'Every person shall be free to speak, write or publish whatsoever he thinks fit provided that this is not contrary to the rules of public order or good morals.'[6] Hersch Lauterpacht's International Bill of Rights proclaimed that 'freedom of speech and expression of opinion in writing and by other means shall not be denied or impaired'.[7]

Article 19 of the Universal Declaration of Human Rights affirms 'Everyone has the right to freedom of opinion and expression; this right includes freedom to hold opinions without interference and to seek, receive and impart information and ideas through any media and regardless of frontiers.' Like all other rights in the Declaration, it is subject to restrictions as framed in Article 29: 'In the exercise of his rights and freedoms, everyone shall be subject only to such limitations as are determined by law solely for the purpose of securing due recognition and respect

[5] Institut de Droit International, 'Declaration of the International Rights of Man', (1941) 35 *American Journal of International Law* 663.

[6] London International Assembly, Report of the Third Commission (Legal Commission) on individual rights, TNA LNU 6/7, art. III.

[7] Hersch Lauterpacht, *An International Bill of the Rights of Man*, New York: Columbia University Press, 1945, p. 71.

for the rights and freedoms of others and of meeting the just requirements of morality, public order and the general welfare in a democratic society.'

The International Covenant on Civil and Political Rights provides a more elaborate formulation of the right: '1. Everyone shall have the right to hold opinions without interference. 2. Everyone shall have the right to freedom of expression; this right shall include freedom to seek, receive and impart information and ideas of all kinds, regardless of frontiers, either orally, in writing or in print, in the form of art, or through any other media of his choice.' Paragraph 3 subjects the rights in paragraph 2, but not the right in paragraph 1, to 'special duties and responsibilities' which allow the possibility of restrictions. Such restrictions must be provided by law and must be necessary for respect of the rights or reputations of others or for the protection of national security or of public order (*ordre public*), or of public health or morals. The fundamental rights of opinion and expression are also affirmed in many of the specialised and regional treaties although the details vary considerably.[8] The text in the Convention on the Rights of the Child is virtually identical to that of the Covenant except that it omits paragraph 1 of Article 19, making no provision for the child's freedom of opinion.[9] Was this nothing more than an oversight? Common experience tells us that children are often very opinionated and there is nothing that the State, their parents, their teachers, or other adults and children can do to restrict or limit this. The African Charter on the Rights and Welfare of the Child declares that '[e]very child who is capable of communicating his or her own views shall be assured the rights to express his opinions freely in all matters and to disseminate his opinions subject to such restrictions as are prescribed by laws'.[10]

The Human Rights Committee did not include freedom of opinion or expression in the list of rights under customary law set out in its General Comment on reservations, issued in 1994.[11] But when it issued its General Comment on freedom of expression, some fifteen years later, the Committee stated that any reservation to Article 19(1), taking account its specific terms as well as the relationship of opinion and thought, as guaranteed by Article 18, would be incompatible with the object and purpose of the Covenant.[12] The Committee cited General Comment 24, on

8 International Convention on the Elimination of All Forms of Racial Discrimination, (1969) 660 UNTS 195, art. 5(d)(viii); International Convention on the Protection of the Rights of all Migrant Workers and Members of their Families, (2003) 2220 UNTS 3, art. 14; Convention on the Rights of Persons with Disabilities, (2008) 2515 UNTS 3, art. 21; European Convention on Human Rights, (1953) 213 UNTS 221, art. 10; American Convention on Human Rights, (1978) 1144 UNTS 123, art. 13; African Charter on Human and Peoples' Rights, (1986) 1520 UNTS 271, art. 9; Arab Charter on Human Rights, art. 24(3); Charter of Fundamental Rights of the European Union, OJ C 326/391, art. 11; African Charter on the Rights and Welfare of the Child, art. 7.

9 Convention on the Rights of the Child, (1990) 1571 UNTS 3, art. 13.

10 African Charter on the Rights and Welfare of the Child, art. 7.

11 General Comment 24, Issues Relating to Reservations Made upon Ratification or Accession to the Covenant or the Optional Protocols thereto, or in Relation to Declarations under art. 41 of the Covenant, CCPR/C/21/Rev.1/Add.6, para. 8.

12 General Comment 34, art. 19: Freedoms of opinion and expression, CCPR/C/GC/34, para. 5.

reservations, as authority for this statement, although it did not specify any particular paragraph. In fact, General Comment 24 does not appear to support such a statement. The Committee's message has thus been somewhat garbled, diminishing its authority in the determination of the status of freedom of opinion and expression under customary international law.

There have been a number of reservations to Article 19 of the Covenant. However, none of these challenge the fundamental principles of freedom of opinion and expression as such, perhaps with the exception of a strange reservation by Pakistan referring to its Constitution and Sharia law that was almost immediately withdrawn after many States objected.[13] The others refer to regulation of broadcasting and cinema[14] and to political activities of public officers and non-nationals.[15] There are no genuine reservations and only three interpretative declarations regarding the freedom of expression provision of the Convention on the Rights of the Child, by Algeria,[16] Belgium,[17] and the Holy See.[18] The broad general reservations to the Convention on the Rights of the Child that refer to national constitutions and Shariah law do not appear, in practice, to contemplate freedom of expression. In any event, the States that have formulated such reservations to the Convention on the Rights of the Child have not made reservations to Article 19 of the International Covenant on Civil and Political Rights. This means that freedom of expression, set out in Article 19 of the Covenant and echoed in Article 13 of the Convention on the Rights of the Child, has been accepted as treaty law by the 197 States that are parties to one or both of these treaties. The objection that States Parties to the Convention have only recognised freedom of expression for children does not seem significant. It would make no sense to accept it for children but deny it to adults.

In any case, further confirmation that States that are not parties to the International Covenant on Civil and Political Rights nevertheless recognise the rights set out in Article 19 are found in the Universal Periodic Review materials: Bhutan,[19] Brunei Darussalam,[20] China,[21] Comoros,[22]

[13] (2010) 2677-2678 UNTS 230-231, C.N.405.2010.TREATIES-17. See the Statement by the Human Rights Committee on Pakistan's reservation at the time of ratification: A/66/40, paras. 48–49.

[14] France, C.N.335.1980.TREATIES-10; Germany, C.N.76.1988.TREATIES-4; Italy, C.N.231.1978.TREATIES-11; Luxembourg, C.N.265.1983.TREATIES-3/8/2; Monaco, C.N.382.1997.TREATIES-5/9; Netherlands, C.N.316.1978.TREATIES-14; Australia, C.N.230.1980.TREATIES-6.

[15] C.N.304.1990.TREATIES-4/11/4.

[16] C.N.135.1993.TREATIES-4.

[17] C.N.320.1991.TREATIES-16.

[18] C.N.112.1990.TREATIES-4.

[19] Bhutan, National report, A/HRC/WG.6/6/BTN/1, paras. 36, 103–105.

[20] Brunei Darussalam, Views on conclusions, A/HRC/27/11/Add.1, para. 113.43; Brunei Darussalam, Report of the Working Group, A/HRC/13/14, para. 85.

[21] China, Report of the Working Group, A/HRC/11/25, para. 71; China, National report, A/HRC/WG.6/17/CHN/1, para. 109.

[22] Comoros, Report of the Working Group, A/HRC/26/11, para. 64; Comoros, Report of the Working Group, A/HRC/41/12, para. 109; Comoros, National report, A/HRC/WG.6/18/COM/1, paras. 138, 143; Comoros, National report, A/HRC/WG.6/32/COM/1, para. 197.

Cuba,[23] Kiribati,[24] Malaysia,[25] Micronesia,[26] Myanmar,[27] Nauru,[28] Oman,[29] Palau,[30] Saint Kitts and Nevis,[31] Saint Lucia,[32] Saudi Arabia,[33] Singapore,[34] Solomon Islands,[35] South Sudan,[36] Tonga,[37] Tuvalu,[38] United Arab Emirates.[39] Moreover, as parties to the Arab Charter on Human Rights, Saudi Arabia and the United Arab Emirates have an applicable treaty obligation. Unquestionably, then, freedom of opinion and expression is universally accepted and is without doubt a norm of customary international law.

1. Freedom of opinion and expression

Freedom of opinion is linked with freedom of expression in the Universal Declaration and in the International Covenant on Civil and Political Rights. Some of the treaties present this in different ways. For example, the African Charter on Human and Peoples' Rights states that '[e]very individual shall have the right to

[23] Cuba, Report of the Working Group, A/HRC/11/22, paras. 21, 118; Cuba, Report of the Working Group, A/HRC/24/16, paras. 16–17; Cuba, National report, A/HRC/WG.6/4/CUB/1, paras. 44–48; Cuba, National report, A/HRC/WG.6/30/CUB/1, paras. 28–30.

[24] Kiribati, National report, A/HRC/WG.6/8/KIR/1, paras. 23, 53.

[25] Malaysia, Report of the Working Group, A/HRC/40/11, paras. 8, 73, Views on conclusions, A/HRC/40/11/Add.1, National report, A/HRC/WG.6/17/MYS/1, paras. 87, 97, 146, and National report, A/HRC/WG.6/31/MYS/1, paras. 30–32.

[26] Micronesia, Report of the Working Group, A/HRC/31/4, para. 8; Micronesia, Report of the Working Group, A/HRC/WG.6/9/FSM/1, paras. 14, 94.

[27] Myanmar, National report, A/HRC/WG.6/23/MMR/1, paras. 34–37.

[28] Nauru, Report of the Working Group, A/HRC/31/7, para. 44; Nauru, Views on conclusions, A/HRC/31/7/Add.1, para. 20; Nauru, National report, A/HRC/WG.6/10/NRU/1, para. 16.

[29] Oman, Report of the Working Group, A/HRC/31/11, para. 12; Oman, National report, A/HRC/WG.6/23/OMN/1, paras. 105–109; Oman, Report of the Working Group, A/HRC/17/7, para. 58; Oman, National report, A/HRC/WG.6/10/OMN/1, p. 5, paras. 55–61.

[30] Palau, National report, A/HRC/WG.6/24/PLW/1, paras. 5, 21.

[31] St Kitts and Nevis, National report, A/HRC/WG.6/10/KNA/1, para. 8.

[32] Saint Lucia, National report, A/HRC/WG.6/10/LCA/1, para. 17.

[33] Saudi Arabia, National report, A/HRC/WG.6/4/SAU/1, paras. 26, 47; Saudi Arabia, Report of the Working Group, A/HRC/11/23, paras. 24, 83; Saudi Arabia, Views on conclusions, A/HRC/11/23/Add.1, paras. 8, 53; Saudi Arabia, Report of the Working Group, A/HRC/40/4, para. 116; Saudi Arabia, Views on conclusions, A/HRC/40/4/Add.1, para. 21; Saudi Arabia, National report, A/HRC/WG.6/31/SAU/1, para. 74.

[34] Singapore, National report, A/HRC/WG.6/11/SGP/1, paras. 141, 145–154; Singapore, Views on conclusions, A/HRC/32/17/Add.1 , paras. 47–50; Singapore, Report of the Working Group, A/HRC/32/17, paras. 72–75.

[35] Solomon Islands, National report, A/HRC/WG.6/11/SLB/1, paras. 23, 24, 82.

[36] South Sudan, National report, A/HRC/WG.6/26/SSD/1, para. 9.

[37] Tonga, National report, A/HRC/WG.6/15/TON/1, paras. 29, 43–48; Tonga, Report of the Working Group, A/HRC/23/4, para. 13; Tonga, National report, A/HRC/WG.6/29/TON/1, paras. 45, 101–109; Tonga, Report of the Working Group, A/HRC/38/5, para. 38; Tonga, Report of the Working Group, A/HRC/8/48, para. 34.

[38] Tuvalu, National report, A/HRC/WG.6/3/TUV/1, paras. 33, 51, 55.

[39] United Arab Emirates, Report of the Working Group, A/HRC/23/13, para. 52; United Arab Emirates, National report, A/HRC/WG.6/29/ARE/1, para. 24; United Arab Emirates, Report of the Working Group, A/HRC/10/75, para. 91(1) and (17); United Arab Emirates, National report, A/HRC/WG.6/15/ARE/1, paras. 20–21.

express and disseminate his opinions within the law'.[40] The American Convention speaks of 'freedom of thought and expression',[41] suggesting, perhaps, that 'thought' and 'opinion' are synonymous. To the extent that there is a relationship between the two freedoms, it seems to be primarily because freedom of expression is used in order to express opinions. Freedom of expression has much broader purposes, however, and may even include mode of dress or clothing as well as the form the expression takes, including the choice of language. The Convention on the Rights of Persons with Disabilities, with 182 States Parties, specifies the exercise of freedom of expression through sign languages, Braille, and other means.[42] There appear to be no reservations to the relevant provision.

In General Comment 34, the Human Rights Committee wrote: 'Freedom of opinion extends to the right to change an opinion whenever and for whatever reason a person so freely chooses. No person may be subject to the impairment of any rights under the Covenant on the basis of his or her actual, perceived or supposed opinions.' It added that forms of opinion enjoyed protection, including opinions of a political, scientific, historic, moral, or religious nature.[43] The Committee referred to one of its decisions, *Mika Miha v. Equatorial Guinea*,[44] as authority for the proposition that '[t]he harassment, intimidation or stigmatisation of a person, including arrest, detention, trial or imprisonment for reasons of the opinions they may hold, constitutes a violation of article 19, paragraph 1'.[45]

Freedom of expression is also bound up with other human rights. The association between free speech and political democracy has always been fundamental. The European Court of Human Rights has said that 'freedom of expression constitutes one of the essential foundations of a democratic society and one of the basic conditions for its progress and each individual's self-fulfilment'.[46] Although freedom of expression may be one of the quintessential civil and political rights, it is not without important relationships to economic, social, and cultural rights. Illiteracy is an obstacle both to the exercise of freedom of expression and the right to receive information, although it is usually approached within the framework of the right to education.[47] Literacy and oral expression are considered to be fundamental elements of primary education and 'essential learning tools'.[48] Without them, freedom of expression cannot be exercised effectively.

[40] African Charter on Human and Peoples' Rights, (1986) 1520 UNTS 271, art. 9(2).
[41] American Convention on Human Rights, (1978) 1144 UNTS 123, art. 13(1).
[42] Convention on the Rights of Persons with Disabilities, (2008) 2515 UNTS 3, art. 21(b).
[43] General Comment 34, art. 19: Freedoms of opinion and expression, CCPR/C/GC/34, para. 9.
[44] *Mika Miha v. Equatorial Guinea*, no. 414/1990, Views, 8 July 1994, CCPR/C/51/D/414/1990, para. 6.8.
[45] General Comment 34, art. 19: Freedoms of opinion and expression, CCPR/C/GC/34, para. 9.
[46] *Rekvényi v. Hungary* [GC], no. 25390/94, § 42, ECHR 1999-III.
[47] See the brief reference to this issue in General Comment 25, The right to participate in public affairs, voting rights and the right of equal access to public service (art. 25), CCPR/C/21/Rev.1/Add.7, para. 12.
[48] General Comment 13, The right to education (art. 13 of the Covenant), E/C.12/1999/10, para. 9.

2. Freedom of information

In addition to freedom of opinion and expression, Article 19 of the Universal Declaration of Human Rights recognises the right 'to seek, receive and impart information'. This right to information is formulated in the same terms in the International Covenant on Civil and Political Rights and, with some variations, in the specialised and regional treaties.[49] The Convention on the Rights of the Child affirms the right 'to information and material from a diversity of national and international sources, especially those aimed at the promotion of [the child's] social, spiritual and moral well-being and physical and mental health'.[50]

In General Comment 34, the Human Rights Committee spoke of a 'right of access to information'.[51] Positive measures are required. States Parties should 'proactively put in the public domain Government information of public interest', and 'ensure easy, prompt, effective and practical access to such information'.[52] The right to seek information includes a right of access to records in the possession of public bodies. The latter encompass all branches of the State (executive, legislative, and judicial) and other public or governmental authorities, at national, regional, or local levels.[53] Protection of the right to privacy imposes limits on the right of access.

3. Restrictions

The Human Rights Committee has spoken of 'narrow restrictions permitted under article 19 of the Covenant'.[54] They must be 'provided by law' and cannot simply be the result of an administrative provision or a vague statutory authorisation. The laws in question are to be formulated with sufficient precision to enable an individual to regulate his or her conduct accordingly.[55] They must be made accessible to the public. Laws cannot confer unfettered discretion for the restriction of freedom of expression on those charged with its execution.[56] According to the Committee,

[49] European Convention on Human Rights, (1953) 213 UNTS 221, art. 10(1); American Convention on Human Rights, (1978) 1144 UNTS 123, art. 13(1); African Charter on Human and Peoples' Rights, (1986) 1520 UNTS 271, art. 9; Arab Charter on Human Rights, art. 32(1); Convention on the Rights of Persons with Disabilities, (2008) 2515 UNTS 3, art. 21; International Convention for the Protection of All Persons from Enforced Disappearance, (2010) 2716 UNTS 3, PP 8; International Convention on the Protection of the Rights of all Migrant Workers and Members of their Families, (2003) 2220 UNTS 3, art. 13(2); Framework Convention for the Protection of National Minorities, CETS 157, art. 9(1).

[50] Convention on the Rights of the Child, (1990) 1571 UNTS 3, art. 17.

[51] General Comment 34, art. 19: Freedoms of opinion and expression, CCPR/C/GC/34, para. 18.

[52] Ibid., para. 19.

[53] Ibid., para. 7.

[54] Russia, Concluding observations, CCPR/C/RUS/CO/7, para. 19; Italy, Concluding observations, CCPR/C/ITA/CO/6, para. 39; Kazakhstan, Concluding observations, CCPR/C/KAZ/CO/2, para. 50.

[55] General Comment 34, art. 19: Freedoms of opinion and expression, CCPR/C/GC/34, para. 25.

[56] Ibid., para. 25, citing General Comment 27, Freedom of movement (art. 12), CCPR/C/21/Rev.1/Add.9, para. 13.

'[l]aws must provide sufficient guidance to those charged with their execution to enable them to ascertain what sorts of expression are properly restricted and what sorts are not'.[57] The requirement of necessity indicates that the restriction must be proportional in severity and intensity to the purpose being sought and may not become the rule. The Committee insists that '[a]ny restriction on the exercise of such freedoms must conform to the strict tests of necessity and proportionality'.[58]

Restriction justified by respect for the rights or reputations of others applies in the case of anti-defamation legislation but it has the potential to undermine freedom of expression, especially in the context of political debate. Other rights justifying restriction include freedom of religion, in the prohibition of blasphemous statements, and the right to equality, where racial and religious hatred is being advocated. Laws may prevent the publication of opinion polls immediately prior to an election so as to protect the integrity of the ballot.[59] Many governments have a tendency to invoke protection of national security to justify far-reaching restrictions on freedom of expression of opposition groups, politicians, and critical media. In a number of cases, the Human Rights Committee has held there to be breaches of freedom of expression.[60] The protection of 'public order' is also listed as a permissible justification for restrictions. However, vague accusations of subversive or dangerous activities raised against critics of a regime and sanctions imposed for this (particularly, arrest) are unacceptable.[61] The 'public health and public morals' ground may shelter restrictions on circulation of misleading information about health-threatening substances (drugs, medicine, poisons, radioactivity, etc.) or practices. Typical examples of interference with freedom of expression to protect public morals include prohibitions of or restrictions on pornographic or blasphemous publications.

Restrictions on freedom of expression are not only permissible but in some cases they are even required by international human rights law. By virtue of an Optional Protocol to the Convention on the Rights of the Child, States Parties are required to ensure that criminal law addresses the production, distribution, dissemination, importing, exporting, offering, selling, and possessing of child pornography.[62] Child pornography is defined as 'any representation, by whatever means, of a child engaged in real or simulated explicit sexual activities or any representation of the

[57] Ibid.

[58] Ibid., para. 22; *Agazade et al. v. Azerbaijan*, no. 2205/2012, Views, 27 October 2017, CCPR/C/118/D/2205/2012, para. 7.4; *Melnikov v. Belarus*, no. 2147/2012, Views, 14 July 2017, CCPR/C/120/D/2147/2012, para. 8.4.

[59] *Jong-Cheol v. Republic of Korea*, no. 968/2001, Views, 27 July 2005, CCPR/C/84/D/968/2001, para. 8.2–8.3.

[60] *Cf., e.g. Mukong v. Cameroon*, no. 458/1991, Views, 27 July 2005, CCPR/C/84/D/968/2001, para. 9.7; *Sohn v. Republic of Korea*, no. 518/1992, Views, 19 July 1995, CCPR/C/54/D/518/1992, para. 8.3.

[61] *Komarovsky v. Belarus*, no. 1839/2008, Views, 25 October 2013, CCPR/C/109/D/1839/2008, para. 9.4; *Coleman v. Australia*, no. 1157/2003, Views, 17 July 2006, CCPR/C/87/D/1157/2003, para. 7.3.

[62] Optional Protocol to the Convention on the Rights of the Child on the sale of children, child prostitution and child pornography, (2002) 2171 UNTS 227, art. 3(1)(c).

sexual parts of a child for primarily sexual purposes'.[63] There have been a few interpretative declarations to the provision,[64] but no genuine reservations. There are 176 States Parties to the Optional Protocol.

The International Convention on the Elimination of All Forms of Racial Discrimination requires States Parties to 'declare an offence punishable by law all dissemination of ideas based on racial superiority or hatred, incitement to racial discrimination as well as all acts of violence or incitement to such acts against any race or group of persons of another colour or ethnic origin'.[65] The Committee on the Elimination of Racial Discrimination has said that 'the prohibition of the dissemination of all ideas based upon racial superiority or hatred is compatible with the right to freedom of opinion and expression'.[66] Along the same lines, Article 20 of the International Covenant on Civil and Political Rights requires the prohibition of propaganda for war and of advocacy of national, racial, or religious hatred that constitutes incitement to discrimination, hostility, or violence. In the list of customary norms set out in General Comment 24, the Human Rights Committee said that States could not 'permit the advocacy of national, racial or religious hatred'.[67] Judge Pinto de Albuquerque has written that there is a principle of customary law and even a norm of *jus cogens* requiring States to criminalise speech or any other form of dissemination of racism, xenophobia, or ethnic intolerance.[68] There have been reservations and interpretative declarations to the provisions in the Covenant and the Convention on Racial Discrimination but their significance has been greatly exaggerated, as explained elsewhere in this study.[69]

The Convention on the Prevention and Punishment of the Crime of Genocide requires the prosecution of 'direct and public incitement to commit genocide'. Although there have been frequent statements suggesting that the principles in

[63] Ibid., art. 2(c).

[64] Belgium, C.N.257.2006.TREATIES-5: 'The expression "child pornography" is understood to mean the visual representation of a child participating in real or simulated sexual activities or the visual representation of the sexual parts of a child, when the dominant characteristic is a description for sexual purposes.' Denmark, C.N.815.2003.TREATIES-19: 'Denmark declares that she interprets the words "any representation" in article 2 (c), of the Protocol to mean "any visual representation". Denmark further declares that the possession of pornographic visual representation of a person, who has completed his or her fifteenth year and who has consented to the said possession, shall not be considered covered by the binding provisions of the Protocol.' Sweden, C.N.63.2007.TREATIES-2: ' ... Sweden interprets the word "any representation" in article 2 (c) of the Protocol as "visual representation".' United States of America, C.N.1360.2002.TREATIES-52: 'The United States understands the term "child pornography", as defined in Article 2(c) of the Protocol, to mean the visual representation of a child engaged in real or simulated sexual activities or of the genitalia of a child where the dominant characteristic is depiction for a sexual purpose.'

[65] International Convention on the Elimination of All Forms of Racial Discrimination, (1969) 660 UNTS 195, art. 4(a).

[66] General Recommendation 15 on art. 4 of the Convention, A/48/18, p. 114, para. 4.

[67] General Comment 24, Issues Relating to Reservations Made upon Ratification or Accession to the Covenant or the Optional Protocols thereto, or in Relation to Declarations under art. 41 of the Covenant, CCPR/C/21/Rev.1/Add.6, para. 8.

[68] *Vona v. Hungary*, no. 35943/10, 9 July 2013, Concurring opinion of Judge Pinto de Albuquerque.

[69] See the discussion at pp. 87–88.

the Convention are enshrined in customary law, the crime of direct and public incitement may be an exception. The Rome Statute of the International Criminal Court incorporates the crime of direct and public incitement to commit genocide. However, in contrast with all other provisions dealing with modes of commission of a crime, the Rome Statute does not extend 'direct and public incitement' to the other crimes within its jurisdiction, namely, aggression, crimes against humanity, and war crimes. In its draft articles on crimes against humanity the International Law Commission did not include a 'direct and public incitement' provision that would correspond to the text in the Genocide Convention.[70] In one of its rare pronouncements on the customary law of human rights, the European Court of Human Rights said there does not appear to be a customary international law norm requiring States to criminalise genocide denial.[71]

* * *

Conclusions. Freedom of opinion and expression is enshrined in customary international law. This includes freedom to hold opinions without interference, and to seek, receive, and impart information.

B. Thought, conscience, and religion

When Georges Clemenceau explained to Polish President Jan Paderewski that the text of the treaty to be adopted at Versailles recognising Poland's independence was to include provisions recognising freedom of religion, he said this was in keeping with various precedents, citing in particular the 1878 Congress of Berlin where the sovereignty and independence of Serbia was affirmed.[72] As Clemenceau noted, Lord Salisbury had affirmed 'the great principle of religious liberty'. Prince Bismarck declared that Germany would admit the independence of Serbia, 'but on condition that religious liberty will be recognised'. Bismarck instructed the drafting committee to link the proclamation of Serbian independence and the recognition of religious liberty.[73] The Treaty of Berlin specified that '[t]he freedom, and outward exercise of all forms of worship shall be assured to all persons belonging to Servia, as well as to foreigners, and no hindrance shall be offered either to the hierarchical organisation of the different communions, or to their relations with their

[70] See William A. Schabas, 'Prevention of Crimes Against Humanity', (2018) 16 *Journal of International Criminal Justice* 702, at p. 726.

[71] *Perinçek v. Switzerland* [GC], no. 27510/08, § 266, 15 October 2015.

[72] Draft of the Covering Letter to be Addressed to M. Paderewski in Transmitting to Him the Treaty to be Signed by Poland under art. 93 of the Treaty of Peace with Germany, FRUS VI, p. 629, (1919) 13 *American Journal of International Law* (supplement) 416, at pp. 417–418.

[73] Protocol No. 8, 28 June 1878, (1877–1878) 69 BFSP 946; Edward Hertslet, *The Map of Europe by Treaty*, Vol. IV, London: HMSO, No. 528, p. 2743.

spiritual chiefs'.[74] The 1919 Treaty with Poland recognised that '[a]ll inhabitants of Poland shall be entitled to the free exercise, whether public or private, of any creed, religion or belief, whose practices are not inconsistent with public order or public morals'.[75] Freedom of religion provisions also appeared in the Declaration prepared by the Institut de Droit International in 1929.[76] The second of Franklin D. Roosevelt's four freedoms was 'freedom of every person to worship God in his own way—everywhere in the world'.[77]

The right to freedom of thought, conscience, and religion is enshrined in Article 18 of the Universal Declaration of Human Rights and in Article 18 of the International Covenant on Civil and Political Rights. The Universal Declaration adds that the right includes freedom to change one's religion or belief, and freedom, either alone or in community with others and in public or private, to manifest religion or belief in teaching, practice, worship, and observance. The Covenant prohibits coercion that impairs the freedom to adopt a religion or belief. It also states that freedom to manifest religion or belief may be subject only to such limitations 'as are prescribed by law and are necessary to protect public safety, order, health, or morals or the fundamental rights and freedoms of others'. Freedom of thought, conscience, and religion is secured in many other specialised and regional human rights treaties.[78] There are several reservations or declarations to the freedom of religion provisions of the International Covenant on Civil and Political Rights and the Convention on the Rights of the Child.

Of States that have not ratified the International Covenant on Civil and Political Rights, several explicitly confirm their recognition of freedom of religion in their reports to the Human Rights Council.[79] Almost all of these States are parties to the

[74] Treaty between Great Britain, Austria-Hungary, France, Germany, Italy, Russia, and Turkey, for the Settlement of the Affairs of the East, signed at Berlin, 13 July 1878, (1877–1878) 69 BFSP 749; Edward Hertslet, *The Map of Europe by Treaty*, Vol. IV, London: HMSO, No. 530, p. 2759, art. XXXV.

[75] Treaty between the Principal Allied and Associated Powers and Poland, (1919) 112 BSP 232, art. II.

[76] Institut de Droit International, 'Declaration of the International Rights of Man', (1941) 35 *American Journal of International Law* 663, art. II.

[77] Congressional Record, 1941, Vol. 87, Pt. I, 6 January 1941.

[78] International Convention on the Elimination of All Forms of Racial Discrimination, (1969) 660 UNTS 195, art. 5(d)(vii); Convention on the Rights of the Child, (1990) 1571 UNTS 3, art. 14; International Convention on the Protection of the Rights of all Migrant Workers and Members of their Families, (2003) 2220 UNTS 3, art. 13; European Convention on Human Rights, (1953) 213 UNTS 221, art. 9; American Convention on Human Rights, (1978) 1144 UNTS 123, art. 12; African Charter on Human and Peoples' Rights, (1986) 1520 UNTS 271, art. 8; Arab Charter on Human Rights, art. 30; Charter of Fundamental Rights of the European Union, OJ C 326/391, art. 10; African Charter on the Rights and Welfare of the Child, art. 9.

[79] Bhutan, National report, A/HRC/WG.6/33/BTN/1, para. 7, Report of the Working Group, A/HRC/42/8, para. 152, and Report of the Working Group, A/HRC/27/8, para. 113; Brunei Darussalam, Views on conclusions, A/HRC/27/11/Add.1 , para. 113.48; China, National report, A/HRC/WG.6/17/CHN/1, para. 59 and National report, paras. 55–58; Comoros, National report, A/HRC/WG.6/18/COM/1, paras. 124–127; Cuba, National report, A/HRC/WG.6/4/CUB/1, paras. 40–43 and Report of the Working Group, A/HRC/11/22, para. 20; Fiji, National report, A/HRC/WG.6/20/FJI/1, paras. 37–38; Malaysia, National report, A/HRC/40/11/Add.1, para. 24 and Report of the Working Group, A/HRC/25/10, para. 66; Micronesia, National report, A/HRC/WG.6/9/FSM/1, para. 14; Myanmar, National report, A/HRC/WG.6/23/MMR/1, paras. 144–149 and National report, A/HRC/WG.6/10/MMR/1, para. 41; Singapore, National report, A/HRC/WG.6/11/SGP/1, para. 23; Solomon Islands,

Convention on the Rights of the Child. In their reports to the Committee on the Rights of the Child, the vast majority use the occasion to affirm their recognition of freedom of religion in general, and not just with respect to children.[80]

In its General Comment on reservations, the Human Rights Committee declared that to deny freedom of thought, conscience, and religion was contrary to customary international law.[81] Although the right is formulated with respect to three categories, thought, conscience, and religion, it is commonly spoken of as 'freedom of religion' and 'freedom of religion or belief'. Submissions in the course of the Universal Periodic Review treat 'thought, conscience, and religion' as a formulaic phrase that in substance only appears to concern religion. In its General Comment on the subject, the Human Rights Committee explained that 'the freedom to hold beliefs' is encompassed, and that theistic, non-theistic, and atheistic beliefs, as well as the right not to profess any religion or belief, are protected.[82] The International Covenant on Civil and Political Rights does not permit derogation from freedom of religion, although this is not the case with the European Convention on Human Rights. In practice, the issue is not the holding of beliefs, religious or other, but their manifestation. The Covenant makes this distinction clear when it specifies that limitations or restrictions may be imposed on manifesting religion or belief. No one can be compelled to reveal his or her inner thoughts or adherence to a religion or belief.

Restrictions on fundamental freedoms are acceptable, according to Article 29(2) of the Universal Declaration of Human Rights: 'In the exercise of his rights and freedoms, everyone shall be subject only to such limitations as are determined by law solely for the purpose of securing due recognition and respect for the rights and freedoms of others and of meeting the just requirements of morality, public order and the general welfare in a democratic society.' The International Covenant makes a significant distinction, codifying the limitation only with regard to manifesting religion and not to the freedom itself. This is an acknowledgement of the protection

National report, A/HRC/WG.6/11/SLB/1, para. 24; United Arab Emirates, National report, A/HRC/WG.6/3/ARE/1, p. 8, Report of the Working Group, A/HRC/10/75, para. 21, Report of the Working Group, A/HRC/23/13, para. 14.

[80] Bhutan, Second periodic report, CRC/C/BTN/2, para. 114; China, Initial report, CRC/C/11/Add.7, paras. 66–67; Cuba, Second periodic report, CRC/C/CUB/2, paras. 182–196; Fiji, Initial report, CRC/C/28/Add.7, para. 94; Kiribati, Initial report, CRC/C/KIR/1, para. 87; Malaysia, Initial report, CRC/C/MYS/1, para. 161; Marshall Islands, Initial report, CRC/C/28/Add.12, para. 56; Micronesia, Initial report, CRC/C/28/Add.5, para. 103; Myanmar, Initial report, CRC/C/8/Add.9, paras. 55–56; Nauru, Initial report, CRC/C/NRU/1, paras. 172–174; Oman, Combined third and fourth periodic reports, CRC/C/OMN/3-4, para. 89; Palau, Initial report, CRC/C/51/Add.3, para. 97; Saint Lucia, Initial report, CRC/C/28/Add.23, paras. 80–81; Singapore, Initial report, CRC/C/51/Add.8, para. 26; Solomon Islands, Initial report, CRC/C/51/Add.6, para. 168; South Sudan, Initial report, CRC/C/SSD/1, para. 84; Tonga, Initial report, CRC/C/TON/1, paras. 246–251; Tuvalu, Initial report, CRC/C/TUV/1, para. 130; United Arab Emirates, Second periodic report, CRC/C/ARE/2, paras. 93–94.

[81] General Comment 23, CCPR/C/21/Rev.1/Add.5, para. 8.

[82] General Comment 22, The right to freedom of thought, conscience and religion, CCPR/C/21/Rev.1/Add.4, para. 2.

of the *forum internum* from any control or restriction. The distinction is not always easy to implement in practice. For example, in some countries compulsory military service has been refused by individuals who argue that it is incompatible with their religion or belief. If the refusal amounts to manifesting their religion, the State may contend that the right is not unrestricted. But if the individual can claim this is part of the *forum internum*, then there can be no limitation.[83]

1. Freedom to change religion

The Universal Declaration of Human Rights states that freedom of thought, conscience, and religion includes the freedom to change one's religion or belief. When the Declaration was being drafted, Saudi Arabia objected to such a freedom. It called for a vote on the provision, which was adopted in the Third Committee of the General Assembly by twenty-seven to five; Afghanistan, Iraq, Pakistan, Saudi Arabia, and Syria voting against.[84] Saudi Arabia was one of eight States to abstain in the final vote on the Universal Declaration. It offered no explanation for its position, although John Humphrey wrote much later that he assumed this was explained by its opposition to recognition of the freedom to change religion.[85]

Reservations to the International Covenant on Civil and Political Rights and to the Convention on the Rights of the Child indicate that some States Parties do not accept the right to change religion, at least as far as Muslims are concerned. Moreover, several of the States that are not party to the Covenant appear to consider that change of religion or apostasy is forbidden by Islamic law.[86] Maldives has

[83] Compare the views of the majority and those of the dissenters in the Human Rights Committee: *Jeong et al. v. Republic of Korea*, nos. 1642-1741/2007, Views, 24 March 2011, CCPR/C/101/D/1642-1741/2007; *Atasoy and Sarkut v. Turkey*, nos. 1853 and 1854/2008, Views, 29 March 2012, CCPR/C/104/D/1853-1854/2008.

[84] Summary Record of the hundred and twenty-eighth meeting [of the Third Committee of the General Assembly], 9 November 1948, *Official Records of the General Assembly*, pp. 405–415. Also Saudi Arabia: Amendment to art. 16 of the Draft Declaration (E/800), A/C.3/247/Rev.1

[85] John P. Humphrey, *Human Rights and the United Nations: A Great Adventure*, Dobbs Ferry, NY: Transnational Publishers, 1984, p. 73. Also: Susan Waltz, 'Universal Human Rights: The Contribution of Muslim States', (2004) 26 *Human Rights Quarterly* 799, at pp. 814–817.

[86] Algeria, C.N.135.1993.TREATIES-4, explained in Algeria, Third and fourth periodic reports, CRC/C/DZA/3-4, para. 390–391; Brunei Darussalam, C.N.478.1995.TREATIES-11, explained in Brunei Darussalam, Combined second and third periodic reports, CRC/C/BRN/2-3, para. 54; Iraq, C.N.235.1994.TREATIES-4, explained in Iraq, Combined second to fourth periodic reports, CRC/C/IRQ/2-4, para. 9; also, para. 41; Jordan, C.N.116.1991.TREATIES-4, explained in Jordan, Combined fourth and fifth periodic reports, CRC/C/JOR/4-5, para. 3; Malaysia, C.N.58.1995.TREATIES-1, explained in Malaysia, Initial report, CRC/C/MYS/1, paras. 6, 161; Maldives, C.N.741.2006.TREATIES-14, explained in Maldives, Core document, HRI/CORE/MDV/2010, paras. 109–11; Mauritania, (2004) 2286 UNTS 271, C.N.789.2004.TREATIES-8, explained in Mauritania, Second periodic report, CCPR/C/MRT/2, p. 9, Mauritania, National report, A/HRC/WG.6/23/MRT/1, para. 8; Morocco, C.N.203.1993.TREATIES-6, withdrawn and modified by C.N.1031.2006.TREATIES-4; Oman, C.N.441.1996.TREATIES-10, explained in Oman, Initial report, CRC/C/78/Add.1, para. 88 and Oman, CRC/C/OMN/3-4, Combined third and fourth periodic reports, para. 89; Qatar, C.N.148.1995.

been quite explicit, reporting to the Human Rights Council that its law does not provide for freedom of religion, the practice of faiths other than Islam, the building of places of worship for other religions and the import of religious icons.[87] These reservations, in one form or another, somewhat weaken the claim that the freedom to change one's religion is a norm of customary international law.[88] On the other hand, as the Human Rights Committee has explained in its General Comment, freedom of religion 'necessarily entails the freedom to choose a religion or belief, including, *inter alia*, the right to replace one's current religion or belief with another or to adopt atheistic views, as well as the right to retain one's religion or belief'.[89] There can be no genuine freedom of religion and belief if an individual's religion is determined at birth and cannot subsequently be changed. States that reject freedom to change one's religion may be required to demonstrate that they have been persistent objectors to the customary norm that is enshrined in Article 18 of the Universal Declaration of Human Rights.

A study of the issue by the Special Rapporteur on freedom of religion or belief referred to earlier pronouncements of United Nations experts[90] and the General Comment of the Human Rights Committee on freedom of religion.[91] The Special Rapporteur was not, strictly speaking, concerned with whether the right to change one's religion was enshrined in customary law. According to the Special Rapporteur, 'within the ambit of freedom of religion or belief, the forum internum, namely, the internal dimension of a person's religious or belief related conviction, enjoys absolute protection. In this regard, the forum internum differs from external manifestation of religion or belief, which can be restricted under certain conditions and in accordance with certain criteria', he wrote. Consequently, said the Special Rapporteur, 'the right to conversion has the rank of an absolutely protected right within freedom of religion or belief and does not permit any limitations or restrictions for any reason'.[92]

TREATIES-4, explained in Qatar, Second periodic report, CRC/C/QAT/2, para. 88 and C.N.262.2018. TREATIES-IV.4, explained in Qatar, Initial report, CCPR/C/QAT/1, paras. 3, 221; Saudi Arabia, C.N.22.1996.TREATIES-1, Saudi Arabia, Combined third and fourth periodic reports, CRC/C/SAU/3-4, paras. 97–98; Singapore, C.N.370.1995.TREATIES-9; Syria, C.N.267.1993.TREATIES-8, explained in Syria, Fifth periodic report, CRC/C/SYR/5, para. 11.

[87] Maldives, National report, A/HRC/WG.6/9/MDV/1/Rev.1, para. 79.

[88] See the thorough discussion of this issue in Brian D. Lepard, *Customary International Law: A New Theory with Practical Applications*, Cambridge: Cambridge University Press, 2010, pp. 346–367.

[89] General Comment 22, The right to freedom of thought, conscience and religion, CCPR/C/21/Rev.1/Add.4, para. 5.

[90] Study of the current dimensions of the problems of intolerance and of discrimination on grounds of religion or belief, Report by Mrs. Elizabeth Odio Benito, Special Rapporteur, E/CN.4/Sub.2/1987/26, para. 21.

[91] General Comment 22, The right to freedom of thought, conscience and religion, CCPR/C/21/Rev.1/Add.4, para. 5.

[92] Elimination of all forms of religious intolerance, A/67/303, para. 19. See also the discussion of conversion by an earlier Special Rapporteur: Report of the Special Rapporteur of the Commission on Human Rights on freedom of religion or belief, Asma Jahangir, A/60/399, paras. 40–68.

The right to change religion is related to proselytising, another aspect of freedom of religion. States that reject the right of persons to change religion, as well as those that simply wish to discourage it, impose restrictions on proselytising. Human rights courts and treaty bodies tread cautiously here, accepting the limitation of activities involving proselytising although condemning the use of criminal sanctions to repress the practice.[93] The term 'teaching' as a form of manifesting religion protected by Article 18 of the Universal Declaration implies 'in principle the right to try to convince one's neighbour'.[94] The European Court of Human Rights has said 'improper proselytising' is not protected by freedom of religion or freedom of expression.[95]

2. Manifesting religion

The Universal Declaration of Human Rights states that freedom of thought, conscience, and religion includes the freedom 'in public or private, to manifest his religion or belief in teaching, practice, worship and observance'. The formulation confirms the distinction that is made between the *forum internum* and the *forum externum*. To the extent that belief is not shared in some fashion with anyone else, it is entirely private and essentially immune from any State interference or violation. Individuals may profess the religion of their parents, or adopt new religions in order to marry or for other reasons yet privately harbour completely different beliefs. The reference in Article 18 of the Universal Declaration to manifesting religion 'in public or private' is somewhat superfluous, because 'private' religious practice is sheltered by the right to privacy. For many, religion and belief is a very private matter, and they also have a right not only to not reveal their faith or religious beliefs but also to not be compelled to do things that may lead to inferences about religious views. The European Court of Human Rights found a violation when there was a presumption that the oath of office of new lawyers would be taken on a Bible, forcing those for whom it was not a sacred text to declare their religion or belief, or the absence of one.[96] The right to manifest religion with others is also linked to the freedoms of peaceful assembly and association.

Freedom to manifest religion or belief in worship, observance, practice, and teaching is a broad concept involving ritual and ceremonial acts that give direct

[93] Armenia, Concluding observations, CCPR/C/ARM/CO/2, para. 24; Uzbekistan, Concluding observations, CCPR/C/UZB/CO/3, para. 707 and CCPR/C/UZB/CO/4, para. 22.

[94] *Ivanova v. Bulgaria*, No. 52435/99, § 78, 12 April 2007; *Jehovah's Witnesses of Moscow v. Russia*, No. 302/02, § 139, 10 June 2010.

[95] *Nasirov et al. v. Azerbaijan*, no. 58717/10, § 65, 20 February 2020; *Kokkinakis v. Greece*, 25 May 1993, § 348, Series A no. 260-A.

[96] *Alexandridis v. Greece*, no. 19516/06, § 38, 21 February 2008. See also *Stavropoulos et al. v. Greece*, no. 52484/18, § 60, 25 August 2020.

expression to belief.[97] To fall within the concept of 'manifest', there must be an intimate link to the religion or belief, for example, as the European Court of Human Rights has explained, 'an act of worship or devotion which forms part of the practice of a religion or belief in a generally recognised form'.[98] It may also extend to customs such as the wearing of distinctive clothing and the observance of dietary rules. International human rights courts have rejected claims by applicants seeking protection of certain acts involving manifesting religion, such as having one's ashes scattered on one's own land,[99] putting a photograph on a graveyard memorial,[100] giving a specific name to a child,[101] an exemption from a general prohibition on divorce,[102] assisted suicide,[103] mandatory participation in a school parade,[104] and refusal to sell contraceptive pills.[105]

3. Religion of children

The religion of children is not addressed in the freedom of religion provision of the Universal Declaration of Human Rights. Article 26, on the right to education, recognises that '[p]arents have a prior right to choose the kind of education that shall be given to their children', which may well imply a right to parochial schooling. Pursuant to Article 18(4) of the International Covenant on Civil and Political Rights, States Parties 'undertake to have respect for the liberty of parents and, when applicable, legal guardians to ensure the religious and moral education of their children in conformity with their own convictions'. Article 14(2) of the Convention on the Rights of the Child formulates this slightly differently, as 'the rights and duties of the parents and, when applicable, legal guardians, to provide direction to the child in the exercise of his or her right in a manner consistent with the evolving capacities of the child'. The Special Rapporteur on freedom of religion or belief has discussed the interplay between these two provisions, explaining that '[w]hereas the International Covenant on Civil and Political Rights focuses on the rights of parents, the Convention on the Rights of the Child combines parental rights and the rights of the child to freedom of religion or belief. That reflects an increased awareness, manifested in the Convention, of the status of the child as a

[97] General Comment 22, The right to freedom of thought, conscience and religion, CCPR/C/21/Rev.1/Add.4, para. 4.

[98] *Eweida and Others v. the United Kingdom*, no. 48420/10, § 82, ECHR 2013 (extracts).

[99] *X. v. Federal Republic of Germany*, no. 8741/79, Commission decision of 10 March 1981, DR 24, p. 137.

[100] *Jones v. the United Kingdom* (dec.), no. 42639/04, 13 September 2005.

[101] *Salonen v. Finland*, no. 27868/95, Commission decision of 2 July 1997.

[102] *Johnston and Others v. Ireland*, 18 December 1986, § 63, Series A no. 112.

[103] *Pretty v. the United Kingdom*, no. 2346/02, § 82, ECHR 2002-III.

[104] *Valsamis v. Greece* and *Efstratiou v. Greece*, 18 December 1996, § 37, *Reports of Judgments and Decisions* 1996-VI.

[105] *Pichon and Sajous v. France* (dec.), no. 49853/99, 2 October 2001.

rights holder.'[106] But the relationship may also be viewed differently, with Article 14(2) amounting to a limitation on the right of the child to choose his or her religion that cannot be justified under the more absolute freedom of thought, conscience, and belief that is recognised in Article 18(1) of the Covenant.

Several States have formulated reservations to Article 14(2) of the Convention on the Rights of the Child, usually premised on the rule in Islamic law whereby children must follow the religion of their father or their parents. A few States have made interpretative declarations upon ratification of the Convention stating they consider that Article 14 gives children the freedom to choose their religion or belief 'as soon as the child is capable of making such choice in view of his or her age or maturity'.[107] The range of views and approaches make it difficult to reach conclusions about the scope of customary law on this issue.

* * *

Conclusions. Freedom of thought, conscience, and religion is enshrined in customary international law. The right necessarily includes freedom to manifest one's religion and freedom to change one's religion.

C. Peaceful assembly

The right to peaceful assembly is assured by Article 20 of the Universal Declaration of Human Rights. This right is also recognised in the International Covenant on Civil and Political Rights,[108] the Convention on the Rights of the Child,[109] and in other specialised and regional treaties.[110] There have been only three reservations to the provision on peaceful assembly in the Covenant.[111] They concern the possibility of certain limitations on the right rather than its essence, and are probably unnecessary given the recognition in the text of Article 21(2) that restrictions on freedom of peaceful assembly may be imposed.[112] Only one reservation has been made to the freedom of assembly provision of the Convention on the Rights of

[106] Report of the Special Rapporteur on freedom of religion or belief, A/70/286, para. 32.

[107] Australia, C.N.335.1990.TREATIES-10. Also Belgium, C.N.320.1991.TREATIES-16.

[108] International Covenant on Civil and Political Rights, (1976) 999 UNTS 171, art. 21.

[109] Convention on the Rights of the Child, (1990) 1571 UNTS 3, art. 15.

[110] International Convention on the Suppression and Punishment of the Crime of Apartheid, (1976) 1015 UNTS 244, art. II(c); International Convention on the Elimination of All Forms of Racial Discrimination, (1969) 660 UNTS 195, art. 5(d)(ix); European Convention on Human Rights, (1953) 213 UNTS 221, art. 11; American Convention on Human Rights, (1978) 1144 UNTS 123, art. 15; African Charter on Human and Peoples' Rights, (1986) 1520 UNTS 271, art. 11; Arab Charter on Human Rights, art. 24(6); Charter of Fundamental Rights of the European Union, OJ C 326/391, art. 12.

[111] Austria, (1978) 1103 UNTS 395; Belgium, (1983) 1312 UNTS 328; Trinidad and Tobago, (1978) 1120 UNTS 488.

[112] Austria, (1978) 1103 UNTS 395; Belgium, (1983) 1312 UNTS 328; Trinidad and Tobago, (1978) 1120 UNTS 488.

the Child,[113] along with two rather innocuous interpretative declarations, one of which has been withdrawn.[114]

Taken together, these confirm the universal recognition of the fundamental right to freedom of peaceful assembly by the 197 States that are parties to one or both of the treaties. Almost all of the States that have ratified the Convention on the Rights of the Child but not the International Covenant on Civil and Political Rights confirm their general recognition of freedom of peaceful assembly, to adults as well as to children, in their reports to the Committee on the Rights of the Child.[115] Those States that have not ratified the International Covenant also provide confirmation of their adherence to freedom of peaceful assembly in their reporting to the Human Rights Council.[116]

An 'assembly' has been defined as 'an intentional and temporary gathering in a private or public space for a specific purpose. It therefore includes demonstrations, inside meetings, strikes, processions, rallies or even sits-in.'[117] Nevertheless, the 'mere fact that an expression occurs in the public space does not necessarily turn such an event into an assembly'.[118] According to the European Court of Human Rights, 'in qualifying a gathering of several people as an assembly, regard must be had to the fact that an assembly constitutes a specific form of communication of ideas, where the gathering of an indeterminate number of persons with the identifiable intention of being part of the communicative process can be in itself an intensive expression of an idea ... Furthermore, an assembly may serve the exchange

[113] Belgium, C.N.320.1991.TREATIES-16.

[114] Luxembourg, C.N.85.1994.TREATIES-1; Myanmar, C.N.160.1991.TREATIES-7, C.N.380.1993. TREATIES-11.

[115] China, Initial report, CRC/C/11/Add.7, para. 69; Cuba, Second periodic report, CRC/C/CUB/2, para. 198; Kiribati, Initial report, CRC/C/KIR/1, para. 87; Malaysia, Initial report, CRC/C/MYS/1, paras. 162–163; Marshall Islands, Initial report, CRC/C/28/Add.12, para. 57; Micronesia, Initial report, CRC/C/28/Add.5, para. 57; Nauru, Initial report, CRC/C/NRU/1, para. 175; Oman, Initial report, CRC/C/78/Add.1, paras. 90–95; Palau, Initial report, CRC/C/51/Add.3, para. 100; St Kitts and Nevis, Initial report, CRC/C/3/Add.51, para. 23; Saint Lucia, Initial report, CRC/C/28/Add.23, para. 87; Singapore, Initial report, CRC/C/51/Add.8, para. 208; Tonga, Initial report, CRC/C/TON/1, para. 252; Tuvalu, Initial report, CRC/C/TUV/1, para. 137.

[116] Brunei Darussalam, Views on conclusions, A/HRC/27/11/Add.1, p. 6; China, Report of the Working Group, A/HRC/25/5, para. 87 and Report of the Working Group (Hong Kong), A/HRC/11/25, para. 100; Comoros, National report, A/HRC/WG.6/5/COM/2, paras. 30–33; Cuba, National report, A/HRC/WG.6/4/CUB/1, para. 49; Malaysia, National report, A/HRC/WG.6/4/MYS/1/Rev.1, para. 9; Micronesia, Report of the Working Group, A/HRC/31/4, para. 8; Myanmar, National report, A/HRC/WG.6/10/MMR/1, para. 42; Nauru Report of the Working Group, A/HRC/31/7, para. 44; Oman, Report of the Working Group, A/HRC/31/11, para. 101; Palau, National report, A/HRC/WG.6/24/PLW/1, para. 5; St Kitts and Nevis National report, A/HRC/WG.6/10/KNA/1, para. 8; Saint Lucia, National report, A/HRC/WG.6/10/LCA/1, para. 17; Singapore, National report, A/HRC/WG.6/11/SGP/1, para. 22; Solomon Islands, National report, A/HRC/WG.6/11/SLB/1, para. 23; South Sudan, National report, A/HRC/WG.6/26/SSD/1, p. 9; Tuvalu, National report, A/HRC/WG.6/16/TUV/1, para. 62; United Arab Emirates, Report of the Working Group, A/HRC/10/75, para. 7.

[117] Report of the Special Rapporteur on the rights to freedom of peaceful assembly and of association, Maina Kiai, A/HRC/20/27, para. 24.

[118] *Tatár and Fáber v. Hungary*, nos. 26005/08 and 26160/08, § 38, 12 June 2012.

of ideas between the speakers and the participants, intentionally present, even if they disagree with the speakers.'[119]

Freedom of peaceful assembly is closely related to freedom of expression and freedom of religion, both of which often require 'assembly' in order to be exercised. Electoral meetings and rallies amount to exercise of the right to participate in government. Church services and marriage, funeral, or religious processions may also be protected under freedom of religion. The High Commissioner for Human Rights has said that the right of peaceful assembly, together with freedom of expression and association, and the right to participate in public affairs, constitute the foundation of all free societies.[120] The Human Rights Committee has said that 'the rejection of a person's right to organise a public assembly on the basis of its content is one of the most serious interferences with the freedom of peaceful assembly'.[121] According to the Committee, the right of peaceful assembly 'is a fundamental human right that is essential for the public expression of an individual's views and opinions and indispensable in a democratic society'.[122] General Comment 37 declares that because political speech enjoys particular protection as a form of expression, 'it follows that assemblies with a political message should enjoy a heightened level of accommodation and protection'.[123]

The right is recognised only for 'peaceful' assemblies. An assembly usually loses its peaceful character when its participants are armed even if weapons are not actually employed. Peaceful forms of civil disobedience, such as 'sit-ins' retain the protection. An assembly remains peaceful even if it is loud and boisterous. An assembly does not lose its peaceful nature, and therefore its protection under the Covenant, merely because it is attacked by the police or other law enforcement authorities, or threatened with violence by opponents. In a Russian case, permission for a picket before the Iranian embassy was denied solely because it addressed the persecution of sexual minorities in Iran. Denial of authorisation had nothing to do with the chosen location, date, time, duration, or manner of the proposed public assembly. The Deputy Prefect said it 'would provoke a negative reaction that could lead to violations of public order'. The Human Rights Committee said that 'an unspecified and general risk of a violent counter-demonstration or the mere possibility that the authorities would be unable to prevent or neutralise such violence is not sufficient to ban a demonstration'.[124] Indeed, States are under a duty to take positive measures to ensure that the right of peaceful assembly may be exercised.[125]

[119] Ibid.

[120] Seminar on effective measures and best practices to ensure the promotion and protection of human rights in the context of peaceful protests, A/HRC/25/32, para. 6.

[121] *Kirsanov v. Belarus*, no. 1864/2009, Views, 20 March 2014, CCPR/C/110/D/1864/2009, para. 9.7.

[122] *Basarevsky and Rybchenko v. Belarus*, nos. 2108 and 2109/2011, Views, 14 July 2016, CCPR/C/117/D/2108/2011-CCPR/C/117/D/2109/2011, para. 9.5; *Poplavny et al. v. Belarus*, no. 2139/2012, Views, 3 November 2016, CCPR/C/118/D/2139/2012, para. 8.5.

[123] General Comment 37, art. 21: right of peaceful assembly, CCPR/C/GC/37, para. 32.

[124] *Alekseev v. Russia*, no. 1873/2009, Views, 25 October 2013, CCPR/C/109/D/1873/2009, para. 9.6.

[125] Ibid.

The International Covenant on Civil and Political Rights and the Convention on the Rights of the Child, in what are essentially identical provisions, provide that this right may be restricted under certain circumstances. Any restrictions must be imposed in conformity with the law and must be necessary in a democratic society in the interests of national security or public safety, public order (*ordre public*), the protection of public health or morals or the protection of the rights and freedoms of others.[126] According to the Human Rights Committee, '[w]hen a State Party imposes restrictions with the aim of reconciling an individual's right to assembly and the aforementioned interests of general concern, it should be guided by the objective of facilitating the right, rather than seeking unnecessary or disproportionate limitations to it'.[127] Extensive restrictions on the right of peaceful assembly were imposed during the COVID-19 pandemic. Some States addressed this by derogating from Article 21 of the International Covenant on Civil and Political Rights.[128] The same States, however, could not derogate from Article 15 of the Convention on the Rights of the Child, as the treaty does not permit this. Surely the derogations were unnecessary because measures restricting gatherings in order to address the pandemic would be restrictions on freedom of peaceful assembly justified by 'the protection of public health'.

* * *

Conclusions. Freedom of peaceful assembly is enshrined in customary international law.

D. Association

Freedom of association in international law can be traced to the peace treaties that concluded the First World War in which 'recognition of the principle of freedom of association' was proclaimed.[129] The Declaration concerning the aims and purposes of the International Labour Organisation, adopted in Philadelphia in 1944, states that freedom of association is 'essential to sustained progress', identifying this as one of the 'fundamental principles' on which the Organisation is based. The

[126] International Covenant on Civil and Political Rights, (1976) 999 UNTS 171, art. 21; Convention on the Rights of the Child, (1990) 1571 UNTS 3, art. 15(2).

[127] *Statkevich et al. v. Belarus*, no. 2133/2012, Views, 29 October 2015, CCPR/C/115/D/2133/2012, para. 9.4.

[128] For example, Moldova , C.N.164.2020.TREATIES-IV.4; Colombia, C.N.131.2020.TREATIES-IV.4; El Salvador, C.N.134.2020.TREATIES-IV.4; Guatemala, C.N.155.2020.TREATIES-IV.4; Peru C.N.133.2020.TREATIES-IV.4; Romania, C.N.146.2020.TREATIES-IV.4; Latvia, C.N.135.2020.TREATIES-IV.4; Chile, C.N.128.2020.TREATIES-IV.4; Palestine, C.N.127.2020.TREATIES-IV.4.

[129] Treaty of Peace between the Allied and Associated Powers and Germany ('Treaty of Versailles'), (1919) TS 4, Part XIII, Preamble; Treaty of St Germain-en-Laye, [1919] TS 11, Part XIII, Preamble; Treaty of Neuilly, [1920] TS 5, Part XII, Preamble; Treaty of Trianon, (1919) 6 LNTS 187, Part XIII, Preamble.

Universal Declaration of Human Rights formulates this more broadly, without confining it to the context of organised labour. This freedom is also recognised in the International Covenant on Civil and Political Rights,[130] the Convention on the Rights of the Child,[131] and in other specialised and regional treaties.[132] The freedom of association provision in the Covenant specifically includes 'the right to form and join trade unions' for the protection of the interests of the worker.[133] The American Convention on Human Rights specifies the right to associate freely 'for ideological, religious, political, economic, labour, social, cultural, sports, or other purposes'.[134] The Human Rights Committee did not include freedom of association in its list of customary law norms.[135]

Austria, Belgium, France, and Germany formulated reservations to the freedom of association provision of the International Covenant on Civil and Political Rights in order to align it with the European Convention on Human Rights.[136] Four other States have made reservations so as to shelter elements of their national legislation that might be inconsistent with freedom of association.[137] There are three interpretative declarations dealing with issues such as prohibition of certain organisations and unions for the police and firefighters.[138] Belgium has made the only reservation to the freedom of association provision in the Convention on the Rights of the Child, more or less repeating its reservation to the Covenant.[139] There have been three rather innocuous interpretative declarations to freedom of association as formulated in the Convention on the Rights of the Child, one of which has been withdrawn.[140] None of these reservations or interpretative declarations

[130] International Covenant on Civil and Political Rights, (1976) 999 UNTS 171, art. 22(1).

[131] Convention on the Rights of the Child, (1990) 1571 UNTS 3, art. 15(1).

[132] International Convention on the Suppression and Punishment of the Crime of Apartheid, (1976) 1015 UNTS 244, art. II(c); International Convention on the Elimination of All Forms of Racial Discrimination, (1969) 660 UNTS 195, art. 5(d)(ix); Convention on the Rights of the Child, (1990) 1571 UNTS 3, art. 15; European Convention on Human Rights, (1953) 213 UNTS 221, art. 11; American Convention on Human Rights, (1978) 1144 UNTS 123, art. 16; African Charter on Human and Peoples' Rights, (1986) 1520 UNTS 271, art. 10; Arab Charter on Human Rights, art. 24(5); Charter of Fundamental Rights of the European Union, OJ C 326/391, art. 12; European Social Charter, ETS 35, Part I(7), art. 5; European Social Charter (Revised), ETS 163, Part I(7), art. 5; ILO Convention 87 concerning Freedom of Association and Protection of the Right to Organise, (1948) 68 UNTS 17; ILO Convention 98 concerning the Right to Organise and Collective Bargaining Convention, (1951) 96 UNTS 257; ILO Convention 189 concerning Decent Work for Domestic Workers, art. 3(2)(a).

[133] International Covenant on Civil and Political Rights, (1976) 999 UNTS 171, art. 22(1). See also European Convention on Human Rights, (1953) 213 UNTS 221, art. 11(1).

[134] American Convention on Human Rights, (1978) 1144 UNTS 123, art. 16(1).

[135] General Comment 24, Issues Relating to Reservations Made upon Ratification or Accession to the Covenant or the Optional Protocols thereto, or in Relation to Declarations under art. 41 of the Covenant, CCPR/C/21/Rev.1/Add.6, para. 8.

[136] Austria, (1978) 1103 UNTS 393; Belgium, (1983) 1312 UNTS 328; France: (1980) 1202 UNTS 395; Germany, (1976) 999 UNTS 29.

[137] Malta, (1990) 1578 UNTS 524; New Zealand, (1978) 1120 UNTS 489; Laos, (2009) 2617 UNTS 285; Republic of Korea, (1990) 1563 UNTS 449; Qatar, C.N.262.2018.TREATIES-IV.4.

[138] Australia, (1980) 1197 UNTS 411; Japan, (1979) 1138 UNTS 456; Monaco, (1997) 1988 UNTS 477.

[139] Belgium, C.N.320.1991.TREATIES-16.

[140] Holy See, C.N.112.1990.TREATIES-4; Luxembourg, C.N.85.1994.TREATIES-1; Myanmar, C.N.160.1991.TREATIES-7, C.N.380.1993.TREATIES-11.

casts any doubt of the commitment of the States concerned to the fundamental principle of freedom of association. Therefore, all of the 197 States that are parties to one or both of the International Covenant on Civil and Political Rights and the Convention on the Rights of the Child recognise freedom of association. Those States that have not ratified the International Covenant provide confirmation in their reporting to the Human Rights Council of their adherence to freedom of association.[141] Similarly, most of the States that have ratified the Convention on the Rights of the Child but not the International Covenant on Civil and Political Rights have confirmed their general recognition of freedom of association, to adults as well as to children, in their reports to the Committee on the Rights of the Child.[142] Several of them are also parties to the key International Labour Organisation Conventions dealing with freedom of association and the right to organise.[143]

The Human Rights Committee has frequently expressed its concerns about legislative measures requiring registration of associations with penalties for those who do not comply.[144] In some cases, it has pointed to the targeting of associations representing specific groups, such as ethnic and sexual minorities.[145] The right to freedom of association comprises not only the right to form an association

[141] Brunei Darussalam, Views on conclusions, A/HRC/27/11/Add.1, para. 6; China, Report of the Working Group, A/HRC/25/5, para. 87 and Report of the Working Group (Hong Kong), A/HRC/11/25, para. 100; Comoros, National report, A/HRC/WG.6/5/COM/2, paras. 30–33; Cuba, National report, A/HRC/WG.6/4/CUB/1, para. 49; Kiribati, National report, A/HRC/WG.6/8/KIR/1, para. 23; Malaysia, National report, A/HRC/WG.6/4/MYS/1/Rev.1, para. 9; Micronesia, Report of the Working Group, A/HRC/31/4, para. 8; Myanmar, National report, A/HRC/WG.6/10/MMR/1, para. 42; Nauru, Report of the Working Group, A/HRC/31/7, para. 44; Oman, Report of the Working Group, A/HRC/31/11, para. 102; Saint Kitts and Nevis, National report, A/HRC/WG.6/10/KNA/1, para. 8; Saint Lucia, National report, A/HRC/WG.6/10/LCA/1, para. 17; Saudi Arabia, Views on conclusions, A/HRC/40/4/Add.1, para. 21; Singapore, National report, A/HRC/WG.6/11/SGP/1, para. 22; Solomon Islands, National report, A/HRC/WG.6/11/SLB/1, para. 23; South Sudan, National report, A/HRC/WG.6/26/SSD/1, para. 9; Tonga, National report, A/HRC/WG.6/29/TON/1, para. 22(c); Tuvalu, National report, A/HRC/WG.6/16/TUV/1, para. 62; United Arab Emirates, Report of the Working Group, A/HRC/10/75, para. 7.

[142] China, Initial report, CRC/C/11/Add.7, para. 69; Comoros, Initial report, CRC/C/28/Add.13, para. 75; Cuba, Initial report, CRC/C/CUB/2, para. 198; Kiribati, Initial report, CRC/C/KIR/1, para. 87; Malaysia, Initial report, CRC/C/MYS/1, paras. 162–163; Marshall Islands, Initial report, CRC/C/28/Add.12, para. 57; Micronesia, Initial report, CRC/C/28/Add.5, para. 57; Nauru, Initial report, CRC/C/NRU/1, para. 175; Oman, Initial report, CRC/C/78/Add.1, paras. 90–95; Palau, Initial report, CRC/C/51/Add.3, para. 100; St Kitts and Nevis, Initial report, CRC/C/3/Add.51, para. 23; Saint Lucia, Initial report, CRC/C/28/Add.23, para. 87; Singapore, Initial report, CRC/C/51/Add.8, para. 208; Tonga, Initial report, CRC/C/TON/1, para. 252; Tuvalu, Initial report, CRC/C/TUV/1, para. 137; United Arab Emirates, Second periodic report, CRC/C/ARE/2, para. 95.

[143] Convention 87 concerning Freedom of Association and Protection of the Right to Organise, (1948) 68 UNTS 17: Comoros, Cuba, Kiribati, Malaysia, Myanmar, St Kitts and Nevis, Saint Lucia, Singapore; Convention 98 concerning the Right to Organise and Collective Bargaining Convention, (1951) 96 UNTS 257: Comoros, Cuba, Kiribati, St Kitts and Nevis, Saint Lucia.

[144] For example, Kazakhstan, Concluding observations, CCPR/C/KAZ/CO/2, paras. 53–54; Kuwait, Concluding observations, CCPR/C/KWT/CO/3, paras. 44–45; Pakistan, Concluding observations, CCPR/C/PAK/CO/1, paras. 39–40; Rwanda, Concluding observations, CCPR/C/RWA/CO/4, paras. 41–42; Togo, Concluding observations, CCPR/CO/76/TGO, para. 19.

[145] Greece, Concluding observations, CCPR/C/GRC/CO/2, paras. 39–40; Sri Lanka, Concluding observations, CCPR/C/LKA/CO/5, para. 22.

but also the right of its members freely to carry out activities of the association.[146] States must also protect the establishment or activities of associations from interference by private parties. Freedom to associate implies freedom not to associate. The Universal Declaration of Human Rights states this explicitly: 'No one may be compelled to belong to an association.'[147] No one may be forced, either directly or indirectly, by the State or by private parties, to join a political party, a religious society, a commercial undertaking, or a sports club. The freedom to join and form associations implies a second aspect too: freedom to choose the organisations to which one wishes to belong.

1. Trade unions and collective bargaining

Freedom to form and join trade unions is 'a special aspect of freedom of association', as the Grand Chamber of the European Court of Human Rights has noted.[148] Trade unions were very engaged in the early stages of the drafting of the International Bill of Rights. The American Federation of Labor, for example, submitted one of the important draft bills of rights at the very outset of the standard-setting work of the United Nations, even before the Commission on Human Rights had been created.[149] The Universal Declaration of Human Rights states that '[e]veryone has the right to form and to join trade unions for the protection of his interests'.[150]

Both Covenants address the issue, although the provisions are not identical. The International Covenant on Civil and Political Rights proclaims that 'everyone has … the right to form and join trade unions for the protection of his interests'.[151] A detailed provision in the International Covenant on Economic, Social and Cultural Rights sets out the scope of the protection.[152] It enshrines '[t]he right of everyone to form trade unions and join the trade union of his choice, subject only to the rules of the organisation concerned, for the promotion and protection of his economic and social interests'. The right, like freedom of association generally, may be subject to restrictions that are prescribed by law and necessary in a democratic society. More specifically, Article 8 of the International Covenant on Economic, Social and Cultural Rights allows for lawful restrictions' where members of the armed forces or of the police or of the administration of the State are concerned. In 2019, on the hundredth anniversary of the establishment of the International

[146] *Korneenko v. Belarus*, no. 1226/2004, Views, 20 July 2012, CCPR/C/105/D/1226/2003, para. 10.2; *Kungurov v. Uzbekistan*, no. 1478/2006, Views, 20 July 2011, CCPR/C/102/D/1478/2006, para. 8.2.

[147] Universal Declaration of Human Rights, A/RES/217 (III), art. 20(2). Also African Charter on Human and Peoples' Rights, (1986) 1520 UNTS 271, art. 10(2).

[148] *Demir and Baykara v. Turkey* [GC], no. 34503/97, § 109, ECHR 2008.

[149] International Bill of Rights, Proposal Submitted by American Federation of Labor, E/CT.2/2.

[150] Universal Declaration of Human Rights, A/RES/217 (III), art. 23(4).

[151] International Covenant on Civil and Political Rights, (1976) 999 UNTS 171, art. 22(1).

[152] International Covenant on Economic, Social and Cultural Rights, (1976) 993 UNTS 3, art. 8.

Labour Organisation, the two treaty bodies charged with implementing the Covenants issued a joint statement describing 'an important commonality' between them, 'reflecting the fact that the right of each individual to freely associate with others, including the right to form and join trade unions, is at the intersection between civil and political rights and economic, social and cultural rights'.[153]

There have been several reservations and a few interpretative declarations to Article 8 of the International Covenant on Economic, Social and Cultural Rights. Most of them are to specific parts of Article 8.[154] Some make the right to trade unions subject to existing national legislation.[155] None of the reservations or interpretative declarations can be said to contest the fundamental right to form trade unions. Of the States not parties to International Covenant on Economic, Social and Cultural Rights, several are parties to other treaties where the right to form and join trade unions is protected. Several of them have ratified one or both of the most relevant International Labour Organisation conventions.[156] Andorra is a party to the European Social Charter (Revised) and has accepted Article 5 on the right to organise. Saudi Arabia and the United Arab Emirates are parties to the Arab Charter on Human Rights which has similar provisions. Of the remaining States, some have confirmed their adhesion to the right to organise trade unions when they report to the Human Rights Council.[157] That the right of everyone to form trade unions and join the trade union of their choice for the promotion and protection of their economic and social interests is enshrined in customary international law does not, therefore, seem to be in any doubt.

The right to form and join trade unions also appears in several regional and specialised treaties.[158] The treaty texts have been interpreted as encompassing not only the existence of trade unions but also features of their activities, in particular

[153] Statement on freedom of association, including the right to form and join trade unions, E/C.12/66/5-CCPR/C/127/4, para. 2.

[154] Algeria, C.N.247.1989.TREATIES-1/13/3 ('comme faisant de la loi le cadre d'intervention de l'Etat pour l'organisation et l'exercice du droit syndical'); France ('it will implement the provisions of article 8 in respect of the right to strike in conformity with article 6, paragraph 4, of the European Social Charter according to the interpretation thereof given in the annex to that Charter'); United Kingdom, C.N.193.1976.TREATIES-6 ('the right not to apply sub-paragraph 1(b) of Article 8 in Hong Kong').

[155] Bangladesh, C.N.541.1998.TREAT1ES-1; China, C.N.262.2001.TREATIES-3; India, C.N.81.1979.TREATIES-2; Mexico, C.N.81.1981.TREATIES-8; Monaco, C.N.382.1997.TREATIES-5/9; New Zealand, C.N.329.1978.TREATIES-15; Norway, C.N.188.1972.TREATIES-7; Qatar, C.N.260.2018.TREATIES-IV.3.

[156] Convention 87 concerning Freedom of Association and Protection of the Right to Organise, (1948) 68 UNTS 17: Belize, Botswana, Comoros, Cuba, Fiji, Kiribati, Malaysia, Mozambique, Myanmar, St Kitts and Nevis, Samoa, Saint Lucia, Singapore, South Sudan, Vanuatu; Convention 98 concerning the Right to Organise and Collective Bargaining Convention, (1951) 96 UNTS 257: Belize, Botswana, Comoros, Cuba, Fiji, Kiribati, Mozambique, Samoa, St Kitts and Nevis, Saint Lucia, Vanuatu.

[157] Botswana, National report, A/HRC/WG.6/3/BWA/1, para. 88; Brunei Darussalam, Views on conclusions, A/HRC/27/11/Add.1, p. 6; United States of America, National report, A/HRC/WG.6/9/USA/1, para. 23.

[158] European Convention on Human Rights, (1953) 213 UNTS 221, art. 11(1); European Social Charter, ETS 35, Part I(7), art. 6(4); European Social Charter (Revised), ETS 163, Part I(7), art. 6(4); Arab Charter on Human Rights, art. 35; Additional Protocol to the American Convention on Human Rights in the area of Economic, Social and Cultural Rights, OASTS 69, art. 8; International Convention on the Protection of the Rights of all Migrant Workers and Members of their Families, (2003) 2220

the right to collective bargaining and the right to strike. One important facet of collective bargaining is the so-called 'closed shop' by which membership in the trade union is compulsory as it has the authority to negotiate binding conditions for all employees. 'No one may be compelled to belong to an association', states Article 20(2) of the Universal Declaration of Human Rights. It was on this point that the European Court of Human Rights held that the 'closed shop' approach, which it said found little support within Council of Europe Member States, was 'not an indispensable tool for the effective enjoyment of trade union freedoms'.[159] As for the right of collective bargaining, the Grand Chamber of the European Court has concluded that it is 'one of the essential elements of the "right to form and to join trade unions for the protection of [one's] interests"', adding that it is understood that States remain free to organise their system so as, if appropriate, to grant special status to representative trade unions.[160]

2. The right to strike

The right to strike is set out explicitly in the International Covenant on Economic, Social and Cultural Rights,[161] the European Social Charter,[162] the Additional Protocol to the American Convention on Human Rights,[163] and the Arab Charter on Human Rights.[164] Kuwait has made a general reservation to the right to strike.[165] Bahrain has reserved the possibility of prohibiting strikes for 'essential services'.[166] Japan has reserved it with respect to certain unspecified services, making a general reference to its national law.[167] Norway declared that its practice of compulsory arbitration 'shall not be considered incompatible with the right to strike, this right being fully recognised in Norway'.[168] With the exception of Kuwait's, none of these reservations challenges the right to strike as such. It is difficult to assess the position of the States that have not ratified one of these treaties because they rarely

UNTS 3, art. 26; International Convention on the Suppression and Punishment of the Crime of Apartheid, (1976) 1015 UNTS 243, art. II(c).

[159] *Sørensen and Rasmussen v. Denmark* [GC], nos. 52562/99 and 52620/99, §§ 72–75, ECHR 2006-I.
[160] *Demir and Baykara v. Turkey* [GC], no. 34503/97, § 154, ECHR 2008.
[161] International Covenant on Economic, Social and Cultural Rights, (1976) 993 UNTS 3, art. 8(1)(d).
[162] European Social Charter (Revised), ETS 163, Part I(7), art. 6(4).
[163] Additional Protocol to the American Convention on Human Rights in the area of Economic, Social and Cultural Rights, OASTS 69, art. 8(1)(b).
[164] Arab Charter on Human Rights, art. 35(3).
[165] C.N.191.1996.TREATIES-1/4.
[166] C.N.947.2007.TREATIES-2.
[167] C.N.132.1979.TREATIES-4.
[168] C.N.188.1972.TREATIES-7.

refer to the right to strike in their reports to the Human Rights Council.[169] Some European States have questioned Andorra about the right to strike, and made recommendations, but there does not seem to be any other evidence of States that are not parties to the Covenant on Economic, Social, and Cultural Rights being challenged on the subject during the Universal Periodic Review.[170]

Despite the silence of some of the relevant treaties on the right to strike as a component of freedom of association, international human rights courts have concluded that the right is comprised within the general right to trade union freedom.[171] After initially rejecting the invitation to find a right to strike within Article 22 of the Covenant,[172] the Human Rights Committee subsequently referred to 'the right to strike' on several occasions, possibly suggesting it considers this to be comprised within the general right to trade union freedom.[173] As recently as 2017, in Concluding Observations on the sixth periodic report of the Dominican Republic, the Committee said: 'The State Party should adopt measures to safeguard workers' freedom of association in practice, including the right to organise, the right to collective bargaining and the right to strike.'[174]

This is also the conclusion of the expert body that monitors the International Labour Organisation conventions. Many decades ago, the International Labour Organisation Committee of Experts said that prohibition of strikes by workers other than public officials acting in the name of the public powers 'may sometimes constitute a considerable restriction of the potential activities of trade unions'. Some years later, it concluded that 'a general prohibition of strikes constitutes a considerable restriction of the opportunities opened to trade unions for furthering and defending the interests of their members (Article 10 of Convention No. 87) and of the right of trade unions to organise their activities'. According to the Committee of Experts, 'the right to strike is one of the essential means available to workers and their organisations for the promotion and protection of their economic and social interests. These interests not only have to do with better working conditions and pursuing collective demands of an occupational nature, but also with seeking

[169] Andorra, National report, A/HRC/WG.6/22/AND/1, para. 93, 100, 102; Comoros, National report, A/HRC/WG.6/18/COM/1, para. 143; Egypt, National report, A/HRC/WG.6/7; Mozambique, National report, A/HRC/WG.6/24/MOZ/1, para. 89.

[170] Sweden, Italy, and Germany in Andorra, Report of the Working Group, A/HRC/30/9, paras. 23, 81, 84.63, 84.64

[171] *Association of Academics v. Iceland*, no. 2451/16, §§ 26–27, 15 May 2018; *National Union of Rail, Maritime and Transport Workers v. the United Kingdom*, no. 31045/10, § 97, ECHR 2014; *Enerji Yapı-Yol Sen v. Turkey*, no. 68959/01, § 24, 21 April 2009.

[172] *J.B. et al. v. Canada*, no. 118/1982, Views, 18 July 1986, A/41/40, p. 151, para. 6.4.

[173] Chile, Concluding observations, CCPR/C/79/Add.104, para. 24; Belarus, Concluding observations, CCPR/C/BLR/CO/5, paras. 54–55; Estonia, Concluding observations, CCPR/C/EST/CO/3, para. 15; Ireland, Comments of the Human Rights Committee, CCPR/C/79/Add.21, para. 17; Dominican Republic, Concluding observations, CCPR/C/DOM/CO/6, para. 32.

[174] Dominican Republic, Concluding observations, CCPR/C/DOM/CO/6, para. 32.

solutions to economic and social policy questions and to labour problems of any kind which are of direct concern to the workers.'[175]

Referring to some of the sources cited above, in 2017 the Special Rapporteur on the rights to freedom of peaceful assembly and association wrote that '[t]he right to strike has been established in international law for decades, in global and regional instruments, and is also enshrined in the constitutions of at least ninety countries. The right to strike has, in fact, become customary international law.'[176] Although the authorities on the right to strike are not as unequivocal as they are for the general right to trade union freedom, it is likely that other courts would follow the lead of the European Court of Human Rights and decide, as a matter of interpretation, that the former is necessarily implied by the latter.

Freedom of association generally, and the component of the freedom concerning trade unions, are subject to restrictions. The International Covenant on Civil and Political Rights specifies that the exercise of these rights may only be restricted if they are prescribed by law and are necessary in a democratic society in the interests of national security or public safety, public order (*ordre public*), the protection of public health or morals or the protection of the rights and freedoms of others. The Covenant makes a specific exception in the case of 'lawful restrictions on members of the armed forces and of the police in their exercise of this right'. A limitation is also implied by Article 4(b) of the International Convention on the Elimination of All Forms of Racial Discrimination. It requires States Parties to 'declare illegal and prohibit organisations, and also organised and all other propaganda activities, which promote and incite racial discrimination' and to 'recognise participation in such organisations or activities as an offence punishable by law'.[177] According to the Committee on the Elimination of Racial Discrimination, it is insufficient for States Parties to make a declaration of illegality of an organisation conditional upon actual promotion or incitement of racism by its members. Vigilance in this respect requires the organisation to be declared illegal and prohibited. 'Participation in these organizations is, of itself, to be punished.'[178]

* * *

Conclusions. Freedom of association is enshrined in customary international law. Collective bargaining and the right to strike are protected by customary international law.

[175] Report of the Committee of Experts on the Application of Conventions and Recommendations, General Survey on Freedom of Association and Collective Bargaining, Report III (Part 4B), International Labour Conference, 81st Session, 1994 (General Survey 1994), p. 66, paras. 147–148.

[176] Report of the Special Rapporteur on the rights to freedom of peaceful assembly and of association, A/71/385, para. 56.

[177] International Convention on the Elimination of All Forms of Racial Discrimination, (1969) 660 UNTS 195, art. 4(b).

[178] General Recommendation 15 on art. 4 of the Convention, A/48/18, p. 114, para. 6.

E. Privacy, family, home, and correspondence

In his 1945 draft declaration of human rights, Hersch Lauterpacht proposed the following: 'The sanctity of the home and the secrecy of correspondence shall be respected.'[179] Lauterpacht said the right had appeared in written constitutions of most modern States where it constituted 'a repudiation of one of the most reprehensible manifestations of tyrannical government'. He pointed to the Fourth Amendment to the Constitution of the United States, which appears to be the ancestor of the notion: 'The right of the people to be secure in their persons, houses, papers, and effects, against unreasonable searches and seizures . . .'. Similar texts are found in the constitutions adopted during the French revolution, and in the case law of English courts.[180] In a creative interpretation of the Fourth Amendment, Louis Brandeis discerned a 'right to privacy', or 'a right to be left alone'.[181]

When John Humphrey canvassed the provisions of national constitutions and various draft human rights declarations and charters in his preparation of an initial draft of the Universal Declaration of Human Rights, he identified a distinct category that he labelled 'Liberty of and respect for private life'. The text that Humphrey proposed read: 'No one shall be subjected to arbitrary searches or seizures, or to unreasonable interference with his person, home, family relations, reputation, privacy, activities, or personal property. The secrecy of correspondence shall be respected.'[182] The American Declaration on the Rights and Duties of Man, adopted several months before the Universal Declaration, contained the following: 'Article IX. Every person has the right to the inviolability of his home. Article X. Every person has the right to the inviolability and transmission of his correspondence.'[183]

The Universal Declaration of Human Rights states that '[n]o one shall be subjected to arbitrary interference with his privacy, family, home or correspondence, nor to attacks upon his honour and reputation. Everyone has the right to the protection of the law against such interference or attacks.' The International Covenant on Civil and Political Rights essentially repeats this provision, the only changes being the addition of 'or unlawful' before 'interference' and 'unlawful' before 'attacks' in the first sentence.[184] Similar provisions on the right to privacy appear in the specialised and regional conventions.[185] Although the texts

[179] Hersch Lauterpacht, *An International Bill of the Rights of Man*, New York: Colombia, 1945, p. 113.

[180] *Entick v. Carrington*, (1765) 2 Wils. 275.

[181] Samuel Warren and Louis Brandeis, 'The Right to Privacy', (1890) 4 *Harvard Law Review* 193; *Olmstead v. United States*, 277 US 438 (1928).

[182] Draft Outline of International Bill of Rights (prepared by the Division of Human Rights), E/CN.4/AC.1/3, pp. 3–4. See also: E/CN.4/W.16, p. 4; E/CN.4/W.18, p. 2.

[183] American Declaration on the Rights and Duties of Man, Final Act of the Ninth International Conference of American States, Res. XXX.

[184] International Covenant on Civil and Political Rights, (1976) 999 UNTS 171, art. 17.

[185] Convention on the Rights of the Child, (1990) 1571 UNTS 3, art. 16; European Convention on Human Rights, (1953) 213 UNTS 221, art. 11; International Convention on the Protection of the Rights of all Migrant Workers and Members of their Families, (2003) 2220 UNTS 3, art. 14; Convention on the Rights of Persons with Disabilities, (2008) 2515 UNTS 3, arts. 22, 23; European Convention on Human

in the Convention on the Rights of the Child and the Convention on the Rights of Persons with Disabilities are limited in scope by the theme of the treaties, in their reports to the treaty bodies States have often confirmed that they respect the right more generally. Such recognition is of particular interest to the extent that States expressing it are not parties to the International Covenant and for whom their only relevant treaty obligations concern children or persons with disabilities.[186] These States also provide confirmation of their recognition of the right to privacy when they report to the Human Rights Council in the course of the Universal Periodic Review.[187] The International Criminal Court has considered that the right to privacy is an 'internationally recognised human right', citing as authority several of the relevant treaty provisions as well as article 12 of the Universal Declaration of Human Rights.[188]

The International Covenant on Civil and Political Rights provision has only one reservation, by Liechtenstein.[189] There is also a declaration of interpretation by Australia that has since been withdrawn.[190] There are no reservations to the right to privacy provision of the Convention on the Rights of Persons with Disabilities.

Rights, (1953) 213 UNTS 221, art. 8; American Convention on Human Rights, (1978) 1144 UNTS 123, art. 11; Arab Charter on Human Rights, art. 21; Charter of Fundamental Rights of the European Union, OJ C 326/391, art. 7; African Charter on the Rights and Welfare of the Child, art. 10.

[186] China, Initial report, CRC/C/11/Add.7, para. 73 and Initial report, CRPD/C/CHN/1, para. 85; Comoros, Initial report, CRC/C/28/Add.13, para. 76; Cuba, Second periodic report, CRC/C/CUB/2, para. 208 and Initial report, CRPD/C/CUB/1, para. 211; Kiribati, Initial report, CRC/C/KIR/1, para. 92 and CRPD/C/KIR/1, para. 94; Initial report, Malaysia, CRC/C/MYS/1, para. 166; Marshall Islands, CRC/C/28/Add.12, para. 52 and Initial report, CRPD/C/MHL/1, para. 101; Micronesia, Initial report, CRC/C/28/Add.5, para. 111; Myanmar, Initial report, CRPD/C/MMR/1, paras. 66–67; Oman, Initial report, CRC/C/78/Add.1, para. 95 and Initial report, CRPD/C/OMN/1, paras. 142–144; Palau, Initial report, CRC/C/51/Add.3, para. 102 and Initial report, CRPD/C/PLW/1, para. 22; St Kitts and Nevis, Initial report, CRC/C/3/Add.51, para. 18(c); Saint Lucia, Initial report, CRC/C/28/Add.23, para. 89; Saudi Arabia, Initial report, CRC/C/61/Add.2, paras. 129–130 and CRPD/C/SAU/1, paras. 145–147; Singapore, Initial report, CRC/C/51/Add.8, paras. 211–212 and Initial report, CRPD/C/SGP/1, paras. 248–250; Tonga, Initial report, CRC/C/TON/1, paras. 258–260; Tuvalu, Initial report CRC/C/TUV/1, para. 140 and Initial report, CRPD/C/TUV/1, para. 139.

[187] Fiji, National report, A/HRC/WG.6/20/FJI/1, para. 8; Marshall Islands, National report, A/HRC/WG.6/9/MHL/1/Rev.1, para. 10(k); Micronesia, A/HRC/WG.6/9/FSM/1, para. 17; Myanmar, National report, A/HRC/WG.6/10/MMR/1, para. 18; St Kitts and Nevis, National report, A/HRC/WG.6/10/KNA/1, para. 8; Saint Lucia, National report, A/HRC/WG.6/10/LCA/1, para. 17; Solomon Islands, National report, A/HRC/WG.6/11/SLB/1, paras. 23–24; South Sudan, National report, A/HRC/WG.6/26/SSD/1, National report, para. 86; United Arab Emirates, National report, A/HRC/WG.6/3/ARE/1, p. 8.

[188] *Prosecutor v. Bemba et al.* (ICC-01/05-01/13), Decision on Requests to Exclude Western Union Documents and other Evidence Pursuant to Article 69(7), 29 April 2016, para. 46; *Prosecutor v. Lubanga* (ICC-01/04-01/06), Decision on the confirmation of charges, 29 January 2007, para. 74–75.

[189] (1998) 2048 UNTS 44 ('the right to respect for family life, as guaranteed by article 17, paragraph 1 of the Covenant, shall be exercised, with regard to aliens, in accordance with the principles at present embodied in the legislation on aliens').

[190] (1980) 1197 UNTS 411 ('Australia accepts the principles stated in article 17 without prejudice to the right to enact and administer laws which, insofar as they authorise action which impinges on a person's privacy, family, home or correspondence, are necessary in a democratic society in the interests of national security, public safety, the economic well-being of the country, the protection of public health or morals or the protection of the rights and freedoms of others.'), (1984) 1379 UNTS 318.

Six States Parties have formulated reservations or declarations respecting Article 16 of the Convention on the Rights of the Child.[191]

Taken as a whole, these materials provide very strong confirmation for recognition of the right to protection against interference with privacy, family, home, and correspondence as a norm of customary international law.

Article 17 of the International Covenant on Civil and Political Rights and several of the other treaties proscribe interference that is either 'arbitrary' or 'unlawful'. It appears that 'arbitrary' refers to interference by the State, through legislation or government action. 'Unlawful', on the other hand, expresses the horizontal obligation requiring the State to protect individuals from interference by others. The Human Rights Committee has explained that '[t]he term "unlawful" means that no interference can take place except in cases envisaged by the law. Interference authorised by States can only take place on the basis of law, which itself must comply with the provisions, aims and objectives of the Covenant.'[192] The Human Rights Committee has said that the notion of 'arbitrariness' is not to be equated with 'against the law'. Rather, it must 'be interpreted more broadly to include elements of inappropriateness, injustice, lack of predictability and due process of law, as well as elements of reasonableness, necessity and proportionality'.[193]

1. Protection of privacy

The right to privacy protects that particular area of individual existence and autonomy that does not touch upon the sphere of liberty and privacy of others. According to the Human Rights Committee, privacy 'refers to the sphere of a person's life in which he or she can freely express his or her identity, be it by entering into relationships with others or alone'.[194] Privacy protects the special, individual qualities of human existence such as a person's manner of appearance and

[191] Algeria, C.N.135.1993.TREATIES-4 (' ... shall be applied while taking account of the interest of the child and the need to safeguard its physical and mental integrity'); Holy See, C.N.112.1990. TREATIES-4 ('that it interprets the Articles of the Convention in a way which safeguards the primary and inalienable rights of parents, in particular insofar as these rights concern ... privacy (Article 16)'); Indonesia, C.N.245.1990.TREATIES-9, since withdrawn, C.N.147.2005.TREATIES-1 (application of art. 16 'in conformity with its constitution'); Kiribati, CN.478.1995.TREATIES-11 (' ... a child's rights as defined in the Convention, in particular the rights defined in [article 16] shall be exercised with respect for parental authority, in accordance with the I-Kiribati customs and traditions regarding the place of the child within and outside the family'); Mali ('The Government of the Republic of Mali declares that, in view of the provisions of the Mali Family Code, there is no reason to apply article 16 of the Convention.'); Poland, C.N.116.1991.TREATIES-4 (similar to Kiribati reservation).

[192] General Comment 16, art. 17 (Right to privacy), A/43/40, Vol. I, p. 181, para. 2.

[193] General Comment 35, art. 9 (Liberty and security of person), CCPR/C/GC/35, para. 12, cited in the context of the right to privacy in *A.B. v. Canada*, no. 2387/2014, Views, 15 July 2016, CCPR/C/117/D/2387/2014, para. 8.7.

[194] *Coeriel et al. v. the Netherlands*, no. 453/1991, Views, 31 October 1994, CCPR/C/52/D/453/1991, para. 10.2; *G. v. Australia*, no. 2172/2012, Views, 17 March 2017, CCPR/C/119/D/2172/2012, para. 7.2.

his or her identity. According to the Grand Chamber of the European Court of Human Rights, 'personal choices as to an individual's desired appearance, whether in public or in private places, relate to the expression of his or her personality and thus fall within the notion of private life'.[195] The European Court of Human Rights has also held that privacy encompasses a person's physical and psychological integrity. Its protection is primarily intended 'to ensure the development, without outside interference, of the personality of each individual in his relations with other human beings'.[196]

Several national courts[197] as well as the United Nations Human Rights Committee have considered that access to abortion falls under the right to privacy.[198] In *Mellet v. Ireland*, the Human Rights Committee addressed the case of a pregnant woman who learned, in the twenty-first week of her pregnancy, that the foetus she was carrying had congenital defects and would die while in utero or shortly after birth. Irish law prohibited abortion, leaving her with the option to carry the foetus to term or travel to another country where she could terminate her pregnancy lawfully. The Committee considered that the interference in the woman's decision as to how best cope with her non-viable pregnancy was unreasonable and arbitrary in violation of her right to privacy.[199] In General Comment 28, the Committee pointed to reproductive functions as an area where States may fail to respect the privacy of women, giving as an example requirements relating to the decision to undertake sterilisation and imposition of a legal duty upon doctors and other health personnel to report cases of women who have undergone abortion.[200] Views on this issue are too diverse to permit useful conclusions about the scope of customary international law.

The right to privacy is an area where technological developments have had a huge impact. Expectations by previous generations of a sphere of anonymity have changed as a result of various forms of collection and transfer of data. For many people, concerns about privacy that once seemed important have become insignificant. Today, in massive numbers individuals seek to share information about their lives and those around them with the virtually limitless audience that social media provide. Whereas once the taking of a photograph was an event surrounded by planning and almost invariably a degree of implied consent, the proliferation of cameras makes the capture and sharing of images essentially uncontrollable.

[195] *S.A.S. v. France* [GC], no. 43835/11, § 107, 1 July 2014.

[196] *Botta v. Italy*, 24 February 1998, § 32, *Reports of Judgments and Decisions* 1998-I; *Von Hannover v Germany (No. 2)* [GC], nos. 40660/08 and 6-641/08, § 95, ECHR 2012-I.

[197] *Roe v. Wade*, 410 US 113 (1973).

[198] *K.L. v. Peru*, no. 1153/2003, Views, 24 October 2005, CCPR/C/85/D/1153/2003, para. 6.4, *L.M.R. v. Argentina*, no. 1608/2007, Views, 29 March 2011, CCPR/C/101/D/1608/2007, para. 9.3.

[199] *Mellet v. Ireland*, no. 2324/2013, Views, 6 September 2016, CCPR/C/116/D/2324/2013, para. 7.8. Also *Whelan v. Ireland*, no. 2425/2014, Views, 12 June 2017, CCPR/C/119/D/2425/2014, para. 7.9.

[200] General Comment 28, Equality of rights between men and women, CCPR/C/21/Rev.1/Add.10, para. 20.

Technology has made intrusions into the private sphere more common and mundane. For many, the sensitivities of the past that were once cherished no longer seem so important.

2. Protection of family life

The notion of 'family' has an important place in international human rights law. The Universal Declaration of Human Rights describes the family as 'the natural and fundamental group unit of society', adding that it 'is entitled to protection by society and the State'.[201] Family is central to the right set out in Article 16 of the Declaration: 'Men and women of marriageable age have the right to marry and to found a family, according to the national laws governing the exercise of this right.' The cluster of issues relating to family life and marriage is not formulated consistently in the international treaties; this points to the need for caution in drawing on these documents in order to identify norms of customary international law.

There are several other references to 'family' in the Universal Declaration of Human Rights. It specifies protection against arbitrary interference with a person's family,[202] the right to 'found a family',[203] a right to 'favourable remuneration' sufficient to provide a worker's family with 'an existence worthy of human dignity',[204] and the right of everyone to 'a standard of living adequate for the health and well-being of himself and of his family'.[205] Parents are given the right to choose the type of education that their children are to be given.[206] In addition, the first recital of the Preamble to the Universal Declaration speaks of 'the inherent dignity and of the equal and inalienable rights of all members of the human family', affirming that it is 'the foundation of freedom, justice and peace in the world'. But here the term 'family' is being used in a broader and more figurative sense.

The protection provided to the family by the Universal Declaration of Human Rights resonates through the regional and specialised human rights treaties.[207] The Convention on the Rights of the Child, in its Preamble, describes the family

[201] Universal Declaration of Human Rights, A/RES/217 A (III), A/810, art. 16(3).
[202] Ibid., art. 12.
[203] Ibid., art. 16(1).
[204] Ibid., art. 23(3).
[205] Ibid., art. 25(1).
[206] Ibid., art. 26(3).
[207] International Covenant on Civil and Political Rights, (1976) 999 UNTS 171, arts. 23 and 17; International Covenant on Economic, Social and Cultural Rights, (1976) 993 UNTS 3, art. 10; European Convention on Human Rights, (1953) 213 UNTS 221, arts. 8 and 12; European Social Charter, ETS 35, Part I(7), art. 16; American Convention on Human Rights, (1978) 1144 UNTS 123, arts. 11 and 17; Convention on the Elimination of All Forms of Discrimination against Women, (1981) 1249 UNTS 13, art. 16; African Charter on Human and Peoples' Rights, (1986) 1520 UNTS 271, art. 18; Arab Charter on Human Rights, art. 38; International Convention on the Protection of the Rights of all Migrant Workers and Members of their Families, (2003) 2220 UNTS 3.

as 'the fundamental group of society and the natural environment for the growth and well-being of all its members and particularly children'. It states that the family 'should be afforded the necessary protection and assistance so that it can fully assume its responsibilities within the community' and recognises that the child, 'for the full and harmonious development of his or her personality, should grow up in a family environment, in an atmosphere of happiness, love and understanding'.[208] Echoing the Universal Declaration and the International Covenant, the Convention on the Rights of Migrant Workers and Members of their Families recognises that the family is 'the natural and fundamental group unit of society and is entitled to protection by society and the State', adding that States Parties are required to take 'appropriate measures to ensure the protection of the unity of the families of migrant workers'.[209]

In practice, however, the formulation about 'the natural and fundamental group unit of society' has not proven to be very significant in international human rights law. It appears that although Article 23(1) has often been invoked in individual petitions, the Human Rights Committee has only once found a violation of Article 23(1) taken alone.[210] Although it frequently concludes that Article 23(1) has been breached, almost invariably this is associated to other provisions of the Covenant, principally Article 17, which protects the right to family life. Recognition of the family as 'the natural and fundamental group unit of society' seems less certain. Although present in the Universal Declaration, the International Covenants,[211] and the American Convention on Human Rights,[212] but absent in the European Convention on Human Rights.[213] In the African Charter the family is described as the 'natural unit and basis of society' and the 'custodian of morals and traditional values recognised by the community'.[214] The Arab Charter on Human Rights repeats the 'fundamental group unit' formulation used in the Universal Declaration but adds that 'it is based on marriage between a man and a woman'.[215]

The Universal Periodic Review materials offer limited support to the notion that the family is 'the natural and fundamental group unit of society'.[216] Of the States

[208] Convention on the Rights of the Child, (1990) 1571 UNTS 3, Preamble, Recitals 5 and 6.

[209] International Convention on the Protection of the Rights of all Migrant Workers and Members of their Families, (2003) 2220 UNTS 3, art. 44(1).

[210] *Husseini v. Denmark*, no. 2243/2013, Views, 24 October 2014, CCPR/C/112/D/2243/2013, para. 9.6.

[211] International Covenant on Civil and Political Rights, (1976) 999 UNTS 171, art. 23(1); International Covenant on Economic, Social and Cultural Rights, (1976) 993 UNTS 3, art. 10(1).

[212] American Convention on Human Rights, (1978) 1144 UNTS 123, art. 17(1); Additional Protocol to the American Convention on Human Rights in the area of Economic, Social and Cultural Rights, OASTS 69, art. 15(1).

[213] It does appear, however, in the European Social Charter, ETS 35, art. 16, where it is described as 'a fundamental unit of society'. Also European Social Charter (Revised), ETS 163, art. 16.

[214] African Charter on Human and Peoples' Rights, (1986) 1520 UNTS 271, art. 18.

[215] Arab Charter on Human Rights, art. 33(1).

[216] The wide range of views can also be seen in Summary of the Human Rights Council panel discussion on the protection of the family, A/HRC/28/40.

that are not parties to the Covenant, only Brunei Darussalam appears to attach any significance to this concept.[217] Saudi Arabia and Oman have made essentially perfunctory reference to provisions in their own constitutions on the importance of the family.[218] Otherwise, family-related issues in the Universal Periodic Review materials appear to be focussed entirely upon negative aspects, notably harmful traditional practices,[219] discriminatory rules of customary law, and archaic legislation,[220] State intervention where families fall short,[221] and domestic violence.[222] Singapore said that it saw 'the family as the foundation safeguarding a child's welfare' but it also addressed the issue of violence in the family.[223]

Similar observations emerge with respect to the Universal Periodic Review more generally. States Parties to the International Covenant and therefore bound by treaty law to protect the family as 'the natural and fundamental group unit of society' almost never refer to this in their reports. The exception is Egypt, which has a virtual obsession with recommending to other States during the Review that they '[c]ontinue to provide, in accordance with [their] obligations under international human rights law, the widest possible protection and support for the family as the natural and fundamental unit of society',[224] of that they '[m]aintain [their] effective protection for the family as the natural and fundamental unit of the society',[225] or '[p]rovide protection to the family, as it is the natural and fundamental group unit of society'.[226] Curiously, none of Egypt's three National reports has addressed the importance of the family.

[217] Brunei Darussalam, Report of the Working Group, A/HRC/13/14, paras. 10, 84. Also A/HRC/WG.6/33/BRN/1, National report, paras. 37–45, 85; National report, A/HRC/WG.6/19/BRN/1, paras. 31–34.

[218] United Arab Emirates, National report, A/HRC/WG.6/3/ARE/1, p. 8; Oman, National report, A/HRC/WG.6/10/OMN/1, para. 15; also para. 47.

[219] Bhutan, Report of the Working Group, A/HRC/27/8, para. 116; South Sudan, Report of the Working Group, A/HRC/34/13, paras. 17, 23; Tuvalu, National report, A/HRC/WG.6/3/TUV/1, para. 27.

[220] Saint Lucia, Report of the Working Group, A/HRC/17/6, para. 53; South Sudan, Report of the Working Group, A/HRC/34/13, para. 77; Tonga, National report, A/HRC/WG.6/15/TON/1, para. 87.

[221] Bhutan, National report, A/HRC/WG.6/19/BTN/2, paras. 26–28; Saint Lucia, Report of the Working Group, A/HRC/17/6, paras. 21–22.

[222] Brunei Darussalam, Views on conclusions, A/HRC/27/11/Add.1, para. 113.57 and Report of the Working Group, A/HRC/13/14, para. 180; Kiribati, National report, A/HRC/WG.6/35/KIR/1, para. 52; Micronesia, Report of the Working Group, A/HRC/31/4, para. 31; Sao Tome and Principe, National report, A/HRC/WG.6/23/STP/1, paras. 120, 132; Saint Lucia, National report, A/HRC/WG.6/23/LCA/1, para. 39; Saudi Arabia, Report of the Working Group, A/HRC/25/3, para. 97(b) and Report of the Working Group, A/HRC/11/23, paras. 84, 86; Singapore, National report, A/HRC/WG.6/11/SGP/1, para. 73; Solomon Islands, Report of the Working Group, A/HRC/18/8, para. 15; Tuvalu, National report, A/HRC/WG.6/3/TUV/1, para. 47; United Arab Emirates, Report of the Working Group, A/HRC/38/14, para. 112.

[223] Singapore, National report, A/HRC/WG.6/11/SGP/1, paras. 73, 77, 82.

[224] Bhutan, Report of the Working Group, A/HRC/27/8, para. 120.43.

[225] Singapore, Report of the Working Group, A/HRC/32/17, para. 166.197. Also Thailand, Report of the Working Group, A/HRC/33/16, para. 159.48.

[226] Germany, Report of the Working Group, A/HRC/39/9, para. 155.166. Also United Kingdom Report of the Working Group, A/HRC/36/9, para. 134.152; Denmark, Report of the Working Group, A/HRC/32/10, para. 120.137.

A recommendation by Bangladesh to Uruguay that it '[e]nsure the protection of and right to family life on the premise that family is the natural and fundamental group of society based upon the stable relationship between a man and a woman'[227] was rejected. Uruguay explained that it 'protects the institution of the family, including through constitutional provisions, on a broad and non-discriminatory basis and rejecting the limiting of the notion of the family on the grounds of gender identity, sexual orientation or any other reason, in accordance with domestic law and the highest international standards on the protection of human rights'.[228] A similar recommendation to Sweden by Belarus[229] was rejected in the following terms: 'While from a broader social perspective, families in all their various manifestations play a crucial role in society, and while they in many central ways can contribute to the protection of children's human rights in accordance with the CRC, Sweden emphasises the fact that human rights are the entitlement of each individual human being. There is, as such, no human rights imperative to strengthen the institution of the family.'[230] The Holy See has made comments about the 'institution of the family', using this as a vehicle to object to same-sex relationships.[231]

The historic role of the family in the provision of life's essentials for its members is declining as more and more responsibility is being taken by the State. This relationship can be seen in Article 25 of the Universal Declaration of Human Rights: 'Everyone has the right to a standard of living adequate for the health and well-being of himself and of his family, including food, clothing, housing and medical care and necessary social services, and the right to security in the event of unemployment, sickness, disability, widowhood, old age or other lack of livelihood in circumstances beyond his control.' The economic and social rights set out in Article 25 belong to the individual, not the family, and they are owed by the State, not the family. But the family may well be the vehicle for their delivery. It is in this sense that States are required to assist families even if there is no obligation to 'strengthen the institution', to borrow the words from Sweden's objection.

Often inequality within the family is enforced by appealing to 'customary law', which is not to be confused with customary international law. As early as 1954, the United Nations General Assembly urged that measures be taken 'with a view to abolishing such customs, ancient laws and practices by ensuring complete freedom

[227] Uruguay, Report of the Working Group, A/HRC/26/7, para. 124.1.

[228] Uruguay, Views on conclusions, A/HRC/26/7/Add.1, p. 7.

[229] Belarus, in Sweden, Draft report of the Working Group, A/HRC/WG.6/8/L.10, para. 96.17. Also Belarus, in Belgium, Report of the Working Group, A/HRC/18/3, para. 103.12.

[230] Sweden, Views on conclusions, A/HRC/15/11/Add.1, p. 4; Belarus, in Slovenia, Report of the Working Group, A/HRC/14/15, para. 53; Belarus, in Côte d'Ivoire, Report of the Working Group, A/HRC/13/, para. 73.

[231] Holy See, in San Marino, Report of the Working Group, A/HRC/28/9, para. 78.37; Holy See, in Colombia, Report of the Working Group, A/HRC/24/6, para. 118.20; Holy See, in Philippines, Report of the Working Group, A/HRC/36/12, para. 133.201; Holy See, in Ethiopia, Report of the Working Group, A/HRC/27/14, para. 155.97; Holy See, in Portugal, Report of the Working Group, A/HRC/27/7, para. 127.48.

in the choice of a spouse; abolishing the practice of the bride-price; guaranteeing the right of widows to the custody of their children and their freedom as to remarriage; eliminating completely child marriages and the betrothal of young girls before the age of puberty and establishing appropriate penalties where necessary; establishing a civil or other register in which all marriages and divorces will be recorded; ensuring that all cases involving personal rights be tried before a competent judicial body ensuring also that family allowances, where these are provided, be administered in such a way as to benefit directly the mother and child'.[232]

Regardless of whether there is enough evidence to conclude that 'the natural and fundamental group of society' falls within the scope of customary international law, there can be much less doubt about the importance of the protection of 'family life'. It is associated in the treaties with 'private life' and there is indeed a close relationship. Just as the individual enjoys a 'private sphere' providing shelter against intrusion by the State, and by others, so the family benefits from an important degree of protection. The Human Rights Committee considers that the notion of 'family' should be given 'a broad interpretation so as to include all those comprising the family as understood in the society in question'. Cultural traditions should be taken into account when defining the term 'family' in a specific situation.[233] The European Court of Human Rights has recognised the existence of family life in the relationship of a single mother and her child,[234] a single father and his adopted son,[235] a father and his son-and law,[236] between siblings,[237] and between grandparents and grandchildren.[238] Noting that 'rapid evolution of social attitudes towards same-sex couples has taken place in many member States', manifested in legislation giving legal recognition to the phenomenon, the European Court said it was 'artificial to maintain the view that, in contrast to a different-sex couple, a same-sex couple cannot enjoy "family life" '. Therefore, 'a cohabiting same-sex couple living in a stable de facto partnership, falls within the notion of "family life", just as the relationship of a different-sex couple in the same situation would'.[239]

Although legal recognition of families will vary considerably from one State to another, the absence of legal recognition should not deny the family and its members the rights to which they are entitled. The same holds true in the case of a family whose configuration may not correspond to the confines of existing legislation.

[232] Status of women in private law; customs, ancient laws and practices affecting the human dignity of women, A/RES/843(IX), art. 1.

[233] *Hopu et al. v. France*, no. 549/1993, Decision, 30 October 1995, CCPR/C/51/D/549/1993, para. 10.3.

[234] Ibid.

[235] *Negrepontis-Giannisis v. Greece*, no. 56759/08, § 55, 3 May 2011.

[236] *Mallah v. France*, no. 29681/08, § 31, 10 November 2011.

[237] *Moustaquim v. Belgium*, 18 February 1991, § 36, Series A no. 193; *Mustafa and Armağan Akın v. Turkey*, no. 4694/03, § 19, 6 April 2010.

[238] *Angela and Rodney Price v. the United Kingdom*, no. 12402/86, Commission decision of 9 March 1988, DR 55, p. 224. Also: *Bronda v. Italy*, 9 June 1998, § 51, *Reports of Judgments and Decisions* 1998-IV.

[239] *Vallianatos et al. v. Greece* [GC], nos. 29381/09 and 32684/09, § 74, ECHR 2013.

According to the Human Rights Committee, protection of the family 'is not necessarily obviated, in any particular case, by the absence of formal marriage bonds, especially where there is a local practice of customary or common law marriage. Nor is the right to protection of family life necessarily displaced by geographical separation, infidelity, or the absence of conjugal relations.'[240]

Protection of 'family life' has taken on considerable importance in the case of migrants, when families find themselves threatened with separation by the application of legislation or as a result of administrative decisions. The Human Rights Committee has said refusal to allow one member of a family to remain on its territory may amount to interference with that person's family life although 'the mere fact that certain members of the family are entitled to remain on the territory of a State Party does not necessarily mean that requiring other members of the family to leave involves such interference.'[241] The Committee says an assessment is to be made of the proportionality of the measure, taking into account, on the one hand, the significance of the reasons for the removal of the person concerned and, on the other hand, of the degree of hardship the family and its members would encounter as a consequence of such removal.[242] To the extent that States have a requirement to protect the institution of the family, they should be obliged to promote its reunification in case of separation and to prevent its breakup, for example in the case of expulsion or deportation.[243] Other issues that may fall within the scope of the protection of 'family life' include child custody and access, removal of children for their own protection, and family visits to prisoners. The Standard Minimum Rules for the Treatment of Prisoners, now known as the Nelson Mandela Rules, declare that '[d]isciplinary sanctions or restrictive measures shall not include the prohibition of family contact. The means of family contact may only be restricted for a limited time period and as strictly required for the maintenance of security and order.'[244] The Grand Chamber of the European Court of Human Rights has found a violation of the right to family life in the refusal of prison authorities to facilitate artificial insemination so that two people, one of whom was detained, could become genetic parents.[245]

[240] *Ngambi v. France*, no. 1179/2003, Decision, 9 July 2004, CCPR/C/81/D/1179/2003, para. 6.4. See also *Z. et al. v. Australia*, no. 2279/2013, Views, 5 November 2015, CCPR/C/115/D/2279/2013, para. 7.2.

[241] *Warsame v. Canada*, no. 1959/2010, Views, 21 July 2011, CCPR/C/102/D/1959/2010, paras. 8.7–8.10; *Winata et al. v. Australia*, no. 930/2000, Views, 26 July 2001, CCPR/C/72/D/930/2000, para. 7.1.

[242] *D.T. et al. v. Canada*, no. 2081/2011, Views, 15 July 2016, CCPR/C/117/D/2081/2011, para. 7.6; *Byahuranga v. Denmark*, no. 1222/2003, Views, 1 November 2004, CCPR/C/82/D/1222/2003, para. 11.7.

[243] *Sahid v. New Zealand*, no. 893/1999, Views, 28 March 2003, CCPR/C/77/D/893/1999, para. 8.2.

[244] United Nations Standard Minimum Rules for the Treatment of Prisoners (the Nelson Mandela Rules), A/RES/70/175, Annex, Rule 43(3).

[245] *Dickson v. the United Kingdom* [GC], no. 44362/04, § 66, ECHR 2007-V; *Kalashnikov v. Russia* (dec.), no. 47095/99, ECHR 2001-XI; *Aliev v. Ukraine*, no. 41220/98, § 187–189, 29 April 2003.

3. Protection of home

According to the Human Rights Committee, protection of the home is to be understood to indicate the place where a person resides or carries out his or her usual occupation.[246] The boundaries of the home encompass the garage and garden.[247] Even a camping trailer or a houseboat is covered. Any intrusion into the home without the consent of the individual affected is an interference. This applies to forced or clandestine trespassing in a physical sense, such as warrantless searches by police or soldiers.[248] According to the European Court of Human Rights, extreme disturbances to the environment may also represent interference with the home.[249] Protection of the home is discussed in greater detail in Chapter 9 under the heading 'Housing'.[250]

4. Protection of correspondence

The term 'correspondence' is used in many of the international legal instruments although in the age of electronic communication it has an archaic ring. Written communication proliferates, but in the form of e-mail, social media, and brief text messages from and to mobile telephones. When postal communication was the rule, the mechanism of correspondence was largely in the hands of State institutions. With the predominance today of electronic communication, the intermediaries for correspondence are private firms such as mobile telephone networks. Responsibility has tended to shift from a vertical relationship between the individual and the State to one that is horizontal, where the State's role is one of regulating private operators rather than delivery itself.

The protection of correspondence relates principally to its secrecy. The earliest drafts of the Universal Declaration of Human Rights referred to the protection of 'secrecy of correspondence'.[251] In the twenty-first century the issue is no longer about postal clerks steaming open envelopes although the issue with electronic communication is fundamentally the same. Any interception of personal communication requires 'rigorous assessment of the legality, necessity and proportionality'.[252] According to the Human Rights Committee, surveillance activities

[246] General Comment 16, para. 5. Also *Naidenova et al. v. Bulgaria*, no. 2073/2011, Views, 25 June 2011, CCPR/C/106/D/2073/2011, para. 14.2.
[247] *Gillow v. the United Kingdom*, 24 November 1986, § 46, Series A no. 109.
[248] *Lumbala Tshidika v. Democratic Republic of the Congo*, no. 2214/2012, Views, 5 November 2015, CCPR/C/115/D/2214/2012, para. 6.7; *Zaier et al. v. Algeria*, no. 2026/2011, 29 October 2014, CCPR/C/112/D/2026/2011, para. 7.10.
[249] *Brânduşe v. Romania*, no. 6586/03, §§ 9–18, 66 and 67, 7 April 2009; *Wałkuska v. Poland* (dec.), no. 6817/04, 29 April 2008; *López Ostra v. Spain*, 9 December 1994, §§ 58–60, Series A no. 303-C.
[250] See *infra*, pp. 305–307.
[251] Draft Outline of International Bill of Rights (prepared by the Division of Human Rights), E/CN.4/AC.1/3, art. 11.
[252] Colombia, Concluding observations, CCPR/C/COL/CO/7, para. 32.

and interference with privacy, including online surveillance for the purposes of State security, must be subject to judicial authorisation as well as effective and independent oversight mechanisms,[253] and affected persons must have proper access to effective remedies in cases of abuse.[254]

The collection of raw or bulk data from intercepted communications and the sharing of such material by intelligence agencies raises concerns.[255] Use of bulk data should be premised upon 'specific and legitimate objectives' and 'the exact circumstances in which such interference may be authorised and the categories of persons likely to be placed under surveillance' should be set out in detail in law.[256] The European Court of Human Rights held that operation of a bulk data capture regime does not in and of itself violate the right to privacy. However, it found that a British system did not provide sufficient oversight and safeguards in the filtering, search, and selection of intercepted communications.[257]

5. Protection against attacks on honour and reputation

The Universal Declaration of Human Rights entitles everyone to protection against unlawful attacks on honour and reputation. The Human Rights Committee held that the right was violated in a case involving regular incidents of harassment, surveillance, and intimidation of the applicants, as well as 'the apparently deliberate intention to damage their honour and reputation and incite public hostility towards them'.[258] Of course, there is no right to preserve the secrecy of conviction for a crime, or to challenge an attack on reputation to which the individuals own actions gave rise.[259] The result is quite different if the person is victim of a wrongful conviction. Where someone was sent to prison for being a 'whistle blower', reporting acts of fraud that he had detected in the course of his work as an accountant for a company, there was a right to be protected against unlawful attacks on honour and reputation.[260]

* * *

[253] Turkmenistan, Concluding observations, CCPR/C/TKM/CO/2, paras. 36–37; Namibia, Concluding observations, CCPR/C/NAM/CO/2, paras. 37–38.

[254] China (Hong Kong Special Administrative Region), Concluding observations, CCPR/C/HKG/CO/2, para. 12; United States of America, Concluding observations, A/69/40 (Vol. I), para. 138.

[255] Sweden, Concluding observations, CCPR/C/SWE/CO/7, para. 36; Switzerland, Concluding observations, CCPR/C/CHE/CO/4, para. 47.

[256] Norway, Concluding observations, CCPR/C/NOR/CO/7, para. 21.

[257] *Big Brother Watch v. the United Kingdom*, nos. 58170/13, 62322/14, and 24960/15, §§ 465–467, 13 September 2018.

[258] *El Hojouj et al. v. Libya*, no. 1958/2010, Views, 21 July 2014, CCPR/C/111/D/1958/2010, para. 6.7.

[259] *M.A.K. v. Belgium*, no. 2148/2012, Decision, 2 June 2017, CCPR/C/119/D/2148/2012, para. 6.10.

[260] *Kerrouche v. Algeria*, no. 2128/2012, Views, 3 November 2016, CCPR/C/118/D/2128/2012, para. 8.6.

Conclusions. Protection against arbitrary interference and against illegal interference with privacy, family, home, or correspondence is enshrined in customary international law. Everyone is also entitled to protection against unlawful attacks on honour and reputation.

F. Marriage

The first draft of the Universal Declaration of Human Rights, prepared by John Humphrey in June 1947, contained the following: 'Everyone has the right to contract marriage in accordance with the laws of the State.'[261] It had little in the way of antecedents. There was no right to marry in any of the proposed declarations other than a line in the Inter-American Juridical Committee draft about interference with family relations and an obligation on the State 'to respect and to protect the reciprocal rights of husband and wife in their mutual relations'.[262] There were also references to marriage in a few Latin American constitutions but nothing resembling a fundamental right.[263] The idea had appeared in a document submitted to the Commission on Human Rights by the Catholic Welfare Association of the United States that dealt with the rights of the family, comprising a right to contract marriage, to make a home, and to have children.[264]

'Men and women of full age, without any limitation due to race, nationality or religion, have the right to marry and to found a family', states Article 16(1) of the Universal Declaration of Human Rights. Recognition of the right to marry and to found a family is repeated, with minor changes, in Article 23 of the International Covenant on Civil and Political Rights,[265] the regional conventions,[266] and in two of the specialised conventions.[267] As for the States that are not parties to the Covenant, their position on the right to marry cannot be clarified from the Universal Periodic Review materials, which tend to focus on the minimum age of marriage to the extent that they deal with the issues at all. This probably concerns the fact that the right of everyone of marriageable age to marry and found a family

[261] Draft Outline of International Bill of Rights (prepared by the Division of Human Rights), E/CN.4/AC.1/3, art. 13.

[262] Draft Declaration of the International Rights and Duties of Man, Formulated by the Inter-American Juridical Committee, E/CN.4/2, art. 10.

[263] Drafting Committee on an International Bill of Human Rights, International Bill of Rights Documented Outline, E/CN.4/AC.1/3/Add.1, pp. 98–99.

[264] Summary Record of the Thirteenth Meeting [of the Commission on Human Rights], E/CN.4/SR.13, p. 6.

[265] International Covenant on Civil and Political Rights, (1976) 999 UNTS 171, art. 23(2).

[266] European Convention on Human Rights, (1953) 213 UNTS 221, art. 12; American Convention on Human Rights, (1978) 1144 UNTS 123, art. 17(2); Arab Charter on Human Rights, art. 33(1); Charter of Fundamental Rights of the European Union, OJ C 326/391, art. 9.

[267] International Convention on the Elimination of All Forms of Racial Discrimination, (1969) 660 UNTS 195, art. 5(2)(iv); Convention on the Rights of Persons with Disabilities, (2008) 2515 UNTS 3, art. 23(1)(a).

is relatively uncontroversial. Were it otherwise, there would be questions and recommendations from States as well as information from United Nations mechanisms and civil society organisations on the subject.

Israel has made general reservations to the right to marry as set out in the International Covenant and the Convention on the Rights of Persons with Disabilities.[268] In its initial report to the Human Rights Committee, Israel referred to the reservation, acknowledging that '[u]nder the religious law applied in matters of marriage and divorce, many couples are prevented from being able to realise their right to marry in Israel, including couples who belong to different religions, or persons who may not marry the person of their choice due to prohibitions deriving from religious law'.[269] Poland has a reservation to the right of disabled persons to marry 'until relevant domestic legislation is amended'.[270] Broad interpretative declarations that make the application of Article 23 of the Covenant subject to religious law have been formulated by Bahrain,[271] Kuwait,[272] and Qatar.[273] While it may be accurate to characterise the interpretative declarations as reservations, in that they seek to reduce the treaty obligations, it is also evident that they are directed at the interpretation of Article 23(2) rather than with the norm as such.[274]

In its General Comment on reservations, the Human Rights Committee said that it would be contrary to customary international law 'to deny to persons of marriageable age the right to marry'.[275] It did not refer to the other marriage-related rights that are enshrined in Article 23 of the Covenant.

These materials, taken as a whole, offer persuasive evidence for the recognition of the right to marry and found a family as a norm of customary international law. Israel's reservations may support a claim that it is a persistent objector, and therefore without obligation despite the existence of the customary norm.

The provisions of the Universal Declaration of Human Rights generally protect the rights of 'everyone'. The right to marry in Article 16 is an exception, ensuring the right to 'men and women'. This has been interpreted by international courts and treaty bodies, relying upon the intent of the drafters of the Universal Declaration, as a limitation of the right to marry to persons of opposite sex.[276] Scrutiny of the *travaux*

[268] (1991) 1651 UNTS 566-567; C.N.568.2012.TREATIES-IV.15.

[269] Israel, Initial report, CCPR/C/81/Add.13, para. 576.

[270] C.N.539.2012.TREATIES-IV.15; Poland, Initial report, CRPD/C/POL/1, para. 286.

[271] C.N.1140.2006.TREATIES-24.

[272] C.N.191.1996.TREATIES-1/4.

[273] C.N.262.2018.TREATIES-1/4.

[274] Kuwait, Second periodic report, CCPR/C/KWT/2, para. 193; Bahrain, Concluding observations, CCPR/C/BHR/CO/1, paras. 17–18; Kuwait, Concluding observations, CCPR/C/KWT/CO/2, para. 10; Kuwait, Concluding observations, CCPR/C/KWT/CO/3, paras. 14–15; Kuwait, Third periodic report, CCPR/C/KWT/3, paras. 40–42.

[275] General Comment 24, Issues Relating to Reservations Made upon Ratification or Accession to the Covenant or the Optional Protocols thereto, or in Relation to Declarations under art. 41 of the Covenant, CCPR/C/21/Rev.1/Add.6, para. 8.

[276] See, *e.g.* *Rees v. the United Kingdom*, 17 October 1986, § 19, Series A no. 106: ' ... the right to marry guaranteed by Article 12 refers to the traditional marriage between persons of the opposite biological sex'. In *Cossey v. the United Kingdom*, 27 September 1990, § 18, Series A no. 184, the European

préparatoires of the Declaration shows such an understanding to be erroneous. The term 'men and women' was inserted to replace 'everyone' upon the request of the Commission on the Status of Women, whose purpose was to strengthen the recognition of equality of the parties to the marriage.[277] An Egyptian amendment to reformulate the provisions so as to state that '[e]veryone has the right to found a family'[278] was rejected, with delegates in the General Assembly explaining that 'it did not take into account the essential concept of the equality of men and women in all questions relating to marriage'.[279] Although attitudes have changed dramatically in recent years, as more and more countries recognise a right to marry regardless of the gender of the two parties, this is far from universal. Strictly speaking, the problem is not one of formulating the norm but rather of interpreting the scope of the words 'men and women'. According to the Inter-American Court of Human Rights, 'international law, including international human rights law, at the current state of its development, does not include special rights for unions between same-sex couples'.[280]

The Universal Declaration of Human Rights confines the right to marry to persons of 'full age'. The treaties replace this with the somewhat tautological term 'marriageable age'. Belgium formulated an interpretative declaration to Article 23(2) of the Covenant 'as meaning that the right of persons of marriageable age to marry and to found a family presupposes not only that national law shall prescribe the marriageable age but that it may also regulate the exercise of that right'.[281] In General Comment 28, the Human Rights Committee linked the establishment of a minimum age for marriage to the issue of consent, recognising that below a certain age children are incapable of providing this and that they are too vulnerable to coercion. In its Concluding Observations, the Committee insisted that States Parties ensure that the minimum age for marriage 'complies with international standards'.[282] A United Nations General Assembly Recommendation adopted in the

Court added that recent developments 'cannot be said to evidence any general abandonment of the traditional concept of marriage'. The position of the European Court remained unchanged two decades later: *Schalk and Kopf v. Austria*, no. 30141/04, § 90, ECHR 2010. The Human Rights Committee has taken a similar view: *Joslin et al. v. New Zealand*, no. 902/1999, Views, 17 July 2002, CCPR/C/75/D/902/1999, paras. 8.2. and 8.3.

[277] See E/CN.4/SR.58, p.10. See also E/CN.4/SR.58, pp. 15–18; E/CN.4/AC.1/SR.38, pp. 12–13; E/CN.4/SR.62, pp. 9–12.

[278] Egypt: Amendments to the Draft Declaration (E/800), A/C.3/264.

[279] Summary Record of the hundred and twenty-fifth meeting [of the Third Committee of the General Assembly], 29 October 1948, *Official Records of the General Assembly*, Third Session, 1948, p. 375.

[280] *State Obligations Concerning Change of Name, Gender Identity, and Rights Derived from a Relationship Between Same-Sex Couples (Interpretation and Scope of Articles 1(1), 3, 7, 11(2), 13, 17, 18, and 24, in relation to Article 1, of the American Convention on Human Rights)*, Advisory Opinion OC-24/17, Series A, No. 24, 24 November 2017, para. 66.

[281] (1983) 1312 UNTS 328.

[282] Iran, Concluding observations, CCPR/C/IRN/CO/3, para. 128; Suriname, Concluding observations, CCPR/C/SUR/CO/3, paras. 15–16; Malawi, Concluding observations, CCPR/C/MWI/CO/1/Add.1, para. 25.

early 1960s set the lower limit for capacity to marry at the age of fifteen.[283] However, half a century later a minimum age agreed to by the General Assembly in 1962 no longer corresponds to international standards. The Human Rights Committee has indicated eighteen years to be 'in accordance with international norms'.[284] Some recommendations to States during the Universal Periodic Review propose that the age of consent to marriage be raised to eighteen, but while it may be a desirable goal, many States authorise marriage of persons aged fifteen or sixteen. For example, several States urged Malaysia to raise the age to eighteen although marriage at a younger age was possible under its legislation.[285] The minimum age for marriage in some States Parties remains different for men and women.[286]

The reports of States that are not parties to the Covenant provide some confirmation that they recognise a rule of customary law requiring that marriage be reserved to those above a certain age, although the information suggests that this is somewhat lower than eighteen. Bahrain said its laws were designed to ensure that any party who wishes to marry, including those under the age of eighteen years, 'has been fully qualified and ready in all aspects to enter into marriage life'.[287] Tonga reported that a male can marry at fifteen with parental consent, although he cannot own land until sixteen or drive a car until twenty-one.[288] It reported upon efforts to increase the age of marriage for women.[289] Malaysia said that the age was eighteen for non-Muslims but that authorisation could be granted to a woman to marry if she had completed her sixteenth year. For Muslim marriages, it was eighteen for men and sixteen for women, again with the possibility of dispensation by a Syariah Judge.[290] But Malaysia also said it was planning to increase the minimum marriageable age to eighteen.[291] South Sudan reported that early and forced marriage of girls under eighteen continued to slow efforts to eliminate discrimination, especially in rural areas.[292] Comoros said marriage was prohibited before the age of eighteen.[293]

[283] Recommendation on Consent to Marriage, Minimum Age for Marriage and Registration of Marriages, A/RES/2018 (XX), Principle II.

[284] Bangladesh, Concluding observations, CCPR/C/BGD/CO/1, para. 14.

[285] For example, Malaysia, Report of the Working Group, A/HRC/40/11, paras. 151.234 (Australia), 151.235 (Austria), 151.237 (Canada) and 151.240 (Hungary). These States permit marriage at sixteen, subject to judicial or parental authorisation, or both.

[286] For example, Côte d'Ivoire, Concluding observations, CCPR/C/CIV/CO/1, para. 11; Israel, Concluding observations, CCPR/C/79/Add.93, para. 29.

[287] Brunei, Views on conclusions, A/HRC/27/11/Add.1, p. 10; Tonga, National report, A/HRC/WG.6/29/TON/1, para. 93 and fn. 20.

[288] Tonga, National report, A/HRC/WG.6/29/TON/1, para. 93.

[289] Ibid., paras. 94–95.

[290] Malaysia, National report, A/HRC/WG.6/31/MYS/1, para. 99, fn. 20.

[291] Malaysia, Report of the Working Group, A/HRC/40/11, paras. 13, 94.

[292] South Sudan, National report, A/HRC/34/13, para. 17.

[293] Comoros, Report of the Working Group, A/HRC/41/12, para. 111; Comoros, Report of the Working Group, A/HRC/26/11, para. 71.

Israel has reported a minimum age of seventeen,[294] and confirmed that prosecutions take place for underage marriages.[295] Israel has signed but not ratified the Convention on Consent to Marriage, Minimum Age for Marriage and Registration of Marriages.[296] Bahrain, which has an interpretative declaration to Article 23 of the International Covenant, has reported to the Human Rights Council on efforts to restrict child marriage.[297] Kuwait has a minimum age for marriage of seventeen for males and fifteen for females.[298] In 1999, Kuwait told the Human Rights Committee that it was in the process of acceding to the Convention on Consent to Marriage.[299] The Convention, which was adopted in 1962, and which specifies that States Parties must set a minimum age for marriage but does not determine what that must be, has been ratified by only fifty-six States.[300]

State practice indicates that in addition to a minimum age, most if not all States impose other restrictions upon marriage, for example prohibiting marriages between close relatives.

The virtual absence of reservations and interpretative declarations to treaty provisions on the right to marry suggests an understanding that the right to marry is not absolute. Like other fundamental rights, it is subject to such restrictions or prohibitions as are reasonable and objective. Nevertheless, prohibition of mixed-race or inter-religious marriages, or restrictions on aliens, naturally represents a violation of the right to marry in conjunction with guarantees of non-discrimination and the right to equality.[301] The Apartheid Convention lists 'the prohibition of mixed marriages among members of various racial groups' as an 'inhuman act' of apartheid.[302] Singapore told the Human Rights Council that it restricts foreign domestic workers from marrying Singaporeans because 'given its space constraints, Singapore could not afford to absorb large numbers of migrants on a permanent basis'.[303] This did not provoke any response during the Universal Periodic Review.

[294] Israel, Second periodic report, CCPR/C/ISR/2001/2, para. 197.

[295] Israel, Third periodic report, CCPR/C/ISR/3, para. 432.

[296] (1964) 521 UNTS 262.

[297] Bahrain, National report, A/HRC/21/6, para. 55; Bahrain, National report, A/HRC/WG.6/1/BHR/1, p. 18.

[298] Kuwait, Concluding observations, CCPR/C/KWT/3, paras. 40–42. Also Kuwait, Concluding observations, CRC/C/KWT/CO/2, para. 25; Kuwait, Concluding observations, CCPR/C/KWT/CO/2, para. 10.

[299] Kuwait, Initial report, CCPR/C/120/Add.1, para. 57.

[300] (1964) 521 UNTS 231, art. 2.

[301] Germany, Report of the Working Group, A/HRC/39/9, para. 155.166. Also United Kingdom Report of the Working Group, A/HRC/36/9, para. 134.152; Denmark, Report of the Working Group, A/HRC/32/10, para. 120.137; Uruguay, Report of the Working Group, A/HRC/26/7, para. 124.1; Uruguay, Views on conclusions, A/HRC/26/7/Add.1, p. 7; Holy See, in San Marino, Report of the Working Group, A/HRC/28/9, para. 78.37; Holy See, in Colombia, Report of the Working Group, A/HRC/24/6, para. 118.20.

[302] International Convention on the Suppression and Punishment of the Crime of Apartheid, (1976) 1015 UNTS 243, art. II(d).

[303] Singapore, Report of the Working Group, A/HRC/18/11, para. 54.

At the European Court of Human Rights there have been several cases where prisoners were denied the right to marry. Early decisions of the European Commission of Human Rights denied the right of prisoners to marry,[304] but views evolved and the Convention organs subsequently accepted the principle.[305]

Nothing explicit in the Universal Declaration or the applicable treaties addresses the issue of polygamy. In General Comment 28, the Human Rights Committee, in surprisingly strong and clear terms, noted that 'equality of treatment with regard to the right to marry implies that polygamy is incompatible with this principle. Polygamy violates the dignity of women. It is an inadmissible discrimination against women.'[306] Calling for a State Party to abolish polygamy, the Human Rights Committee described it as 'an affront to women's dignity' and 'incompatible with the Covenant'.[307] However, in the Universal Periodic Review materials of States that are not parties to the International Covenant on Civil and Political Rights, the issue of polygamy is completely avoided in both the National reports and the recommendations from other States. Only the civil society and United Nations materials refer to the subject.[308]

1. Consent to Marriage

Marriage must be entered into 'only with the free and full consent of the intending spouses', states Article 16(2) of the Universal Declaration of Human Rights. The requirement of full consent by both partners appears in both of the International Covenants.[309] It is also set out in the American Convention on Human Rights[310] and the Arab Charter on Human Rights.[311] The Convention on Consent to Marriage, Minimum Age for Marriage and Registration of Marriages also gives effect to Article 16(2) of the Universal Declaration. Article 1 of the Convention specifies that 'such consent [is] to be expressed by them in person after due publicity and in the presence of the authority competent to solemnise the marriage and of

[304] *X. v. Federal Republic of Germany*, no. 892/60, (1961) 4 *Yearbook of the European Convention on Human Rights* 240, at pp. 254–257, Collection 6, p. 17.

[305] *Hamer v. the United Kingdom*, no. 7114/75, Commission decision of 13 October 1977, DR 10, p. 174; *Draper v. the United Kingdom*, no. 8186/78, Commission decision of 1 May 1979, DR 24, p. 72.

[306] General Comment 28, Equality of rights between men and women (art. 3), CCPR/C/21/Rev.1/Add.10, para. 24.

[307] Algeria, Concluding observations, CCPR/C/DZA/CO/3, para. 20.

[308] Malaysia, Compilation, A/HRC/WG.6/31/MYS/2, para. 70; Saudi Arabia, Summary of Stakeholders' submissions, A/HRC/WG.6/31/SAU/3, para. 36 and Compilation, A/HRC/WG.6/31/SAU/2, para. 54; Singapore, Compilation, A/HRC/WG.6/24/SGP/2, para. 31 and Summary of Stakeholders' submissions, A/HRC/WG.6/24/SGP/3, para. 36; United Arab Emirates, Compilation, A/HRC/WG.6/29/ARE/2, paras. 37, 49.

[309] International Covenant on Civil and Political Rights, (1976) 999 UNTS 171, art. 23(3); International Covenant on Economic, Social and Cultural Rights, (1976) 993 UNTS 3, art. 10(1).

[310] American Convention on Human Rights, (1978) 1144 UNTS 123, art. 17(3).

[311] Arab Charter on Human Rights, art. 33(1).

witnesses, as prescribed by law'.[312] The prohibition of marriage without free and full consent of the intending spouses rules out all forced marriages, whether by the State or by private parties, *i.e.* particularly parents or other family members. Also prohibited is marriage arranged by the parents or other interested parties without the consent of the child, as often occurred in the past and still continues today in some cultures.

As has already been discussed, the requirement of a minimum age for marriage is related to the issue of consent. Vulnerable children are simply unable to provide informed consent. In 1954, the United Nations General Assembly urged States to take all appropriate measures 'eliminating completely child marriages and the betrothal of young girls before the age of puberty and establishing appropriate penalties where necessary'.[313] Article 16(2) of the Convention on the Elimination of All Forms of Discrimination Against Women says that '[t]he betrothal and the marriage of a child shall have no legal effect'.[314]

A woman's consent to marriage may be vitiated if she has been the victim of rape. The Human Rights Committee has warned that free and full consent to marriage may be undermined both by reactionary social attitudes that put pressure on women to marry perpetrators but also laws that provide for extinguishment or mitigation of the perpetrator's criminal responsibility if he marries the victim.[315]

A few States that are not party to one or other of the two Covenants provide information about the consent issue when they report to the Human Rights Council in the context of the Universal Periodic Review. For example, Malaysia told the Council that legislation requires the authorities to confirm that the parties freely consent and also provides for punishment of any person who uses force or threats to compel a person to marry.[316] Saudi Arabia has explained that '[f]orced marriage is forbidden by Islamic sharia law, which holds that a marriage can only be concluded with the woman's consent. Sharia law prohibits a woman being prevented from marrying or forced into marriage against her will.'[317] Moreover, none of the four States that made a general reservation to Article 23 of the International Covenant on Civil and Political Rights has also made a reservation to the provision requiring the free consent of the intending spouses in the International Covenant on Economic, Social and Cultural Rights. Therefore, Bahrain, Israel, Kuwait, and

[312] Convention on Consent to Marriage, Minimum Age for Marriage and Registration of Marriages, (1964) 521 UNTS 262, art. 2.

[313] Status of women in private law: customs, ancient laws, and practices affecting the human dignity of women, A/RES/843 (IX), para. 1.

[314] Convention on the Elimination of All Forms of Discrimination against Women, (1981) 1249 UNTS 13, art. 16(2).

[315] General Comment 28, Equality of rights between men and women (art. 3), CCPR/C/21/Rev.1/Add.10, para. 24.

[316] Malaysia, National report, A/HRC/WG.6/31/MYS/1, para. 100 and fn. 21.

[317] Saudi Arabia, National report, A/HRC/WG.6/31/SAU/1, para. 110.

Qatar have a treaty obligation to ensure that '[m]arriage must be entered into with the free consent of the intending spouses'.

2. Equality

The Universal Declaration of Human Rights specifies that the parties to a marriage 'are entitled to equal rights as to marriage, during marriage and at its dissolution'.[318] Article 16(3) of the Universal Declaration of Human Rights might be considered to be somewhat superfluous. It is merely a specialised formulation of the right to equality and non-discrimination that is at the core of international human rights law and that is undoubtedly customary in nature.

A more elaborate text appears in Article 23(4) of the International Covenant on Civil and Political Rights: 'States Parties to the present Covenant shall take appropriate steps to ensure equality of rights and responsibilities of spouses as to marriage, during marriage and at its dissolution. In the case of dissolution, provision shall be made for the necessary protection of any children.' The American Convention on Human Rights provides something similar[319] and a provision on equality within the marriage was added to the European Convention on Human Rights by Protocol 7.[320] The Arab Charter on Human Rights, on the other hand, replaces the principle of equality with deference to the status quo: 'The laws in force regulate the rights and duties of the man and woman as to marriage, during marriage and at its dissolution.'[321]

The most detailed formulation of equality in marriage is provided in Article 16 of the Convention on the Elimination of All Forms of Discrimination against Women. It requires States Parties to 'take all appropriate measures to eliminate discrimination against women in all matters relating to marriage and family relations ... on a basis of equality of men and women'.[322] Specifically, this includes entry into marriage, choice of a spouse, free and full consent, aspects of parental responsibility including deciding freely and responsibly on the number and spacing of their children, choice of the family name, and exercise of property rights. Several States that have ratified the Covenant without reservation to Article 23(4) have nevertheless formulated reservations to some of the specific provisions of Article 16 of the Women's Convention.[323] This may suggest that some of the components

[318] Universal Declaration of Human Rights, A/RES/217 (III), art. 16(1).

[319] American Convention on Human Rights, (1978) 1144 UNTS 123, art. 17(4).

[320] Protocol 7 to the European Convention on Human Rights, CETS 117, art. 5.

[321] Arab Charter on Human Rights, art. 33.

[322] Convention on the Elimination of All Forms of Discrimination against Women, (1981) 1249 UNTS 13, art. 16(1).

[323] Bangladesh, C.N.289.1984.TREATIES-11, since partially withdrawn, C.N.320.1997.TREATIES-9; Brunei Darussalam, C.N.467.2006.TREATIES-3; Egypt, C.N.306.1981.TREATIES-13; India, C.N.251.1993.TREATIES-5; Iraq, C.N.197.1986.TREATIES-7; Jordan, C.N.257.1992.TREATIES-6; Libya, C.N.132.1989.TREATIES-7; Lebanon, C.N.165.1997.TREATIES-5; Maldives, C.N.251.1993.

of Article 16 are not customary in nature. Some of the reservations to Article 16 of the Women's Convention have provoked objections from States taking the view that to the extent there is any compromise with equality in the marriage this must be contrary to the object and purpose of the Convention, and that Article 16 is a 'core provision' of the treaty.[324] It does not follow, however, that a norm has a claim to being customary international law because some States deem a reservation to it to be inconsistent with the object and purpose of a treaty.

Kuwait has a reservation to Article 16(1)(f) of the Convention on the Elimination of All Forms of Discrimination against Women concerning equal rights of the spouses in matters of child adoption.[325] Thus, Kuwait has accepted the other parts of Article 16 concerning equality in the marriage. As for the Covenant, Kuwait made what it labelled an 'interpretative declaration' that on its own might be understood as a reservation that narrows the scope of Article 23(4).[326] One way or another, Kuwait has recognised the right to equality in the marriage, whether this results from an *a contrario* construction of its reservation to the Women's Convention or a reading of Article 23(4) of the Covenant that disregards its interpretative declaration. On the other hand, broad reservations both to Article 23(4) of the Covenant and to Article 16 of the Women's Convention have been formulated by Algeria,[327] Bahrain,[328] Israel,[329] and Mauritania.[330]

TREATIES-5; Morocco, C.N.251.1993.TREATIES-5; Niger, C.N.966.1999.TREATIES-9; Syria, C.N.267.2003.TREATIES-60; United Kingdom, C.N.108.1986.TREATIES-4.

324 For example, Estonia, to reservations of Oman, C.N.228.2010.TREATIES-5; Italy, to reservation of Qatar, C.N.228.2010.TREATIES-5.

325 C.N.345.1994.TREATIES-7 ('The Government of the State of Kuwait declares that it does not consider itself bound by the provision contained in article 16 (f) inasmuch as it conflicts with the provision of the Islamic Shariah, Islam being the official religion of the State.').

326 C.N.191.1996.TREATIES-1/4 ('The Government of Kuwait declares that the matters addressed by article 23 are governed by personal-status law, which is based on Islamic law. Where the provisions of that article conflict with Kuwaiti law, Kuwait will apply its national law.').

327 C.N.247.1989.TREATIES-1/13/3 (' … interprets the provisions of article 23, paragraph 4, of the Covenant on Civil and Political Rights regarding the rights and responsibilities of spouses as to marriage, during marriage and at its dissolution as in no case impairing the essential foundations of the Algerian legal system … '); C.N.168.1996.TREATIES-4 (' … the provisions of article 16 concerning equal rights for men and women in all matters relating to marriage, both during marriage and at its dissolution, should not contradict the provisions of the Algerian Family Code.').

328 C.N.1140.2006.TREATIES-24 (' … interprets the Provisions of [article 23] as not affecting in any way the prescriptions of the Islamic Shariah … '); C.N.717.2002.TREATIES-20 ('Article 16, in so far as it is incompatible with the provisions of the Islamic Shariah').

329 (1991) 1651 UNTS 566-567; C.N.568.2012.TREATIES-IV.15 ('With reference to Article 23 of the Covenant, and any other provision thereof to which the present reservation may be relevant, matters of personal status are governed in Israel by the religious law of the parties concerned. To the extent that such law is inconsistent with its obligations under the Covenant, Israel reserves the right to apply that law.'); C.N.223.1991.TREATIES-6 ('to Article 16 of the Convention, insofar as the laws of personal status binding on the several religious communities in Israel do not conform with the provisions of that Article').

330 C.N.546.2001.TREATIES-6 (' … each and every one of its parts which are not contrary to Islamic Sharia and are in accordance with our Constitution … '), modified by C.N.505.2014.TREATIES-IV.8 (' … it partially withdraws its general reservation made upon accession, which shall continue to apply in respect of articles 13 (a) and 16 of the Convention.').

Of the States that are not parties to the International Covenant on Civil and Political Rights, fifteen have ratified the Women's Convention without any reservations whatsoever, and are therefore fully bound by Article 16 dealing with equality in the marriage. Two others, China and Cuba, have ratified the Convention with only one reservation, to the dispute settlement provision (art. 29), and not to Article 16 of the Convention concerning marriage. Cook Islands and Fiji have withdrawn the reservations they made at the time of ratification; in any case their reservations did not concern Article 16. Micronesia has a limited reservation to Article 16 that deals with succession to hereditary titles and division of tasks within the marriage.[331]

That leaves six States that are not parties to the International Covenant and that have formulated reservations to Article 16 of the Convention on the Elimination of All Forms of Discrimination against Women or to the Convention as a whole (Brunei Darussalam,[332] Malaysia,[333] Oman,[334] Saudi Arabia,[335] Singapore,[336] and the United Arab Emirates[337]) and four that have not ratified the Convention at all (Holy See, Niue, the Republic of China, and Tonga). The existence of the reservations weakens the claim that the right to equality in the marriage, as formulated in Article 16(3) of the Universal Declaration of Human Rights, Article 23(4) of the International Covenant on Civil and Political Rights, and Article 16 of the Convention on the Elimination of All Forms of Discrimination Against Women, is a norm of customary international law. Yet, to the extent that this is nothing more than a specific formulation of the general right to equality and the prohibition of gender discrimination, the reservations may also be understood as being of relevance to the application of the treaty and the jurisdiction of the treaty bodies but without significance in the assessment of the content of customary international law. This is a situation where there are good arguments on both sides of the divide.

In the implementation of the right to equality in the marriage the Human Rights Committee has said that States 'should ensure that no sex-based discrimination occurs in respect of the acquisition or loss of nationality by reason of marriage, of residence rights, and of the right of each spouse to retain the use of his or her original family name or to participate on an equal basis in the choice of a new family name'.[338] According to the Committee, '[e]quality during marriage implies that husband and wife should participate equally in responsibility and authority within the family'. Furthermore, States should ensure the matrimonial regime 'contains

331 C.N.904.2004.TREATIES-10.
332 C.N.467.2006.TREATIES-3.
333 C.N.250.1995.TREATIES-3.
334 C.N.193.2006.TREATIES-1.
335 C.N.925.2000.TREATIES-8.
336 C.N.358.1995.TREATIES-5.
337 C.N.I223.2004.TREATIES-11.
338 General Comment 28, Equality of rights between men and women (art. 3), CCPR/C/21/Rev.1/Add.10, para. 25.

equal rights and obligations for both spouses with regard to … the ownership or administration of property, whether common property or property in the sole ownership of either spouse. States Parties should review their legislation to ensure that married women have equal rights in regard to the ownership and administration of such property, where necessary.'[339]

* * *

Conclusions. Under customary international law, everyone of marriageable age has the right to marry and found a family. Marriage requires the consent of both parties. The equality of the parties must be recognised at the time of dissolution of the marriage.

G. Mobility and asylum

'Birds fly over the rainbow, why can't I?', asks Dorothy in the *Wizard of Oz*. Of all the species of the animal kingdom, human beings appear to be the only one that lacks full freedom of movement. Liberty of movement is an indispensable condition for the free development of an individual, said the Human Rights Committee in General Comment 27.[340] The same language was adopted by the Inter-American Court of Human Rights.[341] The initial formulation appears in Article 13(1) of the Universal Declaration of Human Rights ('Everyone has the right to freedom of movement and residence within the borders of each state.') It is the only right in the Universal Declaration with such an explicit territorial limitation. The Universal Declaration also specifies that '[e]veryone has the right to leave any country, including his own, and to return to his country'.[342] A very similar text is set out in the International Covenant on Civil and Political Rights. It specifies that '[e]veryone lawfully within the territory of a State shall, within that territory, have the right to liberty of movement and freedom to choose his residence'. The Covenant also affirms the right to leave any country, including 'his own', and states that '[n]o one shall be arbitrarily deprived of the right to enter his own country'.[343] Freedom of movement is recognised in specialised and regional conventions.[344] Some of the

[339] Ibid., para. 25; Concluding observations, Burundi, CCPR/C/BDI/CO/2, para. 11.

[340] General Comment 27, Freedom of movement (art. 12), CCPR/C/21/Rev.1/Add.9, para. 1. See also *Batyrov v. Uzbekistan*, no. 1585/2007, Views, 30 July 2009, CCPR/C/96/D/1585/2007, para. 8.3; *Orazova v. Turkmenistan*, no. 1883/2009, Views, 20 March 2012, CCPR/C/104/D/1883/2009, para. 7.3; *Sayadi et al. v. Belgium*, no. 1472/2006, Views, 29 December 2008, CCPR/C/89/D/1472/2006, para. 10.5.

[341] *Ricardo Canese v. Paraguay*, Judgment (Merits, reparations, and costs), 31 August 2004, Series C, No. 111, para. 115; *Moiwana Community v. Suriname*, Judgment (Preliminary objections, merits, reparations, and costs), 15 June 2005, Series C, No. 124, para. 110.

[342] Universal Declaration of Human Rights, A/RES/217 (III), art. 13(2).

[343] International Covenant on Civil and Political Rights, (1976) 999 UNTS 171, art. 12.

[344] International Convention on the Elimination of All Forms of Racial Discrimination, (1969) 660 UNTS 195, art. 5(2)(i); Convention on the Elimination of All Forms of Discrimination against Women, (1981) 1249 UNTS 13, art. 15(4); International Convention on the Suppression and Punishment of

regional human rights conventions go further than the Covenant in that they expressly prohibit expulsion or exile of a State's own nationals and the collective expulsion of non-nationals.[345] The Migrant Workers Convention also prohibits collective expulsion: 'Each case of expulsion shall be examined and decided individually.'[346]

None of the reservations or declarations to Article 12 of the International Covenant on Civil and Political Rights casts any doubt on the general principle of freedom of movement, and of the right to leave and to return. The only general reservation to Article 12, by Pakistan, stated that the provision was to be applied in conformity with the Constitution.[347] After many objections were submitted, Pakistan withdrew the reservation.[348] A few reservations have made departure from a country conditional upon furnishing proof that outstanding taxes have been paid.[349] Others have invoked specific provisions of domestic law governing issuance of residence permits,[350] restrictions during exceptional circumstances,[351] and ancient texts concerning travel by fallen monarchs.[352] There are also some declarations or reservations of a territorial nature, affecting Macau,[353] and overseas territories of the Netherlands[354] and the United Kingdom.[355]

The freedom of movement provision in the Convention on the Elimination of All Forms of Discrimination against Women corresponds to Article 12(1) of the International Covenant on Civil and Political Rights: 'States Parties shall accord to men and women the same rights with regard to the law relating to the movement

the Crime of Apartheid, (1976) 1015 UNTS 243, art. II(c); Convention on the Rights of the Child, (1990) 1571 UNTS 3, arts. 9, 10; International Convention on the Protection of the Rights of all Migrant Workers and Members of their Families, (2003) 2220 UNTS 3, art. 39; Convention on the Rights of Persons with Disabilities, (2008) 2515 UNTS 3, art. 18; Protocol 4 to the Convention for the Protection of Human Rights and Fundamental Freedoms, securing certain rights and freedoms other than those already included in the Convention and in the first Protocol thereto, CETS 46, arts. 2, 3, and 4; American Convention on Human Rights, (1978) 1144 UNTS 123, art. 22; African Charter on Human and Peoples' Rights, (1986) 1520 UNTS 271, art. 12(1) and (2); Arab Charter on Human Rights, art. 26; Charter of Fundamental Rights of the European Union, OJ C 326/391, art. 45(1).

345 Protocol 4 to the Convention for the Protection of Human Rights and Fundamental Freedoms, securing certain rights and freedoms other than those already included in the Convention and in the first Protocol thereto, CETS 46, arts. 3(1) and 4; American Convention on Human Rights, (1978) 1144 UNTS 123, art. 22(5) and (9); African Charter on Human and Peoples' Rights, (1986) 1520 UNTS 271, art. 12(5); Charter of Fundamental Rights of the European Union, OJ C 326/391, art. 19(1).

346 International Convention on the Protection of the Rights of all Migrant Workers and Members of their Families, (2003) 2220 UNTS 3, art. 22(1).

347 C.N.405.2010.TREATIES-17. See the Statement by the Human Rights Committee on Pakistan's reservation at the time of ratification: A/66/40, paras. 48–49.

348 (2011) 2786 UNTS 97.

349 Trinidad and Tobago, C.N.336.1978.TREATIES-16; Belize, C.N.239.1996.TREATIES-5.

350 Switzerland, C.N.223.1992.TREATIES-7/12.

351 C.N.978.2000.TREATIES-14.

352 Italy, C.N.231.1978.TREATIES-11, since withdrawn, C.N.1291.2005.TREATIES-27; Austria, (1978) 1103 UNTS 393-396.

353 C.N.159.1993.TREATIES-3/8 (Annex), C.N.1156.1999.TREATIES-11.

354 C.N.669.2010.TREATIES-28.

355 C.N.193.1976.TREATIES-6.

of persons and the freedom to choose their residence and domicile.'[356] Although not explicit, it is a reasonable inference that this provision involves recognition of freedom of movement and the right to choose residence and domicile. Most of the States that are not Parties to the International Covenant but that have ratified the Women's Convention have no reservations to the provision in the latter treaty on freedom of movement. However, four relevant reservations to the Women's Convention provision are from States that are not Parties to the International Covenant on Civil and Political Rights. Brunei Darussalam and Saudi Arabia have general reservations to all provisions of the Convention that are not compatible with Islamic law or domestic law.[357] Oman made a general reservation to Article 15(4),[358] but it was withdrawn pursuant to an undertaking during the Universal Periodic Review. Qatar also has a reservation to Article 15(4).[359]

Many of the States that are not parties to the International Covenant on Civil and Political Rights have acknowledged freedom of movement in their reports to the Human Rights Council.[360] Saudi Arabia reported to the Human Rights Council that 'the relevant agencies were authorised to apply the provisions of the Traffic Act equally to both men and women to enhance women's right to freedom of movement'.[361] In an earlier report, it said that migrant workers would be entitled to freedom of movement to the extent that they hold a valid residence permit.[362]

Freedom of movement was not included in the Human Rights Committee's list of rights recognised under customary international law.[363]

These materials, taken as a whole, provide strong evidence that freedom of movement, and freedom to choose residence and domicile, as set out in Article 13 of the Universal Declaration of Human Rights and some of the treaties, are norms

[356] Convention on the Elimination of All Forms of Discrimination against Women, (1981) 1249 UNTS 13, art. 15(4).

[357] Brunei Darussalam, C.N.467.2006.TREATIES-3 ('... reservations regarding those provisions of the said Convention that may be contrary to the Constitution of Brunei Darussalam and to the beliefs and principles of Islam, the official religion of Brunei Darussalam'); Saudi Arabia, ('In case of contradiction between any term of the Convention and the norms of Islamic law, the Kingdom is not under obligation to observe the contradictory terms of the Convention').

[358] C.N.193.2006.TREATIES-1.

[359] C.N.298.2009.TREATIES-1.

[360] China (Hong Kong), National report, A/HRC/WG.6/4/CHN/1, para. 108; Fiji, National report, A/HRC/WG.6/20/FJI/1, para. 8; Kiribati, National report, A/HRC/WG.6/8/KIR/1, para. 23, Views on conclusions, A/HRC/15/3/Add.1, para. 46 and National report, A/HRC/WG.6/21/KIR/1, para. 41; Malaysia, National report, A/HRC/WG.6/4/MYS/1/Rev.1, para. 9; Micronesia, National report, A/HRC/WG.6/9/FSM/1, para. 17; Nauru, Report of the Working Group, A/HRC/17/3, para. 75; Oman, National report, A/HRC/WG.6/10/OMN/1, p. 4 and National report, A/HRC/WG.6/23/OMN/1, para. 95(a); Solomon Islands, National report, A/HRC/WG.6/11/SLB/1, paras. 17, 24, 49; United Arab Emirates, National report, A/HRC/WG.6/3/ARE/1, p. 8.

[361] Saudi Arabia, National report, A/HRC/WG.6/31/SAU/1, para. 103 and Report of the Working Group, A/HRC/40/4, para. 9.

[362] Saudi Arabia, National report, A/HRC/WG.6/4/SAU/1, para. 35.

[363] General Comment 24, Issues Relating to Reservations Made upon Ratification or Accession to the Covenant or the Optional Protocols thereto, or in Relation to Declarations under art. 41 of the Covenant, CCPR/C/21/Rev.1/Add.6, para. 8.

of customary law. There is some question about the position of Brunei Darussalam and Qatar, and these States may contend that they are persistent objectors. As for Saudi Arabia, which has not ratified the relevant universal treaties, it is nevertheless a party to the Arab Charter on Human Rights. Article 26 of that treaty is comparable to Article 13 of the Universal Declaration.

1. Freedom of movement

Freedom of movement, as set out in the Universal Declaration of Human Rights, the International Covenant on Civil and Political Rights, and in the other specialised and regional treaties, is recognised for all who are 'lawfully' within the territory of a State, whether or not the person is a citizen. With very limited exceptions, however, citizens are always 'lawfully' within the territory of their State of nationality. In its General Comment on the position of non-nationals, the Human Rights Committee pointed out that 'in certain circumstances a non-national may enjoy the protection of the Covenant even in relation to entry or residence, for example, when considerations of non-discrimination, prohibition of inhuman treatment, and respect for family life arise'.[364] Non-nationals are also protected from expulsion to the extent that they may be exposed to a real risk to life and personal integrity in the State to which they are being sent.

Freedom of movement means the right to move freely about the entire territory of a State Party. In its Advisory Opinion on the Wall in the Occupied Palestinian Territory, the International Court of Justice found there was a violation of Article 12(1) of the International Covenant on Civil and Political Rights, to the extent that 'the construction of the wall and its associated regime impede the liberty of movement of the inhabitants'.[365] The right of residence may be more restricted, however. Some former Soviet republics continue to retain the *propiska*, a system of compulsory registration of residences.[366] In a case filed against Kazakhstan by a foreign resident who was fined for failing to register the true place of residence, the Human Rights Committee said this was not in itself 'an unreasonable restriction on the author's freedom of movement'.[367] Two dissenting members said that they considered that 'any system that on the one hand obliges all persons legally resident in the country to register their address with the police and on the other hand imposes a penalty—however modest—on any person found to reside at a different

[364] General Comment 15, The position of aliens under the Covenant, A/41/40, para. 5.

[365] *Legal Consequences of the Construction of a Wall in the Occupied Palestinian Territory, Advisory Opinion, ICJ Reports 2004*, p. 136, para. 134; ibid., Separate Opinion of Judge Higgins, para. 25.

[366] Azerbaijan, Concluding Observations, CCPR/C/AZE/CO/3, para. 18; Azerbaijan, Concluding Observations, CCPR/C/AZE/CO/4, paras. 30–31; Kazakhstan, Concluding Observations, CCPR/C/KAZ/CO/2, paras. 41–42; Kazakhstan, Concluding Observations, CCPR/C/KAZ/CO/1, para. 18; Turkmenistan, Concluding Observations, CCPR/C/TKM/CO/2, paras. 28–29.

[367] *L.T. v. Kazakhstan*, no. 2140/2012, Decision, 13 June 2017, CCPR/C/119/D/2140/2012, para. 6.4.

address from that registered, constitutes a restriction on the freedom of choice of place of residence and liberty of movement within the territory of the State concerned'.[368] Internally displaced persons do not enjoy full exercise of their right to freedom of residence. They are defined as 'persons or groups of persons who have been forced or obliged to flee or to leave their homes or places of habitual residence, in particular as a result of or in order to avoid the effects of armed conflict, situations of generalised violence, violations of human rights or natural or human-made disasters, and who have not crossed an internationally recognised border'.[369]

Freedom of movement also includes the right to leave a country and even to emigrate to another country without loss of citizenship. According to the Human Rights Committee, '[f]reedom to leave the territory of a State may not be made dependent on any specific purpose or on the period of time the individual chooses to stay outside the country'.[370] Linked to the exercise of this freedom is the obligation upon the State of nationality to provide travel documents.[371] Although the practice is rather exceptional, some countries still impose a requirement of an exit visa.[372] For example, this may be required of their own nationals as a means of ensuring obligations of military service are honoured. Non-nationals may also be obliged to furnish an exit visa.

The right of a person to enter his or her own country 'recognises the special relationship of a person to that country', states General Comment 27 of the Human Rights Committee.[373] The International Criminal Court has suggested that denying re-entry of refugees to a country may amount to a crime against humanity given that '[u]nder international human rights law, no one may be arbitrarily deprived of the right to enter one's own country'.[374] The Grand Chamber of the European Court of Human Rights held that there was a right under customary international law of displaced persons to return 'voluntarily and in safety to their homes or places of habitual residence as soon as the reasons for their displacement cease to exist'. The Court appeared to consider the right applicable whether or not the displacement had resulted in an international border being crossed. It was presented as a rule of international humanitarian law, indicating that the displacement

[368] Ibid., Dissenting opinion by Olivier de Frouville and Sarah Cleveland, para. 2.

[369] Guiding Principles on Internal Displacement, E/CN.4/1998/53/Add. 2, Introduction, para. 2.

[370] General Comment 27, Freedom of movement (art. 12), CCPR/C/21/Rev.1/Add.9, para. 8.

[371] Ibid., para. 9; *Martins v. Uruguay*, no. 57/1979, Views, 23 March 1982, A/37/40, Annex VIII, p. 157, para. 9.

[372] Equatorial Guinea, Concluding Observations, CCPR/CO/79/GNQ, para. 13; Syria, Concluding Observations, CCPR/CO/71/SYR, para. 21; Uzbekistan, Concluding Observations, CCPR/C/UZB/CO/3, para. 18.

[373] General Comment 27, Freedom of movement (art. 12), CCPR/C/21/Rev.1/Add.9, para. 19.

[374] *Request under Regulation 46(3) of the Regulations of the Court* (ICC-RoC46(3)-01/18), Decision on the 'Prosecution's Request for a Ruling on Jurisdiction under Article 19(3) of the Statute', 6 September 2018, para. 77. In addition to art. 12(4), it referred to International Convention on the Elimination of All Forms of Racial Discrimination, (1969) 660 UNTS 195, art. 5(d)(ii); International Convention on the Suppression and Punishment of the Crime of Apartheid, (1976) 1015 UNTS 243, art. 2(c).

be the consequence of armed conflict. There does not seem to be a requirement that those who return be nationals of the State of origin.[375]

In contrast to Article 3(1) of Protocol 4 to the European Convention on Human Rights and Article 22(5) of the American Convention on Human Rights, the International Covenant on Civil and Political Rights does not contain an express prohibition of expulsion of nationals, but this prohibition follows indirectly from the right to entry. Formulated in the Covenant, the right to enter refers to one's 'own country', in contrast with regional human rights treaties where the right is more limited, applying only to 'nationals'.[376] As the Human Rights Committee has explained, the scope of one's 'own country' is broader than 'country of nationality'. The Committee has held that exercise of the right depends upon 'close and enduring connections between a person and a country'.[377] Examples given in the General Comment include nationals of a country who have been stripped of their nationality in violation of international law, and individuals whose country of nationality had been incorporated in or transferred to another national entity, whose nationality has been denied them. The Committee has pointed to 'a broader interpretation that might embrace other categories of long-term residents, including but not limited to stateless persons arbitrarily deprived of the right to acquire the nationality of the country of such residence'.[378]

2. Restrictions

Like other rights enshrined in the International Covenant as well as in other human rights treaties, freedom of movement is not absolute. A State Party may restrict the exercise of those rights only if the restrictions are provided by law, are necessary to protect national security, public order, public health, or morals or the rights and freedoms of others and are consistent with the other rights recognised in Covenant. In General Comment 27, the Committee noted that 'it is not sufficient that the restrictions serve the permissible purposes; they must also be necessary to protect them' and that 'restrictive measures must confirm to the principle of proportionality; they must be appropriate to achieve their protective

[375] *Sargsyan v. Azerbaijan* [GC], no. 40167/06, § 232, ECHR 2015-IV; *Chiragov et al. v. Armenia* [GC], no. 13216/05, § 97, 16 June 2015.

[376] African Charter on Human and Peoples' Rights, (1986) 1520 UNTS 271, art. 12(2).

[377] Ibid., para. 20. The formulation originates in *Stewart v. Canada*, no. 538/1993, Views, 1 November 1996, CCPR/C/58/D/538/1993, Individual opinion submitted by Ms. Elizabeth Evatt, Ms. Cecilia Medina Quiroga, and Mr. Francisco José Aguilar Urbina, para. 6.

[378] General Comment 27, Freedom of movement (art. 12), CCPR/C/21/Rev.1/Add.9, para. 20.

function'.[379] When Finnish law denied delivery of a passport to persons aged seventeen to thirty unless they could demonstrate that they had done their military service, the Human Rights Committee held this to be necessary for the protection of national security and public order.[380] In a French case, the Committee accepted very far-reaching restrictions on freedom of movement of suspected terrorists as justified on grounds of national security.[381] Permissible restrictions on freedom of internal movement and residency to protect public order include the regulation of vehicle traffic as well as special measures (such as blockades) to maintain public safety. The same applies to restrictions on freedom of movement for reasons of safety (*e.g.* in earthquake, volcanic, landslide, and avalanche zones, but also in the event of internal unrest or threats of terrorist attacks). During the COVID-19 pandemic, several States derogated from Article 12 of the International Covenant because of various measures restricting freedom of movement.[382] This was probably unnecessary because the restrictions on mobility would be justifiable for the purpose of protecting public health.

The United Nations Security Council has imposed travel bans preventing the entry into or the transit through their territories of individuals listed as being suspected of terrorist activity.[383] According to the Human Rights Committee, the obligation of States to comply with Security Council decisions may amount to a 'restriction' on freedom of movement based upon national security or public order.[384] One of the members of the Committee, Nigel Rodley, acknowledged that the Security Council had the authority to 'take measures involving derogation from rights susceptible of derogation' such as freedom of movement, but that it was not easy to see 'why nearly a decade after the first resolution 1267 (1999) and seven years after 9/11 the Council could not have evolved procedures more consistent with the human rights values of transparency, accountability and impartial independent assessment of facts'.[385]

[379] *Batyrov v. Uzbekistan*, no. 1585/2007, Views, 30 July 2009, CCPR/C/96/D/1585/2007, para. 8.3; *Sayadi and Vinck v. Belgium*, no. 1472/2006, Views, 22 October 2008, CCPR/C/94/D/1472/2006, para. 10.5.

[380] *Peltonen v. Finland*, no. 492/1992, Views, 26 July 1994, CCPR/C/51/D/492/1992, paras. 2.1, 6.1, 6.8, 8.2, 8.3, 8.4.

[381] *Celepli v. Sweden*, no. 456/1991, Views, 2 August 1994, CCPR/C/51/D/456/1991, para. 9.2; *Karker v. France*, no. 833/1998, Views, 30 October 2000, CCPR/C/70/D/833/1998, para. 9.2.

[382] For example, Armenia, C.N.114.2020.TREATIES-IV.4; Chile, C.N.128.2020.TREATIES-IV.4; Colombia, C.N.131.2020.TREATIES-IV.4; El Salvador, C.N.134.2020.TREATIES-IV.4; Estonia , C.N.113.2020.TREATIES-IV.4; Guatemala, C.N.117.2020.TREATIES-IV.4; Georgia, C.N.125.2020. TREATIES-IV.4; Kyrgyzstan, C.N.129.2020.TREATIES-IV.4; Latvia, C.N.105.2020.TREATIES-IV.4; Moldova, C.N.164.2020.TREATIES-IV.4; Palestine, C.N.127.2020.TREATIES-IV.4; Romania, C.N.121.2020.TREATIES-IV.4.

[383] S/RES/1390 (2002), para. 2(b).

[384] *Sayadi and Vinck v. Belgium*, no. 1472/2006, Views, 22 October 2008, CCPR/C/94/D/1472/2006, para. 10.7.

[385] Ibid., Individual opinion of Committee member Sir Nigel Rodley (concurring).

3. Asylum

Article 14(1) of the Universal Declaration of Human Rights states that '[e]veryone has the right to seek and to enjoy in other countries asylum from persecution'. It subjects this to an exception, in that it may not be invoked 'in the case of prosecutions genuinely arising from non-political crimes or from acts contrary to the purposes and principles of the United Nations'.[386] The principal vehicles for the implementation of the right to asylum within the international legal order are the Convention relating to the Status of Refugees[387] and the Protocol relating to the Status of Refugees.[388] The Convention has been ratified by 146 States and the Protocol by 147. The right is not reproduced in the International Covenants although it appears in some of the regional human rights treaties that, in effect, incorporate by reference the two specialised treaties dealing with refugees.[389] Some of the other specialised treaties, such as the Istanbul Convention on violence against women, also address specific facets of the right to asylum.[390]

The Refugee Convention and its Protocol offer a limited right to asylum by providing protection to persons who have 'a well-founded fear of being persecuted for reasons of race, religion, nationality, membership of a particular social group or political opinion, is outside the country of his nationality and is unable or, owing to such fear, is unwilling to avail himself of the protection of that country; or who, not having a nationality and being outside the country of his former habitual residence as a result of such events, is unable or, owing to such fear, is unwilling to return to it'.[391] The Convention provides for exceptions similar to those in the Universal Declaration of Human Rights.[392] The General Assembly Declaration on Territorial Asylum, adopted by consensus, affirms that '[a]sylum granted by a State, in the exercise of its sovereignty, to persons entitled to invoke article 14 of the Universal Declaration of Human Rights ... shall be respected by all other States'.[393] Despite the express provision on the right to asylum in the Universal Declaration, it is rarely referred to in the Universal Periodic Review process.[394]

386 Universal Declaration of Human Rights, A/RES/217 (III), art. 13(2).

387 (1954) 189 UNTS 137.

388 (1967) 606 UNTS 267.

389 American Convention on Human Rights, (1978) 1144 UNTS 123, art. 22(7); African Charter on Human and Peoples' Rights, (1986) 1520 UNTS 271, art. 12(3); Arab Charter on Human Rights, para. 28; Charter of Fundamental Rights of the European Union, OJ C 326/391, art. 18. There is also an African Convention: Convention Governing the Specific Aspects of Refugee Problems in Africa, (1974) 1001 UNTS 45.

390 Council of Europe Convention on preventing and combating violence against women and domestic violence, CETS 210, arts. 59–61.

391 Convention relating to the Status of Refugees, (1954) 189 UNTS 137, art. I(A)(2).

392 Ibid., art. I(F).

393 Declaration on Territorial Asylum, A/RES/2312 (XXII), OP 1.

394 Fiji, in Nauru, Report of the Working Group, A/HRC/31/7, para. 76; France, Report of the Working Group, A/HRC/23/3, para. 118; Ghana, in Australia, Report of the Working Group, A/HRC/31/14, para. 136.269; Mozambique, National report, A/HRC/WG.6/10/MOZ/1, para. 58 and National

The right to asylum was the subject of an important judgment of the International Court of Justice dealing with customary international law and 'diplomatic asylum', whereby individuals may obtain sanctuary in an embassy.[395] Colombia cited a South American treaty on the subject and claimed it merely codified a regional custom. The Court dismissed the argument, explaining that the 'limited number of States which have ratified this Convention reveals the weakness of this argument'.[396] The Inter-American Court of Human Rights said the evidence of *opinio juris* was insufficient for the conclusion that customary international law provided for a right of diplomatic asylum.[397] In the *Assange* case, dealing with diplomatic asylum, the United Nations Working Group on arbitrary detention has said that the right to asylum is recognised under customary international law.[398]

The Universal Declaration of Human Rights uses two verbs, 'seek' and 'enjoy', with respect to the right to asylum. There is little evidence to support a right to *seek* asylum, other than the possibility of applying for refugee status once the asylum seeker is already within the jurisdiction of the State where asylum is sought. The right to *enjoy* asylum begins once the individual's status as a refugee within the relatively narrow terms of the Convention has been recognised. Only then do certain rights associated with refugee status become operative, the most important of them being the protection against refoulement. A legal opinion issued by the United Nations Secretariat referred to the text of Article 14(1) of the Universal Declaration but said 'an individual cannot claim a "right" to be granted asylum and no State is obliged to grant asylum under current customary international law'.[399]

Article 33 of the Refugee Convention prevents a State from 'expulsion or return ("refoulement")' of a refugee 'to the frontiers of territories where his life or freedom would be threatened on account of his race, religion, nationality, membership of a particular social group or political opinion'. Protection against refoulement may be refused to a person who is a danger to the security of the country of refuge and by a person convicted of a 'particularly serious crime' who 'constitutes a danger to the community of that country'. The rule set out in Article 33 of the Convention was endorsed by the International Law Commission in its draft articles on the

report, A/HRC/WG.6/24/MOZ/1, para. 42; Togo, in Qatar, Report of the Working Group, A/HRC/42/15, para. 73.

[395] *Colombian-Peruvian asylum case, Judgment, 20 November 1950, ICJ Reports 1950*, p. 266.

[396] Ibid., p. 277.

[397] *The Institution of Asylum and its Recognition as a human right in the Inter-American System of protection (Interpretation and Scope of arts. 5, 22(7), and 22(8) in relation to art. 1(1) of the American Convention on Human Rights)*, Advisory Opinion OC-25/18, 30 May 2018, Series A, No. 25, para. 162.

[398] *Opinion No. 54/2015 concerning Julian Assange (Sweden and the United Kingdom of Great Britain and Northern Ireland)*, A/HRC/WGAD/2015, para. 15.

[399] United Nations, 'Note to the Members of the Senior Management Group of the United Nations Regarding Conditions for the Granting of Political Asylum', *United Nations Juridical Yearbook 2004*, p. 365. For the argument that the right to asylum can be derived from general principles of law, see María-Teresa Gil-Bazo, 'Asylum as a General Principle of International Law', (2015) 27 *International Journal of Refugee Law* 3.

expulsion of aliens.[400] A few States that are not parties to the Refugee Convention and its Protocol acknowledge the principle of non-refoulement of refugees in their reports to the Human Rights Council.[401]

Although there is no serious claim that the Refugee Convention and its Protocol, as a whole, constitute a codification of customary international law, there is nevertheless considerable support for the view that this is the case with respect to the prohibition of refoulement. For example, in 1994, the United Nations High Commissioner for Refugees made a detailed submission to the German Federal Constitutional Court that concluded 'that the principle of non-refoulement has acquired a normative character and constitutes a rule of international customary law'.[402] In 2001, the Executive Committee of the High Commissioner for refugees described non-refoulement as 'the logical complement to the right to seek asylum recognised in the Universal Declaration of Human Rights. It has come to be considered a rule of customary international law binding on all States.'[403] A declaration adopted by the States Parties to the Refugee Convention, in 2002, referred to 'the continuing relevance and resilience of this international regime of rights and principles, including at its core the principle of *non-refoulement*, whose applicability is embedded in customary international law'.[404] The Inter-American Court of Human Rights has said 'the principle of non-refoulement constitutes a norm of customary international law and is, consequently, binding for all States, whether or not they are parties to the 1951 Convention or its 1967 Protocol'. The Court noted that 'this principle is not absolute because it allows for exceptions'.[405]

Other authorities have taken less care to specify that they are referring specifically to refugee law, and that the rule is subject to exceptions. According to the Working Group on Arbitrary Detention, protection against refoulement is recognised under customary international law.[406] Judges of the European Court of Human Rights have echoed this view, describing 'the principle of non-refoulement as a binding

[400] Report of the International Law Commission Sixty-sixth session (5 May–6 June and 7 July–8 August 2014), A/69/10, pp. 28–30.

[401] For example, Bangladesh, Views on conclusions, A/HRC/24/12/Add.1, para. 130.7; Eritrea, National report, A/HRC/WG.6/18/ERI/1, para. 41; Lebanon, National report, A/HRC/WG.6/9/LBN/1, para. 126.

[402] UN High Commissioner for Refugees, The Principle of Non-Refoulement as a Norm of Customary International Law. Response to the Questions Posed to UNHCR by the Federal Constitutional Court of the Federal Republic of Germany in Cases 2 BvR 1938/93, 2 BvR 1953/93, 2 BvR 1954/93, 31 January 1994.

[403] Executive Committee of the High Commissioner's Programme, Note on international protection, A/AC.96/951.

[404] Declaration of States Parties to the 1951 Convention and its 1967 Protocol relating to the Status of Refugees, HCR/MMSP/2001/09, 16 January 2002, para. 4 (italics in the original).

[405] *Rights and Guarantees of Children in the Context of Migration and/or in need of International Protection*, Advisory Opinion OC-21/14, 19 August 2014, Series A, No. 21, para. 211 (internal references omitted); *Pacheco Tineo Family v. Bolivia* (Preliminary objections, merits, reparations, and costs), Judgment, 25 November 2013, Series C, No. 272, para. 151.

[406] *Opinion No. 54/2015 concerning Julian Assange (Sweden and the United Kingdom of Great Britain and Northern Ireland)*, A/HRC/WGAD/2015, para. 15.

rule of international law'.[407] Similarly, a Chamber of the International Criminal Court has referred to the 'the customary rule of non-refoulement'.[408] The Special Rapporteur on extrajudicial, summary, and arbitrary executions spoke of 'the principle of non-refoulement as a matter of customary law'.[409] An example of imprecise invocation of the non-refoulement principle can be seen in a celebrated judgment of the European Court of Human Rights dealing with asylum seekers who were apprehended by the Italian navy and returned to Libya before they could enter Italian territory. The Grand Chamber referred to 'the obligation to fulfil the obligations arising out of international refugee law, including the *non-refoulement* principle'.[410] It then noted that the 'non-refoulement principle' was 'enshrined in Article 19 of the Charter of Fundamental Rights of the European Union', adding that this point had been made in a letter to the Court from the Vice-President of the European Commission.[411] But the European Charter formulates the non-refoulement prohibition only with respect to the death penalty, torture, and inhuman or degrading treatment or punishment.[412] The letter from the European Commission official spoke clearly of return where there is 'a real risk of being subjected to torture or to inhuman or degrading treatment'.[413] Clearly, 'the principle of non-refoulement' under refugee law is not at all equivalent to 'the principle of non-refoulement' where there is a real risk of the death penalty, torture, and ill-treatment, which derives from human rights law and not refugee law.

The Inter-American Commission on Human Rights has raised this a notch, speaking of 'the jus cogens prohibition of refoulement'.[414] The same position has been adopted by the United Nations High Commissioner for Refugees.[415] Judges of the International Criminal Court have also referred to 'the peremptory norm of non-refoulement'.[416] The view finds some academic

[407] *F.G. v. Sweden* [GC], no. 43611/11, 23 March 2016, Joint separate opinion of Judges Ziemele, de Gaetano, Pinto de Albuquerque, and Wojtyczek. Also *Hirsi Jamaa et al. v. Italy* [GC], no. 27765/09, ECHR 2012-II, Concurring opinion of Judge Pinto de Albuquerque.

[408] *Prosecutor v. Katanga et al.* (ICC-01/04-01/07), Decision on an Amicus Curiae application and on the 'Requête tendant à obtenir présentations des témoins DRC-D02-P-0350, DRC-D02-P-0236, DRC-D02-P-0228 aux autorités néerlandaises aux fins d'asile' (arts. 68 and 93(7) of the Statute), 9 June 2011, para. 64. Also paras. 67, 68.

[409] Report of the Special Rapporteur on extrajudicial, summary, or arbitrary executions, A/67/275, para. 87.

[410] *Hirsi Jamaa et al. v. Italy* [GC], no. 27765/09, § 134, ECHR 2012-II.

[411] Ibid., § 135.

[412] Charter of Fundamental Rights of the European Union, OJ C 326/391, art. 19(2).

[413] *Hirsi Jamaa et al. v. Italy* [GC], no. 27765/09, § 34, ECHR 2012-II.

[414] *Djamel Ameziane v. United States of America*, Case 12.865, Report No. 29/20, Merits, 22 June 2020, para. 258. In 1984, a colloquium organised by the Commission had concluded that the principle of non-refoulement of refugees 'should be acknowledged and observed as a rule of jus cogens', Cartagena Declaration on Refugees, 22 November 1984, para. 5, OEA/Ser.L/V/II.66/doc.10, rev. 1, pp. 190–193.

[415] Office of the United Nations High Commissioner for Refugees, Advisory Opinion on the Extraterritorial Application of Non-Refoulement Obligations under the 1951 Convention relating to the Status of Refugees and its 1967 Protocol, 26 January 2007, para. 21.

[416] *Prosecutor v. Katanga et al.* (ICC-01/04-01/07), Decision on the application for the interim release of detained Witnesses DRC- D02-P-0236, DRC-D02-P-0228, and DRC-D02-P-0350, 1 October 2013, para. 30.

endorsement.[417] The Special Rapporteur of the International Law Commission described non-refoulement as 'another principle of international law whose candidacy for peremptory status has ample support'.[418] The Special Rapporteur pointed to a 1996 General Assembly resolution calling upon States to 'respect scrupulously the fundamental principle of non-refoulement, which is not subject to derogation'.[419] This is not a very compelling authority, given the well-known exceptions to the principle set out in Article 33 of the Refugee Convention. Even were it accurate to describe the norm as being not subject to derogation, this does not automatically bring with it the *jus cogens* qualification.[420] The Special Rapporteur reached no conclusion on whether to include non-refoulement among norms of *jus cogens*. Moreover, it is unclear from his discussion whether any distinction was made between refoulement of refugees and refoulement because of a real risk of torture, ill-treatment, and violation of the right to life.[421] Other members of the Commission questioned whether non-refoulement of refugees could be considered a *jus cogens* norm given that the principle is subject to important exceptions.[422]

Besides the refugee context, the principle of non-refoulement may apply to the extent that there is a real risk of serious human rights violations. Refoulement is prohibited by the specialised treaties dealing with torture[423] and enforced disappearance.[424] Neither of these treaties contemplates exceptions to the prohibition of refoulement, in contrast with the Refugee Convention, although the Torture Convention does not extend the non-refoulement obligation to cases of cruel, inhuman, or degrading treatment or punishment.[425] International human rights courts and treaty bodies have developed the doctrine further, considering refoulement to be prohibited where there is a real risk of torture, ill-treatment, and violation of the right to life.[426] The Human Rights Committee has suggested that

[417] Jean Allain, 'The Jus Cogens Nature of Non-refoulement', (2001) 13 *International Journal of Refugee Law* 533; Cathryn Costello and Michelle Foster, 'Non-refoulement as Custom and *Jus Cogens*? Putting the Prohibition to the Test', [2015] *Netherlands Yearbook of International Law* 273; Alice Farmer, 'Non-Refoulement and Jus Cogens: Limiting Anti-Terror Measures that Threaten Refugee Protection', (2008) 23 *Georgetown Immigration Law Journal* 1. *Contra* Aoife Duffy, 'Expulsion to Face Torture? *Non-refoulement* in International Law', (2008) 20 *International Journal of Refugee Law* 373.

[418] Fourth report on peremptory norms of general international law (*jus cogens*) by Dire Tladi, Special Rapporteur, A/CN.4/727, para. 131.

[419] Office of the United Nations High Commissioner for Refugees, A/RES/51/75, para. 3.

[420] See the authorities on this cited *supra*, p. C.2 P32.

[421] Fourth report on peremptory norms of general international law (*jus cogens*) by Dire Tladi, Special Rapporteur, A/CN.4/727, para. 131–135. Also A/CN.4/SR.3465, p. 10.

[422] A/CN.4/SR.3460, p. 16 (Hussein Hassouna); A/CN.4/SR.3461, pp. 14–15 (Aniruddha Rajput).

[423] Convention Against Torture and Other Cruel, Inhuman or Degrading Treatment of Punishment, (1987) 1465 UNTS 85, art. 3.

[424] International Convention for the Protection of All Persons from Enforced Disappearance, (2010) 2716 UNTS 3, art. 16.

[425] See General Comment No.4 (2017) on the implementation of art. 3 of the Convention in the context of art. 22, CAT/C/GC/4, in particular para. 26.

[426] *Kindler v. Canada*, no. 470/1991, Views, 30 July 1993, CCPR/C/48/D/470/1991, para. 13.2; General Comment 31, The Nature of the General Legal Obligation Imposed on States Parties to the Covenant, CCPR/C/21/Rev.1/Add. 13, para. 12; *Husayn (Abu Zubaydah) v. Poland*, no. 7511/13, § 450,

this may also extend to cases of arbitrary detention,[427] and the European Court of Human Rights has stated that it applies where there is a real risk of a 'flagrant denial of a fair trial'.[428] The Human Rights Council's Commission of Inquiry into North Korea wrote that '[t]he obligation not to expel persons to other states where there are substantial grounds for believing that the person would be in danger of being subject to gross human rights violations also emerges from the requirements of customary international law', although no authority is cited.[429] A joint general comment adopted by the Committee on the Protection of the Rights of All Migrant Workers and Members of Their Families and the Committee on the Rights of the Child described the principle of non-refoulement extending to situations where there is 'risk of irreparable harm upon return, including persecution, torture, gross violations of human rights or other irreparable harm'.[430] The International Law Commission draft articles on expulsion of aliens prohibit refoulement of a non-national to 'to a State where his or her life would be threatened on grounds such as race, colour, sex, language, religion, political or other opinion, national, ethnic or social origin, property, birth or other status, or any other ground impermissible under international law' as well as to one where the person 'may be subjected to torture or to cruel, inhuman or degrading treatment or punishment'.[431] The Commission's draft articles on crimes against humanity prohibit refoulement to a State 'where there are substantial grounds for believing that he or she would be in danger of being subjected to a crime against humanity'.[432]

In proceedings before the Human Rights Committee, States have contested application of the principle against refoulement to arbitrary detention,[433] freedom of

24 July 2014; *El Masri v. 'the former Yugoslav Republic of Macedonia'* [GC], no. 39630/09, §§ 218–221, 13 December 2012.

[427] *S. v. Denmark*, no. 2642/2015, Views, 26 March 2018, CCPR/C/122/D/2642/2015, para. 7.5. Note the position of the European Court of Human Rights, in *Othman (Abu Qatada) v. the United Kingdom*, No. 8139/09, § 233, ECHR 2012 (extracts), favouring application of a prohibition of expulsion in cases involving a real risk of a flagrant breach of the prohibition of arbitrary detention: 'A flagrant breach of Article 5 would occur only if, for example, the receiving State arbitrarily detained an applicant for many years without any intention of bringing him or her to trial. A flagrant breach of Article 5 might also occur if an applicant would be at risk of being imprisoned for a substantial period in the receiving State, having previously been convicted after a flagrantly unfair trial.'

[428] *Soering v. the United Kingdom*, 7 July 1989, § 113; Series A no. 161; *Al Nashiri v. Poland*, No. 28761/11, §§ 568–569, 24 July 2014; *Al Nashiri v. Romania*, no. 33234/12, §§ 568–569, 31 May 2018.

[429] Report of the detailed findings of the commission of inquiry on human rights in the Democratic People's Republic of Korea, A/HRC/25/CRP.1, para. 443.

[430] Joint general comment No. 3 (2017) of the Committee on the Protection of the Rights of All Migrant Workers and Members of their Families and No. 22 (2017) of the Committee on the Rights of the Child on the general principles regarding the human rights of children in the context of international migration, CMW/C/GC/3-CRC/C/GC/22, para. 45.

[431] Report of the International Law Commission Sixty-sixth session (5 May–6 June and 7 July–8 August 2014), A/69/10, pp. 59–65.

[432] Report of the International Law Commission Seventy-first session (29 April–7 June and 8 July–9 August 2019), A/74/10, p. 62.

[433] *X. v. Canada*, no. 2280/2013, Views, 22 July 2015, CCPR/C/114/D/2280/2013, para. 6.5.

movement,[434] the right to a fair trial,[435] and to private and family life,[436] freedoms of religion,[437] expression,[438] and peaceful assembly,[439] the rights of the child,[440] the right to education,[441] and the rights of minorities.[442] The United States has contended that the prohibition of refoulement is not contemplated by the International Covenant at all.[443] That, of course, is a quarrel about the interpretation of the Covenant rather than about the existence and scope of non-refoulement under customary international law. But such pronouncements weaken the claim that the prohibition of non-refoulement may be invoked for a broad spectrum of human rights violations.

Under customary international law, the principle of non-refoulement applies with respect to a real risk of violations of the right to life, and the prohibition of torture and ill-treatment and the flagrant denial of a fair trial. It applies to everyone, not just refugees, and without exceptions. With respect to refugees, the principle of non-refoulement is of broader scope, applying to a threat to freedom as well as to life, where this is on account of race, religion, nationality, membership of a particular social group, or political opinion. However, it is subject to exclusions based on national security or a criminal conviction in the country of asylum. Beyond this, it is difficult to extend the principle of non-refoulement under customary international law. There is no broad protection against refoulement on the grounds listed in the Refugee Convention for individuals who are not refugees. It seems that where national legislation permits this, under customary international law even citizens may be returned, deported, or extradited from their own country to a State where there is a well-founded fear of persecution for reasons of race, religion, nationality, membership of a particular social group, or political opinion, providing that there is no real risk of torture, enforced disappearance, ill-treatment, a violation of the right to life, or a flagrant violation of the right to a fair trial. A citizen subject to such a threat could not claim refugee status because the Convention only applies to someone who is 'outside the country of his nationality'.

* * *

[434] *Z.H. v. Denmark*, no. 2602/2015, Views, 27 March 2017, CCPR/C/119/D/2602/2015, paras. 4.7, 6.4.

[435] *Kwok v. Australia*, no. 1442/2005, Views, 23 November 2009, CCPR/C/97/D/1442/2005, para. 9.7.

[436] *A.S.M. et al. v. Denmark*, no. 2378/2014, Views, 18 November 2016, CCPR/C/117/D/2378/2014, para. 4.3.

[437] *B.L. v. Australia*, no. 2053/2011, Views, 16 October 2014, CCPR/C/112/D/2053/2011, para. 4.15; *C.L. v. Denmark*, no. 2753/2016, Views, 26 March 2018, CCPR/C/122/D/2753/2016, paras. 4.4, 7.4.

[438] *K. v. Denmark*, no. 2393/2014, Views, 16 July 2015, CCPR/C/114/D/2393/2014, para. 4.2.

[439] *X. v. Canada*, no. 2366/2014, Views, 5 November 2015, CCPR/C/115/D/2366/2014, para. 8.5.

[440] *A.S.M. et al. v. Denmark*, no. 2378/2014, Views, 18 November 2016, CCPR/C/117/D/2378/2014, para. 4.3; *D.T. et al. v. Canada*, no. 2081/2011, Views, 15 July 2016, CCPR/C/117/D/2081/2011, para. 4.21.

[441] *Y. v. Canada*, no. 2327/2014, Views, 10 March 2016, CCPR/C/116/D/2327/2014, para. 9.6; *M.Z.B.M. v. Denmark*, no. 2593/2015, Views, 3 April 2017, CCPR/C/119/D/2593/2015, paras. 4.4, 6.5.

[442] *J.D. v. Denmark*, no. 2204/2012, Views, 26 October 2016, CCPR/C/118/D/2204/2012, paras. 4.9, 4.16.

[443] United States of America, Concluding Observations, CCPR/C/USA/CO/4, para. 13.

Conclusions. Everyone who is lawfully within a country is entitled to freedom of movement within its borders. Everyone has the right to leave and return to his or her own country. Refoulement of anyone to a country where there is a real risk of violation of the right to life, torture, cruel, inhuman, or degrading treatment or punishment, and a flagrant denial of the right to a fair trial is prohibited by customary international law. Refoulement of a refugee is prohibited.

H. Nationality

Historically, the acquisition and loss of nationality has been viewed as a matter that was quintessentially reserved to national law.[444] Some of the early attempts at codification of human rights attached significance to the issue, especially the phenomenon of statelessness. Of the six articles in the draft declaration adopted by the Institut de Droit International in 1929, the final provision asserted that '[e]xcept for motives based upon its general legislation, no State shall have the right to withdraw its nationality from those whom, for reasons of sex, race, language, or religion, it should not deprive of the guarantees contemplated in the preceding articles.'[445] A similar text appears in the draft declaration adopted in 1943 by the London International Assembly.[446] Hersch Lauterpacht's draft declaration went much further, proclaiming a right to nationality *jus soli*, something going well beyond what is provided in the laws of many countries, both then and today: 'Every person shall be entitled to the nationality of the State where he is born unless and until on attaining majority he declares for the nationality open to him by virtue of descent. No person shall be deprived of his nationality by way of punishment or deemed to have lost his nationality except concurrently with the acquisition of a new nationality.'[447] The explanatory report to the European Convention on Nationality notes that '[w]ith the development of human rights law since the Second World War, there exists an increasing recognition that State discretion in this field must furthermore take into account the fundamental rights of individuals.'[448]

[444] *Nationality Decrees Issued in Tunis and Morocco, Advisory Opinion*, 7 February 1923, PCIJ Series B, No. 4, p. 24.
[445] Institut de Droit International, 'Declaration of the International Rights of Man', (1941) 35 *American Journal of International Law* 663, art. VI.
[446] 'Basic Principles as formulated by the Legal Commission of the London International Assembly', TNA LNU 6/7, art. X.
[447] Hersch Lauterpacht, *An International Bill of the Rights of Man*, New York: Columbia University Press, 1945, p. 71.
[448] Council of Europe, Explanatory Report to the European Convention on Nationality, 6 September 1997, para. 29. See *Ramadan v. Malta*, No. 76136/12, 21 June 2016, Dissenting opinion of Judge Pinto de Albuquerque, para. 7 (internal reference omitted), stating that '[b]eyond the clear and uncontested evidence of a continuing trend in general international law, these principles have gained the status of customary international law'.

The 'right to a nationality' is enshrined in Article 15 of the Universal Declaration of Human Rights, together with the right not to be arbitrarily deprived of nationality and to be denied the right to change nationality. A general right to nationality, applicable to everyone as set out in the Universal Declaration, is not affirmed in the International Covenant on Civil and Political Rights. However, the Covenant guarantees the right to a nationality to 'every child', and in practice this may amount to the same thing.[449] Of the regional treaties, the American Convention on Human Rights faithfully replicates the content of Article 15 of the Universal Declaration, with the specification that '[e]very person has the right to the nationality of the state in whose territory he was born if he does not have the right to any other nationality'.[450] The Arab Charter on Human Rights incorporates the norms in the Universal Declaration of Human Rights.[451] There is nothing on a right to nationality in the African Charter or the European Convention. The European Convention on Nationality declares 'everyone has the right to a nationality'[452] but only three of the forty-seven members of the Council of Europe are Parties. Noting the absence of provisions in the Covenant and the African Charter, the African Court on Human and Peoples' Rights has relied upon Article 15 of the Universal Declaration of Human Rights.[453]

The Convention on the Rights of the Child contains a text similar to that of the International Covenant[454] as well as the right 'to preserve his or her identity, including nationality'.[455] The Convention on the Rights of all Migrant Workers and Members of their Families also recognises that every child has the right to acquire a nationality.[456] The African Charter on the Rights and Welfare of the Child takes this somewhat further, providing that States Parties ensure that 'their Constitutional legislation recognise the principles according to which a child shall acquire the nationality of the State in the territory of which he has been born if, at the time of the child's birth he is not granted nationality by any other State in accordance with its laws'.[457] In any event, such a condition would seem to be implied in the right; the State where the child is born must ensure protection against statelessness.

[449] International Covenant on Civil and Political Rights, (1976) 999 UNTS 171, art. 24(3).

[450] American Convention on Human Rights, (1978) 1144 UNTS 123, art. 20(2).

[451] Arab Charter on Human Rights, art. 29.

[452] European Convention on Nationality, CETS 166.

[453] *Anudo Ochieng Anudo v. United Republic of Tanzania*, No. 012/2015, 22 March 2018, para. 76.

[454] Convention on the Rights of the Child, (1990) 1571 UNTS 3, art. 7(1). Also African Charter on the Rights and Welfare of the Child, art. 6(3).

[455] Convention on the Rights of the Child, (1990) 1571 UNTS 3, art. 8(2).

[456] International Convention on the Protection of the Rights of all Migrant Workers and Members of their Families, (2003) 2220 UNTS 3, art. 29.

[457] African Charter on the Rights and Welfare of the Child, art. 6 *in fine*.

Only two reservations have been made to Article 23(4) of the International Covenant, by the United Kingdom[458] and Liechtenstein.[459] The United Kingdom formulated a similar reservation to the one it submitted upon ratification of the Convention on the Rights of the Child,[460] but it has been withdrawn.[461] Of States that are not party to the Covenant, Malaysia and the United Arab Emirates have formulated reservations to the right of every child to acquire a nationality as set out in the Convention on the Rights of the Child.[462] Based upon the explanations provided by these two countries, the reservations do not manifest any profound disagreement with the principle at stake, although neither State fully recognises *jus soli* or birthright nationality.[463]

Nationality was defined by the International Court of Justice, in the *Nottebohm* case, as 'a legal bond having as its basis a social fact of attachment, a genuine connection of existence, interests and sentiments, together with the existence of reciprocal rights and duties'.[464] It is quite distinct from the notion of 'national origin' or 'ethnic origin'. The right to a nationality has been presented as 'a positive formulation of the duty to avoid statelessness'.[465] Under the Convention on the Reduction of Statelessness, States Parties agree to confer their nationality on persons who are born in their territory who would otherwise be stateless. This must be claimed by the age of twenty-one. To that extent it is similar to the other treaties in that it is confined essentially to children. Moreover, the Statelessness Convention makes eligibility for nationality subject to absence of any conviction of an offence against national security or being sentenced to a term of five years or more.[466] The Convention, which was adopted in 1961, has seventy-five States Parties, half of them having ratified in the decade 2010–2019, suggesting a growing commitment. Sometimes, recommendations during the Universal Periodic Review are directed at ratification of the Convention.[467]

[458] (1976) 1007 UNTS 394, C.N.193.1976.TREATIES-6 ('... the right to enact such nationality legislation as they may deem necessary from time to time to reserve the acquisition and possession of citizenship under such legislation to those having sufficient connection with the United Kingdom or any of its dependent territories ...).

[459] (1998) 2048 UNTS 48-49 (' ... the right to apply the Liechtenstein legislation according to which Liechtenstein nationality is granted under certain conditions ...). It has been withdrawn, (2009) 2629 UNTS 36.

[460] C.N.320.1991.TREATIES-16 (' ... to the acquisition and possession of citizenship ...). Also C.N.163.1997.TREATIES-6.

[461] C.N.980.2008.TREATIES-7.

[462] Malaysia, C.N.58.1995.TREATIES-1 (' ... reservations with respect to [article 7] and declares that the said provisions shall be applicable only if they are in conformity with the Constitution, national laws and national policies of the Government of Malaysia'); United Arab Emirates, C.N.92.1997.TREATIES-1 ('The United Arab Emirates is of the view that the acquisition of nationality is an internal matter and one that is regulated and whose terms and conditions are established by national legislation.').

[463] Malaysia, Initial report, CRC/C/MYS/1, para. 158; Malaysia, Concluding observations, CRC/C/MYS/CO/1, para. 11; United Arab Emirates, Periodic report, CRC/C/ARE/2, para. 32(a).

[464] *Nottebohm Case (second phase), Judgment, 6 April 1955, ICJ Reports 1955*, p. 4, at p. 23.

[465] Council of Europe, Explanatory Report to the European Convention on Nationality, 6 September 1997, para. 32.

[466] Convention on the Reduction of Statelessness, (1975) 989 UNTS 175, arts. 1 and 2.

[467] For example, Canada, in Bhutan, Report of the Working Group, A/HRC/27/8, para. 120.14; Portugal, in Kenya, Report of the Working Group, A/HRC/29/10, para. 143.31; Hungary, in Myanmar,

The pattern of ratification of the relevant treaties and the paucity of reservation to the norm provide compelling evidence of recognition of a right to nationality for children under customary international law. For some rights, there is a logical inference that the right must also be understood to apply to adults, but in the case of nationality this seems presumptuous. The Inter-American Court of Human Rights has said that '[i]t is generally accepted today that nationality is an inherent right of all human beings'.[468] In fact, the only treaty to confirm such a universal principle is the American Convention on Human Rights. The African Commission on Human and Peoples' Rights held that although Kenya was not a party to the Conventions concerning prevention of statelessness, 'it is worthy to note that these conventions outline the position of international customary law on State obligations to prevent statelessness'.[469]

Discrimination on the basis of national origin is prohibited. It is one of the enumerated grounds listed in Article 2 of the Universal Declaration. But discrimination on the basis of nationality is different. Nationality is a prerequisite for the exercise of other rights, notably political rights. A stateless person may thereby be deprived of the right to vote, to stand for elected office, and to work for the public service. The Inter-American Court of Human Rights has explained that '[n]ot only is nationality the basic requirement for the exercise of political rights, it may also have a significant bearing on the individual's legal capacity'.[470] Furthermore, said the Court, '[s]tatelessness deprives an individual of the possibility of enjoying civil and political rights and places him in a condition of extreme vulnerability'.[471] The Convention relating to the Status of Stateless Persons addresses many of the issues concerning equal treatment for stateless persons.[472] It presently has ninety-four States Parties; twenty-eight States ratified the treaty in the decade 2010–2019. The Inter-American Commission of Human Rights has pointed to Article 1.1 of the 1954 Convention where the term 'stateless' is used to describe 'any person who is not considered as a national by any State under the operation of its law'. The Commission said that this definition of statelessness 'is part of customary international law'.[473] There are similar pronouncements from the African Court

Report of the Working Group, A/HRC/17/9, para. 106.13; Sierra Leone, in United Arab Emirates, Report of the Working Group, A/HRC/38/14, para. 50.

[468] *Proposed Amendments to the Naturalisation Provision of the Constitution of Costa Rica*, Advisory Opinion, OC-4/84, 19 January 1984, Series A, No. 4, paras. 32 and 33.

[469] *The Nubian Community in Kenya v. Kenya*, No. 317/2006, 30 May 2016, para. 146. See also, for the view of the African Court on Human and Peoples' Rights, *Robert John Penessis v. Tanzania*, No. 013/2015, Judgment, 28 November 2019, para. 88.

[470] *Proposed Amendments to the Naturalisation Provision of the Constitution of Costa Rica*, Advisory Opinion, OC-4/84, 19 January 1984, Series A, No. 4, paras. 32 and 33.

[471] *Girls Yean and Bosico v. Dominican Republic*, Judgment (Preliminary objections, merits, reparations, and costs), 8 September 2005, Series C, No. 130, para. 142.

[472] Convention relating to the Status of Stateless Persons, (1960) 360 UNTS 117.

[473] Report on the Situation of Human Rights in the Dominican Republic, OEA/Ser.L/V/II, Doc. 45/15, para. 276.

of Human and Peoples' Rights[474] and a judge of the European Court of Human Rights.[475]

* * *

Conclusions. All children have a right to a nationality.

I. Property

Although the right to property, or more precisely the right 'to own property', is enshrined in Article 17 of the Universal Declaration of Human Rights,[476] its status under customary international law seems somewhat uncertain. There is no right to property in either of the International Covenants. This omission might suggest that it was not considered to be of a fundamental character.[477] Nevertheless, the right to property is recognised in the first Protocol to the European Convention on Human Rights,[478] some of the other regional treaties,[479] and the specialised conventions.[480] The Permanent Court of International Justice, in an Advisory Opinion on the minority rights treaty provisions applicable to Poland, held that the term 'civil and political rights' comprised, as a civil right, rights acquired under a contract for the possession or use of property, whether such property be immoveable or moveable'.[481] Like the Covenants, the Convention on the Rights of the Child has no provision on a right to property.

The American Law Institute did not include the right to property in its list of norms of customary international law. The Comment to the Restatement explained that there was 'wide disagreement among states as to the scope and content

[474] *Anudo Ochieng Anudo v. Tanzania*, No. 012/2015, Judgment, 22 March 2018, para. 103, fn. 11.

[475] *Ramadan v. Malta*, no. 76136/12, 21 June 2016, Dissenting opinion of Judge Pinto de Albuquerque, fn. 1.

[476] Universal Declaration of Human Rights, A/RES/217 (III), art. 17. For a rare reference to the provision in international case law, see *Anglo-Iranian Oil Co.* case (jurisdiction), Judgment, 22 July 1952, ICJ Reports 1952, p. 93, Dissenting opinion of Judge Levi Carneiro, p. 168.

[477] William A. Schabas, 'The Omission of the Right to Property in the International Covenants', (1991) 4 *Hague Yearbook of International Law* 135.

[478] Protocol to the Convention for the Protection of Human Rights and Fundamental Freedoms, CETS 9, art. 1 ('... the peaceful enjoyment of his possessions ...'). The heading 'Protection of Property' was added by Protocol 11 to the Convention for the Protection of Human Rights and Fundamental Freedoms, restructuring the control machinery established thereby, CETS 155, Appendix.

[479] Charter of Fundamental Rights of the European Union, OJ C 326/391, art. 17; American Convention on Human Rights, (1978) 1144 UNTS 123, art. 21; African Charter on Human and Peoples' Rights, art. 14; Arab Charter on Human Rights, art. 31.

[480] International Convention on the Elimination of All Forms of Racial Discrimination, (1969) 660 UNTS 195, art. 5(d)(v) and (vi); Convention on the Elimination of All Forms of Discrimination against Women, (1981) 1249 UNTS 13, arts. 15(2) and 16(1); African Charter on the Rights and Welfare of the Child, art. 14; Convention on the Rights of Persons with Disabilities, (2008) 2515 UNTS 3, art. 12(5); Protocol to the African Charter on Human and Peoples' Rights on the Rights of Women in Africa, art. 19(c).

[481] *German Settlers in Poland, Advisory Opinion*, PCIJ, Series B, No. 6, 17 September 1923, p. 23.

of that right, which weighs against the conclusion that a human right to property generally has become a principle of customary law'. It noted that '[a]ll states have accepted a limited core of rights to private property, and violation of such rights, as state policy, may already be a violation of customary law. Invasions of rights in private property that have not achieved the status of customary law may nonetheless violate a particular international agreement or, where the victim is a foreign national, the principles of customary law governing state responsibility to foreign nationals.'[482]

Perhaps even more striking than the failure to include the right to property in the two Covenants is its very infrequent appearance in the Universal Periodic Review materials. There are isolated references to the right to own property without discrimination.[483] Botswana spoke of the 'citizens' right to property' but under the general heading of 'right to housing'.[484] In the context of providing adequate housing, many States promote home ownership.[485] A few States have reported that the right to property is included in the constitution.[486] When Mozambique's National report explained that all land is owned by the State,[487] there were no comments, objections, or recommendations that might indicate a feeling that this was incompatible with a right to own property.[488]

A Commission of Inquiry set up by the Human Rights Council investigated violations of the right to property in Eritrea, relying upon the provision in the African Charter of Human and Peoples' Rights. But it also noted that '[o]ther international human rights treaties leave each State the freedom to regulate private property in its territory' and made no attempt to claim that this was a right under customary law.[489] The Special Rapporteur on food considered the right to property in the context of protection of the rights of 'land users' (and not necessarily owners), focussing specifically on indigenous peoples, smallholders, and herders, pastoralists, and fisherfolk.[490] Noting the 'sometimes highly unequal distribution of land in rural areas', the Special Rapporteur thought that land redistribution might be

[482] Restatement (Third) of the Foreign Relations Law of the United States, St. Paul, MN: American Law Institute, 1987, para. 702, Comment, para. k. See also ibid., Reporter's Notes, para. 9.

[483] Belgium, Report of the Working Group, A/HRC/18/16, para. 61; Tunisia, Report of the Working Group, A/HRC/25/15, para. 136.55; Republic of Korea, Report of the Working Group, A/HRC/23/6, para. 61; France, Report of the Working Group, A/HRC/15/7, para. 56.

[484] Botswana, National report, A/HRC/WG.6/29/BWA/1, para. 141–142.

[485] Singapore, National report, A/HRC/WG.6/11/SGP/1, paras. 44–45; Brunei Darussalam, National report, A/HRC/WG.6/19/BRN/1, paras. 86–89; National report, Guinea, A/HRC/WG.6/8/GIN/1, para. 97

[486] Angola, National report, A/HRC/WG.6/20/AGO/1, para. 6; Micronesia, Report of the Working Group, A/HRC/16/16, para. 8.

[487] Mozambique, National report, A/HRC/WG.6/10/MOZ/1, paras. 69–71.

[488] Mozambique, Compilation, A/HRC/WG.6/10/MOZ/2; Mozambique, Summary, A/HRC/WG.6/10/MOZ/3; Mozambique, Report of the Working Group, A/HRC/17/16.

[489] Report of the detailed findings of the Commission of Inquiry on Human Rights in Eritrea, A/HRC/29/CRP.1, para. 1132.

[490] Report of the Special Rapporteur on the right to food, A/65/281, paras. 10–26.

required'.[491] The relevance of the right to property is not entirely clear. Just as it may strengthen a claim to redistribute land to those without property, it may also be invoked by those who lose their property as a result of redistribution.

During the 1980s, there was a protracted debate within the United Nations General Assembly about the right to property. Competing resolutions advanced capitalist and socialist conceptions of the right, reflecting the quite deliberate ambiguity of Article 17 of the Universal Declaration and its reference to owning property 'alone or in association with others'. The General Assembly debates culminated in an equivocal resolution that described the right to own property as being 'of particular significance in fostering widespread enjoyment of other basic human rights' and noting that it 'contributes to security the goals of economic and social development enshrined in the Charter of the United Nations'.[492] The United Nations Declaration on Social Progress and Development states that '[s]ocial progress and development require ... the establishment, in conformity with human rights and fundamental freedoms and with the principles of justice and the social function of property, of forms of ownership of land and of the means of production which preclude any kind of exploitation of man, ensure equal rights to property for all and create conditions leading to genuine equality among people'.[493] Regularly, resolutions adopted by the United Nations General Assembly call for the restitution of cultural property to the country of origin.[494] But this is a collective right, a 'people's right', not an individual or 'human' right.

Taken as a whole, the evidence the materials provide that the right to property is a norm of customary law is far from overwhelming. An academic study contends that 'review of provisions of international instruments, regional treaties and national constitutions reveal [sic]the universal recognition of the human right to property'.[495] It is a daring conclusion given the absence of the right in the two Covenants and the recognition in several treaties not of a right to property but only of a prohibition of discrimination in ownership or a right to compensation in the event of deprivation of property.

The United Nations Declaration on the Rights of Indigenous Peoples does not refer to any right to own property. Instead, it speaks of 'control by indigenous peoples over developments affecting them and their lands, territories and resources'[496] and of the necessity of remedies to protect against 'dispossessing them of their lands, territories or resources'.[497] Article 26 of the Declaration affirms that

491 Ibid., para. 27.

492 Respect for the right of everyone to own property alone as well as in association with others and its contribution to the economic and social development of Member States, A/RES/45/98, PP 5. See also the Report of the Secretary General on the consultation that preceded adoption of the Resolution: A/45/523.

493 Declaration on Social Progress and Development, A/RES/2532 XXIV), para. 6.

494 For example, Return or restitution of cultural property to the countries of origin, A/RES/73/130.

495 Christophe Golay and Ioana Cismas, 'Legal Opinion: The Right to Property from a Human Rights Perspective', Montreal and Geneva: Rights and Democracy and the Geneva Academy of International Humanitarian Law and Human Rights, 2010, p. 10.

496 United Nations Declaration on the Rights of Indigenous Peoples, A/RES/61/295, PP 10.

497 Ibid., art. 8(b).

indigenous peoples 'have the right to the lands, territories and resources which they have traditionally owned, occupied or otherwise used or acquired'. The Inter-American Court of Human Rights has said that international human rights law guarantees to indigenous peoples 'the right to the collective territory they have used and occupied traditionally, derived from the use and occupation of the land and of the resources necessary for their physical and cultural survival and, also, that the State has the obligation to adopt special measures to recognise, respect, protect and guarantee to their members the right to communal ownership of this territory'.[498] The African Commission on Human and Peoples' Rights found a violation of the right to property provision of the African Charter in a case on removal of the Endorois people from their land in order to build a game reserve and to grant a ruby mining concession. The Commission observed that 'access roads, gates, game lodges and a hotel have all been built on the ancestral land of the Endorois community around Lake Bogoria and imminent mining operations also threatens to cause irreparable damage to the land'.[499] It said that by creating a game reserve, Kenya had 'unlawfully evicted the Endorois from their ancestral land and destroyed their possessions', adding that 'upheaval and displacement of the Endorois from the land they call home and the denial of their property rights over their ancestral land is disproportionate to any public need served by the Game Reserve'.[500]

Intellectual property enjoys special treatment in human rights law, the result of a provision in the Universal Declaration of Human Rights: 'Everyone has the right to the protection of the moral and material interests resulting from any scientific, literary or artistic production of which he is the author.' The text originated in a proposal by France at the very earliest stages of the drafting,[501] and may well have been a bit of a personal obsession of René Cassin. Its inclusion was initially rejected by the Working Group of the Commission on Human Rights,[502] but the idea was revived by Brazil, Mexico,[503] and Cuba[504] as well as France.[505] Intellectual

[498] *Kaliña and Lokono Peoples v. Suriname* , Judgment (Merits, reparations, and costs), 25 November 2015, Series C, No. 309, paras. 124–125. Also *Moiwana Community v. Suriname*, Judgment (Preliminary objections, merits, reparations, and costs), 15 June 2005, Series C, No. 124, para. 133; *Indigenous Community Sawhoyamaxa v. Paraguay*, Judgment (Merits, reparations, and costs), 29 March 2006. Series C, No. 146, 118; *Mayagna (Sumo) Awas Tingni Community v. Nicaragua*, Judgment (Merits, reparations, and costs), 31 August 2001, Series C, No. 79, para. 149; *Indigenous Community Yakye Axa v. Paraguay*. Judgment (Merits, reparations, and costs), 17 June 2005 Series C, No. 125, para. 143.

[499] *Centre for Minority Rights Development (Kenya) and Minority Rights Group International on behalf of the Endorois Welfare Council v. Kenya*, Case No. 276/2003, 4 February 2010, para. 210.

[500] Ibid., para. 214.

[501] Suggestions Submitted by the Representative of France for arts. 7–32 of the International Declaration of Rights, E/CN.4/AC.1/W.2/Rev.1.

[502] E/CN.4/AC.2/SR.9, p. 4; E/CN.4/57, p. 15.

[503] Comments from Governments of the Draft International Declaration of Human Rights, Draft International Covenant on Human Rights and the Question of Implementation, E/CN.4/82/Add.1 and Add 2.

[504] Cuba, France, Mexico: Joint Amendment to art. 25 of the Draft Declaration (E/800), A/C.3/360.

[505] France: Amendment to art. 30 of the Draft International Declaration on Human Rights (Document E/CN.4/95), E/CN.4/125; E/CN.4/SR.70, p. 6.

property is also protected by the International Covenant on Economic, Social and Cultural Rights.[506] The European Court of Human Rights has found that intellectual property is protected by Article 1 of the first Protocol to the Convention.[507] A provision on the issue was incorporated in the American Declaration of the Rights and Duties of Man, which was adopted in April 1948, several months before the Universal Declaration.[508] There is barely a trace of the right to protection of intellectual property in the Universal Periodic Review documents.[509] This makes it difficult to assess the views and the practice of the more than twenty-five States that are not party to the International Covenant on Economic, Social and Cultural Rights. States often report on cultural rights yet totally ignore the issue of protection of intellectual property.[510] There appears to be no evidence of States making recommendations in this area. The United Nations Declaration on the Rights of Indigenous Peoples recognises the right of such peoples 'to maintain, control, protect and develop their intellectual property over such cultural heritage, traditional knowledge, and traditional cultural expressions'.[511]

* * *

Conclusions. Despite recognition in the Universal Declaration of Human Rights, evidence of a customary right to property is weak. Protection of intellectual property is a right under customary international law.

[506] International Covenant on Economic, Social and Cultural Rights, (1976) 993 UNTS 3, art. 15(1)(c).

[507] *Anheuser-Busch v. Portugal* [GC], no. 73049/01, §§ 66–72, 11 January 2007; *Malan v. Moldova*, no. 19247/03, § 34, 29 January 2008.

[508] American Declaration on the Rights and Duties of Man, Final Act of the Ninth International Conference of American States, Res. XXX, art. XIII.

[509] Tanzania, National report, A/HRC/WG.6/12/TZA/1, para. 32, fn. 66; Saint Vincent and the Grenadines, National report, A/HRC/WG.6/11/VCT/1, para. 9, fn.6; Mongolia, National report, A/HRC/WG.6/9/MNG/1, paras. 48–50; Saudi Arabia, National report, A/HRC/WG.6/17/SAU/1, para. 81; Senegal, National report, A/HRC/WG.6/31/SEN/1, para. 143.

[510] Chad, National report, A/HRC/WG.6/31/TCD/1, paras. 62–64; Central African Republic, National report, A/HRC/WG.6/17/CAF/1, paras. 19–23; China, National report, A/HRC/WG.6/17/CHN/1, para. 939; Cuba, National report, A/HRC/WG.6/16/CUB/1, para. 108–110; Democratic People's Republic of Korea, National report, A/HRC/WG.6/19/PRK/1, paras. 68–70; Guinea, National report, A/HRC/WG.6/8/GIN/1, paras. 98–99; Israel, National report, CCPR/C/ISR/4, paras. 126–128; Laos, National report, A/HRC/WG.6/8/LAO/1, paras. 33–36; Lebanon, National report, A/HRC/WG.6/9/LBN/1, paras. 78–79; Malaysia, National report, A/HRC/WG.6/4/MYS/1/Rev.1, paras. 47–51; Mauritania, National report, A/HRC/WG.6/9/MRT/1, paras. 60–63; Morocco, National report, A/HRC/WG.6/13/MAR/1, paras. 62–65; Nauru, National report, A/HRC/WG.6/10/NRU/1, paras. 108–110; Syria, National report, A/HRC/WG.6/12/SYR/1, para. 84; Trinidad and Tobago, National report, A/HRC/WG.6/12/TTO/1, paras. 78–80.

[511] United Nations Declaration on the Rights of Indigenous Peoples, A/RES/61/295, art. 31(1).

7
Political rights

Some human rights are reserved essentially for participation in government. They can be distinguished from rights that are important to political activity, like freedom of expression, freedom of peaceful assembly, and freedom of association, but that also serve to protect many other interests. The Charter of Fundamental Rights of the European Union refers to 'citizens' rights' rather than political rights. Perhaps its drafters were inspired by the 1789 *Déclaration des droits de l'homme et du citoyen* adopted at the dawn of the French Revolution. But that nomenclature has its imperfections, because some fundamental rights that it considers 'citizens' rights' should be ensured for non-citizens as well, such as the right to good administration, the right to access documents, and the right to freedom of movement within the country.

The Secretary-General of the United Nations, Kofi Annan, in his publication *In Larger Freedom*, cited the Universal Declaration of Human Rights for enunciating 'the essentials of democracy'. Annan wrote that '[e]ver since its adoption, it has inspired constitution-making in every corner of the world, and it has contributed greatly to the eventual global acceptance of democracy as a universal value. The right to choose how they are ruled, and who rules them, must be the birthright of all people, and its universal achievement must be a central objective of an Organisation devoted to the cause of larger freedom.'[1]

A. Participation in government

The Universal Declaration of Human Rights proclaims the right of everyone 'to take part in the government of his country, directly or through freely chosen representatives'.[2] The International Covenant on Civil and Political rights modifies this somewhat, describing it as a right to take part not 'in the government of his country' but 'in the conduct of public affairs'. The Covenant also specifies that this is a right of 'every citizen', replacing the arguably broader concept of 'his country' in the Declaration.[3] Similar texts are found in the regional conventions[4]

[1] In larger freedom: towards development, security, and human rights for all, A/59/2005, para. 148.
[2] Universal Declaration of Human Rights, A/RES/217 (III), art. 21(1).
[3] International Covenant on Civil and Political Rights, (1976) 999 UNTS 171, art. 25(1).
[4] Protocol to the Convention for the Protection of Human Rights and Fundamental Freedoms, CETS 9, art. 3; American Convention on Human Rights, (1978) 1144 UNTS 123, art. 23(1)(a); African

The Customary International Law of Human Rights. William A. Schabas, Oxford University Press.
 DOI: 10.1093/oso/9780192845696.003.0008

and some specialised treaties.[5] The Convention on the Rights of Migrant Workers and Members of their Families recognises a right of migrants to participate in the public affairs of the State of origin, and to vote and be elected there.[6] Unfortunately political rights are not set out in the Convention on the Rights of the Child, probably based upon the misconception that young persons, unlike adults (!), lack the maturity to make wise and informed decisions about who shall represent them.

The Human Rights Committee has described the conduct of public affairs as 'a broad concept which relates to the exercise of political power, in particular the exercise of legislative, executive and administrative powers. It covers all aspects of public administration and the formulation and implementation of policy at international, national, regional and local level.'[7] At the core of this right is the electoral process and similar manifestations, such as referendums and plebiscites. Nevertheless, as the Committee has explained, citizens also participate in the conduct of public affairs 'by exerting influence through public debate and dialogue with their representatives or through their capacity to organise themselves. This participation is supported by ensuring freedom of expression, assembly and association.'[8]

The Universal Declaration of Human Rights specifies the need for 'periodic and genuine elections which shall be by universal and equal suffrage and shall be held by secret vote or by equivalent free voting procedures'.[9] The International Covenant on Civil and Political Rights develops this principle somewhat, removing any alternative to the secret ballot, and recognising that elections include not only the right to vote but also 'to be elected'.[10] After repeating the text of the Covenant, the American Convention adds that '[t]he law may regulate the exercise of the rights and opportunities referred to in the preceding paragraph only on the basis of age, nationality, residence, language, education, civil and mental capacity, or sentencing by a competent court in criminal proceedings'.[11] Protocol 1 to the European Convention on Human Rights requires 'free elections at reasonable intervals by secret ballot, under conditions which will ensure the free expression of the opinion of

Charter on Human and Peoples' Rights, (1986) 1520 UNTS 271, art. 13(1); Arab Charter on Human Rights art. 24(2).

[5] International Convention on the Elimination of All Forms of Racial Discrimination, (1969) 660 UNTS 195, art. 5(c); Convention on the Elimination of All Forms of Discrimination against Women, (1981) 1249 UNTS 13, art. 7(b); Convention on the Rights of Persons with Disabilities, (2008) 2515 UNTS 3, art. 29.

[6] International Convention on the Protection of the Rights of all Migrant Workers and Members of their Families, (2003) 2220 UNTS 3, art. 41(1).

[7] General Comment 25, The right to participate in public affairs, voting rights, and the right of equal access to public service (art. 25), CCPR/C/21/Rev.1/Add.7, para. 5.

[8] Ibid., para. 8. See, for example, *Beydon et al. v. France*, no. 1400/2005, Views, 31 October 2005, CCPR/C/85/D/1400/2005, para. 4.5.

[9] Universal Declaration of Human Rights, A/RES/217 (III), art. 21(3).

[10] International Covenant on Civil and Political Rights, (1976) 999 UNTS 171, art. 25.

[11] American Convention on Human Rights, (1978) 1144 UNTS 123, art. 23(2).

the people in the choice of the legislature'.[12] The Arab Charter recognises the right of every citizen '[t]o stand for election or choose his representatives in free and impartial elections, in conditions of equality among all citizens that guarantee the free expression of his will'.[13] There is nothing on the subject in the African Charter on Human and Peoples' Rights, although the African Union has made up for the silence with a very advanced instrument on democratic elections, the African Charter on Democracy, Elections and Governance. The Human Rights Committee did not include participation in government through genuine periodic elections in the list of customary law norms it proposed in General Comment 24.[14] The Venice Commission of the Council of Europe has frequently cited Article 21 of the Universal Declaration of Human Rights with the observation that it is considered to be a statement of customary international law.[15]

There have been a few reservations to Article 25 of the International Covenant on Civil and Political Rights that are of general scope but they do not appear to undermine the general commitment to the general principle of public participation in government, and all but one has been withdrawn.[16] There have also been a number of reservations to Article 25(b). Australia reserved the possibility of taking into account factors like sources of revenue in establishing electoral boundaries;[17] the reservation was withdrawn.[18] Kuwait made a reservation restricting to men the right to vote and stand for election.[19] It was withdrawn after a request from the Human Rights Committee.[20] Kuwait's reservation excluding members of the armed forces or the police from application of the right to vote and stand for election remains in effect.[21] Mexico has a reservation denying to ministers of

[12] Protocol to the Convention for the Protection of Human Rights and Fundamental Freedoms, CETS 9, art. 3.

[13] Arab Charter on Human Rights, art. 24(3).

[14] General Comment 24, Issues Relating to Reservations Made upon Ratification or Accession to the Covenant or the Optional Protocols thereto, or in Relation to Declarations under Article 41 of the Covenant, CCPR/C/21/Rev.1/Add.6, para. 8.

[15] Opinion on the balance of powers in the Constitution and the Legislation of the Principality of Monaco, adopted by the Venice Commission at its 95th Plenary Session (Venice, 14–15 June 2013), CDL-AD(2013)018-e, para. 9; Report on Constituency Delineation and Seat Allocation, Adopted by the Council for Democratic Elections at its 60th meeting (Venice, 7 December 2017) and by the Venice Commission at its 113th Plenary Session (Venice, 8–9 December 2017), CDL-AD(2017)034-e, para. 42; Draft report on Constituency Delineation and Seat Allocation, CDL(2017)033-e, para. 40; Adopted Final Opinion on the Law on Government Cleansing (Lustration Law) of Ukraine as would result from the amendments submitted to the Verkhovna Rada on 21 April 2015, adopted by the Venice Commission at its 103rd Plenary Session (Venice, 19–20 June 2015), CDL-AD(2015)012-e, para. 17.

[16] Pakistan, C.N.405.2010.TREATIES-17, subsequently modified by C.N.590.2011.TREATIES-40. See the Statement by the Human Rights Committee on Pakistan's reservation at the time of ratification: A/66/40, paras. 48–49. Belgium, C.N.113.1983.TREATIES-4, subsequently withdrawn, C.N.463.1998.TREATIES-5.

[17] C.N.230.1980.TREATIES-6.

[18] C.N.273.1984.TREATIES-20.

[19] C.N.423.2016.TREATIES-IV.4. See Kuwait, Concluding observations, CCPR/C/KWT/CO/3, para. 5.

[20] Kuwait, Concluding observations, Kuwait, CCPR/C/KWT/CO/2, para. 7; Kuwait, Concluding observations, CCPR/CO/63/KWT/1, para. 4.

[21] C.N.191.1996.TREATIES-1/4.

religion the right to vote and to participate in political activity more generally.[22] Reservations to Article 25(b) also remain in force for the two Chinese territories that are subject to the Covenant, Macau[23] and Hong Kong.[24]

Some States that are not parties to the International Covenant nevertheless confirm their recognition of fundamental rights to take part in government through genuine periodic elections. Not surprisingly, there is a certain correspondence between the failure of some States to ratify the Covenant and the level of democratic development. Yet the submissions to the Human Rights Council within the context of the Universal Periodic Review contain valuable information about progressive reforms of systems of governance. Some of the States that have not ratified the Covenant nevertheless have relatively well-entrenched traditions of electoral democracy.[25] In others, democratic structures are more of a work in progress, although the States in question sometimes appear to profess their commitment to progressive reform. Nevertheless, there are probably too many States with deficient practice to permit a firm conclusion that the right to political democracy set out in Article 21 of the Universal Declaration of Human Rights is a norm of customary international law. It is safer to speak of a legal rule that is 'crystallising' or 'emerging'.

In its first report to the Human Rights Council, Saudi Arabia stated that although it was 'not yet' a party to the International Covenant on Civil and Political Rights, many of its provisions were being implemented. To demonstrate this, it explained that '[i]n the Kingdom, the first municipal elections were monitored by observers who ascertained their fairness'.[26] Saudi Arabia reported that '[i]n 2005, the Kingdom held its first free elections for the appointment of representatives of local municipalities'.[27] In a subsequent report, it pointed to the participation of women in national decision-making.[28] The United Arab Emirates has also taken steps towards greater public participation in governance, according to its reports to the Human Rights Council. It has described this as 'a gradual process of expansion of political participation'.[29]

[22] C.N.81.1981.TREATIES-8.

[23] C.N.159.1993.TREATIES-3/8 (Annex). See China (Macau), Concluding observations, CCPR/C/CHN-MAC/CO/1, para. 7.

[24] C.N.193.1976.TREATIES-6. See China (Hong Kong), Concluding observations, CCPR/C/CHN-HKG/CO/3, para. 6.

[25] Singapore, National report, A/HRC/WG.6/24/SGP/1, para. 10; Singapore, National report, A/HRC/WG.6/11/SGP/1, para. 10–13; Singapore, Views on conclusions, A/HRC/32/17/Add.1, para. 51; Singapore, Views on conclusions, A/HRC/18/11/Add.1, para. 14.

Saint Lucia, National report, A/HRC/WG.6/10/LCA/1, paras. 11–14; Malaysia, National report, A/HRC/WG.6/17/MYS/1, para. 105; Malaysia, Working Group Report, A/HRC/25/10, para. 7; Sao Tome and Principe, Report of the Working Group, A/HRC/31/17, para. 87; Sao Tome and Principe, National report, A/HRC/WG.6/23/STP/1, paras. 31–33; Sao Tome and Principe, National report, A/HRC/WG.6/10/STP/1, paras. 6–11; Tuvalu, National report, A/HRC/WG.6/3/TUV/1, para. 11.

[26] Saudi Arabia, National report, A/HRC/WG.6/4/SAU/1, para. 18.

[27] Ibid., para. 47.

[28] Saudi Arabia, Report of the Working Group, A/HRC/25/3, para. 12.

[29] United Arab Emirates, Report of the Working Group, A/HRC/38/14, para. 9. Also United Arab Emirates, National report, A/HRC/WG.6/29/ARE/1, para. 31; United Arab Emirates, Report of the Working Group, A/HRC/10/75, para. 14.

Since the Universal Periodic Review began in 2008, Tonga has moved from what was essentially an absolute monarchy to a form of parliamentary democracy, as its reports and the reaction from other States indicate.[30] Beginning in 2008, Bhutan has also moved towards a form of constitutional monarchy with periodic elections and universal suffrage.[31] Comoros provides another example of a State that has undergone major reform in electoral governance since the Universal Periodic Review began.[32] In 2016, Oman reported to the Human Rights Council that constitutional amendments had given extensive legislative and regulatory powers to the Council of Oman 'in order to affirm the importance of political participation and the democratic process'. According to the report, '[f]ree and transparent elections for the Shura Council had been held recently'.[33] The only comment was a positive one, from Canada, which welcomed efforts during the Shura Council elections to strengthen the participation of women.[34] Myanmar has also introduced measures that strengthen democratic governance since Universal Periodic Review began.[35] Its report to the Council spoke of a 'crucial time in Myanmar for transition to a democratic system'.[36] Most of these States cannot claim to be exemplary models of a thriving democracy but the measures they have taken, and their reports on them to the Human Rights Council, tend to confirm their recognition of a customary norm of international law requiring participation by citizens in government through periodic elections.

The only exception appears to be Brunei Darussalam, which identifies itself to the Human Rights Council as a monarchy.[37] There are no visible initiatives towards the introduction of elections and democratic governance.[38] The Universal Periodic Review materials on Brunei Darussalam are rather silent about democratic governance, with the exception of comments from non-governmental organisations,[39] which might suggest that other States do not consider the absence of elections to be an important issue. Brunei reported to the Human Rights Council that Legislative Council membership was increased from twenty-nine to thirty-three members which, for the first time, included two women.[40] Syria congratulated Brunei on the

[30] Tonga, National report, A/HRC/WG.6/29/TON/1, paras. 38–44; Tonga, Report of the Working Group, A/HRC/38/5, paras. 17, 34, 48, 73, 83, 88–90; Tonga, National report, A/HRC/WG.6/15/TON/1, paras. 8–23; Tonga, Compilation, A/HRC/WG.6/29/TON/2, para. 8; Tonga, Report of the Working Group, A/HRC/8/48, para. 10.

[31] Bhutan, Report of the Working Group, A/HRC/42/8, para. 9; Bhutan, National report, A/HRC/WG.6/33/BTN/1, paras. 28–30; Bhutan, Report of Working Group, A/HRC/27/8, paras. 8, 114; Bhutan, Views on conclusions, A/HRC/27/8/Add.1, paras. 31–32.

[32] Comoros, National report, A/HRC/WG.6/18/COM/1, paras. 2, 140, 142.

[33] Oman, Report of the Working Group, A/HRC/31/11, para. 10.

[34] Ibid., para. 122.

[35] Myanmar, Report of the Working Group, A/HRC/17/9, paras. 8–10.

[36] Myanmar, National report, A/HRC/WG.6/10/MMR/1, para. 30.

[37] Brunei Darussalam, Report of the Working Group, A/HRC/27/11, para. 18.

[38] Brunei Darussalam, Report of the Working Group, A/HRC/13/14, paras. 8–9; Brunei Darussalam, Summary of stakeholders' submissions, A/HRC/WG.6/33/BRN/3, para. 29.

[39] Brunei Darussalam, Summary of stakeholders' submissions, A/HRC/WG.6/33/BRN/3, para. 29.

[40] Brunei Darussalam, National report, A/HRC/WG.6/19/BRN/1, para. 6.

'election' of women to the Legislative Council,[41] but the word was not well chosen because the Legislative Council is appointed, not elected.[42]

China and Cuba do not have a multiparty system but both States insist that they provide forms of democratic governance that are consistent with international human rights law. Explaining that 'there was not one single model of democracy or an agreed formula in that regard', Cuba reported that elections are 'held periodically and in absolute freedom, in accordance with the electoral law', and that they have been 'characterised by the existence of automatic and public electoral registries, popular appointment of candidates and high turnout levels'.[43] Cuba noted that in recent elections, 53% of members of Parliament were women and 41% were black or mulatto.[44] It has described the increasing of popular participation in elections and decision-making processes as one of its 'human rights priorities'.[45] China has reported to the Human Rights Council that it endeavours 'to promote democracy, enhance democratic institutions, improve the system of people's congresses, and reinforce political consultations among the political parties. A system of grassroots self-government has been established, involving rural villagers' committees and urban neighbourhood committees. A Chinese-style democracy is characterised by democratic election, democratic consultation and democratic self-government.'[46]

According to the Human Rights Committee, 'restrictions on political activity outside the only recognised political party amount to an unreasonable restriction of the right to participate in the conduct of public affairs'.[47] In its General Comment on Article 25 of the Covenant, the Committee re-affirmed that 'party membership should not be a condition of eligibility to vote, nor a ground of disqualification', that 'the right of persons to stand for election should not be limited unreasonably by requiring candidates to be members of parties or of specific parties', and that 'political parties and membership in parties play a significant role in the conduct of public affairs and the election process'.[48] In Concluding Observations concerning North Korea's periodic report, the Human Rights Committee cited Article 25 of the Covenant as well as the General Comment, saying it had taken note of the explanation from the delegation that because 'there has been no popular manifestation of any desire to create new political parties, no regulation or legislation governing the creation and registration of political parties is currently envisaged'. The Committee said that 'this situation runs counter to the provisions of article

[41] Brunei Darussalam, Report of the Working Group, A/HRC/27/11, para. 26.

[42] Brunei Darussalam, National report, A/HRC/WG.6/6/BRN/1, paras. 7–8.

[43] Cuba, Report of the Working Group, A/HRC/24/16, para. 6. See also Cuba, National report, A/HRC/WG.6/4/CUB/1, paras. 8–24; Cuba, National report, A/HRC/WG.6/30/CUB/1, paras. 33–37.

[44] Cuba, Report of the Working Group, A/HRC/39/16, paras. 9–10.

[45] Cuba, National report, A/HRC/WG.6/16/CUB/1, para. 163(d).

[46] China, Report of the Working Group, A/HRC/11/25, para. 10. Also China, National report, A/HRC/WG.6/4/CHN/1, para. 9; China, National report, A/HRC/WG.6/17/CHN/1, paras. 51–52.

[47] *Bwalya v. Zambia*, no. 314/1988, Views, 27 July 1993, CCPR/C/48/D/314/1988, para. 6.6.

[48] General Comment 25, The right to participate in public affairs, voting rights, and the right of equal access to public service (art. 25), CCPR/C/21/Rev.1/Add.7, paras. 10, 17, and 26.

25 of the Covenant, as it may adversely affect the rights of citizens to participate in the conduct of public affairs through freely chosen representatives'.[49] Referring to treaty provisions that regulate the status of political parties, including the International Covenant on Civil and Political Rights, the European Convention on Human Rights, the Convention on the Elimination of All Forms of Discrimination against Women, and the Convention on the Rights of Persons with Disabilities, the Venice Commission of the Council of Europe said that 'the rights and protections articulated in the above legally binding documents are already to be found in the Universal Declaration of Human Rights (UDHR), which has acquired the status of customary international law'.[50]

* * *

Conclusions. A customary international legal norm recognising a right to democratic governance, in the sense of the right of citizens to participate in government through periodic elections, is in the process of emerging.

B. Equal access to the public service

The right of equal access to the public service is set out in the provision of the Universal Declaration of Human Rights dealing with elections and participation in government, although in reality it is quite distinct in nature. The right is also recognised in the International Covenant on Civil and Political Rights[51] and in some regional and specialised treaties.[52] The Arab Charter presents it as a right of access to 'public office', which is not quite the same thing.[53] The reports to the Human Rights Council by States that are not parties to the International Covenant on Civil and Political Rights do not address this issue directly. Frequently, they note efforts, and accomplishments, directed at increasing the participation of women in various organs of government.[54] There is therefore considerable evidence to

49 Democratic People's Republic of Korea, Concluding observations, CCPR/CO/72/PRK, para. 25. See also Libya, Concluding observations, CCPR/C/79/Add.101, para. 15; Equatorial Guinea, Concluding observations, CCPR/CO/79/GNQ, para. 12.

50 Draft Guidelines on Political Party Regulation, CDL-EL(2017)003-e, para. 43.

51 International Covenant on Civil and Political Rights, (1976) 999 UNTS 171, art. 25(c).

52 American Convention on Human Rights, (1978) 1144 UNTS 123, art. 23(1)(c); African Charter on Human and Peoples' Rights, (1986) 1520 UNTS 271, art. 13(2); International Convention on the Elimination of All Forms of Racial Discrimination, (1969) 660 UNTS 195, art. 5(c); Convention on the Elimination of All Forms of Discrimination against Women, (1981) 1249 UNTS 13, art. 7.

53 Arab Charter on Human Rights, art. 33.

54 China, Report of the Working Group, A/HRC/11/25, para. 20; Comoros, Report of the Working Group, A/HRC/26/11, para. 71; Malaysia, in Comoros, Report of the Working Group, A/HRC/26/11, para. 110.48; Micronesia, Report of the Working Group, A/HRC/31/4, para. 12; Myanmar, Report of the Working Group, A/HRC/17/9, para. 47; Oman, National report, A/HRC/WG.6/10/OMN/1, para. 106; Saint Lucia, Report of the Working Group, A/HRC/17/6, para. 54; Saudi Arabia, Report of the Working Group, A/HRC/25/3, para. 12; Singapore, National report, A/HRC/WG.6/24/SGP/1, para. 53; Solomon Islands, National report, A/HRC/WG.6/24/SLB/1, paras. 71–74; South Sudan, National

support inclusion of equal access to the public service, and to public office, in the list of norms of customary international law.

The Human Rights Committee considers that temporary special measures may be required to ensure that there is equal access to public service for women. It has explained that '[b]asing access to public service on equal opportunity and general principles of merit, and providing secured tenure, ensures that persons holding public service positions are free from political interference or pressures'.[55] Most individual cases decided by the Human Rights Committee under Article 25(c) of the Covenant concern dismissal and non-reinstatement of civil servants on political grounds,[56] including the removal of judges.[57]

* * *

Conclusions. There is a right of access to the public service without discrimination.

report, A/HRC/WG.6/26/SSD/1, paras. 51, 53 and Report of the Working Group, A/HRC/34/13, para. 69; Tonga, National report, A/HRC/WG.6/15/TON/1, paras. 75, 94 and Report of the Working Group, A/HRC/38/5, paras. 16–17; Tuvalu, National report, A/HRC/WG.6/16/TUV/1, para. 10.

[55] General Comment 25, The right to participate in public affairs, voting rights, and the right of equal access to public service (art. 25), CCPR/C/21/Rev.1/Add.7, para. 23.

[56] *Aduayom, Diasso, and Dobou v. Togo*, nos. 422, 423, and 424/1990, Views, 30 June 1994, CCPR/C/51/D/422/1990, 423/1990 and 424/1990, para. 7.6; *Gedumbe v. Democratic Republic of Congo*, no. 641/1995, Views, 10 July 1997, CCPR/C/60/D/641/1995, para. 5.2; *Mazou v. Cameroun*, no. 630/1995, Views, 6 July 1998, CCPR/C/63/D/630/1995, para. 8.4.

[57] *Mundyo Busyo et al. v. Democratic Republic of Congo*, no. 933/2000, Views, 31 July 2003, CCPR/C/78/D/933/2000, para. 5.2; *Pastukhov v. Belarus*, no. 814/1998, Views, 17 September 2003 CCPR/C/78/D/814/1998, para. 7.3; *Bandaranayake v. Sri Lanka*, no. 1376/2005, Views, 24 July 2008, CCPR/C/93/D/1376/2005, para. 6.4.

8
Justice

There are several references to 'justice' in the Charter of the United Nations. The Preamble speaks of establishing 'conditions under which justice and respect for the obligations arising from treaties and other sources of international law can be maintained'. Article 1(1), setting out the Purposes of the United Nations, refers to 'conformity with the principles of justice and international law'. Article 2(3), dealing with the Principles of the United Nations, states that Members are to settle disputes by peaceful means, 'in such a manner that international peace and security, and justice, are not endangered'. The principal judicial organ of the United Nations is named the International Court of *Justice*. All of these references seem addressed to justice at the international level.

In human rights law, justice is first and foremost about the relationship between the individual and the State. It governs both the entitlement of everyone to being treated in a just manner by the organs of the State and the right to have the State's judicial system properly and fairly resolve disputes with others. It largely overlaps with another important notion, the rule of law, which is affirmed in the Preamble of the Universal Declaration of Human Rights: 'Whereas it is essential, if man is not to be compelled to have recourse, as a last resort, to rebellion against tyranny and oppression, that human rights should be protected by the rule of law . . . '.

The opening words of the Universal Declaration of Human Rights speak of recognition of the inherent dignity and of the equal and inalienable rights of all members of the human family being 'the foundation of freedom, justice and peace in the world'. These words are repeated in the first paragraph of the preambles of the two International Covenants on human rights. The International Covenant on Civil and Political Rights also refers to 'the interests of justice'[1] and 'miscarriage of justice'.[2]

Rights grouped under the heading 'justice' address both procedural and substantive dimensions. At the procedural level, they are concerned with fairness of judicial proceedings. At the substantive level, the main issue is the 'principle of legality' by which criminal law should be both foreseeable and accessible. Finally, the right of access to justice itself is vital to the protection of fundamental rights.

[1] International Covenant on Civil and Political Rights, (1976) 999 UNTS 171, art. 14(1) and (3)(d).
[2] Ibid., art. 14(6).

The Customary International Law of Human Rights. William A. Schabas, Oxford University Press.
 DOI: 10.1093/oso/9780192845696.003.0009

A. Effective remedy and right of access to justice

'Everyone has the right to an effective remedy by the competent national tribunals for acts violating the fundamental rights granted him by the constitution or by law', states Article 8 of the Universal Declaration of Human Rights. The right to an effective remedy is also set out in Article 2(3) of the International Covenant on Civil and Political Rights as well as in specialised[3] and regional[4] human rights treaties. There do not appear to be any reservations to Article 2(3) of the International Covenant. There is no provision on the right to a remedy in the International Covenant on Economic, Social and Cultural Rights,[5] the Convention on the Elimination of All Forms of Discrimination against Women, the Convention on the Rights of the Child, and the Convention on the Rights of Persons with Disabilities.

Detailed provisions of some of the treaties contemplate remedies for specific violations. An example is the right of habeas corpus, by which a person who claims to be the victim of arbitrary or unlawful detention may challenge this before a court.[6] The Human Rights Committee has offered the right to appeal from a conviction, provided for in Article 14(5) of the Covenant, as an example of *lex specialis* with regard to the right to a remedy.[7]

The provisions in the International Covenant and the Arab Charter acknowledge the right to a remedy with respect to 'rights or freedoms as herein recognized'. The text in the European Convention on Human Rights is similar, limiting the right to 'an effective remedy before a national authority' to '[e]veryone whose rights and freedoms as set forth in this Convention are violated'. The American Convention on Human Rights is more faithful to the terms of the Universal Declaration in that it recognises the right to a remedy for breaches of fundamental rights granted by the constitution or by law. Similarly, the African Charter recognises the 'right to an appeal to competent national organs against acts of violating his fundamental

[3] International Convention on the Elimination of All Forms of Racial Discrimination, (1969) 660 UNTS 195, art. 6; Convention against Torture and Other Cruel, Inhuman and Degrading Treatment or Punishment, (1984) 1465 UNTS 85, art. 14; Convention on the Rights of the Child, (1990) 1571 UNTS 3, art. 39; International Convention for the Protection of All Persons from Enforced Disappearance, (2010) 2716 UNTS 3, arts. 8(2), 20(2), 23(2).

[4] European Convention on Human Rights, (1953) 213 UNTS 221, art. 13; American Convention on Human Rights, (1978) 1144 UNTS 123, art. 25; African Charter on Human and Peoples' Rights, (1986) 1520 UNTS 271, art. 7(a); Arab Charter on Human Rights, art. 23; Charter of Fundamental Rights of the European Union, OJ C 326/391, art. 47.

[5] See the reference by the Committee on Economic, Social and Cultural Rights to art. 2(3) of the International Covenant on Civil and Political Rights: General Comment 3, The nature of States Parties' obligations (art. 2, para. 1, of the Covenant), E/1991/23, p. 83, para. 5.

[6] International Convention on the Elimination of All Forms of Racial Discrimination, (1969) 660 UNTS 195, art. 4; European Convention on Human Rights, (1953) 213 UNTS 221, art. 5(4); Arab Charter on Human Rights, art. 14(6). Habeas corpus is discussed *supra*, at p. C.4 P98

[7] General Comment 32, art. 14: Right to equality before courts and tribunals and to a fair trial, CCPR/C/GC/32, para. 58; *Terrón v. Spain*, no. 1073/2002, Views, 5 November 2004, CCPR/C/82/D/1073/2002, para. 6.6.

rights as recognised and guaranteed by conventions, laws, regulations and customs in force'.

The incomplete reflection within several of the human rights treaties of the right set out in Article 8 of the Universal Declaration of Human Rights and the total absence of the right in several of the major instruments is troublesome from the standpoint of identifying customary norms. Many States would probably reject the proposition that they must ensure that there are legal remedies for breaches of norms that are themselves not codified. Despite the lack of compelling evidence similar to what exists for many substantive rights, it nevertheless seems reasonable to recognise the customary nature of the right defined in Article 8 of the Declaration, where it is specified that it applies to fundamental rights granted by the constitution or by law. Of course, the term 'law' in Article 8 necessarily includes customary international law. Perhaps the solution is to treat the right to an effective remedy as a corollary of the substantive right in much the same way as international courts and tribunals have treated the prohibition of refoulement as a corollary of the right to life and the prohibition of torture and ill-treatment.

In 2005, the General Assembly adopted the Basic Principles and Guidelines on the Right to a Remedy and Reparation for Victims of Gross Violations of International Human Rights Law and Serious Violations of International Humanitarian Law.[8] It must be borne in mind that this is only a partial implementation of Article 8 of the Universal Declaration of Human Rights because its application is limited to 'gross' violations of human rights. The Basic Principles and Guidelines prohibit statutory limitation in the case of 'gross violations' whereas it would obviously be completely at odds with State practice to contend that there can be no statutory limitation for any human rights violation. The General Assembly Basic Principles and Guidelines anchor the right to a remedy in the 'obligation to respect, ensure respect for and implement international human rights law', explaining that this 'emanates from: (*a*) Treaties to which a State is a party; (*b*) Customary international law'.[9]

The right to an effective remedy dictates that individuals have 'accessible and effective remedies to vindicate those rights' and that such remedies should be 'appropriately adapted so as to take account of the special vulnerability of certain categories of person, including in particular children'.[10]

[8] Basic Principles and Guidelines on the Right to a Remedy and Reparation for Victims of Gross Violations of International Human Rights Law and Serious Violations of International Humanitarian Law, A/RES/60/147, Annex.

[9] Ibid., para. 1.

[10] General Comment 31, The Nature of the General Legal Obligation Imposed on States Parties to the Covenant, CCPR/C/21/Rev.1/Add. 13, para. 15. See Martin Scheinin, 'The Human Rights Committee's Pronouncements on the Right to an Effective Remedy—an illustration of the Legal Nature of the Committee's Work under the Optional Protocol', in Nisuke Ando, ed., *Towards Implementing Universal Human Rights*, Leiden/Boston: Martinus Nijhoff, 2004, pp. 101–116.

Recognition of a right to a remedy may be seen as a sign of deference to national jurisdictions, as they are deemed to be the means by which violations of fundamental rights are addressed and remedied. The counterpart of this norm, for States that are subject to international petition mechanisms, is the rule whereby domestic remedies must be exhausted as a condition of admissibility for recourse to the international court or quasi-judicial body.[11]

The 'right to access justice' is understood as a right to a judicial remedy before an independent court of law.[12] The right of access to justice is not set out explicitly in the Universal Declaration of Human Rights or, for that matter in the principal human rights treaties. Nevertheless, in many respects it is closely related to the right to the effective remedy enshrined in Article 12 of the Declaration. In a sense, it is narrower because the right to justice is confined to judicial remedies whereas the right to an effective remedy is also achieved through administrative mechanisms and legislative changes. At the same time, the right of access to justice is closer to Article 12 of the Declaration than many of the treaty provisions because it is not limited to 'rights and freedoms as herein recognised' or even to 'fundamental rights granted ... by the constitution or by law'. The right of access to justice applies to the determination of all rights and obligations and in that sense is distinct from the right to an effective remedy.[13]

The right of access to a court was recognised by the European Court of Human Rights through a creative interpretation of the fair trial provision in the European Convention on Human Rights. The Court noted that Article 6(1) of the Convention 'does not state a right of access to the courts or tribunals in express terms'. Rather, it enunciates distinct rights that 'stem from the same basic idea and which, taken together, make up a single right not specifically defined in the narrower sense of the term'.[14] The Court said it was 'inconceivable' that Article 6(1) could offer a detailed description of procedural guarantees yet that it 'should not first protect that which alone makes it in fact possible to benefit from such guarantees, that is, access to a court. The fair, public and expeditious characteristics of judicial proceedings are of no value at all if there are no judicial proceedings.'[15] It described the right as 'inherent', explaining that this was not 'an extensive interpretation forcing new obligations on the Contracting States: it is based on the very terms of the first sentence of Article 6 § 1 read in its context and having regard to the object and purpose of the Convention, a law-making treaty'.[16]

[11] For example, Optional Protocol to the International Covenant on Civil and Political Rights, (1976) 999 UNTS 171, para. 2; European Convention on Human Rights, (1953) 213 UNTS 221, art. 35(1).

[12] Francesco Francioni, 'The Rights of Access to Justice under Customary International Law', in Francesco Francioni, ed., *Access to Justice as a Human Right*, New York: Oxford University Press, 2007, pp. 1–55, at p. 4.

[13] *Golder v. the United Kingdom*, 21 February 1975, § 33, Series A no. 18.

[14] Ibid., § 28.

[15] Ibid., § 35.

[16] Ibid., § 36; *Enea v. Italy* [GC], no. 74912/01, § 104, ECHR 2009.

The logic of the European Court can be extended to the context of customary international law. As recognition of the right of access is inherent in the right to fair, public, and expeditious judicial proceedings for the determination of rights and obligations, the issue to be considered is whether there is a right under customary law to such proceedings. The chapter that follows considers this issue and reaches a positive conclusion.

Antonio Cassese, sitting as president of the Special Tribunal for Lebanon, in an *ex parte* proceeding, held that '[t[he right of access to justice is regarded by the whole international community as essential and indeed crucial to any democratic society. It is therefore warranted to hold that the customary rule prescribing it has acquired the status of a peremptory norm (jus cogens).'[17] He acknowledged that 'there are few judicial pronouncements or State declarations suggesting that the right at issue has been elevated to this rank'.[18] Cassese relied upon a judgment of the Inter-American Court of Human Rights stating that '[a]ccess to justice is a peremptory norm of international law and, as such, gives rise to obligations erga omnes for the States to adopt all necessary measures to ensure that such violations do not remain unpunished, either by exercising their jurisdiction to apply their domestic law and international law to prosecute and, when applicable, punish those responsible, or by collaborating with other States that do so or attempt to do so'.[19] The Inter-American Court case dealt with the illegal and arbitrary detention, torture, and forced disappearance of several individuals. It is not at all clear from the context that the Inter-American Court intended its pronouncement to encompass rights and obligations in general, or all fundamental rights. Cassese also referred to the separate opinion of Judge Antonio Cançado Trindade, who wrote: 'By correctly affirming that the right for justice to be done is a peremptory norm of jus cogens, I consider that the Court has shown that there are reasons to continue hoping: because, in the end, sooner or later, ... the law reacts—as testified by this judgment of the Inter-American Court. Nowadays, the universal juridical conscience has awoken to acknowledge human suffering judicially and to seek its reparation by the guarantee of the primacy of justice in human relations.'[20]

The Grand Chamber of the European Court of Human Rights has rejected the argument that a right of access to justice is a norm of *jus cogens*.[21] In a concurring opinion, Judge Pinto de Albuquerque disagreed with the Court's 'abrupt conclusion'. He acknowledged that the right of access to a court in civil proceedings was 'certainly not absolute, since it may be subject to limitations permitted

[17] *El Sayed* (CH/PRES/2010/01), Order assigning Matter to Pre-Trial Judge, President of the Special Tribunal of Lebanon, 15 April 2010, para. 29.

[18] Ibid.

[19] *Goiburú et al. v. Paraguay*, Judgment (Merits, reparations, and costs), 22 September 2006, Series C, No. 153, para. 131.

[20] Ibid., Separate opinion of Judge A.A. Cançado Trindade, para. 68.

[21] *Al-Dulimi and Montana Management Inc. v. Switzerland* [GC], no. 5809/08, § 136, 21 June 2016.

by implication'. However, he said, 'the limitations applied must not restrict the access left to the individual in such a way or to such an extent that the very essence of the right is impaired'.[22] Judge Pinto de Albuquerque, supported by three of his colleagues, said the development of international humanitarian and criminal law warranted upholding the right of access to a court in criminal matters as a non-derogable right, adding that this was 'compatible with the emergence of this right as an intransgressible norm of jus cogens'.[23] He said that 'deprivation of access to a court in order to challenge punitive confiscation measures breaches a jus cogens norm'.[24] Gregor Nolte said that European practice suggests the right of access to a court may be an example of regional *jus cogens*.[25]

According to General Comment 32 of the Human Rights Committee, equality before courts and tribunals includes equal access to justice, and ensures that the parties to the proceedings in question are treated without any discrimination.[26] For example, the Committee found an instance of sex discrimination and a violation of the right to equality before the courts because the Peruvian Civil Code entitled only the husband to represent matrimonial property before the courts.[27] Access to courts 'must also be available to all individuals, regardless of nationality or statelessness, or whatever their status, whether asylum seekers, refugees, migrant workers, unaccompanied children or other persons, who may find themselves in the territory or subject to the jurisdiction' of a State.[28]

* * *

Conclusions. Everyone has the right to an effective remedy by the competent national tribunals for acts violating fundamental rights. Customary law recognises a right of access to the courts for the exercise of rights and obligations.

B. Fair trial

The right to a fair trial is set out in Article 11(1) of the Universal Declaration of Human Rights: 'Everyone is entitled in full equality to a fair and public hearing by an independent and impartial tribunal, in the determination of his rights and obligations and of any criminal charge against him.' This general proposition has

[22] Ibid., Concurring opinion of Judge Pinto de Albuquerque, joined by Judges Hajiyev, Pejchal, and Dedov, § 33.

[23] Ibid., para. 34.

[24] Ibid., para. 37.

[25] A/CN.4/SR.3461, p. 4.

[26] General Comment 32, art. 14: Right to equality before courts and tribunals and to a fair trial, CCPR/C/GC/32, para. 8.

[27] *Ato del Avellanal v. Peru*, no. 202/1986, Views, 28 October 1988, CCPR/C/34/D/202/1986, paras. 2.1, 10.1, 11.

[28] General Comment 32, art. 14: Right to equality before courts and tribunals and to a fair trial, CCPR/C/GC/32, para. 9.

been expanded in the human rights treaties into detailed enumerations of the components of a fair trial, with particular attention directed to criminal proceedings where the liberty of the accused person is at stake.[29] Even more extensive codifications of principles applicable to a fair trial are set out in a variety of instruments that have been endorsed by such authoritative bodies as the United Nations General Assembly.[30]

When the general formulation in Article 11(1) has been transformed into treaty provisions, courts and treaty bodies have tended to exclude certain forms of litigation, such as administrative and disciplinary proceedings, on the ground that they do not amount to determinations of 'rights and obligations' or 'criminal charges'.[31] But from the standpoint of customary international law, to the extent that a right to a fair trial is recognised it does not seem proper that this concept should be restricted by such technical restrictions derived from narrow and literal interpretations of legal texts.

Where a mechanism to adjudicate legal disputes is provided by law, be it to determine eligibility for refugee status, a charge of plagiarism in a student assignment, or an accusation of voluntary homicide, the proceedings must always be 'fair'. What this requires specifically, however, will vary depending upon the circumstances. It is obvious that over time there has been enormous evolution in terms of what fairness requires. Fair trial standards that might have been deemed acceptable half a century ago are no longer adequate, and the development can be expected to continue.

In the enumeration of customary norms presented in its General Comment on reservations, the United Nations Human Rights Committee did not list the right to a fair trial. Referring to the fair trial provision of the International Covenant on Civil and Political Rights, the Committee said that 'reservations to particular clauses of article 14 may be acceptable [but] a general reservation to the right to a fair trial would not be'.[32] In the General Comment, adopted in the early 1990s, the Committee surely understated the importance of the right to a fair trial. Later,

[29] European Convention on Human Rights, (1953) 213 UNTS 221, art. 6; International Covenant on Civil and Political Rights, (1976) 999 UNTS 171, art. 14; American Convention on Human Rights, (1978) 1144 UNTS 123, art. 8; African Charter on Human and Peoples' Rights, (1986) 1520 UNTS 271, art. 7; Arab Charter on Human Rights, art. 13; Charter of Fundamental Rights of the European Union, OJ C 326/391, arts. 47, 48(2).

[30] For example, Standard Minimum Rules for the Administration of Juvenile Justice ('Beijing Rules'), A/RES/40/33, Annex; Basic Principles on the Independence of the Judiciary, A/CONF.121/22/Rev.1, p. 58, endorsed by Human rights in the administration of justice, A/RES/40/146, para. 2; Basic Principles on the Role of Lawyers, A/CONF.144/28/Rev.l, p. 117; Guidelines on the Role of Prosecutors, A/CONF.144/28/Rev.l, p. 188.

[31] *Kazantzis v. Cyprus*, no. 972/2001, Views, 19 September 2003, CCPR/C/78/D/972/2001, para. 6.5; *Ferrazzini v. Italy* [GC], no. 44759/98, §§ 16-19, ECHR 2001-VII.

[32] General Comment 24, Issues Relating to Reservations Made upon Ratification or Accession to the Covenant or the Optional Protocols thereto, or in Relation to Declarations under art. 41 of the Covenant, CCPR/C/21/Rev.1/Add.6, para. 8. See also General Comment 32, art. 14: Right to equality before courts and tribunals and to a fair trial, CCPR/C/GC/32, para. 5.

in subsequent General Comments, it seems to have elevated the importance of the right. In its General Comment on states of emergency, it said that States could never 'deviat[e] from fundamental principles of fair trial, including the presumption of innocence',[33] and in its General Comment on fair trial rights it confirmed that any such departure was 'prohibited at all times'.[34]

The right to a fair trial under customary international law has also been recognised by the Appeals Chamber of the International Criminal Tribunals.[35] The Inter-American Commission has said '[i]t is beyond question' that 'core rights', including the right to a fair trial, 'have attained the status of customary, and indeed peremptory, norms of international law'.[36] The United States Supreme Court has referred to 'the barest of the trial protections recognised in customary international law'.[37] The Appeals Chamber of the Special Tribunal for Lebanon, somewhat carelessly, spoke of 'the jus cogens character of fair trial'.[38] The footnote reference states '[a]s recognised by the unanimous Appeals Chamber in Interlocutory Decision on the Applicable Law, para.·76' but that authority speaks of *nullum crimen sine lege* and not the right to a fair trial.[39]

1. Full equality

The Universal Declaration of Human Rights requires a trial 'in full equality'. This is a specific manifestation of the more general right to equality and the protection against discrimination, discussed elsewhere in this study and to which readers are referred.[40] In specialised conventions aimed at eliminating discrimination against certain groups of persons, the right to equal treatment before the courts without distinction as to race, colour, national origin, heritage, or sex is expressly emphasised.[41] The establishment of special court systems for some categories of persons, such as juveniles or military personnel, is not in principle prohibited by

33 General Comment 29, art. 4: Derogations during a State of Emergency, CCPR/C/21/Rev.1/Add.11, para. 11.

34 General Comment 32, art. 14: Right to equality before courts and tribunals and to a fair trial, CCPR/C/GC/32, para. 11.

35 *Prosecutor v. Kayishema and Ruzindana* (ICTR-95-1-A), Appeal Judgment, 4 December 2001, para. 51; *Prosecutor v. Aleksovski* (IT-94-14/1-A), Appeal Judgment, 24 March 2000, para. 104.

36 *Mario Aflredo Lares-Reyes et al. v.* United States, Case 12.379, Report No. 19/02, Merits, 27 February 2002, para. 46, fn. 23.

37 *Hamdan v. Rumsfeld*, 548 US 557 (2006).

38 *Prosecutor v. Ayyash et al.* (STL-11-01/AC.AR90.1), Decision on the Defence Appeals against the Trial Chamber's 'Decision on the Jurisdiction and Legality of the Tribunal', 24 October 2012, para. 68.

39 *Unnamed defendant* (STL-11-01/I), Interlocutory Decision on the Applicable Law: Terrorism, Conspiracy, Homicide, Perpetration, Cumulative Charging, 16 February 2011, para. 76.

40 *Supra* Chapter 5.

41 International Convention on the Elimination of All Forms of Racial Discrimination, (1969) 660 UNTS 195, art. 5(a); Convention on the Elimination of All Forms of Discrimination against Women, (1981) 1249 UNTS 13, art. 15(2).

the requirement of 'full equality' provided that the distinction is rooted in reasonable and objective grounds.[42] Justice can be very costly for those who attempt to assert their rights before the courts. In this respect, social and economic inequalities mean that in practice access to the courts is limited to those with adequate means. Recognition of a customary law rule that justice is required 'in full equality' may well be interpreted so as to require State-funded counsel and waiver of court costs that are often imposed on litigants.[43]

2. Fair and public hearing

The Universal Declaration of Human Rights requires that a hearing be 'fair'. Although international law treaties have set out specific features of the requirements of 'fairness' with respect to criminal trials, there is little guidance when issues of justice before courts dealing with 'rights and obligations' or administrative matters are concerned. International human rights courts and treaty bodies have developed a notion of 'equality of arms',[44] but this does not advance the discussion very much, as the notions that it encompasses can also be derived from the principles of 'full equality' and 'fair trial'. It is also difficult to develop detailed content for the concept of a fair trial under customary international law because there are significant differences in national practice that are deeply rooted in cultural traditions. It is important to bear in mind that 'fair hearing' is a holistic concept necessitating an overall assessment of proceedings. Isolated violations of procedural rules do not necessarily result in a condemnation of the trial as a whole as being unfair. But it is also the case that a trial may appear to observe all of the procedural rules in a technical sense yet nevertheless be profoundly unfair in its essence.

The European Court of Human Rights has recognised the phenomenon of a 'flagrant denial of justice', describing it as 'a stringent test of unfairness'. The Court has said that a flagrant denial of justice goes beyond 'mere irregularities or lack of safeguards in the trial procedures'. What is required, it says, is a breach of the principles of fair trial 'which is so fundamental as to amount to a nullification, or destruction

[42] *Kavanagh v. Ireland*, no. 819/1998, Views, 4 April 2001, CCPR/C/71/D/819/1998, para. 10.2.

[43] *Lindon v. Australia*, no. 646/1995, Views, 25 November 1998, CCPR/C/64/D/646/1995, para. 6.4; *Y.B. v. Russia*, no. 1983/2010, Views, 23 April 2014, CCPR/C/110/D/1983/2010, para. 9.4; General Comment 32, art. 14: Right to equality before courts and tribunals and to a fair trial, CCPR/C/GC/32, para. 11.

[44] *Zhuk v. Belarus*, no. 1910/2009, Views, 30 October 2013, CCPR/C/109/D/1910/2009 para. 8.5; *Proskurnikov v. Russia*, no. 48364/11, §§ 16–18, 1 September 2020; *A. and Others v. the United Kingdom* [GC], no. 3455/05, § 204, ECHR 2009; *Reinprecht v. Austria*, no. 67175/01, § 31, ECHR 2005-XII; *Mooren v. Germany* [GC], no. 11364/03, § 124, 9 July 2009; *Prosecutor v. Orić* (IT-03-68-AR73.2), Interlocutory decision on length of defence case, 20 July 2005, para. 7; *Prosecutor v. Nyiramasuhuko et al.* (ICTR-98-42-AR73), Decision on witness list, 21 August 2007, para. 26; *Prosecutor v. Lubanga* (ICC-01/04-01/06), Additional Observations by Judge Perrin de Brichambaut, 14 June 2019, para. 9.

of the very essence, of the right guaranteed'.[45] Examples might include 'conviction *in absentia* with no subsequent possibility to obtain a fresh determination of the merits of the charge; a trial which is summary in nature and conducted with a total disregard for the rights of the defence; detention without any access to an independent and impartial tribunal to have the legality of the detention reviewed and deliberate and systematic denial of access to a lawyer, especially for an individual detained in a foreign country'.[46]

A Pre-Trial Chamber of the International Criminal Court referred to several human rights treaties and humanitarian law instruments in holding that the right to a fair trial includes respect for equality of arms, an adversarial procedure, reasoned judgments, and the inadmissibility of evidence illegally obtained.[47]

If detailed description of the 'fair hearing' principle remains elusive, the requirement of a 'public hearing' is straightforward. Publicity ensures the transparency of proceedings, thereby providing 'an important safeguard for the interest of the individual and of society at large', as the Human Rights Committee has explained.[48] It is not only a right of the parties to proceedings but also one closely related to the protection of the rule of law, which is an interest of the public as a whole. Like many rules, it is subject to exceptions and restrictions. This qualified nature of the right is further confirmed by the not insignificant number of reservations formulated with respect to Article 14(1) of the International Covenant concerning aspects of the public hearing requirement.[49] Limited access of the public to hearings involving children is quite normal.[50] Justification for a degree of secrecy is also presented in trials involving sexual crimes, so as to protect 'public morals' or the privacy of those involved, and in terrorism trials, with national security providing the rationale. But these are exceptions to the general rule and must be applied narrowly. Even where the hearing is closed to the public, there is a strong imperative that the judgment be openly available.[51] The Universal Periodic Review materials confirm that States

[45] *Sejdovic v. Italy* [GC], no. 56581/00, § 84, ECHR 2006-II; *Othman (Abu Qatada) v. the United Kingdom*, no. 8139/09, § 258, ECHR 2012 (extracts); *Al Nashiri v. Poland*, no. 28761/11, § 563, 24 July 2014.

[46] *Al Nashiri v. Poland*, no. 28761/11, § 562, 24 July 2014; *Othman (Abu Qatada) v. the United Kingdom*, no. 8139/09, § 259, ECHR 2012 (extracts).

[47] *Prosecutor v. Al Hassan* (ICC-01/12-01/18), Rectificatif à la Décision relative à la confirmation des charges portées contre Al Hassan Ag Abdoul Aziz Ag Mohamed Ag Mahmoud, 13 November 2019, para. 384.

[48] General Comment 32, art. 14: Right to equality before courts and tribunals and to a fair trial, CCPR/C/GC/32, para. 28.

[49] Denmark, (1976) 999 UNTS 290 and C.N.194.2014.TREATIES-IV.4; Liechtenstein, (1998) 2048 UNTS 48; Finland, (1976) 999 UNTS 292; Switzerland, (1985) 1392 UNTS 568; Belgium, (1992) 1678 UNTS 394–395.

[50] International Covenant on Civil and Political Rights, (1976) 999 UNTS 171, art. 14(1).

[51] European Convention on Human Rights, (1953) 213 UNTS 221, art. 6(1); International Covenant on Civil and Political Rights, (1976) 999 UNTS 171, art. 14(1); *Prosecutor v. Al Hassan* (ICC-01/12-01/18), Rectificatif à la Décision relative à la confirmation des charges portées contre Al Hassan Ag Abdoul Aziz Ag Mohamed Ag Mahmoud, 13 November 2019, para. 384. That is, not merely for the parties to the trial. The Human Rights Committee refers to a right of the society at large, General Comment 13, A/39/40, p. 143, para. 6.

that are not parties to the International Covenant recognise the right to public trial, subject to the usual exceptions.[52]

3. Independent and impartial tribunal

Justice must be delivered by an independent and impartial tribunal. According to the Human Rights Committee, this 'is an absolute right that is not subject to any exception'.[53] A tribunal (or court) must be established by law in such a way as to be independent of other branches of government, something that may be achieved by a range of measures, including a secure appointment for a term of significant length without the threat of arbitrary removal together with salary and working conditions that are conducive to independence. It is necessary to protect judges against conflicts of interest and intimidation. Impartiality of the tribunal is closely associated with the guarantee of a fair trial in full equality. It has two aspects. First, 'judges must not harbour preconceptions about the matter put before them, and ... must not act in ways that promote the interests of one of the parties'.[54] Second, the tribunal must also appear to a reasonable observer to be impartial. In other words, judges must not only be impartial, they must also be seen to be impartial.[55] The Universal Periodic Review materials confirm that States that are not parties to the International Covenant recognise the requirement that tribunals be independent and impartial.[56]

4. Presumption of innocence

The presumption of innocence is explicitly affirmed in Article 11 of the Universal Declaration of Human Rights as well as in virtually all detailed provisions in human

[52] China, National report, A/HRC/WG.6/4/CHN/1, para. 52; Cuba, National report, A/HRC/WG.6/4/CUB/1, para. 32; Myanmar, National report, A/HRC/WG.6/10/MMR/1, paras. 104, 107; Oman, National report, A/HRC/WG.6/10/OMN/1, para. 67; Saudi Arabia, National report, A/HRC/WG.6/4/SAU/1, para. 1 and National report, A/HRC/WG.6/17/SAU/1, para. 31; Sudan, National report, A/HRC/WG.6/11/SDN/1, para. 37.

[53] *Gonzalez del Rio v. Peru*, No. 263/1987, para. 5.2; General Comment 32, art. 14: Right to equality before courts and tribunals and to a fair trial, CCPR/C/GC/32, para. 19.

[54] *Karttunen v. Finland*, No. 387/1989, Views, 23 October 1992, UN Doc. CCPR/C/46/D/387/1989, para. 7.2; General Comment 32, art. 14: Right to equality before courts and tribunals and to a fair trial, CCPR/C/GC/32, para. 21.

[55] *Lagunas Castedo v. Spain*, no. 1122/2002, Views, 20 October 2008, CCPR/C/94/D/1122/2002, para. 9.7; *Jenny v. Austria*, no. 1437/2005, Views, 9 July 2008, CCPR/C/93/D/1437/2005, para. 9.4.

[56] China, National report, A/HRC/WG.6/4/CHN/1, para. 53 and Report of the Working Group, A/HRC/11/25, para. 10; Cuba, National report, A/HRC/WG.6/4/CUB/1, para. 32; Myanmar, National report, A/HRC/WG.6/10/MMR/1, paras. 104, 107; Oman, Report of the Working Group, A/HRC/31/11, para. 11 and National report, A/HRC/WG.6/10/OMN/1, paras. 66–67; Saudi Arabia, National report, A/HRC/WG.6/4/SAU/1, para. 1; Singapore, National report, A/HRC/WG.6/11/SGP/1, para. 114; Solomon Islands, National report, A/HRC/WG.6/11/SLB/1, para. 26.

rights treaties that concern criminal justice. Moreover, it is also recognised in most national constitutions. Several States that are not parties to the International Covenant on Civil and Political Rights affirm, in reporting to the Human Rights Council, that they ensure respect of the presumption of innocence.[57] Although the enumeration of customary norms in the Human Rights Committee's General Comment on reservations excluded the right to a fair trial, as an exception it declared that it would be contrary to customary international law 'to presume a person guilty unless he proves his innocence'.[58] The Committee has said that there can be no 'deviating from fundamental principles of fair trial, including the presumption of innocence'.[59] In one sense, the presumption of innocence is nothing more than a general principle of law by which the claimant of a right has a burden to prove the case: *ei incumbit probatio qui dicit, non qui negat*. In criminal law, where the freedom of the individual is at stake, this presumption applies with particular vigour. As a principle, its place within customary international law is assured.

In a criminal trial, not only does the presumption dictate that the prosecution has the burden to prove the guilt of the accused but that this be done to a very high standard of certainty. According to the Human Rights Committee, '[t]he presumption of innocence, which is fundamental to the protection of human rights, imposes on the prosecution the burden of proving the charge, guarantees that no guilt can be presumed until the charge has been proved beyond reasonable doubt, ensures that the accused has the benefit of doubt, and requires that persons accused of a criminal act must be treated in accordance with this principle'.[60] One facet of the presumption of innocence is the privilege against self-incrimination. The European Court of Human Rights has referred to a 'right not to incriminate oneself',[61] explaining that it is primarily concerned with 'respecting the will of an accused person to remain silent'.[62]

For some crimes, it is not necessarily contrary to the presumption of innocence to infer certain facts from the proof of other facts. For example, the possession of

[57] Cuba, National report, A/HRC/WG.6/4/CUB/1, paras. 32(f), 36–37; Micronesia, Report of the Working Group, A/HRC/31/4, para. 8; Nauru, National report, A/HRC/WG.6/10/NRU/1, para. 20; Oman, National report, A/HRC/WG.6/10/OMN/1, para. 15; Saudi Arabia, National report, A/HRC/WG.6/4/SAU/1, para. 16; Solomon Islands, National report, A/HRC/WG.6/11/SLB/1, para. 27; South Sudan, Report of the Working Group, A/HRC/34/13, para. 9; Tuvalu, National report, A/HRC/WG.6/3/TUV/1, para. 36; Sudan, National report, A/HRC/WG.6/11/SDN/1, para. 37; United Arab Emirates, National report, A/HRC/WG.6/3/ARE/1, p. 10.

[58] General Comment 24, Issues Relating to Reservations Made upon Ratification or Accession to the Covenant or the Optional Protocols thereto, or in Relation to Declarations under art. 41 of the Covenant, CCPR/C/21/Rev.1/Add.6, para. 8.

[59] General Comment 29, art. 4: Derogations during a State of Emergency, CCPR/C/21/Rev.1/Add.11, para. 11; also, para. 16.

[60] General Comment 32, art. 14: Right to equality before courts and tribunals and to a fair trial, CCPR/C/GC/32, para. 30.

[61] *Saunders v. the United Kingdom*, 17 December 1996, § 69, *Reports of Judgments and Decisions* 1996-VI.

[62] Ibid.

a very large quantity of prohibited drugs suggests the conclusion that the accused person was a trafficker, even in the absence of direct evidence that trafficking took place. Such exceptions must rest upon reasonable inferences and should not be overly broad.[63] Proof of intent, which is an essential component of criminal justice, generally rests on the entirely reasonable inference that persons intend the consequences of their acts. Should an accused person challenge this presumption, arguing for example that the act was unintended due to intoxication, mental illness, or for some other similar reason, requiring that the accused provide evidence to counter the reasonable inference does not breach the presumption of innocence.

There are other corollaries of the presumption of innocence. Collective guilt is incompatible with the presumption of innocence. Criminal liability is premised upon individual accountability. The presumption of innocence applies not only during the trial but also prior to it, when the 'suspect' has not yet become the 'accused'.[64] Detention prior to conviction should be the exception and not be the general rule, and should be justified by criteria such as the likelihood of appearance at trial. In the courtroom, defendants should not normally be shackled or placed in cages, as this suggests that they are dangerous criminals, thereby weakening the presumption of innocence.[65]

Public authorities should protect the presumption of innocence by refraining from comments on pending proceedings that suggest an accused person is guilty.[66] According to the European Court of Human Rights, the presumption of innocence 'is aimed at preventing the undermining of a fair criminal trial by prejudicial statements made in close connection with those proceedings'.[67] It does not 'prevent the authorities from informing the public of criminal investigations in progress, but it requires that they do so with all the discretion and circumspection necessary if the presumption of innocence is to be respected'.[68]

[63] *Radio France et al. v. France*, no. 53984/00, § 71, ECHR 2004-II; *Salabiaku v. France*, 7 October 1988, § 28, Series A no. 141-A; *Willcox and Hurford v. the United Kingdom*, (dec.), nos. 43759/10 and 43771/12, § 96, 8 January 2013.

[64] Directive (EU) 2016/343 of the European Parliament and of the Council of 9 March 2016 on the strengthening of certain aspects of the presumption of innocence and of the right to be present at the trial in criminal proceedings, Official Journal of the European Union 11.3.2016 L 65/1, art. 2.

[65] *Karimov and Nursatov v. Tajikistan*, nos. 1108 and 1121/2002, Views, 27 March 2007, CCPR/C/89/D/1108 and 1121/2002, para. 7.4; *Zinsou v. Benin*, no. 2055/2011, Views, 18 July 2014, CCPR/C/111/D/2055/2011, para. 7.3.

[66] *Cedeño v. Venezuela*, no. 1940/2010, Views, 29 October 2012, CCPR/C/106/D/1940/2010, para. 7.4; *Kovaleva v. Belarus*, no. 2120/2011, Views, 29 October 2012, CCPR/C/106/D/2120/2011, para. 11.4; *Włoch v. Poland* (dec.), no. 27785/95, 30 March 2000; *Baragiola v. Switzerland*, no. 17265/90, Commission decision of 21 October 1993, (1993) 36 YB 90, DR 75, p. 76; *Berns and Ewert v. Luxembourg*, no. 13251/87, Commission decision of 6 March 1991, (1991) 34 YB 65, DR 68, p. 147. Also: General Comment 13, A/39/40, p. 143, para. 7; General Comment 32, art. 14: Right to equality before courts and tribunals and to a fair trial, CCPR/C/GC/32, para. 30.

[67] *G.C.P. v. Romania*, no. 20899/03, § 54, 20 December 2011.

[68] *Allenet de Ribemont v. France*, 10 February 1995, § 38, Series A no. 308.

5. Guarantees necessary for the defence

With reference to criminal trials only, the International Covenant on Civil and Political Rights provides a detailed list of minimum guarantees. They apply to all States Parties to the Covenant, of course, and several of the provisions have not been subject to any reservation. The Covenant provides for the right of a person charged with a criminal offence to be informed promptly and in detail in a language which the person understands of the nature and cause of the charge; to have adequate time and facilities for the preparation of the defence and to communicate with counsel of the person's choice; to be tried without undue delay; to examine, or have examined, the witnesses for the prosecution and to obtain the attendance and examination of witnesses for the defence behalf under the same conditions as witnesses for the prosecution; and not to be compelled to testify against himself or herself or to confess guilt.

The customary law study of the International Committee of the Red Cross confirmed the rule that '[n]o one may be convicted or sentenced, except pursuant to a fair trial affording all essential judicial guarantees'.[69] It must be borne in mind that the norms of international humanitarian law apply to civilians in an occupied territory, prisoners of war and other 'protected persons', and there is no automatic transposition to the law governing criminal justice in peacetime. The International Committee identified the following components of the fair trial under customary international law: trial by an independent, impartial and regularly constituted court; presumption of innocence; information on the nature and cause of the accusation; right to defend oneself or to be assisted by a lawyer of one's own choice; right to free legal assistance if the interests of justice so require; right to sufficient time and facilities to prepare the defence; right of the accused to communicate freely with counsel; trial without undue delay; right of the accused to examine and to have examined witnesses; assistance of an interpreter, if the accused cannot understand the language used in the proceedings; the right to be present at trial; not to be compelled to testify or to confess guilt; public trial; *ne bis in idem*.[70]

The Inter-American Commission has said '[i]t is beyond question' that 'core rights', including the right to due process and to a fair trial, 'have attained the status of customary, and indeed peremptory, norms of international law'.[71] In a dissenting opinion, Judge Pinto de Albuquerque of the European Court of Human Rights wrote that the guarantee against double jeopardy (*ne bis in idem*) is a rule of

[69] Jean-Marie Henckaerts and Louise Doswald-Beck, *Customary International Humanitarian Law*, Vol. I, Cambridge: Cambridge University Press, 2005, p. 352.

[70] Ibid., pp. 352–371. See also *Prosecutor v. Al Hassan* (ICC-01/12-01/18), Rectificatif à la Décision relative à la confirmation des charges portées contre Al Hassan Ag Abdoul Aziz Ag Mohamed Ag Mahmoud, 13 November 2019, para. 384.

[71] *Mario Alfredo Lares-Reyes et al. v. United States*, Case 12.379, Report No. 19/02, Merits, 27 February 2002, para. 46, fn. 23.

customary international law.[72] The Venice Commission of the Council of Europe said that the right to a fair trial, protection against double jeopardy, and *nullum crimen sine lege* were 'likely to have acquired the status of customary international law'.[73] According to the United States Supreme Court, customary international law guarantees a limited number of fair trial protections such as the principle that an accused must be present for trial and must be informed of the evidence against him or her.[74] Antonio Cassese, writing as President of the Special Tribunal for Lebanon, referred to 'very broad recognition of the right to communicate freely and privately with counsel by the international community', concluding that this was 'now accepted in customary international law as one of the fundamental human rights relating to due process'.[75] In the same order, he said 'the right of access to the criminal file' was also enshrined in custom.[76]

Some provisions in Article 14 of the International Covenant on Civil and Political Rights have provoked reservations, notably with respect to the obligation to provide funded defence counsel,[77] the right to an appeal from a conviction,[78] the right to compensation for a miscarriage of justice,[79] and the protection against double jeopardy (*ne bis in idem*).[80] Virtually all of these reservations concern exceptions rather than the rules themselves and do little if anything to undermine their inclusion in a list of norms of customary international law.

The position with respect to the specific rights respecting criminal trials set out in Article 14 is more difficult to establish for States that have not ratified the International Covenant on Civil and Political Rights, Many have not provided detailed information in their submissions to the Human Rights Council, satisfying themselves (and, apparently, other Member States), with general pronouncements

[72] *A. and B. v. Norway* [GC], no. 24130/11 and 29758/11, 15 November 2016, Dissenting opinion of Judge Pinto de Albuquerque, paras. 6–15; *Mihalache v. Romania* [GC], no. 54012/10, 8 July 2019, Concurring opinion of Judge Pinto de Albuquerque, para. 47.

[73] Amicus Curiae Brief for the Constitutional Court of Georgia on the non ultra petita rule in criminal cases, adopted by the Venice Commission at its 103rd Plenary Session (Venice, 19–20 June), CDL-AD(2015)016-e, para. 42.

[74] *Hamdan v. Rumsfeld*, 548 US 557 (2006).

[75] *Unnamed applicants* (CH/PRES/2009/01/rev), Order on Conditions of Detention, 21 April 2009, para. 16.

[76] Ibid., para. 44.

[77] Barbados, (1976) 999 UNTS 288; Belize, (1996) 1927 UNTS 503; Guyana, (1977) 1035 UNTS 351, C.N.51.1977.TREATIES-2; Gambia, (1979) 1130 UNTS 349; United Kingdom, (1976) 1007 UNTS 394, C.N.193.1976.TREATIES-6; Switzerland, (1992) 1678 UNTS 395.

[78] Denmark, (1992) 1678 UNTS 395; Republic of Korea, (1990) 1563 UNTS 450; Norway, (1976) 999 UNTS 297–298, C.N.188.1972.TREATIES-7; Trinidad and Tobago, (1978) 1120 UNTS 48; Italy, (1978) 1106 UNTS 369; C.N.265.1983.TREATIES-3/8/2 (Luxembourg); (1978) 1120 UNTS 489 (the Netherlands); Switzerland, (1992) 1678 UNTS 395; Belgium, (1983) 1312 UNTS 329; Germany, (1976) 999 UNTS 293–294.

[79] Australia, (1980) 1197 UNTS 412; Bahamas, C.N.1043.2008.TREATIES-30; Belize, (1996) 1927 UNTS 503–504; Guyana, C.N.51.1977.TREATIES-2; Malta, C.N.304.1990.TREATIES-4/11/4; Bangladesh, C.N.609.2000.TREATIES-8.

[80] Denmark, (1976) 999 UNTS 290 and (1979) 1144 UNTS 387; Republic of Korea, (1990) 1563 UNTS 450; Netherlands, C.N.316.1978.TREATIES-l4; Sweden, (1976) 999 UNTS 299; Bahrain, C.N.1140.2006.TREATIES-24.

about how they guarantee the right to a fair trial, or referring only to some of the detailed rights.[81] In the course of the Universal Periodic Review, some of these States have confirmed their recognition of the right to counsel, including funded counsel in the case of indigence[82] and the right of a convicted person to appeal the verdict to a higher court.[83] The Universal Periodic Review materials confirm that States that are not parties to the International Covenant accept the right to counsel, including funded counsel in the case of indigence[84] and the protection against double jeopardy.[85]

For example, Myanmar told the Human Rights Council that its justice system provided 'the right of cross-examination in accordance with the Evidence Act, the right to produce witnesses, right of appeal to defend through legal assistance at government expense on behalf of poor person [sic] accused of offences punishable with death. The court may not convict the accused without sufficient evidence.'[86] During the review, New Zealand called upon Myanmar to '[r]epeal laws that are not in compliance with international human rights law and review its legal system to ensure compliance with the rights to due process and a fair trial and respect for the rule of law', but without further specification as to what the laws that were inconsistent with international human rights law.[87] Canada recommended that Myanmar undertake '[t]horough reform of the judiciary to ensure compliance with due process and fair trial standards, including independence and impartiality', a comment that is really about compliance with international standards rather than their identification.[88] Similarly, Sweden said it should 'ensure that all trial proceedings conform to international fair trial standards, including the right to a fair and public trial by a competent, independent and impartial tribunal, access to legal counsel of one's choosing, the presumption of innocence, and the opportunity

[81] For example, Tonga, National report, A/HRC/WG.6/15/TON/1, para. 29.

[82] China, National report, A/HRC/WG.6/4/CHN/1, para. 54; Comoros, National report, A/HRC/WG.6/32/COM/1, paras. 23–24; Micronesia, National report, A/HRC/WG.6/9/FSM/1, para. 20; Sao Tome and Principe, National report, A/HRC/WG.6/23/STP/1, para. 12; Singapore, National report, A/HRC/WG.6/11/SGP/1, para. 113 and National report, A/HRC/WG.6/11/SGP/1, paras. 115, 116; South Sudan, Report of the Working Group, A/HRC/34/13, para. 9; Tuvalu, National report, A/HRC/WG.6/3/TUV/1, para. 36; Saudi Arabia, National report, A/HRC/WG.6/4/SAU/1, para. 16; Sudan, National report, A/HRC/WG.6/11/SDN/1, para. 37.

[83] Cuba, National report, A/HRC/WG.6/4/CUB/1, para. 32; Malaysia, National report, A/HRC/WG.6/31/MYS/1, para. 18; Myanmar, National report, A/HRC/WG.6/10/MMR/1, paras. 104, 107.

[84] China, National report, A/HRC/WG.6/4/CHN/1, para. 54; Comoros, National report, A/HRC/WG.6/32/COM/1, paras. 23–24; Micronesia, National report, A/HRC/WG.6/9/FSM/1, para. 20; Singapore, National report, A/HRC/WG.6/11/SGP/1, para. 113 and National report, A/HRC/WG.6/11/SGP/1, paras. 115, 116; South Sudan, Report of the Working Group, A/HRC/34/13, para. 9; Tuvalu, National report, A/HRC/WG.6/3/TUV/1, para. 36; Saudi Arabia, National report, A/HRC/WG.6/4/SAU/1, para. 16; Sudan, National report, A/HRC/WG.6/11/SDN/1, para. 37.

[85] Cuba, National report, A/HRC/WG.6/4/CUB/1, para. 36; Micronesia, National report, A/HRC/WG.6/9/FSM/1, para. 19; Singapore, National report, A/HRC/WG.6/11/SGP/1, para. 23; Tonga, National report, A/HRC/WG.6/15/TON/1, para. 29.

[86] Myanmar, National report, A/HRC/WG.6/10/MMR/1, para. 107.

[87] Myanmar, Report of the Working Group, A/HRC/17/9, para. 107.5.

[88] Ibid., para. 107.37.

to appeal through a process of judicial review'.[89] In sum, these exchanges do not indicate that Myanmar has any significant dispute about the basic principles that underpin the right to a fair trial; although that does not necessarily mean that in its practice it observes all of them. The same assessment emerges from an examination of China's appearance before the Human Rights Council. Under the heading 'The right to a fair trial', its first Universal Periodic Review report presented a summary description that addressed issues such as independence and impartiality of the tribunal, the right to public trial, and the right to defence counsel.[90] During the Review itself, China told the Council that it 'ensures implementation of human rights guarantees in the judicial field'.[91] One State, Slovakia, said China should provide the 'right to a fair trial',[92] a recommendation that China accepted.[93]

Therefore, there is good evidence that the specific fair trial guarantees listed in Article 14(3) of the International Covenant on Civil and Political Rights are also recognised as customary international law. The same can be said of other guarantees set out in Article 14, notably the protection against double jeopardy (art. 14(7)) and the right to appeal from a conviction (art. 14(5)).

* * *

Conclusions. Everyone charged with an offence has the right to a fair and public hearing by an independent and impartial tribunal where the presumption of innocence is respected. Guarantees of a full defence include being informed promptly of the nature and cause of the charge, having adequate time and facilities to prepare a defence, to be assisted by counsel including funded counsel in the case of an indigent defendant, to be tried without undue delay, to be present at trial, to examine witnesses, to have an interpreter if necessary, and to exercise a right to silence. A person may not be tried twice for the same offence. A convicted person has the right to appeal to a higher court.

C. Principle of legality—*nullum crimen nulla poena sine lege*

Long before it was codified in the Universal Declaration of Human Rights, the principle of legality was enshrined in domestic constitutions. Article 8 of the French *Déclaration des droits de l'homme et du citoyen*, adopted on 26 August 1789, affirms that 'no one shall suffer punishment except it be legally inflicted in virtue of a law passed and promulgated before the commission of the offense'. In international law, it may have first arisen at the Paris Peace Conference in 1919. Delegates from

89 Ibid., para. 107.41.
90 China, National report, A/HRC/WG.6/4/CHN/1, para. 54.
91 China, Report of the Working Group, A/HRC/25/5, para. 85.
92 Ibid., para. 186.55.
93 China, Views on conclusions, A/ HRC/25/5/Add.1, p. 5.

the United States objected to plans to prosecute violations of the 'laws and principles of humanity' that were too uncertain to have any place in a court of criminal justice.[94] They said they 'were of the opinion that an act could not be a crime in the legal sense of the word, unless it were made so by law, and that the commission of an act declared to be a crime by law could not be punished unless the law prescribed the penalty to be inflicted'.[95]

'No one shall be held guilty of any penal offence on account of any act or omission which did not constitute a penal offence, under national or international law, at the time when it was committed', states Article 11(2) of the Universal Declaration of Human Rights. Similar formulations appear in the International Covenant on Civil and Political Rights[96] and in specialised and regional treaties.[97] The principle of legality is consecrated in a familiar Latin expression: *nullum crimen nulla poena sine lege*. In those treaties that provide for derogation, it is consistently deemed a non-derogable right.[98] Of States that are not parties to the International Covenant or to regional treaties that provide for the norm, a few indicate their adherence in reports to the Human Rights Council[99] or to the Committee on the Rights of the Child.[100] The principle of legality is also recognised in the customary law study of the International Committee of the Red Cross.[101] Nevertheless, the Human Rights Committee did not include the principle of legality in the list of customary norms in General Comment 24.[102] The absence of questions or recommendations by other States during the Universal Periodic Review suggests a lack of any concern that the rule against retroactive prosecution is not being respected in those States.

[94] 'Memorandum of Reservations Presented by the Representatives of the United States to the Report of the Commission on Responsibilities', (1920) 14 *American Journal of International Law* 127, at p. 134.

[95] Ibid., p. 145.

[96] International Covenant on Civil and Political Rights, (1976) 999 UNTS 171, art. 15. Also Second Optional Protocol to the International Covenant on Civil and Political Rights, aiming at the abolition of the death penalty, (1991) 1642 UNTS 414, art. 6.

[97] Convention on the Rights of the Child, (1990) 1571 UNTS 3, art. 40(2)(a); European Convention on Human Rights, (1953) 213 UNTS 221, art. 7; American Convention on Human Rights, (1978) 1144 UNTS 123, art. 9; African Charter on Human and Peoples' Rights, (1986) 1520 UNTS 271, art. 7(2); Arab Charter on Human Rights, art. 15; Charter of Fundamental Rights of the European Union, OJ C 326/391, art. 49(1) and (2).

[98] International Covenant on Civil and Political Rights, (1976) 999 UNTS 171, art. 4; European Convention on Human Rights, (1953) 213 UNTS 221, art. 7; American Convention on Human Rights, (1978) 1144 UNTS 123, art. 27(2).

[99] Cuba, National report, A/HRC/WG.6/4/CUB/1, paras. 34, 36; Malaysia, National report, A/HRC/WG.6/4/MYS/1/Rev.1, para. 9; Myanmar, National report, A/HRC/WG.6/10/MMR/1, para. 40; Saudi Arabia, Views on conclusions, A/HRC/40/4/Add.1, para. 22; Singapore, National report, A/HRC/WG.6/11/SGP/1, para. 23.

[100] Malaysia, Initial report, CRC/C/MYS/1, paras. 64, 327; Oman, Initial report, CRC/C/78/Add.1, paras. 218–219.

[101] Jean-Marie Henckaerts and Louise Doswald-Beck, *Customary International Humanitarian Law*, Vol. I, Cambridge: Cambridge University Press, 2005, pp. 371–372.

[102] General Comment 24, Issues Relating to Reservations Made upon Ratification or Accession to the Covenant or the Optional Protocols thereto, or in Relation to Declarations under art. 41 of the Covenant, CCPR/C/21/Rev.1/Add.6, para. 8.

The United Nations Working Group on Arbitrary Detention said that a retroactive increase of a sentence after a prisoner has fully served the sentence imposed at the time of conviction breaches Article 15 of the International Covenant on Civil and Political Rights 'and customary international law'.[103] The *lex mitior* principle, by which a convicted person is entitled to benefit from the lesser penalty if the law has been changed since the commission of the alleged act, is also widely recognised.[104]

The principle of legality has been identified as a peremptory norm (*jus cogens*) by the Appeals Chamber of the Special Tribunal for Lebanon[105] and judges of the European Court of Human Rights.[106] Judge Ammoun of the International Court of Justice described it as one of 'the most sacred principles of criminal law'.[107] However, the history of the norm suggests a more moderate and less absolute understanding of the rule than the *jus cogens* designation would require. Nazi defendants invoked the principle of legality when they were tried before the International Military Tribunal.[108] The final judgment dismissed their objection, stating that 'it is to be observed that the maxim *nullum crimen sine lege* is not a limitation of sovereignty, but is in general a principle of justice'.[109] In the Eichmann trial, judges referred with approval to Hans Kelsen, writing in 1944: 'There is no rule of general customary international law forbidding the enactment of norms with retrospective force, so-called *ex post facto* laws.'[110] They wrote that 'if it is the contention of counsel for the appellant that we must apply international law as it is, and not as it ought to be from the moral point of view, then we must reply that precisely from a *legal* point of view no such rule of international law is to be found'.[111] Both the European Convention on Human Rights and the International Covenant on Civil and Political Rights include what is sometimes called the 'Nuremberg

[103] Report of the Working Group on Arbitrary Detention, Addendum, Follow-up mission to Germany, A/HRC/30/36/Add.1, 10 July 2015.

[104] International Covenant on Civil and Political Rights, (1976) 999 UNTS 171, art. 15; Explanation Relating to the Charter of Fundamental Rights, *Official Journal of the European Union*, OJ C 303/34, 14 December 2007; *Ilnseher v. Germany* [GC], nos. 10211/12 and 27505/14, 4 December 2018, Dissenting opinion of Judge Pinto de Albuquerque, joined by Judge Dedov, para. 75.

[105] *Unnamed defendant* (STL-11-01/I), Interlocutory Decision on the Applicable Law: Terrorism, Conspiracy, Homicide, Perpetration, Cumulative Charging, 16 February 2011, para. 76.

[106] *Maktouf and Damjanović v. Bosnia and Herzegovina* [GC], nos. 2312/08 and 34179/08, ECHR 2013-IV, Concurring opinion of Judge Pinto de Albuquerque, joined by Judge Vučinić, para. 9; *Ilnseher v. Germany* [GC], nos. 10211/12 and 27505/14, 4 December 2018, Dissenting opinion of Judge Pinto de Albuquerque, joined by Judge Dedov, para. 75.

[107] *Legal Consequences for States of the Continued Presence of South Africa in Namibia (South West Africa) notwithstanding Security Council Resolution 276 (1970), Advisory Opinion, ICJ Reports 1971*, p. 16, Separate Opinion of Judge Ammoun, Vice-President, p. 71.

[108] Motion adopted by all defence counsel, 19 November 1945, (1948) 1 IMT 168-170.

[109] (1948) 22 IMT 203, p. 462. Hans Kelsen, 'Will the Judgment in the Nuremberg Trial Constitute a Precedent in International Law?', (1947) 1 *International Law Quarterly* 153, at p. 165.

[110] Hans Kelsen, *Peace through Law*, Chapel Hill: University of North Carolina Press, 1944, p. 87. See also Hans Kelsen, 'Will the Judgment in the Nuremberg Trial Constitute a Precedent in International Law?', (1947) 1 *International Law Quarterly* 153, at p. 165.

[111] *A.G. Israel v. Eichmann*, (1968) 36 ILR 5 (DC), para. 7(3) (emphasis in the original).

clause',[112] which somewhat attenuates the general formulation of the principle of legality: 'This Article shall not prejudice the trial and punishment of any person for any act or omission which, at the time when it was committed, was criminal according to the general principles of law recognised by civilised nations.'[113]

Resisting a strictly positivistic application of the principle, the European Court of Human Rights has required only that the criminal offence be 'accessible' and 'foreseeable' to the accused person at the time of the punishable act, upholding prosecutions based upon unwritten norms, in particular when they concern serious crimes that violate human dignity.[114] Along the same lines, Judge Cançado Trindade of the International Court of Justice wrote that '[t]he imperative of the preservation of human dignity stands well above pleas of non-retroactivity'.[115] In 2018, Uruguay proposed that the draft articles on crimes against humanity being finalised by the International Law Commission include a provision based on Article 15(2) of the International Covenant on Civil and Political Rights, describing it as an '[e]xception to the nullum crimen sine lege principle in criminal law'.[116]

The modern day focus on prosecution of historic atrocity crimes highlights the importance of the requirement, spelled out in Article 11(2) of the Universal Declaration, that the crime be recognised under either national or international law. The term 'international law' invites reference to both treaty law and customary international law. Indeed, most of the debate arises in the context of retroactive prosecution for offences recognised under international law. Sometimes this is because there is no domestic equivalent of the crime, or because the domestic equivalent is time barred. It may also arise as a result of government decisions to stigmatise the act, which may well be punishable as an ordinary crime, by labelling it using the language of international criminal law. Because international criminal law is an extremely dynamic field, with sometimes quite dramatic changes in its scope, determining when certain conduct became recognised as an international crime under customary international law is not always straightforward.[117]

* * *

Conclusions. No one shall be held guilty of any criminal offence on account of any act or omission which did not constitute a criminal offence, under national or

[112] Triestino Mariniello, 'The "Nuremberg Clause" and Beyond: The Legality Principle and Sources of International Criminal Law in the European Court's Jurisprudence', (2013) 82 *Nordic Journal of International Law* 221.

[113] European Convention on Human Rights, (1953) 213 UNTS 221, art. 7(2); International Covenant on Civil and Political Rights, (1976) 999 UNTS 171, art. 15(2).

[114] *C.R. v. the United Kingdom*, 22 November 1995, § 42, Series A no. 335-C.

[115] *Questions relating to the Obligation to Prosecute or Extradite (Belgium v. Senegal), Judgment, ICJ Reports 2012*, p. 422, Separate Opinion of Judge Cançado Trindade, para. 149.

[116] Crimes against humanity, Comments and observations received from Governments, international organisations and others, A/CN.4/726, p. 20.

[117] See, for example, *Kononov v. Latvia* [GC], no. 36376/04, ECHR 2010-IV; *Drėlingas v. Lithuania*, no. 28859/16, 12 March 2019.

international law, at the time when it was committed. Nor shall a heavier penalty be imposed than the one that was applicable at the time when the criminal offence was committed. If, subsequent to the commission of the offence, provision is made by law for the imposition of the lighter penalty, the offender shall benefit thereby.

D. Children and criminal justice

The Convention on the Rights of the Child provides a detailed enumeration of fair trial rights that comprise the minimum fair trial guarantees set out in Article 14 of the International Covenant on Civil and Political Rights. Article 40 of the Convention has had only a few reservations, principally to the requirement that a child 'alleged as or accused of having infringed the penal law' is entitled, '[i]f considered to have infringed the penal law, to have this decision and any measures imposed in consequence thereof reviewed by a higher competent, independent and impartial authority or judicial body according to law'.[118] There is also a reservation to the requirement of legal assistance in 'cases involving minor offences'.[119] The very broad general reservations made by certain States do not in reality appear to have any bearing on the rights set out in Article 40. Therefore, as a general proposition it can be said that the content of Article 40 of the Convention on the Rights of the Child sets out norms of customary law applicable to criminal prosecutions of children.

Pursuant to paragraph 1 of Article 40 the Convention on the Rights of the Child, States recognise 'the right of every child alleged as, accused of, or recognised as having infringed the penal law to be treated in a manner consistent with the promotion of the child's sense of dignity and worth, which reinforces the child's respect for the human rights and fundamental freedoms of others and which takes into account the child's age and the desirability of promoting the child's reintegration and the child's assuming a constructive role in society'.[120] Perhaps no better example can be provided than the total prohibition under customary international law of both capital punishment and irreducible life imprisonment for crimes committed by children.[121] The Standard Minimum Rules for the Administration of

[118] Convention on the Rights of the Child, (1990) 1571 UNTS 3, art. 40(2)(v). Reservations have been formulated by Belgium, C.N.320.1991.TREATIES-16; Denmark, C.N.151.1991.TREATIES-6; France; Monaco, C.N.203.1993.TREATIES-6; Netherlands, C.N.58.1995.TREATIES-1; Republic of Korea, C.N.295.1991.TREATIES-14.

[119] Convention on the Rights of the Child, (1990) 1571 UNTS 3, art. 40(2)(iii), by the Netherlands, with respect to the Netherlands Antilles, C.N.525.1997.TREATIES-12/1.

[120] Convention on the Rights of the Child, (1990) 1571 UNTS 3, art. 41(1).

[121] Ibid., art. 37(a). See Helmut Sax and William A. Schabas, 'Article 37, Prohibition of Torture, Prohibition of Death Penalty and Life Imprisonment and the Deprivation of Liberty', in André Alen, Johan Vande Lanotte, Eugeen Verhellen, Fiona Ang, Eva Berghmans and Mieke Verheyde, eds., *A Commentary on the United Nations Convention on the Rights of the Child*, Leiden/Boston: Martinus Nijhoff, 2006.

Juvenile Justice, known as the Beijing Rules, provide the most detailed framework in this area.[122] They are intended as minimum standards of universal application and furnish a useful guide to the content of customary international law, in particular the general principle set out in Article 40(1). Assessing whether all of the detailed provisions of the Beijing Rules meet the criteria for them to be deemed customary international law is beyond the scope of this study.

International law imposes an initial requirement that States establish a minimum age for criminal responsibility below which children shall be presumed not to have the capacity to infringe the penal law.[123] In reality, there are few examples of States that have not done this.[124] The minimum age is set bearing in mind the physical and mental immaturity of children.[125] Treaty law does not specify the precise age, which varies considerably from one State to another. Sometimes States[126] and treaty bodies[127] call for the age of responsibility to be increased so as to conform to 'international standards' but without specifying what the standard actually is. States have also urged that the age is set 'in accordance with the Convention on the Rights of the Child', yet the treaty does not propose an age.[128]

The Committee on the Rights of the Child has said that a minimum age of criminal responsibility below the age of twelve years is not internationally acceptable.[129] The Committee on the Rights of the Child told Saint Lucia that it should ensure that the age was set at twelve in all relevant legislation.[130] According to the Human Rights Committee, ten years is 'too low'.[131] In the course of the Universal Periodic Review, Thailand agreed to raise the age to twelve from ten[132] after this was recommended by France[133] and Sierra Leone.[134] Thailand had earlier increased the age from seven to ten, but was told by the Committee on the Rights of the Child that

[122] The United Nations Standard Minimum Rules for the Administration of Juvenile Justice (The Beijing Rules), A/RES/40/33, Annex.

[123] Convention on the Rights of the Child, (1990) 1571 UNTS 3, art. 40(3)(a).

[124] For example, Micronesia, Report of the Working Group, A/HRC/16/16, paras. 61.36–61.38.

[125] General Comment 32, art. 14: Right to equality before courts and tribunals and to a fair trial, CCPR/C/GC/32, para. 43.

[126] For example, Botswana, in United States, Report of the Working Group, A/HRC/32/10, para. 120.128; Lithuania, in Kenya, Report of the Working Group, A/HRC/29/10, para. 142.114; Uruguay, in Thailand, Report of the Working Group, A/HRC/33/16, para. 158.126; Sierra Leone, in Brunei Darussalam, Report of the Working Group, A/HRC/27/11, para. 113.74; Turkey, in Brunei Darussalam, Report of the Working Group, A/HRC/13/14, para. 34.

[127] Concluding observations, Barbados, CCPR/C/GRD/CO/1, para. 18; Concluding observations, Brunei Darussalam, CRC/C/BRN/CO/2-3, para. 70(a) and CRC/C/15/Add.219, para. 56(b); United Arab Emirates, CRC/C/ARE/CO/2, para. 71(a).

[128] Canada, in Oman, Report of the Working Group, A/HRC/17/7, para. 90.41; Portugal, in Brunei Darussalam, Report of the Working Group, A/HRC/13/14, para. 15; Uruguay, in Myanmar, Report of the Working Group, A/HRC/17/9, para. 107.12; Peru, in Brunei Darussalam, Report of the Working Group, A/HRC/42/11, para. 121.204.

[129] Saudi Arabia, Concluding observations, CRC/C/SAU/CO/3-4, para. 44(a).

[130] Saint Lucia, Concluding observations, CRC/C/LCA/CO/2-4, para. 63(a).

[131] Malawi, Concluding observations, CCPR/C/MWI/CO/1/Add.1, para. 18.

[132] Thailand, Report of the Working Group, A/HRC/33/16, para. 161(b)(i).

[133] Ibid., para. 158.128.

[134] Ibid., para. 158.125.

this was still below international standards, and that it should be set at 'an internationally acceptable age and in no circumstances below the age of twelve years'.[135] When Sudan reported that the age in its criminal law was twelve, France recommended this be increased so as to comply with Sudan's international obligations.[136] Some States report increases in the age to fourteen[137] and fifteen.[138] The Human Rights Committee criticised Hungary when it lowered the age from fourteen to twelve.[139] When Belize reported that children between twelve and fourteen could be held to be criminally responsible if 'found to have the appropriate maturity to understand the nature and consequences of their criminal conduct', the Human Rights Committee said it should raise the minimum age of criminal responsibility in accordance with international standards.[140] Taken together, and despite some inconsistencies, these sources indicate that the age of criminal responsibility under customary international law cannot be lower than twelve.

The Convention on the Rights of the Child sets out a number of substantive and procedural rules that essentially echo provisions in other treaties, especially Article 14 of the International Covenant on Civil and Political Rights.[141] This part of the Convention also confirms the customary status of those provisions, as there cannot be any logic in accepting such rules of fundamental fairness for juveniles yet denying them to adults. These include the prohibition of retroactive crimes; the presumption of innocence; the right to be informed promptly of the charges; to have assistance in the preparation of a defence; to be judged expeditiously by a competent, independent, and impartial tribunal; protection against self-incrimination; to summon witnesses; and to the free services of an interpreter. A few aspects are tailored to the needs of juvenile justice, such as the requirement that parents or guardians also be informed of the offence where this is appropriate. In one contentious case, the Human Rights Committee found there was a violation of the International Covenant because the age of the applicant, who was fifteen, 'placed him in a vulnerable position' and 'unimpeded access by his parent or legal guardian or legal representative could have played a crucial role in protecting his rights throughout the criminal proceedings'.[142] Furthermore, as an exception to

135 Thailand, Concluding observations, CRC/C/THA/CO/3-4, paras. 79–80.

136 Sudan, Report of the Working Group, A/HRC/18/16, para. 83.123.

137 Malta, Concluding observations, CCPR/C/MLT/CO/2, para. 3(c); Georgia, Concluding observations, CCPR/C/GEO/CO/4, para. 3(e); Cyprus, Concluding observations, CCPR/C/CYP/CO/4, para. 3(c); Kuwait, Concluding observations, CCPR/C/KWT/CO/3, para. 3(b); Indonesia, Concluding observations, CCPR/C/IDN/CO/1, para. 3(b); Malta, Concluding observations, CCPR/C/MLT/CO/2, para. 3(c).

138 Kuwait, Concluding observations, CCPR/C/KWT/CO/3, para. 3(b).

139 Hungary, Concluding observations, CCPR/C/HUN/CO/6, paras. 29–30.

140 Belize, Concluding observations, CCPR/C/BLZ/CO/1/Add.1, paras. 36–37.

141 Convention on the Rights of the Child, (1990) 1571 UNTS 3, art. 40(2).

142 *Berezhnoy v. Russia*, no. 2107/2011, Views, 5 December 2016, CCPR/C/118/D/2107/2011, para. 9.7. See also General Comment 32, art. 14: Right to equality before courts and tribunals and to a fair trial, CCPR/C/GC/32, para. 42.

the norm for adults, there is no requirement the hearing be public.[143] Moreover, the Convention enshrines the right of a juvenile '[t]o have his or her privacy fully respected at all stages of the proceedings'.[144]

There is no treaty requirement for States to establish separate courts for young offenders, and it is therefore difficult to claim that this is an obligation imposed by customary international law. According to the Human Rights Committee, States should establish an appropriate juvenile criminal justice system, 'in order to ensure that juveniles are treated in a manner commensurate with their age'.[145] They must guarantee that criminal trials against juveniles are conducted differently than those of adults, this being normally accomplished by juvenile courts.[146]

Children who are detained either pending criminal proceedings or in the service of a sentence should be segregated from adults, unless it is in the child's best interest not to do so, according to the Convention on the Rights of the Child.[147] Nevertheless, there have been far too numerous reservations to the relevant provisions to permit the conclusion that there is a customary norm.[148]

* * *

Conclusions. States must establish a minimum age for criminal responsibility of twelve or higher. Children detained while awaiting trial should be segregated from adults.

[143] See also International Covenant on Civil and Political Rights, (1976) 999 UNTS 171, art. 14(1).

[144] Convention on the Rights of the Child, (1990) 1571 UNTS 3, art. 40(2)(vii).

[145] General Comment 32, art. 14: Right to equality before courts and tribunals and to a fair trial, CCPR/C/GC/32, para. 43.

[146] Special courts and procedures are also noted by the Human Rights Committee in General Comment 13, A/39/40, p. 143, para. 16.

[147] Convention on the Rights of the Child, (1990) 1571 UNTS 3, art. 37(c). Also International Covenant on Civil and Political Rights, (1976) 999 UNTS 171, arts. 10(2)(b) and (3).

[148] Australia, C.N.230.1980.TREATIES-6, C.N.335.1990.TREATIES-10; Austria, (1978) 1103 UNTS 393; Bangladesh, C.N.609.2000.TREATIES-8; Belgium, C.N.113.1983.TREATIES-4; Canada, C.N.320.1991.TREATIES-16; Denmark, C.N.10.1972.TREATIES-1; Finland, C.N.210.1975. TREATIES-7; Iceland, C.N.189.1979.TREATIES-6; Ireland, C.N.344.1989.TREATIES-2/17/4; Japan, C.N.123.1994.TREATIES-2; Luxembourg, C.N.265.1983.TREATIES-3/8/2; Malaysia, C.N.58.1995. TREATIES-1; Netherlands, C.N.58.1995.TREATIES-1; New Zealand, C.N.329.1978.TREATIES-15, C.N.135.1993.TREATIES-40; Norway, C.N.188.1972.TREATIES-7; Singapore, C.N.370.1995. TREATIES-9; Sweden, C.N.198.1971.TREATIES-6; Trinidad and Tobago, C.N.193.1976.TREATIES-6; United Kingdom, C.N.320.1991.TREATIES-16; United States of America, C.N.250.1992. TREATIES-14.

9

Economic, social, and cultural rights

The peace treaties that concluded the First World War declared that universal peace could only be established 'if it is based upon social justice'.[1] The treaties provided for the establishment of the International Labour Organisation, whose mission included the regulation of working conditions, the prevention of unemployment, protection against sickness, disease and injury, the protection of children, young persons, women, and older persons. It is surely significant, then, that economic and social rights were central to the first initiatives in the development of international human rights law. Two decades later, 'freedom from want' was one of the four freedoms proposed by Franklin D. Roosevelt in his 1941 State of the Union Speech. Later that year, in the Atlantic Charter, Roosevelt and Churchill affirmed the 'desire to bring about the fullest collaboration between all nations in the economic field with the object of securing, for all, improved labour standards, economic advancement, and social security'. In 1944, Roosevelt developed this slogan into what has been called the 'Second Bill of Rights', explaining that 'true individual freedom cannot exist without economic security and independence. "Necessitous men are not free men." People who are hungry and out of a job are the stuff of which dictatorships are made.' Roosevelt listed several rights, including the right to a useful and remunerative job, to a decent home, to adequate medical care, to adequate protection from the economic fears of old age, sickness, accident, and unemployment, and the right to a good education.[2]

Economic and social rights were not addressed in some of the early attempts at drafting a declaration of human rights, by the Institut de Droit International, in 1929,[3] the London International Assembly, in 1943,[4] and by Hersch Lauterpacht, in 1945.[5] Reflecting Roosevelt's understanding of human rights, an internal draft declaration prepared in the Department of State in 1943 listed, as Article II, 'the right to enjoy such minimum standards of economic, social and cultural well-being as

[1] Treaty of Peace between the Allied and Associated Powers and Germany ('Treaty of Versailles'), (1919) TS 4, Part XIII, Preamble; Treaty of St Germain-en-Laye, [1919] TS 11, Part XIII, Preamble; Treaty of Neuilly, [1920] TS 5, Part XII, Preamble; Treaty of Trianon, (1919) 6 LNTS 187, Part XIII, Preamble.

[2] Congressional Record, 1944, Vol. 90, Pt. 2, 11 January 1944.

[3] Institut de Droit International, 'Declaration of the International Rights of Man', (1941) 35 *American Journal of International Law* 663.

[4] 'Basic Principles as formulated by the Legal Commission of the London International Assembly', TNA LNU 6/7.

[5] Hersch Lauterpacht, *An International Bill of the Rights of Man*, New York: Columbia University Press, 1945, pp. 70–71.

The Customary International Law of Human Rights. William A. Schabas, Oxford University Press.
 DOI: 10.1093/oso/9780192845696.003.0010

the resources of the country, effectively used, are capable of sustaining', ahead of the right to equality and the right to life.[6] Economic and social rights also had an important place in the draft declarations proposed by Panama and Cuba for inclusion in the Charter of the United Nations,[7] and in the submissions early in the drafting of the Universal Declaration of Human Rights.[8]

Economic, social, and cultural rights are set out in six articles of the Universal Declaration of Human Rights.[9] Their status in the catalogue of human rights was soon challenged by wealthy States. They considered that these rights did not belong in the international covenant that was being drafted to complement the Universal Declaration of Human Rights. In 1950, the Economic and Social Council asked the General Assembly to take a policy decision on the inclusion of economic, social, and cultural rights in the draft covenant.[10] The General Assembly confirmed that 'the enjoyment of civil and political freedoms and of economic, social and cultural rights are interconnected and interdependent', and that 'when deprived of economic, social and cultural rights, man does not represent the human person whom the Universal Declaration regards as the idea of the free man'.[11] Unhappy with such a result, the opponents of including economic, social, and cultural rights in the Covenant resumed the battle the following year. In 1952, the General Assembly, by a vote of twenty-seven in favour to twenty opposed, decided to draft two covenants, one on civil and political rights and the other on economic, social, and cultural rights.[12] The two Covenants were ultimately adopted by the General Assembly together, as if they are twins, but in reality they are more like cousins.

There is a lack of symmetry in the two Covenants that implies that civil and political rights are more fundamental than economic and social rights. Much has been done since the adoption of the Covenants to correct this distortion. Yet, the historic relegation of economic, social, and cultural rights to a second-class status continues to the present day. It has also infected discussion of the content of customary law and of *jus cogens* norms. Examples of customary and peremptory norms focus

[6] 'Bill of Rights', in *Postwar Foreign Policy Preparation 1939–1945*, Washington: Department of State, 1949, p. 483.

[7] Cuba: Declaration of the International Rights and Duties of the Individual, Doc. 2 G/14 (g), 2 May 1945, III UNCIO 500-502, art. V; Panama: Declaration of Essential Human Rights, Doc. G/7 (g)(2), VI UNCIO 546-549, arts. 11–15.

[8] Cuba, Draft Declaration of Human Rights, E/HR/1, arts. 8–14; Statement of Essential Human Rights Presented by the Delegation of Panama, E/HR/3, arts. 11–15; Draft Declaration of the International Rights and Duties of Man Formulated by the Inter-American Juridical Committee, E/CN.4/2, arts. 14, 16, 17; Proposal Submitted by American Federation of Labor, E/CT.2/2, art. IV(3) and (4).

[9] Universal Declaration of Human Rights, A/RES/217 (III), arts. 22–27.

[10] Report of the Commission on Human Rights, Sixth Session, E/RES/303 (XI), Part I.

[11] Draft International Covenant on Human Rights and measures of implementation: future work of the Commission on Human Rights, A/RES/421 (V), Part E, Preamble.

[12] Preparation of two Draft International Covenants on Human Rights A/RES/543 (VI), para. 1.

on such issues as the prohibition of torture, slavery, and arbitrary detention, and generally neglect economic, social, and cultural rights as candidates. It is the contention of this study that many economic, social, and cultural rights have as strong a claim to customary status as classic civil and political rights.

One of the distinctions between the two Covenants concerns the nature of the obligations of States Parties. Whereas the International Covenant on Civil and Political Rights requires a State 'to respect and to ensure to all individuals within its territory and subject to its jurisdiction the rights recognised in the present Covenant',[13] the International Covenant on Economic, Social and Cultural Rights imposes an obligation 'to take steps, individually and through international assistance and co-operation, especially economic and technical, to the maximum of its available resources, with a view to achieving progressively the full realisation of the rights recognised in the present Covenant'.[14] In a very general sense, the reporting by States to the Human Rights Council pursuant to the Universal Periodic Review, whether or not they are parties to one or both of the Covenants, tends to reflect these understandings of the nature of such obligations. This is also evident in the questions and recommendations of States during the Universal Periodic Review. Whereas immediate compliance with civil and political rights is expected, there is an expectation that many obligations of an economic and social nature depend upon available resources and are subject to progressive implementation.

For example, Bhutan was urged to 'ensure non-discrimination of members of the LGBT community', implying immediate compliance, and to 'improve the situation of women farmers', indicating a progressive obligation.[15] Several States called upon Brunei Darussalam to repeal immediately corporal punishments such as stoning and amputation[16] and end criminalisation of consensual same-sex activity,[17] while others said it should '[c]ontinue enhancing its programmes on the economic participation of women and youth'[18] and 'further raise people's living standards'.[19] Saudi Arabia received recommendations to 'guarantee due process'[20] and 'adopt a moratorium on the death penalty',[21] as well as to '[c]ontinue efforts to strengthen the quality of education'.[22]

[13] International Covenant on Civil and Political Rights, (1976) 999 UNTS 171, art. 2(1).
[14] International Covenant on Economic, Social and Cultural Rights, (1976) 993 UNTS 3, art. 2(1).
[15] Bhutan, Report of the Working Group, A/HRC/42/8, paras. 157.24, 157.64.
[16] Brunei Darussalam, Report of the Working Group, A/HRC/42/11, paras. 121.37, 121.39–121.340.
[17] Ibid., paras. 121.38, 121.40, 121.41.
[18] Ibid., para. 121.101.
[19] Ibid., para. 121.105.
[20] Saudi Arabia, Report of the Working Group, A/HRC/40/4, para. 122.49.
[21] Ibid., paras. 122.94–122.96, 122.101–122.105.
[22] Ibid., para. 122.199.

A. Social security

The right to 'social security' was proclaimed in the Atlantic Charter, signed by the American President and the British Prime Minister in August 1941.[23] It is set out in the first of the provisions of the Universal Declaration of Human Rights in the field of economic, social, and cultural rights. The Declaration adds that everyone is entitled to realisation of the right to social security 'through national effort and international co-operation and in accordance with the organisation and resources of each State, of the economic, social and cultural rights indispensable for his dignity and the free development of his personality'.[24] Furthermore, everyone is entitled to the 'right to security in the event of unemployment, sickness, disability, widowhood, old age or other lack of livelihood in circumstances beyond his control'.[25] The International Covenant on Economic, Social and Cultural Rights is more succinct: 'The States Parties to the present Covenant recognise the right of everyone to social security, including social insurance.'[26] There is a requirement that working mothers be accorded 'paid leave or leave with adequate social security benefits' during a reasonable period before and after childbirth.[27] The right to social security also appears in several specialised and regional treaties.[28]

There are no reservations to Article 9 of the International Covenant on Economic, Social and Cultural Rights that cast doubt on the recognition by States Parties of the principle of the right to social security.[29] This is confirmed in their periodic reports to the Committee on Economic, Social and Cultural Rights by those States that have formulated reservations.[30]

States that have not ratified the International Covenant on Economic, Social and Cultural Rights consistently report on various social security schemes that they

[23] Joint Statement by President Roosevelt and Prime Minister Churchill, 14 August 1941', FRUS 1941 I, pp. 367-369, recital five.

[24] Universal Declaration of Human Rights, A/RES/217 (III) , art. 22.

[25] Ibid., art. 25.

[26] International Covenant on Economic, Social and Cultural Rights, (1976) 993 UNTS 3, art. 9.

[27] Ibid., art. 10(2).

[28] International Convention on the Elimination of All Forms of Racial Discrimination, (1969) 660 UNTS 195, art. 5(e)(iv); Convention on the Elimination of All Forms of Discrimination against Women, (1981) 1249 UNTS 13, arts. 11(1)(e) and 14(2)(c); Convention on the Rights of the Child, (1990) 1571 UNTS 3, art. 26(4); International Convention on the Protection of the Rights of all Migrant Workers and Members of their Families, (2003) 2220 UNTS 3, art. 27; Additional Protocol to the American Convention on Human Rights in the area of Economic, Social and Cultural Rights, OASTS 69, art. 9; European Social Charter, CETS 35, arts. 12–14; European Social Charter (revised), CETS 163, arts. 12–14; Arab Charter on Human Rights, art. 36.

[29] Reservations or declarations have been formulated by France, C.N.335.1980.TREATIES-10 (' ... not to be interpreted as derogating from provisions governing the access of aliens to employment ... ') and by Monaco, C.N.382.1997.TREATIES-5/9 (' ... should not be constituting an impediment to provisions governing access to work by foreigners ... ').

[30] France, Fourth periodic report, E/C.12/FRA/4, paras. 306–333; Monaco, Initial report, E/1990/5/Add.64, paras. 110–157.

operate.[31] One of them, Saint Lucia, cited Article 22 of the Universal Declaration of Human Rights as the basis for its national social security system.[32]

Taken as a whole, these materials provide very strong evidence that the right to social security is a norm of customary international law.

The Committee on Economic, Social and Cultural Rights considers that the right to social security 'encompasses the right to access and maintain benefits, whether in cash or in kind, without discrimination in order to secure protection, inter alia, from (a) lack of work-related income caused by sickness, disability, maternity, employment injury, unemployment, old age, or death of a family member; (b) unaffordable access to health care; (c) insufficient family support, particularly for children and adult dependents'.[33] The Committee explains that social security, 'through its redistributive character, plays an important role in poverty reduction and alleviation, preventing social exclusion and promoting social inclusion'.[34]

The General Comment explains that implementation of the right requires that 'a system, whether composed of a single scheme or variety of schemes, is available and in place to ensure that benefits are provided for the relevant social risks and contingencies. The system should be established under domestic law, and public authorities must take responsibility for the effective administration or supervision of the system.' Such schemes must be sustainable so that they may cover both present and future generations.[35] The Committee on Economic, Social and Cultural Rights lists nine principal branches of social security: health care; sickness; old age; unemployment; employment injury; family and child support; maternity; disability; survivors and orphans.[36]

* * *

Conclusions. Everyone, as a member of society, has the right to social security and is entitled to realisation, through national effort and international co-operation and in accordance with the organisation and resources of each State, of the economic, social, and cultural rights indispensable for his dignity and the free development of his or her personality.

[31] Andorra, National report, A/HRC/WG.6/22/AND/1, paras. 14–15 and National report, A/HRC/WG.6/9/AND/1, paras. 70–78; Singapore, National report, A/HRC/WG.6/11/SGP/1, paras. 59–60 and Report of the Working Group, A/HRC/18/11, para. 51; United Arab Emirates, National report, A/HRC/10/75, para. 11 and National report, A/HRC/WG.6/3/ARE/1, pp. 8, 12, 17, 24; St Kitts and Nevis, Report of the Working Group, A/HRC/17/12, para. 34; Saudi Arabia, National report, A/HRC/WG.6/4/SAU/1, paras. 11, 47; Sudan, National report, A/HRC/18/16/Add.1, para. 30 and National report, A/HRC/WG.6/11/SDN/1, paras. 51–53; Bhutan, National report, A/HRC/WG.6/19/BTN/1, para. 117; Brunei Darussalam, National report, A/HRC/WG.6/33/BRN/1, para. 94.

[32] Saint Lucia, National report, A/HRC/WG.6/10/LCA/1, para. 67.

[33] General Comment No. 19, The right to social security (art. 9), E/C.12/GC/19, para. 2.

[34] Ibid., para. 3.

[35] Ibid., para. 11.

[36] Ibid., paras. 12–21.

B. Right to work

The 'right to work is enshrined in Article 23(1) of the Universal Declaration of Human Rights: 'Everyone has the right to work, to free choice of employment, to just and favourable conditions of work and to protection against unemployment.' It is also recognised in many international human rights treaties, including the International Covenant on Economic, Social and Cultural Rights,[37] African Charter of Human and Peoples' Rights,[38] the Protocol of San Salvador,[39] the Arab Charter on Human Rights,[40] the European Social Charter,[41] the Apartheid Convention,[42] the Charter of Fundamental Rights of the European Union,[43] and the specialised anti-discrimination conventions.[44] The Convention on the Elimination of All Forms of Discrimination against Women describes the right to work as an inalienable right of all human beings.[45]

There are no reservations to Article 6 of the International Covenant on Economic, Social and Cultural Rights that would cast doubt on the recognition by States Parties of the essence of the right to work.[46] This is confirmed in the reports of these States to the Committee on Economic, Social and Cultural Rights.[47]

The right to work has also been acknowledged in reports under the Universal Periodic Review mechanism from States that have not ratified the International Covenant on Economic, Social and Cultural Rights and that do not appear to have any treaty obligations on the subject.[48] For example, Saudi Arabia stated that 'the

[37] International Covenant on Economic, Social and Cultural Rights, (1976) 993 UNTS 3, art. 6.

[38] African Charter on Human and Peoples' Rights, (1986) 1520 UNTS 271, art. 15.

[39] Additional Protocol to the American Convention on Human Rights in the area of Economic, Social and Cultural Rights, OASTS 69, art. 6.

[40] Arab Charter on Human Rights, art. 34.

[41] European Social Charter, ETS 35, Part I; European Social Charter (Revised), ETS 163, Part I.

[42] International Convention on the Suppression and Punishment of the Crime of Apartheid, (1976) 1015 UNTS 244, art. II(c).

[43] Charter of Fundamental Rights of the European Union, OJ C 326/391, art. 15.

[44] Convention on the Rights of Persons with Disabilities, (2008) 2515 UNTS 3, art. 27; International Convention on the Elimination of All Forms of Racial Discrimination, (1969) 660 UNTS 195, art. 5(e)(1); Convention on the Elimination of All Forms of Discrimination against Women, (1981) 1249 UNTS 13, art. 11(1)(a).

[45] Convention on the Elimination of All Forms of Discrimination against Women, (1981) 1249 UNTS 13, art. 11(1).

[46] Reservations or interpretative declarations have been formulated by France, C.N.335.1980. TREATIES-10 ('… not to be interpreted as derogating from provisions governing the access of aliens to employment … '); Monaco, C.N.382.1997.TREATIES-5/9 (' … should not be constituting an impediment to provisions governing access to work by foreigners … '); United Kingdom, C.H.193.1976. TREATIES-6 ('… reserve the right to interpret article 6 as not precluding the imposition of restrictions, based on place of birth or residence qualifications, on the taking of employment in any particular region or territory for the purpose of safeguarding the employment opportunities of workers in that region or territory … ').

[47] France, Fourth periodic report, E/C.12/FRA/4, paras. 117–235; Monaco, Initial report, E/1990/5/Add.64, paras. 17–37.

[48] Andorra, National report, A/HRC/WG.6/9/AND/1, paras. 58–63; United Arab Emirates, National report, A/HRC/WG.6/3/ARE/1, pp. 10, 17; Samoa, National report, A/HRC/WG.6/11/WSM/1, paras. 90–93; Saint Lucia, National report, A/HRC/WG.6/23/LCA/2, paras. 39–40; St Kitts and Nevis, A/HRC/31/16/Add.1, Views on conclusions, para. 20.

right to work is a basic human right'.[49] The right to work is also guaranteed in many national constitutions.[50]

These materials, taken together, provide compelling evidence that the human right to work is a norm of customary international law.

The Committee on Economic, Social and Cultural Rights has explained that the right to work 'should not be understood as an absolute and unconditional right to obtain employment'. Rather, it imposes upon States an obligation to adopt policies aimed at full employment, including the establishment of vocational guidance and training programmes. Clearly, the nature of the work is not unqualified. It must be 'decent' work, meaning that it must respect fundamental human rights, ensure a safe working environment, and provide adequate remuneration permitting workers to support themselves and provide for their families.[51]

The right to 'free choice of employment' implies, according to the Committee on Economic, Social and Cultural Rights, 'not being forced in any way whatsoever to exercise or engage in employment'.[52] Article 6 of the Covenant formulates this as 'the opportunity to gain his living by work which he freely chooses or accepts'. One of the early treaties of the International Labour Organisation, adopted in 1929, defines forced labour as 'all work or service which is exacted from any person under the menace of any penalty and for which the said person has not offered himself voluntarily'.[53] This aspect of the right to work is closely linked to the prohibition of servitude, which is associated with the guarantee against slavery.

The right to work necessarily implies the right to protection against unemployment. Modern capitalist economies are premised on maintaining a minimum level of unemployment as a mechanism to ensure competition for employment. This cannot easily be reconciled with recognition of a right to work although the practice is sufficiently widespread and accepted that it may be difficult to insist this violates customary international law. Yet unemployment in many countries reaches levels that go well beyond any possible economic justification, especially for youth and vulnerable groups or those traditionally subject to discrimination on racial, gender, and other prohibited grounds.

The right to just and favourable conditions of work has several aspects, described in detail in Article 7 of the International Covenant on Economic, Social and Cultural Rights. The first is the right to 'decent' remuneration 'for themselves and their families', a formulation that acknowledging wages must do more than merely

[49] Saudi Arabia, National report, A/HRC/WG.6/4/SAU/1, para. 47.

[50] Central African Republic, National report, A/HRC/WG.6/17/CAF/1, para. 14; Saudi Arabia, National report, A/HRC/WG.6/4/SAU/1, para. 11; United Arab Emirates, National report, A/HRC/WG.6/3/ARE/1, para. 2.1; Tonga, National report, A/HRC/WG.6/2/TON/1, para. 42.

[51] General Comment No. 18, art. 6 of the International Covenant on Economic, Social and Cultural Rights, E/C.12/GC/18, para. 7.

[52] The right to work, General Comment No. 18, E/C.12/GC/18, para. 6.

[53] Convention 29 concerning Forced or Compulsory Labour, 1930, art. 2(1). Also Convention 105 concerning the Abolition of Forced Labour, (1959) 320 UNTS 291.

provide subsistence of an individual. Article 23(3) of the Universal Declaration of Human Rights speaks of remuneration capable of ensuring 'an existence worthy of human dignity'. Wages must be 'fair', and there must be equal remuneration for work of equal value. The second aspect is the assurance of safe and healthy working conditions. The third aspect listed by the International Covenant is described as '[e]qual opportunity for everyone to be promoted in his employment to an appropriate higher level, subject to no considerations other than those of seniority and competence'. This does not appear to be anything more than the protection against discrimination guaranteed more generally under customary international law. Finally, the right to work includes a right to rest, leisure, and reasonable limitation of working hours and periodic holidays with pay, as well as remuneration for public holidays.

There is an important social dimension to the right to work that goes beyond the rights of the individual. The United Nations Declaration on Social Progress and Development states that '[s]ocial development requires the assurance to everyone of the right to work and the free choice of employment' and that '[s]ocial progress and development require the participation of all members of society in productive and socially useful labour'.[54] According to the Committee on Economic, Social and Cultural Rights, the right to work is 'essential for realising other human rights and forms an inseparable and inherent part of human dignity. Every individual has the right to be able to work, allowing him/her to live in dignity.' Moreover, '[t]he right to work contributes at the same time to the survival of the individual and to that of his/her family, and insofar as work is freely chosen or accepted, to his/her development and recognition within the community'.[55]

Labour or trade unions protect the 'collective dimension' of the right to work.[56] The existence of such institutions is assured by recognition of freedom of association. Two components of the activities of unions are, to a greater or lesser degree, protected by labour legislation in most countries. These are the right to collective bargaining and the right to strike.[57]

* * *

Conclusions. Under customary international law, everyone has the right to work, to free choice of employment, to just and favourable conditions of work, and to protection against unemployment. Everyone, without any discrimination, has the right to equal pay for equal work. Everyone who works has the right to just and favourable remuneration ensuring for himself and his family an existence

[54] Declaration on Social Progress and Development, A/RES/2532 (XXIV), para. 6.

[55] General Comment No. 18, art. 6 of the International Covenant on Economic, Social and Cultural Rights, E/C.12/GC/18, para. 1.

[56] Ibid., para. 2.

[57] The customary nature of these rights is discussed *supra*, pp. 214–216.

worthy of human dignity, and supplemented, if necessary, by other means of social protection.

C. Adequate standard of living

Article 25(1) of the Universal Declaration of Human Rights states that '[e]veryone has the right to a standard of living adequate for the health and well-being of himself and of his family, including food, clothing, housing and medical care and necessary social services'. The International Covenant on Economic, Social and Cultural Rights partially reproduces this provision in Article 11, recognising, 'the right of everyone to an adequate standard of living for himself and his family, including adequate food, clothing and housing, and to the continuous improvement of living conditions'. Health care is addressed in a separate provision of the Covenant.[58]

The only reservations to Article 11 are by France and Monaco.[59] These reservations do not cast doubt on the recognition by these two States of the principle of the right to food, to clothing, to housing, and to medical care, as the reports of these States to the Committee on Economic, Social and Cultural Rights confirm.[60]

1. Food

The right to food is listed in Article 25(1) of the Universal Declaration of Human Rights as a component of 'the right to a standard of living adequate for the health and well-being of himself and of his family'. The International Covenant on Economic, Social and Cultural Rights, specifies that the right to food includes an obligation '[t]o improve methods of production, conservation and distribution of food by making full use of technical and scientific knowledge, by disseminating knowledge of the principles of nutrition and by developing or reforming agrarian systems in such a way as to achieve the most efficient development and utilisation of natural resources'. It adds that '[t]aking into account the problems of both food-importing and food-exporting countries', States Parties to the Covenant are 'to ensure an equitable distribution of world food supplies in relation to need'.[61]

58 International Covenant on Economic, Social and Cultural Rights, (1976) 993 UNTS 3, art. 12.

59 Reservations or declarations have been formulated by France, C.N.335.1980.TREATIES-10 (' … not to be interpreted as derogating from provisions governing the access of aliens to employment … '); Monaco, C.N.382.1997.TREATIES-5/9 (' … should not be constituting an impediment to provisions governing access to work by foreigners … ').

60 France, Fourth periodic report, E/C.12/FRA/4, paras. 380–428; Monaco, Initial report, E/1990/5/Add.64, paras. 209–224.

61 International Covenant on Economic, Social and Cultural Rights, (1976) 993 UNTS 3, art. 11(2).

Specialised and regional treaties also recognise the right to food.[62] The Convention on the Rights of the Child affirms a right to 'adequate and nutritious foods'.[63] The human right to food is also confirmed by the prohibition of starvation as a method of warfare[64] and its prosecution as a war crime under international law.[65]

Some of the States that have not ratified the International Covenant on Economic, Social and Cultural Rights explicitly acknowledge the right to food in their reports to the Human Rights Council.[66] Others appear to prefer the expression 'food security'.[67] Most of them address issues of access to food in their reports, and none contests or challenges the place of access to food within the general scheme of the protection of human rights.

These materials, taken together, offer strong confirmation that the right to food is a norm of customary international law.

The right to food might also be formulated as 'freedom from hunger', but while this may be at the core there are other dimensions that must not be overlooked or neglected. In its General Comment on the right to food, the Committee on Economic, Social and Cultural Rights declared that the right was realised by both 'physical and economic access at all times to adequate food or means for its procurement'.[68] The Committee said that the core content of a right to adequate food consisted of 'availability of food in a quantity and quality sufficient to satisfy the dietary needs of individuals, free from adverse substances, and acceptable within a given culture'.[69] Consequently, the diet as a whole must contain 'a mix of nutrients for physical and mental growth, development and maintenance,

[62] Convention on the Rights of Persons with Disabilities, (2008) 2515 UNTS 3, art. 28(1); Arab Charter on Human Rights, art. 38.; Additional Protocol to the American Convention on Human Rights in the area of Economic, Social and Cultural Rights, OASTS 69, art. 12.

[63] Convention on the Rights of the Child, (1990) 1571 UNTS 3, art. 24(2)(c); also art. 27(3).

[64] Additional Protocol to the 1949 Geneva Conventions and Relating to the Protection of Victims of International Armed Conflicts, (1979) 1125 UNTS 3, art. 54(1); Additional Protocol to the 1949 Geneva Conventions and Relating to the Protection of Victims of Non-International Armed Conflicts, (1979) 1125 UNTS 3, art. 14; Jean-Marie Henckaerts and Louise Doswald-Beck, *Customary International Humanitarian Law*, Vol. I, Cambridge: Cambridge University Press, 2005, p. 186.

[65] Rome Statute of the International Criminal Court (2002) 2187 UNTS 689, art. 8(2)(b)(xxv) and 8(2)(e)(xix). Art. 8(2)(e)(xix) was adopted in December 2019, by Resolution on amendments to art. 8 of the Rome Statute of the International Criminal Court, ICC-ASP/18/Res.5, and is not yet in force.

[66] Mozambique, National report, A/HRC/WG.6/10/MOZ/1, paras. 103–110; Kiribati, National report, A/HRC/WG.6/35/KIR/1, paras. 91–92 ; Tonga, Report of the Working Group, A/HRC/8/48, para. 60; Saudi Arabia, National report, A/HRC/WG.6/31/SAU/1, para. 140.

[67] Brunei Darussalam, in Saudi Arabia, Report of the Working Group, A/HRC/40/4, para. 28; Nauru, National report, A/HRC/WG.6/10/NRU/1, paras. 102–105; Tuvalu, National report, A/HRC/WG.6/16/TUV/1, paras. 10, 25, 75; Malaysia, in Brunei Darussalam, Report of the Working Group, A/HRC/42/11, para. 121.136; South Sudan, National report, A/HRC/WG.6/26/SSD/1, paras. 63–65; Samoa, Report of the Working Group, A/HRC/18/14, para. 24; Nauru, Report of the Working Group, A/HRC/17/3, para. 24; Botswana, Report of the Working Group, A/HRC/38/8, para. 37; United States of America, National report, A/HRC/WG.6/22/USA/1, para. 100; Federated States of Micronesia, A/HRC/WG.6/23/FSM/1, para. 14.

[68] General Comment 12, The right to adequate food (art. 11), E/C.12/1999/5, para. 6.

[69] Ibid., para. 8.

and physical activity that are in compliance with human physiological needs at all stages throughout the life cycle and according to gender and occupation'.[70]

2. Clothing

The right to 'clothing' is set out in Article 25(1) of the Universal Declaration of Human Rights and in Article 11(1) of the International Covenant on Economic, Social and Cultural Rights, where it is a component of the right to an adequate standard of living. It also appears in similar lists of components of the right to an adequate standard of living in some of the specialised and regional treaties. Article 28(1) of the Convention on the Rights of Persons with Disabilities refers to the right to an 'adequate standard of living' for disabled persons and their families 'including adequate food, clothing and housing'.[71] Clothing seems to have been overlooked in the standard of living provisions of other treaties, including the International Convention on the Elimination of All Forms of Racial Discrimination,[72] the Convention on the Elimination of All Forms of Discrimination against Women,[73] as well as in the Vienna Declaration and Programme of Action of 1993.[74]

The right to clothing can be found in some of the earliest efforts at codification of fundamental human rights. The Cuban draft bill of rights, submitted to the first session of the United Nations General Assembly in February 1946, contained the following: 'The right to hygienic living conditions and to clothing suitable for the climate in which he lives'.[75] Subsequently, it appeared within an enumeration in the early drafts of the Universal Declaration of Human Rights—'adequate food, clothing, housing and medical care'[76]—and remained there without further discussion or debate.

The right to clothing has attracted little attention. In its General Comment on the right to health, the Committee on Economic, Social and Cultural Rights referred, but only in a footnote, to 'adequate protective clothing' for workers in order to reduce the risk of occupational accidents.[77] Otherwise, it does not appear to have devoted any attention to the subject in its general comments. Perfunctory

[70] Ibid., para. 9.

[71] Convention on the Rights of the Child, (1990) 1571 UNTS 3, art. 27(3); Convention on the Rights of Persons with Disabilities, (2008) 2515 UNTS 3, art. 28(1); Arab Charter on Human Rights, art. 38.

[72] International Convention on the Elimination of All Forms of Racial Discrimination, (1969) 660 UNTS 195, art. 5(e).

[73] Convention on the Elimination of All Forms of Discrimination against Women, (1981) 1249 UNTS 13, art. 14(2)(h).

[74] Vienna Declaration and Programme of Action, A/CONF.157/23, para. 31.

[75] Draft Declaration on Human Rights and Letter of Transmittal, E/HR/1, para. 12.

[76] E/CN.4/AC.2/SR.8, p. 10.

[77] General Comment 14, The right to the highest attainable standard of health (art. 12 of the International Covenant on Economic, Social and Cultural Rights), E/C.12/2000/4, para. 46, fn. 25.

references to 'clothing' in the Universal Periodic Review materials confirm the lack of interest in the issue.[78]

Although a neglected right, it cannot be said that it is a controversial one. Perhaps the lack of attention only reflects the fact that there are few violations. That is not a reason to reject inclusion of the right to clothing in the catalogue of customary human rights norms.

3. Housing

The right to housing is one of the components that is associated with the right to an adequate standard of living, set out in Article 25(1) of the Universal Declaration of Human Rights and Article 11(1) of the International Covenant on Economic, Social and Cultural Rights. Specialised and regional treaties also recognise the right to housing.[79]

Several States that are not parties to the International Covenant on Economic, Social and Cultural Rights affirm their recognition of the right to housing.[80] The first heading under the title 'Economic, social and cultural rights' in Saudi Arabia's National report was: 'Housing: Efforts have been directed towards providing suitable housing for every citizen.'[81] Saint Lucia describes 'affordable housing as a basic right for its people'.[82] Mozambique formulates it as 'a fundamental right', noting that it is enshrined in the country's Constitution.[83] United Arab Emirates affirms that '[t]he State supplies and creates suitable housing for citizens'.[84] South Sudan reported that its Transitional Constitution sets out a right to decent housing.[85] Under the heading 'Adequate Housing', Brunei Darussalam says it is 'committed to improve the quality of life in Brunei by providing sustainable and affordable housing for the citizen'.[86] In its reports, the United States has described activities intended

[78] For example, China, National report, A/HRC/WG.6/4/CHN/1, para. 30.

[79] Convention on the Rights of Persons with Disabilities, (2008) 2515 UNTS 3, art. 28(1); Arab Charter on Human Rights, art. 38; International Convention on the Protection of the Rights of all Migrant Workers and Members of their Families, (2003) 2220 UNTS 3, art. 43(1)(d); Convention on the Elimination of All Forms of Discrimination against Women, (1981) 1249 UNTS 13, art. 14(2)(h); European Social Charter (Revised), CETS 163, art. 31; International Convention on the Elimination of All Forms of Racial Discrimination, (1969) 660 UNTS 195, art. 5(e)(iii); Convention on the Rights of the Child, (1990) 1571 UNTS 3, art. 24(2)(c) and art. 27(3).

[80] Botswana, National report, A/HRC/WG.6/29/BWA/1, paras. 14–15; Tuvalu, National report, A/HRC/WG.6/30/TUV/1, para. 20 and Report of the Working Group, A/HRC/39/8, para. 16; Saudi Arabia, National report, A/HRC/WG.6/31/SAU/1, para. 17; Singapore, National report, A/HRC/WG.6/11/SGP/1, paras. 3, 43–46, 157.

[81] Saudi Arabia, National report, A/HRC/WG.6/17/SAU/1, para. 76.

[82] Saint Lucia, National report, A/HRC/WG.6/23/LCA/1, para. 7. Also Saint Lucia, National report, A/HRC/WG.6/10/LCA/1, paras. 96–99.

[83] Mozambique, National report, A/HRC/WG.6/10/MOZ/1, para. 111 and A/HRC/WG.6/24/MOZ/1, paras. 66–67.

[84] United Arab Emirates, National report, A/HRC/WG.6/3/ARE/1, pp. 25–26.

[85] South Sudan, Report of the Working Group, A/HRC/34/13, para. 15.

[86] Brunei Darussalam, National report, A/HRC/WG.6/33/BRN/1, para. 19.

to eliminate homelessness as well as discrimination in housing.[87] St Kitts and Nevis reported on its commitment 'to providing adequate and affordable housing that will improve the quality and standard of life of its people'.[88]

Adequate housing must deliver more than four walls and a roof, according to the Office of the High Commissioner for Human Rights.[89] First and foremost, it must provide shelter from the elements as well as privacy and security. But the right to adequate housing also requires the availability of services, materials, facilities, and infrastructure so as to ensure that residents have facilities essential to a dignified life including health, security, comfort, and nutrition. Elements of adequate housing include access to safe drinking water, sanitary and washing facilities, and facilities for cooking and light, as well as heat where this is required by the climate.[90] Even when these criteria are met, housing may not be adequate if the environment is unsuitable, due for example to pollution by industry, hazards such as flooding, disease, and ambient noise, and proximity to armed conflict.

Housing necessitates protection by the law in the form of 'legal security of tenure'. This may take many different forms short of unconditional ownership including rental (public and private) accommodation, cooperative housing, lease, owner-occupation, emergency housing, and informal settlements, including occupation of land or property. Whatever the form of tenure, according to the Committee on Economic, Social and Cultural Rights, 'all persons should possess a degree of security of tenure which guarantees legal protection against forced eviction, harassment and other threats'.[91] In a contentious case involving the right to housing, the Committee said that for an eviction to be compatible with the right to housing, 'it must be provided for by law and carried out as a last resort, and the persons concerned must have had prior access to an effective judicial remedy, in order to ascertain that the measure in question is duly justified, for example, in cases where there is no legal title for the tenancy. In addition, there must be a real opportunity for genuine and effective prior consultation between the authorities and the persons concerned, there must be no alternative means or measure less injurious to the right to housing available, and the persons concerned must not be left in or exposed to a situation that constitutes a violation of other human rights.'[92]

Housing must be affordable, something that is closely related to the right to employment and to wages that are adequate. Those without resources for whatever reason must be provided with adequate housing. Writing with respect to the

87 United States of America, Report of the Working Group, A/HRC/30/12, paras. 115–117. Also United States, National report, A/HRC/WG.6/9/USA/1, paras. 45–46, 74–76.

88 St Kitts and Nevis, National report, A/HRC/WG.6/10/KNA/1, para. 74.

89 *The Right to Adequate Housing, Fact Sheet No. 21/Rev.1*, Geneva: Office of the High Commissioner for Human Rights, 2009, p. 3.

90 General Comment 4, The right to adequate housing (art. 11(1) of the Covenant), E/1992/23, p. 114, para. 8(b).

91 Ibid., para. 8(a).

92 *López Albán et al. v. Spain*, no. 37/2018, Views, 11 October 2019, E/C.12/66/D/37/2018, para. 8.3.

right to access to housing as guaranteed in the South African Constitution, the Constitutional Court of South Africa noted that 'there is a difference between the position of those who can afford to pay for housing, even if it is only basic though adequate housing, and those who cannot. For those who can afford to pay for adequate housing, the state's primary obligation lies in unlocking the system, providing access to housing stock and a legislative framework to facilitate self-built houses through planning laws and access to finance. Issues of development and social welfare are raised in respect of those who cannot afford to provide themselves with housing. State policy needs to address both these groups.'[93] Closely related to affordability is the location itself, which must offer access to employment, health care, child care, education, and cultural and recreational facilities.

4. Health and medical care

The right to health and to medical care is set out in Article 25(1) of the Universal Declaration of Human Rights as a component of 'the right to a standard of living adequate for the health and well-being of himself and of his family'. A much more detailed formulation of the right to health appears in Article 12 of the International Covenant on Economic, Social and Cultural Rights. States Parties to the Covenant recognise 'the right of everyone to the enjoyment of the highest attainable standard of physical and mental health'. Several steps to be taken 'to achieve the full realisation of this right' are set out, including reduction of the stillbirth-rate and of infant mortality; the improvement of all aspects of environmental and industrial hygiene; the prevention, treatment, and control of epidemic, endemic, occupational, and other diseases; and the creation of conditions that assure medical service and medical attention to all in the event of sickness. There appear to be no reservations to Article 12 of the International Covenant on Economic, Social and Cultural Rights.

The right to health is set out in many other international instruments, including the International Convention on the Elimination of All Forms of Racial Discrimination,[94] the Convention on the Elimination of All Forms of Discrimination against Women,[95] the Convention on the Rights of the Child,[96] the Convention on the Rights of Persons with Disabilities,[97] and in several regional human rights instruments.[98]

[93] *South Africa et al. v. Grootboom et al.*, [2000] ZACC 19, para. 36.

[94] International Convention on the Elimination of All Forms of Racial Discrimination, (1969) 660 UNTS 195, art. 5(e)(iv).

[95] Convention on the Elimination of All Forms of Discrimination against Women, (1981) 1249 UNTS 13, arts. 11.1(f) and 12.

[96] Convention on the Rights of the Child, (1990) 1571 UNTS 3, art. 24.

[97] Convention on the Rights of Persons with Disabilities, (2008) 2515 UNTS 3, art. 25.

[98] African Charter on Human and Peoples' Rights, (1986) 1520 UNTS 271, art. 16; Arab Charter on Human Rights, art. 39; Additional Protocol to the American Convention on Human Rights in the area of Economic, Social and Cultural Rights, OASTS 69, art. 10; European Social Charter, CETS 35, art. 11;

Of the States that have not ratified the International Covenant on Economic, Social and Cultural Rights, almost all have addressed issues of health care in their reports to the Human Rights Council, confirming their view that it falls within their obligations under international human rights law.[99] Several of them refer explicitly to the 'right to health'.[100] For example, Myanmar 'recognised that everyone has the right to have a standard of living adequate for the health and well-being of himself and his family. The right to health is also closely related to, and dependent upon, the realisation of other human rights.'[101] A rare exception is the United States, which does not speak of a 'right to health' in its submissions to the Human Rights Council. Nevertheless, in its first National report the United States described recent legislation, known colloquially as 'Obamacare', explaining that it represented 'great strides towards the goal that all Americans have access to quality, affordable health care'.[102] In its third National report, the United States referred to the objective of making 'quality, affordable health care available to all'.[103]

The Constitution of the World Health Organisation describes health as 'a state of complete physical, mental and social well-being and not merely the absence of disease or infirmity'. In its General Comment on the right to health, the Committee on Economic, Social and Cultural Rights said health was 'a fundamental human right

European Social Charter (revised), CETS 163, art. 11; Charter of Fundamental Rights of the European Union, OJ C 326/391, art. 35; African Charter on the Rights and Welfare of the Child, art. 14.

[99] Andorra, National report, A/HRC/WG.6/9/AND/1, paras. 73–78; Bhutan, Report of the Working Group, A/HRC/WG.6/33/BTN/1, paras. 41–53 and National report, A/HRC/WG.6/19/BTN/1, para. 51; Botswana, National report, A/HRC/WG.6/3/BWA/1, para. 41 and Report of the Working Group, A/HRC/WG.6/15/BWA/1, paras. 80–82; Brunei Darussalam, National report, A/HRC/13/14, para. 13, National report, A/HRC/WG.6/19/BRN/1, paras. 75–85, and Report of the Working Group, A/HRC/27/11, para. 9; Kiribati, National report, A/HRC/WG.6/35/KIR/1, paras. 108–110; Vanuatu, National report, A/HRC/WG.6/32/VUT/1, paras. 62–63; Malaysia, Views on conclusions, A/HRC/40/11/Add.1, para. 11; Micronesia, National report, A/HRC/WG.6/9/FSM/1, para. 106 and National report, A/HRC/WG.6/9/FSM/1, para. 59; Nauru, National report, A/HRC/WG.6/10/NRU/1, paras. 83–88; St Kitts and Nevis, National report, A/HRC/WG.6/23/KNA/1, paras. 60–64; Saint Lucia, National report, A/HRC/WG.6/23/LCA/1, para. 27, National report, A/HRC/WG.6/23/LCA/1, paras. 49–58 and Report of the Working Group, A/HRC/31/10, para. 25; Saudi Arabia, Report of the Working Group, A/HRC/25/3, para. 20, National report, A/HRC/WG.6/17/SAU/1, para. 77 and National report, A/HRC/WG.6/4/SAU/1, para. 47; Singapore, National report, A/HRC/WG.6/11/SGP/1, paras. 39–42 and Views on conclusions, A/HRC/32/17/Add.1, paras. 11–13; Tonga, National report, A/HRC/WG.6/29/TON/1, para. 22; Tuvalu, National report, A/HRC/WG.6/3/TUV/1, para. 37 and Report of the Working Group, A/HRC/39/8, paras. 14; United Arab Emirates, National report, A/HRC/WG.6/29/ARE/1, para. 65 and A/HRC/WG.6/3/ARE/1, para. 5.2.

[100] Andorra, National report, A/HRC/WG.6/9/AND/1, paras. 70, 74, 104; Bhutan, Report of the Working Group, A/HRC/WG.6/33/BTN/1, paras. 41–53; Botswana, Report of the Working Group, A/HRC/WG.6/15/BWA/1, para. 32; Kiribati, National report, A/HRC/WG.6/35/KIR/1, paras. 102–107; Malaysia, Report of the Working Group, A/HRC/25/10, para. 6; Nauru, Report of the Workiong Group, A/HRC/17/3/Add.1, para. 41; St Kitts and Nevis, Report of the Working Group, A/HRC/31/16/Add.1, paras. 25–26; Saint Lucia, National report, A/HRC/WG.6/23/LCA/1, para. 49; Samoa, National report, A/HRC/WG.6/11/WSM/1, paras. 82–87; United Arab Emirates, National report, A/HRC/WG.6/29/ARE/1 para. 25; Vanuatu, Report of the Working Group, A/HRC/41/10, paras. 13, 90.30.

[101] Myanmar, National report, A/HRC/WG.6/10/MMR/1, para. 82.

[102] United States of America, National report, A/HRC/WG.6/9/USA/1, para. 70.

[103] United States of America, National report, A/HRC/WG.6/36/USA/1, para. 62.

indispensable for the exercise of other human rights'. It continued: 'Every human being is entitled to the enjoyment of the highest attainable standard of health conducive to living a life in dignity.'[104] Medical care that is accessible to all, whether this is obtained privately or furnished by the government, is absolutely fundamental to the protection of the right to health. In other words, those without means to obtain quality medical care must be provided with it. It is a right and not an obligation, and individuals are always free to deny their consent to medical care. However, the availability of medical care is only one component of the right to health. It also requires access to safe and potable water as well as to adequate sanitation, proper nutrition, and appropriate housing. The collective dimension of the right to health was highlighted by the great pandemic of 2020. Proper medical care for those infected with the virus was an entitlement derived from the right to health but it was also essential to the prevention of its spread. Treatment of those with the disease was essential to prevention for those who had been spared.

5. Water and sanitation

Despite the absence of any specific mention of water or sanitation, Article 25(1) of the Universal Declaration of Human Rights and Article 11(1) of the International Covenant on Economic, Social and Cultural Rights affirm the right to an 'adequate' standard of living, 'including' food, clothing, and housing. Prefacing the components of an adequate standard of living with the word 'including' confirms that the list is not exhaustive. 'Water is a limited natural resource and a public good fundamental for life and health. The human right to water is indispensable for leading a life in human dignity', wrote the Committee on Economic, Social and Cultural Rights in its General Comment on the subject.[105]

A right to water and sanitation appears in a few specialised treaties.[106] International humanitarian law treaties describe 'drinking water installations'[107] as being indispensable to the survival of the civilian population. The Arab

[104] General Comment 14, The Right to the Highest Attainable Standard of Health (art. 12), E/C.12/2000/4, para. 1.

[105] General Comment 15, The right to water (arts. 11 and 12 of the International Covenant on Economic, Social and Cultural Rights), E/C.12/2002/11, para. 1.

[106] Convention on the Elimination of All Forms of Discrimination against Women, (1981) 1249 UNTS 13, art. 14(2)(h) provides a right to 'sanitation, electricity and water supply' for women in rural areas; Convention on the Rights of the Child, (1990) 1571 UNTS 3, art. 24(2)(c) guarantees 'clean drinking-water'; Convention on the Rights of Persons with Disabilities, (2008) 2515 UNTS 3, art. 26(1)(a) ensures the right to 'clean water'.

[107] Additional Protocol to the 1949 Geneva Conventions and Relating to the Protection of Victims of International Armed Conflicts, (1979) 1125 UNTS 3, art. 54(2); Additional Protocol to the 1949 Geneva Conventions and Relating to the Protection of Victims of Non-International Armed Conflicts, (1979) 1125 UNTS 3, art. 14. Also Jean-Marie Henckaerts and Louise Doswald-Beck, *Customary International Humanitarian Law*, Vol. I, Cambridge: Cambridge University Press, 2005, p. 193.

Charter on Human Rights requires 'provision of ... safe drinking water for all'.[108] Acknowledging that there is no 'right to water' as such enshrined in the European Convention on Human Rights, the European Court of Human Rights has nevertheless recognised that 'without water the human person cannot survive. A persistent and long-standing lack of access to safe drinking water can therefore, by its very nature, have adverse consequences for health and human dignity effectively eroding the core of private life and the enjoyment of a home.'[109]

Resolutions of the United Nations General Assembly, adopted by near unanimity, have affirmed 'that the human rights to safe drinking water and sanitation, as components of the right to an adequate standard of living, are essential for the full enjoyment of the right to life and all human rights'. Furthermore, 'the human right to safe drinking water entitles everyone, without discrimination, to have access to sufficient, safe, acceptable, physically accessible and affordable water for personal and domestic use, and that the human right to sanitation entitles everyone, without discrimination, to have physical and affordable access to sanitation, in all spheres of life, that is safe, hygienic, secure, socially and culturally acceptable and that provides privacy and ensures dignity, while reaffirming that both rights are components of the right to an adequate standard of living'.[110] The General Assembly has designated 19 November as 'World Toilet Day'.[111]

Many States refer explicitly to the 'right to water' in national reports to the Human Rights Council[112] or when questioning other States during the Universal Periodic Review.[113] In an investment arbitration case, Argentina raised a defence of necessity based upon the importance of water 'to the life and health of the population ... Because of the fundamental role of water in sustaining life and health and the consequent human right to water, it maintains that in judging the conformity of governmental actions with treaty obligations this Tribunal must grant Argentina a broader margin of discretion in the present cases than in cases involving other commodities and services.'[114]

[108] Arab Charter on Human Rights, art. 39(2)(c).

[109] *Hudorović et al. v. Slovenia*, nos. 24816/14 and 25140/14, § 116, 10 March 2020.

[110] The human rights to safe drinking water and sanitation, A/RES/72/178, paras. 1–2. It was adopted by a recorded vote of 183 in favour, one against (Kyrgyzstan), with two abstentions (South Africa, Turkey): A/72/PV.73, p. 20. See also The human right to safe drinking water and sanitation, A/RES/70/169; The human right to safe drinking water and sanitation, A/RES/68/157; The human right to water and sanitation, A/RES/64/292.

[111] Sanitation for All, A/RES/67/291.

[112] Benin, National report, A/HRC/WG.6/28/BEN/1, paras. 47–50; Eritrea, National report, A/HRC/WG.6/18/ERI/1, paras. 75–76; Vanuatu, Report of the Working Group, A/HRC/26/9, para. 49; Samoa, Report of the Working Group, A/HRC/18/14, para. 66; Senegal, National report, A/HRC/WG.6/31/SEN/1, para. 127; Angola, National report, A/HRC/WG.6/20/AGO/1, para. 6; Maldives, National report, A/HRC/WG.6/9/MDV/1/Rev.1, para. 15.

[113] Libya, in Guyana, Report of the Working Group, A/HRC/15/14, para. 69.26; Germany, in Guyana, Report of the Working Group, A/HRC/15/14, para. 51; Bolivia, in United States of America, Report of the Working Group, A/HRC/30/12, para. 176.312.

[114] *Suez, Sociedad General de Aguas de Barcelona S.A., and Vivendi Universal S.A. v. The Argentine Republic*, ICSID Case No. ARB/03/19, Decision on Liability, 30 July 2010, para. 252.

The United Kingdom has declared that 'right to water and the right to sanitation are *not* free-standing rights or rights under customary international law'.[115] The United States has said it recognises that the right to water and sanitation is derived from the right to an adequate standard of living but that it does not consider General Assembly resolutions on the right to be legally binding.[116]

The significance of water to an 'adequate standard of living' goes well beyond potable drinking water. It is also necessary for food production and to ensure environmental hygiene. Water contamination and diseases linked to water are often the consequence of inadequate sanitation. Moreover, in addition to personal and domestic uses water may be essential for securing livelihoods, and for recreation and culture. Nevertheless, the Committee on Economic, Social and Cultural Rights insists that priority be given to water resources necessary for the prevention of starvation and disease.[117]

Describing sanitation as a largely neglected topic, the Committee on Economic, Social and Cultural Rights has said it is 'fundamental for human survival and to enabling humans to live a life in dignity'.[118] Sanitation has been defined as 'a system for the collection, transport, treatment and disposal or re-use of human excreta and associated hygiene'. According to the Committee, everyone, without discrimination, must be provided physical and affordable access to sanitation 'in all spheres of life, which is safe, hygienic, secure, socially and culturally acceptable, provides privacy and ensures dignity'.[119]

* * *

Conclusions. Everyone has the right to an adequate standard of living, including food, clothing, housing, medical care, water, sanitation, and necessary social services, and the right to security in the event of unemployment, sickness, disability, widowhood, old age, or other lack of livelihood.

D. Education

There may be no better case for recognition of a fundamental human right as a matter of customary international law than the right to education. Until relatively recently in human history, education was reserved for the wealthy, for elites. Although basic skills, such as literacy and numeracy, have existed for 5,000 years or more, it is estimated that by 1820 only 12% of the world's population could read

[115] 'United Kingdom's position', Annex to A/HRC/21/9 (emphasis in the original).
[116] United States of America, Views on conclusions, A/HRC/30/12/Add.1, para. 12.
[117] General Comment No. 15 (2002), The right to water (arts. 11 and 12 of the International Covenant on Economic, Social and Cultural Rights), E/C.12/2002/11, para. 6.
[118] Statement on the right to sanitation, E/C.12/2010/1, paras. 1, 7.
[119] Ibid., para. 8.

and write. In the twentieth century these abilities became commonly available to the majority. UNESCO has reported that in 2016, 86% of the global adult population had basic reading and writing skills, and that the youth literacy rate was 91%. Literacy and numeracy are directly related to education from which much of the world's population, historically, was excluded. It is believed that in 1870 only one person in four attended school. In its Millennium Development Goals, the United Nations General Assembly resolved that by 2015 'children everywhere, boys and girls alike, will be able to complete a full course of primary schooling and that girls and boys will have equal access to all levels of education'.[120] Although that ambition was not achieved, there has been significant progress and success is within sight.

Education is addressed in the minorities treaties adopted following the First World War, but with respect to the language of instruction rather than the right as such.[121] The Cuban proposal for a draft declaration of human rights submitted at the first session of the General Assembly included not only the right to education but also a rationale: 'The right to education which will enable him to improve himself in every respect and will lead to his becoming a useful member of society and sharing in all the material and spiritual benefits of civilisation.'[122]

'Everyone has the right to education', proclaims Article 26 of the Universal Declaration of Human Rights. 'Education shall be free, at least in the elementary and fundamental stages. Elementary education shall be compulsory.' The Universal Declaration goes on to specify that '[t]echnical and professional education shall be made generally available and higher education shall be equally accessible to all on the basis of merit'. The International Covenant on Economic, Social and Cultural Rights recognises the right, specifying that education 'shall be directed to the full development of the human personality and the sense of its dignity, and shall strengthen the respect for human rights and fundamental freedoms'. Education is to 'enable all persons to participate effectively in a free society, promote understanding, tolerance and friendship among all nations and all racial, ethnic or religious groups, and further the activities of the United Nations for the maintenance of peace'. Exceptionally, the Covenant requires that at the primary level this be enforceable immediately, where it is to be both compulsory and free.[123] Many other specialised and regional treaties affirm a right to education.[124] The only Member

[120] United Nations Millennium Declaration, A/RES/55/2, para. 19.

[121] For example, Treaty between the Principal Allied and Associated Powers and Poland, (1919) 112 BSP 232, arts. 8–10. See the discussion *supra*, pp. 160–161.

[122] Draft Declaration on Human Rights, E/HR/1, art. 8.

[123] International Covenant on Economic, Social and Cultural Rights, (1976) 993 UNTS 3, arts. 13 and 14.

[124] International Convention on the Elimination of All Forms of Racial Discrimination, (1969) 660 UNTS 195, art. 5(e)(v); Convention on the Elimination of All Forms of Discrimination against Women, (1981) 1249 UNTS 13, art. 10; Convention on the Rights of the Child, (1990) 1571 UNTS 3, art. 28; UNESCO Convention against Discrimination in Education, (1962) 429 UNTS 92, art. 4; African Charter on the Rights and Welfare of the Child, art. 13; Convention on the Rights of Persons with Disabilities, (2008) 2515 UNTS 3, art. 24; International Convention on the Protection of the Rights of all Migrant Workers and Members of their Families, (2003) 2220 UNTS 3, art. 30; Protocol to the

State of the United Nations that is not a party to the Convention on the Rights of the Child, the United States of America, has confirmed recognition of a right to education in its reports to the Human Rights Council.[125] Judgments of the International Criminal Court have recognised the right to education as one of the 'fundamental rights' encompassed within the definition of the crime against humanity of persecution.[126]

To the basic right to free compulsory primary education, formulated in Article 28(1)(a) of the Convention on the Rights of the Child, reservations or declarations have been formulated by Malaysia (since withdrawn),[127] Samoa,[128] and Singapore.[129] But in its most recent report to the Human Rights Council, Samoa indicated that education was now free at all government primary schools.[130] Singapore's reservation notes that 'in practice virtually all children attend primary school'. There are several reservations to Article 13 of the International Covenant on Economic, Social and Cultural Rights,[131] but all of them by States that have

Convention for the Protection of Human Rights and Fundamental Freedoms, CETS 9, art. 2; Additional Protocol to the American Convention on Human Rights in the area of Economic, Social and Cultural Rights, OASTS 69, art. 13; African Charter on Human and Peoples' Rights, (1986) 1520 UNTS 217, art. 17(1); Arab Charter on Human Rights, art. 41; Charter of Fundamental Rights of the European Union, OJ C 326/391, art. 14.

125 United States of America, National report, A/HRC/WG.6/9/USA/1, paras. 47–49.

126 *Situation in the People's Republic of Bangladesh/Republic of the Union of Myanmar* (ICC-01/19), Decision Pursuant to Article 15 of the Rome Statute on the Authorisation of an Investigation into the Situation in the People's Republic of Bangladesh/Republic of the Union of Myanmar, 14 November 2019, para. 101. Also *Situation in Burundi* (ICC-01/17-X), Public Redacted Version of "Decision Pursuant to Article 15 of the Rome Statute on the Authorization of an Investigation into the Situation in the Republic of Burundi", ICC-01/17-X-9-US-Exp, 25 October 2017, 9 November 2017, para. 132; *Prosecutor v. Lubanga* (ICC-01/04-01/06), Dissenting opinion of Judge Odio-Benito, 10 July 2012, para. 21.

127 C.N.58.1995.TREATIES-1 (' … declares that [article 28(1)(a)] shall be applicable only if they are in conformity with the Constitution, national laws and national policies of the Government of Malaysia'); C.N.474.2010.TREATIES-4.

128 C.N.396.1994.TREATIES-8 (' … whilst recognising the importance of providing free primary education as specified under article 28 (1)(a) … the Government of Western Samoa thus reserves the right to allocate resources to the primary level sector of education in Western Samoa in contrast to the requirement of article 28 (1)(a) to provide free primary education').

129 C.N.370.1995.TREATIES-9 (' … (a) does not consider itself bound by the requirement to make primary education compulsory because such a measure is unnecessary in our social context where in practice virtually all children attend primary school; and (b) reserves the right to provide primary education free only to children who are citizens of Singapore').

130 National report, Samoa, A/HRC/WG.6/25/WSM/1, para. 68.

131 Algeria, C.N.247.1989.TREATIES-1/13/3 (paras. 3 and 4 'can in no case impair its right freely to organize its educational system'); Bangladesh, C.N.541.1998.TREAT1ES-1 ('Bangladesh accepts the provisions embodied in [article] 13 of the Covenant in principle, it will implement the said provisions in a progressive manner, in keeping with the existing economic conditions and the development plans of the country'); Barbados, C.N.5.1973.TREATIES-1 ('The application of article 13 (2) (a) of the Covenant, in so far as it relates to primary education; since, while the Barbados Government fully accepts the principles embodied in [article 13(2)(a)] and undertakes to take the necessary steps to apply them in their entirety, the problems of implementation are such that full application of the principles in question cannot be guaranteed at this stage.'); France, C.N.335.1980.TREATIES-10 (' … not to be interpreted as derogating from provisions … or as establishing residence requirements for the allocation of certain social benefits'); India, C.N.81.1979.TREATIES-2 (' … reserves its right to apply its law relating to foreigners …); Madagascar, C.N.54.1991.TREATIES-2 (' … reserves the right to postpone the application of article 13, paragraph 2,

made no reservation to the right to education in the Convention on the Rights of the Child. Consequently, despite reservations to the Covenant, they have accepted a legal norm requiring compulsory free primary education and the other components of the right set out in the Convention on the Rights of the Child. Moreover, none of the reservations to Article 13 of the Covenant actually challenges the obligation to provide compulsory free primary education. Rather, the reservations express difficulty in immediate implementation of the norm. There are only two reservations to certain aspects of the right to education provision of the Convention on the Rights of Persons with Disabilities.[132]

In reports to the Human Rights Council under the Universal Periodic Review mechanism, no country has suggested that it is not obliged to respect the right set out in Article 26(1) of the Universal Declaration. Indeed, those with the least impressive rates of literacy and numeracy seem especially determined to ensure universal primary education.[133] States that have not ratified the International

of the Covenant, more particularly in so far as relates to primary education, since, while the Malagasy Government fully accepts the principles embodied in the said paragraph and undertakes to take the necessary steps to apply them in their entirety at the earliest possible date, the problems of implementation, and particularly the financial implications, are such that full application of the principles in question cannot be guaranteed at this stage'); Malta, C.N.304.1990.TREATIES-4/11/4 ('... having regard to the fact that the population of Malta is overwhelmingly Roman Catholic, it is difficult also in view of limited financial and human resources, to provide such education in accordance with a particular religious or moral belief in cases of small groups, which cases are very exceptional in Malta'); Monaco, C.N.382.1997.TREATIES-5/9 ('... not to be interpreted as derogating from provisions ... or as establishing residence requirements for the allocation of certain social benefits'); South Africa, C.N.23.2015.TREATIES-IV.3 ('... will give progressive effect to the right to education, as provided for in Article 13 (2) (a) and Article 14, within the framework of its National Education Policy and available resources'); Turkey C.N.1207.2003.TREATIES-4 ('... reserved the right to interpret and apply the provisions of the paragraph (3) and (4) of Article 13 ... in accordance to the provisions under the Article 3, 14 and 42 of the Constitution of the Republic of Turkey'); United Kingdom, C.N.193.1976.TREATIES-6 ('... maintain the right to postpone the application of subparagraph (a) of paragraph 2 of article 13, and article 14, in so far as they require compulsory primary education, in the Gilbert Islands, the Solomon Islands and Tuvalu'); Zambia, C.N.82.1984.TREATIES-l/5/2 ('reserves the right to postpone the application of article 13 (2) (a) of the Covenant, in so far as it relates to primary education; since, while the Government of the Republic of Zambia fully accepts the principles embodied in the same article and undertakes to take the necessary steps to apply them in their entirety, the problems of implementation, and particularly the financial implications, are such that full application of the principles in question cannot be guaranteed at this stage').

[132] Suriname, C.N.158.2017.TREATIES-IV.15 (' ... Suriname recognises the right of persons with disabilities to education and determines to guarantee free primary education for every person. Accordingly, it declares that it shall not for the time being guarantee the application of the provision 24 paragraph 2 (b) on the condition that the educational system is still far from inclusive education'); United Kingdom, C.N.360.2009.TREATIES-15 ('The United Kingdom reserves the right for disabled children to be educated outside their local community where more appropriate education provision is available elsewhere. Nevertheless, parents of disabled children have the same opportunity as other parents to state a preference for the school at which they wish their child to be educated.')

[133] Afghanistan, National report, A/HRC/WG.6/32/AFG/1, paras. 83–94; Benin, National report, A/HRC/WG.6/28/BEN/1, paras. 66–72; Burkina Faso, National report, A/HRC/WG.6/30/BFA/1, para. 95–97; Central African Republic, National report, A/HRC/WG.6/31/CAF/1, para. 40–42; Chad, National report, A/HRC/WG.6/31/TCD/1, paras. 57–58; Comoros, National report, A/HRC/WG.6/32/COM/1, paras. 135–145; Côte d'Ivoire, National report, A/HRC/WG.6/33/CIV/1, para. 59–62; Ethiopia, National report, A/HRC/WG.6/33/ETH/1, paras. 91–97; The Gambia, National report, A/HRC/WG.6/34/GMB/1, paras. 125–136; Guinea, National report, A/HRC/WG.6/35/GIN/1, paras.

Covenant on Economic, Social and Cultural Rights nevertheless acknowledge it as a right in their reports to the Human Rights Council.[134]

Taken as a whole, these materials confirm universal recognition of a right to education at the primary level and free of charge. In terms of obligations upon the State, this means that measures must be adopted in order to enforce attendance at school. There is a duty upon children to attend school and one upon parents to ensure this. There may be other aspects of the right to education that are also customary in nature, including making secondary and technical education generally available and accessible to all, making higher education accessible on the basis of individual capacity, and ensuring that standards of education are equivalent in public educational institutions of the same level.

1. Prohibition of discrimination in education

The right to education must be ensured without discrimination. This is nothing more than a corollary of the general right to equality and prohibition of discrimination, but one that is acutely significant to the right to education. It is a constituent part of the customary right to education. As the Committee on Economic, Social and Cultural Rights has insisted, 'protection from discrimination in the field of education is an underlying and basic principle of human rights law'.[135] Stunning inequalities persist, with even the wealthiest countries still confronting the effects of

34–50; Guinea Bissau, National report, A/HRC/WG.6/35/GNB/1, paras. 49–68; Haiti, National report, A/HRC/WG.6/26/HTI/1, paras. 71–79; Iraq, National report, A/HRC/WG.6/34/IRQ/1, paras. 146–154; Liberia, National report, A/HRC/WG.6/22/LBR/1, para. 62; Mali, National report, A/HRC/WG.6/29/MLI/1, paras. 44–45; Mauritania, National report, A/HRC/WG.6/23/MRT/1, paras. 121–140; Niger, National report, A/HRC/WG.6/24/NER/1, pp. 23–24; Senegal, National report, A/HRC/WG.6/31/SEN/1, pp. 94–118; Sierra Leone, National report, A/HRC/WG.6/24/SLE/1, paras. 71–72, 76–80; South Sudan, National report, A/HRC/WG.6/26/SSD/1, paras. 66–71.

[134] Andorra, National report, A/HRC/WG.6/9/AND/1, paras. 80–86; Bhutan, National report, A/HRC/WG.6/33/BTN/1, paras. 31–32; Botswana, National report, A/HRC/WG.6/3/BWA/1, paras. 32–36; Brunei Darussalam, National report, A/HRC/WG.6/33/BRN/1, paras. 119–132; Kiribati, National report, A/HRC/WG.6/35/KIR/1, paras. 111–121; Malaysia, National report, A/HRC/WG.6/4/MYS/1/Rev.1, paras. 30–38; Micronesia, National report, A/HRC/WG.6/9/FSM/1, paras. 39–45; National report, Mozambique, A/HRC/WG.6/10/MOZ/1, paras. 72–79; Myanmar, National report, A/HRC/WG.6/10/MMR/1, paras. 90–98; Nauru, National report, A/HRC/WG.6/10/NRU/1, paras. 54–55; Saudi Arabia, National report, A/HRC/WG.6/4/SAU/1, pp. 18–19, National report, A/HRC/WG.6/17/SAU/1, para. 80, and Report of the Working Group, A/HRC/25/3, paras. 18, 62; Singapore, National report, A/HRC/WG.6/11/SGP/1, paras. 35–38; South Sudan, National report, A/HRC/WG.6/26/SSD/1, paras. 66–71; St Kitts and Nevis, National report, A/HRC/WG.6/10/KNA/1, paras. 29–35; Saint Lucia, National report, A/HRC/WG.6/10/LCA/1, paras. 36–43; Tonga, National report, A/HRC/WG.6/2/TON/1, para. 48; Tuvalu, National report, A/HRC/WG.6/3/TUV/1, paras. 38–39; United Arab Emirates, National report, A/HRC/WG.6/3/ARE/1, pp. 8, 18, 23 and A/HRC/WG.6/15/ARE/1, para. 65; United States of America, National report, A/HRC/WG.6/9/USA/1, para. 68 and A/HRC/WG.6/22/USA/1, paras. 103–104; Vanuata, National report, A/HRC/26/9, paras. 12–13.

[135] General Recommendation 36 on the right of girls and women to education, CEDAW/C/GC/36, para. 6.

racial discrimination in access to their elite educational institutions. The UNESCO Convention against Discrimination in Education, adopted in 1960, acknowledges three exceptions to the prohibition of discrimination in which separate educational systems are allowed: for pupils of the two sexes, for religious and linguistic reasons, and private educational systems.[136] In practice, tolerance of these exceptions has contributed to inequality at all levels of education and continues to do so.

According to the Committee on Economic, Social and Cultural Rights, girls and women are disproportionately prevented from claiming and enjoying their basic human right to education. Factors for this include 'barriers to access for girls and women from disadvantaged and marginalized groups, exacerbated by poverty and economic crises, gender stereotyping in curricula, textbooks and teaching processes, violence against girls and women in and out of school and structural and ideological restrictions to their engagement in male-dominated academic and vocational fields'.[137] The Committee has also confirmed that the 'adoption of temporary special measures intended to bring about de facto equality for men and women and for disadvantaged groups is not a violation of the right to non-discrimination with regard to education, so long as such measures do not lead to the maintenance of unequal or separate standards for different groups, and provided they are not continued after the objectives for which they were taken have been achieved'.[138]

2. Aims of education

The Universal Declaration of Human Rights states that education is to be directed 'to the full development of the human personality and to the strengthening of respect for human rights and fundamental freedoms. It shall promote understanding, tolerance and friendship among all nations, racial or religious groups, and shall further the activities of the United Nations for the maintenance of peace.'[139] The International Covenant on Economic, Social and Cultural Rights builds upon this, adding that education should be directed to the sense of dignity of the human personality, 'shall enable all persons to participate effectively in a free society'[140]. Article 29(1) of the Convention on the Rights of the Child develops this still further:

[136] UNESCO Convention against Discrimination in Education, (1962) 429 UNTS 92, art. 2.

[137] General Recommendation 36 on the right of girls and women to education, CEDAW/C/GC/36, para. 4.

[138] General Comment 13, The right to education (art. 13 of the Covenant), E/C.12/1999/10, para. 32.

[139] Universal Declaration of Human Rights, A/RES/217 (III), art. 26(2). See also UNESCO Convention against Discrimination in Education, (1962) 429 UNTS 92, art. 5(1)(a).

[140] International Covenant on Economic, Social and Cultural Rights, (1976) 993 UNTS 3, art. 13(1).

1. States Parties agree that the education of the child shall be directed to:
   (a) The development of the child's personality, talents and mental and physical abilities to their fullest potential;
   (b) The development of respect for human rights and fundamental freedoms, and for the principles enshrined in the Charter of the United Nations;
   (c) The development of respect for the child's parents, his or her own cultural identity, language and values, for the national values of the country in which the child is living; the country from which he or she may originate, and for civilisations different from his or her own ...

According to the Committee on the Rights of the Child, Article 29(1) brings to the right to education 'a qualitative dimension which reflects the rights and inherent dignity of the child' but that also 'insists upon the need for education to be child-centred, child-friendly and empowering, and it highlights the need for educational processes to be based upon the very principles it enunciates'.[141] There have been only three reservations to Article 29,[142] two of them now withdrawn.[143] Perhaps account might also be taken of the reservations to the Convention that invoke national legislation generally or Islamic law although it seems doubtful, given the text of Article 29, that this could be very relevant if at all. Consequently, it is a reasonable conclusion that the requirement that education be directed to the purposes set out in Article 26(2) of the Universal Declaration of Human Rights, as complemented by Article 13(2) of the International Covenant on Economic, Social and Cultural Rights and Article 29 of the Convention on the Rights of the Child, constitutes a norm of customary international law.

3. Private schools and parental choice in education

The right of parents 'to choose the kind of education that shall be given to their children' is acknowledged in Article 26(3) of the Universal Declaration of Human Rights. Although formulated in an apparently absolute fashion, it must be understood in the context of the previous paragraph of the Declaration where there is an obligation to provide education that is directed at 'strengthening of respect for human rights and fundamental freedoms', promoting 'understanding, tolerance

[141] General Comment 1, art. 29(1): The aims of education, CRC/GC/2001/1, para. 2.

[142] Indonesia, C.N.245.1990.TREATIES-9 (art. 29 will be applied 'in conformity with its constitution'); Thailand, C.N.94.1992.TREATIES-7 (art. 29 will be applied 'subject to the national laws, regulations and prevailing practices in Thailand'); Turkey, C.N.14 8.1995.TREATIES-4 (' ... the right to interpret and to apply the provisions of [article 29] in conformity with the work and spirit of the Constitution of the Republic of Turkey and of the Treaty of Lausanne of 24 July 1923').

[143] Indonesia, C.N.147.2005.TREATIES-1; Thailand, C.N.163.1997.TREATIES-6.

and friendship among all nations, racial or religious groups, and furthering the activities of the United Nations for the maintenance of peace'. The right of parents to intervene in the education of their children is set out more elaborately in Article 13(4) of the International Covenant on Economic, Social and Cultural Rights as 'the liberty of individuals and bodies to establish and direct educational institutions, subject always to the observance of the principles set forth in paragraph 1 of this article and to the requirement that the education given in such institutions shall conform to such minimum standards as may be laid down by the State'. There is a similar recognition in the Convention on the Rights of the Child of the right of 'individuals and bodies' to establish and direct schools.[144]

Several treaties recognise the rights of parents to exercise control over the education of their children, but some of them only in a limited manner that does not imply a right to establish independent parochial schools. The International Covenant on Civil and Political Rights requires that States Parties 'undertake to have respect for the liberty of parents and, when applicable, legal guardians to ensure the religious and moral education of their children in conformity with their own convictions'.[145] The first Protocol to the European Convention on Human Rights provides for the right of parents to ensure such education and teaching 'in conformity with their own religious and philosophical convictions'.[146] Similar texts are found in some of the other instruments.[147] The Charter of Fundamental Rights of the European Union extends the rights of parents to ensuring education 'in conformity with their religious, philosophical and pedagogical convictions'.[148]

The UNESCO Convention against Discrimination in Education addresses separate and private education, but in a provision prefaced with the words '[w]hen permitted in a State . . . '. The Convention says that private or separate schools shall not be deemed discriminatory under certain conditions, for example by segregating boys and girls, for 'religious or linguistic reasons' and, more generally '[t]he establishment or maintenance of private educational institutions, if the object of the institutions is not to secure the exclusion of any group but to provide educational facilities in addition to those provided by the public authorities'.[149]

[144] Convention on the Rights of the Child, (1990) 1571 UNTS 3, art. 29(2). Also Additional Protocol to the American Convention on Human Rights in the area of Economic, Social and Cultural Rights, OASTS 69, art. 13(5).

[145] International Covenant on Civil and Political Rights, (1976) 999 UNTS 171, art. 18(4).

[146] Protocol to the Convention for the Protection of Human Rights and Fundamental Freedoms, CETS 9, art. 2.

[147] International Covenant on Economic, Social and Cultural Rights, (1976) 993 UNTS 3, art. 13(3); International Convention on the Protection of the Rights of all Migrant Workers and Members of their Families, (2003) 2220 UNTS 3, art. 12(4); American Convention on Human Rights, (1978) 1144 UNTS 123, art. 12(4); Additional Protocol to the American Convention on Human Rights in the area of Economic, Social and Cultural Rights, OASTS 69, art. 13(4); African Charter on the Rights and Welfare of the Child, arts. 9(3), 11(4); Arab Charter on Human Rights, art. 30(3).

[148] Charter of Fundamental Rights of the European Union, OJ C 326/391, art. 14(3).

[149] UNESCO Convention against Discrimination in Education, (1962) 429 UNTS 92, art. 2.

The only State that does not have a treaty obligation recognising the right of 'individuals and bodies' to establish and direct schools is the United States of America. Its reports to the Human Rights Council have only addressed issues that concern public educational institutions.[150] Nevertheless, private education at all levels is very highly developed in the United States. The United States is a signatory to the International Covenant on Economic, Social and Cultural Rights and the Convention on the Rights of the Child and is therefore obliged to refrain from acts which would defeat their object and purpose.[151]

There is therefore much evidence, essentially based upon the universality of treaty provisions, to confirm that the right of parents to choose the education they wish for their children is recognised under customary law, subject of course to respecting the progressive objectives of education. The right of 'individuals and bodies' to establish and direct educational institutions also seems to be customary in nature although there is no suggestion that the implementation is entitled to rely upon public funds.

* * *

Conclusions. Everyone has the right to universal primary education that is compulsory and free of charge. The right must be recognised without any discrimination based on race, gender or other grounds. Education shall promote understanding, tolerance and friendship among all nations, racial or religious groups, and shall further the activities of the United Nations for the maintenance of peace. Parents have the right to participate in decisions about the education that their children receive.

E. Cultural rights

Within the overall scheme of international human rights law, cultural rights are a neglected category. They are sometimes dropped altogether in the peculiarly abbreviated but not uncommon references to 'socioeconomic rights'. That they be included in the Universal Declaration of Human Rights apparently results from an American suggestion: 'Among the categories of rights which the United States suggests should be considered is the right "to enjoy minimum standards of economic, social and cultural wellbeing".'[152] The Universal Declaration of Human Rights addresses cultural rights in a single provision, Article 27, which is composed of two paragraphs. The first concerns participation in cultural life, enjoyment of the arts,

[150] United States of America, National report, A/HRC/WG.6/9/USA/1, paras. 47–49; United States of America, National report, A/HRC/WG.6/22/USA/1, paras. 30–32, 37, 103–104.
[151] Vienna Convention on the Law of Treaties, (1980) 1155 UNTS 31, art. 18(a).
[152] United States Proposals Regarding an International Bill of Rights, E/CN.4/4, p. 2.

and benefiting from scientific advancement. The second is directed at protection of the intellectual property of a scientific, literary, or artistic nature. Cultural rights are also relevant to the right to education. Article 24 of the Universal Declaration, which provides a right to rest and leisure, serves the purpose of facilitating participation in culture and the arts. The principles in Article 27 of the Universal Declaration find a more elaborate expression in Article 15 of the International Covenant on Economic, Social and Cultural Rights. Furthermore, Article 27 of the International Covenant on Civil and Political Rights protects the right of members of minority groups to enjoy their culture. Cultural rights are also addressed in the regional human rights treaties.[153]

Although Article 27 of the Universal Declaration is obviously the template, there is great variation in the formulations of the right to culture in human rights treaties. The diversity of texts contributes in two ways to the identification of customary international law: it tends to confirm that the protection of cultural life is entrenched within custom and it provides a broad range of elements and approaches that may then be taken into consideration in the interpretation and application of the customary norm. For example, the International Convention for the Elimination of All Forms of Racial Discrimination protects the right 'to equal participation in cultural activities'.[154] Somewhat differently, the Convention for the Elimination of All Forms of Discrimination against Women enshrines a right 'to participate fully in recreational activities, sports and all aspects of cultural life'.[155] The Charter of Fundamental Rights of the European Union 'recognises and respects the rights of the elderly to lead a life of dignity and independence and to participate in social and cultural life'.[156] Pursuant to the International Covenant on Civil and Political Rights, members of ethnic, religious, and linguistic minorities shall not be denied the right 'to enjoy their own culture'.[157]

The Convention on the Rights of the Child provides for the right of the child 'to engage in play and recreational activities appropriate to the age of the child and to participate freely in cultural life and the arts'.[158] The most detailed provision in the specialised treaties is found in the Convention on the Rights of Persons with Disabilities under the heading 'Participation in cultural life, recreation, leisure and sport'. Persons with disabilities are entitled 'to take part on an equal basis with others in cultural life'. This involves access to cultural materials, television programmes,

[153] Additional Protocol to the American Convention on Human Rights in the area of Economic, Social and Cultural Rights, OASTS 69, art. 14; Arab Charter on Human Rights, art. 42; African Charter on Human and Peoples' Rights, (1986) 1520 UNTS 271, art. 17(1).

[154] International Convention on the Elimination of All Forms of Racial Discrimination, (1969) 660 UNTS 195, art. 5(e)(vi).

[155] Convention on the Elimination of All Forms of Discrimination against Women, (1981) 1249 UNTS 13, art. 13(c).

[156] Charter of Fundamental Rights of the European Union, OJ C 326/391, art. 25.

[157] International Covenant on Civil and Political Rights, (1976) 999 UNTS 171, art. 27; Convention on the Rights of the Child, (1990) 1571 UNTS 3, art. 30.

[158] Convention on the Rights of the Child, (1990) 1571 UNTS 3, art. 31.

films, theatre, museums, libraries and tourism services, cultural monuments, and measures enabling them 'to have the opportunity to develop and utilise their creative, artistic and intellectual potential, not only for their own benefit, but also for the enrichment of society'.[159]

The International Covenant on Economic, Social and Cultural Rights presents a succinct formulation: 'The States Parties to the present Covenant recognise the right of everyone: (a) To take part in cultural life . . . '.[160] In its General Comment on the subject, the Committee on Economic, Social and Cultural Rights said that the expression 'cultural life' referred to culture 'as a living process, historical, dynamic and evolving, with a past, a present and a future'.[161] The Committee explained that culture 'encompasses, inter alia, ways of life, language, oral and written literature, music and song, non-verbal communication, religion or belief systems, rites and ceremonies, sport and games, methods of production or technology, natural and man-made environments, food, clothing and shelter and the arts, customs and traditions through which individuals, groups of individuals and communities express their humanity and the meaning they give to their existence, and build their world view representing their encounter with the external forces affecting their lives'.[162] The Committee has insisted that 'cultures have no fixed borders. The phenomena of migration, integration, assimilation and globalisation have brought cultures, groups and individuals into closer contact than ever before, at a time when each of them is striving to keep their own identity.'[163]

There are no reservations to Article 15 of the International Covenant on Civil and Political Rights, Article 31 of the Convention on the Rights of the Child, and Article 30 of the Convention on the Rights of Persons with Disabilities.[164] Accordingly, every Member State of the United Nations is a party to one of the cultural rights provisions and most are parties to at least two of them. The one exception, the United States of America, is not a party to any of the three treaties. This is quite ironic as it was the United States that first proposed the inclusion of a cultural rights provision in the International Bill of Rights, as explained above. The Universal Periodic Review materials provide no insight into its position concerning cultural rights under international law. The United States is a signatory to

[159] Convention on the Rights of Persons with Disabilities, (2008) 2515 UNTS 3, art. 30.

[160] International Covenant on Economic, Social and Cultural Rights, (1976) 993 UNTS 3, art. 15(1)(a).

[161] General Comment 21, Right of everyone to take part in cultural life (art. 15, para. 1 (a), of the International Covenant on Economic, Social and Cultural Rights), E/C.12/GC/21, para. 11.

[162] Ibid., para. 13. See also the thematic reports of the Special Rapporteur on cultural rights, A/HRC/14/36, A/HRC/31/59.

[163] General Comment No. 21. Right of everyone to take part in cultural life (art. 15, para. 1 (a), of the International Covenant on Economic, Social and Cultural Rights), E/C.12/GC/21, para. 41.

[164] Malaysia has a declaration to art. 30 of the Convention on the Rights of Persons with Disabilities that confirms its recognition of the right to culture, C.N.488.2010.TREATIES-19: 'Malaysia recognises the participation of persons with disabilities in cultural life, recreation and leisure as provided in article 30 of the said Convention and interprets that the recognition is a matter for national legislation.'

all three of the treaties and is therefore obliged to refrain from acts that would defeat their object and purpose.[165]

States that are not parties to the International Covenant on Economic, Social and Cultural Rights sometimes refer to the subject in reporting to the Human Rights Council as part of the Universal Periodic Review. For example, Tonga told the Council that although it had not ratified the Covenant, its principles were incorporated within national law and include the right to take part in cultural life.[166] Myanmar reported that '[e]very citizen shall, in accord with the law, have the rights to freely develop literature, culture, arts, customs and tradition they cherish'.[167] Some States appear to view the right to culture as being directed to the protection of their traditional culture[168] or those of ethnic minorities.[169] But this only reflects the more general pattern in the Universal Periodic Review, which is to ignore the right to participate in cultural life, although there are some exceptions.[170]

Cultural heritage receives special protection under international humanitarian law and international criminal law.[171] According to the Special Rapporteur in the field of cultural rights, the prohibition of acts of deliberate destruction of cultural heritage of major value for humanity is a norm of customary international law.[172] Article 4 of the UNESCO Convention Concerning the Protection of the World Cultural and Natural Heritage declares the 'duty of ensuring the identification, protection, conservation, presentation and transmission to future generations' with respect to buildings and monuments of cultural heritage, defined as being 'outstanding universal value from the point of view of history, art or science'.[173]

Taken as a whole, these materials confirm the customary legal status of the right to participate in the cultural life of the community, to enjoy the arts and to share in scientific advancement and its benefits.

The Special Rapporteur in the field of cultural rights of the Human Rights Council has identified several clusters that are protected by the right to

[165] Vienna Convention on the Law of Treaties, (1980) 1155 UNTS 31, art. 18(a).

[166] Tonga, National report, A/HRC/WG.6/29/TON/1, para. 22, National report, A/HRC/WG.6/15/TON/1, para. 139 and Report of the Working Group, A/HRC/38/5, para. 7.

[167] Myanmar, National report, A/HRC/WG.6/10/MMR/1, para. 34.

[168] Nauru, National report, A/HRC/WG.6/10/NRU/1, paras. 108–110.

[169] Malaysia, National report, A/HRC/WG.6/4/MYS/1/Rev.1, paras. 47–51.

[170] Cuba, National report, A/HRC/WG.6/4/CUB/1, paras. 45–46, National report, A/HRC/WG.6/30/CUB/1, paras. 104–109; China, National report, A/HRC/WG.6/17/CHN/1, para. 39; Tajikistan, National report, A/HRC/WG.6/12/TJK/1, paras. 172–177; Korea (DPRK), National report, A/HRC/WG.6/19/PRK/1, paras. 68–70; Mongolia, National report, A/HRC/WG.6/9/MNG/1, paras. 48–50.

[171] Convention for the Protection of Cultural Property in the Event of Armed Conflict with Regulations for the Execution of the Convention, (1956) 249 UNTS 215; Jean-Marie Henckaerts and Louise Doswald-Beck, *Customary International Humanitarian Law*, Vol. I, Cambridge: Cambridge University Press, 2005, pp. 127–138; Rome Statute of the International Criminal Court (2002) 2187 UNTS 689, arts. 8(2)(b)(ix), 8(2)(e)(ix).

[172] Report of the Special Rapporteur in the field of cultural rights, A/HRC/31/59, para. 59, citing Francesco Francioni and Federico Lanzerini, 'The Destruction of the Buddhas of Bamiyan and International Law', (2003) *14 European Journal of International Law* 619, at p. 635.

[173] Convention Concerning the Protection of the World Cultural and Natural Heritage.

culture: human creativity in all its diversity and the conditions for it to be exercised, developed, and made accessible; free choice, expression, and development of identities, which include the right to choose not to be a part of particular collectives, as well as the right to exit a collective, and to take part on an equal basis in the process of defining it; the rights of individuals and groups to participate, or not to participate, in the cultural life of their choice and to conduct their own cultural practices; the right to interact and exchange, regardless of group affiliation and of frontiers; the rights to enjoy and have access to the arts, to knowledge, including scientific knowledge, and to an individual's own cultural heritage, as well as that of others; and the rights to participate in the interpretation, elaboration, and development of cultural heritage and in the reformulation of cultural identities.[174]

The Universal Declaration of Human Rights affirms the right 'to enjoy the arts'.[175] The phrase traces its origin to the Secretariat draft of the Universal Declaration of Human Rights which was prepared by John Humphrey in June 1947.[176] Some of the drafters thought the entire text on cultural rights might more properly belong in the Preamble.[177] The reference to 'enjoying the arts' remained in the substantive provisions without debate or amendment.[178] The notion of enjoying the arts is not reprised in the International Covenant on Economic, Social and Cultural Rights or in any of the regional treaties. The Convention on the Rights of the Child recognises the right of children 'to participate freely in cultural life and the arts'.[179] The Committee on the Rights of the Child has said that '[c]ultural and artistic expression is articulated and enjoyed in the home, school, streets and public spaces, as well as through dance, festivals, crafts, ceremonies, rituals, theatre, literature, music, cinema, exhibitions, film, digital platforms and video'.[180] In an observation that is as valid for adults as it is for children, the Committee said 'it is through cultural life and the arts that children and their communities express their specific identity and the meaning they give to their existence, and build their world view representing their encounter with external forces affecting their lives'.[181]

The right to enjoy the arts does not seem to have ever been considered during the Universal Periodic Review, by States, by 'stakeholders', or by United Nations bodies. A report by the Special Rapporteur in the field of cultural rights addressed the subject, but only indirectly, focussing on censorship. She wrote that all persons 'enjoy the right to freedom of artistic expression and creativity, which includes

[174] Cultural rights: Tenth anniversary report, A/HRC/40/53, para. 15.

[175] Universal Declaration of Human Rights, A/RES/217 (III), art. 27(1).

[176] Draft Outline of International Bill of Rights (prepared by the Division of Human Rights), E/CN.4/AC.1/3.

[177] E/CN.4/AC.1/SR.15, p. 3; Report of the Drafting Committee to the Commission on Human Rights, E/CN.4/21, p. 81.

[178] Ibid., p. 81.

[179] Convention on the Rights of the Child, (1990) 1571 UNTS 3, art. 31.

[180] General Comment 17 on the right of the child to rest, leisure, play, recreational activities, cultural life and the arts (art. 31), CRC/C/GC/17, para. IV.A.(f).

[181] Ibid.

the right to freely experience and contribute to artistic expressions and creations, through individual or joint practice, to have access to and enjoy the arts, and to disseminate their expressions and creations'.[182] However, as it is presented in the Universal Declaration the right is broader because it belongs not only to those who 'create' but also to those who merely 'enjoy'. Alongside the general tendency to disregard the right to 'enjoy the arts' within international human rights law stand the commitments of governments to support cultural institutions such as theatres, art galleries, libraries, and concert halls, as well as provision of education and training in dance, music, and drama within universities and specialised institutions. But this may not be enough to cement the claim that States treat this as an international obligation within the field of human rights.

The right to share in scientific advancement and its benefits also appears in Article 27(1) of the Universal Declaration of Human Rights. Formulated somewhat differently, as the right to enjoy the benefits of scientific progress and its applications, it is also set out explicitly in the International Covenant on Economic, Social and Cultural Rights.[183] The Covenant adds an obligation upon States 'to respect the freedom indispensable for scientific research and creative activity'.[184] There is similar language in the Protocol to the American Convention on Human Rights and the Arab Charter on Human Rights.[185] The subject of scientific progress or advancement is ignored in the Universal Periodic Review materials, aside from occasional references to the significance of science in public education.[186]

The Special Rapporteur in the field of cultural rights of the Human Rights Council, using the abbreviated term 'the right to science', has said it consists of access to the benefits of science by everyone, without discrimination, opportunities for all to contribute to the scientific enterprise and freedom indispensable for scientific research, participation of individuals and communities in decision-making, and an enabling environment fostering the conservation, development, and diffusion of science and technology.[187] The Declaration on the Use of Scientific and Technological Progress, adopted in 1975 by the United Nations General Assembly, underscores the need for scientific and technological developments to be used in a manner consistent with fundamental human rights, explaining that they can also give rise to social problems and have harmful consequences.[188]

There is a tension between the human right to benefit from scientific progress and the protection of intellectual property, a matter addressed in the second

[182] The right to freedom of artistic expression and creativity, A/HRC/23/34, para. 85.
[183] International Covenant on Economic, Social and Cultural Rights, (1976) 993 UNTS 3, art. 15(1)(b).
[184] Ibid., art. 15(3).
[185] Additional Protocol to the American Convention on Human Rights in the area of Economic, Social and Cultural Rights, OASTS 69, art. 14; Arab Charter on Human Rights, art. 42.
[186] Oman, Report of the Working Group, A/HRC/31/11, para. 13.
[187] The right to enjoy the benefits of scientific progress and its applications, A/HRC/20/26, para. 25.
[188] Declaration on the Use of Scientific and Technological Progress, A/RES/3384 (XXX).

paragraph of Article 27 of the Universal Declaration of Human Rights: 'Everyone has the right to the protection of the moral and material interests resulting from any scientific, literary or artistic production of which he is the author.' How can everyone benefit if scientific developments remain the private property of those who are responsible for them and who monopolise their exploitation? According to the Special Rapporteur, '[t]he potential of intellectual property regimes to obstruct new technological solutions to critical human problems such as food, water, health, chemical safety, energy and climate change requires attention.'[189] The protection of intellectual property is also set out in Article 15 of the International Covenant on Economic, Social and Cultural Rights, in other international human rights instruments,[190] and in specialised treaties.[191]

* * *

Conclusions. Everyone has the right to participate in cultural life, to enjoy the arts, and to benefit from scientific progress. Deliberate destruction of cultural heritage of major value for humanity is prohibited by customary international law.

[189] The right to enjoy the benefits of scientific progress and its applications, A/HRC/20/26, para. 56.

[190] Additional Protocol to the American Convention on Human Rights in the area of Economic, Social and Cultural Rights, OASTS 69, art. 14(1)(c); Arab Charter on Human Rights, art. 42(2).

[191] See the discussion under 'Right to property', *supra*, pp. 257–261.

10
Solidarity

There is a category of fundamental rights that is only very partially reflected in the Universal Declaration of Human Rights and in the two International Covenants. In the late 1970s, Karel Vasek famously proposed a taxonomy of human rights that he labelled the 'three generations'.[1] The first generation comprises the classic civil and political rights of the Enlightenment while the second consists of the economic and social rights set out in Roosevelt's 'second bill of rights'. The third generation includes the right to self-determination, the right to a healthy environment, and the right to development. Sometimes this category has also been described as 'peoples' rights'. The African Charter of Human and Peoples' Rights, adopted in 1981, includes several so-called 'peoples' rights'. But the term can be traced back further to common Article 1 of the International Covenants, which proclaims 'the inalienable right of all peoples to self-determination and to control over their natural wealth and resources'. The distinction between peoples' rights and human rights may take on significance in the application and enforcement of specific human rights treaties. For example, the Human Rights Committee has declined jurisdiction in dealing with individual petitions that rely upon Article 1 of the Covenant, holding that the first Optional Protocol only provides a petition procedure for claims that individual rights set out in Part III of the Covenant (Arts. 6 to 27) have been violated.[2]

The 'third-generation rights' have also been called 'solidarity rights'. As one of its final initiatives, the Commission on Human Rights adopted a resolution on international solidarity in which it '[r]*ecognise[d]* that the so-called "third-generation rights" closely interrelated to the fundamental value of solidarity need further progressive development within the United Nations human rights machinery in order to be able to respond to the increasing challenges of international cooperation in this field'.[3] The terminology is controversial, and some even question whether 'peoples' rights' belong within the universe of human rights.[4] Whatever the label,

[1] Karel Vasak, 'Human Rights: A Thirty-Year Struggle', (1977) 30 *UNESCO Courier* 11.

[2] *Lubicon Lake Band v. Canada*, no. 167/1984, Views, 26 March 1990, CCPR/C/38/D/167/1984, paras. 13.3 and 32.1; *Sanila-Aikio v. Finland*, no. 2668/2015, Decision, 14 February 2019, CCPR/C/124/D/2668/2015, para. 8.6.

[3] Human rights and international solidarity, E/CN.4/RES/2005/55, para. 5. See also Human rights and international solidarity, A/HRC/RES/12/9, para. 6; Human rights and international solidarity, A/HRC/RES/23/12, para. 9.

[4] Philip Alston, *Peoples' Rights*, Oxford: Oxford University Press, 2001; James Crawford, ed., *The Rights of Peoples*, Oxford: Oxford University Press, 1988.

The Customary International Law of Human Rights. William A. Schabas, Oxford University Press.
 DOI: 10.1093/oso/9780192845696.003.0011

a discussion of customary international law would not be complete if these rights were not considered.

A. Peace

The preamble of the Charter of the United Nations begins by affirming a determination 'to save succeeding generations from the scourge of war, which twice in our lifetime has brought untold sorrow to mankind'. The two World Wars of the twentieth century are estimated to be responsible for a total of about 80 million deaths. This is an average of about 8 million deaths per year at a time when the world's population was approximately a quarter of what it is now. It is the equivalent, in today's numbers, of more than 30 million people a year or close to 100,000 victims every single day.

Such an assessment helps in appreciating the huge achievement that represents the end of World Wars. Of course, it is impossible to know if this is a permanent development, like the eradication of smallpox and the bubonic plague, or whether we are simply in the midst of a protracted ceasefire. International law has made no small contribution to the end of large scale global conflicts. The resort to force to settle international disputes is prohibited by the Charter of the United Nations, whose mechanisms and institutions have ensured that this is implemented, albeit with some terrible exceptions, for three quarters of a century. The crime of aggression was prosecuted at the Nuremberg and Tokyo trials, and is enshrined in the jurisdiction of the International Criminal Court.

The African Charter on Human and Peoples' Rights recognises that '[a]ll peoples shall have the right to national and international peace and security'.[5] No equivalent is be found in the Universal Declaration of Human Rights and the other major human rights treaties with the exception, perhaps, of the International Covenant on Civil and Political Rights which declares that propaganda for war shall be prohibited by law.[6] The Women's Protocol to the African Charter contains a provision on the 'right to peace' that requires increased participation in a range of areas relating to the maintenance of peace. It also declares that 'States Parties shall take the necessary measures to reduce military expenditure significantly in favour of spending on social development in general, and the promotion of women in particular'.[7]

In 1984, the General Assembly adopted the 'Declaration on the Right of Peoples to Peace'.[8] Paragraph 1 '[s]olemnly proclaims that the peoples of our planet have a

[5] African Charter on Human and Peoples' Rights, (1986) 1520 UNTS 271, art. 23(1).
[6] International Covenant on Civil and Political Rights, (1976) 999 UNTS 171, art. 20(1).
[7] Protocol to the African Charter on Human and Peoples' Rights on the Rights of Women in Africa, art. 10.
[8] Declaration on the Right of Peoples to Peace, A/RES/39/11.

sacred right to peace'. There were no negative votes but there were thirty-four abstentions, mainly from western countries.[9] Following study of the question by the Human Rights Council,[10] in 2016 the General Assembly adopted the 'Declaration on the Right to Peace', of which paragraph 1 states: 'Everyone has the right to enjoy peace such that all human rights are promoted and protected and development is fully realised.'[11] The language in the resolution firmly situates it within the framework of the protection of human rights but stops short of proclaiming a human right to peace. An earlier resolution of the Human Rights Council had stated 'that human rights include social, economic and cultural rights and the right to peace, a healthy environment and development'[12] but the formulation did not appear in the Council's final resolution. The General Assembly Resolution adopting the Declaration was controversial, however, with a recorded vote of 131 in favour, to thirty-four against, and nineteen abstentions.[13] Other than Japan and the Republic of Korea, all of the opponents were associated with the Western European and Other or Eastern European Groups.

The right to peace is also related to the condemnation of aggression, punishable as a crime of international concern pursuant to the Rome Statute.[14] In the *Nicaragua* case, the International Court of Justice described the prohibition of aggression as a norm of customary international law and 'a fundamental or cardinal principle of such law'.[15] The International Law Commission included the 'prohibition of aggression' in its draft list of *jus cogens* norms.[16] In its third General Comment on the right to life, the Human Rights Committee affirmed that '[w]ars and other acts of mass violence continue to be a scourge of humanity resulting in the loss of lives of many thousands of lives every year. Efforts to avert the risks of war, and any other armed conflict, and to strengthen international peace and security, are among the most important safeguards for the right to life.'[17]

A study of customary law is not the place to debate the merits of recognising a human right to peace.[18] That the 'enjoyment of peace' is fundamental to the

[9] A/39/PV.57, para. 206.

[10] Promotion of the right to peace, A/HRC/RES/20/15.

[11] Declaration on the Right to Peace, A/RES/71/189.

[12] Promotion of the right to peace, A/HRC/RES/17/16, PP 17.

[13] A/71/PV.65, p. 26

[14] Rome Statute of the International Criminal Court, (2002) 2187 UNTS 689, art. 8 *bis*.

[15] *Military and Paramilitary Activities in and against Nicaragua (Nicaragua v. United States of America), Merits, Judgment, ICJ Reports 1986*, p. 14, para. 190. See also *Certain Activities Carried Out by Nicaragua in the Border Area (Costa Rica v. Nicaragua), Provisional Measures, Order of 8 March 2011, ICJ Reports 2011*, p. 6, Separate Opinion of Judge *ad hoc* Dugard, para. 15.

[16] Report of the International Law Commission, Seventy-first session (29 April–7 June and 8 July–9 August 2019), A/74/10, p. 147.

[17] General Comment 36, art. 6: right to life, CCPR/C/GC/36, para. 69 (internal references omitted).

[18] For the author's views, see: William A. Schabas, 'The Human Right To Peace', in Asbjørn Eide, Jakob Th. Möller, and Ineta Ziemele, eds., *Making Peoples Heard, Essays on Human Rights in Honour of Gudmundur Alfredsson*, Leiden/Boston: Martinus Nijhoff, 2011, pp. 43–57; William A. Schabas, 'Freedom from Fear and the Human Right to Peace', in David Keane and Yvonne McDermott, eds., *The Challenge of Human Rights; Past, Present and Future*, Cheltenham, UK and Northampton, MA: Edward Elgar, 2012, pp. 36–51.

protection and promotion of human rights does not seem to be disputed. Article 28 of the Universal Declaration of Human Rights states that '[e]veryone is entitled to a social and international order in which the rights and freedoms set forth in this Declaration can be fully realised'. A human right to peace may prove important, for example, by facilitating a balancing of the competing interests of justice for victims and the resolution of armed conflict in circumstances where amnesty is required in order to reach a peace agreement.[19] In contrast with other 'peoples' rights' or 'third generation rights', such as the right to a healthy environment and the right to development, the right to peace has little resonance in the Universal Periodic Review materials.[20]

* * *

Conclusions. The elements that are necessary in order to affirm the recognition of a human right to peace under customary international law are probably insufficient.

B. Healthy environment

The right to enjoyment of a safe, clean, healthy, and sustainable environment does not appear in the Universal Declaration of Human Rights and the two International Covenants. The African Charter on Human and Peoples' Rights declares: 'All peoples shall have the right to a general satisfactory environment favourable to their development.'[21] The Arab Charter on Human Rights includes 'the right to a healthy environment' under the general rubric of an adequate standard of living.[22] The Charter of Fundamental Rights of the European Union contains a provision entitled 'Environmental protection': 'A high level of environmental protection and the improvement of the quality of the environment must be integrated into the policies of the Union and ensured in accordance with the principle of sustainable development.'[23] The Additional Protocol to the American Convention on Human Rights affirms that '[e]veryone shall have the right to live in a healthy environment and to have access to basic public services' and that States Parties are to 'promote the protection, preservation, and improvement of the environment'.[24]

According to the Human Rights Council, more than 100 States have recognised some form of a right to a healthy environment in international agreements, their constitutions, legislation, or policies.[25] Initiatives aimed at the adoption of

[19] See, for example, *Massacres of El Mozote and nearby places v. El Salvador*, Judgment (Merits, reparations, and costs), 25 October 2012, Series C, No. 252, Concurring opinion of Judge Diego García-Sayán.
[20] Cuba, in United States of America, Report of the Working Group, A/HRC/16/11, para. 92.215.
[21] African Charter on Human and Peoples' Rights, (1986) 1520 UNTS 271, art. 24.
[22] Arab Charter of Human Rights, art. 38.
[23] Charter of Fundamental Rights of the European Union, OJ C 326/391, art. 37.
[24] Additional Protocol to the American Convention on Human Rights in the area of Economic, Social and Cultural Rights, OASTS 69, art. 11.
[25] Human rights and the environment, A/HRC/RES/37/8, PP 17.

an additional protocol to the European Convention on Human Rights on the subject have not come to fruition, but that may be explained by the view that the Convention is already sufficient to address the issue.[26]

Aspects of environmental protection have been developed in the case law and other materials of international human rights courts and treaty bodies, relying upon the right to life[27] and the right to privacy.[28] In its third General Comment on the right to life, the Human Rights Committee explained that '[e]nvironmental degradation, climate change and unsustainable development constitute some of the most pressing and serious threats to the ability of present and future generations to enjoy the right to life'. It said that obligations under international environmental law should inform an understanding of the right to life: 'Implementation of the obligation to respect and ensure the right to life, and in particular life with dignity, depends, inter alia, on measures taken by States Parties to preserve the environment and protect it against harm, pollution and climate change caused by public and private actors'. This requires the adoption of measures to ensure sustainable use of natural resources and the development and implementation of substantive environmental standards. States must provide notification to other States about 'natural disasters and emergencies and cooperate with them, provide appropriate access to information on environmental hazards and pay due regard to the precautionary approach'.[29]

The Inter-American Court of Human Rights has identified 'an undeniable relationship between the protection of the environment and the realization of other human rights, in that environmental degradation and the adverse effects of climate change affect the real enjoyment of human rights'.[30] It has emphasised the special importance of the relationship between a healthy environment and human rights in cases that deal with territorial rights of indigenous and tribal peoples, where the protection of natural resources is essential.[31] For the Inter-American

[26] Recommendation 1885 (2009), Drafting an additional protocol to the European Convention on Human Rights concerning the right to a healthy environment; Reply adopted by the Committee of Ministers on 8 July 2009 at the 1063rd meeting of the Ministers' Deputies, CM/AS(2009)Rec1862 final, para. 9; Opinion of the CDDH on Recommendation 1883 (2009), The challenges posed by climate change and Recommendation 1885 (2009) Drafting an additional protocol to the European Convention on Human Rights concerning the right to a healthy environment, DH-DEV(2010)03, Appendix III, para. 3.

[27] *Teitiota v. New Zealand*, no. 2728/2016, Views, 24 October 2019, CCPR/C/127/D/2728/2016; Cabo Verde, Concluding observations, CCPR/C/CPV/CO/1/Add.1, paras. 17–18.

[28] *López Ostra v. Spain*, 9 December 1994, §§ 58–60, Series A no. 303-C; *Fägerskiöld v. Sweden* (dec.), no. 37664/04, 26 February 2008; *Galev et al. v. Bulgaria* (dec.), no. 18324/04, 29 December 2009; *Di Sarno et al. v. Italy*, no. 30765/08, § 113, 10 January 2012.

[29] General Comment 36, art. 6: right to life, CCPR/C/GC/36, para. 62.

[30] *The Environment and Human Rights (State obligations in relation to the environment in the context of the protection and guarantee of the rights to life and to personal integrity: interpretation and scope of articles 4(1) and 5(1) in relation to articles 1(1) and 2 of the American Convention on Human Rights*, Advisory Opinion OC-23/17, Series A, No. 23, 15 November 2017, para. 47. Also *Kawas Fernández v. Honduras*, Judgment (Merits, reparations, and costs), 3 April 2009, Series C, No. 196, para. 148.

[31] Ibid. Also *Yakye Axa Indigenous Community v. Paraguay*, Judgment (Merits, reparations, and costs), 17 June 2005. Series C, No. 125, para. 137; *Sawhoyamaxa Indigenous Community v. Paraguay*, Judgment (Merits, reparations, and costs), 29 March 2006. Series C, No. 146, para. 118; *Saramaka*

Commission on Human Rights, 'several fundamental rights require, as a necessary precondition for their enjoyment, a minimum environmental quality, and are profoundly affected by the degradation of natural resources'.[32] Similarly, the African Commission on Human and Peoples' Rights has noted the significance of economic and social rights to the extent that 'the environment affects the quality of life and the safety of the individual'.[33]

Many submissions to the Human Rights Council in the course of the Universal Periodic Review address the question of climate change and its impact upon human rights.[34] Some speak explicitly of a human right to a clean and healthy

People v. Suriname, Judgment (Preliminary objections, merits, reparations, and costs), 28 November 2007, Series C, No. 172, paras. 121 and 122; *Kaliña and Lokono Peoples v. Suriname*, Judgment (Merits, reparations, and costs), Series C, No. 309, 25 November 2015, para. 173.

[32] *Indigenous and Tribal Peoples' Rights over their Ancestral Lands and Natural Resources—Norms and jurisprudence of the inter-American human rights system*, 30 December 2009, OEA/Ser.L/V/II, Doc. 56/09, para. 190.

[33] *Social and Economic Rights Centre (SERAC) and Centre for Economic and Social Rights (CESR) v. Nigeria*, No. 155/96, Decision, 27 October 2001, para. 51.

[34] Algeria, in Guyana, Report of the Working Group, A/HRC/15/14, paras. 33, 69.24; Australia, in Maldives, Report of the Working Group, A/HRC/16/7, para. 63; Azerbaijan, in Tuvalu, Report of the Working Group, A/HRC/24/8, para. 55 and in Maldives, Report on the Working Group, A/HRC/16/7, para. 45; Bahrain, in Comoros, Report of the Working Group, A/HRC/12/16, para. 23; Bangladesh, in Bhutan, Report of the Working Group, A/HRC/42/8, para. 91; Barbados, in Vanuatu, Report of the Working Group, A/HRC/41/10, para. 55; Bhutan, National report, A/HRC/WG.6/33/BTN/1, paras. 59–70, 163 and Report of the Working Group, A/HRC/42/8, paras. 9, 22, 155; Bolivia, in United States of America, Report of the Working Group, A/HRC/16/11, para. 92.222; Brazil, in Solomon Islands, Report of the Working Group, A/HRC/18/8, para. 38 and Tuvalu, Report of the Working Group, A/HRC/39/8, paras. 16, 43; Brunei Darussalam, Report of the Working Group, A/HRC/13/14, para. 16; Canada, in Micronesia, Report of the Working Group, A/HRC/16/16, para. 28 and in Nauru, Report on the Working Group, A/HRC/17/3, para. 79.84; Chad, National report, A/HRC/WG.6/31/TCD/1, paras. 34–38; China, in Guyana, Report of the Working Group, A/HRC/15/14, para. 37 and Kiribati, Report of the Working Group, A/HRC/15/3, para. 35; Chile, in Kiribati, Report of the Working Group, A/HRC/15/3, para. 53 and Solomon Islands, Report of the Working Group, A/HRC/18/8, para. 58; Comoros, National report, A/HRC/WG.6/18/COM/1, paras. 103–110, National report, A/HRC/WG.6/32/COM/1, paras. 29–37, Report of the Working Group, A/HRC/26/11, para. 29 and Report of the Working Group, A/HRC/41/12, para. 8; Costa Rica, in Nauru, Report of the Working Group, A/HRC/31/7, para. 73; Cuba, in Kiribati, Report of the Working Group, A/HRC/15/3, para. 29 and Guyana, Report of the Working Group, A/HRC/15/14, para. 36; Djibouti, in Nauru, Report of the Working Group, A/HRC/31/7, para. 85.53; Ecuador, in Solomon Islands, Report of the Working Group, A/HRC/18/8, para. 81.34; Ethiopia, National report, A/HRC/WG.6/33/ETH/1, paras. 37–38; Fiji, in Bhutan, Report of the Working Group, A/HRC/42/8, paras. 128, 158.52 and Brunei Darussalam, Report of the Working Group, A/HRC/42/11, paras. 47, 121.107; Finland, in Maldives, Report of the Working Group, A/HRC/16/7, para. 100.124; Georgia, in Micronesia, Report of the Working Group, A/HRC/31/4, para. 48; Ghana, in Tuvalu, Report of the Working Group, A/HRC/39/8, para. 101.72; Guyana, Views on conclusions, A/HRC/15/14/Add.1, para. 18 and Report of the Working Group, A/HRC/15/14, paras. 10, 31; Haiti, in Saint Lucia, Report of the Working Group, A/HRC/31/10, para. 88.121 and Tuvalu, Report of the Working Group, A/HRC/39/8, para. 101.69; Hungary, in Micronesia, Report of the Working Group, A/HRC/16/16, para. 45 and Saint Vincent and the Grenadines, Report of the Working Group, A/HRC/18/15, para. 46; Iceland, in Vanuatu, Report of the Working Group, A/HRC/41/10, para. 74; India, in Maldives, Report on the Working Group, A/HRC/16/7, para. 39; Indonesia, in Kiribati, Report of the Working Group, A/HRC/15/3, para. 59 and Nauru, Report of the Working Group, A/HRC/31/7, para. 85.54; Ireland, in Solomon Islands, Report of the Working Group, A/HRC/18/8, para. 34; Israel, in Nauru, Report on the Working Group, A/HRC/17/3, para. 69; Italy, in Solomon Islands, Report of the Working Group, A/HRC/32/14, para. 71; Jamaica, in Tuvalu, Report of the Working Group, A/HRC/39/8, para. 101.73; Kenya, National report, A/HRC/WG.6/8/KEN/1, para. 99; Kiribati, National report, A/HRC/WG.6/35/KIR/1, paras. 17–19, 47–49, 66–68, 83–84 and Report

environment.[35] Many of them do not recognise a right to a healthy environment as such but nor do they reject the idea that issues of climate change and environmental protection belong within the protection of human rights. Even the United

of the Working Group, A/HRC/15/3, paras. 19–21, 44; Korea (ROK), in Tuvalu, Report of the Working Group, A/HRC/39/8, para. 101.108 and Tonga, Report of the Working Group, A/HRC/38/5, para. 93.25; Laos, National report, A/HRC/WG.6/8/LAO/1, para. 72; Maldives, National report, A/HRC/WG.6/9/MDV/1/Rev.1, para. 137.138 and in Nauru, Report of the Working Group, A/HRC/31/7, para. 35; Malaysia, in Comoros, Report of the Working Group, A/HRC/12/16, paras. 39, 44; Mauritius, in Nauru, Report on the Working Group, A/HRC/17/3, para. 68; Mexico, in Comoros, Report of the Working Group, A/HRC/12/16, para. 29 and Tuvalu, Report of the Working Group, A/HRC/39/8, para. 74; Micronesia, National report, A/HRC/WG.6/23/FSM/1, paras. 13, 92–100, National report, A/HRC/WG.6/9/FSM/1, paras. 96–101 and Report of the Working Group, A/HRC/31/4, para. 16; Mongolia, National report, A/HRC/WG.6/9/MNG/1, paras. 21–26; Morocco, in Kiribati, Report of the Working Group, A/HRC/15/3, para. 58 and Maldives, in Nauru, Report of the Working Group, A/HRC/31/7, para. 37; Mozambique, in Comoros, Report of the Working Group, A/HRC/41/12, para. 74; Myanmar, in in Solomon Islands, Report of the Working Group, A/HRC/32/14, paras. 83, 99.55; Namibia, in Nauru, Report of the Working Group, A/HRC/31/7, para. 38 and Micronesia, Report of the Working Group, A/HRC/31/4, para. 56; Nauru, Report of the Working Group, A/HRC/31/7, para. 82, Report on the Working Group, A/HRC/17/3, para. 24, and Views on conclusions, A/HRC/17/3/Add.1, paras. 38, 46; Nepal, in Tuvalu, Report of the Working Group, A/HRC/39/8, para. 77; New Zealand, in Vanuatu, Report of the Working Group, A/HRC/12/14, para. 38; Nicaragua, in Tuvalu, Report of the Working Group, A/HRC/24/8, para. 28; Pakistan, in Samoa, Report of the Working Group, A/HRC/33/6, para. 62; Niger, National report, A/HRC/WG.6/10/NER/1, paras. 80–86; Qatar, National report, A/HRC/WG.6/19/QAT/1, para. 11; Palau, Report of the Working Group, A/HRC/18/5, para. 12; Papua New Guinea, National report, A/HRC/WG.6/11/PNG/1, paras. 82–83; Philippines, in Kiribati, Report of the Working Group, A/HRC/15/3, paras. 60, 66.82 and Nauru, Report of the Working Group, A/HRC/31/7, para. 85.56; Poland, in Palau, Report of the Working Group, A/HRC/18/5, para. 31; Portugal, in Report of the Working Group, A/HRC/41/12, para. 79; Saint Lucia, National report, A/HRC/WG.6/23/LCA/1, para. 59 and Report of the Working Group, A/HRC/31/10, para. 83; Saint Vincent and the Grenadines, Report of the Working Group, A/HRC/18/15, paras. 16, 63; Samoa, Report of the Working Group, A/HRC/18/14, para. 25.26; Seychelles, in Vanuatu, Report of the Working Group, A/HRC/41/10, para. 32; Sierra Leone, in Nauru, Report of the Working Group, A/HRC/31/7, paras. 51, 85.58; Slovenia, in Vanuatu, Report of the Working Group, A/HRC/41/10, para. 34; Solomon Islands, National report, A/HRC/WG.6/11/SLB/1, paras. 39, 57–59, Report of the Working Group, A/HRC/18/8, paras. 7, 24 and in Nauru, Report of the Working Group, A/HRC/31/7, para. 85.55; Singapore, Views on conclusions, A/HRC/32/17/Add.1, para. 36 and in Tuvalu, Report of the Working Group, A/HRC/24/8, para. 32; Slovakia, in Tuvalu, Report of the Working Group, A/HRC/24/8, para. 39; Somalia, in Comoros, Report of the Working Group, A/HRC/26/11, para. 110.98; Spain, in Kiribati, Report of the Working Group, A/HRC/15/3, para. 34 and Maldives, in Nauru, Report of the Working Group, A/HRC/31/7, para. 54; Sudan, in Report of the Working Group, A/HRC/41/12, para. 90; Tanzania, National report, A/HRC/WG.6/12/TZA/1, para. 75; Thailand, in Micronesia, Report of the Working Group, A/HRC/16/16, para. 61.73; Timor Leste, in Micronesia, Report of the Working Group, A/HRC/31/4, para. 24; Togo, in Tuvalu, Report of the Working Group, A/HRC/39/8, para. 87; Tonga, Report of the Working Group, A/HRC/38/5/Add.1, para. 2; Trinidad and Tobago, in Nauru, Report of the Working Group, A/HRC/31/7, para. 57; Turkey, in Maldives, Report of the Working Group, A/HRC/16/7, para. 65; Tuvalu, National report, A/HRC/24/8 A/HRC/WG.6/3/TUV/1, paras. 3, 42, 56–57, 75, Report of the Working Group, A/HRC/24/8, paras. 6, 9–11 and National report, A/HRC/WG.6/30/TUV/1, paras. 81–83, 88; Uganda, National report, A/HRC/WG.6/12/UGA/1, paras. 90–91 and in Eritrea, Report of the Working Group, A/HRC/26/13, para. 122.198; Ukraine, in Tonga, Report of the Working Group, A/HRC/38/5, para. 82; United Kingdom, in Micronesia, Report of the Working Group, A/HRC/31/4, para. 25; Uruguay, in Saint Vincent and the Grenadines, Report of the Working Group, A/HRC/18/15, para. 47; Vanuatu, Report of the Working Group, A/HRC/12/14, para. 9; Venezuela, in Micronesia, Report of the Working Group, A/HRC/31/4, para. 28 and in United States of America, Report of the Working Group, A/HRC/16/11, para. 92.51; United States of America, National report, A/HRC/WG.6/22/USA/1, paras. 109–112, Views on Conclusions, A/HRC/30/12/Add.1, para. 12 and in Micronesia, Report of the Working Group, A/HRC/16/16, para. 31; Viet Nam, in Bhutan, Report of the Working Group, A/HRC/42/8, para. 83.

[35] Benin, National report, A/HRC/WG.6/14/BEN/1, para. 57; Comoros, National report, A/HRC/WG.6/18/COM/1, paras. 103–110; Cuba, in Tuvalu, Report of the Working Group, A/HRC/39/8,

States addresses environmental issues in its Universal Periodic Review reports.[36] The large number of States that express concern about these issues at the Human Rights Council demonstrates not only their importance but also the strength of opinion that these are matters falling within the scope of human rights obligations. This is all the more impressive given the relative silence of international human rights treaties on the subject. Micronesia, in its National report to the Human Rights Council, explained that '[c]limate change has dramatically impacted not only the people's right to life, food, water, property, quality standard of living, and self-determination, but also the survival of a cultural heritage and patrimony of Micronesians'.[37] Tuvalu stated that '[t]he increasing frequency in which effects of climate change had been felt [had] been well documented worldwide. Those effects threatened the full and effective enjoyment by Tuvaluans of their rights to life, water and sanitation, food, health, housing, self-determination, culture and development.'[38] Ireland underscored 'the need for the international community to address the human rights dimensions of climate change'.[39] Samoa described 'the impact of climate change on the enjoyment of human rights of Samoans' as affecting food security, the right to water, access to health, the right to life, the right to an adequate standard of living, and freedom of movement, due to internal displacements.[40] Canada commended Maldives for its efforts 'to promote human rights internationally, particularly human rights and climate change'.[41] Bhutan said that although its commitments to global agreements on the environment and climate change 'would remain steadfast', it was concerned that 'global actions were inadequate to prevent further global temperature rises'.[42] It related climate change to the right to health, where the impact 'was becoming visible with the emergence of new patterns of vector-borne diseases, such as malaria, dengue, chikungunya

para. 101.71; Tanzania, National report, A/HRC/WG.6/12/TZA/1, para. 31; Morocco, National report, A/HRC/WG.6/13/MAR/1, para. 66; Andorra, National report, A/HRC/WG.6/9/AND/1, paras. 1, 87–89 and Report of the Working Group, A/HRC/16/8, para. 7; Lesotho, National report, A/HRC/WG.6/8/LSO/1, para. 9; Central African Republic, National report, A/HRC/WG.6/17/CAF/1, para. 14; Mongolia, National report, A/HRC/WG.6/9/MNG/1, para. 21; Senegal, National report, A/HRC/WG.6/31/SEN/1, para. 5; Ethiopia, National report, A/HRC/WG.6/33/ETH/1, para. 37; Uganda, National report, A/HRC/WG.6/12/UGA/1, paras. 90–91; Côte d'Ivoire, National report, A/HRC/WG.6/33/CIV/1, para. 47; Kazakhstan, National report, A/HRC/WG.6/7/KAZ/1, paras. 111–117; Lebanon, National report, A/HRC/WG.6/9/LBN/1, para. 4; Indonesia, in Kiribati, Report of the Working Group, A/HRC/15/3, para. 59; Solomon Islands, National report, A/HRC/WG.6/11/SLB/1, para. 39; Kuwait, National report, A/HRC/WG.6/8/KWT/1, p. 21; India, National report, A/HRC/WG.6/13/IND/1, para. 8.

36 United States of America, National report, A/HRC/WG.6/36/USA/1, para. 71.
37 Micronesia, National report, A/HRC/WG.6/9/FSM/1, para. 97.
38 Tuvalu, Report of the Working Group, A/HRC/39/8, para. 16.
39 Tuvalu, Report of the Working Group, A/HRC/24/8, para. 73.
40 Samoa, Report of the Working Group, A/HRC/18/14, para. 66.
41 Maldives, Report of the Working Group, A/HRC/16/7, para. 54.
42 Bhutan, Report of the Working Group, A/HRC/42/8, para. 22.

and water-borne diseases'.[43] Tonga 'continues to grapple with the ever-increasing threats of climate change that have recently brought an onslaught of more severe and more frequent natural disasters'.[44] Germany said it was 'working towards a comprehensive approach to addressing climate change in collaboration with United Nations agencies and other countries'.[45]

The Human Rights Council has recognised that 'while the human rights implications of environmental damage are felt by individuals and communities around the world, the consequences are felt most acutely by those segments of the population that are already in vulnerable situations'.[46] It has also noted 'the particular vulnerability of children to the effects of environmental harm, including to air pollution, water pollution, climate change, exposure to chemicals, toxic substances and waste, and loss of biodiversity, and that environmental harm may interfere with the full enjoyment of a vast range of the rights of the child'.[47]

Decades ago, the International Law Commission described as *jus cogens* obligations 'of essential importance for the safeguarding and preservation of the human environment, such as those prohibiting massive pollution of the atmosphere or of the seas'.[48] In 1991, the Commission identified wilful and severe damage to the environment as a crime against the peace and security of mankind.[49] But in 2019, it opted not to include this in its list of peremptory norms, following considerable debate on the subject.[50] Special Rapporteur Dire Tladi noted that despite 'the importance of the subject matter and the catastrophic consequence that could result from the destruction of the environment', he thought there was 'little evidence of the required "acceptance and recognition of the international community of States as a whole" that the environmental norms (or some of them) have acquired peremptory status, notwithstanding this empirical fact of the importance of environmental rules for the very survival of humanity and the planet'.[51]

* * *

Conclusions. There is compelling evidence for a human right to a safe, clean, healthy, and sustainable environment under customary international law.

[43] Bhutan, National report, A/HRC/WG.6/19/BTN/2, para. 43.

[44] Tonga, Views on conclusions, A/HRC/38/5/Add.1, para. 2.

[45] Germany, Report of the Working Group, A/HRC/39/9, para. 153.

[46] Human rights and the environment, A/HRC/RES/37/8, PP 11.

[47] Ibid., PP 15.

[48] *Yearbook ... 1976*, Vol. II (Part 2), pp. 95–96.

[49] *Yearbook ... 1991*, Vol. II (Part 2), p. 107.

[50] A/CN.4/SR.3461, p. 9 (Charles Jalloh); A/CN.4/SR.3459, p. 20 (Marja Lehto); A/CN.4/SR.3460, p. 7 (Nilüfer Oral); A/CN.4/SR.3460, p. 16 (Hussein Hassouna); A/CN.4/SR.3462, p. 12 (Carlos Arguëllo Gomez).

[51] Fourth report on peremptory norms of general international law (*jus cogens*) by Dire Tladi, Special Rapporteur, A/CN.4/727, para. 136.

C. Self determination

The right to self-determination of peoples occupies a special place in international human rights law by the importance it is given as Article 1 common to the two International Covenants. Paragraph 1 of common Article 1 states: '1. All peoples have the right of self-determination. By virtue of that right they freely determine their political status and freely pursue their economic, social and cultural development.' The African Charter on Human and Peoples' Rights contains a similar provision.[52] Recognition of self-determination as a 'right' can be traced to the Declaration on the Granting of Independence to Colonial Countries and Peoples of 14 December 1960.[53] This was the seminal text adopted at the height of decolonisation that inspired the drafters of the Covenant. A decade later, the Declaration on Principles of International Law concerning Friendly Relations and Co-operation among States of 24 October 1970 affirmed the content of the right of political self-determination and, in particular, the ways in which it can be applied.[54] Using language echoing Article 1 of the Covenant, the 2008 United Nations Declaration on the Rights of Indigenous Peoples affirms that '[i]ndigenous peoples have the right to self-determination. By virtue of that right they freely determine their political status and freely pursue their economic, social and cultural development.'[55]

The right to self-determination was addressed in the Vienna Declaration and Programme of Action. After two paragraphs that essentially reproduced the text of common Article 1 of the Covenants, the Declaration stated:

> Taking into account the particular situation of peoples under colonial or other forms of alien domination or foreign occupation, the World Conference on Human Rights recognises the right of peoples to take any legitimate action, in accordance with the Charter of the United Nations, to realise their inalienable right of self-determination. The World Conference on Human Rights considers the denial of the right of self-determination as a violation of human rights and underlines the importance of the effective realisation of this right. In accordance with the Declaration on Principles of International Law concerning Friendly Relations and Cooperation Among States in accordance with the Charter of the United Nations, this shall not be construed as authorizing or encouraging any

[52] African Charter on Human and Peoples' Rights, (1986) 1520 UNTS 271, art. 20.

[53] Declaration on the granting of independence to colonial countries and peoples, A/RES/1514 (XV).

[54] Declaration on Principles of International Law concerning Friendly Relations and Co-operation among States in accordance with the Charter of the United Nations, A/RES/2625 (XXV).

[55] United Nations Declaration on the Rights of Indigenous Peoples, A/RES/61/295, para. 3. See Malgosia Fitzmaurice, 'The Question of Indigenous Peoples' Rights: a Time for Reappraisal', in Duncan French, ed., *Statehood and Self-Determination*, Cambridge: Cambridge University Press, 2013, pp. 349–376; Joshua Castellino, 'Conceptual Difficulties and the Rights of Indigenous Peoples', in N. Ghanea and A. Xanthaki, eds., *Minorities, Peoples and Self-Determination*, Leiden/Boston: Martinus Nijhoff, 2005, pp. 55–74.

> action which would dismember or impair, totally or in part, the territorial integrity or political unity of sovereign and independent States conducting themselves in compliance with the principle of equal rights and self-determination of peoples and thus possessed of a Government representing the whole people belonging to the territory without distinction of any kind.[56]

Nevertheless, there are very few references to the 'right to self-determination' in the Universal Periodic Review materials. Although that in no way should be taken to indicate a rejection or repudiation of the right to self-determination, this might suggest that many States do not consider it to fall within the scope of international human rights law. On the other hand, for most States, including those not party to the Covenants, self-determination may simply not be an issue of significance and for that reason it does not warrant any observations in reports to the Human Rights Council.

Sudan devoted a paragraph to the subject in one of its reports to the Human Rights Council. Sudan explained that self-determination is a constitutional right that had been exercised by the people of Southern Sudan through a referendum to determine their future status. The referendum was organised under international and local monitoring, with the people of Southern Sudan, including members of the diaspora, deciding whether they wanted either a united Sudan or secession. Sudan explained that the ballot was conducted in 'a prevailing atmosphere of freedom and security and no instances of violence were detected'.[57] Within the context of the right to self-determination, customary international law recognises a right of 'remedial secession' in circumstances where a people are victims of gross human rights violations, severe repression, and an inability to validly exercise the right to self-determination in an internal sense.[58]

The International Law Commission included 'the right of self-determination' in the draft list of peremptory norms that it adopted in 2019.[59]

* * *

Conclusions. Customary international law recognises a right of peoples, including indigenous peoples, to self-determination. The right is *jus cogens*.

[56] Vienna Declaration and Programme of Action, A/CONF.157/23, para. 2.

[57] Sudan, National report, A/HRC/WG.6/11/SDN/1, para. 45.

[58] *Reference re Secession of Quebec*, [1998] 2 SCR 217, para. 134. See also the discussion in *Chiragov et al. v. Armenia* [GC], no. 13216/05, 16 June 2015, Partly concurring, partly dissenting opinion of Judge Ziemele, §§ 17–27; ibid., Dissenting opinion of Judge Pinto de Albuquerque, §§ 38–49.

[59] Report of the International Law Commission, Seventy-first session (29 April–7 June and 8 July–9 August 2019), A/74/10, p. 207. For the debate, see A/CN.4/SR.3460, pp. 9–10 (Sean Murphy); A/CN.4/SR.3460, p. 12 (Ernesto Petrić); A/CN.4/SR.3460, pp. 12–13 (Sean Murphy); A/CN.4/SR.3465, pp. 6–7 (Dire Tladi); A/CN.4/SR.3462, p. 6 (Gilberto V. Saboia); A/CN.4/SR.3462, p. 16 (Concepción Escobar Hernández); Fourth report on peremptory norms of general international law (*jus cogens*) by Dire Tladi, Special Rapporteur, A/CN.4/727, paras. 108–115.

D. Development

The right to development does not appear in the Universal Declaration of Human Rights or in the International Covenant on Civil and Political Rights. Nevertheless, there are indications of this right in the International Covenant on Economic, Social and Cultural Rights. Article 2(1) sets out the scope of the Covenant: 'Each State Party to the present Covenant undertakes to take steps, individually and through international assistance and co-operation, especially economic and technical, to the maximum of its available resources, with a view to achieving progressively the full realisation of the rights recognised in the present Covenant by all appropriate means, including particularly the adoption of legislative measures.' The right to development is set out explicitly in the African Charter on Human and Peoples' Rights, where it is a 'peoples' right' rather than a human right: '1. All peoples shall have the right to their economic, social and cultural development with due regard to their freedom and identity and in the equal enjoyment of the common heritage of mankind. 2. States shall have the duty, individually or collectively to ensure the exercise of the right to development.'[60]

The Declaration on the Right to Development, adopted by the United Nations General Assembly in 1986, set out 'an inalienable human right by virtue of which every human person and all peoples are entitled to participate in, contribute to, and enjoy economic, social, cultural and political development, in which all human rights and fundamental freedoms can be fully realised'.[61] The World Conference on Human Rights 'reaffirm[ed] the right to development, as established in the Declaration on the Right to Development, as a universal and inalienable right and an integral part of fundamental human rights'. Recalling the Declaration on the Right to Development, it states that 'the human person is the central subject of development', adding that although development facilitates the enjoyment of all human rights, 'the lack of development may not be invoked to justify the abridgement of internationally recognised human rights'. The World Conference said that '[l]asting progress towards the implementation of the right to development requires effective development policies at the national level, as well as equitable economic relations and a favourable economic environment at the international level'.[62] On the twenty-fifth anniversary of the adoption by the General Assembly of the Declaration on the Right to Development, the chairman of the human rights treaty bodies issued a statement observing that the right to development 'finds clear resonance in various human rights treaty provisions, which emphasise the multi-faceted, multi-dimensional and complex nature of

[60] African Charter on Human and Peoples' Rights, (1986) 1520 UNTS 271, art. 22.
[61] Declaration on the Right to Development, A/RES/41/128, para. 1.
[62] Vienna Declaration and Programme of Action, A/CONF.157/23, para. 10.

development processes and the need for development to be inclusive, equitable and sustainable'.[63]

States frequently refer to the 'right to development' in the Universal Periodic Review materials.[64] In surveying the recognition of the right to development within the context of the Universal Periodic Review, there is a very noticeable absence of the countries of the Global North. The 2016 resolution of the Human Rights Council establishing the position of Special Rapporteur on the right to development was proposed by Venezuela and China, and was adopted on a recorded vote with thirty-four in favour, two opposed, and eleven abstentions.[65]

[63] The 25th anniversary of the Declaration on the Right to Development, Joint Statement of Chairpersons of the UN Treaty Bodies, 1 July 2011.

[64] Algeria, in Cuba, Report of the Working Group, A/HRC/11/22, paras. 52, 130(57); Angola, in China, Report of the Working Group, A/HRC/11/25, para. 49; Bangladesh, in Mauritania, Report of the Working Group, A/HRC/16/17, para. 90.56; Belarus, in Cuba, Report of the Working Group, A/HRC/11/22, para. 87; Bhutan, in Cuba, Report of the Working Group, A/HRC/11/22, para. 63; Brazil, National report, A/HRC/WG.6/13/BRA/1, para. 1; Cambodia, in Cuba, Report of the Working Group, A/HRC/24/16, para. 170.53; China, National report, A/HRC/WG.6/17/CHN/1, paras. 4, 5, 25, 87; Cuba, National report, A/HRC/WG.6/16/CUB/1, para. 162; Ecuador, in Cuba, Report of the Working Group, A/HRC/11/22, para. 75; Eritrea, in China, Report of the Working Group, A/HRC/25/5, para. 186.190; Gabon, in China, Report of the Working Group, A/HRC/25/5, para. 76; Gambia, National report, A/HRC/WG.6/34/GMB/1, paras. 137–140; Guinea, National report, A/HRC/WG.6/35/GIN/1, paras. 12, 135, 150; Honduras, in Saudi Arabia, Report of the Working Group, A/HRC/40/4, para. 60; Iran, National report, A/HRC/WG.6/20/IRN/1, paras. 65–73; Jordan, in Malaysia, Report of the Working Group, A/HRC/40/11, para. 151.89; Korea (DPRK), in Cuba, Report of the Working Group, A/HRC/11/22, para. 54; Kuwait, in Oman, Report of the Working Group, A/HRC/17/7, para. 27; Laos, in Cuba, Report of the Working Group, A/HRC/11/22, paras. 60, 130(7); Lebanon, in China, Report of the Working Group, A/HRC/25/5, para. 186.249; Malawi, National report, A/HRC/WG.6/9/MWI/1, paras. 41–42; Micronesia, National report, A/HRC/WG.6/23/FSM/2, paras. 44–45; Morocco, National report, A/HRC/WG.6/13/MAR/1, para. 78; Myanmar, National report, A/HRC/WG.6/10/MMR/1, paras. 76–81; Namibia, in Cuba, Report of the Working Group, A/HRC/24/16, para. 170.220; Oman, National report, A/HRC/WG.6/10/OMN/1, para. 27; Palestine, in Cuba, Report of the Working Group, A/HRC/11/22, paras. 100, 130(57); Paraguay, in Botswana, Report of the Working Group, A/HRC/23/7, para. 101; Philippines, in Cuba, Report of the Working Group, A/HRC/11/22, para. 83; Qatar, in Oman, Report of the Working Group, A/HRC/17/7, para. 22; Saint Vincent and the Grenadines, National report, A/HRC/18/15, paras. 14, 36; Saudi Arabia, National report, A/HRC/WG.6/31/SAU/1, paras. 94–97; Sierra Leone, in China, Report of the Working Group, A/HRC/25/5, paras. 141, 186.252; Singapore, in China, Report of the Working Group, A/HRC/11/25, para. 29; Solomon Islands, National report, A/HRC/WG.6/11/SLB/1, para. 39; South Africa, in Mozambique, Report of the Working Group, A/HRC/32/6, para. 78; Sri Lanka, in China, Report of the Working Group, A/HRC/25/5, para. 148; Sudan, National report, A/HRC/WG.6/11/SDN/1, paras. 83, 108; Suriname, National report, A/HRC/WG.6/11/SUR/1, para. 2; Syria, in Comoros, Report of the Working Group, A/HRC/12/16, para. 46; Viet Nam, in Myanmar, Report of the Working Group, A/HRC/17/9, para. 104.20; United Arab Emirates, National report, A/HRC/WG.6/29/ARE/1, para. 23; Uzbekistan, in China, Report of the Working Group, A/HRC/11/25, para. 44; Vanuatu, National report, A/HRC/WG.6/32/VUT/1, para. 67.71; Venezuela, in China, Report of the Working Group, A/HRC/11/25, para. 89; Viet Nam, National report, A/HRC/WG.6/18/VNM/1, para. 22.

[65] The Right to Development, A/HRC/RES/33/14. *In favour*: Algeria, Bangladesh, Bolivia, Botswana, Burundi, China, Congo, Côte d'Ivoire, Cuba, Ecuador, El Salvador, Ethiopia, Ghana, India, Indonesia, Kenya, Kyrgyzstan, Maldives, Mexico, Mongolia, Morocco, Namibia, Nigeria, Panama, Paraguay, Philippines, Qatar, Russian Federation, Saudi Arabia, South Africa, Togo, United Arab Emirates, Venezuela, Viet Nam; *Against*: France, United Kingdom; *Abstaining*: Albania, Belgium, Georgia, Germany, Latvia, Netherlands, Portugal, Republic of Korea, Slovenia, Switzerland, the former Yugoslav Republic of Macedonia.

Although it is sometimes presented as a 'peoples' right' rather than a human right, resolutions of the Human Rights Council use formulations like 'the enjoyment of human rights, be they economic, social and cultural, or civil and political, in particular the right to development'[66] and 'the full realisation of all human rights for all, including the right to development',[67] leaving no doubt about where the right to development belongs. The Advisory Committee of the Human Rights Council has observed that many elements of the right to development are reflected in the provisions and jurisprudence of the human rights instruments. It offered many examples: self-determination; fair distribution of resources; equality and non-discrimination, particularly on grounds of sex, age, race, and disability; active, free, and meaningful participation; accountability and transparency; substantive rights relating to an adequate standard of living, including food, water and sanitation, housing, health services, education, employment, and enjoyment of culture; freedom of expression, assembly, and association; and international assistance and cooperation.[68]

Beyond generalisations about the right to development, mainly with respect to the implementation of economic, social, and cultural rights, it is invoked particularly with regard to the issues of repatriation of illicit funds,[69] foreign debt[70] and unilateral coercive measures.[71]

* * *

Conclusions. Customary international law recognises that all peoples have a right to economic, social, cultural, and political development.

[66] The negative impact of the non-repatriation of funds of illicit origin to the countries of origin on the enjoyment of human rights, and the importance of improving international cooperation, A/HRC/RES/22/12, PP 10.

[67] Ibid., PP 15.

[68] Contribution of development to the enjoyment of human rights, A/HRC/41/50, para. 4.

[69] The negative impact of the non-repatriation of funds of illicit origin to the countries of origin on the enjoyment of human rights, and the importance of improving international cooperation, A/HRC/19/38, PP 6, 8, 9, 15.

[70] The effects of foreign debt and other related international financial obligations of States on the full enjoyment of all human rights, particularly economic, social, and cultural rights, A/HRC/RES/40/8, para. 13.

[71] Human rights and unilateral coercive measures, A/HRC/RES/34/13, PPs 5, 12, paras. 12, 19, 21.

Conclusion

The future of the customary law of human rights

The creation and identification of customary law is a process very much like the development of judicial precedent, described by Benjamin N. Cardozo as 'the power of the beaten track'.[1] Cardoza's metaphor was adopted by Robert Jackson in his report to the American President on the 1945 London Conference, where the legal framework of the Nuremberg trial was adopted.[2] By its very nature, custom eludes codification. Its existence is often difficult to prove. But by the same token, it has an inherent dynamism enabling it sometimes to evolve more quickly than treaty law. Academic research, including this study, can help to 'beat the track'. Evidence is marshalled to indicate where custom exists and where it is 'crystallising' or 'emerging'. It can also point to exaggerated claims based upon insufficient proof, where noble aspirations sometimes embellish reality.

The methodological premise of this study is that recent developments, both in treaty ratification and in universal monitoring, greatly facilitate the identification of custom in the area of human rights, providing evidence of the two requisite elements, State practice and *opinio juris*. As the narrative portion indicates, in Chapter 1, one of the peculiarities of international human rights law is the pioneering role played by treaties. This contrasts with the pattern of development of other areas of public international law, including the cognate field of international humanitarian law, where norms first emerged as a matter of custom. Only later were treaties crafted in order to facilitate observance of the rules and assist in the settlement of disputes. The trajectory of human rights law was quite different. It first developed within national legal systems, notably in constitutional or constitutionalised instruments. During this early phase, it was largely impervious to internationalisation. Human rights law was viewed as essentially an internal matter. For this reason, the common examples of early initiatives in the international law of human rights are of situations where reciprocal rights of States were involved, such as the slave trade and the regulation of international armed conflict. A quantum

[1] Benjamin Cardozo, *The Growth of the Law*, New Haven: Yale University Press, 1924, p. 62. Perhaps Cardozo was inspired by Oliver Wendell Holmes Jr., 'The Path of the Law', (1897) 10 *Harvard Law Review* 457.

[2] 'Report to the President by Mr. Justice Jackson, October 7, 1946', in Robert H. Jackson, ed., *Report of Robert H. Jackson, United States Representative to the International Conference on Military Trials*, Washington: US Government Printing Office, 1949, pp. 432–440, at p. 437.

The Customary International Law of Human Rights. William A. Schabas, Oxford University Press.
 DOI: 10.1093/oso/9780192845696.003.0012

leap was required so that what was quintessentially domestic in nature, namely how a State treated its own citizens, could move to the global stage, becoming a matter of international concern. This process only really began with the establishment of the United Nations, although early stirrings can be identified a generation earlier, at the end of the First World War.

Frustration with what was perceived as the slow pace of standard setting within the United Nations, in the form of treaties, prompted efforts to define a parallel body of human rights law in the form of customary law. Initially, the case for customary legal norms in the field of human rights was built on a confused foundation, involving important components of natural law and a rejection of the traditional methodology for the identification of international custom. The early efforts to enumerate norms of customary human rights law, principally the Third Restatement of the American Law Institute and General Comment 24 of the Human Rights Committee, in the final decades of the twentieth century, were more in the form of pronouncements or proclamations than careful analysis of the practice of States and of their recognition of legal obligation (*opinio juris*).

New elements and factors, unavailable twenty or thirty years ago, have emerged that greatly assist in the identification of customary international law in the area of human rights. First is the growing realisation that the Universal Declaration of Human Rights provides a source of legal obligation. It has moved beyond the cautious words of its Preamble, where it is described as a 'common standard of achievement', and the modest ambitions of most of its authors. Second is the near-universality of several of the human rights treaties. Six of them now have in excess of 170 States Parties. Virtually every State on the planet has ratified one or more of these treaties. This makes for a complex mosaic of overlapping rights and obligations. Careful analysis permits the identification of many areas where there is universal agreement. To some extent, reservations weaken the treaty regime but their significance tends to be overstated. Reservations are generally directed at sheltering limited exceptions to a particular norm rather than challenging its essence. Finally, for more than a decade the Human Rights Council has been engaged in its Universal Periodic Review of all United Nations Member States. It has generated a rich body of material whereby both the practice and the recognition of legal obligation by States can be assessed. This is of particular significance for the relatively small number of States that have left only a small footprint in terms of treaty ratification. Their participation in the Universal Periodic Review permits insights into areas that were previously completely opaque.

The very nature of customary international law has dictated a cautious approach to its identification. This study has sought to eschew overly prescriptive conclusions about the content of customary norms. The spectrum of rights has been analysed in light of these new materials, bearing in mind also the very limited pronouncements about customary international law by international and national courts, human rights expert mechanisms, and political bodies like the General

Assembly and the Human Rights Council. In the course of this research, the author toyed with developing a quantitative analytical tool, by which points would be assessed based upon such factors as the number of treaty norms that had been ratified, references in the reports to the Human Rights Council, and claims of the existence of a customary norm in case law. On reflection, it was felt that this would give the project a pretence of scientific method that is inappropriate to the identification of custom. It is more helpful to assemble the relevant materials, then weigh their importance using words like 'probably' or 'unlikely' or 'compelling'.

Many of the observations will be uncontroversial. There was no need for an academic study to demonstrate that torture is prohibited by customary international law. A pronouncement by the International Court of Justice settles that issue. But for other rights, the situation is not as clear. Moreover, scholars, activists, lawyers, and judges have not previously had a resource where these materials were compiled, enabling them to reach their own conclusions, or to develop arguments for one side or the other in the context of litigation. There are frequent opportunities to invoke customary law before courts and tribunals although they are likely to remain overshadowed by treaty-based institutions like the regional human rights courts and the treaty bodies. The main international human rights courts and treaty bodies have very generally avoided discussion of the content of the customary international law of human rights. This is a missed opportunity. Customary law also plays an important role in human rights advocacy and political debate. Not only can it fill the gaps left by the treaties, it can also provide support to claims of genuine universality, applicable to the States that have yet to ratify important treaties.

The metaphor of the 'beaten track' should make it clear that this is an area where law is constantly developing. For example, much as the author would have been pleased to declare that the abolition of capital punishment is a norm of customary international law, intellectual rigour makes it difficult to sustain such a position. Hopefully the assessment can be revisited if there is ever a second edition of this work because there can be little doubt that the norm is crystallising. Economic, social, and cultural rights is an area where it was not really necessary to beat a path. Upon inspection, the evidence for custom seems clear enough. Yet there has been an unfortunate tendency to neglect rights to health, housing, education, work, water and sanitation, leisure, and cultural life by those who have made pronouncements about the content of the customary law of human rights.

Recently, some have suggested that States may have a preference for the development of non-conventional forms of human rights law.[3] Stagnation in the development of treaties is accompanied by a 'turn to informality'.[4] Obviously, there are

[3] Laurence R. Helfer and Ingrid B. Wuerth, 'Customary International Law: An Instrument Choice Perspective', (2016) 37 *Michigan Journal of International Law* 563.

[4] Joost Pauwelyn, Ramses A. Wessel and Jan Wouters, 'When Structures Become Shackles: Stagnation and Dynamics in International Lawmaking', (2014) 25 *European Journal of International Law* 733.

areas of human rights law where development of treaty law has proven difficult if not impossible. There are no serious initiatives aimed at conventions dealing with the rights of national minorities, or indigenous peoples, or corporate social responsibility, for example. Codification has essentially ceased with the adoption of so-called 'non-binding' declarations and resolutions. Yet lurking within so-called 'soft-law' texts are legal obligations of a customary nature.

The Universal Periodic Review mechanism has been invoked in this study as a source of evidence of custom. But although this is nowhere stated explicitly, custom may also be understood as the legal foundation of the Review. Officially, of course, 'the basis' is defined with reference to the Charter of the United Nations, the Universal Declaration of Human Rights, and the treaties that have been ratified by the State in question. However, neither the State under consideration nor the many States that participate actively refer to these sources in their assessment of compliance with human rights norms. The only significant references to treaties consist of recommendations that they be ratified if this is not already the case. Thus, the real 'basis' of the review is a somewhat nebulous body of international norms about which there appears to be a shared understanding.

For many decades, the Charter-based human rights activities of the United Nations have been rooted in this uncodified body of law, in obvious distinction with the treaty-based systems. The legal pronouncements were made by experts most of whom were pursuing an agenda of progressive development. The Universal Periodic Review is different because it is controlled by States. As a result, it is inherently more conservative than the special procedures and other expert mechanisms. But this also means that the consensus that emerges about the norms of international human rights in the course of the Universal Periodic Review is assuredly much closer to the core of customary international law.

Even a path that has been beaten—and it is rather immodest to suggest that the task has been accomplished by this study—can quickly become overgrown. A beaten path needs regular traffic or it will soon be lost. The objective of this study has been to begin a conversation about customary law rather than provide a comprehensive compilation. Many of the preliminary conclusions in this study most certainly warrant more detailed examination. Eventually, some of them may be contested in court proceedings.

An important feature of international human rights law is the limited availability of judicial remedies; where they exist, such as in the territory of the Council of Europe, they apply to a rather limited palette of norms. The International Court of Justice has been able to pronounce itself on customary human rights law, but only in rather unique circumstances and with respect to what is arguably the least controversial norm in the entire catalogue, the prohibition of torture. This is not to say that courts lack the potential for significant development of customary international law. The European Court of Human Rights can certainly fit customary international law within the sources that it consults for the purposes of interpretation, pursuant to Article 31(3)(c) of the Vienna Convention on the Law of Treaties, although it has yet to seize this opportunity. But for the foreseeable future the debate about customary law will mainly take place elsewhere, in the special procedures of the Human Rights Council, in political forums like the Human Rights Council and the General Assembly, and of course within the framework of the Universal Periodic Review. In so many respects, customary international law has great and still untapped potential to enrich the protection and promotion of human rights, and to contribute to its progressive development.

Bibliography

Abi-Saab, Georges, 'La Coutume dans tous ces états ou le dilemme du développement du droit international général dans un monde éclaté', in Roberto Ago, ed., *Le droit international à l'heure de sa codification. Etudes en l'honneur de Roberto Ago*, Vol. I, Milan: Giuffre, 1987, pp. 55–65.

Adak, Hülya, 'The Legacy of André Nikolaievitch Mandelstam (1869–1949) and the Early History of Human Rights', (2018) *70 Zeitschrift für Religions—und Geistesgischichte* 117.

Adams, Dean, 'The Prohibition of Widespread Rape as a Jus Cogens', (2005) 6 *San Diego International Law Journal* 357.

Akehurst, Michael, 'Custom as a Source of International Law', (1974–1975) 47 *British Yearbook of International Law* 1.

Aldrich, George H., 'Customary International Humanitarian Law—An Interpretation on Behalf of the International Committee of the Red Cross', (2005) *76 British Yearbook of International Law* 503.

Alfredsson, Gudmunder and Asbjørn Eide, eds., *The Universal Declaration of Human Rights, A Common Standard of Achievement*, The Hague/Boston/London: Martinus Nijhoff, 1999.

Allain, Jean, 'The *Jus Cogens* Nature of *Non-refoulement*', (2001) 13 *International Journal of Refugee Law* 533.

Allain, Jean, *Slavery in International Law: Of Human Exploitation and Trafficking*, Leiden: Martinus Nijhoff, 2012.

Alston, Philip, *Peoples' Rights*, Oxford: Oxford University Press, 2001.

Alston, Philip, 'The Universal Declaration at 35: Western and Passée or Alive and Universal', (1982) 31 *ICJ Review* 60.

Alvarez-Jiménez, Alberto, 'Methods for the Identification of Customary International Law in the International Court of Justice's Jurisprudence: 2000–2009', (2011) 60 *International and Comparative Law Quarterly* 681.

Ambos, Kai and Anina Timmermann, 'Terrorism and Customary International Law', in Ben Saul, ed., *Research Handbook on International Law and Terrorism*, Cheltenham: Edward Elgar, 2014, pp. 20–38.

Arajärvi, Noora, 'Between Lex Lata and Lex Ferenda? Customary International (Criminal) Law and the Principle of Legality', (2010–2011) 15 *Tilburg Law Review* 163.

Arajärvi, Noora, *The Changing Nature of Customary International Law: Methods of Interpreting the Concept of Custom in International Criminal Tribunals*, London: Routledge, 2014.

Arajärvi, Noora, 'The Requisite Rigour in the Identification of Customary International Law: A Look at the Reports of the Special Rapporteur of the International Law Commission', (2017) 19 *International Community Law Review* 9.

Arajärvi, Noora, 'The Role of the International Criminal Judge in the Formation of Customary International Law', (2007) 1 *European Journal of Legal Studies* 2.

Arangio-Ruiz, Gaetano, 'Customary law: A few more thoughts about the theory of "spontaneous" international custom', in Nicolas Angelet, Eric David and Pierre Klein, eds., *Droit du pouvoir, pouvoir du droit: Mélanges offerts à Jean Salmon*, Brussels: Bruylant, 2007, pp. 93–123.

Aust, Helmut Philipp, 'From Diplomat to Academic Activist: André Mandelstam and the History of Human Rights', (2014) *25 European Journal of International Law* 1105.

Baker, Roozbeh (Rudy) B., 'Customary International Law in the 21st Century: Old Challenges and New Debates', (2010) 21 *European Journal of International Law* 173.

Baker, Roozbeh (Rudy) B., 'Customary International Law: A Reconceptualization', (2016) 41 *Brooklyn Journal of International Law* 439.

Bantekas, Ilias and Lutz Oette, *International Human Rights, Law and Practice*, 3rd. ed., Cambridge: Cambridge University Press, 2020.

Barberis, Julio A., 'Reflexions sur la coutume internationale', (1990) *36 Annuaire Français de Droit International* 9.

Bassiouni, M. Cherif, 'Enslavement as an International Crime', (1991) *23 New York University Journal of International Law and Politics* 445.

Bassiouni, M. Cherif, 'International Crimes: "Jus Cogens" and "Obligatio Erga Omnes"', (1996) 59 *Law and Contemporary Problems* 63.

Baxter, Richard, 'Multilateral Treaties as Evidence of Customary International Law', (1965) 41 *British Yearbook of International Law* 275.

Baxter, Richard, 'Treaties and Customs', (1970) 129 *Receuil des cours* 27.

Baylis, Elena A., 'General Comment 24: Confronting the Problem of Reservations to Human Rights Treaties', (1999) *17 Berkeley Journal of International Law* 277.

Bederman, David J., 'Acquiescence, Objection and the Death of Customary International Law', (2010) 21 *Duke Journal of Comparative and International Law* 31.

Bederman, David J., *Custom as a Source of Law*, New York: Cambridge University Press, 2010.

Bellia, Anthony J. Jr., 'Re-Examining Customary International Law and the Federal Courts: An Introduction', (2010) 85 *Notre Dame Law Review* 1787.

Bellinger, John B. III and W.J. Haynes II, 'A US Government Response to the International Committee of the Red Cross Study: Customary International Humanitarian Law', (2007) 89 *International Review of the Red Cross* 443.

Benvenisti, Eyal, 'Customary international law as a judicial tool for promoting efficiency', in Eyal Benvenisti and Moshe Hirsch, eds., *The Impact of International Law on International Cooperation: Theoretical Perspectives*, Cambridge: Cambridge University Press, 2004, pp. 85–116.

Bianchi, Andrea, 'Human Rights and the Magic of Jus Cogens', (2008) 19 *European Journal of International Law* 491.

Blokker, Niels, 'International Organisations and Customary International Law', (2017) 14 *International Organisation Law Review* 1.

Blutman, Laszlo, 'Conceptual Confusion and Methodological Deficiencies: Some Ways that Theories of Customary International Law Fail', (2014) 25 *European Journal of International Law* 529.

Borchard, Edwin, 'Historical Background of International Protection of Human Rights', (1946) *243 Annals of the American Academy of Political and Social Science* 112.

Borgwardt, Elizabeth, *A New Deal for the World, America's Vision for Human Rights*, Cambridge, MA and London: Harvard University Press, 2005.

Boucher, David, 'The Recognition Theory of Rights, Customary International Law and Human Rights', (2011) 59 *Political Studies* 753.

Bourgeois, Hanna and Jan Wouters, 'Methods of identification of international custom: A new role for *opinio juris*?', in Riccardo Pisillo Mazzeschi and Pasquale De Sena, eds., *Global Justice, Human Rights and the Modernization of International Law*, Cham, Switzerland: Springer, 2018, pp. 69–111.

Bradley, Curtis A., ed., *Custom's Future, International Law in a Changing World*, New York: Cambridge University Press, 2016.

Bradley, Curtis A. and Jack L. Goldsmith, 'The Current Illegitimacy of International Human Rights Litigation', (1997) 66 *Fordham Law Review* 319.

Bradley, Curtis A. and Jack L. Goldsmith, 'Customary International Law as Federal Common Law: A Critique of the Modern Position', (1997) 110 *Harvard Law Review* 816.

Bradley, Curtis A. and Jack L. Goldsmith, 'Federal Courts and the Incorporation of International Law', (1998) 111 *Harvard Law Review* 2260.

Bradley, Curtis A. and Mitu Gulati, 'Withdrawing from International Custom', (2010) 120 *Yale Law Journal* 202.

Briggs, Herbert W., 'The Colombian-Peruvian Asylum Case and Proof of Customary International Law', (1951) 45 *American Journal of International Law* 728.

Brown, Philip Marshall, 'The New York Session of the Institut de Droit International', (1930) *24 American Journal of International Law* 126.

Brownlie, Ian, *Principles of Public International Law*, 6th ed., Oxford: Oxford University Press, 2003.

Brownlie, Ian, *The Rule of Law in International Affairs: International Law at the Fiftieth Anniversary of the United Nations*, The Hague: Martinus Nijhoff, 1998.

Buergenthal, Thomas, 'Human Rights', in Rüdiger Wolfrum, ed., *The Max Planck Encyclopaedia of Public International Law*, Oxford: Oxford University Press, 2012, pp. 1021–1031.

Bufalina, A., 'The Principle of Legality and the Role of Customary International Law in the Interpretation of the ICC Statute', (2015) 14 *The Law and Practice of International Courts and Tribunals* 233.

Bugnion, Francois, 'Droit international humanitaire coutumier', (2007) 17 *Swiss Review of International and European Law* 165.

Bullard, Madeleine Grey, 'Child Labor Prohibitions are Universal, Binding, and Obligatory Law: The Evolving State of Customary International Law Concerning the Unempowered Child Labourer', (2001) 24 *Houston Journal of International Law* 139.

Burgers, Jan Herman, 'The Road to San Francisco: The Revival of the Human Rights Idea in the Twentieth Century', (1992) *14 Human Rights Quarterly* 447.

Byers, Michael, 'Conceptualising the Relationship between Jus Cogens and Erga Omnes Rules', (1997) 66 *Nordic Journal of International Law* 211.

Byers, Michael, *Custom, Power and the Power of Rules: International Relations and Customary International Law*, Cambridge: Cambridge University Press, 1999.

Byers, Michael, 'Introduction: Power, Obligation, and Customary International Law', (2001) 11 *Duke Journal of International and Comparative Law* 81.

Cançado Trindade, Antonio A., 'Enforced Disappearances of Persons as a Violation of Jus Cogens: The Contribution of the Inter-American Court of Human Rights', (2012) 81 *Nordic Journal of International Law* 507.

Cannizzaro, Enzo, ed., *The Present and Future of Jus Cogens*, Rome: Sapienza Università Editrice, 2015.

Caplan, Lee M., 'State Immunity, Human Rights, and Jus Cogens: A Critique of the Normative Hierarchy Theory', (2003) 97 *American Journal of International Law* 741.

Cardozo, Benjamin, *The Growth of the Law*, New Haven: Yale University Press, 1924.

Carozza, Paolo, 'Human Dignity and Judicial Interpretation of Human Rights: A Reply', (2008) *19 European Journal of International Law* 931.

Carraro, Valentina, 'The United Nations Treaty Bodies and Universal Periodic Review: Advancing Human Rights by Preventing Politicization', (2017) 39 *Human Rights Quarterly* 943.

Carty, Anthony, 'The Need to be Rid of the Idea of General Customary Law', (2018) 112 *AJIL Unbound* 319.

Cassese, Antonio, *Human Rights in a Changing World*, Cambridge: Polity, 1990.

Cassese, Antonio, *International Law in a Divided World*, Cambridge: Cambridge University Press, 1986.

Cassin, René, 'La déclaration universelle et la mise en œuvre des droits de l'homme', (1951) *79 Recueil des cours* 241.

Castellino, Joshua, 'Conceptual Difficulties and the Rights of Indigenous Peoples', in N. Ghanea and A. Xanthaki, eds., *Minorities, Peoples and Self-Determination*, Leiden/ Boston: Martinus Nijhoff, 2005, pp. 55–74.

Cataldi, Giuseppe, 'Immunités juridictionnelles des États étrangers et droit de l'homme : quel équilibre entre les valeurs fondamentales de l'ordre national et le droit international coutumier ?', in James Crawford, Abdul Koroma, Said Mahmoudi and Alain Pellet, eds., *The International Legal Order, Current Needs and Possible Responses, Essays in Honour of Djamchid Momtaz*, The Hague: Brill, 2017, pp. 571–590.

Charlesworth, Hillary, 'Customary International Law and the Nicaragua Case', (1984–1987) 11 *Australian Yearbook of International Law* 1.

Charlesworth, Hillary and Christine Chinkin, 'The Gender of Jus Cogens', (1993) 15 *Human Rights Quarterly* 63.

Charlesworth, Hilary and Emma Larking, eds., *Human Rights and the Universal Periodic Review*, Cambridge: Cambridge University Press, 2014.

Charney, Jonathan I., 'The Persistent Objector Rule and the Development of Customary International Law', (1985) 56 *British Yearbook of International Law* 11.

Charpentier, Jean, 'Le droit des peuples a disposer d'eux-mêmes et le droit international positif', (1985) 2 *Revue québécoise de droit international* 195.

Chibundu, Maxwell O., 'Making Customary International Law Through Municipal Adjudication: A Structural Inquiry', (1999) 39 *Virginia Journal of International Law* 1069.

Chimni, Bhupinder S., 'Customary International Law: A Third World Perspective', (2018) 112 *American Journal of International Law* 1.

Christenson, Gordon A., 'Jus Cogens: Guarding Interests Fundamental to International Society', (1988) 28 *Virginia Journal of International Law* 585.

Christenson, Gordon A., 'The World Court and Jus Cogens', (1987) 81 *American Journal of International Law* 93.

Christopher, Darcie L., 'Jus Cogens, Reparation Agreements, and Holocaust Slave Labor Litigation', (2000) 31 *Law and Policy in International Business* 1227.

Cohen, Harlan G., 'From Fragmentation to Constitutionalization', (2012) 25 *Pacific McGeorge Global Business and Development Law Journal* 381.

Cohen-Jonathan, Gérard, 'Les droits de l'homme, une valeur internationalisée', (2001) *1 Droits fondamentaux* 157.

Conklin, William, 'The Peremptory Norms of the International Community', (2012) 33 *European Journal of International Law* 837.

Costello, Cathryn and Michelle Foster, 'Non-Refoulement as Custom and Jus Cogens? Putting the Prohibition to the Test', (2016) 47 *Netherlands Yearbook of International Law* 273.

Costelloe, Daniel, *Legal Consequences of Peremptory Norms in International Law*, Cambridge: Cambridge University Press, 2017.

Cowell, Frederick, 'Understanding the Legal Status of Universal Periodic Review Recommendations', (2018) 7 *Cambridge International Law Journal* 164.

Crawford, James, ed., *The Rights of Peoples*, Oxford: Oxford University Press, 1988.

Cunningham, Andrew, 'The European Convention on Human Rights, Customary International Law and the Constitution', (1994) 43 *International and Comparative Law Quarterly* 537.

Czapliński, Władysław 'Customary international law as a basis of an individual criminal responsibility', in Bartlomiej Krzan, ed., *Prosecuting International Crimes: A Multidisciplinary Approach*, Leiden: Brill, 2016, pp. 53–69.

Dahlman, Christian, 'The Function of Opinio Juris in Customary International Law', (2012) 82 *Nordic Journal of International Law* 327.

D'Amato, Anthony, 'It's a Bird, it's a Plane, it's *Jus Cogens*', (1990) 6 *Connecticut Journal of International Law* 1.

D'Amato, Anthony, *The Concept of Custom in International Law*, Ithaca, NY: Cornell University Press, 1971.

D'Amato, Anthony, 'The Concept of Human Rights in International Law', (1982) 82 *Columbia Law Review* 1110.

D'Amato, Anthony, 'The Concept of Special Custom in International Law', (1969) 63 *American Journal of International Law* 211.

D'Amato, Anthony, 'Human Rights as Part of Customary International Law: A Plea for Change of Paradigms', (1996) 25 *Georgia Journal of International and Comparative Law* 47.

Danilenko, Gennady M., 'International Jus Cogens: Issues of Law-Making', (1991) 2 *European Journal of International Law* 42.

Danilenko, Gennady M., 'The Theory of International Customary Law', (1988) 31 *German Yearbook of International Law* 9.

d'Aspremont, Jean, 'The decay of modern customary international Law in spite of scholarly heroism', in Giuliana Ziccardi Capaldo, ed., *Global Community Yearbook of International Law and Jurisprudence 2015*, New York: Oxford University Press, 2016, p. 9.

d'Aspremont, Jean, 'Jus Cogens as a Social Construct Without Pedigree', (2016) 47 *Netherlands Yearbook of International Law* 85.

d'Aspremont, Jean, 'A Postmodernization of Customary International Law for the First World?', (2018) 112 *AJIL Unbound* 293.

de la Vega, Connie, 'Customary international law', in David Forsythe, ed., *Encyclopaedia of Human Rights*, Vol. 1, Oxford: Oxford University Press, 2009, pp. 451–455.

de Schutter, Olivier, *International Human Rights Law, Cases, Materials, Commentary*, 3rd ed., Cambridge: Cambridge University Press, 2019.

Decaux, Emmanuel, *Les formes contemporaines de l'esclavage*, Leiden/Boston: Martinus Nijhoff, 2009.

den Heijer, Maarten and Harmen van der Wilt, 'Jus Cogens and the Humanization and Fragmentation of International Law', (2016) 47 *Netherlands Yearbook of International Law* 3.

Deplano, Rossana, 'Assessing the Role of Resolutions in the ILC Draft Conclusions on Identification of Customary International Law', (2017) 14 *International Organizations Law Review* 227.

de Souza, M.L., 'The Role of State Consent in the Customary Process', (1995) 44 *International and Comparative Law Quarterly* 521.

de Visscher, Charles, 'Positivism et "jus cogens"', (1971) 75 *Revue générale de droit international public* 5.

de Wet, Erika, 'Jus cogens and obligations erga omnes', in Dinah Shelton, ed., *Oxford Handbook on Human Rights*, Oxford: Oxford University Press, 2013, pp. 541–562.

de Wet, Erika, 'The Prohibition of Torture as an International Norm of Jus Cogens and Its Implications for National and Customary Law', (2004) 15 *European Journal of International Law* 98.

Dicke, Klaus, 'The Founding Function of Human Dignity in the Universal Declaration of Human Rights', in Kretzmer, David and Eckart Klein, eds., *The Concept of Human Dignity in Human Rights Discourse*, The Hague: Kluwer Law International, 2002, pp. 111–120.

Dinstein, Yoram, 'The ICRC Customary Humanitarian Law Study', (2006) 36 *Israel Yearbook on Human Rights* 6.

Dinstein, Yoram, 'The Interaction between Customary and International Law and Treaties', (2006) 322 *Recueil des cours* 243.

Dodge, William S., 'Corporate Liability Under Customary International Law', (2012) 43 *Georgetown Journal of International Law* 1045.

Dodge, William S., 'Jurisdiction, State Immunity, and Judgments in the Restatement (Fourth) of US Foreign Relations Law', (2020) *19 Chinese Journal of International Law* 101.

Domb, Fania, '*Jus Cogens* and Human Rights', (1976) 6 *Israel Yearbook on Human Rights* 104.

Dominguez Redondo, Elvira, 'The Universal Periodic Review—Is There Life Beyond Naming and Shaming in Human Rights Implementation?', (2012) *34 New Zealand Law Review* 673.

Dominguez Redondo, Elvira, 'The Universal Periodic Review of the UN Human Rights Council: An Assessment of the First Session', (2008) *7 Chinese Journal of International Law* 21.

Dominguez Redondo, Elvira, *In Defence of Politicization of Human Rights, The UN Special Procedures*, Oxford: Oxford University Press, 2020.

Drumbl, Mark A., 'A hard look at the soft theory of international criminal law', in Leila Nadya Sadat and Michael P. Scharf, eds., *The Theory and Practice of International Criminal Law: Essays in Honor of M. Cherif Bassiouni*, Leiden: Martinus Nijhoff, 2008, pp. 1–18.

Duffy, Aoife, 'Expulsion to Face Torture? Non-Refoulement in International Law', (2008) *20 International Journal of Refugee Law* 373.

Dumberry, Patrick, *The Formation and Identification of Rules of Customary International Law in International Investment Law*, Cambridge: Cambridge University Press, 2016, pp. 14–59.

Dunbar, Norman C.H., 'The Myth of Customary International Law', (1983) 8 *Australian Yearbook of International Law* 1.

Dunbar, Robert, 'The Council of Europe's European Charter for Regional or Minority Languages', in Kristin Henrard and Robert Dunbar, eds., *Synergies in Minority Protection*, Cambridge: Cambridge University Press, 2008, pp. 1556–1586.

Dupuy, Réné-Jean, 'Coutume sage et coutume sauvage', in Charles Rousseau, ed., *Mélanges offerts à Charles Rousseau: la communauté internationale*, Paris: Pedone, 1974, pp. 75–87.

Eide, Asbjørn, 'The Council of Europe's Framework Convention for the Protection of National Minorities', in Kristin Henrard and Robert Dunbar, eds., *Synergies in Minority Protection. European and International Law Perspectives*, Cambridge: Cambridge University Press, 2008, pp. 119–154.

Eide, Asbjørn, Gudmunder Alfredsson, Göran Melander, Lars Adam Rejof and Allan Rosas, eds., *The Universal Declaration of Human Rights: A Commentary*, Oslo: Scandinavian University Press, 1992.

Ermacora, Felix, 'The Protection of Minorities before the United Nations', (1985) *182 Recueil des cours* 250.

Espaliu Berdud, C., 'De la vie et de la mort des normes impératives en droit international', (2013) 47 *Revue belge de droit international* 209.

Farmer, Alice, 'Non-Refoulement and Jus Cogens: Limiting Anti-Terror Measures that Threaten Refugee Protection', (2008) 23 *Georgetown Immigration Law Journal* 1.

Ferrari-Bravo, Luigi, 'Méthodes de recherche de la coutume internationale dans la pratique des États', (1985) 192 *Recueil des cours* 1.

Finch, George A., 'The International Rights of Man', (1941) *35 American Journal of International Law* 662.

Fischer, Hugo, 'The Suppression of Slavery in International Law', (1950) 3 *International Law Quarterly* 28.

Fitzmaurice, Malgosia, 'The Question of Indigenous Peoples' Rights: A Time for Reappraisal', in Duncan French, ed., *Statehood and Self-Determination*, Cambridge: Cambridge University Press, 2013, pp. 349–376.

Fitzpatrick, Joan, 'The Relevance of Customary International Norms to the Death Penalty in the United States', (1995/96) *25 Georgia Journal of International and Comparative Law* 165, at p. 168.

Focarelli, Carlo, 'Promotional Jus Cogens: A Critical Appraisal of Jus Cogens' Legal Effects', (2008) 77 *Nordic Journal of International Law* 429.

Foot, Rosemary, 'Torture: The Struggle Over a Peremptory Norm in a Counter-Terrorist Era', (2006) 20 *International Relations* 131.

Francioni, Francesco, 'Customary International Law and the European Convention on Human Rights', (1999) IX *Italian Yearbook of International Law* 11.

Francioni, Francesco, 'The rights of access to justice under customary international law', in Francesco Francioni, ed., *Access to Justice as a Human Right*, New York: Oxford University Press, 2007, pp. 1–55.

Francioni, Francesco, and Federico Lanzerini, 'The Destruction of the Buddhas of Bamiyan and International law', (2003) *14 European Journal of International Law* 619.

Frulli, Micaela, 'The Contribution of International Criminal Tribunals to the Development of International Law: The Prominence of Opinio Juris and the Moralization of Customary Law', (2015) 14 *The Law and Practice of International Courts and Tribunals* 80.

Gaja, Giorgio, 'Jus Cogens beyond the Vienna Convention', (1982) 172 *Recueil des cours* 271.

Gaja, Giorgio, 'Le riserve al Patto sui diritti civili e politici e il diritto consuetudinario', (1996) *79 Rivista di diritto internazionale* 451.

Galand, Alexandre Skander, 'Approaching Custom Identification as a Conflict Avoidance Technique: *Tadić* and *Kupreškić* Revisited', (2018) 31 *Leiden Journal of International Law* 403.

Gallant, Kenneth S., 'Use of Comparative Law in Determining the Customary International Law of Human Rights', (2012) 24 *Florida Journal of International Law* 429.

Gal-Or, Noemi, 'The Formation of a Customary International Crime: Global Terrorism Human (In) Security', (2015) 14 *International Criminal Law Review* 665.

García-Mora, Manuel R., 'The Colombian-Peruvian Asylum Case and the Doctrine of Human Rights', (1951) 37 *Virginia Law Review* 927.

Gearty, Conor and Costas Douzinas, eds., *Cambridge Companion to Human Rights Law*, Cambridge: Cambridge University Press, 2012, p. 138.

Geiger, Rudolf, 'Customary international law in the jurisprudence of the international court of justice: A critical appraisal', in Ulrich Fastenrath, Rudolf Geiger, Daniel-Erasmus Khan, Andreas Paulus, Savine von Schorlemer and Christoph Vedder, eds., *From Bilateralism to Community Interest: Essays in Honour of Judge Bruno Simma*, Oxford: Oxford University Press, 2011, pp. 673–694.

Glennon, Michael, 'Peremptory Nonsense', in Stephan Breitenmoser, Bernhard Ehrenzeller, Marco Sassoli, Walter Stoffel and Beatrice Wagner Pfeifer, eds., *Human Rights, Democracy and the Rule of Law: Liber Amicorum Luzius Wildhaber*, Baden-Baden: Nomos, 2007, pp. 1265–1272.

Golay, Christophe and Ioana Cismas, *Legal Opinion: The Right to Property from a Human Rights Perspective*, Montreal and Geneva: Rights and Democracy and the Geneva Academy of International Humanitarian Law and Human Rights, 2010.

Gómez Robledo, Antonio, 'Le ius cogens international: sa génèse, sa nature, ses fonctions', (1981) 172 *Recueil des cours* 9.

Goodman, Ryan, 'Congressional Support for Customary International Human Rights as Federal Common Law: Lessons of the Torture Victim Protection Act', (1998) 4 *ILSA Journal of International and Comparative Law* 455.

Gormley, W. Paul, 'The right to life and the rule of non-derogability: Peremptory norms of jus cogens', in Bertrand Ramcharan, ed., *The Right to Life in International Law*, Dordrecht: Martinus Nijhoff, 1985, pp. 120–159.

Gradoni, Lorenzo, 'L'attestation du droit international pénal coutumier dans la jurisprudence du Tribunal pour l'ex Yougoslavie: « régularités » et « règles »', in Mireille Delmas-Marty, Emanuela Fronza and Elisabeth Lambert-Abdelgawad, eds., *Les sources du droit international penal*, Paris: Société de législation comparée, 2004, pp. 24–27.

Green, James A., 'Persistent objector teflon? Customary international human rights law and the United States in international adjudicative proceedings', in James A. Green and Christopher Waters, eds., *Adjudicating International Human Rights: Essays in Honour of Sandy Ghandhi*, The Hague: Brill Nijhoff, 2015, pp. 167–191.

Grotius, Hugo, *On the Law of War and Peace*, Oxford: Clarendon Press, 1925.

Guggenheim, Paul, 'Les deux éléments de la coutume en droit international', in *La technique et les principles du droit public: Etudes en l'honneur de Georges Scelle*, Vol. I, Paris, Librairie générale de droit et de jurisprudence, 1950, pp. 275–284.

Gunning, Isabelle R., 'Modernizing Customary International Law: The Challenge of Human Rights', (1991) 31 *Virginia Journal of International Law* 211.

Guzman, Andrew, 'Saving Customary International Law', (2005) 27 *Michigan Journal of International Law* 115.

Guzman, Andrew and Jerome Hsiang, 'Reinvigorating customary international law', in Curtis A. Bradley, ed., *Custom's Future, International Law in a Changing World*, New York: Cambridge University Press, 2016, pp. 275–304.

Haggenmacher, Peter, 'La doctrine des deux élements du droit coutumier dans la pratique de la Cour internationale', (1986) 90 *Revue générale de droit international public* 5.

Hameed, Asif, 'Unravelling the Mystery of Jus Cogens in International Law', (2014) 84 *British Yearbook of International Law* 52.

Hannikainen, Lauri, *Peremptory Norms (Jus Cogens) in International Law: Historical Development, Criteria, Present Status*, Helsinki: Lakimiesliiton Kustannus, Finnish Lawyers' Publishing Company, 1988.

Hannum, Hurst, 'The Status of the Universal Declaration of Human Rights in National and International Law', (1995/96) 25 *Georgia Journal of International and Comparative Law* 287.

Heintschel von Heinegg, R., 'Criminal international law and customary international law', in Andreas Zimmermann, ed., *International Criminal Law and the Current Development of Public International Law*, Berlin: Duncker and Humblot, 2003, pp. 27–47.

Helfer, Laurence R. and Ingrid B. Wuerth, 'Customary International Law: An Instrument Choice Perspective', (2016) 37 *Michigan Journal of International Law* 563.

Heller, Kevin Jon, 'Specially-Affected States and the Formation of Custom', (2018) 112 *American Journal of International Law* 191.

Henckaerts, Jean-Marie, 'Study on Customary International Humanitarian Law: A Contribution to the Understanding and Respect for the Rule of Law in Armed Conflict', (2005) 87 *International Review of the Red Cross* 175.

Henckaerts, Jean-Marie and Els Debuf, 'The ICRC and the clarification of customary international law', in Brian D. Lepard, ed., *Reexamining Customary International Law*, Cambridge: Cambridge University Press, 2017, pp. 161–188.

Henckaerts, Jean-Marie and Louise Doswald-Beck, *Customary International Humanitarian Law*, Cambridge: Cambridge University Press, 2005.

Henkin, Louis, 'Human Rights and State "Sovereignty"', (1995–96) 25 *Georgia Journal of International and Comparative Law* 31.

Higashi, Jutaro, 'The Role of Resolutions of United Nations General Assembly in the Formative Process of International Customary Law', (1982) 25 *Japanese Annual of International Law* 11.

Hoffman, Paul L., 'The "Blank Stare Phenomenon": Proving Customary International Law in U.S. Court', (1995–96) 25 *Georgia Journal of International and Comparative Law* 181.

Holmes, Oliver Wendell Jr., 'The Path of the Law', (1897) 10 *Harvard Law Review* 457.

Humphrey, John P., *Human Rights and the United Nations: A Great Adventure*, Dobbs Ferry, NY: Transnational Publishers, 1984, p. 65.

Humphrey, John P., 'The International Bill of Rights: Scope and Implementation', (1976) 17 *William and Mary Law* Review 527.

Humphrey, John P., 'The universal declaration of human rights: Its history, impact and juridical character', in Bertrand G. Ramcharan, ed., *Human Rights: Thirty Years After the Universal Declaration*, The Hague: Martinus Nijhoff, 1979, pp. 21–37.

Institut de Droit International, 'Declaration of the International Rights of Man', (1941) 35 *American Journal of International Law* 663.

International Law Association, 'London Statement of Principles Applicable to the Formation of General Customary International Law', (2000) 69 *ILA Report of Conference*, pp. 712–790.

Janis, Mark W., 'Nature of Jus Cogens', (1988) 3 *Connecticut Journal of International Law* 359.

Jennings, Robert Y., 'What is International Law and How Do We Tell It When We See It?', (1981) 37 *Annuaire Suisse de Droit International* 59.

Jhabvala, Farrokh, 'The Drafting of the Human Rights Provisions of the UN Charter', (1997) *44 Netherlands International Law Review* 1.

Jia, Bing Bing, 'The Relations between Treaties and Custom', (2010) 9 *Chinese Journal of International Law* 81.

Johnson, Katie A., 'Identifying the *jus cogens* Norm in the *jus ad bellum*', (2021) 70 *International and Comparative Law Quarterly* 29.

Kadelbach, Stefan, 'Genesis, Function and Identification of *Jus Cogens* Norms', (2016) 46 *Netherlands Yearbook of International Law* 147.

Kadelbach, Stefan, 'Jus cogens, obligations erga omnes and other rules—the identification of fundamental norms', in Christian Tomuschat and Jean-Marc Thouvenin, eds., *The Fundamental Rules of the International Legal Order*, Leiden/Boston: Martinus Nijhoff, 2006, pp. 21–40.

Kammerhofer, Jörg, 'Uncertainty in the Formal Sources of International Law: Customary International Law and Some of Its Problems', (2004) 15 *European Journal of International Law* 523.

Kedian, Kathleen M., 'Customary International Law and International Human Rights Litigation in United States Courts: Revitalizing the Legacy of *The Paquete Habana*', (1999) 40 *William and Mary Law Review* 1395.

Kelly, J. Patrick, 'The Twilight of Customary International Law', (2000) 40 *Virginia Journal of International Law* 449.

Kelsen, Hans, *Peace through Law*, Chapel Hill: University of North Carolina Press, 1944.

Kelsen, Hans, 'Théorie du droit international coutumier', (1939) 1 *Revue internationale de la théorie du droit, Nouvelle Série* 253.

Kelsen, Hans, 'Will the Judgment in the Nuremberg Trial Constitute a Precedent in International Law?', (1947) *1 International Law Quarterly* 153.

Kenny, Cóman and Yvonne McDermott, 'The Expanding Protection of Members of a Party's own Armed Forces under International Criminal Law', (2019) 68 *International and Comparative Law Quarterly* 943.

Kirakosyan, Yeghishe, 'Finding custom: The ICJ and the international criminal courts and tribunals compared', in Larissa van den Herik and Carsten Stahn, eds., *The Diversification and Fragmentation of International Criminal Law*, The Hague: Martinus Nijhoff, 2012, pp. 149–161.

Kirgis, Frederic I. Jr., 'Custom on a Sliding Scale', (1987) 81 *American Journal of International Law* 146.

Klabbers, Jan, 'The Curious Condition of Custom', (2002) 8 *International Legal Theory* 29.

Klein, David F., 'A Theory for the Application of the Customary International Law of Human Rights by Domestic Courts', (1988) 3 *Yale Journal of International Law* 332.

Kleinlein, Thomas, '*Jus Cogens* as the "Highest Law"? Peremptory Norms and Legal Hierarchies', (2016) 47 *Netherlands Yearbook of International Law* 173.

Kolb, Robert, 'La détermination du concept de jus cogens', (2014) 118 *Revue Générale de Droit International Public* 5.

Kolb, Robert, *Peremptory International Law—Jus Cogens: A General Inventory*, Oxford and Portland: Hart, 2015.

Kolb, Robert, 'Selected Problems in the Theory of Customary International Law', (2003) 50 *Netherlands International Law Review* 119.

Koskenniemi, Martti, *From Apology to Utopia: The Structure of Legal Argument (Reissue with new Epilogue)*, Cambridge: Cambridge, University Press, 2006.

Koskenniemi, Martti *The Politics of International Law*, Oxford: Oxford University Press, 2011.

Koskiennemi, Martti, 'The Pull of the Mainstream', (1990) 88 *Michigan Law Review* 1946.

Krieger, Heike, 'A Conflict of Norms: The Relationship Between Humanitarian Law and Human Rights Law in the ICRC Customary Law Study', (2006) 11 *Journal of Conflict and Security Law* 265.

Ku, Julian G., 'Customary International Law in State Courts', (2001) 42 *Virginia Journal of International Law* 265.

Kunz, Josef L., 'The Nature of Customary International Law', (1953) 47 *American Journal of International Law* 662.

Kunz, Josef L., 'The United Nations Declaration of Human Rights', (1949) 43 *American Journal of International Law* 316.

Lamond, Grant, 'Legal Sources, the Rule of Recognition, and Customary Law', (2014) 59 *American Journal of Jurisprudence* 25.

Lau, H., 'Rethinking the Persistent Objector Doctrine in International Human Rights Law', (2005) 6 *Chicago Journal of International Law* 495.

Lauren, Paul Gordon, *The Evolution of Human Rights, Visions Seen*, Philadelphia: University of Pennsylvania Press, 1998.

Lauterpacht, Elihu, *The Life of Hersch Lauterpacht*, Cambridge: Cambridge University Press, 2010.

Lauterpacht, Elihu and Daniel Bethlehem, 'The Scope and Content of the Principle of Non-Refoulement: Opinion', in Erika Feller, Volker Türk and Frances Nicholson, eds., *Refugee Protection in International Law: UNHCR's Global Consultations on International Protection*, Cambridge: Cambridge University Press, 2003, pp. 87–177.

Lauterpacht, Hersch, *An International Bill of the Rights of Man*, New York: Columbia University Press, 1945.

Lauterpacht, Hersch, *International Law and Human Rights*, London: Stevens and Sons, 1950.

Lauterpacht, Hersch, *Oppenheim's International Law*, Vol. I, 8th ed., London: Longmans, Green, 1955.

Lauterpacht, Hersch, 'The Universal Declaration of Human Rights', (1948) 25 *British Yearbook of International Law* 354.

Lepard, Brian D., *Customary International Law: A New Theory with Practical Applications*, Cambridge: Cambridge University Press, 2010.

Lepard, Brian D., 'Determining the customary law status of specific human rights', *Customary International Law: A New Theory with Practical Applications*, Cambridge: Cambridge University Press, 2010, pp. 331–345.

Lepard, Brian D., 'Toward a new theory of customary international human rights law', in Brian D. Lepard, ed., *Reexamining Customary International Law*, Cambridge: Cambridge University Press, 2017, pp. 233–265.

Lerner, Natan, *Group Rights and Discrimination in International Law*, Dordrecht/Boston/London: Martinus Nijhoff, 1991.

Lillich, Richard, 'The Growing Importance of Customary International Human Rights Law', (1996) 25 *Georgia Journal of International and Comparative Law* 1.

Linderfalk, Ulf, 'The Effect of *Jus Cogens* Norms: Whoever Opened Pandora's Box, Did You Ever Think About the Consequences?', (2007) 18 *European Journal of International Law* 853.

Linderfalk, Ulf, 'Reservations to treaties and norms of jus cogens—a comment on human rights committee general comment no. 24', in Ineta Ziemele, ed., *Reservations to Human Rights Treaties and the Vienna Convention Regime*, Dordrecht: Springer, 2004, pp. 213–234.

Linderfalk, Ulf, 'Understanding the Jus Cogens Debate: The Pervasive Influence of Legal Positivism and Legal Idealism', (2016) 47 *Netherlands Yearbook of International Law* 51.

Linderfalk, Ulf, *Understanding Jus Cogens in International Law and International Legal Discourse*, Cheltenham, UK: Edward Elgar, 2020.

MacBride, Sean, 'The New Frontiers of International Law', *UNESCO Courier*, (January 1968), p. 26.

McCrudden, Christopher, 'Human Dignity and Judicial Interpretation of Human Rights', (2008) *19 European Journal of International Law* 655.

McDougal, Myres S., Harold Lasswell, and Lung-Chu Chen, *Human Rights and World Public Order*, New Haven: Yale University Press, 1980.

McGregor, Lorna, 'State Immunity and Jus Cogens', (2006) 55 *International and Comparative Law Quarterly* 437.

McMahon, Edward and Marta Ascherio, 'A Step Ahead in Promoting Human Rights? The Universal Periodic Review of the UN Human Rights Council', (2012) *18 Global Governance* 231.

McMillan, Margaret, *Paris 1919, Six Months That Changed the World*, New York: Random House, 2001.

Malik, Habib C., ed., *The Challenge of Human Rights, Charles Malik and the Universal Declaration*, Oxford: Centre for Lebanese Studies, 2000.

Mandsager, Dennis, 'U.S. Joint Letter from John Bellinger III, Legal Adviser, U.S. Department of State, and William J. Haynes, General Counsel, U.S. Department of Defense to Dr. Jakob Kellenberger, President, International Committee of the Red Cross, Regarding Customary International Law Study', (2007) 46 *International Legal Materials* 514.

Mandelstam, André, 'La déclaration des droits internationaux de l'homme adoptée par l'Institut de Droit International', (1930) *5 Revue de Droit International* 59.

Mariniello, Triestino, 'The "Nuremberg Clause" and Beyond: The Legality Principle and Sources of International Criminal Law in the European Court's Jurisprudence', (2013) *82 Nordic Journal of International Law* 221.

Mathias, Stephen, 'The Work of the International Law Commission on Identification of Customary International Law: A View from the Perspective of the Office of Legal Affairs', (2016) 15 *Chinese Journal of International Law* 17.

Mazower, Mark, 'The Strange Triumph of Human Rights', (2004) 47 *The Historical Journal* 379.

Mejia-Lemos, Diego G., 'Some Considerations Regarding "Instant" International Customary Law, Fifty Years Later', (2015) 55 *Indian Journal of International Law* 85.

Meltzer, Nils, *Interpretive Guidance on the Notion of Direct Participation in Hostilities under International Humanitarian Law*, Geneva: International Committee of the Red Cross, 2009.

Mendelson, Maurice, 'The Formation of Customary International Law', (1998) 272 *Recueil des cours* 155.

Mendelson, Maurice, 'State acts and omissions as explicit or implicit claims', in International Law Association, *Report of the Sixty-Fifth Conference, Cairo, Egypt*, London: International Law Association, 1993, pp. 370–379.

Mendelson, Maurice, 'The Subjective Element in Customary Law', (1995) 66 *British Yearbook of International Law* 177.

Meron, Theodor, 'A Hierarchy of Human Rights', (1986) *80 American Journal of International Law* 1.

Meron, Theodor, 'The Geneva Conventions as Customary Law', (1987) 81 *American Journal of International Law* 348.

Meron, Theodor, *Human Rights and Humanitarian Norms as Customary Law*, Oxford: Clarendon Press, 1989.

Meron, Theodor, *The Humanisation of International Law*, Leiden/Boston: Martinus Nijhoff, 2006, pp. 403–404.

Miller, David Hunter, *The Drafting of the Covenant*, Vol. I, New York: G.P. Putnam, 1928.

Mitchell, David S., 'The Prohibition of Rape in International Humanitarian Law as a Norm of Jus Cogens: Clarifying the Doctrine', (2005) 15 *Duke Journal of Comparative and International Law* 219.

Müllerson, Rein, 'The interplay of objective and subjective elements in customary law', in Karel Wellens, ed., *International Law: Theory and Practice: Essays in Honour of Eric Suy*, The Hague: Martinus Nijhoff, 1998, pp. 161–165.

Murphy, Daniel T., 'The Restatement (Third)'s Human Rights Provisions: Nothing New, But Very Welcome', (1990) 24 *International Lawyer* 917.

Murphy, Sean, 'Identification of Customary International Law and Other Topics: The Sixty-Seventh Session of the International Law Commission', (2015) 109 *American Journal of International Law* 822.

Murphy, Sean, 'Peremptory Norms of General International Law (*Jus Cogens*) and Other Topics: The Seventy-First Session of the International Law Commission', (2020) 114 *American Journal of International Law* 68.

Neal, Mary, 'Respect for Human Dignity as "Substantive Basic Norm"', (2014) 10 *International Journal of Law in Context* 26.

Neuman, Gerald L., 'Sense and Nonsense About Customary International Law: A Response to Professors Bradley and Goldsmith', (1997) 66 *Fordham Law Review* 371.

Norman, George and Joel P. Trachtman, 'The Customary International Law Game', (2005) 99 *American Journal of International Law* 541.

Nowak, Manfred, *Introduction to the International Human Rights Regime*, Leiden/Boston: Martinus Nijhoff, 2003.

O'Boyle, Michael and Michelle Lafferty, 'General principles and constitutions as sources of human rights law', in Dinah Shelton ed., *The Oxford Handbook of International Human Rights Law*, Oxford: Oxford University Press, 2013, pp. 194–221.

Ochoa, Christiana, 'The Individual and Customary International Law Formation', (2007) 48 *Virginia Journal of International Law* 119.

O'Connell, Mary Ellen, 'Jus cogens: International law's higher ethical norms', in Donald Earl Childress III, ed., *The Role of Ethics in International Law*, Cambridge: Cambridge University Press, 2012, pp. 78–101.

Odermatt, Jed, 'The Development of Customary International Law by International Organisations', (2017) 66 *International and Comparative Law Quarterly* 491.

Oeter, Stefan, 'Ius cogens und der Schutz der Menschenrechte', in Stephan Breitenmoser, Bernhard Ehrenzeller, Marco Sassoli, Walter Stoffel, and Beatrice Wagner Pfeifer, eds., *Human Rights, Democracy and the Rule of Law: Liber Amicorum Luzius Wildhaber*, Baden-Baden: Nomos, 2007, pp. 499–521.

O'Mahony, Conor, 'There is No Such Thing as a Right to Dignity', (2012) *10 International Journal of Constitutional Law* 551.

Oppenheim, Lassa, *International Law, A Treatise*, Vol. I, *Peace*, London: Longmans, Green, 1905.

Oppenheim, Lassa, 'The Science of International Law: Its Task and Method', (1908) *2 American Journal of International Law* 313.

Orakhelashvili, Alexander, 'Audience and Authority—The Merit of the Doctrine of Jus Cogens', (2016) 47 *Netherlands Yearbook of International Law* 115.

Orakhelashvili, Alexander, 'Natural Law and Customary Law', (2008) 68 *Zeitschrift für ausländisches, öffentliches Recht und Völkerrecht* 69.

Orakhelashvili, Alexander, *Peremptory Norms in International Law*, Oxford: Oxford University Press, 2008.

Parker, Karen and Lyn Beth Neylon, 'Jus Cogens: Compelling the Law of Human Rights', (1989) 12 *Hastings International and Comparative Law Review* 411.

Parks, W. Hays, 'The ICRC Customary Law Study: A Preliminary Assessment', (2005) 99 *Proceedings of the Annual Meeting (American Society of International Law)* 208.

Paulus, Andreas and Matthias Lippold, 'Customary Law in the Postmodern World (dis) Order', (2018) 112 *AJIL Unbound* 308.

Paulus, Andreas, 'Jus Cogens in a Time of Hegemony and Fragmentation—An Attempt at a Re-appraisal', (2005) 74 *Nordic Journal of International Law* 295.

Paust, Jordan, 'The Complex Nature, Sources and Evidences of Customary Human Rights', (1996) 25 *Georgia Journal of International and Comparative Law* 147.

Paust, Jordan, 'Customary International Law and Human Rights Treaties *are* Law of the United States', (1998–1999) 20 *Michigan Journal of International Law* 301.

Paust, Jordan, 'Customary International Law: Its Nature, Sources and Status as Law of the United States', (1990) 12 *Michigan Journal of International Law* 59.

Pauwelyn, Joost, Ramses A. Wessel and Jan Wouters, 'When Structures Become Shackles: Stagnation and Dynamics in International Lawmaking', (2014) *25 European Journal of International Law* 733.

Pellet, Alain, 'Article 38', in Andreas Zimmermann, Karin Oellers-Frahm, Christian Tomuschat and Christian J. Tams eds., *The Statute of the International Court of Justice: A Commentary*, 2nd ed., Oxford: Oxford University Press, 2012, pp. 731–870.

Perreau-Saussine, Amanda and James B. Murphy, eds., *The Nature of Customary Law: Philosophical, Historical and Legal Perspectives*, Cambridge: Cambridge University Press, 2007.

Petersen, Niels, 'Customary Law Without Custom? Rules, Principles, and the Role of State Practice in International Norm Creation', (2007) 23 *American University International Law Review* 275.

Petersen, Niels, 'The International Court of Justice and the Judicial Politics of Identifying Customary International Law', (2017) *28 European Journal of International Law* 357.

Petsche, Markus A., 'Jus Cogens as a Vision of the International Legal Order', (2010) 29 *Penn State International Law Review* 233.

Pictet, Jean, *Development and Principles of International Humanitarian Law*, Dordrecht: Martinus Nijhoff, 1985.

Pocar, Fausto, 'International Criminal Justice and the Unifying Role of Customary Law', (2016) 21 *Uniform Law Review* 171.

Pollock, Frederick, *Principle of Contract at Law and Equity*, London: Stevens and Sons, 1876.

Posner, Eric and Jack Goldsmith, 'A Theory of Customary International Law', (1999) 66 *University of Chicago Law Review* 1113.

Predescu, Nicoleta-Ramona, 'Human Dignity—A Right or a Principle of Human Rights', [2018] *Conferinta Internationala de Drept, Studii Europene si Relatii Internationale* 137.

Pronto, Arnold N., '"Human-rightism" and the Development of General International Law', (2007) 20 *Leiden Journal of International Law* 753.

Quinn, Molly C., 'Life without Parole for Juvenile Offenders: A Violation of Customary International Law', (2007) *St. Louis University Law Journal* 283.

Ramcharan, Bertrand G., 'The law-making process: From declaration to treaty to custom to prevention', in Dinah Shelton ed., *The Oxford Handbook of International Human Rights Law*, Oxford: Oxford University Press, 2013, pp. 499–526.

Rassam, A. Yasmine, 'Contemporary Forms of Slavery and the Evolution of the Prohibition of Slavery and the Slave Trade Under Customary International Law', (1999) 39 *Virginia Journal of International Law* 303.

Rasulov, Akbar, 'The Life and Times of the Modern Law of Reservations: The Doctrinal Genealogy of General Comment No. 24', (2009) *14 Austrian Review of International and European Law* 103.

Rauter, Thomas, *Judicial Practice, Customary International Criminal Law and Nullum Crimen Sine Lege*, Cham, Switzerland: Springer, 2017.

Redgwell, C.J., 'Reservations to Treaties and Human Rights Committee General Comment No. 24(52)', (1997) *46 International and Comparative Law Quarterly* 390.

Redman, Renee Colette, 'The League of Nations and the Right to be Free from Enslavement: The First Human Right to be Recognized as Customary International Law', (1994) 17 *Chicago-Kent Law Review* 759.

Reisman, W. Michael, 'The Cult of Custom in the Late 20th Century', (1987) 17 *California Western International Law Journal* 133.

Retter, Marc, 'Jus Cogens: Towards an International Common Good?', (2011) 2 *Transnational Legal Theory* 537.

Roberts, Anthea Elizabeth, 'Comparative International Law? The Role of National Courts in Creating and Enforcing International Law', (2011) *60 International and Comparative Law Quarterly* 57, at p. 69.

Roberts, Anthea Elizabeth, 'Traditional and Modern Approaches to Customary International Law: A Reconciliation', (2001) 95 *American Journal of International Law* 757.

Roberts, Anthea Elizabeth, 'Who Killed Article 38(1)(b)? A Reply to Bradley and Gulati', (2010) 21 *Duke Journal of Comparative and International Law* 173.

Robinson, Jacob, *Human Rights and Fundamental Freedoms in the Charter of the United Nations, A Commentary*, New York: Institute of Jewish Affairs, 1946.

Rodley, Nigel S., 'Human Rights and Humanitarian Intervention: The Case Law of the World Court', (1989) 38 *International and Comparative Law Quarterly* 321.

Rousseau, Jean-Jacques, *Du contrat social, in Œuvres complètes, Vol. III*, Paris: Gallimard, 1964.

Sands, Philippe, 'Treaties, Custom and the Cross-fertilisation of International Law', (1999) 1 *Yale Human Rights and Development Law Journal* 85.

Santalla Vargas, Elizabeth, 'In Quest of the Practical Value of Jus Cogens Norms', (2016) 47 *Netherlands Yearbook of International Law* 211.

Sarkin, Jeremy, 'Why the Prohibition of Enforced Disappearance Has Attained *Jus Cogens* Status in International Law', (2012) 81 *Nordic Journal of International Law* 537.

Saul, Matthew, 'Identifying Jus Cogens Norms: The Interaction of Scholars and International Judges', (2015) 5 *Asian Journal of International Law* 1.

Sax, Helmut and William A. Schabas, 'Article 37, Prohibition of Torture, Prohibition of Death Penalty and Life Imprisonment and the Deprivation of Liberty', in André Alen, Johan Vande Lanotte, Eugeen Verhellen, Fiona Ang, Eva Berghmans and Mieke Verheyde, eds., *A Commentary on the United Nations Convention on the Rights of the Child*, Leiden/Boston: Martinus Nijhoff, 2006.

Schabas, William A., *The Abolition of the Death Penalty in International Law*, 3rd ed., Cambridge: Cambridge University Press, 2003.

Schabas, William A., 'Customary law or judge-made law: Judicial creativity at the UN criminal tribunals', in M. Cherif Bassiouni, Jose Doria and Hans-Peter Gasser, eds., *The Legal Regime of the International Criminal Court*, The Hague: Brill, 2009, pp. 75–102.

Schabas, William A., 'Le droit coutumier, les normes impératives (*jus cogens*), et la Cour européenne des droits de l'homme', (2020) *Revue québécoise de droit international* 681.

Schabas, William A., 'Les droits des minorités: Une déclaration inachevée', in *Déclaration universelle des droits de l'homme 1948–98, Avenir d'un idéal commun*, Paris: La Documentation française, 1999, pp. 223–242.

Schabas, William A., *The European Convention on Human Rights, A Commentary*, Oxford: Oxford University Press, 2015.

Schabas, William A., 'Freedom from Fear and the Human Right to Peace', in David Keane and Yvonne McDermott, eds., *The Challenge of Human Rights: Past, Present and Future*, Cheltenham, UK and Northampton, MA: Edward Elgar, 2012, pp. 36–51.

Schabas, William A., 'The Human Right To Peace', in Asbjørn Eide, Jakob Th. Möller, and Ineta Ziemele, eds., *Making Peoples Heard, Essays on Human Rights in Honour of Gudmundur Alfredsson*, Leiden/Boston: Martinus Nijhoff, 2011, pp. 43–57.

Schabas, William A., 'The Omission of the Right to Property in the International Covenants', (1991) *4 Hague Yearbook of International Law* 135.

Schabas, William A., 'Prevention of Crimes Against Humanity', (2018) *16 Journal of International Criminal Justice* 702.

Schachter, Oscar, 'Entangled treaty and custom', in Yoram Dinstein, ed., *International Law at a Time of Perplexity: Essays in Honour of Shabtai Rosenne*, Dordrecht: Kluwer, 1989, pp. 717–738.

Schachter, Oscar, 'International Law in Theory and Practice: General Course in Public International Law', (1982) 178-V *Recueil des cours* 21.

Schachter, Oscar, 'New custom: Power, opinio juris and contrary practice', in J. Makarczyk, ed., *Theory of International Law at the Threshold of the 21st Century: Essays in Honour of Krzysztof Skubiszewski*, The Hague: Kluwer Law International, 1996, pp. 531–540.

Scharf, Michael P., 'Accelerated Formation of Customary International Law', (2014) 20 *ILSA Journal of International and Comparative Law* 305.

Scharf, Michael P., *Customary International Law in Times of Fundamental Change, Recognizing Grotian Moments*, Cambridge: Cambridge University Press, 2013.

Scharf, Michael P., 'Seizing the Grotian Moment: Accelerated Formation of Customary International Law in Times of Fundamental Change', (2010) 43 *Cornell International Law Journal* 439.

Scheinin, Martin, 'The Human Rights Committee's Pronouncements on the Right to an Effective Remedy—an illustration of the Legal Nature of the Committee's Work under the Optional Protocol', in Nisuke Ando, ed., *Towards Implementing Universal Human Rights*, Leiden/Boston: Martinus Nijhoff, 2004, pp. 101–116.

Scheinin, Martin, 'Reservations by States under the International Covenant on Civil and Political Rights and Its Optional Protocols, and the Practice of the Human Rights Committee', in Ineta Ziemele, ed., *Reservations to Human Rights Treaties and the Vienna Convention Regime*, Dordrecht: Springer, 2004, pp. 41–58.

Schlütter, Birgit, *Developments in Customary International Law: Theory and the Practice of the International Court of Justice and the International ad hoc Criminal Tribunals for Rwanda and Yugoslavia*, The Hague: Brill/Nijhoff, 2010.

Schwarzenberger, Georg, 'International Jus Cogens', (1965) 43 *Texas Law Review* 455.

Schwebel, Stephen M., 'The Effect of Resolutions of the U.N. General Assembly on Customary International Law', (1979) 73 *Proceedings of the Annual meeting (American Society of International Law)* 301.

Schwelb, Egon, 'The Influence of the Universal Declaration of Human Rights on International and National Law', (1959) 53 *Proceedings of the American Society of International Law* 217.

Schwelb, Egon, 'The International Court of Justice and the Human Rights Clauses of the Charter', (1972) *68 American Journal of International Law* 337.

Schwelb, Egon, 'Some Aspects of International Jus Cogens as Formulated by the International Law Commission', (1967) 61 *American Journal of International Law* 946.

Scobbie, Iain, 'The Invocation of Responsibility for the Breach of "Obligations under Peremptory Norms of General International Law"', (2002) 13 *European Journal of International Law* 1201.

Scoble, Andrew M., 'Enforcing the Customary International Law of Human Rights in Federal Court', (1986) 74 *California Law Review* 127.

Sellers, Patricia Viseur, 'Sexual Violence and Peremptory Norms: The Legal Value of Rape', (2002) 34 *Case Western Reserve Journal of International Law* 287.

Sender, Omri and Michael Wood, 'The emergence of customary international law: Between theory and practice', in Catherine Brölmann and Yannick Radi, eds., *Research Handbook on the Theory and Practice of International Lawmaking*; Cheltenham: Edward Elgar, 2016, pp. 133–159.

Shavers, Anna Williams, 'Using customary international law to improve women's lives', in Brian D. Lepard, ed., *Reexamining Customary International Law*, Cambridge: Cambridge University Press, 2017, pp. 266–308.

Sheeran, Scott and Sir Nigel Rodley, eds., *Routledge Handbook of International Human Rights*, London and New York: Routledge, 2013.

Shelton, Dinah, 'Sherlock Holmes and the Mystery of Jus Cogens', (2016) 47 *Netherlands Yearbook of International Law* 23.

Shimazu, Naoko, *Japan, Race and Equality: The Racial Equality Proposal of 1919*, London: Routledge, 2009.

Siebert-Fohr, Anja, 'Modern concepts of customary international law as a manifestation of a value-based international order', in Andreas Zimmermann and Rainer Hofmann, eds., *Unity and Diversity in International Law*, Berlin: Duncker and Humblot, 2006, pp. 257–283.

Simma, Bruno, 'International Human Rights and General International Law: A Comparative Analysis', (1993) 4 *Collected Courses of the Academy of European Law* 153.

Simma, Bruno, 'Remarks by Bruno Simma', (1988) *82 Proceedings of the Annual Meeting (American Society of International Law)* 377.

Simma, Bruno and Philip Alston, 'The Sources of Human Rights Law: Custom, Jus Cogens, and General Principles', (1992) 12 *Australian Yearbook of International Law* 82.

Sohn, Louis B., '"Generally Accepted" International Rules', (1986) 61 *Washington Law Review* 1073.

Sohn, Louis B., 'The Human Rights Law of the Charter', (1977) 12 *Texas International Law Journal* 129.

Sohn, Louis B., 'The International Law of Human Rights: A Reply to Recent Criticisms', (1981) 9 *Hofstra Law Review* (1981) 347.

Sohn, Louis B., 'John A. Sibley Lecture: The Shaping of International Law', (1978) 8 *Georgia Journal of International and Comparative Law* 1.

Sohn, Louis B., 'The New International Law: Protection of the Rights of Individuals rather than States', (1982) 32 *American University Law Review* 1.

Stephens, Beth, 'Litigating Customary International Human Rights Norms', (1995–96) 25 *Georgia Journal of International and Comparative Law* 191.

Stern, Brigitte, 'La coutume au coeur du droit international: quelques réflexions', in Paul Reuter, ed., *Mélanges offerts à Paul Reuter: le droit international, unité et diversité*, Paris: Pedone, 1981, pp. 479–499.

Stern, Brigitte, 'Custom at the Heart of International Law', (2001) 11 *Duke Journal of Comparative and International Law* 89.

Swaine, Edward T., 'Rational Custom', (2002) 52 *Duke Law Journal* 559.

Takemura, Hitomi, 'Inconvenient Truths about the Identification of Customary International Law in International Criminal Law', (2019) 62 *Japanese Yearbook of International Law* 312.

Talmon, Stefan, 'Determining Customary International Law: The ICJ's Methodology between Induction, Deduction and Assertion', (2015) 26 *European Journal of International Law* 417.

Tams, Christian J., 'Meta-Custom and the Court: A Study in Judicial Law-Making', (2015) 14 *The Law and Practice of International Courts and Tribunals* 51.

Tan, Yudan, 'The Identification of Customary Rules in International Criminal Law', (2018) 34 *Utrecht Journal of International and European Law* 104.

Tasioulas, John, 'Custom, jus cogens, and human rights', in Curtis A. Bradley, ed., *Custom's Future: International Law in a Changing World*, New York: Cambridge University Press, 2016, pp. 95–116.

Tasioulas, John, 'In Defence of Relative Normativity: Communitarian Values and the Nicaragua Case', (1996) 16 *Oxford Journal of Legal Studies* 85.

Tasioulas, John, 'Opinio Juris and the Genesis of Custom: A Solution to the Paradox Comment', (2007) 26 *Australian Yearbook of International Law* 199.

Terman, Rochelle, and Erik Voeten, 'The Relational Politics of Shame: Evidence from the Universal Periodic Review', (2018) *13 Review of International Organizations* 1.

Tesón, Fernando R., 'Fake custom', in Brian D. Lepard, ed., *Reexamining Customary International Law*, Cambridge: Cambridge University Press, 2017, pp. 86–110.

Thirlway, Hugh, 'Human Rights in Customary Law: An Attempt to Define Some of the Issues', (2015) 28 *Leiden Journal of International Law* 495.

Thirlway, Hugh, *International Customary Law and Codification*, Leiden: Sijthoff, 1972.

Thirlway, Hugh, *The Sources of International Law*, Oxford: Oxford University Press, 2014.

Tistounet, Eric, *The Human Rights Council*, Cheltenham: Elgar, 2020.

Tomka, Peter, 'Custom and the International Court of Justice', (2013) 12 *The Law and Practice of International Courts and Tribunals* 195.

Treves, Tullio, 'Customary international law', in Rüdiger Wolfrum, ed., *The Max Planck Encyclopedia of Public International Law*, Vol. IV, Oxford: Oxford University Press, 2012, pp. 937–957, at p. 945.

Trimble, Phillip R., 'A Revisionist View of Customary International Law', (1986) 33 *UCLA Law Review* 665.

Tunkin, Grigory I., 'Jus Cogens in Contemporary International Law', (1971) 3 *University of Toledo Law Review* 107.

Tunkin, Grigory I., 'Remarks on the Juridical Nature of Customary Norms of International Law', (1961) 49 *California Law Review* 419.

van Zyl Smit, Dirk and Catherine Appleton, *Life Imprisonment, A Global Human Rights Analysis*, Cambridge, MA: Harvard University Press, 2019.

Vasak, Karel, 'Human Rights: A Thirty-Year Struggle', (1977) 30 *UNESCO Courier* 11.

Verdross, Alfred, 'Jus Dispositivum and Jus Cogens in International Law', (1966) 60 *American Journal of International Law* 55.

Villiger, Mark E., *Customary International Law and Treaties: A Manual on the Theory and Practice of the Interrelation of Sources*, 2nd ed., The Hague/Boston: Kluwer Law International, 1997.

Walden, Raphael M., 'Customary International Law: A Jurisprudential Analysis', (1978) 13 *Israel Law Review* 86.

Walden, Raphael M., 'The Subjective Element in the Formation of Customary International Law', (1977) 12 *Israel Law Review* 344.

Waldock, Humphrey, 'Human Rights in Contemporary International Law and the Significance of the European Convention', (1965) 11 *International and Comparative Law Quarterly* Supp. 1.

Waltz, Susan, 'Universal Human Rights: The Contribution of Muslim States', (2004) *26 Human Rights Quarterly* 799.

Warren, Samuel and Louis Brandeis, 'The Right to Privacy', (1890) 4 *Harvard Law Review* 193.

Weil, Prosper, 'Towards Relative Normativity in International Law', (1983) *77 American Journal of International Law* 413.

Weill, Sharon, Kim Thuy Seelinger, and Kerstin Bree Carlson, eds., *The President on Trial*, Oxford: Oxford University Press, 2020.

Weisburd, A. Mark, 'The Effect of Treaties and Other Formal International Acts on the Customary Law of Human Rights', (1995/96) 25 *Georgia Journal of International and Comparative Law* 99.

Weisburd, A. Mark, 'The Emptiness of the Concept of Jus Cogens, as Illustrated by the War in Bosnia-Herzegovina', (1995) 17 *Michigan Journal of International Law* 1.

Weissbrodt, David and Anti-Slavery International, *Abolishing Slavery and its Contemporary Forms*, HR/PUB/02/4, United Nations, 2002, p. 3.

Weller, Mark, ed., *The Rights of Minorities in Europe, A Commentary on the European Framework Convention for the Protection of National Minorities*, Oxford: Oxford University Press, 2005.

Wells, Herbert G., *The Rights of Man*, London: Penguin, 1940.

White, Emily Kidd, 'There is No Such Thing as a Right to Human Dignity: A Reply to Conor O'Mahony', (2012) *10 International Journal of Constitutional Law* 575.

Whiteman, Marjorie, 'Jus Cogens in International Law with a Projected List', (1977) 7 *Georgia Journal of International and Comparative Law* 609.

Wolfke, Karol, *Custom in Present International Law*, Dordrecht: Martinus Nijhoff Publishers, 1993.

Wood, Michael, 'Editorial Comments: The Present Position within the ILC on the Topic "Identification of Customary International Law": In Partial Response to Sienho Yee, Report on the ILC Project on "Identification of Customary International Law"', (2016) 15 *Chinese Journal of International Law* 3.

Worster, William T., 'The Inductive and Deductive Methods in Customary International Law Analysis: Traditional and Modern Approaches', (2014) 45 *Georgetown Journal of International Law* 445.

Wouters, Jan and Cedric Ryngaert, 'Impact on the process of the formation of customary international law', in Menno Kamminga and Martin Scheinin, eds., *The Impact of Human Rights Law on General International Law*, Oxford: Oxford University Press, 2009, pp. 111–132.

Wouters, Jan and Sten Verhoeven, 'The Prohibition of Genocide as a Norm of *Ius Cogens* and its Implications for the Enforcement of the Law of Genocide', (2005) 5 *International Criminal Law Review* 401.

Wuerffel, Kristin N., 'Discriminating among Rights: A Nation's Legislating a Hierarchy of Human Rights in the Context of International Human Rights Customary Law', (1998) 33 *Valparaiso University Law Review* 369.

Wyler, Eric, 'From "State Crime" to Responsibility for "Serious Breaches of Obligations under Peremptory Norms of International Law"', (2002) 13 *European Journal of International Law* 1147.

Yee, Sienho, 'Report on the ILC Project on "Identification of Customary International Law"', (2015) 14 *Chinese Journal of International Law* 375.

Young, Ernest A., 'Sorting Out the Debate Over Customary International Law', (2002) 42 *Virginia Journal of International Law* 365.

Ziemele, Ineta, 'Customary international law in the case law of the European Court of Human Rights', in *The Judge and International Custom*, Strasbourg: Council of Europe, 2012, pp. 73–85.

Ziemele, Ineta, 'Customary International Law in the Case Law of the European Court of Human Rights—The Method', (2013) 12 *The Law and Practice of International Courts and Tribunals* 243.

Zimmermann, Andreas, 'Sovereign Immunity and Violations of International Jus Cogens—Some Critical Remarks', (1995) 16 *Michigan Journal of International Law* 433.

Index

For the benefit of digital users, indexed terms that span two pages (e.g., 52–53) may, on occasion, appear on only one of those pages.

Footnotes are indicated by n. following the paragraph number